This excellent volume examines Paul's theology and practice of mission. Its scope is wide and touches upon many areas of Pauline studies that have caused and continue to cause controversy. Through close study of Acts and the Apostle's epistles, Dr Reymond seeks to bring the reader through these to a deeper understanding of Paul's missionary method and practice but, above all, to the world-changing content of his message. Throughout the work the author never takes his eye off the content of Paul's preaching and teaching and the need for that same Gospel to be taken around the world in the twenty-first century. It is undoubtedly an inspiring and thought-provoking work.

Dr. Paul Gardner
Vicar, Hartford, England

This is quite a book! It tackles a big subject and grapples with it in a big way. Scholars, ministers, theological students and many general Christian readers will find much to stimulate and instruct them here. Professor Reymond is both a New Testament scholar and a theologian, roles not always combined. He writes with admirable clarity and never evades issues, either exegetical or theological. His own theology is never in doubt and he contends vigorously, fairly and ably for Paul's teaching as supporting Protestantism, Conservative Evangelicalism, Calvinism, Presbyterianism and Amillennialism. A most unusual feature is a well-reasoned argument for Pauline authorship of Hebrews. He will not persuade every reader on every issue, but he compels serious thought. He ends with an impassioned call for Christians to take Christ's call to mission seriously, just as Paul did.

Dr Geoffrey Grogan
Glasgow Bible College

Like some of his predecessors with whom I group him, Drs. Warfield and Hodge to mention only two of the best known, Dr. Reymond has applied his considerable skill in systematic theology to the study of the writings of the Apostle Paul. Or one might say that his theology being so informed as it is by his study of that great figure, he has now returned to his mentor to let him speak for himself in his own milieu, that is, in his writings as well as in the Book of Acts. The approach that my former colleague takes is the fascinating aspect of this study. He is not writing about Paul as the great theologian, albeit he does do that, but about him as the great missionary/theologian. That is, he places his writings exactly where Paul writes them, i.e. in the midst of his great missionary endeavor. And the goal of the writer is not only to understand Paul and his writings, but his desire is for this work to be a catalyst for others to carry Paul's great statement of the gospel to places where the gospel has not yet gone or has not gone fully enough. Dr. Reymond is feeding the mind and the heart simultaneously in the same way that Paul originally did. And that in itself is the reason to get this book and read it and thereby be discipled by the Apostle of whom it speaks.

Dr. George W. Knight III,
Greenville Presbyterian Theological Seminary
Taylors, South Carolina

Those who have read and appreciated Robert Reymond's *A New Systematic Theology of the Christian Faith*, will be delighted with this new volume on the apostle Paul. There are five particularly notable features. First, he is unashamedly evangelical in his approach to Scripture and expounds the text without constantly feeling the need to defend its authenticity and authority. Second, the detailed analysis of Paul's letters in the context of the missionary journeys, rather than in some detached literary fashion, adds greatly to one's understanding of the letters themselves. Third, the fact that Reymond inserts additional background material into the volume at appropriate points is hugely helpful (for example, 'excursus on travel in Paul's day' or 'excursus on the Jewish synagogue'). Fourth, the way in which Part Two of the book expounds Paul's missionary theology is a marvellous reminder that the letters of the apostle were not written to provide material for biblical scholars but to aid the advancement of the gospel. Fifth, Reymond's biblical and theological exposition of particular themes, for example, on canonicity, imputation, justification and the Holy Spirit, is superb and stimulating.

Dr A.T.B. McGowan
Principal, Highland Theological College,
Dingwall, Scotland

Robert Reymond has written a useful survey of Paul's missionary life and theology. While breaking little new scholarly ground, the book helps students of the Bible to grasp the historical sequence of Paul's missionary work and introduces the main themes of Paul's teaching about God's work in his Son. The approach to the New Testament materials reflects a high view of their divine origin and authority. Of particular note is a serious defense of the now generally abandoned view that Paul was the author of Hebrews.

Dr. Douglas Moo
Trinity Evangelical Divinity School, Chicago

In this compelling presentation of Paul's theology, Dr. Reymond exposes the great missionary heart of the beloved apostle. Enriched by insights from the field of systematic theology, this volume expounds the important truth that the vibrancy and resilience of Paul's missionary efforts were rooted in and motivated from the depths and breadths of a profound theological vision. As few other works in his generation have done, Dr. Reymond's book will give its readership a fresh introduction to the vitality of that lesson.

Dr. Fowler White
Knox Theological Seminary, Fort Lauderdale

Paul
Missionary Theologian

Robert L. Reymond

Mentor

© Robert L. Reymond
ISBN 185792 497 5

Published in 2000 by Christian Focus Publications, Geanies House,
Fearn, Ross-shire, Scotland,
IV10 5QN, Great Britain.

Cover design by Owen Daily

CONTENTS

Preface — 9

Part 1 – Paul's Missionary Labours

1. Introduction to Paul's Life and Letters — 17
2. Luke's Acts — 31
3. Saul, Zealot Jew — 45
4. Saul's Conversion, Call, New Eschatological Vision, and Gospel — 55
5. Saul's First Evangelistic Efforts and His First Two Post-conversion Trips to Jerusalem — 89
6. Paul's First Missionary Journey, Peter's Later Hypocrisy and Paul's *Letter to the Galatians* — 115
7. The Jerusalem Conference — 139
8. Paul's Second Missionary Journey, His Fourth Post-conversion (uneventful) Trip to Jerusalem and His Thessalonian Correspondence — 153
9. Paul's Third Missionary Journey, His Fifth Post-conversion (very eventful) Trip to Jerusalem, His Corinthian Correspondence, and His *Letter to the Romans* — 177
10. Paul's Journey to Caesarea and to Rome, His First Roman Imprisonment and His Prison Letters from Rome — 215
11. Paul's Release from Prison, His 'Fifth' Missionary Journey, His Second Roman Imprisonment, the *Letter to the Hebrews*, the Pastoral Letters and His Martyrdom — 245
12. The Divine Authority and Canonicity of the Pauline Correspondence — 293

Part 2 – Paul's Missionary Theology

	Paul's Missionary Theology	307
13.	Sin and 'Man in Adam'	315
14.	The Sovereignty of God in Salvation	331
15.	God the Father's Salvific Work	343
16.	The Person of Christ	355
17.	The Old Testament Roots of the Pauline Gospel	373
18.	God the Son's Salvific Work	385
19.	The Holy Spirit's Person and Salvific Work	405
20.	The Doctrine of Justification	421
21.	The Pauline Ethic: the Christian and the Decalogue	469
22.	The Church	493
23.	Baptism and the Lord's Supper	507
24.	The Pauline Eschatology	529
25.	Lessons from Paul's Ministry for Today's Missionaries	557
Appendix	Representative Greek Words Describing Paul's Preaching Activity	589
Bibliography		596
Persons Index		609
Scripture Index		614
Subject Index		631

Dedicated

to

my students who,

following in Paul's footsteps,

have "boldly gone where

no man has gone before"

Chronology of Paul's Life
(dates are at times not certain)

c. 32-33	Paul's conversion
c. 32-35	Paul's early evangelistic ministy in Nabatean Arabia
c. 35-36	Paul's first post-conversion visit to Jerusalem
c. 36-45	Paul's 'silent years' of ministry in Syria/Cilicia
c. 45-46	The beginning of Paul's ministry in Antioch Syria
c. 46	Paul's second post-conversion 'famine relief visit' to Jerusalem
c. 47-48	Paul's first missionary journey in Cyprus and South Galatia
c. 48-49?	Paul's *Letter to the Galatians*
c. 49	Paul's third post-conversion visit to the Jerusalem Conference
c. 49-50	Paul's second missionary journey through Asia Minor to Macedonia and Achaia
c. 50	Paul's *Epistles to the Thessalonians*
c. 50-52	Paul's ministry in Corinth
c. 52	Paul's fourth (quick) post-conversion visit to Jerusalem
c. 52-55	Paul's third missionary journey and ministry in Ephesus
c. 55-56	Paul's *Epistles to the Corinthians*
c. 56-57	Paul's travels in Macedonia, Illyricum, and Achaia
c. 57	Paul's *Letter to the Romans*
c. 57	Paul's fifth and last post-conversion visit to Jerusalem
c. 57-59	Paul's imprisonment at Caesarea
c. 59	Paul's 'fourth missionary journey' to Rome begins
c. 60	Paul's arrival in Rome
c. 60-62	Paul's 'house arrest' and ministry in Rome
c. 60-62	Paul's *Epistles to the Colossians, Philemon, Ephesians,* and *Philippians*
c. 62	Paul's release from 'house arrest'
c. 62-63?	Paul's 'fifth missionary journey', possibly to Spain, but certainly to Crete, Nicopolis, Ephesus, Macedonia, Troas, Corinth, and Miletus
c. 62-63?	Paul's *First Epistle to Timothy*
c. 63?	Paul's *Epistle to Titus*
c. 63?	Paul's second arrest and second imprisonment in Rome
c. 64?	Paul's *Epistle to the Hebrews*
c. 65?	Paul's *Second Epistle to Timothy*
c. 65?	Paul's martyrdom in Rome

PREFACE

The question may quite properly be asked, 'Why another book about Paul? Haven't hundreds upon hundreds of books already been written about Paul's life and ministry?' Yes, and hundreds of commentaries have been written on his letters and well over fifty-seven hundred journal articles about him as well.[1] So if I thought that this book was just 'another book about Paul' I would be the first to say, 'Ignore it.' But sharing as I do the opinion of Jeffrey L. Sheler who opines: '[Paul's] impact on the shaping of [the] post-Easter faith makes the search for ever clearer portraits of the man a worthy endeavor',[2] I think this book will provide such a portrait of the man and his ministry and say some things that most 'Paul studies' that are being made available to the Bible student today do not say.

First, the reader should know that it is classically orthodox in its approach to Holy Scripture—unlike so many studies out there such as Günther Bornkamm's *Paul*,[3] Michael Grant's *Saint Paul*,[4] C. K. Barrett's *Paul: An Introduction to His Thought*,[5] and the pertinent sections in Raymond E. Brown's *An Introduction to the New Testament*[6] that routinely question the accuracy and authenticity of Luke's Acts and of at least some of Paul's letters and without any warrant at times virtually rewrite New Testament history and Paul's theology.

Second, the reader should know that while I was concerned to portray Paul primarily in his role as a missionary I was also concerned to

---

1. Bruce M. Metzger's *Index to Periodical Literature on the Apostle Paul*, second edition (Leiden: E. J. Brill, 1970), lists three thousand and thirteen entries. Twenty-three years later Watson E. Mills's *An Index to Periodical Literature on the Apostle Paul* (Leiden: E. J. Brill, 1993) added an additional twenty-seven hundred entries. And seven more years of journal articles since 1993 must be added to that!

2. Jeffrey L. Sheler, 'Reassessing an Apostle' in *U. S. News & World Report* 126.13 (April 5, 1999), 55.

3. Günther Bornkamm, *Paul*, translated by D. M. G. Stalker (New York: Harper & Row, 1971).

4. Michael Grant, *Saint Paul* (New York: Charles Scribner's Sons, 1976).

5. C. K. Barrett, *Paul: An Introduction to His Thought* (Louisville, Kentucky: Westminster/John Knox, 1994).

6. Raymond E. Brown, for example—very likely the most important Roman Catholic biblical scholar in the world before his death in 1998—in his *An Introduction to the New Testament* (Anchor Bible Reference Library; New York: Doubleday, 1997), accepts historical errors in Luke-Acts and regards the 'we' passages in Acts as sources possibly from Paul's companions, but the author of Acts should not be included among these companions nor should the author be looked to for information about Paul's theology. As for the Pauline literature, he regards Colossians, Ephesians, 2 Thessalonians, 1 and 2 Timothy, and Titus to be pseudonymous 'deutero-Pauline' material and not directly from the hand of Paul.

represent as correctly as I could at least the main themes of his missionary theology (which for the most part I have treated separately and in some detail in Part Two), for we must be under no delusion about one simple fact: if the apostle Paul went astray in his theology, then certainly the Protestant church, if not the entire Christian church, is in serious error because it has primarily followed Paul's lead in its theological formulations.

One should not draw the conclusion from my last statement that in following Paul Christianity in general and Protestantism in particular have in some significant ways departed from Jesus' teaching. Let me say plainly at the outset of our study: *Paul is not the founder of Christianity. Jesus is.* For just as Paul taught that Jesus was God incarnate (Rom 9:5; Titus 2:13; Phil 2:6; Col 1:15-20; 2:9; Heb 1:8), so also did Jesus teach about himself before Paul did.[7] Just as Paul represented Jesus' death as a sacrificial death, that is, as a death laid down in the stead of others for the remission of sin (Acts 20:28; Rom 3:25; 5:6, 8, 9; 1 Cor 5:7; 15:3; Eph 1:7; 5:2; Col 1:20), so also did Jesus before him (Matt 20:28; 26:28; Mark 10:45; 14:24; Luke 22:19-20; John 10:11, 15). Just as Paul spoke of salvation in terms of justification by faith (Acts 13:38-39; Rom 1:16-17; 3:24-25; 5:9; Phil 3:9), so also spoke Jesus before him, though not as often or as explicitly: '[On the day of judgment] by your words *you will be acquitted* [or 'justified', δικαιωθήσῃ], and by your words you will be condemned [καταδικασθήσῃ]' (Matt 12:37; note our Lord's employment of the antonyms of acquittal or justification and condemnation). He elucidates his teaching in his parable of the Pharisee and the tax collector (Luke 18:9-14), declaring that it was the latter—who had simply prayed sincerely: 'God, *have mercy* [ἱλάσθητί] on me, the sinner'—who 'went home *justified* [δεδικαιωμένος].'[8] Finally, just as Paul insisted that faith in Jesus and his saving mission was the only instrument which would bring about justification or right standing before God (Rom 3:22, 28; 4:5; Gal 2:16; Phil 3:9), so also did Jesus

---

7. For the evidence see my *A New Systematic Theology of the Christian Faith* (Nashville: Thomas Nelson, 1998), 214-37.

8. Jesus' first verb, ἱλάσθητι, is the aorist passive imperative form from ἱλάσκομαι, 'to propitiate', meaning 'be propitious, show mercy'. But since its root is the same as that which underlies ἱλασμός, 'propitiation' (1 John 2:2; 4:10), and ἱλαστήριον, 'propitiation' (Rom. 3:25) and 'mercy seat' (LXX, Ex. 25:16; Lev 16:5; Heb 9:5), I would suggest that Jesus' publican is praying: 'Look upon me—the sinner that I am—with mercy, as you do when you look at the sinner through the shed blood on the mercy seat.' Jesus' second verb, δεδικαιωμένος, is the perfect passive participle from δικαιόω, 'to justify', meaning literally 'having been justified'. Here Jesus teaches the *instantaneous* justification of the penitent sinner through a simple prayer of faith that looks for forgiveness on the ground of the shed blood of the sacrifice—the same as Paul's teaching!

teach before him: 'Just as Moses lifted up the snake in the desert, so the Son of Man must be lifted up, that *everyone who believes in him* may have eternal life. For God so loved the world that he gave his one and only Son, that *whoever believes in him* shall not perish but have eternal live...Whoever believes in [God's Son] is not condemned [but is justified, since the opposite of condemnation is justification]' (John 3:14-16, 18; see also John 6:29, 40, 47; 11:25-26; Luke 24:47).[9] But if Paul did not err, particularly in his understanding and explication of the gospel (which position I will argue throughout the study), then historic Protestantism is essentially correct in its theology of justification by grace alone through faith alone in the finished work of Jesus Christ and conversely the Roman Catholic Church and the Eastern Orthodox churches are in serious error precisely with respect to this central tenet of the Christian gospel. All this is just to say that to follow Paul is to follow Christ; to disagree with Paul or to misinterpret Paul is to disagree with or to misinterpret Christ whose inspired apostle Paul was.

Third, as an incidental feature in the book, moving against the majority opinion of New Testament scholars in this age, I argue the case once again for the Pauline authorship of the Letter to the Hebrews which at one time was the classical view of the church but which has fallen upon hard times in our day.

Finally, when I wrote these chapters originally in 1989 as lectures for seminary students at Covenant Theological Seminary in St. Louis, Missouri,[10] my purpose then was not to make them so scholarly that

---

9. I would refer the reader to David Wenham, *Paul: Follower of Jesus or Founder of Christianity?* (Grand Rapids: Eerdmans, 1995), who in my opinion successfully argues that Paul was a faithful follower of Christ and therefore that he did not distort the teaching of Jesus Christ.

See also J. Gresham Machen's somewhat dated but still very valuable *The Origin of Paul's Religion* (Reprint of 1925 edition; Grand Rapids: Eerdmans, 1965), Chapter Four, 'Paul and Jesus' (117-69), in which he shows (1) that Paul regarded himself as a disciple of Jesus, (2) that he was so regarded by Jesus' intimate friends, (3) that he had abundant sources of information about Jesus (117-42), and (4) that Paul shared with Jesus the same view of the Kingdom of God (160-61), the same doctrine of the fatherhood of God (161-64), the same doctrines of salvation by God's free grace and a final judgment before the judgment-seat of Christ (164), the same essential ethic of love as the fulfilling of the law (164-65), and most significant of all, the same religion of redemption in and by the death and resurrection of Jesus (166-69).

John M. G. Barclay, 'Jesus and Paul' in *Dictionary of Paul and His Letters*, edited by Gerald F. Hawthorne, Ralph P. Martin, and Daniel G. Reid (Downers Grove, Ill.: InterVarsity, 1993), also concludes from his research: 'There is sufficient evidence to show that, whether consciously or otherwise, Paul did develop the central insights of the teaching of Jesus and the central meaning of his life and death in a way that truly represents their dynamic and their fullest significance' (502).

10. This fact explains why there are so many references in the book to F. F. Bruce's

only the Paul scholar would appreciate them. For example, I did not treat in detail the nineteenth-century Hegelian theory of Ferdinand Christian Baur (d. 1860) and his Tübingen school,[11] which theory was opposed at the time by August Neander (d. 1850), that resolved all of the New Testament writings into *Tendenzschriften* ('tendency writings' that were more or less conscious falsifications of history into fiction in the interest of a party) that pitted Jewish or primitive Christianity represented by Peter on the one hand against Gentile or progressive Christianity represented by Paul on the other. It is enough to say here that the Tübingen school's views, in their pristine form, fell under the weight of their own anti-supernaturalism[12] and also through the later scholarship of J. B. Lightfoot, W. Lütgert, W. Bousset and R. Reitzenstein of the History of Religions School, and Dieter Georgi. But Baur's position in a much less radical form has seen something of a revival in recent times in C. K. Barrett's two essays, 'Paul and the "Pillar" Apostles'[13] and 'Cephas and Corinth.'[14] So after one hundred and fifty years of scholarly research and writing, the net effect of Barrett's work is the destruction of the notion that a general consensus has been reached concerning the identity and theology of Paul's opponents, whose identity, as Barrett quite correctly observes, 'constitutes one of the crucial

---

Paul: Apostle of the Heart Set Free (Grand Rapids: Eerdmans, 1996 reprint) and Martin Franzmann's *The Word of the Lord Grows* (St. Louis: Concordia, 1961). Both were required textbooks for the course, and I used my lectures to assist my students in their reading of them. I still highly recommend both books as the best treatments on Paul for the lay reader.

11. See F. C. Baur, 'Die Christuspartie in der korinthischen Gemeinde,' *Tübingen Zeitschrift für Theologie* 5 (1831): 61-206. Interested students may consult Herman Ridderbos' brief discussion of F.C. Baur's views in his *Paul: An Outline of His Theology*, translated by John R. DeWitt (Grand Rapids: Eerdmans, 1975), 16-17. Most evangelical New Testament introductions also treat Baur and the Tübingen school.

12. One has only to compare Peter's sermon in Acts 2 and Paul's sermon in Acts 13 to discern how much they agreed in all essential matters.

13. C. K. Barrett, 'Paul and the "Pillar" Apostles' in *Studia Paulina in honorem J. de Zwaan*, edited by J. N. Sevenster and W. C. van Unnik, (Haarlem: Erven F. Bohn, 1953), 1-19.

14. C. K. Barrett, 'Cephas and Corinth' in *Abraham unser Vater: Juden und Christen im Gespräch über die Bibel. Festschrift für Otto Michel zum 60. Geburtstag*, edited by Otto Betz, Martin Hengel, Peter Schmidt (Leiden: E. J. Brill, 1963); republished in C. K. Barrett, *Essays on Paul* (Philadelphia: Westminster, 1982), 28-39. In this essay Barrett argues that Peter had visited Corinth, that either he or someone acting in his name was the 'man' who was building on Paul's foundation in 1 Corinthians 3:10-17, and accordingly that a 'Cephas Party' had risen in Corinth in opposition to Paul. Barrett draws a distinction, however, between the original Jerusalem apostle (Gal 2:9) and the 'super apostles' of Corinth (2 Cor 11:5), and contends that Paul, out of respect for the former, opposed only the latter. Barrett sees the key to this situation in Corinth as that which had occurred earlier in Antioch: While Peter's heart was in the right place, he had again allowed his name and authority to be used by Judaizers against Paul, and Paul found himself once again in the uncomfortable position of having to deal with those who wanted to destroy his work in Peter's name without repudiating Peter himself.

questions for the understanding of the New Testament and the origins of Christianity'.[15] The Baur and anti-Baur positions by 1980 seemed equally well-fortified with arguments and counter-arguments and at a stalemate.

Nor did I interact in those original lectures in any great detail with what is currently the most debated topic among Paul scholars (which has carried the Baur–anti-Baur debate forward)—namely, Paul's understanding of the law and more specifically the meaning of his key phrase, 'works of law' (ἔργα νόμου), by which phrase he summed up what he so strongly opposed, namely, justification by works of law—that is raging today between Protestant Pauline scholars, particularly German Lutheran scholars such as Rudolf Bultmann's followers, on the one hand, and the 'new perspective' views of E. P. Sanders, James D. G. Dunn and their followers, on the other.

Bypassing such debates in any great detail at that time,[16] I set as my primary goal for the entire lecture series (1) simply to take Luke's Acts and Paul's letters as they stand and, with a minimum of speculation, including even the 'sanctified' kind, to confront my students with the biblical facts about this great pioneer missionary whose single ambition in ministry was 'to preach the gospel where Christ was not known, so that I would not be building on someone else's foundation' (Rom 15:20), or, as he says in another place, to 'finish the race and complete the task the Lord Jesus has given me—the task of testifying to the gospel of God's grace' (Acts 20:24), and (2) thereby to motivate them to love and to admire him and his life's work as I did with the hope and prayer that the Holy Spirit would call some of them to follow Paul's example in the world mission program which he launched, the purpose of which was to evangelize and to Christianize the entire world. Those lectures remained in their original form for almost a decade while I continued to read the literature until recently when I did a complete revision of them for my students in a course on Paul that I offered at Knox Theological Seminary in Fort Lauderdale, Florida. The students' responses in both seminaries to the lectures as I was giving them prompted me to think that they might prove to be of blessing to Christ's people and moved me

---

15. C. K. Barrett, 'Paul's Opponents in II Corinthians' in *New Testament Studies* 17 (1971), 233; republished in *Essays on Paul*, 60; see also P. W. Barnett, 'Opponents of Paul' in *Dictionary of Paul and His Letters* (edited by G. F. Hawthorne, R. P. Martin, G. Reid; Downers Grove, Ill.: InterVarsity, 1993), 644-53.

16. I did, however, offer my studied opinions in class about these matters at appropriate places along the way, and I have treat the current debate between the classical Protestant view of Paul's statements on the law and the view of the 'new perspective' theologians in Chapter Twenty of this book.

to revise them for a third time for an adult Sunday School class I taught in 1999 at Coral Ridge Presbyterian Church in Fort Lauderdale. That class's interaction with them convinced me that they should be revised for yet a fourth time into their present form for the larger Christian reading public. In this revision I followed the practice of footnoting the more technical material so as not to impede the student who desires simply to follow the flow of Luke's history of Paul without much interruption. This is not to suggest that the student should ignore the footnotes completely since many of them are informational and many contain significant bibliographical data for purposes of further research.

Readers should be aware that my original agenda has remained unchanged, however. They should know that, having spent with my family my first sabbatical on the mission field in South Korea and Japan and having led groups of seminary students on cross-cultural mission efforts to Jamaica, I wrote this book with the needs of mission agencies, missionaries, and missionary candidates in mind. It is my hope that it will become a 'staple' in college and seminary courses on Christian mission to provide students and mission candidates both with their biblical basis for becoming 'world Christians' and in the life of Paul their best human exemplar of what it means to be a 'world Christian' and a communicator of God's law-free gospel. It is my prayer that it will be used of God to help foster a resurgence of interest among students and lay readers to serve Christ in our time in a transnational and/or transcultural way and that many readers will actually be challenged, as together we follow Paul along the roads of the Roman provinces of Asia, Macedonia, Greece, Rome, and possibly even Spain, to join that honored band of men and women who through the centuries have heard their Master's summons 'to open their eyes and to look at the fields which are ripe for harvest' (John 4:35) and as a result have left their native lands, homes, families and all the other 'lesser things' of life to carry the gospel of the unsearchable riches of Christ to those who have never heard Paul's 'good news' that 'through Jesus the forgiveness of sins is proclaimed' and that 'through him everyone who believes is justified from everything [he] could not be justified from by the law of Moses' (Acts 13:38-39). If only one reader responds to Christ's summons to serve him in his cause as a result of reading this book my labors will not have been in vain. And I can assure him now that his life will become as enriched and as exciting (and possibly as painful) as Paul's became.

PART ONE

PAUL'S MISSIONARY LABOURS

Method of Presenting Paul's Missionary Journeys

In the course of following Paul from his conversion and call by Jesus Christ on the Damascus Road 'to carry [his] name before the Gentiles and their kings and before the people of Israel' (Acts 9:15) to the third milestone of the Ostian Way outside the city of Rome where he finished his earthly race as a martyr, we shall behold in Paul (1) a Jew, once a zealot in the strictest sect of Judaism, suddenly overwhelmed by divine grace and spiritually transformed, and thereby captured forever by the cause of Christ (Eph 3:7-8; 1 Tim 1:12-17); (2) a Jew who was convinced that Christ had 'set [him] apart for the gospel of God...to call people from among all the Gentiles to the obedience that comes from faith' (Rom 1:1, 5; Gal 1:15-16), (3) a Jew fired with a heavenly passion 'to be a minister of Christ Jesus to the Gentiles with the priestly duty of proclaiming the gospel of God, so that the Gentiles might become an offering acceptable to God, sanctified by the Holy Spirit' (Rom 15:16), indeed, (4) a Jew directed by the driving ambition—an ambition which he found outlined in Isaiah 52:15, a text descriptive of the Messiah's own *universalistic* vision: 'Those who were not told about him will see, and those who have not heard will understand' (Rom 15:21)—'to preach the gospel where Christ was not known, so that [he] would not be building on someone else's foundation' (Rom 15:20). Surely, when we study Paul, we study one of the greatest trophies, if not *the* greatest trophy, of divine grace the world has ever seen and the greatest pioneer missionary the church has ever known.

In this first section of our study, after we examine Paul's life as Saul the Pharisee and chief persecutor of the church in order better to understand who he was and why he felt compelled to do the things that he did, we will present Paul's five missionary journeys in the historical order in which he made them, highlighting and describing as we go the major cities where he conducted his ministry and noting the significant advances in his mission strategy when they occur. We will also treat in some detail the twists and turns that emerged in the relationship between the mother church in Jerusalem and the Gentile churches which were created by its mission to the nations through Paul's mission labors.

My Sources for Paul's Missionary Journeys

Assuming the historicity, accuracy and inspiration of Luke's Acts and Paul's letters, I will draw my description of Paul's journeys (and to a certain extent in Part One his missionary theology) primarily from these two biblical sources, integrating these two primary sources wherever it is possible to do so. Of course, while it is true that we will be reading in Paul's letters only one side of several historical/theological dialogues, it is also true, as all Paul scholars are more or less agreed, that by placing Paul's letters in their historical context and by detecting through careful exegesis the allusions in them to the other sides of the several dialogues, we will be able both to reconstruct, at least in broad outline, the dialogues themselves and thereby to discern the contours of his opponents' theologies against which he contends.

Where I deem it necessary, I will also draw upon the relevant ancient extra-biblical sources for their descriptions of the major cities, the geography and customs, and the political situations which existed within the provinces of the Roman Empire in which Paul conducted his missionary activity.

INTRODUCTION TO PAUL'S LIFE AND LETTERS

> I dreamed that, with a passionate complaint,
>   I wished me born amid God's deeds of might,
>   And envied those who saw the presence bright
> Of gifted Prophet and strong-hearted Saint,
> Whom my heart loves, and fancy strives to paint,
>   I turned, when straight a stranger met my sight,
>   Came as my guest, and did awhile untie
> His lot with mine, and lived without restraint.
> Courteous he was, and grave—so meek in mien,
>   It seemed untrue, and told a purpose weak:
>   Yet in the mood, he could with aptness speak,
> Or with stern force, or show of feelings keen,
>   Marking deep craft, methought, or hidden pride:
>   Then came a voice—'St. Paul is at thy side!'
>   —From *Lyra Apostolica*, John Henry Newman

The Importance of Paul and His Missionary Ministry

It is not overstating the case to assert that the Apostle Paul is the most influential Christian who ever lived. Every 'Paul scholar', sooner or later, expresses sincere admiration for the man and a deep appreciation of his unparalleled significance with respect to the theology and spread of the Christian faith. For example, J. Gresham Machen writes:

> The Christian movement...in 35 A.D....would have appeared to a superficial observer to be a Jewish sect. Thirty years later it was plainly a world religion. This establishment of Christianity as a world religion, to almost as great an extent as any great historical movement can be ascribed to one man, was the work of Paul.[1]

Geerhardus Vos avers that Paul's writings reveal 'the genius of the greatest constructive mind ever at work on the data of Christianity'.[2] Michael Grant declares:

---

1. J. Gresham Machen, *The Origin of Paul's Religion*, (reprint of 1925 edition; Grand Rapids: Eerdmans, n.d.), 7-8.
2. Geerhardus Vos, *The Pauline Eschatology* (Grand Rapids: Baker, 1979 reprint of 1930 edition), 149.

Paul is one of the most perpetually significant men who have ever lived. Without the spiritual earthquake that he brought about, Christianity would probably never have survived at all. Yet his importance also extends very widely beyond and right outside the religious field. For he has also exercised a gigantic influence, for generation after generation, upon non-religious events and ways of thinking—upon politics and sociology and war and philosophy and that whole intangible area in which the thought-processes of successive epochs become formed.

He has to be considered, therefore, not only as a religious figure of exceptional power, but as one of the outstanding makers of the history of mankind.[3]

F. F. Bruce asserts:

The spread of Christianity cannot be imagined apart from [Paul's] work ...he devoted all [the wealth of his inherited powers, natural abilities, and gifts of the Holy Spirit] to the task of Gentile evangelization; and, latecomer though he was among the Apostles, he 'worked harder than any of them, though [he added] it was not I, but the grace of God which is with me' (1 Cor. 15:10).[4]

James D. G. Dunn declares:

...within that [first] generation [of Christian theologians] it was [Paul] more than any other single person who ensured that the new movement stemming from Jesus would become a truly international and intellectually coherent religion. Paul has indeed been called the 'second founder of Christianity,' who has, compared with the first, 'exercised beyond all doubt the stronger...influence' [Wrede]. Even if that should be regarded as an overblown assessment of Paul's significance [and it should be, RLR] the fact remains that Paul's influence and writings have shaped Christianity as the writings/theology of no other single individual have...if theology is measured in terms of articulation of Christian belief, then Paul's letters laid a foundation for Christian theology which has never been rivaled or superseded.

Hence also the claim that he is the *greatest* Christian theologian of all time...Paul's status within the New Testament canon in itself gives Paul's theological writings a preeminence which overshadows all the Christian theologians who followed.[5]

---

3. Michael Grant, *Saint Paul* (New York: Charles Scribner's Sons, 1976), 1.
4. F. F. Bruce, *Commentary on the Book of the Acts* (Grand Rapids: Eerdmans, 1954), 196-97.
5. James D. G. Dunn, *The Theology of Paul the Apostle* (Grand Rapids: Eerdmans, 1998), 2-3.

Introduction to Paul's Life and Letters

Specifically with reference to the significance of Paul's mission labors, Martin Hengel, powerfully arguing that Paul was the first Christian theologian precisely because he was the first Christian missionary,[6] writes:

> ...the success of the earliest Christian mission...was unique in the ancient world...[Paul's] mission [was] an unprecedented happening, in terms both of the history of religion in antiquity and of later church history...With Paul, for the first time we find the specific aim of engaging in missionary activity throughout the world. [As a result, what he did] has remained unparalleled over the subsequent 1900 years.[7]

Finally, Robert Jewett observed in 1988 that

> the awareness is dawning in current scholarship that Paul should be understood not simply as a theologian and a writer of letters but as a self-supporting missionary actively engaged in cooperative projects with a number of groups and individuals.[8]

This book, based upon Luke's account of Paul's four missionary journeys in Acts, Paul's own account of his fifth and final missionary journey drawn from his Pastoral Letters, and his fourteen extant letters[9] which appear among the twenty-seven literary pieces of the New Testament will provide a study of the man, his missionary efforts, and his missionary theology. It is, of course, an understatement to say that his letters – as the Apostle himself – are an exceedingly important part of Christianity.

Paul's Missionary Letters

'In the whole range of literature there is nothing like St. Paul's letters. Other correspondence may be more voluminous, more elaborate, more studiously demonstrative. But none is so faithful a mirror of the writer' (J. B. Lightfoot). Concerning their genre, the Pauline letters are just that – highly personal letters written either to members of his mission

---

6. Martin Hengel, 'The Origins of the Christian Mission' in *Between Jesus and Paul: Studies in the Earliest History of Christianity* (London: SCM, 1983), 49-50.

7. Hengel, 'The Origins of the Christian Mission,' 48, 49, 52.

8. Robert Jewett, 'Paul, Phoebe, and the Spanish Mission' in *The Social World of Formative Christianity and Judaism. Essays in Tribute to H. C. Kee*, edited by J. Neusner, S. S. Frerichs, P. Borgen and R. Horsley (Philadelphia: Fortress, 1988), 142.

9. I side with those New Testament scholars who believe that Paul wrote the Epistle to the Hebrews.

teams or to the mission churches he had planted; and as personal letters, they reflect the style of the man and his times and circumstances. The following descriptions of his letters and their style by several highly knowledgeable scholars will help us grasp, in quick compass, something of what is in store for us as we study them.[10] About these letters Philip Schaff writes:

> They presuppose throughout the Gospel history, and often allude to the death and resurrection of Christ as the foundation of the church and the Christian hope. They were composed amidst incessant missionary labors and cares, under trial and persecution, some of them from prison, and yet they abound in joy and thanksgiving. They were mostly called forth by special emergencies, yet they suit all occasions. Tracts for the times, they are tracts for all times. Children of the fleeting moment, they contain truths of infinite moment. They compress more ideas in fewer words than any other writings.... They discuss the highest themes which can challenge an immortal mind—God, Christ, and the Spirit, sin and redemption, incarnation, atonement, regeneration, repentance, faith and good works, holy living and dying, the conversion of the world, the general judgment, eternal glory and bliss. And all this before humble little societies of poor, uncultured artisans, freemen and slaves. And yet they are of more real and general value to the church than all the systems of theology from Origen to Schleiermacher—yea, than all the confessions of faith. For eighteen hundred years they have nourished the faith of Christendom, and will continue to do so to the end of time.[11]

R. D. Shaw writes:

> Like true letters, those of St. Paul were occasional in their origin. He did not compose them as studies in theology, or as treatises on Christian doctrine which he desired to give to the world; even the Epistle to the Romans is only an apparent, not a real, exception. Events of moment to him and his converts called them into being. He was appealed to on some point of faith or conduct, and he replied. Or, he heard good news, or received tokens of affection, and he wrote to express his joy, to encourage, and to exhort. Again, he heard of the presence of teachers who calumniated him, denied his authority, and undermined the faith of his followers. This drew forth his bold definition of doctrine, his impassioned defences of the gospel, and his no less impassioned apologies for his own life.

---

10. For a brief but very informative treatment of methods, materials, and amanuenses employed in letter writing in antiquity see Ben Witherington III, *The Paul Quest: The Renewed Search for the Jew of Tarsus* (Downers Grove, Ill.: InterVarsity, 1998), 99-115.

11. Philip Schaff, *A History of the Christian Church* (New York: Charles Scribner's Sons, 1910), I, 741.

Introduction to Paul's Life and Letters

These things naturally affected the style in which the Epistles were composed. There never was a writer whose style more clearly reflected the mood and purpose of the hour. It completely reveals the man, and its rapid changes are just the lights and shadows flitting over his face. It indicates the pulses of his feeling, shows him quivering with nervous excitement and anxiety, or flashing with indignation, jubilant with Christian triumph, or calm with the hidden depths of Christian peace. It is not polished or careful as to form, rather the reverse; it not seldom labours under the burden of thought, becomes involved, digresses, goes off at a word, draws clause out of clause in telescopic fashion as one new idea suggests another, until the main purpose is almost forgotten, and there is either a violent turn to recover it, or an abrupt conclusion and a new start altogether. Sometimes the Apostle seems verily to wrestle with words, struggling to express some great idea that almost passes knowledge. [In his letters] 'there is a disproportion between thought and language, the thought straining the language until it cracks in the process —a shipwreck of grammar...as the sentences are whirled through the author's mind—a growth of words and thoughts out of and into each other often to the utter entanglement of the argument which is framed out of them' [Stanley]. Paul was also fond of expressing the most spiritual conceptions in poetic and concrete symbols; delighted, like a true Hebrew, in elaborate parallelisms and antitheses; loved to startle his readers with a paradox, or to confound his opponents with a dilemma. A born debater, he frequently uses the quick thrust of short, sharp sentences, the rapid fire of triumphant interrogation; spiritually minded, he rejoices to wind up a paragraph with an outburst of praise or prayer; and a child of feeling, he sometimes suffers the depression of the moment to display itself in passages that are sombre and heavy, without lilt or gleam.... Sometimes he wrote in peace and gladness, at other times under the keenest tension, when his thoughts were fire and his words were battles.... [In his epistles] we have to do with a genius so sensitive and versatile, that nice balancing of probabilities of authorship, and narrowing and fixing of dates, must never be made to depend too exclusively on our conceptions of what might or might not have been its product.

It is unlikely that the Apostle wrote any of the Epistles we possess entirely with his own hand. He made his mark or sign in them; as he says in doing so, 'In every Epistle so I write' [2 Thess 3:17]; but he seems usually to have dictated his message to a friend or amanuensis. This also left traces on the style. We feel we are all the time listening to a *speaker*—one whom we may imagine walking up and down his room, while the pen of the shorthand writer flies swiftly over the parchment to keep pace with the utterance. All the Epistles have this air of being spoken, reported, and passed on without much revisal. Hence the broken sentences, the occasional obscurity, the natural digressions, as well as the freedom and buoyancy by which they are so much distinguished.

We could scarcely have imagined a literary form less likely to be chosen to convey a great religious revelation to the world. Yet its advantages are obvious. How living it makes the page! How vivid, natural, and full of human interest! Such records do not seem handwritten, but heart-written: as Luther said, 'They are not dead words; they are living creatures, and have hands and feet.' Here, we perceive, is a man who has lived the great life and understands it; who believes and therefore speaks; who thinks, and says what he thinks; who is filled with the Spirit, and speaks as he is moved by the Holy Ghost.[12]

In the same vein Dean Alford may be quoted:

[With Paul's first Christian literary effort] commenced that invaluable series of letters in which, while every matter relating to the faith is determined once for all with demonstration of the Spirit and power, and every circumstance requiring counsel at the time, so handled as to furnish precepts for all time, the whole heart of this wonderful man is poured out and laid open. Sometimes he pleads, and reminds, and conjures, in the most earnest strain of fatherly love: sometimes, playfully rallies his converts on their vanities and infirmities: sometimes, with deep and bitter irony, concedes that he may refute, and praises where he means to blame. The course of the mountain torrent is not more majestic nor varied. We have the deep still pool, the often returning eddies, the intervals of calm and steady advance, the plunging and foaming rapids, and the thunder of the headlong cataract. By turns fervid and calm, argumentative and impassioned, he wields familiarly and irresistibly the varied weapons of which Providence has taught him the use. With the Jew he reasons by Scripture citation, with the Gentile by natural analogies: with both, by the testimony of conscience to the justice and holiness of God. Were not the Epistles of Paul among the most eminent of inspired writings, they would long ago have been ranked as the most wonderful of uninspired.[13]

Philip Schaff characterizes Paul's literary style this way:

Paul's style is manly, bold, heroic, aggressive, and warlike; yet at times tender, delicate, gentle, and winning. It is involved, irregular, and rugged, but always forcible and expressive, and not seldom rises to more than poetic beauty, as in the triumphant paean at the end of the eighth chapter of Romans, and in the ode on love (1 Cor. 13). His intense earnestness and overflowing fulness of ideas break through the ordinary rules of

---

12. R. D. Shaw, *The Pauline Epistles* (Edinburgh: T. & T. Clark, 1909), 7-10.
13. Dean Alford, *Edinburgh Review* (Jan-April 1853), 112.

grammar. His logic is on fire. He abounds in skilful arguments, bold antitheses, impetuous assaults, abrupt transitions, sudden turns, zigzag flashes, startling questions and exclamations. He is dialectical and argumentative; he likes logical particles, paradoxical phrases, and plays on words. He reasons from Scripture, from premises, from conclusions; he drives the opponent to the wall without mercy and reduces him *ad absurdum*, but without indulging in personalities. He is familiar with the sharp weapons of ridicule, irony, and sarcasm, but holds them in check and uses them rarely. He varies the argument by touching appeals to the heart and bursts of seraphic eloquence. He is never dry or dull, and never wastes words; he is brief, terse, and hits the nail on the head. His terseness makes him at times obscure.... His words are as many warriors marching on to victory and peace; they are like a mountain torrent rushing in foaming rapids over precipices, and then calmly flowing over green meadows, or like a thunderstorm ending in a refreshing shower and bright sunshine.

Paul created the vocabulary of scientific theology and put a profounder meaning into religious and moral terms than they ever had before. We cannot speak of sin, flesh, grace, mercy, peace, redemption, atonement, justification, glorification, church, faith, love, without bearing testimony to the ineffaceable effect which that greatest of Jewish rabbis and Christian teachers has had upon the language of Christendom.[14]

One more thing may be said here, and it is this: Without his realizing it when he wrote his missionary letters, Paul raised the Greek literary art form of letter writing to a level of universality which it had never enjoyed before. In this connection F. F. Bruce writes:

Of all the New Testament authors, Paul is the one who has stamped his own personality most unmistakably on his writings. It is especially for this reason that he has his secure place among the great letter-writers in world literature—not because he composed his letters with a careful eye to stylistic propriety and the approving verdict of a wider public than those for whom they were primarily intended, but because they express so spontaneously and therefore so eloquently his mind and his message. 'He is certainly one of the great figures in Greek literature,' said Gilbert Murray; and a greater Hellenist even than Murray, Ulrich von Wilamowitz-Moellendorff, described him as 'a classic of Hellenism'. Paul, he said, did not directly take over any of the elements of Greek education, yet he not only writes Greek but thinks Greek; without realizing it, he serves as the executor of Alexander the Great's testament by carrying the gospel to the Greeks.

14. Schaff, *History*, I, 753-54.

At last, at last, [he writes] once again someone speaks in Greek out of a fresh inward experience of life. That experience is his faith, which makes him sure of his hope. His glowing love embraces all mankind: to bring them salvation he joyfully sacrifices his own life, yet the fresh life of the soul springs up wherever he goes. He writes his letters as a substitute for his personal activity. This epistolary style is Paul, Paul himself and no other.

No mean tribute from a Hellenist of Hellenists to one who claimed to be a Hebrew of Hebrews![15]

In another place in the same work Bruce writes:

Something of Paul's native impetuousness is apparent in his epistolary style. His letters were regularly dictated to an assistant. At times the torrent of his thought rushes forward so swiftly that it outstrips the flow of his words, and his words have to leap over a gap now and then so as to catch up on his thought. How the scribe managed to keep up with his words we can only surmise. Time and again Paul starts a sentence that never reaches a grammatical end, for before he is well launched on it a new thought strikes him and he turns aside to deal with that. When he comes back on to the main track, the original start of the sentence has been forgotten. All this means that Paul is not the smoothest of authors, or the easiest to follow, but it does give us an unmistakable impression of the man himself. He has something worth saying, and in saying it he communicates something of himself; there is nothing artificial or merely conventional about the way he says it. And what he has to say is so important – for readers of the twentieth century as much as for those of the first – that the effort to understand him is abundantly rewarding.[16]

Paul's letters to his aides and young churches, then, whose theological articulations at all points emerged from within the context of his mission labors, are extremely personal, and afford a very complete revelation of their author. Without realizing it perhaps, by them he also gave the Christian church the theology which has dominated all of its thought forms to this day, in both its Christology and its soteriology, in both its ecclesiology and its eschatology. He was a man of God in the truest sense—perhaps the most gifted, the most loyal, the most heroic, certainly the hardest working man that Christ ever sent forth to labor for him in the whitened harvest fields

---

15. F. F. Bruce, *Paul, Apostle of the Heart Set Free* (Grand Rapids: Eerdmans, 1996 reprint of the 1977 edition), 15-16.
16. Bruce, *Paul*, 456-57.

of the world. Paul was a man 'Christ-possessed', a man 'intoxicated with Christ', who had 'resolved to know nothing among men but Jesus Christ and him crucified' (1 Cor 2:2); who declared that 'to [him], to live is Christ' (Phil 1:21); who declared that Christ's headship over the church and his status as the 'firstborn from among the dead' required that 'in everything he should have the preeminence' (Col 1:18); who gloried only in Christ's cross work (Gal 6:14); who 'considered whatever was to his profit [before his conversion] as "loss" [ζημία] for the sake of Christ'—what is more, who considered everything as 'loss' compared to the surpassing greatness of knowing Christ Jesus his Lord, for whose sake, he said, 'I have suffered loss of [ἐζημιώθην] all things [apparently his parents had disinherited him; all his old teachers and friends had disowned him]. I consider them "dung" [σκύβαλον] that I may gain Christ and be found in him, not having a righteousness of my own that comes through the Law, but that which is through faith in Christ—the righteousness that comes from God and is by faith' (Phil 3:7-9); who said, 'One thing I do: Forgetting what is behind, and straining toward what is ahead, I press on toward the goal to win the prize for which God has called me heavenward in Christ Jesus' (3:13-14); and who testified: 'I consider my life worth nothing to me, if only I may finish the race and complete the task the Lord Jesus has given me—the task of testifying to the gospel of God's grace' (Acts 20:24). Paul is saying in this last verse that self-preservation did not rank high on his list of earthly priorities; his highest priority was to be obedient to his Lord and his gospel of sovereign grace. Quite evidently, all of the native gifts, worldly learning, physical and mental energies, tireless zeal, personal genius, and unflagging persistence which he had directed earlier to the elevation and spread of the 'traditions' of Pharisaic Judaism,[17] he now consecrated to a new end—to serve Jesus Christ his Lord and to declare to the entire then-known world the fulness of the blessing of the gospel of Christ.

The scholarly commendations above from a later age should not obscure the fact, however, that Paul in his own day

---

17. On the basis of Galatians 5:11 ('if I still preach circumcision'), many authorities believe that before his conversion Paul had involved himself in the Pharisaic mission effort to bring Gentiles into obedience to the law. Jesus made mention of this mission effort in his denunciation of the Pharisees when he said: 'Woe to you, teachers of the law and Pharisees, you hypocrites! You travel over land and sea to win a single convert, and when he becomes one, you make him twice as much a son of hell as you are' (Matt 23:15).

was one of the most hated men in the ancient world; and not without reason. It was natural for Jews to think of him as a traitor. He had betrayed their Law and therewith their national identity; he seemed to have renounced the natural responsibility that he owed his fellow-countrymen by constituting himself an 'apostle to the Gentiles'. Many even of the Jews who had become Christians thought he had given away too much in doing this: if Gentiles were to be admitted to the people of God they should join the people in the proper way. But if Paul was a bad Jew neither was he a proper Gentile. In becoming a Christian he had not ceased to think of pagan religions as Jews did. The pagans had their many gods and many lords, but 'for us there is one God, the Father, from whom come all things and to whom our own being leads, and one Lord Jesus Christ, through whom all things, including ourselves, come into being' (1 Cor. 8:6). Small wonder, to Paul, that pagan idolatry led to the horrors of pagan immorality (Rom 1:24-31); and small wonder that he was not able—and indeed never attempted—to make himself universally popular.

[Accordingly,] diverse attitudes to Paul have persisted through the ages, though in varying proportions. He has been hated and loved, understood and misunderstood, sometimes more hated, not very often more loved....

...The Pauline literature is shot through with controversy....it [is] apparent [from his letters] that, though he did not seek it, he was unable to avoid controversy. It was in controversy rather than in any other context that his theology was shaped and developed....[18]

His letters are a record of the life and development of the early church, and mirror for us many aspects of the conflicts which the church in *every* age must endure. They present us with the doubts, the fears, the failures, the errors, the joys, the hopes, the aspirations, the achievements, and the heroic endurance of his converts, their ideals that spurred them, the questions that troubled them, the environments that antagonized them, and the pulls of this age that tempted them.

Furthermore, his letters are a noble testimony to the Lord Jesus Christ whom he worshiped as God and served as Lord. They presuppose that unique Life about which the Gospels would later inform us, elucidate certain divine characteristics of that Life on a grander scale than anywhere else in Christian literature (see, for example, Col 1:15-19; Phil 2:6-11), and illustrate the marvellous

---

18. C.K. Barrett, *Paul: An Introduction to His Thought* (Louisville, Kentucky: Westminster/John Knox, 1994), 1-2, 6, 20.

Introduction to Paul's Life and Letters 27

power that had begun to flow from that Life through 'earthen vessels' into the world. Of course, it is true that there are many things that we would never know about Jesus if we had only Paul's letters as the sources of our information about him. For example, we would not know that Jesus had been born of a virgin, had been baptized by John, had been tempted of Satan, had carried on a ministry in Galilee, had taught in parables, had healed the sick and performed other signs, or had been transfigured. In fact, we would not even learn from Paul's letters what events led up to Jesus' crucifixion. Our knowledge about Christ would be restricted rather narrowly to his messianic investiture as the Seed of David, his sinless obedience to his Father, and to his crucifixion, death, burial, and resurrection.[19] But while they do not tell us much about Christ's earthly life, it is equally true that Paul's letters nevertheless are 'our earliest literary authority for the historical Jesus'.[20] And his letters, we must also never forget, while reflecting the language and style of the man, were at the same time the words of a Spirit-inspired apostle of Christ and therefore the Word of God for his church (1 Thess 2:13; 5:27; 2 Thess 2:15; 1 Cor 2:13; Col 4:16; 2 Tim 3:16-17; 2 Pet 3:15-16).

Our Approach in This Study of Paul

Precisely because all this is so—because so much of this 'Christ-intoxicated man' and the times and circumstances engaging him as he labored to plant churches and then dictated his letters to them lie behind the printed words which we find in our Bible—it would be the worst kind of mistake to proceed to a study of his letters in the artificial order in which they appear in our Bible. We can never understand them unless we pay respect to the times and circumstances out of which they sprang. Clearly, then, the best way to study them is

---

19. The fact that Paul does not provide his readers with minute details about Jesus' life and teaching has provided many critical scholars the ground to conclude that Paul was not interested in the historical Jesus and knew little about him, and therefore that Paul became more the founder of Christianity as we know it than a faithful follower of Jesus. We will argue in this study that Paul was a true apostle of Jesus Christ and accordingly that what he taught was in fact Jesus' gospel. The interested reader may also want to consult David Wenham's *Paul: Follower of Jesus or Founder of Christianity?* (Grand Rapids: Eerdmans, 1995), which in my opinion successfully argues that Paul was the former of these alternatives and defends him from the charge that he made Christianity into a religion different from the one intended by Jesus.

20. Bruce, *Paul*, 95; see, for example, Romans 1:3; 15:3; Galatians 3:16; 4:4; 1 Corinthians 11:23-25; 15:4-8; 2 Corinthians 10:1; Philippians 2:5-7; 1 Thessalonians 2:15.

to honor their historical order, beginning with none of them before us and gratefully[21] and humbly receiving each of them as they come from his pen in the order in which he dictated them, and to consider their canonicity only after we have them all before us.

This will necessitate then that we relate them, as carefully and as accurately as modern scholarship will allow, to his entire life—to his conversion and early years as an evangelist, to his missionary journeys, to his trip to Rome, to his first Roman imprisonment and release, to his ministry after his release, and finally to his second Roman imprisonment. This incarceration eventually brought him to that site near the third milestone on the Ostian Way where he laid down his life for the Faith which he steadfastly kept to the end, to that place where today stands not far away a basilica in which two ancient slabs bear the simple engraving: 'To Paul, Apostle and Martyr,' to which Paul himself would doubtless have insisted on adding: 'But to God be the glory forever and ever. Amen.'

The Relationship of Paul's Letters to Luke's Acts and An Indication of their Place and Time of Writing

Since the order of the Pauline letters is artificially arranged in our English Bible according (generally) to length, from longest to shortest, before we consider the Pauline material in detail, we will provide the following basic historical categories of his fourteen letters:

I. THE 'PEDESTRIAN [or "PERIPATETIC"] LETTERS' (those related to his first three missionary journeys)

A. Galatians – written from Antioch in Syria (Acts 11:29; 12:25; 14:26-28; see Gal 2:1-10) around A.D. 48 or 49.
Note: Paul's *first* letter is to be related to his *first* missionary journey [Acts 13:4–14:26].

B. 1 Thessalonians – written from Corinth (Acts 17:16; 18:1, 5-8; see 1 Thess 1:1; 3:1, 2, 6) around A.D. 50-51.

---

21. Why do I say 'gratefully' receive them one by one? Because we will have more—much more—of Paul's mind at the end of this study than many of the first Gentile Christians of the first century ever had, who, after Paul had left their area, maybe had access to the Old Testament in its Septuagint form and to some scanty oral traditions about Jesus, but who would never possess more than maybe one or two (if any) of his letters at the most (The Corinthian Christians were indeed blessed; they received four letters from him!), not to mention no Gospels, no other New Testament epistles, not even the book of Acts! Try to imagine how

Introduction to Paul's Life and Letters 29

> 2 Thessalonians – written from Corinth (Acts 18:11 [see 20:1-2]; 2 Thess 1:1), some weeks after the first letter.
>
> Note: These two letters are to be related to his *second* missionary journey [Acts 15:36–18:22]; they are sometimes called the 'eschatological letters' or 'early letters'.

C. 1 Corinthians – written from Ephesus (Acts 19:1, 10 [see also 19:20-21; 20:1-2]; 1 Cor 16:5, 8, 10) around A.D. 55-56.

> 2 Corinthians – Macedonia (Acts 20:1-2; see 2 Cor 2:12, 13; 8:6; 12:18 [see also 7:5-7, 13, 14]) around A.D. 55-56.
>
> Romans – written from Corinth (Acts 18:18; 20: 3, 16; see Rom 15:25, 26; 16:1) around A.D. 57.
>
> Note: These *three* letters are to be related to his *third* missionary journey [Acts 18:23-21:15]; they, together with Galatians, are sometimes called the 'doctrinal letters', 'soteriological letters', or 'major letters'.

II. THE 'PRISON LETTERS', all written during Paul's two-year imprisonment in Rome between A.D. 60 and early 62, Acts 28:31 (some authorities have proposed Caesarea as the site of origin for these 'prison letters', Acts 24:27; but I do not agree).

A. Colossians (Col 4:7-10).

B. Philemon (vv. 1, 9, 10, 13, 24; see Col 4:7-10, 14, 17; Eph 6:21).

C. Ephesians (3:1; 4:1; 6:20).

D. Philippians (1:7, 13, 16, 25; 2:24; 4:22).

> Note: These *four* letters, all written in Rome, are to be related to Paul's '*fourth* missionary journey' [Acts 23:23–28:31]; they are sometimes called the 'Christological letters'.

III. THE 'PASTORAL LETTERS' AND THE LETTER TO THE HEBREWS, written after Paul's release from his first imprisonment in Rome (Acts 28:30) sometime between A.D. 63-65 during both his 'fifth missionary journey' and his second Roman imprisonment, which release, missionary journey, and imprisonment go beyond the history recorded in Acts which concludes with Paul's first imprisonment in

---

difficult it would be to understand Paul's letters, even if you had all of them, if you did not have the historical framework of Luke's Acts within which to place them. For years they were completely dependent on the exalted Christ to give to his church living apostles (who would periodically visit and nurture them), prophets and glossolalists (with, of course, their translators), evangelists, and pastor/teachers (and the fellowship of one another, Acts 2:42).

Rome. The 'Pastoral Letters' are sometimes called the 'ecclesiological letters'.

A. 1 Timothy – written from 'somewhere in Macedonia' to Timothy in Ephesus (1 Tim 1:3).

B. Titus – written from 'somewhere in Macedonia' to Titus on Crete (Titus 1:5).

C. Hebrews – written probably during Paul's second Roman imprisonment (Heb 13:24) before his martyrdom in A.D. 65.

D. 2 Timothy – from Rome to Timothy in Ephesus just before his martyrdom in A.D. 65 (2 Tim 1:16-18; 4:18-19).

Of course, there are other letters in the New Testament in additiion to the ones written by Paul,[22] namely, the so-called General Epistles, which might be better termed the 'Jewish Epistles'. For when one studies James, 1 Peter, and most likely 2 Peter and Jude as well, one will soon become aware that he is looking through literary 'windows' at predominantly Jewish Christianity with the peculiar problems that Jewish Christians faced in the first century. In short, these 'general letters' provide a window for observing Jewish Christianity of the first century in a way that Paul's travels and letters simply cannot afford us, and our knowledge of the total picture of first-century Christianity would be somewhat skewed if we did not have the 'General Epistles'. But when one studies Paul's letters at any length, he will become aware that he is looking through literary 'windows' at predominantly Gentile mission churches (these churches, of course, had Jews in them) which Paul as the 'apostle to the Gentiles' (Gal 2:7-8; Rom 11:13) had founded and which demanded letters which treated peculiarly 'Gentile' concerns. The one exception here is, of course, his letter to the Jewish church in Jerusalem.

So let us begin *our* journey! In the following ten chapters we have provided an overview of this great pioneer missionary's life and ministry, relating as accurately as we can his letters to Luke's history of his mission labors. Then in Chapter Twelve we have addressed the issue of the canonical status of Paul's letters.

---

22. We know that Paul wrote other letters in addition to the ones just mentioned (see 1 Cor 5:9; Col 4:16).

CHAPTER TWO

LUKE'S ACTS
The Second Volume of Luke's 'History of Christian Origins'

Since Luke's Acts is the church's only (at times) eye-witness historical overview of the missionary travels and ministry of the Apostle Paul (7:58; 8:1a, 3; 9:1ff.) it is necessary that we say something about this important work at the outset of our study of Paul. The first thing that must be underscored is that Luke's Acts is a portion of Holy Scripture and is therefore inerrant and trustworthy in what it records concerning Paul's ministry. In 1 Timothy 5:18 Paul places Luke's Gospel within the venue of 'the Scripture' (ἡ γραφή) and altogether on a par with Deuteronomy. This suggests that Luke's Acts – the second volume of Luke's history of Christian origins – which originally circulated together with his Gospel until the four canonical Gospels were gathered together into a separate collection, thereby separating Acts away from Luke's Gospel, is 'Scripture' as well. And about such 'Scripture' Paul later stated that it 'is God-breathed [θεόπνευστος] and is useful for teaching, rebuking, correcting, and training in righteousness' (2 Tim 3:16).

Its Title

Though Luke's second volume has been known as 'The Acts of the Apostles' since the late second century, I sincerely doubt that Luke himself would have named it so. He refers to it, by the implication in his use of the numerical adjective 'first' (πρῶτον) in Acts 1:1, simply as a 'word' (λόγον), that is, an 'account'; see also Luke's use of διήγησις, 'narrative', in Luke 1:1).[1] F. F. Bruce says the title gives

---

1. Many suggestions have been offered regarding the literary genre of Luke's Acts: ancient historiography (H. J. Cadbury), historical novel, that is, historical fiction (R. I. Pervo), biographical 'succession narrative' on the analogy of Diogenes Laertius's *Lives of the Philosophers* (C. H. Talbert), 'general history' (D. E. Aune), 'scientific treatise' on the analogy of Greek technical and professional writing on medicine, mathematics, and engineering (L. C. A. Alexander), Hellenistic historiography (G. L. Sterling), historical monograph, political history, etc. After all is said and done, I believe Luke's descriptive word (διήγησις), intending a long narrative account of many events, places his Gospel and Acts within the genre of ancient apologetic historiography, that is, historiography written for an apologetic purpose.

an 'exaggerated impression'.[2] Martin Franzmann observes that it is an 'inaccurate'[3] description of the content for the following reasons:

A. Of the apostles only Peter ('the apostle to the circumcision') and Paul ('the apostle to the Gentiles') are major figures in Acts (even so Acts speaks of Paul as an 'apostle' only twice, 14:4, 14). The Apostle John appears a few times (1:13; 3:1-4:23; 8:14; 12:2) and then disappears forever, while the Apostle James, son of Zebedee, appears only as one who was present in the upper room on the Day of Pentecost and as a martyr (1:13; 12:2).

B. Men who are not apostles (Stephen, Philip, Barnabas, Silas, Agabus) play semi-major roles in the narrative.

C. The very term 'apostle', as defined by Jesus and as used by the apostles themselves, should have excluded such a title. For the apostle by definition is nothing of himself and everything only by virtue of the commission given him by his Lord. This book is not a record of human greatness; it is an account of the geographic spread and growth of the divine Word, telling the story of the men involved only because and in so far as men are instrumental in the spread of that divine Word.

If it is a book of 'acts' at all, I think Luke intended his readers to see it as a record of the missionary activity and words of the exalted Christ through the creative power of his Spirit and his Word (1:1). Where his Word is spoken, even though it should be by 'defeated' men in prison, there Christ the King, the Lord of the Church, is gathering his people, the church. Note Luke's *six summarizing statements* in the work itself (6:7; 9:31; 12:24; 16:5; 19:20; 28:31), each concluding what seems to be its preceding 'panel' of material:[4]

In the case of Luke/Acts, Luke's purpose was to trace and defend, in the words of Joel B. Green, 'the unfolding of the divine purpose, from Israel to the life and ministry of Jesus to the early church with the inclusion of Gentile believers as full participants, and thus to legitimate the Christian movement of which Luke himself was a part' ('Acts of the Apostles' in *Dictionary of the Later New Testament & Its Development*, edited by Ralph P. Martin and Peter H. Davids [Downers Grove, Ill.: InterVarsity, 1997], 8).

2. F. F. Bruce, *The Book of the Acts* (Revised edition; The New International Commentary on the New Testament; Grand Rapids: Eerdmans, 1988), 5.

3. Martin Franzmann, *The Word of the Lord Grows* (St. Louis: Concordia, 1961), 204.

4. I am indebted for this insight, as well as for many others in this book, to Martin Franzmann, under whom I studied at Concordia Seminary, St. Louis, Missouri.

A. 1:1–6:7: The Word creates a church in Jerusalem. (6:7: 'So the word of God spread. The number of disciples in Jerusalem increased rapidly, and a large number of priests became obedient to the faith.')

B. 6:8–9:31: The Word triumphs over all persecution, going to Samaria and eventually to Damascus, converting there the archfoe of the church. (9:31: 'Then the church throughout Judea, Galilee and Samaria enjoyed a time of peace. It was strengthened; and encouraged by the Holy Spirit, it grew in numbers, living in the fear of the Lord.')

C. 9:32–12:24: The Word becomes a light to the Gentiles, with Peter converting Cornelius, and Barnabas and Saul building a strong Gentile church in Syrian Antioch. Christ's servant Peter is delivered from his would-be destroyer. (12:24: 'But the word of God continued to increase and spread.')

D. 12:25–16:5: The Word unites Jew and Gentile in one, liberated church, Paul conducting his first missionary journey, and the controversy with the Judaizers being resolved at the Jerusalem Council. (16:5: 'So the churches were strengthened in the faith and grew daily in number.')

E. 16:6–19:20: The Word goes forth both in conflict and in triumph to Asia, Macedonia, and Achaia (Paul's second and third missionary journeys). (19:20: 'In this way the word of the Lord spread widely and grew in power.')

F. 19:21–28:31: The Word shows its power in human weakness: Paul the prisoner witnessing 'before rulers and authorities' (Luke 12:11) and bringing his gospel to Rome itself, indeed, into the very household of Caesar (Phil 4:22). (28:31: 'Boldly and without hindrance he preached [in Rome] the kingdom of God and taught about the Lord Jesus Christ.')

Its Purpose

Although Acts shows that Paul's main opposition throughout his missionary endeavors came from the Jewish authorities[5] and that the

---

5. According to Luke's Acts it was the Jewish authorities primarily that fomented the disturbances, discord, and riots that broke out when Jews and Gentile God-fearers responded to the gospel that Paul preached in Damascus, 9:23-24; in Jerusalem, 9:29; in Pisidian Antioch, 13:45, 50; in Iconium, 14:2; in Lystra, 14:19; in Thessalonica, 17:5; in Berea, 17:13; in

Roman authorities throughout his ministry exonerated him at every turn of being a political revolutionary or an enemy of Rome,[6] both of which facts would have been of interest to any fair tribunal in Rome, I do not think that Luke wrote Acts originally and primarily as part of a legal defense for Paul at his trial in Rome. As Bruce notes: '...there is much in Acts...that would have been quite irrelevant forensically— whether it be...the detailed account of Paul's voyage and shipwreck or...the pervasive emphasis on the dominant role of the Holy Spirit in the expansion of the gospel.'[7]

Though Acts has also often been characterized as such, it was not intended either to be primarily a history of the early church or a history of early Christian missions, for while it does indeed recount history, indeed, extremely helpful history for understanding Paul's letters, it is inadequate as a history of either. In fact, Acts makes no

---

Corinth, 18:6, 12-13; 20:3; 21:11; and again in Jerusalem, 21:27; and it was the Sanhedrin that prosecuted Paul before Felix (24:1-9) and Festus (25:2-3, 7) in Caesarea. On only two occasions in Acts (at Philippi, 16:16-21, and at Ephesus, 19:23-27) did hostilities come to Paul's mission team from Gentiles, and on both occasions, as Bruce notes, 'the reason was a real or imagined threat to property interests' (*The Book of the Acts*, 9, fn 31).

In light of Israel's historical experience and Judaism's understanding of the law's purpose, first-century Palestinian and Hellenistic Judaism's concern for strict observance of the law and its hostility toward Paul's gospel is understandable. For Old Testament history had made it abundantly clear that Israel's worship of Baal, Moloch, and Astarte in particular and its covenant disobedience in general had brought on the Assyrian and Babylonian exiles (Amos 5:26-27); see Acts 7:43). And the books of Ezra (see chaps. 9–10, Nehemiah (see chaps. 8–10, 13), and Malachi (see 4:4-6) had made it equally clear that the first leaders of the Second Jewish Commonwealth and Second Temple Judaism had resolved that they would never again permit the Jewish people to become idolatrous and unfaithful to the law with impunity. Hence when Paul came to synagogues of the Diaspora and began to declare that temple and law, specifically the laws concerning circumcision, dietary laws, and seventh-day Sabbath-keeping, were not essential to covenant faithfulness, it is understandable that the synagogue leaders became alarmed and viewed Paul's teachings as heresy and blasphemy.

6. Throughout Luke's portrayal of Paul's activities in Acts he brings forward a variety of both Roman and Jewish officials who either show good will toward Paul or admit that no basis existed for the accusations Paul's Jewish adversaries brought against him: at Paphos in Cyprus the Roman proconsul Sergius Paulus accepted his message (13:6-12); at Philippi the chief magistrates of the city apologized for illegally beating Paul and Silas (16:37-39); at Corinth Gallio, the proconsul of Asia, dismissed the charges brought by the Jewish authorities against Paul (18:12-17); at Ephesus the Asiarchs, leading citizens of the province of Asia, befriended Paul and the chief executive officer of the city absolved him before the mob of the charge of public sacrilege (19:31, 35-41); in Palestine Felix and Festus, both Roman procurators, in succession found him innocent of the crimes of which the Sanhedrin accused him (24:22-23; 25:1-12, 24-25); Herod Agrippa II and his sister Bernice agreed with Festus that Paul had done nothing deserving death or imprisonment (26:30-32); and in Rome, though under constant surveillance, Paul was permitted to carry on his missionary activities for two years without hindrance (28:30-31).

7. F. F. Bruce, *The Book of the Acts*, 12-13.

mention of and shows no express awareness of the existence of any of Paul's letters,[8] ignores a trip that Paul made from Ephesus to Corinth, and concludes his 'account' with Paul's first imprisonment, saying nothing about his 'fifth missionary journey', his second imprisonment and his martyrdom.

I would urge that its primary purpose was to provide a certain 'most excellent Theophilus' ('dear to God') a kerygmatic (that is, proclamatory) witness to the ever-continuing, ever-advancing (see Luke's 'that which Jesus *began* to do and teach', Acts 1:1) impact of the Word of the risen Christ, Lord of the church, upon the alien world. As such, it is also a continuation of the story of the triumphant Christ of Luke's Gospel (1:1), vividly displaying the ongoing conquest of his Word and his works in the Gentile world, with the Kingdom of God finally penetrating Rome, the very capital of the empire (Acts 28:16), and indeed, as we already observed, into the Roman Caesar's very household (Phil 4:22). For Luke, the full significance of the central happenings at Jerusalem was not worked out in history until Paul preached in Rome. But once his gospel had reached Rome Luke at last felt at liberty to lay down his pen, the gospel – penetrating as it did into Caesar's very household – having in type triumphed over *all* the empires of this world.[9]

Its Record of the Primitive *Kerygma*

Referring to Acts as we just did as a '*kerygmatic* [proclamatory] witness', a word should be said about its *kerygma* (Gr. 'proclamation'). Acts gives to us samples of early Christian evangelistic preaching to the non-Christian world. The New Testament word for this particular activity is *kerygma* (κήρυγμα). By *kerygma* (over against

---

8. Although Acts makes no mention of Paul writing any letters to his churches, it is possible, because Luke almost certainly knew of at least some of Paul's letters, that he may have used them in writing Acts as one of his sources for his historical reconstruction of Paul's travels and activities. Of course, he was himself also actually present at times on some of Paul's journeys (see his three 'we' passages, Acts 16:10-17; 20:5-21:18; 27:1-28:16) and had ample opportunity to talk to Paul about his mission activities. See Jacques Dupont, *The Sources of Acts*, translated by K. Pond (London: Darton, Longman & Todd, 1964).

9. See Joel B. Green, 'Acts of the Apostles' in *Dictionary of the Later New Testament & Its Development*, 16-17, for an excellent overview of recent proposals for Luke's purpose in writing Acts. Green himself proposes that Luke's purpose in Luke/Acts was 'to strengthen the Christian movement in the face of opposition by ensuring them in their interpretation and experience of the redemptive purpose of God and by calling them to continued faithfulness and witness in God's salvific project' (17).

didache, διδαχή) I have reference to the content of the primitive gospel, specifically the components of the message of God's mighty redemptive act in Christ in which he calls people to the decision of repentance and faith and to membership in the community of faith, that is, in the church. C. H. Dodd writes:

> The New Testament writers draw a clear distinction between preaching and teaching.... Teaching (*didaskein*) is in a large majority of cases ethical instruction.... Preaching [*kerussein*], on the other hand, is the public proclamation of Christianity to the non-Christian world.... Much of our preaching in the Church at the present day would not have been recognized by the early Christians as *kerygma*. It is teaching, or exhortation (*paraklesis*), or it is what they called *homilia*, that is, the more or less informal discussion of various aspects of Christian life and thought, addressed to a congregation already established in the faith.... While the Church was concerned to hand on the teaching of the Lord, it was not by this that it made converts. It was by *kerygma*, says Paul, not by *didache*, that it pleased God to save men.[10]

What was the content of this primitive *kerygma*? From his analyses of the several sermons recorded in Acts Dodd suggests that the following were the main components of the apostolic *kerygma*:

A. The Age of Fulfillment has come (see Mark 1:15a). The *kerygma* connects the events of Jesus' life and ministry to the history of Israel as the climax of God's redemptive activity. (This is the truth element in C. H. Dodd's concept of the 'realized eschatology' of the New Testament.)

B. This 'realized eschatology' has occurred in the ministry, death, and resurrection of Jesus (see Mark 1:15b).

C. Jesus has been exalted to the right hand of God as Lord and Judge.

For other significant discussions of Luke's purpose in writing Acts, see C. K. Barrett, *The Acts of the Apostles* (2 vols.; International Critical Commentary; Edinburgh: T. & T. Clark, 1994); C. J. Hemer, *The Book of Acts in the Setting of Hellenistic History*, edited by C. H. Gempf (Wissenschaftliche Untersuchungen zum Neuen Testament 49; Tubingen: J. C. B. Mohr, 1989); I. Howard Marshall, *The Acts of the Apostles* (Tyndale New Testament Commentary; Grand Rapids: Eerdmans, 1980); Martin Hengel, *Acts and the History of Earliest Christianity* (Philadelphia: Fortress, 1979).

10. C. H. Dodd, *The Apostolic Preaching and Its Developments* (New York: Harper & Row, 1964), 7-8.

D. The Holy Spirit in the church is the sign of Christ's present exaltation and glory.

E. The Messianic Age will reach its consummation in the return of Christ.

F. The summons of men to repentance, and the offer of forgiveness, the Spirit, and salvation (the life of the Age to Come) to all who enter the elect community (see Mark 1:15c).

We have only to analyze for ourselves the sample sermons of Peter and Paul in Acts and the epistles to discern these elements and the emphases of the primitive gospel as it was proclaimed by the early church. In doing so, we may better discern (1) whether our own evangelistic preaching today includes the content that it should, and (2) why, perhaps, our evangelistic efforts are not as effective as they might be.

A. Peter's preaching

1. Acts 2:14-39 (to the Jews gathered in Jerusalem). The elements here are the following:

> The Scripture has been fulfilled (16-21, 25-28);
> God has borne witness to Christ's messiahship by performing miracles, wonders, and signs through him (22);
> Christ is of the seed of David (30);
> By divine design the Jews crucified their Messiah (23);
> But God has raised him from the dead (24, 32);
> We apostles are witnesses to Christ's resurrection (32);
> God has exalted him by making him both Lord and Messiah (34-36);
> Christ has certified his own lordship by pouring forth God's Spirit (33);
> Repent and believe the gospel for the forgiveness of your sins (38).

2. Acts 3:13-26 (to the Jews of Jerusalem). The elements here are the following:

> The God of Israel has glorified his servant Jesus (13a);
> You Jews handed God's servant over to be killed, you disowned him before Pilate, you disowned the holy and righteous One; and you killed the author of life (13b-14);

But God has raised him from the dead (15b, 26);
We apostles are witnesses of his resurrection (15c);
Christ has also certified this fact by healing this lame man (16);
The Scripture has been fulfilled (21-24);
God has exalted Jesus by taking him to heaven where he will remain until the time comes for God to restore all things, as he promised long ago in the prophets (21);
Therefore, repent and turn to God, for God has sent him first to you (26), that your sins may be wiped out (19, 26).

3. Acts 4:10-12 (to the Sanhedrin and everyone else in Israel). The elements here are the following:

You rulers and elders in Israel have crucified Jesus of Nazareth, the Christ (10);
But God has raised him from the dead (10);
We apostles are witnesses of his resurrection (20);
Christ has also certified this fact by healing this lame man (10);
The Scriptures have been fulfilled (11);
God has exalted him by making him – the rejected Stone – the Capstone of the corner (11);
Therefore, he is the only Savior of men (12).

4. Acts 5:30-32 (to the Sanhedrin). The elements here are as follows:

You killed Jesus by hanging him on a tree (30b);
But the God of Israel raised him from the dead (30a);
God has exalted him to his own right hand as Prince and Savior that he might give repentance and forgiveness to Israel (31)
We apostles are witnesses of these things, and so is the Holy Spirit who is given to those who obey him (32).

5. Acts 10:36-43 (to Cornelius, a 'God-fearer', and his household). The elements here are as follows:

God has sent a message of the good news of peace to Israel through Jesus Christ (36);
God anointed Jesus of Nazareth with the Holy Spirit and power, who then went around doing good and healing all who were under the power of the devil because God was with him (38);
We apostles are witnesses of everything he did (39a);
The Jews killed him by hanging him on a tree (39b);

But God raised him from the dead on the third day and caused him to be seen (40);

We apostles are witnesses of Christ's resurrection (41);

God has exalted him as Lord of all (36);

God has commanded us to preach and to testify that God has appointed Jesus Christ to be the Judge of the living and the dead (42);

The Scriptures have been fulfilled (43a);

Therefore, everyone who believes in him receives the forgiveness of sins through his name (43b).

B. Paul's preaching

1. Acts 13:17-41 (to the Jews and 'God-fearers' of Pisidian Antioch). The elements here are as follows:

God has sent to Israel the good news of the message of salvation (26, 32);

God has brought to Israel the Savior Jesus, as he promised our fathers (23, 32);

Jesus is of the seed of David (23, 34);

The rulers of Israel condemned him and in their doing so the Scriptures were fulfilled (27, 29);

The rulers of Israel crucified him and laid him in a tomb (29);

But God raised him from the dead (30), and in doing so fulfilled Psalm 2, Psalm 16, and Isaiah 55:3 (33-37);

For many days after his resurrection his apostles saw him, from Galilee to Jerusalem (31);

His apostles are now his witnesses (31);

Therefore, everyone who believes in Jesus receives the forgiveness of sins and is justified from everything one could not be justified from by the law of Moses (38-39) (note here Paul's proclamation of the doctrine of justification by faith alone in Christ alone);

Take care that the judgment for unbelief predicted by the prophets does not happen to you (40-42).

2. Acts 17:22-31 (to Epicurean and Stoic philosophers at the Areopagus). Paul begins his message by finding a point of contact with these philosophers – the altar erected 'to an unknown God'; for them an act of religious devotion, for Paul an act by their own admission of religious ignorance. The elements here are as follows:

The 'unknown God' whom you Greeks acknowledge you worship in ignorance made the world and everything in it (24);

> He lives in heaven and needs nothing from you; indeed, it is he who gives to all men life and breath and everything else (25);
> All the nations of men have descended from the first man he created; and he has providentially continued to govern the nations, determining their times and places for soteric reasons (26-28);
> You are therefore God's creatures, unlike him in your creatureliness (29);
> In the past God did nothing to rectify your ignorance of him but now he commands you and all other people to repent (30);
> He has set a day when he will judge the world with justice by the Man he has appointed for this task (31a);
> And he has given proof that he will judge the world by this Man by raising him from the dead (31b);
> (The Areopagus stopped Paul when he mentioned the resurrection of the dead, whereupon he left the Council. But some, we are told, believed Paul and repented [33]).

3. Romans 1:2-4; 2:16; 8:34; 9:5; 10:8-9 (to the world at large). The elements here are as follows:

> The gospel was promised by God in the prophetic writings of the Holy Scripture (1:2);
> The gospel concerns God's Son who was a descendant of David according to the flesh (1:3) but who is over all, the ever-blessed God, according to the Spirit (1:4; see 9:5);
> Christ Jesus has died (3:24-26; 8:34a);
> Christ Jesus has been raised from the dead (1:4; 8:34b);
> God has declared him by his resurrection to be the Son of God (1:4);
> God has exalted him to his own right hand where he intercedes for his own (8:34c);
> God shall judge the secrets of men someday by Jesus Christ (2:16);
> Therefore, if you confess with your mouth Jesus as Lord and believe in your heart that God has raised him from the dead, you will be saved (10:8-9).

4. 1 Corinthians 15:3-4 (to the world at large). The elements here are as follows:

> Christ Jesus died for our sins according to the Scriptures;
> Christ Jesus was buried;
> Christ Jesus was raised on the third day according to the Scriptures;
> Christ Jesus appeared to Cephas *et al.* who were to serve as his witnesses.

From our analyses, having expanded somewhat on Dodd's list of components, we see that the primitive *kerygma* consisted of the following components:

A. Old Testament prophecy has been fulfilled, and the Messianic Age *in its grace modality* has been inaugurated by the coming of Christ.[11]

B. Christ was born of the seed of David, showing that he was of royal and thus of messianic descent.

C. Christ died for our sin according to the Scriptures, to deliver us from this present evil age.

D. Christ was buried.

E. God raised Christ from death after three days, again according to the Scriptures.

F. We apostles are witnesses of these things.

G. God has seated Christ at his own right hand as Son of God and Lord of the living and the dead.

H. He will return as Judge and Savior of men.

I. Repent of your sins and believe in him for the forgiveness of sins!

These sermonic components the apostles placed at the very cutting edge of their gospel proclamation in the first century. But though all of them may be found in the primitive apostolic preachments, it is also apparent from a careful analysis of these sermons that one component of the apostolic *kerygma* received the primary emphasis.

Somewhat surprisingly, it is not the earthly ministry of Jesus, not even the expiatory significance of the death of Jesus, that receives the primary emphasis in the church's proclamation to the non-Christian world. It is true, the expiatory significance of Christ's death is there (1 Cor 15:3), but, as Bruce rightly points out, it is 'not a prominent feature in [the early speeches in Acts]; in fact the one speech in Acts where it does find expression is Paul's speech to the

---

11. See my treatment of Christ's explanatory unfolding of the Old Testament's eschatological hope by his 'already [of grace]' and 'not yet [of power]' aspects of the Kingdom of God in *A New Systematic Theology of the Christian Faith* (Nashville: Thomas Nelson, 1998), 991-99.

elders of the Ephesian church, whom he exhorts "to feed the church of God which he purchased with the blood of his beloved one".[12] But even this example, it should be noted, was addressed to Christians.

Rather, it is the resurrection of Jesus that receives primary emphasis.[13] Recognizing this, Wilbur M. Smith declares:

> The Book of Acts testifies...that it was by the preaching of the resurrection of Christ that the world was turned upside down. The first sermon on the Day of Pentecost was but a proving from the prophetic Scriptures, and from the fact of the empty tomb, and the risen Lord, that God had made this person Jesus, whom the Jews had crucified, both Lord and Christ. The early apostles took seriously the fact that they had been commissioned to be 'witnesses of these things' (Luke 24:46-47).... It was to this fact that Paul constantly alluded in the various defenses he was compelled to make before the rulers of Palestine and Syria: 'touching the hope of the resurrection of the dead I am called in question' (Acts 23:6; 24:15; 25:9; 26:8, 23).[14]

George Eldon Ladd writes:

> ...the resurrection [of Jesus] stands as the heart of the early Christian message. The first recorded Christian sermon was a proclamation of the fact and significance of the resurrection (Acts 2:14-36). Peter said almost nothing about the life and earthly career of Jesus (Acts 2:22). He made no appeal to the character and personality of Jesus as one who was worthy of devotion and discipleship. He did not recall Jesus' high ethical teachings nor try to demonstrate his superiority to the many rabbinic teachers among the Jews. He made only passing reference to the mighty deeds that had marked Jesus' ministry as evidence that God's blessings had rested on him (Acts 2:22). *The all-important thing was the fact that Jesus who had been executed as a criminal had been raised from the dead (Acts 2:24-32)*. It is not on the basis of Jesus' incomparable life or

---

12. F. F. Bruce, *Paul: Apostle of the Heart Set Free* (Grand Rapids: Eerdmans, 1996 reprint), 89. In Luke's Acts Christ's 'blood', theological shorthand for his sacrificial death, is mentioned only once (20:28); the fact that he was 'killed' is mentioned only once (3:15); the fact that he was 'crucified' is mentioned only twice (2:36; 4:10); the 'tree' upon which he died is referred to only three times (5:30; 10:39; 13:29); and his 'cross' is not mentioned at all. But his 'resurrection' is spoken of ten times; the fact that he had been 'raised' from the dead is mentioned fourteen times; and the apostolic 'witness' to this momentous event is referred to about ten times. The emphasis in the primitive church's *kerygma* is clearly on the fact of Christ's resurrection and its implications.

13. See my defense of the historicity of Jesus' resurrection in *A New Systematic Theology of the Christian Faith*, 565-75.

14. Wilbur M. Smith, 'Resurrection,' *Baker's Dictionary of Theology*, edited by Everett F. Harrison (Grand Rapids: Baker, 1960), 453.

excellent teachings or awe-inspiring works that Peter makes his appeal, but simply because God had raised him from the dead and exalted him to his own right hand in heaven. On the ground of this fact, Peter calls upon Israel to repent, to receive the forgiveness of sins, and to be baptized in the name of Jesus Christ (Acts 2:38).

The primary function of the apostles in the earliest Christian fellowship was not to rule or govern [this task rested with the eldership], but to bear witness to the resurrection of Jesus (Acts 4:33).... Throughout the sermons in [the book of Acts; see 'resurrection' – 1:22; 2:31; 4:2; 17:18, 32; 23:6; 24:21; 'raised up' – 2:24, 30; 3:15, 26; 4:10; 5:30; 10:40; 13:30, 33, 34, 37; 17:3, 31; (25:19), 26:8, 23], the resurrection continues to be a central theme....

In short, the earliest Christianity did not consist of a new doctrine about God nor of a new hope of immortality nor even of new theological insights about the nature of salvation. It consisted of the recital of a great event, of a mighty act of God: the raising of Christ from the dead.[15]

In sum, it was the proclamation by and with the Spirit's power (1 Cor 2:4), not of the cross *per se*, but of God's mighty act of raising Jesus from death three days after his crucifixion—together with its implications for men—that turned the first-century world upside down for Christ! While Peter and Paul did not ignore the fact of Christ's death by crucifixion, it was Christ's resurrection from the dead that they emphasized in the *kerygma*. In none of these early preachments did they stop to elucidate for their auditors the full significance of the death of Christ. Rather, they stressed that God had reversed the verdict of men by raising from the dead a certain person—even Jesus of Nazareth—who had been crucified as a criminal. Then they began to expound upon the significance of this titanic event. It may even be said that it was the *implications* which they drew from the momentous event of Christ's resurrection that shook the first-century world to its depths (see Acts 17:6), namely, that

A. Christ's resurrection was the means to his enthronement in heaven as the sovereign Lord of men (Acts 2:36; 10:42).[16]

B. Christ's resurrection 'powerfully declared [Christ] to be the Son of God on his divine side' (Rom 1:4).[17]

---

15. George Eldon Ladd, *A Theology of the New Testament* (1987 reprint; Grand Rapids: Eerdmans, 1974), 317.
16. See my exposition of the historicity and significance for him and for us of Jesus' ascension in my *A New Systematic Theology of the Christian Faith*, 575-81.

C. Christ's resurrection shows him to be the only Savior of men (Acts 4:12) and by implication renders all of the other religions of the world as false and unworthy of men's devotion.

D. Christ's resurrection shows that God has set his seal of approval, his endorsement, upon Christ's atoning work (Rom 4:25; Heb 7:24-25).

E. Christ's resurrection makes him the new 'temple site' or place to meet God (John 2:19, 21; Mark 14:58).

F. Christ's resurrection assures Christians of the truthfulness of his teaching (Matt 16:21) and becomes their encouragement to be faithful to him unto death (2 Tim 2:8).

G. Christ's resurrection as the 'firstfruits' or 'first portion' of the final resurrection guarantees and assures Christians and all other men that they too will be raised from the dead someday, the former to ever-=lasting bliss and glory, the latter to everlasting perdition (John 5:28-29; Acts 24:15; Rom 8:19ff.; 1 Cor 15:20ff.; 1 Thess 4:14; 1 Pet 1:3-4).

H. Christ's resurrection and ascension to Lordship has placed him in the role of Judge of all men whom he will judge at his coming in the Last Day (Acts 17:31).

While the first-century pagan might remain unimpressed by the announcement that Jesus had died on a Roman cross (had not thousands done so in addition to Christ?), he could not remain neutral regarding the announcement that God had raised Jesus from the dead. Either God had or he had not done so—there was no room for neutrality here! This aspect of the primitive gospel proclamation demanded the pagan's attention and response. If he regarded and rejected as nonsense this feature of the church's *kerygma*, the apostles were prepared to inform him that he did so at the peril of his own soul for he was denying the exalted Lord who would someday judge him (Acts 13:40-41, 46-47, 51; 28:25-28). If he accepted the facticity of this event, the apostles were prepared to explain to him that he was accepting the divine Savior who had vicariously died for him to save him from his sin.

---

17. See my exegesis and exposition of Romans 1:4 in my *A New Systematic Theology of the Christian Faith*, 238-45.

CHAPTER THREE

SAUL, ZEALOT JEW

Oh the regret, the struggle and the failing!
Oh the days desolate and useless years!
Vows in the night, so fierce and unavailing!
Sting of my shame and passion of my tears.
— From 'Saint Paul,' Frederick W.H. Myers

Pre-Christian Saul of Tarsus

The earliest physical description we have of Saul/Paul the man comes from the *Acts of Paul and Thecla*, one of three parts of the second-century work, *Acts of Paul*, in the New Testament Apocrypha, which states that he was 'a man of small stature, with a bald head and bow legs, who carried himself well. His eyebrows met in the middle, and his nose was rather large and he was full of grace, for at times he seemed a man and at times he had the face of an angel.'[1] The sixth-century Byzantine historian John Malalas added that he had a thick grey beard, light bluish eyes, and a fair and florid complexion; and that he was a man who often smiled.[2]

Saul of Tarsus was the product of three civilizations or cultures. As a Jew of the Diaspora[3] born probably during the first years of the Christian Era (since he was a νεανίας – 'a young man [from about

---

1. Bruce J. Malina and Jerome H. Neyrey, *Portraits of Paul: An Archaeology of Ancient Personality* (Louisville, Kentucky: Westminster John Knox, 1996), 128-52, and Ben Witherington III, *The Paul Quest: The Renewed Search for the Jew of Tarsus* (Downers Grove, Ill.: InterVarsity, 1998), 42-44, argue on the basis of their analysis of ancient physiognomics that this description was not intended to be so much a physical description of Paul as it was intended to be a sketch of Paul's character as 'an ideal male figure' (Malina and Neyrey) or as a 'good and honorable man' (Witherington).

2. John Malalas, *Chronographia*, 10.

3. Greek διασπορά, 'dispersion' from the verb διασπείρω, 'to scatter', refers first to the deportations of Jews carried out by the Assyrians (2 Kgs 17:6-23) and the Babylonians (Dan 1:1-14; 2 Kgs 24:14-15; 25:11) and then, as now, to the ensuing *voluntary* Jewish communities scattered throughout the Graeco-Roman world who were involved in mercenary activities, agriculture, and the merchandising of skilled arts and crafts. Of the eight or so million Jews living in the world in the first century A.D. around two-thirds of them lived outside Palestine. Around two million Jews lived in Asia Minor and Babylonia (Josephus, *Antiquities of the Jews*, 11.5.2; see Sepharad [Sardis] in Obad 20). A high percentage of the population in such

the 24th to the 40th year]'[4] – around A.D. 33 at Stephen's stoning, Acts 7:58), he came under both Roman and Hellenistic influence. Born both a citizen of Tarsus[5] and a Roman citizen (Acts 22:28),[6] he lived (probably) throughout his early childhood in Tarsus, capital of the Roman imperial province of Cilicia,[7] and there, in addition to his father teaching him how to make tents (σκηνοποιός[8]) which may

---

great cities of Syria as Antioch and Damascus were Jewish. Jewish colonies were also located in the cities of Greece and the Greek isles of the eastern Mediterranean, in Macedonia, and in Carthage in North Africa. Philo reports that one million Jews lived in Egypt (see Jer 41:17-18; 44:1ff.), mainly in Alexandria where they constituted one-eighth of the population and controlled two of the city's five wards (*In Flaccum*, 6.8). Josephus reports that Jews, as an extension of their Egyptian population, also moved west into Cyrenaica (*Antiquities*, 14.7.2). In the capital city of Rome at this time some forty to sixty thousand Jews lived – about as many as lived in Jerusalem itself (Philo, *Legatio ad Gaium* 36; but see M. Hengel, *The 'Hellenization' of Judaea in the First Century After Christ* [Philadelphia: Trinity, 1989], 10, who estimates the Jewish population of Jerusalem in the first century to have been around one hundred thousand). These Jewish communities, enjoying the privilege of *religio licita* as they did, had their synagogues and openly practiced their religion, and many of these dispersed Jews both paid the annual half-shekel Temple tax and made annual pilgrimages to Jerusalem at festival times (see Acts 2:9-11).

4. BAGD, νεανίας, *A Greek-English Lexicon of the New Testament and Other Early Christian Literature* (Chicago: Chicago University Press, 1958), 534. Ben Witherington III notes in his *The Paul Quest*, since the word was used most often for unmarried men and since most Jewish men usually married no later than their twenties or thirties, that it is likely that Luke intended a man thirty or younger (306).

5. Being a citizen of Tarsus was not the same as being a citizen of Rome. Being a citizen of Tarsus meant that one was a member of one of the socio-politico-religious 'tribes' around which the city was organised. Most likely the 'tribe' of which Saul's people were members was composed of Jewish citizens.

6. As a Roman citizen Paul would have had three Latin names – his *cognomen* or family name which was probably *Paulus*, his *nomen* or name of the founding member of his gens or tribe, and his *praenomen*, about the last two of which we know nothing. 'Saul' (שאול) was his Hebrew name, as was also the name of the first king of Israel who was from the tribe of Benjamin as was Paul.

As for his privileges as a Roman citizen, he had the right of *provocatio*, the right to appeal after trial, *muneris publici vacatio*, exemption from imperial duties such as military service, *reiectio*, the right as an accused to reject one court in favor of another, and the exemption, usually honored but not always, from flogging. For F. F. Bruce's discussion of Paul's Roman citizenship, how he probably obtained it, and its privileges, see *Paul: Apostle of the Heart Set Free* (1996 reprint; Grand Rapids: Eerdmans, 1977), 37-40.

7. Tarsus, with the standing in Paul's day of a Greek city-state as well as being the capital of Cilicia, was a shipping center and could boast of its own university which was noted for its courses in philosophy, its Stoic philosophers, and medicine. Its temple of Aesculapius, the god of healing, served as a hospital and clinic for the medical students. For Bruce's discussion of the city of Tarsus, see his *Paul*, chapter 3.

8. See the entry σκηνοποιός in BAGD, 755, for a helpful discussion of this *hapax legomenon*. Born as he was in Tarsus which was known for its *cilicium* (named for the Roman province), a cloth woven from the hair of the black goats of the Taurus region which was used to make protective coverings against inclement weather including the famous black tents of Tarsus which were popular throughout the empire, it is not surprising that Saul would have been taught the trade of tent-making.

have been the family occupation (Acts 18:3),[9] he learned to speak fluently both Aramaic (ἡ ʽΕβραΐς διάλεκτος, Acts 21:40; 22:2; see 26:14) which he spoke at home, and Greek (ʽΕλληνιστὶ, Acts 21:37) which he would have spoken perhaps on the streets of Tarsus. It seems likely that from his early years in Tarsus and from his travel throughout the Empire he probably learned some Latin as well, for he would someday inform the Roman Christians that he had already evangelized 'Illyricum' (using the Latin name of the province rather than the Greek 'Illyria,' Rom 15:19), and that he was planning to evangelize Spain (Rom 15:24; see 2 Cor 10:15-16), both of these areas of the Empire (Illyricum and Spain) being territories where Latin was the principal spoken language.[10]

Furthermore, 'it is scarcely conceivable,' Philip Schaff writes, 'that a man of universal human sympathies, and so wide awake to the problems of thought, as he, should have...taken no notice of the vast treasures of Greek philosophy, poetry, and history.'[11] He apparently knew Greek philosophy well enough to challenge the 'wise man' (σοφός), the 'scholar' (γραμματεύς), and the 'debater' or 'skillful reasoner' (συζητητής) of Greek Corinth to demonstrate their wisdom to him (1 Cor 1:20). We know that he had some acquaintance with the Greek poets because he cites Menander (*Thais*, 218; 1 Cor 15:33), Epimenedes (*de Oraculis*, Tit 1:12), and Aratus (*Phaenomena* 5) or Cleanthes (Acts 17:28), and alludes to Pindar (Acts 17:26).

But in spite of the Roman and Hellenistic influences which were surely there, Saul was, above all, *a Jew* ('circumcised on the eighth day, of the people of Israel, of the tribe of Benjamin, a Hebrew of Hebrews,' Phil 3:5).[12] His father, himself a Pharisee and apparently of some means, saw to that. Though he was 'born [γεγεννημένος] in Tarsus', Saul was 'brought up [ἀνατεθραμμένος] in this city [Jerusalem]'[13] and 'under Gamaliel [of the rabbinic school of Hillel]

---

9. See 1 Thess 2:9; 2 Thess 3:8; 1 Cor 4:12; 9:1-18; 2 Cor 6:5; 11:23, 27; and Acts 18:3; 20:34-35, where we read that on his missionary journeys Paul supported himself by the work of his hands.

10. See A. Souter, 'Did St. Paul Speak Latin?' *Expositor* (1911), 8, 1, 337-42; also F.F. Bruce, *Paul*, 315-17, for his discussion of Paul's likely familiarity with Latin.

11. Philip Schaff, *History of the Christian Church* (New York: Charles Scribner's Sons, 1910), I, 290. Very likely he would have received some formal education in these matters even in Jerusalem.

12. For Bruce's discussion of Saul's 'Jewishness', see *Paul*, chapter 5.

13. In the fact that a sister of Paul was living in Jerusalem many years later (Acts 23:16) we may find a hint that perhaps the entire family moved to Jerusalem in Saul's early childhood, making available to him there the training of which he speaks. W. C. van Unnik argues in his

thoroughly trained [πεπαιδευμένος] in the law of our fathers' (Acts 22:3). And since, as Martin Hengel has argued, there was no region of the Roman Empire that was not a 'Hellenized region', including the region of Judea,[14] Paul, trained as a youth in Jerusalem as he was, could have and very likely would have also received *even in Jerusalem* instruction in Greek rhetoric, Greek literature and Greek philosophy so that he might be able to communicate well with Diaspora Jews coming to Jerusalem.[15] In sum, though born in Tarsus, at least some if not all of Saul's formative years—during which time he received his education—were spent in Jerusalem.

His religion was Judaism, and about his commitment to it he would later write: "I was advancing in Judaism beyond many Jews of my own age, *being more exceedingly [than they] a zealot* [περισσοτέρως ζηλωτὴς] for the tradition of my fathers' (Gal 1:14).

Paul's use of 'zealot' (ζηλωτὴς) in Galatians 1:14 and Acts 22:3 and 'zeal' (ζῆλος) in Philippians 3:6 ('as for zeal, persecuting the church') should not be glossed over quickly. As far as we know, Saul was never involved in the political movement seeking Rome's overthrow, but rooted in the consciousness of the Jewish zealot was the conviction that Israel's God, whose very name is 'Zealot' (קַנָּא, Ex 34:14), was a 'jealous' or 'zealot' God (Ex 20:5; 34:14; Deut 4:24; 5:9; 6:15; the Hebrew word underlying our English 'jealous' in these verses [קַנָּא], as is true also of the Greek, means both 'jealous' and 'zealous'). Then in Israel's history certain 'heroes of zeal' were singled out for their 'zeal' in preserving Yahweh's honor:

(1) Yahweh commends Phinehas who, seeing an Israelite man bring a Midianite woman into his tent, ran them both through with his spear: 'he was zealous [בְּקַנְאוֹ]...for my honor [קִנְאָתִי] among them, so that in my zeal [בְּקִנְאָתִי] I did not put an end to them...he

---

Tarsus or Jerusalem: The City of Paul's Youth, translated by G. Ogg (London: Epworth, 1962) on the basis of Paul's use of ἀνατρέφω and the punctuation in Acts 22:3 that his family moved to Jerusalem while he was in his infancy. For the contrary view that Saul spent his early years in Tarsus, see Nigel Turner, *Grammatical Insights into the New Testament* (Edinburgh: T. & T. Clark, 1965), 83-85.

14. Martin Hengel, *The 'Hellenization' of Judaea in the First Century after Christ* (Philadelphia: Trinity Press International, 1989).

15. For a brief but good discussion of this matter, see 'Paul's Education', in Ben Witherington III, *The Paul Quest: The Renewed Search for the Jew of Tarsus* (Downers Grove, Ill.: InterVarsity, 1998), 94-98. Though Paul avoids the more florid displays of Greek oratory in his speech (1 Cor 2:1-4), his letters employ such rhetorical devices as chiasmus (1 Cor 3:17), litotes (Rom 1:28), alliteration (2 Cor 6:3), climax (Rom 8:29-30), oxymoron (2 Cor 6:9), and paranomasia (2 Cor 3:2).

was zealous [קִנֵּא] for the honor of his God' (Num 25:6-13; see Ps 106:30-31; Sir 45:23-24; 1 Macc 2:54);

(2) Yahweh commended Jehu for his 'zeal [בְּקִנְאָתִי] for the Lord' in killing Ahab's descendents (2 Kgs 10:16-17, 30);

(3) later Jewish tradition commended Simeon and his brothers for avenging the rape of their sister Dinah (Gen 34:25-26): 'thy beloved sons burned with zeal for you [O Yahweh] and abhorred the pollution of their blood' (Judith 9:2-4; for its commendation of Levi's zeal in the same incident, see Jub 30:8 and Test. of Levi 6:3); and

(4) it commended Elijah for the zeal he displayed in the slaying of the prophets of Baal (1 Kgs 18:40; see Sir 48:2-3; 1 Macc 2:58). These men were commended for their violent deeds especially against fellow Jews. Jesus too exhibited the zeal of Psalm 69:9 when he cleansed the Temple (John 2:17). This kind of zeal was doubtless what Paul meant when he referred to his life in Judaism as the life of a 'zealot' who burned 'beyond measure' (καθ' ὑπερβολὴν, Gal 1:13) with 'persecuting zeal' for the honor of 'the tradition of the fathers' against its enemies.[16]

Saul the Pharisee

With regard to the law, *his particular type of Judaism was Pharisaism* (see his 'I am a Pharisee, a son of Pharisees,' Acts 23:6),[17] which party he himself would later describe as the '*strictest* [ἀκριβεστάτην] *party* of our religion' (26:5), and which demanded rigid observance of *every* precept of the *twofold* written and traditional law. He was, if not already a rabbi, certainly on his way to becoming one; and he

---

16. See M. Hengel, *The Zealots: An Investigation into the Jewish Freedom Movement in the Period from Herod I until 70 A.D.*, translated by David Smith (Edinburgh: T. & T. Clark, 1989), 146-228. After his conversion Paul turned his zeal toward Christ's service (2 Cor 11:2; Phil 3:12, 14) and taught that the Christian should be a 'zealot [ζηλωτὴν] to do right' (Tit 2:14; see also 1 Cor 12:31; 14:1, 12, 39; 2 Cor 7:7, 11; 9:2).

17. The Pharisees (οἱ Φαρισαῖοι, the Greek transliteration of the Hebrew הַפְּרוּשִׁים = Aramaic פְּרִישַׁיָּא, meaning 'separated ones'), according to Josephus, were one of three 'philosophical' sects (the Sadducees and Essenes being the other two) that existed during the governorship of Jonathan (160-143 B.C.), brother and successor to Judas Maccabaeus (*Antiquities of the Jews*, 13.5.9; 18.1.2-3; *Wars of the Jews*, 2.8.14). Josephus estimated their number in Herod the Great's day (c. 7 B.C.) to be around six thousand (*Antiquities*, 17.2.4). Over against the Sadducees the Pharisees believed in the resurrection of the dead. Their 'separation' may have had to do originally with their opposition to the Hasmonaeans, but it is more likely that the term was intended to describe their 'strict separation from everything which might convey moral or ceremonial impurity' (Bruce, *Paul*). 'In their study of the law they built up a body of interpretation and application which in due course acquired a validity equal to that of the written law.... The purpose of this oral law – "the tradition of the elders,"

was possibly even a member of the Jewish Sanhedrin (see his statement, 'and when [Christians] were put to death, I *cast my pebble* [κατήνεγκα ψῆφον] against them,' Acts 26:10).[18] If he was the latter, then he must have been thirty or more at the time of Stephen's martyrdom or close in age to Jesus himself. Paul describes what he perceived his spiritual state as a Pharisee to have been during his pre-Christian period in the following ways:

Acts 22:3-4: 'Under Gamaliel I was thoroughly trained in the law of our fathers and was just as zealous for God as any of you are today. I persecuted the followers of this Way to their death, arresting both men and women and throwing them into prison, as also the high priest and all the council can testify.'

Acts 26:4-5: 'The Jews all know the way I have lived ever since I was a child, from the beginning of my life in my own country, and also in Jerusalem. They have known me for a long time and can testify, if they are willing, that according to the strictest party of our religion, I lived as a Pharisee.'

Galatians 1:13-14: 'For you have heard of my previous way of life in Judaism, how intensely I persecuted the church of God and tried to destroy it. I was advancing in Judaism beyond many Jews of my own age and was extremely zealous for the traditions of my fathers.'

Philippians 3:4-6: 'If anyone else thinks he has reasons to put confidence in the flesh, I have more: circumcised on the eighth day, of the people of Israel, of the tribe of Benjamin, a Hebrew of Hebrews; in regard to the law, a Pharisee; as for zeal, persecuting the church; as for legalistic righteousness, faultless.'

---

as it is called in the Gospels (Mark 7:5) – was to adapt the ancient prescriptions to the changing situations of later days and so guard them from being dismissed as obsolete or impracticable. There were differing schools of interpretation among the Pharisees, but they all agreed on the necessity of applying the written law in terms of the oral law' (Bruce, *Paul*). Paul understood himself then as a member of the scholarly class who taught the twofold (written and oral) law.

Paul declared that before his conversion, 'according to the strictest [ἀκριβεστάτην] party of our religion, I lived as a Pharisee' (Acts 26:5). His description here agrees exactly with Josephus' descriptions, who regularly describes the Pharisees as the party of ἀκρίβεια, who interpreted the laws or customs μετ᾽ ἀκριβείας (*Wars*, 2.8.14). For Bruce's full discussion of Pharisaism, see his *Paul*, 44-47.

18. Many New Testament scholars state, if Saul was in fact a member of the Sanhedrin, that he would have had to be married. Perhaps he had married since marriage was normally expected of pious Jewish men anyway when they came of age. But in light of 1 Corinthians 7:8, it is clear that at the time of his missionary journeys he was 'free' of any marriage bond. Perhaps his wife, if indeed he had married, had died. F. F. Bruce thinks it 'more probable...that his wife left him when he became a Christian: that when he "suffered the lost of all things" for the sake of Christ he lost his wife too' (*Paul*, 270).

Romans 7:9-11: 'Once I was alive apart from law; but when the commandment came, sin sprang to life and I died. I found that the very commandment that was intended to bring life actually brought death. For sin, seizing the opportunity afforded by the commandment, deceived me, and through the commandment put me to death.' (Here the Christian Paul is describing that pre-salvation period of his life when, still a committed Pharisee, he became aware of his sinfulness before the law and came under deep conviction of his sinfulness. Romans 7:14-25 continues to describe that condition in graphic terms.[19])

As for the work he was about as a Pharisee, he may have already become or planned to become a missionary to Gentiles, doubtless propagating the strictest expression of Judaic thought,[20] in order to bring the Gentiles into complete obedience to the law (see Isa 43:10-12, 21; Matt 23:15). Martin Hengel declares: 'We have to give serious consideration to the possibility that, before he became a Christian, the "Hillelite" Paul was committed to the Jewish mission.'[21] His question in Galatians 5:11, 'If I am *still* [ἔτι] preaching circumcision, why am I *still* [ἔτι] being persecuted?,' very likely indicates that prior to his conversion to Christianity he had already involved himself

---

19. See my *A New Systematic Theology of the Christian Faith* (Nashville: Thomas Nelson, 1998), Appendix F, for the argument.

20. It used to be thought that Palestinian Judaism was more rigidly conservative than Diaspora Judaism, with the former insisting on circumcision for all whereas the latter was satisfied if God-fearing Gentiles confessed faith in the one God of Israel and observed a minimum of ritual commandments (such as Sabbath observance) and the basic ethical requirements of the law, and requiring circumcision only for those Gentiles who desired to become proselytes. More recent scholarship, while not denying that there were differences between the two expressions of Judaism with Diaspora Judaism being more inclined to assimilate the Greek mindset and culture than was the Judaism of the homeland, now recognizes that variety was present in both: Diaspora Judaism could be both lax and strict in its observance of Torah just as in Palestinian Judaism, the cleavage between these strict and lax expressions in both cases being along Judaic/Hellenistic lines. See M. Stern, 'The Jewish Diaspora' in *The Jewish People in the First Century: Historical Geography, Political History, Social, Cultural and Religious Life*, edited by S. Safrai and M. Stern (2 vols.; Philadelphia: Fortress, 1974), 1.117-83, and J. Alvin Sanders, 'Dispersion' in *The Interpreter's Dictionary of the Bible* (Nashville: Abingdon, 1962), 1.854-56.

21. M. Hengel, 'Die Ursprünge der christlichen Mission' in *New Testament Studies 18* (1971-72), 23. Saul himself would furnish classic testimony years later in his letter to the Romans of Judaism's consciousness of its obligation to missionarize the nations in accordance with Isaiah 42:6; 43:10-12: '...if you [the Jew] are convinced that you are a guide for the blind, a light for those who are in the dark, an instructor of the foolish, a teacher of infants...' (2:19-20); he then concludes his point by referring to the fact of the marked discrepancy between the Jew's claim and his God-dishonoring conduct: 'God's name is blasphemed among the Gentiles because of you' (2:24). G. Bornkamm, *Paul* (New York: Harper & Row, 1971), 12, also remarks:

in such activity. If so, as Bruce states, 'then it would serve as a background for his new vocation to proclaim Christ among the Gentiles – the law being displaced in his plan of missionary campaign, as it was in his personal life, by the crucified and exalted Jesus.'[22]

There is clear indication from Romans 7:9-11, as we have already suggested, that at some point in his experience as a Pharisee he had begun to be plagued by a consciousness of sin *within* him, that is, that he had transgressed the tenth commandment pertaining to covetousness, with the 'good' that he wanted to do being always corrupted by the evil within him and the evil that he sought to avoid being always present in his heart. Paul's zeal for persecution, then, may have been the effort of a misguided conscience to do something for God which would compensate for the evil in his soul. Perhaps his original 'coveteousness', which both 'killed' and spiritually demoralized him, came in connection with his inability to 'stand up against [Stephen's] wisdom or the Spirit by whom he spoke', and his envy of Stephen's exegetical gifts and insights (see Acts 6:9-10).

Saul the Visionary Persecutor

Being the zealous Pharisee that he was, Saul 'was exceptionally farsighted, and realized as clearly as Stephen did the fundamental incompatibility between [Judaism and Christianity]. The temporizing policy of his master Gamaliel (Acts 5:34-39) was not for him: he saw that no compromise was logically possible, and if the old order was to be preserved, the new faith must be stamped out.'[23]

> If Stephen saw the logic of the situation more clearly than the [Jerusalem] apostles [and apparently he did], [Saul] saw it more clearly than Gamaliel.

...we have good grounds for believing that when the Diaspora Jew Paul chose to become a Pharisee, he also decided to be a Jewish missionary to the Gentiles along the lines taken by [Pharisaic] orthodoxy, and was actually such before becoming a Christian. This is suggested by the fact that later on, when his Judaizing opponents in Galatia maintained the need for circumcision, they exploited the apostle's former activities against him. He said in reply: 'But if I, brethren, *still* preach circumcision, why am I *still* persecuted? In that case the stumbling block of the cross has been removed' (Gal. 5:11). This most probably means that had he continued in the kind of missionary preaching that the Judaizers were now propagating afresh, but with which Paul had long ago broken, he would have been spared persecution at the hands of the Jews – but at the cost of the gospel of the cross.

22. Bruce, *Paul*, 129.
23. Bruce, *The Book of the Acts* (Revised edition; The New International Commentary on the New Testament; Grand Rapids: Eerdmans, 1988), 161.

In the eyes of Stephen and [Saul] alike, the new order and the old were incompatible. If Stephen argued, 'The new has come; therefore the old must go', [Saul] for his part argued, 'The old must stay; therefore the new must go'. Hence the uncompromising rigour with which he threw himself into the work of repression.[24]

Besides, he was quite confident that Christians 'were not merely misguided enthusiasts whose sincere embracing of error called for patient enlightenment; they were deliberate imposters, proclaiming that God had raised from the tomb to be Lord and Messiah a man whose manner of death was sufficient to show that the divine curse rested on him [see Deut 21:22-23]'.[25] Bruce writes:

> ... that Jesus of Nazareth could be the expected Messiah, as his disciples maintained, was out of the question.... The conclusive argument was simply this: Jesus had been crucified. A crucified Messiah was a contradiction in terms.... A crucified Messiah was worse than a contradiction in terms; the very idea was an outrageous blasphemy.... No heed could be paid to [his followers] when they supported their affirmation by the claim that Jesus had come back from the dead and appeared to them. In making this claim they were either deceivers or self-deceived, for none of the arguments which they used for Jesus' messiahship could stand against the one irrefragable argument on the other side: a crucified man could not conceivably be the elect one of God.[26]

He himself would later acknowledge that in preaching a crucified Messiah he was preaching something which was a 'stumbling block' (σκάνδαλον) to Jews (1 Cor 1:23). And he would later explain the 'curse' under which Christ died (Deut 21:22-23), which he had originally viewed as clear and positive proof that Jesus could in no sense have been the Messiah, as being the very means by which Jesus the Messiah redeemed us: 'Christ redeemed us from the curse of the law,' he writes, 'by becoming a curse for us, for it is written, "Cursed is everyone who is hung on a tree" ' (Gal 3:13).

---

24. Bruce, *Paul*, 70.
25. Bruce, *Acts*, 163.
26. Bruce, *Paul*, 70-71.

Saul the Right Man for the Gentile Mission

Saul, in the divine wisdom, was certainly the right man to meet the special need facing the church in the first century A.D.—the bridging of the major cultures in the Roman Empire and the avoidance at the same time of an irreconcilable breach between Jewish and Gentile members of Christ's community. Because he was (in the best sense of the phrase) the 'cosmopolitan, Renaissance man' that he was, he would be willing and able to move among Greeks and utter pagans, eating with them and addressing their philosophical questions, and to build churches comprised mainly of Gentiles. But precisely because Saul was ever the fervent Jew that he was,[27] 'he would be the last man to break ruthlessly with Judaic Christianity, even when the question of the relationship between Gentile and Jew in the church made fellowship between Jew and Gentile agonizingly difficult, for he remained in the highest sense a Hebrew of the Hebrews to the last (see Rom. 9:1-5).'[28]

We must never represent God's choice of Saul for the task to which he called him as God having been reduced to looking around, somewhat helplessly, for the best man to do a specific job he had in mind. If God wanted a man to do the particular job that Paul did and to write the specific letters that Paul wrote, he prepared a Paul throughout his entire life to be that particular man. Paul himself realized this: '[God] set me apart from birth [for this task]' (Gal 1:15; see also Isa 49:1-2; Jer 1:5; Luke 1:13-17). In the same way God is even now preparing and equipping certain men and women, unknown to them, to accomplish great works for him!

---

27. Even after Paul became a Christian and had given his entire life to his Savior's service, unlike many converts to a new faith who turn their backs completely on the faith they left, Paul did not abandon the Jewish nation or its spiritual heritage. When he asked the question, 'What advantage, then, is there in being a Jew, or what profit is there in circumcision?', though the logic of his argument would have led one to expect the answer, 'None at all,' his own answer was 'Much, in every way' (Rom 3:1-2; see Rom 9:1-5). And though the glory of the Yahwism of the Old Testament could not compare with the Christian way of the New Testament (2 Cor 3:11) which possessed the 'greater glory' (2 Cor 3:11; see 3:8 and also his whole argument in Hebrews), he could still declare that, in its own way, the Old Testament dispensation was glorious (2 Cor 3:7, 11; see Rom 9:4).

Paul identified himself with Israel, speaking of Abraham as 'our forefather', of Isaac as 'our father', and of 'all our fathers' (Rom 4:1; 9:10; 1 Cor 10:1). He could wish that he himself were cursed and cut off from Christ if his rejection would avail for his Jewish kinsmen's salvation (Rom 9:1-5).

28. Martin Franzmann, *The Word of the Lord Grows* (St. Louis: Concordia, 1961), 47.

CHAPTER FOUR

SAUL'S CONVERSION, CALL, NEW ESCHATOLOGICAL VISION, AND GOSPEL

We sing the glorious conquest before Damascus gate,
    When Saul, the church's spoiler, came breathing threats and hate;
The rav'ning wolf rushed forward full early to the prey;
    But lo! the Shepherd met him, and bound him fast today.

O glory most excelling that smote across his path!
    O light that pierced and blinded the zealot in his wrath!
O voice that spake unto him the calm, reproving word!
    O love that sought and held him the bondman of his Lord!

O Wisdom ord'ring all things in order strong and sweet,
    What nobler spoil was ever cast at the victor's feet?
What wiser masterbuilder e'er wrought at thine employ
    Than he, till now so furious thy building to destroy?

Lord, teach thy church the lesson, still in her darkest hour
    Of weakness and of danger, to trust Thy hidden pow'r:
Thy grace by ways mysterious the wrath of man can bind,
    And in Thy boldest foeman Thy chosen saint can find.
                                —John Ellerton

F. F. Bruce has very rightly observed that 'no single event, apart from the Christ-event itself, has proved so determinant for the course of Christian history as the conversion and commissioning of Paul. For any who accepts Paul's own explanation of his Damascus-road experience, it would be difficult to disagree with the observation of an eighteenth-century writer[1] that "the conversion and apostleship of St. Paul alone, duly considered, was of itself a demonstration sufficient

---

1. Lord George Lyttleton, *Observations on the Conversion and Apostleship of St. Paul* (London: R. Dodsley, 1747), paragraph 1. Lyttleton's eighty-page pamphlet, later published as 'The Conversion of St. Paul' in *Infidelity* [New York: American Tract Society, n. d. [1840?]), argued that Paul's conversion could be explained in only one of four ways: (1) he was an imposter who reported what he knew was false; or (2) he was an enthusiast driven by an overheated imagination and was therefore self-deceived; or (3) he was deceived by the fraud

to prove Christianity to be a divine revelation." '[2]

What Lord Lyttleton meant by his remark is that the entire 'Paul phenomenon' – that is, the man together with his literary corpus—is inexplicable apart from the resurrection of Christ. The conversion of Saul of Tarsus, Christ's 'boldest foeman', in a real sense becomes then the fourth great strand of biblical evidence—joining before it (1) the fact of the empty tomb, (2) Jesus' numerous post-crucifixion appearances to his disciples, and (3) their sudden transformation from fearful friends to fearless 'kerygmatics'—for the reality of Christ's resurrection and the supernatural origin and character of Christianity.[3]

Saul's Involvement in Stephen's Martyrdom

> Saint, did I say? with your remembered faces,
>   Dear men and women, whom I sought and slew!
> Ah when we mingle in the heavenly places
>   How will I weep to Stephen and to you!
>   From 'St. Paul,' Frederic H. W. Myers

Stephen was a Hellenist[4] Christian. Being 'less entangled in the prejudices of Hebrew nationality than his Aramaic brethren', he seems to have understood better at first than the Jerusalem apostles the implications of the radicality of the universal grace of the Christian gospel.[5] Accordingly, unlike the Jerusalem Christian leadership who

---

of others; or (4) what he said about his conversion was true, and therefore the Christian religion is a divine revelation. He argued, of course, for the fourth explanation.

2. F. F. Bruce, *Paul: Apostle of the Heart Set Free* (Grand Rapids: Eerdmans, 1996 reprint of the 1977 edition), 75.

3. See Philip Schaff, *History of the Christian Church* (New York: Charles Scribner's Sons, 1910), I, 307-16; J. Gresham Machen, *The Origin of Paul's Religion* (Grand Rapids: Eerdmans, 1965 reprint of 1925 edition); Richard N. Longenecker, *Paul, Apostle of Liberty* (New York: Harper & Row, 1964); and Seyoon Kim, *The Origin of Paul's Gospel* (second edition; Tübingen: J. C. B. Mohr, 1984), for helpful discussions of false explanations of the 'Paul phenomenon'.

4. See Ἑλληνιστῶν in Acts 6:1 and all of the Greek proper names in Acts 6:5, including Στέφανος, 'Stephen.' BAGD, *A Greek-English Lexicon of the New Testament and Other Early Christian Literature* (Second edition; Chicago: University of Chicago, 1979), 252, translating Ἑλληνιστής simply as 'a Hellenist', states that the word denotes a Greek-speaking Jew in contrast to one speaking a Semitic language. The word occurs only twice in the New Testament: in Acts 6:1 the 'Hellenists' are Greek-speaking Jews who had become Christians; in Acts 9:29 the 'Hellenists' are Greek-speaking Jews who, as non-Christian Jews who apparently felt the need to distance themselves from the Hellenist Christians, attempt to kill the converted Saul of Tarsus.

5. See W. J. Conybeare and J. S. Howson, *The Life and Epistles of St. Paul* (Grand

remained, while inwardly free, at least in outward form essentially Judaic,[6] Stephen 'took the fight to the enemy', urging the Hellenistic Jews of the Synagogue of the Freedmen (very likely Saul's synagogue), in their search for righteousness, to transfer their allegiance away from personal obedience to the Mosaic law and to Temple ritual to Jesus Christ who was the fulfillment and embodiment respectively of these two central features of Judaism (Acts 6:9-10). This teaching brought him (possibly through a report of Saul himself) to the attention of and finally under the condemnation of the Sanhedrin.

In his defense (Acts 7), in keeping with his Lord's earlier 'radical' declaration that the time would come when men would worship God neither in Samaria nor in Jerusalem but rather would worship him in spirit and truth (John 4:21-24), Stephen reviewed Israel's own history beginning with Abraham and traced God's dealings with the nation through Joseph, Moses, David, and Solomon, highlighting the fact that God had dealt with each of these great patriarchs of Israel in some place *other than the Jerusalem Temple*. He concluded this part of his defense with Isaiah's ringing declaration: 'Heaven is my throne, and the earth is my footstool. What kind of house will you build for me? says the Lord. Or where will my resting place be? Has not my hand made all these things?' He then charged the Sanhedrin, like Israel of old who had persecuted and killed God's prophets, with betraying and murdering the Messiah, and he stated that though Israel had the law, the nation had not obeyed it, the implication being that

---

Rapids: Eerdmans, 1971 reprint), 57. Precisely because he was not entangled as a Hellenist in the 'traditions of the fathers' to the degree that Saul was, not to mention the fact that he had become a Christian, would have made Stephen in Saul's opinion a legitimate target for persecution. Martin Hengel, *The Zealots* (Edinburgh: T. & T. Clark, 1989), has argued that Saul, being the zealot that he was, would have considered the Christian Hellenists (first in Jerusalem and later in Damascus), because of their criticism of Torah and Temple, as accursed lawbreakers (72-84).

6. The Jerusalem church leaders observed the law, as all good Jews did, in such points at least at first as the distinction between clean and unclean foods (Acts 10:14) as well as shunning fellowship with Gentiles (Acts 10:27-28; 11:2-3; Gal 2:12). They observed the traditional hours of prayer, both in Jerusalem and when they were away from the holy city (Acts 3:1; 10:9, 30), taught in the Temple precincts (Acts 5:20), endorsed the prescribed purification rites and vows which in turn involved the paying of a Temple tax (Acts 21:23-24), and, most significantly, even commended the rite of circumcision for Jewish male Christian children and urged obedience to the law of Moses and the customs of the Jews (Acts 21:21-24). Thus the church would have been looked upon by the Jewish religious authorities as a Jewish sect or synagogue, strange and monstrously in error certainly but a Jewish sect or synagogue nonetheless. Perhaps the religious authorities considered the church as the 'Nazarene Synagogue' or the 'Synagogue of the Galileans'.

the law was powerless to produce holy living.

It is in connection with Stephen's defense and execution that Luke first introduces us to Saul (Acts 7:58 and 8:1, 3). Saul was very likely present and heard Stephen's defense. Contrary to Günther Bornkamm's opinion that 'Paul can hardly have been present at the stoning of Stephen: the connection is clearly of Luke's own making',[7] Luke informs us that, Stephen having been found guilty of blasphemy against the Temple and its institutions, Saul guarded the garments of the witnesses who stoned Stephen to death, 'giving approval' (συνευδοκῶν) to his death. Apparently Saul did not cast a stone; he left the actual execution to those who had been witnesses against Stephen, as Deuteronomy 17:7 and the Mishna, *Sanhedrin* 6.1-4, prescribed.[8]

But Saul never forgot the part that he had played in Stephen's martyrdom (Acts 22:20) and the fact that he had tried 'to destroy the church. Going from house to house [and from city to city], he dragged off men and women and put them in prison' (Acts 8:3; see 22:4, 19-20; 26:10-12; 1 Tim 1:13-16).[9] Of course, we must note that in doing so Saul was not acting the part of a vigilante; he had sought and received authority from the Jewish religious leadership in Israel to solve the 'Christian problem' for them (Acts 9:1-2; 22:5; 26:10).

---

7. Günther Bornkamm, *Paul*, translated by D. M. G. Stalker (New York: Harper & Row, 1971), 15.

8. Bruce observes that 'when Judaea became a Roman province in A. D. 6, the Jewish administration was deprived of capital jurisdiction, which the prefect reserved for himself. In one area, however, capital jurisdiction was left with the Sanhedrin: that was in cases affecting the sanctity of the temple. Where that sanctity was violated...the Jewish authorities were empowered to execute their own law [see Josephus, *Wars of the Jews*, 6.2.4]. The penalty for blasphemy was death by stoning [Lev 24:10-16], and this penalty was carried out against Stephen' (*Paul*, 68).

9. From the two facts that the apostles were able to stay in Jerusalem during Saul's persecution (Acts 8:1) and that some of the Christians—'men of Cyprus and Cyrene' (Acts 11:20)—who were scattered because of his persecution began preaching to pagan Greeks (Ἕλληνας, the reading of P^{74} ℵ^c A D* 1518, with Eusebius and Chrysostom), we may infer with some assurance that Saul's persecution was directed mainly at Hellenist Christians among whose leadership was Stephen himself. F. F. Bruce, *The Book of the Acts* (Revised edition; The New International Commentary on the New Testament; Grand Rapids: Eerdmans, 1988), observes: 'From this time onward the Jerusalem church appears to have been a predominantly "Hebrew" body' (162), adding in fn. 10: 'That is, until its dispersal c. A.D. 66, and even more so in exile after that.'

Saul's Conversion

The Acts accounts of Saul's conversion on his way to Damascus are recorded in Acts 9:1-19 (Luke's historical account in the third person), 22:3-16, and 26:2-18 (these last two passages being Luke's reports of Paul's personal accounts in the first person).[10] Paul's own references to his conversion may be found in Galatians 1:15-16, 1 Corinthians 9:1; 15:8-10, Philippians 3:4-11, and 1 Timothy 1:12-16. In a sentence, Saul's conversion was effected *objectively* by the glorified Christ's sudden appearance to him on the Damascus Road.[11] Romans 7:7-25 is the only passage in Paul's writings that addresses his spiritual turmoil at the time; it suggests that God had prepared him *subjectively* for this encounter by previously bringing him under deep conviction of his sin and convincing him of his impotence regarding true and full obedience to the law of God.[12]

Saul's trip to Damascus was not the first such trip by any means (see Acts 26:11-12); it was, however, his last such trip! This momentous event that reshaped the history of the world occurred probably at one of four reputed sites, perhaps near the squalid little Syrian village called Mezze, located about five miles south of Damascus.[13]

---

10. Because the Acts 9 account of Paul's conversion is the most familiar of the three accounts to most beginning Bible students, I would suggest that the three accounts might be read upon occasion in reverse order in order that the Bible student may become more familiar with the later accounts and thus gain a better picture of all that happened on that momentous occasion.

11. See Bruce Corley, 'Interpreting Paul's Conversion – Then and Now' in *The Road to Damascus: The Impact of Paul's Conversion on His Life, Thought, and Ministry*, edited by Richard N. Longenecker (Grand Rapids: Eerdmans, 1997), 1-17. Corley provides an illuminating history of the church's attempts to understand what happened that day on the Damascus Road under the headings: 'The Heretical Paul: Marcion and the Ebionites', 'The Vanquished Paul: Augustine and Medieval Piety', 'The Thundering Paul: Luther, Calvin, and the Puritans', and 'The Ecstatic Paul: Enlightenment and Modern Criticism.' Corley concludes that the Damascus Road event was neither simply an 'alteration' (a gradual change of life that grows out of the past) nor simply a 'transformation' (a cognitive change of life that reconceives the past). It was also more than simply a call. It was both a 'conversion' experience and a call – a sudden change of life that rejects the past, or at least some aspects of it, and takes a new direction.

12. See Robert H. Gundry, 'The Moral Frustration of Paul Before His Conversion: Sexual Lust in Romans 7:7-25' in *Pauline Studies: Essays Presented to Professor F. F. Bruce on His 70th Birthday*, edited by Donald A. Hagner and Murray J. Harris (Grand Rapids: Eerdmans, 1980), 228-45, who urges that 'we may call [the passage] the biography of Everyman if we like, but here Everyman's biography is the autobiography of Paul' (229). He also answers all of the major objections to this view. I concur with Gundry's argument. See my 'Whom Does the Man in Romans 7:14-25 Represent?' in *A New Systematic Theology of the Christian Faith* (Nashville, Tenn.: Thomas Nelson, 1998), Appendix F, 1127-32.

13. See my *Jesus, Divine Messiah: The New Testament Witness* (Philipsburg, N. J.:

Krister Stendahl has argued that Saul's experience of meeting the glorified Christ on the Damascus Road, since it involved no change of religion or change of Gods but only a change in assignments, was a call rather than a conversion.[14] The traditional understanding of Saul's Damascus Road experience as a conversion experience is due, according to Stendahl, more to the West's introspective readings of Augustine and Luther than it does to the New Testament documents.[15]

Saul, however, would later describe his experience much more radically than simply the receiving of a new assignment. In 1 Corinthians 15:8 he speaks of it as of the nature of an 'irregular birth' – he was 'one abnormally born' (an ἔκτρωμα[16]). In Philippians 3:12, he speaks of it as an 'arrest' – he 'was apprehended [κατελήμφθην] by Christ Jesus'. In Galatians 1:13 he speaks of his 'previous [ποτε] life in Judaism',[17] setting his former religious experience off over

---

Presbyterian and Reformed, 1990), Chapter 5, for my discussion of the historical objectivity of Jesus' appearance to Saul. Paul later classified it as the last [ἔσχατον πάντων] of Jesus' post-resurrection appearances (1 Cor 15:8).

14. Krister Stendahl, *Paul Among Jews and Gentiles and Other Essays* (Philadelphia: Fortress, 1976), 7-23.

15. Is Stendahl correct when he declares that Western theology has introspectively read the conversion experiences of Augustine and Luther back into Luke's Acts and Paul's letters? I would urge that not only has the Western church not read Augustine and Luther back into Paul; neither Augustine nor Luther read their own conversion experience directly and singularly in the light of Paul's.

While it is true that Augustine in his *Retractations* of A. D. 396 argued that Saul's 'fierce, savage, and blind will' was suddenly 'turned from [its] fierceness and set on the right way towards faith,' and then in his *Confessions* of c. A. D. 400 saw himself in his new evaluation of Paul, it must be noted that what he found in common between himself and Paul was not a troubled conscience but a vanquished will. Interpreting Romans 7:14-25 as he did as the experience of Paul the Christian, not Saul the persecutor, the previous comparison was not open to him.

Not even Luther, with whom Paul's conversion has been so often compared in modern church history, was converted to Christ the way Paul was. There was much time and distance between the lightning bolt that drove Luther into the Augustinian monastery at Erfurt and his later 'tower experience' at Wittenberg in which he came to understand the meaning of the 'righteousness of God' in Romans 1:17 and thus was finally delivered from his hostility toward God. Luther himself seems to have had relatively little interest in Paul's conversion as a topic of reflection and preaching, nor does he draw an analogy between his own spiritual struggle with a 'troubled conscience' and Paul's experience. His view of Romans 7:14-25, holding as he did Augustine's interpretation of the passage, would not permit him to do so.

16. Bruce (*Paul*, 86) understands Paul's descriptive term to mean 'an abortion'. George Eldon Ladd (*A Theology of the New Testament* [Grand Rapids: Eerdmans, 1974], 367-68) takes it to mean 'an abnormal birth' in the sense that Christ appeared to Saul 'after [he] had ceased to appear to the other disciples'.

17. The term Ἰουδαϊσμός ('Judaism') only occurs twice in the New Testament—in Galatians 1:13-14. It first appears in 2 Macabbees 2:21; 8:1; 14:38, apparently having been coined to express opposition to 'Hellenism' (2 Mac 4:13). In every instance it denotes the national Jewish religion and way of life.

against 'the church of God [τὴν ἐκκλησίαν τοῦ θεοῦ]', implying by this contrast that the one living and true God was in the church but not in Judaism. In Philippians 3:4-8 he declares that he had come to regard his prior 'Judaic' reasons for confidence in the flesh as 'rubbish' (σκύβαλα), which suggests a radical and complete break with his 'Judaic' past. And in transferring his confidence as he did, in his search for personal righteousness before God, away from personal obedience to the Mosaic law and the temple ritual to the cross-work of Jesus Christ who was the fulfillment and embodiment respectively of these two central features of the Old Testament, Saul in fact created a new religious pattern for others to follow. For while it is true that Saul continued to think of himself as a Jew, his radical reinterpretation of the Mosaic covenant and its law as a 'glorious anachronism (2 Cor 3; see Gal 4)'[18] and his rejection of the Gentile's need for circumcision for salvation did in fact constitute for him a religious conversion—a conversion away from Second Temple 'Judaism', the man-made deconstruction of Old Testament Yahwism (see Mark 7:6-8), to New Covenant Yahwism, the fulfillment of Old Testament religion, which fulfillment later came to be called 'Christianity'.[19] Of course, his conversion *initially* was more principial than substantive: firstly, since it originally amounted in content to little more than his new conscious faith in Jesus Christ as the Son of God and Jewish Messiah (Acts 9:20, 22) plus the logical implicates of that new faith; and since, secondly, the maturation of his thought as a Christian apostle had to await the spiritual struggles and controversies of the mission field for its fullest development. Of course, his conversion to Christ was also *accompanied* by his call to be the apostle to the nations.[20]

---

18. The phrase is Ben Witherington III's, found in his *The Paul Quest: The Renewed Search for the Jew of Tarsus* (Downers Grove, Ill.: InterVarsity, 1998), 78.

19. Bible students should draw a distiction between the religion of the Old Testament and Judaism. The former is rightly designated Yahwism—the worship and service that Yahweh required in the Abrahamic and Mosaic covenants—while Judaism is the postexilic deconstruction of Old Testament Yahwism that the rabbinic schools erected around the law in such sources as the Babylonian Talmud in order to make Yahwism compatible with and applicable to the Jews' lack of access to land and to Temple. The two are *not* the same and are *not* compatible, as Jesus so clearly declared (Mark 7:6-8), the former urging 'the commands of God', the latter urging 'the traditions of men' which nullified (ἀκυροῦντες) the Word of God (7:13; see also Jesus' condemnation of Judaism's handling of the Word of God in Matt 15:3-9 and Matt 23). On the other hand, 'new covenant' Christianity is simply the administrative extension and unfolding of the Abrahamic covenant, which is just to say that the spiritual blessings which Christians enjoy today under Jeremiah's 'new covenant' (31:31-34) are founded on the Abrahamic covenant.

I. Rationalizing explanations

Three extreme rationalizations of the event are that Saul either suffered an epileptic seizure of some kind or a sun stroke or, seeing a flash of lightning which blinded him and being thrown from his horse when it became startled and bolted from under him at the same flash of lightning (actually, Luke's accounts say nothing about Paul being on a horse), struck his head on the ground and in the daze that followed imagined that he had seen the Lord. But these explanations have not commended themselves generally even to the critical mind.

More popular is the view that, under the stress of his fanatical persecution of the church, Saul suffered a mental breakdown on the road to Damascus, and in this broken mental state imagined that the Lord of the very ones he was persecuting had called upon him to desist in his persecution and instead to serve him.

Probably the most popular naturalistic explanation is that Saul was subconsciously being conditioned by the logic of the Christian position and his observance of the dynamic quality of Christians' lives and patient fortitude under oppression. Then, it is said, when he underwent that 'mood-changing' crisis experience on the road to Damascus, the precise nature and cause of which scholarship is not able to recover (so there is an agnostic aspect to this suggestion), he became convinced because of this prior sub-conscious pre-conditioning of mind that he should become a follower of Christ rather than his persecutor. In support of this explanation, it is urged that the risen Christ's purported statement to Saul, 'It is hard for you to kick against the goads' (Acts 26:14), may mean that 'Paul had been resisting a better conviction, gradually forming in his mind, that the disciples might be right about Jesus and he might be wrong...,'[21] in other words, that for some time he had been stifling ('kicking against') serious doubts of conscience about the propriety of his attitude toward Christ ('the goads') by engaging himself in ever more feverish activity in persecution but this resistance to these doubts had not brought him peace and the 'goads' of conscience continued to afflict him. But near Damascus the subconscious conviction that had been afflicting him was at last allowed to come

---

20. See Janet Meyer Everts, 'Conversion and Call of Paul' in *Dictionary of Paul and His Letters*, edited by Gerald F. Hawthorne, Ralph P. Martin, and Daniel G. Reid (Downers Grover, Ill.: InterVarsity, 1993), 156-63.

21. Machen, *The Origin of Paul's Religion*, 60.

to the surface, to overcome his resistance to Christ, and to begin to rule his life. However, with Machen I would urge, since Paul would later say in 1 Timothy 1:13 that he had persecuted the church 'in ignorance and unbelief [ἀγνοῶν...ἐν ἀπιστίᾳ]', that Paul was 'not conscious of any goad which before his conversion was forcing him into the new faith.... The meaning [of Jesus' statement] may be simply that the will of Christ is resistless; all opposition is in vain, the appointed hour of Christ has arrived...all resistance [in that moment],...all hesitation, is as hopeless as for the ox to kick against the goad; instant obedience alone is in place.'[22]

It should be apparent that all psychologico/psychoanalytical explanations of Saul's Damascus Road experience leave too many questions unanswered. In addition to the impossibility of psychoanalyzing a person who lived almost two thousand years ago with any degree of clinical accuracy, what real evidence is there that Saul suffered a mental breakdown, or that his conscience had been troubling him? (While we have already suggested, on the basis of Roman 7:7-25, that he was deeply troubled by the knowledge of his inate sinfulness, it is equally certain that he was not laboring under any guilt springing from his activities of persecution, for he knew he was acting under the auspices of the Sanhedrin, and he believed that he was serving God by such 'zealot' activity.) What was the nature of the crisis experience that triggered his conversion? Such questions as these, and many more besides, must be answered satisfactorily before any credence can be given to these theories.

Then there is the view of Rudolf Bultmann who believed that all such depictions of 'Biblical supernaturalism' are actually reflections of either Gnostic mythology or Jewish Apocalyptic. But his own explanation of Saul's conversion is wholly unsatisfactory in that it fails to come to terms to any degree with the historical character of the Acts narrative itself: 'Not having been a personal disciple of Jesus, *he was won to the Christian faith by the kerygma of the Hellenistic church.*'[23] But neither is James D. G. Dunn's view much better when

---

22. Machen, *The Origin of Paul's Religion*, 61, 62. So too Herman Ridderbos who writes in his *Paul and Jesus*, translated by David H. Freeman (Nutley, N. J.: Presbyterian and Reformed, 1977): 'The expression is simply an indication of the fruitlessness of Paul's terrible persecution of Jesus and his church' (45), and 'By σκληρόν ['hard, difficult'] nothing else is meant than that Paul set himself against Jesus, as this was revealed in his persecution of the church, and that his opposition to Jesus was fruitless and pernicious' (140, fn. 20).

23. Rudolf Bultmann, *Theology of the New Testament*, trans. Kendrick Grobel (London: SCM, 1971), I, 187; emphasis original.

he concludes that it is impossible to know for sure whether Jesus was '"out there", alive and making himself known to Paul'. All that one can say with any certainty, Dunn continues, is that 'Paul himself was convinced that what he saw was external to him' but it may have been 'after all, all "in the mind" '.[24]

II. The biblical evidence

Such conclusions, as I have said, frankly fail to come to terms with Luke's historical narrative regarding Paul's conversion (recounted in the third person) in Acts 9 or with Paul's later accounts (told in the first person) in Acts 22 and 26 which he gave on the solemn occasions of defending his office and actions under the auspices of the Roman commander and before high government dignitaries respectively. There are pertinent data which indicate that his conversion was not mentally induced. We are expressly informed that, while Saul alone saw the glorified Jesus, the men who were traveling with him both heard a voice (9:7), though they did not understand its words (22:9), and saw the brilliant light (22:9; 26:13-14). And while it is true that Paul would later call the event a 'vision from heaven' (26:19), which description itself imputes an *ab extra* character to it ('*from* heaven'), the accounts make it clear that his conversion was not subjectively self-induced in the sub-conscious but, rather, that it resulted from an initiating action external to him (9:3-4; 22:6-7; 26:13-14). Indeed, the ascended Christ represents *himself* as the initiator in 26:16: 'I have appeared to you [ὤφθην σοι].' And Ananias will say later that God had chosen Saul 'to see the Righteous One and to hear words from his mouth' (22:14).

When all the facts in Acts 9:1-28, 22:1-21, 26:4-23, and Galatians 1:13-17; 1 Corinthians 9:1; 15:8-10 are considered, Longenecker's judgment seems clearly justified:

> Only the Damascus encounter with Christ was powerful enough to cause the young Jewish rabbi to reconsider the death of Jesus; only his meeting with the risen Christ was sufficient to demonstrate that God had vindicated the claims and work of the One he was opposing. Humanly speaking, Paul was immune to the Gospel. Although he was ready to follow evidence to its conclusion, he was sure that no evidence could overturn the verdict of the cross; that is, that Christ died the death of a criminal. But...the eternal God 'was pleased,' as Paul says by way of

---

24. James D. G. Dunn, *Jesus and the Spirit* (Philadelphia: Westminster, 1975), 107-08.

reminiscence, 'to reveal his Son to me' (Gal 1:16). Thus Paul was arrested by Christ, and made his own (Phil 3:12).[25]

The Date of Saul's Conversion (c. A.D. 32-33)

The date of Saul's conversion is a studied guess based upon the following facts and inferences:

A. According to Acts 11:28 a succession of droughts and poor harvests occurred during the reign of Claudius Caesar (A.D. 41-54). One of the resultant famines was specially severe in Judea during the procuratorships of Cuspius Fadus and his successor Tiberius Julius Alexander. This 'severe famine' occurred around A.D. 46.[26]

B. Very likely about this same time the church at Antioch sent Barnabas and Saul to Jerusalem on what has been called Saul's 'famine relief visit' (Acts 11:29-30).

C. If we equate this 'famine relief visit' with the visit to Jerusalem that Paul discusses in Galatians 2:1-10 (the evidence for which equation I will provide in the next chapter), and if we view the 'three years' reference in Galatians 1:18 and the 'fourteen years' reference in Galatians 2:1 as running concurrently rather than consecutively (also to be argued later), then we may conclude that Paul was converted fourteen years before his 'famine relief visit' to Jerusalem around A.D. 46, that is to say, about A.D. 32. Of course, since

---

25. Richard N. Longenecker, *The Ministry and Message of Paul* (Grand Rapids: Zondervan, 1971), 34-35. I would add to Longenecker's suggested reason for Saul's immunity to the gospel the additional reason that faith in Christ's obedience for salvation was surely for him incompatible with his Judaic inclination to rely upon his own obedience to the law for salvation (see Jacques Dupont, 'The Conversion of Paul, and Its Influence on His Understanding of Salvation by Faith,' *Apostolic History and the Gospel*, eds. W. Ward Gasque and Ralph P. Martin [Exeter: Paternoster, 1970], 178-94). As we show in Chapter Twenty, E. P. Sanders has argued in his *Paul and Palestinian Judaism* (Philadelphia: Fortress Press, 1977) that Palestinian Judaism was not a religion of legalistic works-righteousness wherein right standing before God was earned by good works in a system of strict justice. One can indeed find references in the literature of the period to God's election of Israel and to His grace and mercy. But Palestinian Judaism also taught that the elect man was obligated, even though he would do so imperfectly, to obey the law in order to *remain* in the covenant. Thus the legalistic principle was still present and ultimately governed the soteric status of the individual. Paul rightly saw that any obligation to accomplish a 'works-righteousness' on the sinner's part would negate the principle of *sola gratia* altogether (Rom 11:6). For a more detailed critical analysis of Sanders' thesis, see Chapter Twenty and Karl T. Cooper, 'Paul and Rabbinic Soteriology,' *Westminster Theological Journal 44* (1982), 123-39.

26. See Bruce, *Paul*, 150.

'fourteen years' could mean twelve full years and parts of the years at both ends, we have to allow for the possibility that he was converted somewhat later, hence the 'c. A.D. 32-33' suggestion above.

An Apologetic for the Historicity and Authenticity of Saul's Conversion

I. Paul's argument in Galatians for the validity of his apostleship based upon his own history

In support of the historicity of Paul's conversion, the validity of his apostleship, and the 'revealedness' of the gospel he proclaimed, we can produce no better argument than the one which he himself adduced in Galatians 1:13–2:21 where he defends his apostolic authority and message against the Judaizers who had come to South Galatia, denied his apostolic authority, and proclaimed 'another gospel' to his converts. The issue we are now facing is, in one sentence: What was the ultimate origin of Paul's apostolic commission and the gospel he proclaimed? It is evident that he could have obtained his gospel and the authority to preach it from only one of three possible sources:

A. His Judaistic training? Did he obtain his apostolic authority and the law-free gospel he was preaching after his conversion from his *previous* life in Judaism? To ask the question is to answer it. Certainly not! Paul himself describes that experience in Judaism for us five different times:

Galatians 1:13-14 (the passage under discussion): 'For you have heard of my previous way of life in Judaism, how intensely I persecuted the church of God and tried to destroy it. I was advancing in Judaism beyond many Jews of my own age and was extremely zealous for the traditions of my fathers.'

Acts 22:3: 'I am a Jew, born in Tarsus of Cilicia, brought up in this city at the feet of Gamaliel, thoroughly trained in the law of our fathers, being zealous for God....'

Acts 26:4-5: 'The Jews all know the way I have lived ever since I was a child, from the beginning of my life in my own country, and also in Jerusalem. They have known me for a long time and can testify, if they are willing, that according to the strictest sect of our religion, I lived as a Pharisee.'

Philippians 3:4-6: 'If anyone else thinks he has reasons to put confidence in the flesh, I have more: circumcised on the eighth day, of the people of Israel, of the tribe of Benjamin, a Hebrew of the Hebrews; in regard to the law, a Pharisee; as for zeal, persecuting the church; as for legalistic righteousness, faultless.'

1 Timothy 1:13: '...I was once a blasphemer and a persecutor and a violent man....'

It should be evident from these autobiographical descriptions that Paul was not proclaiming as the Christian apostle and missionary what he had learned from his life in Judaism. Just to the contrary, as the Christian apostle and missionary he directed men's trust away from Torah and Temple and personal law-keeping where his own confidence had resided as a Pharisee and toward Jesus Christ for salvation.

B. Apostolic training and apostolic authorization? Did he then obtain the gospel he was preaching and the authority to preach it *after* his conversion, if not at the feet of Gamaliel, at the feet of the apostles? Listen to Paul again:

> ... when God...was pleased to reveal his Son to me..., I did not consult any man nor did I go up to Jerusalem to see those who were apostles before I was, but I went immediately into Arabia and later returned to Damascus. (Gal 1:15-17)

In this connection, there is separate corroborating evidence if Paul intended by his reference to 'Arabia' to refer to the Nabataean Kingdom, that Paul did not simply devote himself to a life of quiet contemplation in Arabia after his conversion, but in fact immediately began to missionarize the populace there. He informs us in 2 Corinthians 11:32-33 that 'the governor under King Aretas guarded the city of Damascus in order to seize me'. But one does not stir up the kind of trouble with civil authorities that he alludes to in the passage just cited merely by quiet meditation. This would suggest that long before he made any contact with the Jerusalem apostles Paul had already engaged himself in Gentile evangelism.[27]

Then Paul informs us under a self-imposed oath (see Gal 1:20: 'I assure you before God that what I am writing to you is no lie') that three years passed after his conversion before he finally met any of the apostles. Even then it was only Peter and James he met, and that

---

27. See Günther Bornkamm, *Paul*, translated by D. M. G. Stalker (New York: Harper & Row, 1971), 27, and Bruce, *Paul*, 81, both of whom urge that Paul engaged himself in Arabia immediately in preaching Jesus as the Christ.

it was for the space of only fifteen days (Gal 1:18-19). This was doubtless the visit Luke records in Acts 9:26-28, and while it is likely that it was at this time that he 'received' the precise details of the 'tradition' about Jesus' post-resurrection appearances, particularly those to Peter and James, which he later 'delivered' to the Corinthians in 1 Corinthians 15:5-7, it is evident, since the apostles had no opportunity to do so, that they conferred no authority on him at that time. Furthermore, Paul assures his reader: 'I was personally unknown to the churches of Judea' (Gal 1:22). Then Paul declares that another eleven years passed (I am assuming here the correctness of the South Galatia theory with respect to Paul's first missionary trip, the case for which I will argue later) before he saw the apostles again, this time on the occasion of his so-called 'famine-relief' visit to Jerusalem recorded in Acts 11:27-30. On this occasion, Paul informs us, 'I set before [the apostles] the gospel that I preach among the Gentiles' (Gal 2:2). The outcome of this presentation, which surely would have included his view of Christ and justification, was that the apostles 'added nothing to my message' (2:6), but to the contrary, he writes, they saw 'that I had been entrusted with the gospel' (2:7), that 'God who was at work in Peter as an apostle to the circumcision was also at work in me [as an apostle] to the Gentiles' (2:8), and accordingly they 'gave me the right hand of fellowship' (2:10). In other words, they again conferred no authority on him but rather only acknowledged the authority which was already his, by virtue of which authority he had been engaged in his apostolic ministry among the Gentiles for fourteen years.

We conclude, then, that throughout this entire fourteen-year period (see Gal 2:1)—during the three-year period preceding his first visit to Jerusalem and during the eleven-year period preceding his second visit to Jerusalem—and beginning immediately after his conversion (Acts 9:20) Paul, apart from any human authorization, was 'proclaiming Jesus, that this one is the Son of God' (Acts 9:20), 'proving that this one is the Messiah' (9:22), 'speaking out boldly in the name of the Lord' (9:27), and 'preaching the faith that he once tried to destroy' (Gal 1:23)—an apostolic ministry that only after fourteen years had transpired was personally and officially acknowledged to be authentic by the original apostles.

C. Divine call and authorization? If Paul was not preaching what he had learned during his life in Judaism antecedent to his conversion, it is equally clear from his review of the first fourteen years of his apostolic ministry that he was not preaching what he had learned from the original apostles subsequent to his conversion either. Nor had they conferred the authority on him to execute his ministry as an apostle. In fact, if any instruction was done, he writes in Galatians 2:11-14, it was he, during an incident which arose later in Antioch (more about this incident later), who had to rebuke Peter publicly for the latter's actions which would have compromised the law-free gospel[28] and which could well have led to the permanent division of the church. We may infer that Peter had accepted his rebuke (see Peter's later comments at the Jerusalem Council in Acts 15:7-11 and his still later description of Paul in 2 Peter 3:15).

All this means that the gospel he was proclaiming and the authority with which he was proclaiming it, he received neither from his Judaistic training before his conversion nor from any apostolic indoctrination after his conversion. The only remaining alternative is that *he was proclaiming the gospel which he had received, as he says, in and by his conversion experience itself* – 'by revelation from Jesus Christ' (Gal 1:12)!

---

28. F. F. Bruce popularized the expression, 'law-free gospel' by its several occurences in his *Paul*. But when he employed the expression he intended to say that the gospel liberates the Christian from the law not only with respect to its condemning character (in justification) but also with respect to it as a rule of life (in sanctification). He writes:

> In the Reformed tradition derived from Geneva, it has frequently been said that, while the man in Christ is not under law as a means of salvation, he remains under it as a rule of life. In its own right, this distinction may be cogently maintained as a principle of Christian theology and ethics, but it should not be imagined that it has Pauline authority. According to Paul, the believer is *not* under law as a rule of life – unless one thinks of the law of love, and that is a completely different kind of law, fulfilled not by obedience to a code but by the outworking of an inward power. When Paul says, 'sin will have no dominion over you, since you are not under law but under grace' (Romans 6:14), it is the on-going course of Christian life that he has in view, not simply the initial justification by faith. (*Paul*, 192).

I too employ the expression 'law-free gospel' in this book, but I do not intend to imply by it that the gospel delivers the Christian man or woman from his or her obligation to obey God's moral law as that law comes to expression in the ten commandments and in Christ's own pattern of life. Nowhere does Paul, when rightly understood, suggest such a thing. What I intend by 'law-free gospel' is what Paul intended when concerning justification he stated that a 'man is not justified by observing the law, but by faith in Jesus Christ...because by observing the law no one will be justified' (Gal 2:16) and that 'a man is justified by faith apart from observing the law' (Rom 3:28). But clearly the Christian continues to live under the law as the covenant rule of life.

I would refer the reader to Chapters Twenty and Twenty-One for full discussions of both these issues, for they are at the heart of the Reformed faith in its opposition to Roman Catholicism and to antinomianism respectively.

I do not mean to suggest by these remarks that Saul had known nothing before his conversion about Jesus Christ or about the church's doctrinal teaching concerning him. He knew some things well enough, and as the church's persecutor he had confronted them often enough. What I do mean is that Jesus' post-ascension appearance to Saul on the Damascus Road forced upon him an entirely new 'hermeneutical grid' through which he had to filter not only his understanding of Jesus' person and work but also his own previous Judaistic instruction concerning law and grace.[29] In sum, for Saul of Tarsus his encounter with Jesus Christ meant a completely new 'hermeneutical paradigm shift'.

Nor do I mean to suggest by these remarks that Paul did not grow in his understanding of Christ during those fourteen years, for indeed, he continued to grow in his knowledge of Christ to the very end of his life (see Eph 4:11-13; Phil 3:10-14). What I do mean is that in all his 'growing up' in his understanding of Christ he never 'grew away' from that first clear 'vision from heaven', as James Stalker so poignantly suggests when he writes: 'His whole theology is nothing but the explication of his own conversion.'[30]

II. Rational arguments showing 'the impossibility of the contrary', that is, showing the impossibility of another explanation for his radical transformation being better than the explanation offered by Luke and Paul himself.

A. Was Saul's conversion due to a sunstroke, a hallucination, or an epileptic seizure? As I said above, some have proposed these as causes for his radical transformation. (Speaking tongue in cheek, one could wish that some such malady would occur among more people, for whatever it was, it transformed the Jewish zealot into the great Christian 'apostle of the heart set free'.) Of course, none of these produced Saul's change. His travel companions also saw the blazing light and with him fell to the ground (Acts 22:9; 26:13-14), and they too heard the sound of a voice though they did not understand what the voice was saying to Saul (Acts 9:7; 22:9).

---

29. See J. Gresham Machen, *The Origin of Paul's Religion* (Grand Rapids: Eerdmans, 1965 reprint of 1925 edition), 144ff.

30. James Stalker, *The Life of St. Paul* (Edinburgh: T. & T. Clark, 1889), 40. See particularly here also Margaret E. Thrall, 'The Origin of Pauline Christology,' *Apostolic History and the Gospel*, eds. W. Ward Gasque and Ralph P. Martin (Exeter: Paternoster, 1970), 304-16.

B. Was Saul's conversion simply the expression of the wild and extravagant fanaticism of one who was given to serious psychological mood swings? Some have proposed this. But completely apart from the difficulty (really, the impossibility) of psychoanalyzing someone's mental state two thousand years after his death with any degree of accuracy, anyone who considers the wisdom, the prudence, the calmness and serenity which Paul evidenced under extremely difficult circumstances, and, above all, his humility (which characteristic is inconsistent with fanaticism) which he displayed in his letters will find it impossible to believe that his 'transformation' was due simply to a major bipolar mood swing.

C. Was Saul simply a religious charlatan who changed his religious allegiance for purposes of self-interest? Some have proposed this. But one may pose four questions here:

1. Is it possible that the prospect or the ostentation of some new learning produced his transformation? It is impossible to believe that Saul, zealot that he was for the traditions of the fathers, would have cast aside all that he had been taught by Gamaliel, or what he had learned through long years of study, in favor of the opinions of fishermen of Galilee whom he had scarcely seen and who had never been educated in the approved schools of Jewish learning.

2. Is it possible that the love of power prompted his change? It is impossible to believe that he who was already at the 'center of Jewish power' abdicated in a moment the authority which he already possessed for authority over a 'little flock' whose 'Shepherd' had been executed, who themselves were being led as lambs to the slaughter, and whose 'new authority' could only promise him that he too would be marked out for the same knife which he himself had drawn against them.

3. Is it possible that the love of wealth provoked his conversion? It is impossible to believe, whatever may have been his own worldly possessions at that time, that the prospect of wealth would have been a factor in his conversion, for it was apparent that he was joining himself to those who at that time were certainly poor, and

the prospect before him was that which he actually came to know and realize, namely, never having much and having to minister to his necessities with the labor of his own hands as a tentmaker.

4. Is it possible that the prospect of fame and world-wide prestige led him to become a follower of Jesus Christ? It is impossible to believe that his prophetic powers at that time were so great and miraculous that he could look beyond the shame and scorn which then rested on the servants of the crucified Christ and see that glory which Christendom now heaps upon the memory of Paul.

In light of Paul's argument drawn from Galatians 1–2 and the impossibility of all the contrary alternatives, the historicity of his conversion just as Luke's Acts reports it is placed beyond all reasonable doubt. Accordingly, we shall proceed with our study supported by the well-grounded conviction that Saul was converted on the Damascus Road precisely the way Luke's Acts reports that he was. And though we have said it already, it bears repeating: the conversion of Saul of Tarsus is the fourth great strand of biblical evidence – joining the fact of the empty tomb, Jesus' numerous post-crucifixion appearances to his disciples, and their sudden transformation from fearful friends to fearless 'kerygmatics' – for the historicity and reality of Christ's resurrection and the supernatural origin and character of Christianity.

Saul's Theological Deductions from His Conversion Encounter with Jesus Christ

Saul deduced from his conversion encounter with Jesus of Nazareth on the Damascus Road at least six new perceptions.[31] And I would submit that it would not have taken him very long, certainly not three years (see Gal 1:17), to deduce these things from the momentous experience he had just undergone; for a man of Saul's native genius aided by the Spirit, three days (see Acts 9:9) would have been quite sufficient. In fact, Ladd declares that 'all the essentials of Paul's theology – Jesus as the Messiah, the gospel for the Gentiles, justification by faith as against works of the Law – are contained in his Damascus Road experience.'[32] Bruce concurs, writing: 'Paul's

---

31. Ladd, *Theology*, 368.   32. Ladd, *Theology*, 369.

Damascus-road experience...contained within itself the totality of his apostolic message.'³³ What are these six things? He would have inferred

A. That the Hellenist Christian Stephen, just as he, had in fact earlier seen 'heaven open and the Son of Man standing at the right hand of God' (Acts 7:56), and accordingly, that his Christian proclamation was indeed correct: Jesus was in fact the long-awaited Messiah, wrongly crucified but divinely exonerated from all wrongdoing and 'powerfully shown to be the Son of God' by the resurrection from the dead (Rom 1:4). In sum, Saul's theology and Christology were in principle corrected.

B. That the Hellenist Christian Stephen and the church of which he was a part and which he himself had been persecuting were indeed the people of the Messiah after all;

C. That if a people who did not observe the law as the Pharisees prescribed were in fact the Messiah's people, then salvation was apparently not by law-keeping; rather, it was a gift. In this connection, Ladd writes:

> The realization that Jesus really was the Messiah was revolutionizing to Saul's evaluation of the entire meaning of the Law, for it was his very zeal for the Law that had made him hate the Christians and their alleged Messiah. Jesus had not been condemned by irreligious, immoral men, but by conscientious devout Jews who believed they were defending God's Law. It was Judaism at its best that put Jesus on the cross. If Paul's effort to establish righteousness by the Law had itself blinded him to the true righteousness of God in the Messiah (Rom. 10:3), then the Law could not be a way of righteousness. Judaism must be wrong in understanding the Law as the way of righteousness. It was this certainty that brought Paul to the conviction that Christ was the end of the Law as a way of righteousness (Rom. 10:4).³⁴

D. That if the Messianic salvation was being bestowed on Hellenistic Jews apart from law-keeping, then this salvation must be universal and appropriate to Gentiles as Gentiles as well.³⁵ In sum, points C. and D. show that Saul's soteriology in principle was corrected.

---

33. Bruce, *Paul*, 188.
34. Ladd, *Theology*, 368-69.
35. Even though Genesis 17:9-14 (see also Ex 4:24-26; Lev 12:3; Josh 5:2-9) states that circumcision was to be an 'everlasting covenant' (בְּרִית עוֹלָם) for God's people (in which

E. That if his persecution of Christians was at the same time a persecution of the Messiah himself, then there must be an intimate union between them and him, on the order of the relationship between a body and its head. In sum, his ecclesiology was in principle formed. Finally,

---

fact the Judaizers doubtless found their chief support), over the course of his ministry as the Christian apostle Paul erected at least six arguments in defense of the idea that Gentiles could be the people of God as *Gentiles* apart from circumcision and 'works of law':

(1) the Spirit's presence in the lives of the uncircumcised Galatians—reflected also (if Paul knew about the event) by the Spirit's presence in Cornelius' earlier salvation apart from circumcision (Acts 10:44-45; 11:15-18)—showed that circumcision was unnecessary for membership in the covenant (Gal 3:1-5);

(2) the Mosaic covenant of which Paul regarded circumcision a part *if* and *when* it was viewed as necessary for salvation (Rom 2:25; otherwise he regarded it as the sign of the Abrahamic Covenant, Rom 4:11)—designed as it was for the Mosaic age until the Abrahamic promise reached its fulfillment in the 'new covenant' (Jer 31:31-34; Ezek 36:26-27)—was no longer operative now that Christ had come (Gal 3:15-4:7);

(3) if one believes he must be circumcised in order to be saved, then he must understand that he must keep perfectly the *entire* law as well (Gal 3:10; 5:2-6; see Rom 2:25-27), but since no one can perfectly perform the 'works of law', Christ redeemed Christians from the law's curse in order that the blessing of Abraham might come to the Gentiles apart from works of law through faith in Christ (Gal 3:10-14);

(4) God had obviously placed his authenticating *imprimatur* on Paul's proclamation of his law-free gospel by doing signs and wonders among the Gentiles through him (Acts 15:12; see 2 Cor 12:12);

(5) Abraham's justification in Genesis 15:6 prior to his circumcision in Genesis 17:23-24 some fourteen years later clearly shows that he was already righteous in God's sight prior to his circumcison which was intended as really only the confirming 'sign' and 'seal' of his righteousness by faith apart from circumcision (Rom 4:9-12); and

(6) Paul's own spiritual union with the death and resurrection of Christ was for him a *spiritual* circumcision, and these same great events have become for every believer in union with Christ his spiritual circumcision (Col 2:11-14), which is the only circumcision that really matters (Rom 2:28-29).

A Judaizer still might have insisted that no argument Paul could mount could be allowed to overthrow the fact that God had said that circumcision was to be an *everlasting* covenant. But Paul apparently believed that just as the Passover Feast, also said by God to be an 'everlasting ordinance [עוֹלָם חֻקַּת]' (Ex 12:17), as a type, was 'everlasting' only for the duration of the age of promise and thus was fulfilled in and by Christ who was the antitypical 'Passover' (1 Cor 5:7), so also circumcision, also a type, was 'everlasting' only for the duration of the age of promise and thus was fulfilled by its antitype, Christian baptism (Col 2:11-12). And he would have been right to believe so, for from his exposition Allan A. Macrae,'עוֹלָם III,' *Theological Wordbook of the Old Testament*, edited by R. Laird Harris, Gleason L. Archer Jr., and Bruce K. Waltke (Chicago: Moody, 1980), concludes: 'That neither the Hebrew [עוֹלָם] nor the Greek [αἰών] word in itself contains the idea of endlessness is shown both by the fact that they sometimes refer to events or conditions that occurred at a definite point in the past, and also by the fact that sometimes it is thought desirable to repeat the word, not merely saying "forever", but "forever and ever" ' (2.673).

F. That the Messianic kingdom must already be, in some sense, a present reality.[36] In sum, he received in principle a 'new eschatology' which had been his Lord's before him.[37] This last point requires further elucidation.

Saul's New 'Eschatological Dualism'

The fact that Jesus was indeed the Messiah after all required Saul to revise his Judaistic understanding of redemptive history and to begin to work theologically within the framework of what Ladd calls an 'apocalyptic [eschatological] dualism'[38] and what Herman Ridderbos calls the 'redemptive-historical, eschatological' frame of reference.[39] To comprehend what is intended here, one has to know something about what Saul had believed about redemptive history as a Pharisee prior to his conversion.

> He continued to look forward to the Day of the Lord, the appearance of the Messiah in power and glory, to establish his eschatological Kingdom [just as the prophets had predicted]. Paul does not surrender the Jewish scheme of the two ages and the evil character of the present age (Gal. 1:4). ...from the point of view of nature, history, and culture, the Kingdom of God remains an eschatological hope.[40]

But if Jesus is the Messiah and has brought to his people the messianic salvation, something has radically changed. What is now different? It is this: While the present evil age obviously continues (Gal 1:4), *the Kingdom of God of the Eschaton in its salvific modality has already become a present reality (into which the Messiah's people have been brought, Col 1:13) even if the world cannot see it (see Mark 4:11-12)*. This is clear from the following affirmations found in Paul's Acts sermons and his letters:

A. That Jesus in some sense *has already entered upon his messianic reign at and by his resurrection and ascension* (see Acts 13:30-41 [see also here Acts 2:22-36]; 1 Cor 15:23-25; Col 1:13). The Messiah, in other words, is reigning now, and will continue to reign until he

---

36. Ladd, *Theology*, 369.
37. See footnote 46.
38. Ladd, *Theology*, 369-75, 550.
39. Herman Ridderbos, *Paul, An Outline of His Theology*, translated by John R. DeWitt (Grand Rapids: Eerdmans, 1975), 44-66.
40. Ladd, *Theology*, 369.

has put all his enemies (including death) under his feet! (The Corinthians passage also suggests that Jesus' present reign extends in unbroken continuity from his ascension to the Great White Throne Judgment of Revelation 20).

B. That the eschatological resurrection of the dead, which in his thinking as a Pharisee belonged entirely to the Age to Come, *has already begun* in Jesus' resurrection, whose resurrection is the 'firstfruits' (ἀπαρχή) of the resurrection of all men (1 Cor 15:21-23). Ladd remarks: 'The important point here is that the resurrection of Christ is the beginning of the resurrection as such, and not an isolated event.'[41]

C. That the eschatological outpouring of the Spirit, predicted by Joel for the 'last days' (2:28-32; see Acts 2:17-21), *has already begun* with the giving of the Spirit to Christians as the sealing 'down payment' (ἀρραβών) guaranteeing the consummation of the transaction unto the 'day of redemption' (2 Cor 1:22; 5:5; Eph 1:14; 4:30).

D. That *eschatological* 'life in the Spirit', accordingly, *has already begun.*[42] The author of Hebrews (whom I will argue later is Paul) implies in this connection that true Christians have already truly 'tasted of the powers of the Age to Come' (Heb 6:5; see John 5:24-25).[43] In other words, as Richard B. Gaffin, Jr. observes, 'the Christian life in its entirety is essentially and necessarily resurrection life...believers at the core of their being will never be more resurrected than they already are.'[44]

E. That judicial acquittal (δικαιοσύνη, δικαίωμα, δικαίωσις), properly the affirmative side of the eschatological judgment by the righteous Judge of all the earth at the End of the Age, *has already occurred* for Christians through their faith in the justifying death and resurrection of Christ (Rom 5:1, 9; 4:25; Gal 2:16).[45] In other words,

---

41. Ladd, *Theology*, 369-70.
42. Ladd, *Theology*, 370-71.
43. While the entire pericope of Hebrews 6:4-6 describes only those with a non-saving 'temporary' faith (see Matt 13:20-21), surely true Christians would also enjoy the specific 'eschatological' blessing spoken of in 6:5.
44. Richard B. Gaffin, Jr., '"Life-Giving Spirit": Probing the Center of Paul's Pneumatology,' *JETS 41/4* (December 1998), 585.
45. Ladd, *Theology*, 374.

because of the imputed righteousness of Jesus Christ which they receive when they place their faith in his work on their behalf, Christians have, as it were, already passed through the final judgment and have been acquitted because they will never be more righteous in God's sight then than they are right now.

It was this new eschatological vision (eschatological dualism) that spurred Paul later to write: 'When *the time had fully come* [ἦλθεν τὸ πλήρωμα τοῦ χρόνου], God sent forth his Son' (Gal 4:4). That is to say, with the termination of the age of promise, the age of fulfillment began with God's sending both his Son's forerunner and his Son (Mal 3:1; 4:5-6; Matt 11:10; Luke 1:17) into the world. In these acts God inaugurated eschatology.

It was this new eschatological vision that spurred Paul later to use such radical expressions as 'Before the faith came [Πρὸ τοῦ δὲ ἐλθεῖν τὴν πίστιν]' (Gal 3:23) and 'when the faith came [ἐλθούσης δὲ τῆς πίστεως]' (Gal 3:25), expressions which might even suggest that Paul believed that there had been no faith in the Old Testament (which representation of Paul would constitute an error of massive proportions in light of Genesis 15:6, Habakkuk 2:4, and Hebrews 11) but which he doubtless intended as metonymies for the eschatological realities of the gospel 'epoch' of faith in Jesus Christ.

It was this new eschatological vision that spurred Paul later to speak about Christ's person and work as the 'revelation of [the] mystery [ἀποκάλυψις μυστηρίου]'. What does he mean? In Jesus' 'mystery [μυστήριον] of the kingdom' parables (Matthew 13)[46] and elsewhere (for example, Matt 19:28; 25:31-46), he laid the groundwork for the New Testament's 'eschatological dualism' by teaching that the Kingdom of God would indeed yet come in *power and glory* as the Old Testament prophets had predicted but that it

---

46. By his 'mystery of the kingdom' parables, Jesus had already taught that the present expression of the kingdom in its grace modality, unlike its future power modality, (1) can be resisted and rejected ('four soils', Matt 13:3-9, 18-23), (2) will tolerate the existence of the opposing kingdom of evil ('wheat and tares', Matt 13:24-30, 36-43), (3) though small and insignificant in its inception, is not to be despised, for it will someday cover the earth ('mustard seed' and 'leaven', Matt 13:31-33), (4) in its growth is irresistible, that is to say, that though it will use men in its employ, its growth will not depend in any ultimate sense upon the labor of men ('growing seed', Mark 4:26-29), (5) though despised by the world, is the most valuable thing a man could ever obtain ('hidden treasure' and 'pearl', Matt 13:44-45), and finally, (6) will not always tolerate opposition from the kingdom of evil, for the citizens of that kingdom will someday be destroyed ('net', Matt 13:47-50).

would first appear in *grace*, indeed, *had already come* in his own person and ministry (see Mark 1:15; Luke 11:20; 17:20-21). About its initial appearance in grace, Jesus declared (Matt. 13:17): 'I tell you the truth, many prophets and righteous men longed to see what you see but did not see it, and to hear what you hear but did not hear it.' Matthew then made this comment on Jesus' 'mystery of the kingdom' parables:

> Jesus spoke all these things to the crowd in parables; he did not say anything to them without using a parable. So was fulfilled what was spoken through the prophet [Asaph, Ps 78:2]: 'I will open my mouth in parables, I will *utter* [that is, reveal] things *hidden* [κεκρυμμένα] since the creation of the world.' (Matt 13:34-35)

In other words, Jesus taught that a particular kind of 'Kingdom-coming' which had been 'hidden since the creation of the world', that is, which had hitherto not been revealed *in redemptive history*, had appeared at his first coming with expanded grace to the nations *before* the Kingdom finally comes with power and glory at the end of the world.

Now in perfect concert with his Lord, Paul would later describe the redemptive events that had dawned in the appearing of Christ as the 'revelation of the *mystery*', the 'making known' of that which until *now* (νῦν) had been 'kept secret' or 'hidden'. For example:

1 Corinthians 2:7-8: '...we speak[47] of God's *secret wisdom* [σοφίαν ἐν μυστηρίῳ], a wisdom that has been hidden [ἀποκεκρυμμένην] and that God destined for our glory before time began. None of the rulers of this age understood it, for if they had, they would not have crucified the Lord of glory';

---

47. From the relationship which Paul draws between God's *revelation* of the 'mystery' and his own *preaching* of God's 'mystery' (see his 'we speak of God's wisdom in mystery', 1 Cor 2:7-8; his 'proclamation...according to the revelation of the mystery', Rom 16:25-26; his 'the mystery...was given to me for you', Eph 3:3-5; his 'the commission...to present to you...the mystery', Col 1:25-26; and his 'the preaching entrusted to me', Tit 1:2-3), it is evident that the 'revelation of the mystery' was the very content of Paul's 'gospel'; it was the proclaimed propositional content of the ministry entrusted to him. This means that Paul's missionary preaching, teaching and writing were taken up into the great eschatological event of the appearing of the kingdom of God in its grace modality; they were rightly and in the fullest sense the proclamation and unveiling of the *eschatological* gospel, that is, the proclamation and unveiling of Christ's lordship and the salvation to be found in submission to his lordship. I would submit that the same is true of all biblically-based missionary preaching and teaching

Saul's Conversion, Call,... 79

Romans 16:25-26: '... the *proclamation* [κήρυγμα] of Jesus Christ, according to the *revelation* [ἀποκάλυψιν] of the *mystery* [μυστηρίου] *hidden* [σεσιγημένου] for long ages past, but *now revealed* [φανερωθέντος νῦν]....';

Ephesians 1:9-10: 'He made known to us the *mystery* [μυστήριον] of his will according to his good pleasure, which he purposed in Christ to be put into effect *when the times will have reached their fulfillment* [εἰς οἰκονομίαν τοῦ πληρώματος]';

Ephesians 3:3-5: 'Surely you have heard about the administration of God's grace that was given to me for you, that is, the *mystery* [μυστήριον] made known to me by *revelation* [ἀποκάλυψιν].... In reading this, then, you will be able to understand my insight into the *mystery* [μυστηρίῳ] of Christ, which *was not made known* [οὐκ ἐγνωρίσθη] to men in other generations as it *has now been revealed* [νῦν ἀπεκαλύφθη] by the Spirit to God's holy apostles and prophets';

Colossians 1:25-26: '... by the commission God gave me *to present* to you the word of God *in its fulness* [πληρῶσαι]—the *mystery* [μυστήριον] that *has been kept hidden* [ἀποκεκρυμμένον] for ages and generations, but *is now disclosed* [νῦν ἐφανερώθη] to the saints. To them God has chosen to *make known* [γνωρίσαι] among the Gentiles the glorious riches of this *mystery* [μυστηρίου], which is Christ in you, the hope of glory';

2 Timothy 1:9b-10: 'This grace was given us in Christ Jesus before the beginning of time, but it has *now been revealed* [φανερωθεῖσαν νῦν] through the appearing of our Savior, Christ Jesus, who *has destroyed* [καταργήσαντος] death and has brought [eschatological] life and immortality to light through the gospel';

---

by virtue of the authority such preaching and teaching inherently derive from the divine gospel's intrinsic authority.
   This means that today, to the degree that the preacher's preaching is the proclamation of the one gospel of God, his preaching is just to that same degree the *eschatological* 'unveiling' of the kingdom of God in its grace modality. It is the *eschatological* proclamation of the 'already' aspect of the end-time kingdom of God. And to the degree that his teaching is explication or exposition of the one gospel of God, his teaching is just to that same degree the *eschatological* 'unveiling' of the kingdom of God in its grace modality. It is the *eschatological* teaching of the 'already' aspect of the end-time kingdom of God. My writing at this very moment is an *eschatological* explication of the kingdom of God in its grace modality. This *eschatological* feature of the gospel governed Paul in his theological thinking and motivated him to service. Just so should this feature which is present in all true gospel proclamation also govern and motivate the preacher and missionary of the twenty-first century!

Titus 1:2-3: 'God, who does not lie, promised [the hope of eternal life] before the beginning of time, and at his appointed season he *brought* his word *to light* [ἐφανέρωσεν] through the *preaching* [κηρύγματι] entrusted to me.'

Accordingly, Paul would later declare: 'I tell you, *now* [νῦν, that is, during "this gracious Eschaton" before "the judgment Eschaton"] is the time of God's favor; *now* [νῦν] is the day of salvation' (2 Cor 6:2).

It was this new eschatological vision that spurred Paul later—knowing as he did that the very idea of 'newness' is eschatological (see 'new heavens and a new earth', Isa 65:17; 2 Pet 3:11; Rev 21:1; a 'new song' for the redeemed, Isa 42:10; Rev 5:9; 14:3; a 'new thing', Isa 43:19)—to say of the one who is 'in Christ' that he is 'a *new* creation; the old has gone, *the new has come!*' (2 Cor 5:17) and that a '*new* man' had been created that is comprised of all who are in Christ, whether Jew or Gentile (Eph 2:15). Christians, in sum, are already 'people of the Eschaton'!

It was this new eschatological vision that spurred Paul later to speak of Christians as those 'on whom the fulfillment [τὰ τέλη; lit, "ends"] of the ages has come [κατήντηκεν]' (1 Cor 10:11), and to represent them as those concerning whose existence a radical definitive transformation has occurred, namely, a radical breach with the power of sin, with their new resurrection life now to be lived under the new mastery of the Christ (see Rom 6:17; 1 Cor 6:11).

In sum, with the appearance of Jesus the Messiah in redemptive history, the *eschatological* Kingdom of God also entered earth history in its redemptive modality 'before the Eschaton' and is even now present in earth history (see Matt 13; Luke 11:20); *eschatological* eternal life is already present in Christ; the *eschatological* resurrection has already begun in Jesus' resurrection; the *eschatological* Spirit has already been given to the church and *eschatological* life in the Spirit has already begun; and finally, the verdict of the *eschatological* judgment has already been handed down for all those who put their trust in Christ, and God has already forensically acquitted his people.[48]

This 'passing away of the old' does not mean, however, the end of this age; the 'old age' continues until Christ's second appearance (his παρουσία), at which time, through the cataclysmic overthrow

---

48. For Bruce's insights in this connection, see *Paul*, 97-100.

of the kingdom of evil, the knowledge of the glory of the Lord will cover the earth as the waters cover the places of the seas (Hab 2:14). But this age does *not* remain intact; the 'new age' has broken in upon it; the King's people are advancing upon the enemy's territory (Matt 16:18), and in Christ men may be spiritually delivered from this present evil age (Gal 1:4) and even now be brought into the gracious kingdom of his Son (Col 1:13). This is in order that they may no longer conform themselves to the old age but may 'be transformed by the *renewing* of their minds' (Rom 12:2).

All this meant for Paul, in keeping with the basic 'redemptive-historical, eschatological' structure of Jesus' eschatological dualism, that into the midst of *this* present evil age – this 'already' *before* the dawn of the Age to Come – the *salvific* aspects of the Age Still to Come had already *graciously* intruded themselves 'before the time'. 'In a surprising [totally unexpected] way *visible only to faith* the end of the old aeon and the dawn of the new have come upon the [Christian] community,'[49] and Christians are no longer citizens of this age but are already citizens of the Age to Come. They are already subjects in the 'Kingdom of God and of Christ'. 'The new world and its salvation are already present, but they are hidden in the midst of the old world.'[50] Quite correctly and insightfully does Ladd write:

> The events of the eschatological consummation are not merely detached events lying in the future about which Paul speculates. They are rather redemptive events that have already begun to unfold within history. The blessings of the Age to Come no longer lie exclusively in the future; they have become objects of present experience. *The death of Christ is an eschatological event.* Because of Christ's death, the justified man stands already on the age-to-come side of the eschatological judgment, acquitted of all guilt. By virtue of the death of Christ, the believer has already been delivered from this present evil age (Gal. 1:4). He has been transferred from the rule of darkness and now knows the life of the Kingdom of Christ (Col. 1:13). In his cross, Christ has already defeated the powers of evil that have brought chaos into the world (Col. 2:14f.).
>
> *The resurrection of Christ is an eschatological event.* The first act of the eschatological resurrection has been separated from the eschatological consummation and has taken place in history. Christ has already abolished death and displayed the life and immortality of the Age to Come in an event that occurred within history (II Tim.

---

49. Ladd, *Theology*, 372.
50. Ladd, *Theology*, 486.

1:10). Thus the light and the glory of the Age to Come have already shined in this dark world in the person of Jesus Christ (II Cor. 4:6).

Because of these eschatological events, the believer lives the life of the new age. *The very phrase describing the status of the believer, 'in Christ,' is an eschatological term.* To be 'in Christ' means to be in the new age and to experience its life and powers. 'If any one is in Christ, he is a new creation; the old has passed away, behold, the new has come' (II Cor. 5:17). The believer has already experienced death and resurrection [in Christ] (Rom. 6:3-4). He has even been raised with Christ and exalted to heaven (Eph. 2:6), sharing the resurrection and ascension life of his Lord.

Yet the experience of this new life of the Age to Come is not a secular event of world history, it is known only to believers. This good news of the new life is hidden to unbelievers. Their eyes are blinded so that they cannot behold it (II Cor. 4:4 [see also Mark 4:11-12]). They are still in the darkness of this present evil age.

[But because the consummating stage of the Age to Come is still future and has not yet dawned] the believer lives in a tension of experienced and anticipated eschatology. He is already in the Kingdom of Christ (Col. 1:13), but he awaits the coming of the Kingdom of God (I Cor. 15:50). He has already experienced the new life (II Cor. 2:16), but he looks forward to the inheritance of eternal life (Gal. 6:8). He has already been saved (Eph. 2:5), but he is still awaiting his salvation (Rom. 13:11). He has been raised into newness of life (Rom. 6:4), yet he longs for the resurrection (II Cor. 5:4).[51]

Jesus' eschatological dualism, grounded in his own person and coming—this is the eschatological vision that revolutionized Saul's thinking when he was converted and, I submit, that governed his missionary endeavors and controlled the theology expressed in his letters to his aides and his mission churches.

We may summarize what we have said to this point about Paul's theology this way: Just as the Old Testament declared that its predicted 'last days' were to be the times of the Messiah, and just as Jesus spoke of this age—the Old Testament's predicted *salvific* 'last days' —as the age of the Kingdom's end-time *salvific* work, with the age to come being the Kingdom's consummating and eternal state, so we have seen that Paul maintained this perspective as well. In fact, Herman Ridderbos with rich insight states: 'It can be rightly said that Paul does nothing but explain the eschatological reality which

---

51. Ladd, *Theology*, 551-52.

in Christ's teaching is called the Kingdom.'[52] And Geerhardus Vos states: 'To unfold Paul's eschatology [in terms of the two ages, namely, this age and the age to come] is to set forth his theology as a whole,' not just his teaching on Christ's return.[53] But by his interpreting what is commonly regarded as soteriology eschatologically in the way he did, Paul, without distorting in any way the basic structure of Jesus' eschatological perspective, makes it clear that with Jesus' death and resurrection the future age (which *will* be fully realized in solid existence) had in principle *already* been realized. It has been realized now in heaven with Jesus' present reign and on earth salvifically in the church.[54] I would conclude then that Paul's eschatological paradigm is similar to his Lord's – an eschatological dualism.

Saul's Gospel

What did Saul's new eschatological vision have to do with the gospel he proclaimed? In a word, everything. How did his new eschatological vision affect the content of Saul's gospel? As he himself might have said: 'Much, in every way.' The verb εὐαγγελίζειν ('to proclaim good news') and its cognate noun εὐαγγέλιον ('good news') had a linguistic history both in the Septuagint and in pagan Greek literature before they ever came into the New Testament.[55] With respect to its Septuagint background, for example, the verb occurs at Isaiah 40:9:

> Go up on a high mountain,
>   O Zion, *herald of good tidings* [ὁ εὐαγγελιζόμενος].
> Lift up your voice with strength,
>   O Jerusalem, *herald of good tidings* [ὁ εὐαγγελιζόμενος],
>   lift it up, do not be afraid,
>   say to the towns of Judah,
>   'Behold your God!'

It occurs also in Isaiah 52:7 (which Paul cites in Romans 10:15 as being descriptive of the New Testament gospel proclamation):

---

52. Herman Ridderbos, *When the Time Had Fully Come: Studies in New Testament Theology* (Grand Rapids: Eerdmans, 1957), 48-49.
53. Vos, *The Pauline Eschatology*, 11.
54. Vos, *The Pauline Eschatology*, 38.
55. Sixty of the seventy-six occurrences of εὐαγγέλιον in the New Testament are found in Paul's writings.

> How beautiful on the mountains
>> are the feet *of those who bring good news* [εὐαγγελιζομένου],
> who proclaim peace,
>> *who bring good tidings* [ὃς εὐαγγελιζόμενος ἀγαθά],
>> who proclaim salvation,
> who say to Zion,
>> 'Your God reigns!' (See also Nahum 1:15)

These verses show that Isaiah's concept of the 'good news' that these 'beautiful feet' bring entails the proclamation of both Yahweh's coming to and his enthronement on Zion and the concomitant dethronement of all the pagan gods (see Isaiah's 'Behold your God!' and 'Your God reigns!'). His enthronement also holds out the promise of his people's release from exile, for which idea one may go to Isaiah 61:1-2, which prophecy Jesus declared in Luke 4:17-21 was to be fulfilled by his mission:

> The Spirit of the Sovereign Lord is upon me,
> because the Lord has anointed me
> *to preach good news* [εὐαγγελίσασθαι] to the poor.
> He has sent me to bind up the brokenhearted,
>> to proclaim freedom for the captives
>>> and release from darkness for the prisoners,
>> to proclaim the year of the Lord's favor.

In pagan Greco-Roman literature the plural form (only) of εὐαγγέλιον is a technical term used within the context of the Caesar cult to designate the announcement of the birth or accession of an emperor or the achieving of a great victory. The coming of a new ruler meant the promise of peace and a new start for the world. An inscription from around 9 B.C. found in Priene on the coast of Asia Minor illustrates well these points when it speaks of Octavian Caesar (Augustus) who became the first Roman emperor in 31 B.C.:

> The providence which has ordered the whole of our life, showing concern and zeal, has ordained the most perfect consummation for human life by giving to it Augustus, by filling him with virtue for doing the work of a benefactor among men, and by sending in him...a saviour for us and those who come after us, to make war to cease, to create order everywhere...; the birthday of the god [Augustus] was the beginning for the world of the *glad tidings* [εὐανγελίων] that have come to men through him....[56]

These usages highlight the *confrontational* character of the gospel. By his death, resurrection, and ascension Christ has inherited the title above all titles – that of Lord (Phil 2:9-11). In the Roman world of Paul's day the word κύριος ('lord') was regularly used to denote the politico-social superior above all other superiors, even the Roman emperor. From the Roman perspective there was only one lord of the world, the Roman Caesar. But according to the Christian gospel, he and all other kings now have a rival Lord who wears a crown that out-rivals all the lords of the earth, before whom every knee will bow and every tongue will confess his Lordship to the glory of God the Father. Therefore, 'to do the work of an evangelist' (2 Tim 4:5) is not simply to tell people 'how to be saved'; to 'evangelize' is to proclaim, to announce, from the housetops that Jesus Christ is Lord of lords. And to announce that Jesus Christ reigns as King and Lord of the universe is to announce to the Caesars of this world that they do not. To proclaim Christ's Lordship is to *confront* all the petty pretensions of the religious and secular pagan lords of this world with his true and sovereign Kingship which demands heart submission. As Paul would later assert, his apostleship in the service of God's gospel concerning his Son was intended 'to call people from all the Gentiles to the obedience that comes from faith' (Rom 1:1-5).

Nor is the 'proclamation of the gospel' merely the recounting of a salvific system whereby people are saved, that is, the delineating of an *ordo salutis* or an *ordo applicatio*. True, its proclamation results in people being saved. But the proclamation of the gospel is the proclamation that the crucified and risen Jewish Messiah is Lord and King of the universe and that in that capacity he has authoritatively summoned the whole world to repentance (Acts 17:30) and obedience to his scepter through faith in him (Rom 1:5).

Nor is the 'proclamation of the gospel' the mere 'offering' of Christ's saving benefits to those who apathetically may or may not want them. Paul would no more have said to his auditors: 'If you would like to have an experience of living under an emperor, you might try the Jewish Messiah,' than Caesar's herald would have said:

---

56. *Priene Inscriptions*, edited by F. Hiller von Gärtringen, 105, 40f. Note the similarity between the last sentence of the Priene inscription and the opening statement, 'The beginning of the good news,' in Mark 1:1. See also H. G. Liddell and R. Scott, εὐαγγέλιον, *A Greek-English Lexicon*, revised by H. S. Jones (Oxford: Clarendon, 1940), with Supplement (1968), and G. H. R. Horsley, *New Documents Illustrating Early Christianity* (North Ryde: The Ancient History Documentary Research Center, 1981-), 3.12-15.

'You might try Nero.' Just as Caesar's herald would have announced: 'Nero has ascended the throne of Rome and has become your emperor; submit to his imperial authority,' so also by his gospel Paul proclaimed: 'Christ by his deeds has become the Lord of the universe and your sovereign King! You must submit to him if you would be delivered from the bonds that enslave you!' In short, the 'good news' concerning God's Son is the proclamation that through his death and resurrection in a very human, even Jewish, life the living God in the person of Jesus Christ has become the sovereign King of the world and demands the obedience of mankind. And only to those who from the heart submit in faith to his authority will he grant the gift of eternal life; all others in his wrath he will destroy.[57]

The Demographic Extent of Saul's Apostolic Call

The Damascus Road experience was, for Saul, not only the occasion of his conversion; it was also the occasion of his apostolic call to proclaim Christ's lordship *both to Israel and to the nations*. To Ananias, the risen Christ declared: 'This man is my chosen instrument to carry my name *before the Gentiles and their kings and before the people of Israel*. I will show him how much he must suffer for my name' (Acts 9:15-16). Ananias communicated Christ's words to Saul accurately though in somewhat different terms: 'The God of our fathers has chosen you to know his will and to see the Righteous One and to hear words from his mouth. You will be his witness to *all men* of what you have seen and heard' (22:15). This call the Lord Jesus confirmed to him directly in an ecstatic trance three years later in Jerusalem, in the Temple: 'Quick! Leave Jerusalem immediately, because they will not accept your testimony about me...Go; I will send you far away *to the Gentiles*' (Acts 22:18, 21).[58]

Paul in his defense before King Herod Agrippa II years later, by citing Christ directly, abbreviated the terms of Christ's call to him this way: 'I have appeared to you to appoint you as a servant and as

---

57. I am indebted to N. T. Wright, *What Saint Paul Really Said* (Grand Rapids: Eerdmans, 1997), 41-45, for some of the insights of this section.

58. Paul had perhaps come to Jerusalem three years after his conversion (Gal 1:18), after having evangelized Damascus and Arabia, not only to become acquainted with the apostles, but also to make Jerusalem his mission headquarters. If these were his plans, they were not to be, for the glorified Christ informed him that he should 'leave Jerusalem immediately' and go away to the Gentiles. Accordingly, as we shall see, after a lengthy stay at Tarsus, he made Antioch on the Orontes his mission headquarters.

a witness of what you have seen of me and what I will show you. I will rescue you *from your own people and from the Gentiles. I am sending you to open their eyes and turn them [Jews and Gentiles] from darkness to light*, and from the power of Satan to God, so that they may receive forgiveness of sins and a place among those who are sanctified by faith in me' (Acts 26:15-18). And lest Agrippa should conclude that this 'gospel' to which Christ had called him—to be proclaimed to both Israel and the Gentile nations—was a *de novo* proclamation not rooted firmly in the covenantal theology of the Old Testament scriptures, in this same defense before Agrippa Paul also declared unequivocally: 'It is because of my hope in *what God has promised our fathers* that I am on trial today. It is *the promise our twelve tribes are hoping to see fulfilled* as they earnestly serve God day and night...I have had God's help to this very day, and so I stand here and testify to small and great alike. *I am saying nothing beyond what the prophets and Moses said would happen – that the Messiah would suffer and, as the first to rise from the dead, would proclaim light to his own people and to the Gentiles*' (Acts 26:6-7, 22-23).[59]

To the magnificent story of Saul's 'obedience to this heavenly vision' we will now turn. First to his kinsman according to the flesh we will hear him declare

(1) that God in the coming of Jesus Christ had moved history from the age of Old Testament promise into the age of New Testament fulfillment, in short, that what the prophets had predicted had already begun to see fulfillment,

(2) that the Messianic age had appeared in its grace modality and was summoning Israel to repudiate its misguided efforts to achieve a righteousness before God by works of law and to receive by faith the benefits of the Messiah's obedience, death-work, and resurrection for righteousness and pardon,

(3) that since Christ is the end of the law for righteousness right standing before God is law-free, making the observance by Israel of its ancient ceremonial laws, dietary laws, and circumcision unnecessary for acceptance by him (though never necessary for salvation, their observance was still permissible as long as their observance was not being done for meritorious purposes), and

(4) that the power modality of the Eschaton was still to appear at

---

59. See my chapter, 'The Unity of the Covenant of Grace' in *A New Systematic Theology of the Christian Faith*, 503-44.

the return of Jesus Christ, at which time the resurrection of the dead, the judgment of all mankind, and the transformation of created nature into a new heaven and a new earth would occur.

Then to all the forms of paganism we will hear him declare

(1) from Old Testament revelation, over against their many gods and their divinization of creation, the knowledge of the true God and the goodness of creation;

(2) from the biblical doctrines of creation, fall, and redemption, over against their mythologies, the true story of the world;

(3) from the ultimate lordship of Jesus Christ, over against all their lesser and petty lords, a radical challenge to the powers of world empire;

(4) from the propitiatory sacrifice of Jesus Christ, over against all their efforts to placate the gods by their cultic sacrifices, true justification and pardon for sin;

(5) from the Christian world-and-life view, over against the flawed wisdom in even the magisterial philosophies of Greece, the nature of true wisdom, and

(6) from the Decalogue as the covenant way of life, over against their self-destructive modes of living, what it means to live a truly human life.

And to both groups we will hear him declare that God in and by the church, which is the body of Christ, God has made both Jew and Gentile 'one new man' and fellow-heirs, fellow-members of Christ's body, and fellow-sharers of the promises of God, making peace between them.

CHAPTER FIVE

SAUL'S FIRST EVANGELISTIC EFFORTS AND HIS FIRST TWO POST-CONVERSION TRIPS TO JERUSALEM (c. A.D. 33-46) (ACTS 9:20-12:25)

> He who can part from country and from kin,
>   And scorn delights, and tread the thorny way,
> A heavenly crown, through toil and pain, to win –
>   He, who reviled, can tender love repay,
>   And, buffeted, for bitter foes can pray –
>   He who, upspringing at his Captain's call,
> Fights the good fight, and when at last the day
>   Of fiery trial comes, can nobly fall –
> Such were a saint – or more – and such the holy Paul!
>   Anon., cited by P. Schaff,
>   *History of the Christian Church*, 1.316

With the exalted Christ's power and blessing now resting upon him and his new faith in the Christ with its eschatological implications redirecting his life's course and energies, Saul of Tarsus began that missionary work which, though he never realized it at the time, would make him a major figure in human history and his name a revered household name among Christians throughout the world.

Saul's Damascene (Acts 9:20-22) and Arabian (Galatians 1:17; 2 Corinthians 11:32-33) Evangelistic Efforts (c. A.D. 33-35).

Although only newly converted to the Way[1] which he had come to

---

1. 'The Way' (ἡ ὁδός) was the term used by the early followers of Jesus for the Christian movement (Acts 9:2; 19:9, 23; 22:4; 24:14, 22; see also 16:17; 18:25-26). Some scholars find the origin for this term in the Zadokite Work and other documents of the Qumran community, but it is not necessary to resort to such an origin. Jesus himself had claimed to be 'the Way' (ἡ ὁδός) to the Father and thus to heaven (John 14:6), and the word naturally came to designate 'the true way' or 'the right way' of faith and life to God and to salvation which he had initiated.

Damascus to persecute, Saul spent several days with the Damascus disciples, and

(1) '*immediately* [εὐθέως] in the synagogues *preached* [ἐκήρυσσεν] Jesus, that he is the Son of God' (Acts 9:20),[2]

(2) '*grew more and more powerful* [ἐνεδυναμοῦτο] and *baffled* [συνέχυννεν] the Jews living in Damascus, *offering proof* [συμβιβάζων] that [Jesus] is the Christ' (Acts 9:22), and

(3) 'in Damascus...*preached fearlessly* [ἐπαρρησιάσατο] in the name of Jesus' (Acts 9:27).

Sometime during the period denoted by Luke's 'many days' in Acts 9:23, Saul journeyed south into (Petran?[3]) Arabia (Gal 1:17; see Galatians 4:25 for an indication of how extensive 'Arabia' was regarded at the time). What did he do there? Some say he went there for quiet reflection and to reorient his mind Christocentrically in light of his Damascus Road experience; others contend that he went to preach Christ. Which? I suggest the latter (though the first could also have occurred), for the following two reasons:

A. '...probably his three days of blindness in Damascus had been sufficient for his mind to be reorientated. The implication of his own narrative [in Galatians] relates his Arabian visit rather closely to his call to preach Christ among the Gentiles [compare 1:17 and 1:16]; the point of his reference to it in writing to his Galatian converts is to underline the fact that he began to discharge this call before he went up to Jerusalem to see the apostles there, so that none could say that it was they (or any other authorities on earth) who commissioned him to be the Gentiles' apostle.'[4]

---

2. The title, 'the Son of God', in Acts 9:20 is the only occurrence of this Christological title in Acts. F. F. Bruce (*The Book of the Acts* [Revised edition; The New International Commentary on the New Testament; Grand Rapids: Eerdmans, 1988]) declares that it is 'no merely official title', but represents an advance on the way in which Jesus' messiahship had been proclaimed in Acts to this point, expressing Jesus' 'unique relationship and fellowship with the Father' (190). I would urge, however, that Jesus was believed on and proclaimed as the unique, divine Son of God from the very beginning of the church's proclamation; see my *Jesus, Divine Messiah: The New Testament Witness* (Phillipsburg, N. J.: Presbyterian and Reformed, 1990).

3. Josephus in his *Jewish Wars* 5.159-60 and *Antiquities of the Jews* 5.82 writes that Arabia can be seen from the tower of Psephinus in Jerusalem on a clear day. In his *Antiquities* 18.109 Josephus speaks of Arabia Petrea meaning 'the Arabia that belongs to Petra'.

4. F. F. Bruce, *Paul: Apostle of the Heart Set Free* (Grand Rapids: Eerdmans, 1996 reprint of the 1977 edition), 81.

B. 'By "Arabia" in this context we naturally understand the Nabataean kingdom, which was readily accessible from Damascus. At this time it was ruled by Aretas IV (9 B.C.-A.D. 40).... It certainly appears from a piece of evidence elsewhere in his correspondence that it was not simply a quiet retreat that Paul sought in Arabia. In a later reminiscence he recalls a humiliating experience from his early Christian days: "At Damascus the ethnarch [ἐθνάρχης] of King Aretas guarded the city of the Damascenes in order to seize me, but I was let down in a basket through a window in the wall, and escaped his hands" (2 Corinthians 11:32f.)....[5] But why should the Nabataean ethnarch take this hostile action against Paul, if Paul spent his time in Arabia in quiet contemplation? If, on the other hand, he spent his time there in preaching, he could well have stirred up trouble for himself and attracted the unfriendly attention of the authorities.'[6]

So in Damascus the peril from Jewish (and only occasionally Gentile) quarters began (Acts 9:20) which dogged Paul's steps for the remainder of his life. Jewish hostility here was only the first instance of what the glorified Lord had told Ananias was to be Saul's lot when he said: 'Go to the house of Judas on Straight Street and ask for a man named Saul of Tarsus... Go! This man is my chosen instrument to carry my name before the Gentiles and their kings and before the

---

5. Luke refers to this escape in Acts 9:23-25. He informs us that the Jewish leaders in Damascus were also in some way involved in the conspiracy to seize Paul and to kill him, no doubt partly because of what they regarded as his treason toward his earlier faith and because he had been preaching in their synagogues that the crucified Jesus was the divine Son of God (Acts 9:20).
    Why does Paul refer to this incident at all in 2 Corinthians? His mention of it occurs in a section (11:16–12:10) where he begins, with real reticence but also in high drama, to itemize the things about which he reluctantly boasts over against the things about which the opposing 'false apostles' at Corinth boasted. He mentions it as one example of the 'weaknesses' in which he gloried. How was it that? He had gone to Damascus in full political power and prestige, authorized to imprison Jewish Christians; he had departed from Damascus with so little power and prestige with men that he had to escape those who would have killed him by hiding in a basket and being let down through a window in the wall of the city. Ministers today could learn from this: in what do *they* glory? In their great strengths and gifts or in their equally great (if not greater) weaknesses which alone enable Christ's power to rest upon them (see 12:9-10)?
6. Bruce, *Paul*, 81-82. So also Martin Hengel and Anna Maria Schwemer, *Paul Between Damascus and Antioch: The Unknown Years*, translated by John Bowden (Louisville, Kentucky: Westminster John Knox, 1997), 106-26, who suggest that Saul would have preached in the synagogues of the larger cities of the Nabataean kingdom such as Petra and, basing their suggestion upon Galatians 4:25, perhaps as far south as Hegra which place name may have suggested to Paul his allegory on Hagar.

people of Israel. *I will show him how much he must suffer for my name'* (Acts:9:11-16).

One last matter should be addressed again before we move on. In response to the question, does the assertion that Saul was preaching in Arabia mean that almost immediately after his conversion he had worked out the main lines of his gospel proclamation of justification by faith alone? I would answer in the affirmative as do Hengel and Schwemer also, who write:

> Paul formulates his doctrine of justification for the first time in principle, in the letters we have, in Gal. 2, but he emphatically states that he had put this forward at the time in Antioch in the face of Peter and the assembled community as the 'truth of the gospel'.... The fact that Paul definitively parted company even with Barnabas after this dispute shows that what was being discussed was not Antiochene community tradition, but exclusively the theological question of truth as the apostle understood it. Here he had all the Antiochene Jewish Christians, i.e. the leading men in the community, against him. [And he had preached the doctrine of justification by faith in Christ in Pisidian Antioch on his first missionary journey (Acts 13:38-39) even before the incident involving Peter in Antioch on the Orontes and also before he wrote Galatians. – RLR]
>
> [We (the authors) have already argued in *Paul Between Damascus and Antioch*, 4.2] that the core of [Paul's thought], that 'in Christ' the Gentiles become sons of God and therefore are also the seed of Abraham, will have been part of Paul's message to the Gentile godfearers already in Damascus (and Arabia) and later in Cilicia and Syria.[7]

Saul's First (of Five) Recorded Post-Conversion Visit to Jerusalem in Luke's Acts (Acts 9:26-30; 22:17-21; Galatians 1:18-19) (c. A.D. 35–36).

Luke refers to Saul's first visit to Jerusalem after his conversion in Acts 9:26-30 (his 'after many days' in Acts 9:23 covers the same period as Paul's 'after three years' in Galatians 1:18).[8] He informs us that when Saul first came to Jerusalem the disciples at first were afraid of him, not believing that he really was a Christian. But Joseph, a Levite from Cyprus whom the apostles had early on begun to call 'Barnabas, which means "Son of Consolation" ' (Acts 4:36), brought

---

7. Hengel and Schwemer, *Paul Between Damascus and Antioch*, 292.
8. See 1 Kings 2:38-39 (NASV) for a precise parallel of the 'time' phrases here: 'Shimei lived in Jerusalem *many days*. But it came about at the end of *three years* that two of the servants of Shimei ran away to Achish....'

him to the apostles (τοὺς ἀποστόλους), and related to them, first, that Saul *had seen* (εἶδεν) the Lord, second, that the Lord *had spoken* (ἐλάλησεν) to him, and third, that in Damascus Saul had '*preached fearlessly* [ἐπαρρησιάσατο] in the name of Jesus'. 'So Saul stayed with them and moved about freely in Jerusalem, *speaking boldly* [παρρησιαζόμενος] *in the name of the Lord*. He talked and debated *with* [συνεζήτει] the Hellenists [τοὺς Ἑλληνιστάς; were these Greek-speaking Jews members of his old synagogue?], but they tried to kill him' (Acts 9:29).

He still would have continued his ministry there, but the Lord spoke to him in an ecstatic trance (ἐν ἐκστάσει) while he was praying in the temple and commanded him to leave the city: 'Go, I will send you far away to the Gentiles' (Acts 22:17-21).[9] So just as the Damascus Christians came to Paul's rescue earlier, so now the Jerusalem Christians also, for his safety, took him to the port city of Caesarea and sent him off to Tarsus. Paul refers to his destination at this time as 'the regions of Syria and Cilicia' (Gal 1:21), which is his description of the one united imperial province ('Syria/Cilicia') whose chief cities were Antioch on the Orontes and Tarsus respectively.

Luke pauses at this point to give his readers his second (the first for this book) progress report in Acts: 'Then the church throughout Judea, Galilee and Samaria enjoyed a time of peace. It was strengthened; and encouraged by the Holy Spirit, it grew in numbers, living in the fear of the Lord' (9:31). While it may already be obvious to the perceptive reader, it still bears pointing out that the 'church' about which Luke speaks here is 'the original Jerusalem church, now dispersed and decentralized,' but confined to Jewish and semi-Jewish people.[10]

In Galatians 1:18-19 Paul also refers to this first Jerusalem visit, giving us some details in addition to those in Luke's account. He informs us, first, that he went up to Jerusalem 'to get acquainted with' (ἱστορῆσαι, more likely intending its precise classical sense, 'to make inquiry of'[11]) Peter, since Paul would doubtless have been interested in Peter's firsthand eye- and ear-witness account of the earthly life

---

9. Bruce, *Paul*, 94.
10. Bruce, *Acts*, 196.
11. BAGD, ἱστορέω, *A Greek-English Lexicon of the New Testament and Other Early Christian Literature* (Second edition; Chicago: University of Chicago, 1979): 'visit for the purpose of coming to know someone or someth.', 'to get information from' (383). See also James D. G. Dunn, *Jesus, Paul, and the Law* (Louisville, Kentucky:

and ministry of Jesus; second, that this visit took place three years after his conversion, during which three-year period, as we have already noted, he had already been engaged in Gentile evangelism; third, that this visit lasted two weeks (hardly time enough for Paul to have become a disciple of Peter as the Judaizing opposition in South Galatia would likely later contend); and fourth, that during his visit, besides Peter, he saw only James, the Lord's brother.[12]

It was doubtless at this time that Paul 'received [παρέλαβον]' from Peter and James the 'Jerusalem tradition' which he had 'passed on [παρέδωκα]' to the Corinthians (see 1 Cor 15:3-5).[13] Bruce notes: 'In that list [in 1 Corinthians 15:3-5] two individuals are mentioned by name as having seen the risen Christ, and only two [Peter and

Westminster/John Knox, 1990), who argues that, having made the point that three years had passed *before* he met any of the original apostles, 'Paul was quite ready to acknowledge his indebtedness to Peter for further information—no doubt primarily background information about the ministry of Jesus while on earth as well perhaps as the very beginnings of the new movement centred on the risen Christ' (112-13). It should not go unnoticed that while he 'inquired of' (ἱστορῆσαι) Peter (Gal. 1:18), he only 'saw' (εἶδον) James (Gal 1:19).

12. Bruce (*Paul*, 84) writes: '...where Luke generalizes [Acts 9:27], Paul is specific, and makes it plain he met only two of [the apostles].' These men, by themselves, hardly constituted a legitimate source of his apostolic commission.

13. New Testament scholars in increasing numbers are advocating that Paul's statements in 1 Corinthians 15:3-5 (the first written account of the resurrection appearances since 1 Corinthians was written prior to the canonical Gospels) reflect the contents of a quasi-official early Christian creed much older than 1 Corinthians itself (which letter was written probably in the spring of A.D. 55 from Ephesus) which circulated within the *Palestinian* community of believers. Günther Bornkamm, for example, refers to Paul's enumeration of the appearances of the risen Christ in 1 Corinthians 15:3-7 as 'the oldest and most reliable Easter text...formulated long before Paul'. He says of this 'old form' that it 'reads almost like an official record' (*Jesus of Nazareth* [New York: Harper and Brothers, 1960], 182). See also Wolfhart Pannenberg, *Jesus—God and Man* (Philadelphia: Westminster, 1968), 90-91. Excellent treatments of this generally accepted view may be found in George E. Ladd, 'Revelation and Tradition in Paul,' *Apostolic History and the Gospel*, eds. W. Ward Gasque and Ralph P. Martin (Exeter: Paternoster, 1970), 223-30, particularly 224-25; Grant R. Osborne, *The Resurrection Narratives: A Redactional Study* (Grand Rapids: Baker, 1984), 221-25; and Gary R. Habermas, *Ancient Evidence for the Life of Jesus* (Nashville: Thomas Nelson, 1984), 124-27.

This insight is based upon (1) Paul's references to his 'delivering' to the Corinthians what he had first 'received', terms suggesting that he had passed on to them a piece of 'tradition', (2) the stylized parallelism of the 'delivered' material itself (see the four ὅτι clauses and the repeated κατὰ τὰς γραφάς phrases in the first and third of them), (3) the Aramaic 'Cephas' for Peter, suggesting a Palestinian milieu for this tradition, (4) the traditional description of the disciples as 'the Twelve', and (5) the omission of the appearances to the women from the list. If Paul, in fact, had 'received' some of this 'tradition', for example, that concerning Jesus' appearances to Peter and to James (referred to in 15:5, 7; see also Acts 13:30-31) directly from Peter and James themselves during his first visit to Jerusalem three years after his conversion (see Acts 9:26-28; Gal

James].... It is no mere coincidence that these should be the only two apostles whom Paul claims to have seen during his first visit to Jerusalem after his conversion.'[14]

Paul apparently regarded James in some sense as an apostle (or 'apostolic man'), according to the most probable sense of his statement (*contra* J. Gresham Machen who translates Paul's statement: 'Another of the apostles I did not see – only, I did see James').[15] But it seems to me that James must be regarded in some sense as an apostle to satisfy Luke's plural ἀποστόλους in Acts 9:27. And we know that Paul thought of others beside the original Twelve as 'apostles', for he draws a distinction between the 'Twelve' and 'all the apostles' in 1 Corinthians 15:5, 7.

Saul's 'Syria/Cilicia Evangelization' (Acts 9:30; Galatians 1:22-23) (c. A.D. 36-45)

How long Paul was in and around Tarsus in Syria/Cilicia cannot be determined with precision. Perhaps he was there as long as nine to ten years.[16] But what he did there is not in doubt. He tells us in Galatians 1:22-23 that while he 'was personally unknown to the churches of Judea', the people of Judea 'only kept on hearing [μόνον ἀκούοντες ἦσαν]' that he '*is preaching* [εὐαγγελίζεται] the faith

---

1:18-19), which is quite likely, then this pericope reflects what those who were the earliest eye-witnesses to the events that had taken place in Jerusalem were teaching on *Palestinian* soil within *five to eight years* after the *crucifixion*. This clearly implies that the material in 1 Corinthians 15:3b-5 is based on *early Palestinian* eyewitness testimony and is hardly the reflection of legendary reports arising much later within the so-called Jewish Hellenistic or Gentile Hellenistic communities of faith. There simply was not enough time, with the original disciples still present in Jerusalem to correct false stories that might arise about Jesus, for legendary accretions of this nature to have risen and to have become an honored feature of the 'tradition'.

The presence and characteristics of this 'early confession' raise serious questions in turn concerning the contention of many Bultmannian scholars that the appearance stories in the canonical Gospels are 'legendary' stories based upon non-Palestinian sources. The facts strongly suggest otherwise – that the appearance stories in the Gospels are not legendary accounts, as these Bultmannians contend.

14. Bruce, *Paul*, 84-5.

15. J. Gresham Machen, *Machen's Notes on Galatians*, edited by John H. Skilton (Philadelphia: Presbyterian and Reformed, 1972), 78.

16. This length of time for Saul in Syria/Cilicia is the eleven-year period which transpired between Paul's first and second visits to Jerusalem (Gal 1:18; 2:1) minus the full year of ministry in Antioch (Acts 11:26). See also F. F. Bruce, *New Testament History* (London: Nelson, 1969), 245. Hengel and Schwemer, *Paul Between Damascus and Antioch*, suggest a much shorter time – from c. 36/37 to c. 39/40 – but a longer mission for Paul in Syrian Antioch (c. 41 to 46/47) than the one year or so that I allow based on Acts 11:26.

he once tried to destroy'. He doubtless made tents (Acts 18:3) to support himself while he carried on his evangelistic ministry. Indeed, it may have been mainly while he was making tents that he evangelized those who would listen to him.

During these years Paul was probably disinherited by his family for joining the followers of Jesus (Phil 3:8), and during these years he very probably endured some of the suffering he itemizes in 2 Corinthians 11:23-27 such as the five times he received from the Jews thirty-nine lashes,[17] since none of these lashings are reported in Acts or by Paul elsewhere, and the three times he was beaten with rods (by Gentiles?).

One other significant piece of Pauline history should be noted here. If Paul's labors in the province of 'Syria/Cilicia' did extend from about A.D. 36 to A.D. 45, as I have suggested, then it was during this time that the mysterious vision he refers to in 2 Corinthians 12:2-9 also occurred.[18] His account of this incident occurs in the section, referred to earlier, where he is itemizing the things about which he would boast if he had to boast about something. He had carried around with him what he tells us there for all that time and had said nothing about it, and he would have said nothing about it even there had not 'the false apostles' (οἱ ψευδαπόστολοι, 2 Cor 11:13) questioned his apostolic authority and infected his church at Corinth with their false teaching. Around A.D. 42 (fourteen years before A.D. 55 or 56, the calculated date of writing of 2 Corinthians, to be established later), Paul was caught up to Paradise in some unknown state (see his 'Whether it was in the body or out of the body I do not know'), and he heard 'things too

---

17. With respect to these scourgings, according to the Mishna's 'Treatise on Punishments' (מכות, 'Stripes'), after the upper body of the subject of the scourging was stripped bare of all clothing, his hands were tied to a stake, and with a scourge of two thongs the executioner, with all of the force of one hand, struck the subject thirteen times on the breast, thirteen times on the right shoulder, and thirteen times on the left. While the subject was being scourged, the chief judge read aloud Deuteronomy 28:58-59, then Deuteronomy 29:9, and finally, Psalm 78:38-39. The readings might be repeated but were so timed as to be completed exactly with the completion of the punishment. A second judge counted the blows, and a third exclaimed 'Strike him' before each blow. The potential for serious, if not fatal, physical harm from such a scourging can be drawn from the brief addition: '*If the criminal die under the infliction*, the executioner is not accounted guilty unless he gives by mistake a single blow too many, in which case he is banished.' See Michael L. Rodkinson (ed.), *New Edition of the Babylonian Talmud* (Boston: New Talmud Society, 1918), 9.50.

When one examines numerous offences listed in the treatise for which this punishment was assigned (מכות, 3.1-4), it is difficult to identify even one offence of which Paul would have been guilty. Of course, where the will to punish exists, the pretext for such is not long in being found.

18. See Acts 18:9ff. and 23:11 for additional visions he received.

Saul's First Evangelistic Efforts and First Two Trips

sacred to put into words [ἄρρητα ῥήματα], things that a man is not permitted to tell.' To keep him from becoming conceited because of 'the surpassing greatness of the revelations' (τῇ ὑπερβολῇ τῶν ἀποκαλύψεων) which he received on that occasion – what must heaven be like! – the glorified Christ blessed Paul by giving to him 'a thorn in the flesh, a messenger of Satan, to torment' him. In spite of his thrice-expressed entreaty to Christ to remove the thorn, Christ refused to remove it, declaring: 'My grace is sufficient for you, for my power is made perfect in [your] weakness.' So Paul boasted, but not in what he had seen and heard, but in his 'thorn in the flesh' which may have been chronic ophthalmia.[19] I mention the occurrence of this 'heavenly journey' here, not only because it fits here historically, but also because in its own unique way it makes us aware of the extremely difficult physical circumstances under which Paul labored throughout all of his recorded missionary travels in Acts and the Pastoral Letters.

It was also during this period – in A.D. 44, to be precise – that King Herod Agrippa died,[20] having earlier beheaded James, the brother of John, and imprisoned Peter who was miraculously delivered from prison and from almost certain martyrdom (see Acts 12).

At this juncture Luke offers his third progress report concerning the advance of the gospel: 'But the word of God continued to increase and spread' (12:24).

Saul's Antiochene Labors (Acts 11:25-26) (c. A.D. 45-46)

Some unnamed Hellenistic Jewish Christians from Cyprus and Cyrene, forced to leave Jerusalem because of the 'Sauline' persecution that began in Jerusalem after Stephen's martyrdom, had travelled to Antioch on the Orontes.

Excursus on Antioch on the Orontes

Seleucus I Nicator, who defeated Antigonus, one of Alexander the Great's generals, at the battle of Ipsus in 301 B.C. and claimed Antigonus's portion of Alexander's divided Greek empire, founded Antioch on the Orontes in 300 B.C. as the capital of the Seleucid monarchy and named it after his father Antiochus. The city (modern Antakya), situated some

---

19. I must ask again, do we boast in our weaknesses which alone make it possible for Christ to manifest his power through us?

20. See Josephus, *Antiquities*, 19. 50: 'the fifty-fourth year of his life and the seventh year of his reign.'

ten miles upriver from its port city, Seleucia, and another five miles from the river's mouth, covered an area of approximately one by two miles and was laid out on a Hippodamian grid plan (streets crossing at right angles forming rectangular blocks of 367 feet by 190 feet). In Roman times, continuing a building program begun in 67 B.C. by Marcius Rex and Pompey, Julius Caesar conducted a building program there commencing in 47 B.C., building an aqueduct to bring water into the city from Mount Silpius on the east, a theater and an amphitheater, the *Kaisareion*, perhaps the oldest basilica dedicated to the cult of Rome in the east, and rebuilding the Pantheon. Augustus Caesar visited the city twice and also conducted extensive building projects which he funded from the treasury he found in Egypt after the defeat of Antony and Cleopatra in 31 B.C. Tiberius Caesar completed the building of several temples which Augustus had begun. And Herod the Great erected colonnades on both sides of its main street running the full length of the city northeast to southwest which cut the city in half and paved this street with polished stone. Gaius Caesar (Caligula) responded to an earthquake which devastated the city in A.D. 37, both renovating and building new buildings. The city established its own Olympic Games in A.D. 43. These facts indicate the strategic importance that Rome attached to this capital of the Roman province of Syria.

At first the city's population was Greek but in later years many Syrians and many Jews (Josephus, *Wars of the Jews*, 7.3.3) also settled there. These Jews possessed equal rights with the Greeks and established their own synagogue worship. Under Roman rule the city prospered and became the military and commercial gateway to the Orient. In New Testament times Antioch ranked next to Rome and Alexandria in size, with its population, according to Strabo (*Geography* 16.2.5), numbering about three hundred thousand. Antioch was known for its moral laxity and the worship of Artemis and Apollo (actually new names for Astarte and his consort), but 'most of all [the city] was famous for the worship of Daphne whose temple stood five miles out of the town amidst its laurel groves. The legend was that Daphne was a mortal maid with whom Apollo fell in love. He pursued her, and to save her Daphne was changed into a laurel bush. The priestesses of the Temple of Daphne were sacred prostitutes and, nightly, in these laurel groves the pursuit was reenacted by the worshippers and the priestesses. "The morals of Daphne" was a phrase that all the world knew for loose and lustful living.'[21]

With Paul's arrival in Antioch the beginning of a new chapter in the history of the city was about to be written, for it was to become the birthplace of Gentile Christianity and the sending center for the Pauline mission enterprise and Paul's teaching of justification through faith in Christ apart from works of law.

Saul's First Evangelistic Efforts and First Two Trips

According to Luke, these Hellenist Jewish Christians began to evangelize Gentiles at Antioch:

> Now those who had been scattered by the persecution in connection with Stephen traveled as far as Phoenicia, Cyprus, and Antioch, telling the message only to [Diaspora, and therefore, 'Hellenist'] Jews. Some of them, however, men from Cyprus and Cyrene, went to Antioch and began to speak to Greeks ["Ελληνας] also, telling them the good news about the Lord Jesus. The Lord's hand was with them, and a great number of people believed and turned to the Lord. (Acts 11:19-21)[22]

Luke's words here, though simple in themselves, nonetheless record a quantum leap forward in Gentile evangelization. Merrill C. Tenney declares:

> The Cypriote and Cyrenian believers who preached at Antioch departed from the general exclusive procedure of their fellows by preaching to Greek Gentiles. Luke's comment here indicates that his presentation of [this period] emphasized the exceptions rather than the usual procedure of preaching. Antioch, which was evangelized in [this] period, was so exceptional that it became the fountainhead of an entirely new missionary enterprise.[23]

This remarkable work of evangelization at Antioch had probably begun between A. D. 33 and A. D. 35. This Lukan bit of information also highlights a not-always-recognized truth, namely, that 'Paul is not quite the lone genius in pioneering Gentile missions and in establishing Gentile churches free from the Law that some romanticizing accounts make him out to be'.[24] Bruce comments on Acts 11:20-21:

> ...in Antioch some daring spirits ... took a momentous step forward. If the gospel was so good for Jews, might it not be good for Gentiles also? At any rate, they would make the experiment. So they began to make known to the Greek population of Antioch the claims of Jesus as Lord and Savior....
> This enterprise met with instant success. The Gentiles took to the Christian message as the very thing they had been waiting for, as something that exactly suited their case, and a large number of them believed the gospel and yielded their allegiance to Jesus as Lord.[25]

---

21. William Barclay, *The Acts of the Apostles* (Philadelphia: Westminster, zzz), 94.

22. I would argue that "Ελληνας, meaning 'Greeks', and not "Ελληνιστὰς, 'Hellenist Jews', should be the preferred reading in Acts 11:20 from the fact that the latter are already referred to in 11:19.

23. Merrill C. Tenney, *New Testament Survey* (Grand Rapids: Eerdmans, 1961), 251-52.

24. Martin Franzmann, *The Word of the Lord Grows* (St. Louis: Concordia, 1961), 48.

The Jerusalem church sent Barnabas to investigate this missionary effort. Concluding that the evident hand of God's blessing was upon the Antioch experiment and selflessly recognizing the need for learned and stable leadership which he himself could not provide, he journeyed to Tarsus to find Saul who was uniquely suited for just such a mission, 'and when he found him, he brought him to Antioch. So for a whole year Barnabas and Saul met with the church and taught great numbers of people. The disciples were first called Christians [Χριστιανούς] at Antioch' (11:26).[26]

Saul's Second Post-Conversion Visit to Jerusalem (the 'Famine Relief Visit') and the Demarcation of Mission Fields (Acts 11:27-30; 12:25; Galatians 2:1-10) (c. A.D. 46)

In response to the Spirit-directed prediction of Agabus, a Jerusalem prophet who had come to Antioch, that 'a severe famine would spread over the entire Roman world' (Acts 11:28), which famine occurred during the reign of Claudius Caesar (A.D. 41-54) with Judea being particularly hard hit between A.D. 45 and 48,[27] the Christians at Antioch, each according to his ability, decided to help the Judean church with a money gift to buy food (which would have doubtless been quite high in price due to its scarcity).

The Antioch church sent its gift to the Jerusalem elders by Barnabas and Saul (Acts 11:30) around A.D. 46.[28] Upon the completion of their mission, Barnabas and Saul returned to Antioch, bringing John Mark,

---

25. F. F. Bruce, *Acts*, 225. To sum up, before Paul began his missionary travels among the Gentiles in Acts 13, Philip had already preached to the Ethiopian eunuch (Acts 8), Peter had already brought Cornelius into the church (Acts 12), and certain unnamed Jews from Cyprus and Cyrene had already founded the predominantly Gentile church at Antioch (Acts 12).

26. For the other two New Testament occurrences of Χριστιανός see Acts 26:28 and 1 Peter 4:16. As with 'Vitellian', Othonian', 'Herodian' or 'Caesarian' the Latin suffix '-ian' (from *-ianus*) means 'servant of' or 'follower of.' The term seems to have been a term full of reproach because it is used of Christians in the New Testament only by non-Christians, that is, by the citizens of Antioch, by the younger Agrippa, and as the language of indictment when one suffers 'as a Christian'. For early occurrences in non-Christian literature see Josephus, *Antiquities of the Jews*, 18.64; Pliny, *Epistles*, 10.96-97; Tacitus, *Annals*, 15.44.3-4; and Suetonius, *Nero*, 16.2.

27. See Josephus, *Antiquities*, 20.51-53, 101.

28. Martin Franzmann, *The Word of the Lord Grows*, 48, observes: 'How great Paul's influence was [at Antioch] and how graciously ecumenical it must have been, we can measure by the fact that it was Paul whom the brethren chose to go with Barnabas to bring relief to the brethren in Judea during the famine....'

Barnabas' cousin (Col 4:10), with them (Acts 12:25).

Luke tells us in Acts 11:30 that Barnabas and Saul visited Jerusalem in order to complete his account of Agabus' prophecy. But actually, their visit occurred after the events of Acts 12, since Herod died in A.D. 44: 'Their return, though not their setting out, is related in chronological order... the sentence [in 12:25] provides the transition from 11:30, where Barnabas and Saul go to Jerusalem, to 13:1, where they are in Antioch again.'[29]

We will now address two rather complex but related matters: firstly, the question of the relationship between the 'famine relief visit' of Acts 11:30 and the visit Paul describes in Galatians 2:1-10; secondly, the precise intention of the demarcation of mission fields outlined in Galatians 2:7-9.

I. Paul's 'famine relief visit' identical with his visit described in Galatians 2:1-10

It is to this 'famine relief visit' of Acts 11:27-30, I would submit, that Paul refers in Galatians 2:1-10. If this connection is correct, then it is apparent that Paul, with Barnabas and Titus, an uncircumcised Greek Christian, accompanying him, also used the opportunity provided by this 'famine relief visit', to do two other things: firstly, to contact the Jerusalem apostles in order to lay before them the substance of his law-free gospel that he had been proclaiming among the Gentiles (we gather from what he writes that, not surprisingly, they found it acceptable), and secondly, to arrange a 'demarcation of mission fields',[30] no doubt because of plans in mind for forthcoming missionary endeavors. The agreed-upon result was that Cephas[31] and the Jerusalem church would evangelize Jews, Paul would evangelize Gentiles.

With respect to the first matter on his mind, that is, Saul's desire to discuss with the Jerusalem leaders his law-free gospel, apparently he

---

29. Bruce, *Acts*, 243.
30. Bruce's term in *Paul*, 152-54.
31. Only twice in his letters—both occurrences to be found here in Galatians 2:7-9—does Paul employ 'Peter' as his designation for this leading apostle. Of the other eight references to Peter in Paul's writings (Gal 1:18; 2:9, 11, 14; 1 Cor 1:12; 3:22; 9:5; 15:5; note specifically Gal 2:9, 11, 14) Paul speaks of him by the Aramaic 'Cephas'. His use of 'Peter' in Galatians 2:7-8 would suggest an accommodation to the wording of an actual agreement (possibly the minutes) drawn up at the meeting in Jerusalem. See Bruce's discussion of Paul's account, *Paul*, 153-54.

had gone up to Jerusalem on this occasion with some anxiety regarding what the Jerusalem church leaders would say about his ministry in Syria/Cilicia and in Antioch, for after making it clear that he had gone up 'according to a revelation', thereby excluding by this comment any suggestion that he had been summoned by the Jerusalem apostolate to appear before it,[32] he states: 'I laid before [ἀνεθέμην] them [the Jerusalem church leaders] the gospel which I preach among the Gentiles, but privately [κατ' ἰδίαν]...for fear that I am running [now, and will continue to do so in the future] or had run [in the past] my race *in vain* [εἰς κενὸν]' (Gal 2:2). What does he mean by this strange and striking statement? F. F. Bruce explains it as follows:

> ...there is certainly cause for surprise in the implication of his statement that, failing the recognition by the Jerusalem authorities that the gospel he preached was the authentic gospel, his apostolic service would have been, and would continue to be, fruitless. It is certainly not implied that, if this recognition had been withheld, Paul would have changed his mind about the gospel he preached or changed his method of presenting it. A gospel received by direct revelation is not to be modified out of deference to any human authority. What Paul was concerned about was not the validity of his gospel but its practicability. His commission was not derived from Jerusalem, but it could not be effectively discharged except in fellowship with Jerusalem. A cleavage between his Gentile mission and the mother-church in Jerusalem would be disastrous for the progress of the gospel: the cause of Christ would be divided, and all the devotion with which Paul had thus far prosecuted his apostolate to the Gentiles, and hoped to go on prosecuting, would be frustrated.[33]

On this question James D. G. Dunn, in accord with Bruce, writes:

> How is it that Paul in the same breath [Gal 2:2] can both assert his independence of the Jerusalem apostles and yet also acknowledge that

---

32. Paul's four phrases describing the Jerusalem church leaders in the Galatians 2:1-10 pericope as 'the ones reputed [to be something]' (τοῖς δοκοῦσιν, Gal 2:2), 'the ones reputed to be something [τῶν δοκούντων εἶναί τι] – what they once were [ὁποῖοί ποτε ἦσαν] makes no difference to me [now] [note the shift in tense from the previous imperfect to the present tense]; God shows no partiality' (Gal 2:6ab), 'the ones reputed [to be something] [οἱ δοκοῦντες] added nothing to me' (Gal 2:6c), and 'the ones reputed to be pillars' (οἱ δοκοῦντες στῦλοι εἶναι, Gal 2:9), both separately and collectively also appear to be 'distancing' phrases, intended to distance Paul's apostolic authority from the authority of the Jerusalem apostolate and to make it quite clear that the original apostles were not the source of Paul's authority to preach the gospel of Christ.

33. Bruce, *Paul*, 152.

the effectiveness of his work depended on their approval of his gospel? We cannot put this seeming contradiction less strongly without lessening the force of Paul's own language. What was it that was at stake here? Not, it would appear, Paul's conviction as to the *truth* of his gospel; such an admission would run too sharply counter to the firm assertions of Galatians 1. Nor does it seem to meet the force of 2.2c to argue that Paul's concern was simply for the future unity of the whole church, or that he feared the future depredations of Judaizers; 2.2c seems rather to envisage the possibility of a decision made by the Jerusalem apostles which would at a stroke nullify the effectiveness of his past and current missionary work. It was this *effectiveness* of his gospel which Paul was concerned for. Presumably he had been preaching that acceptance of the good news of Jesus Christ without circumcision brought Gentiles into the people of God, made them heirs of God's promise to Abraham together with believing Jews.... But Jerusalem's refusal to acknowledge the validity of this proclamation would render it ineffective (not false), because as a result, whether Paul liked it or not, the churches he had already founded would be distinct from believing Israel; and adverse decision by the Jerusalem apostles would make it impossible for Gentile churches to be seen in their true continuity with the religion of Israel, of the prophets, of Jesus' first disciples.

In short, in laying his gospel before the Jerusalem apostles what he sought was not so much their approval (without which his gospel would have no validity) as their recognition of his gospel's validity (without which his gospel would lose its effectiveness).[34]

Robert H. Stein agrees with the above assessments, but he goes even farther than Bruce and Dunn in spelling out the dire consequences which would have ensued from a wrong decision by the Jerusalem apostolate at this meeting:

Certainly [Paul] did not believe that the truthfulness of his message was at stake or that it could be affected by anything the [Jerusalem church leaders] decided, for his gospel was not of human origin nor even from a human source (Gal 1:1, 11) but directly from Christ himself (Gal 1:12). If an angel from heaven could not change that gospel, how much less could the Jerusalem [church leaders].

[What Paul feared] was the splitting of the church. [For] Paul would, of course, continue to preach the gospel (1 Cor 9:16), but the church would be irreconcilably divided [if the Jerusalem leaders made a wrong decision about his law-free gospel]. In fact, since out of Jerusalem there would [then] be coming forth a different gospel, which in fact was no

---

34. Dunn, *Jesus, Paul, and the Law*, 115-16.

gospel at all (Gal 1:6-7), they might not even be able to be considered a true church. The mother church would itself have become apostate! Finally, Paul no doubt feared that the divine purpose of uniting Jew and Gentile and the destruction of the dividing wall [between Jew and Gentile] through the death of Christ might be thwarted by actions of the [Jerusalem leaders] (Eph 2:11-21).[35]

These prospects, it would seem, are what created for Paul his apprehensions as he renewed his acquaintance with the Jerusalem leaders for the second time. Would they acknowledge his law-free gospel as the true gospel and as *their* own gospel? Would they accept his apostolic calling as being as authentic as their own? As it was, and again I would stress, not surprisingly, everything turned out well. The Jerusalem leaders recognized not only Paul's gospel as the authentic gospel but also that his vocation as an apostle, though authentic like their own, was, unlike theirs, primarily to be directed to the task of reaching the nations for Christ.

II. The Imprecise Terms of the Demarcation of Mission Fields

With respect to the second matter, that is, Paul's interest in and desire to arrange a 'division of labor' between himself and the Jerusalem leadership, it is not entirely clear from Paul's description of this 'division of labor' whether the Jerusalem church leaders intended for Paul (or whether they just assumed that Paul intended) to evangelize Gentiles *through the ministrations of the Diaspora synagogues* located throughout the then-known world or whether they intended for him to preach to Gentiles directly, *apart from the Diaspora synagogues*. In fact, it is not clear from his description whether Paul himself knew precisely what missionary policy and pattern he would follow. (As a matter of fact, we know that Paul regularly went immediately to the synagogues in the cities he visited and found the nucleus of his churches mainly among the God-fearing Gentiles who attended the services of worship there.) Bruce observes that the agreement, at least as Paul states it, 'concealed one or two unobserved ambiguities'.[36] Were the terms of the division of labor to be interpreted *geographically* (the Gentile world versus Palestine) or *ethnically* (Gentiles versus Jews)? 'Either way,' writes Bruce, 'it must have

---

35. R. H. Stein, 'Jerusalem,' *Dictionary of Paul and His Letters* (Downers Grove, Ill., InterVarsity, 1993), 468.
36. Bruce, *Paul*, 154.

been difficult to define the boundaries of the two mission fields.' Did the agreement intend that the Jerusalem leaders could not leave Palestine and evangelize Jews, say, in Corinth or Ephesus or Rome or evangelize Gentiles in Palestine? And did the agreement take into account that Paul would in time be barred by the Diaspora synagogues from visiting them or that he would be ejected from synagogues in Gentile cities? Would the Jerusalem leaders have given precisely the same account of the matter as Paul does in Galatians 2? Did they intend for Paul to 'integrate' Gentiles and Jews into 'one assembly', or did they intend that he would form 'Christian synagogues' comprised of Jews and 'Christian churches' comprised of Gentiles? Without a clear understanding about such matters, 'this could constitute a fruitful source of misunderstanding, unless entire mutual confidence was maintained between the two parties to the agreement.'[37]

All things considered, it is best to conclude that the field of labor for neither Paul nor the Jerusalem Church leaders should be interpreted *exclusively* as either geographic or ethnic. But while the demarcation of missionary spheres both for Paul and for the Jerusalem church is best understood as being *primarily* geographic, that is, the Gentile world for Paul versus Palestine and the Jewish Diaspora for the Jerusalem church leaders respectively, the purpose of designating these areas was more to bring focus to the responsibilities of Paul and the Jerusalem church than to impose strict limitations on them.

In any event, such undefined issues as these just mentioned were to be raised in a striking way on his first missionary journey, and it became the occasion for the whole complex of issues which later faced the Jerusalem Council of Acts 15.

Defense of the 'South Galatia' Hypothesis

By asserting as I have the identity between the 'famine relief visit' and the visit Paul mentions in Galatians 2:1-10 I am assuming that 'Galatia' in Galatians 1:2 means the Roman province of Galatia, which comprehended not only the territory actually occupied by the old Galatian people but also other lands including the territory in which lay the cities evangelized by Paul and Barnabas on their first missionary journey.[38]

---

37. Bruce, *Paul*, 155.
38. 'Galatia' is the name that was given originally to the territory in north central Asia Minor where the invading Gauls settled in the third century before Christ and where an independent Gallic kingdom was maintained for many years. The Gallic population

This is known as the *South Galatia Hypothesis*, championed by such authorities as Sir William Ramsay, F. F. Bruce, R. A. Cole, Martin Franzmann, Ronald Y. K. Fung, Donald Guthrie, C. J. Hemer, Herman N. Ridderbos, Merrill C. Tenney, and the majority of English-speaking interpreters.[39] Others take 'Galatia' to mean the actual Galatian territory, the land occupied by the Galatians (ancient Gauls) in north central Asia Minor, whose chief cities were Tavium, Pessinus, and Ancyra. This view—the classic view—known as the *North Galatia Hypothesis* and championed by the great commentator J. B. Lightfoot, James Moffatt, J. Gresham Machen (provisionally), Günther Bornkamm, W. G. Kümmel, Willi Marxsen, and many other scholars predominantly but not exclusively in Germany,[40] contends that Paul wrote Galatians on his third missionary journey to churches he had founded on his second missionary journey in such cities as the three just mentioned, and that the visit Paul alludes to in Galatians 2:1-10 is his third visit to Jerusalem at the time of the Jerusalem Conference recorded in Acts 15.

Why do I believe that Paul is referring in Galatians 2:1-10 to his second visit to Jerusalem (the 'famine relief visit' of Acts 11:30) and not to his third visit (the Jerusalem Conference of Acts 15) and that

---

was gradually absorbed into the other peoples living there and Rome took possession of the territory in 25 B.C. The Romans incorporated this territory into a larger division of land which they made a province and called by the name of Galatia. 'Galatia' under Roman rule could refer then either to the original territory which the Gauls had founded or the name could refer to the whole Roman province. I will argue that Paul is using the term as a reference to the Roman province which included the cities of Pisidian Antioch, Iconium, Derbe, and Lystra.

39. William M. Ramsay, *A Historical Commentary on St. Paul's Epistle to the Galatians* (New York: G. P. Putnam's Sons, 1900), xi, 478; F. F. Bruce *Paul*, 179; R. A. Cole, *The Epistle of Paul to the Galatians* (Tyndale New Testament Commentaries; Grand Rapids: Eerdmans, 1977), 15-20; Martin Franzmann, *The Word of the Lord Grows*, 60-61; Ronald Y. K. Fung, *The Epistle to the Galatians* (The New International Commentary on the New Testament; Grand Rapids: Eerdmans, 1988), 1-3; Donald Guthrie, *New Testament Introduction* (Downers Grove, Ill.: InterVarsity, 1970), 450-56; C. J. Hemer, 'Acts and Galatians Reconsidered' in *Themelios* (New Series 2; 1976-77), 81-88; Herman N. Ridderbos, *The Epistle of Paul to the Churches of Galatia* (The New International Commentary on the New Testament; Grand Rapids: Eerdmans, 1953), 22-31; Merrill C. Tenney, *New Testament Survey*, 265-68.

40. J. B. Lightfoot, *St. Paul's Epistle to the Galatians* (London: Macmillan, 1890), 18-35; James Moffatt, *Introduction to the Literature of the New Testament* (Third edition; New York: Charles Scribner's Sons, 1918), 90-101; J. Gresham Machen, *The Origin of Paul's Religion* (Grand Rapids: Eerdmans, 1965 reprint of 1925 edition), 78-98, Günther Bornkamm, *Paul*, 32, 82-3; P. Feine, J. Behm, (completely reedited by) W. G. Kümmel, *Introduction to the New Testament*, translated by A. J. Mattill, Jr. (Revised edition; Nashville: Abingdon, 1975), 296-98; Willi Marxsen, *Introduction to the New Testament*, translated by G. Buswell (Philadelphia: Fortress, 1968), 46.

he wrote his letter to the Galatians from Antioch or on his way to Jerusalem just prior to the Jerusalem Conference in Acts 15? I do so for the following eighteen reasons:

1. Proponents of the North Galatia Hypothesis contend that the Roman province of Galatia had no fixed, official title (i.e., 'Galatia') at the time of Paul's writing his letter to the Galatians. Paul therefore, they urge, could not with propriety call the churches at Pisidian Antioch, Iconium, Lystra and Derbe 'churches of Galatia' as he does (Gal 1:2) or address the men of Pisidian Antioch and the Lycaonian cities of Lystra and Derbe as 'Galatians' as he does (3:1) just because they lived in a province *popularly* known as Galatia.

Advocates of the South Galatia Hypothesis ask, What other single term could Paul have used which would have more accurately covered all of the churches he founded on his first missionary journey if he had wanted to write a letter to all of them? There does not seem to be a better one. Moreover, for Paul to use the provincial designation for these churches would not have seemed strange; Galatia had been a Roman province since 25 B.C. Furthermore, the use of provincial names seems to follow Paul's general practice (regardless of Luke's practice whose use of 'Galatia' in Acts 16:6 and 18:23 may be 'provincial' rather than ethnic as well).[41]

2. The North Galatia Hypothesis would require that one believe that Paul wrote Galatians to churches located in cities such as Tavium, Pessinus, and Ancyra about which Acts and the rest of the New

---

41. James M. Scott, *Paul and the Nations: The Old Testament and Jewish Background of Paul's Mission to the Nations with Special Reference to the Destination of Galatians* (Tübingen: J. C. B. Mohr [Paul Siebeck], 1995), has advanced and argued the intriguing thesis that Paul conducted his missionary labors with the Jewish geography of the Genesis 10 'Table of Nations' in mind, and that he would have therefore identified the 'Galatians' (Γαλάται), as did Josephus, with Gomer, the first son of Japheth, whose descendants settled in the territory roughly equivalent to the later Roman province of Galatia. Scott concludes from this that Paul probably wrote to the churches of south Galatia or, in Jewish terminology, to the descendants of Ashkenaz, the firstborn son of Gomer, who had settled in the southern portion of the province.

While Scott presents a strong case, his thesis, of course, can be endlessly debated. And while Scott's thesis does not prove the South Galatia Hypothesis, it does remove what is perhaps the most significant obstacle to the theory, namely, the argument that Paul's use of 'Galatia' (Γαλατία) must be restricted, according to Greco-Roman usage, to the ethnic people living in north Galatia and cannot refer to the territory of the Roman province of Galatia which included the southern portion of that region. If Scott is right, 'Galatia' would have simply been for Paul a reference to the territory that had been occupied by the descendants of Gomer which was roughly equivalent to the later Roman province.

Testament are completely silent rather than to churches about which Acts informs us. It is true, of course, that it is possible that this is what has happened, but it is harder to believe that this is what has happened than to believe that the letter is written to churches about which we know something.

3. Advocates of the North Galatia Hypothesis cannot adequately explain why the Judaizers in their campaign to 'Judaize' Paul's churches by-passed the South Galatian churches which he clearly had founded and established on his first and second missionary journeys respectively – which are readily accessible from Antioch – and went into the wild, less civilized, and more remote regions of North Galatia with their 'revisionist gospel'.

4. The contention of the proponents of the North Galatia hypothesis, since Galatians and Romans both treat the doctrine of justification by faith alone, that Galatians would most likely have been written around the same time as the letter to the Romans in the mid-fifties, is extremely weak, to say the least. Paul's letters were 'occasional' letters; he wrote them *whenever* the need arose, and merely because these two letters happen to have 'justification' vocabulary in them is no indication that they were written in temporal proximity to each other. Paul could have used (see Acts 13:39) and doubtless would have used such vocabulary *whenever* his opponents were Judaizers.

5. If Paul's letter to the Galatians was written after the Jerusalem Conference in Acts 15, why does he not refer to the 'Apostolic Decree' which came out of its deliberations since it dealt definitively, precisely, and officially with one of the major issues Paul is addressing in his letter to the Galatians? Tenney quite justifiably asserts:

> If Galatians were not written until after Paul toured the Galactic territory on his second or third journey, and consequently long after the council of Jerusalem, it is difficult to explain why he made no appeal to the decision of that council in settling the controversy of law versus grace. ...it could have been quite useful in convincing the Galatians that the teaching of the Judaizing faction was insupportable. The fact that no action of the council is so much as mentioned probably indicates that it had not yet taken place.[42]

Advocates of the North Galatia Hypothesis respond by saying that this is precisely what he is doing, simply in 'other terms', in

---

42. Tenney, *New Testament Survey*, 267.

Galatians 2:1-10. But proponents of the South Galatia Hypothesis believe that it is a stretch to see a reference to the 'Apostolic Decree' in the Galatians 2 passage. Besides, the identity of this Galatians 2 Jerusalem visit (whether it is the Acts 11 visit or the Acts 15 visit) is precisely the point at issue, and it will not do simply to appeal to the passage itself. The matter must be settled on other grounds outside of the disputed passage itself.

6. The most natural reading of Galatians 1:21-24 is that Paul intended to teach that between the two Jerusalem visits referred to in Galatians 1 and 2 he had been *only* in the regions of Syria and Cilicia (which regions could and probably did include his ministry in Antioch with Barnabas), *not* in Syria/Cilicia, and also in Jerusalem on the famine-relief visit, and also back in Antioch, and also in all the sites that he visited on his first missionary journey, and then back again in Antioch.

7. According to Galatians 2:1 Paul went up to Jerusalem on the occasion recorded there 'by revelation' (κατὰ ἀποκάλυψιν), but according to Acts 15:2 he went up to Jerusalem on the occasion recorded there by commission of the Antioch church (see ἔταξαν, 'they determined').

8. It is difficult to see how a meeting which Paul describes as a private meeting in Galatians 2:2 can be identified with the very public meeting described by Luke in Acts 15. Of course, one could argue that the private meeting occurred before or during the public meeting but it is difficult to understand why Paul would have spoken only of the smaller private meeting and told the Galatian church nothing about the highly significant decisions reached in the larger public meeting.

9. Luke's Acts implies that after Peter's miraculous deliverance from prison in Acts 12 and his departure from Jerusalem to 'another place' (Acts 12:17; incidentally, many Roman Catholic exegetes identify this 'other place' as Rome, but this is simply a dogmatic conjecture which biblical and historical data overturn), he turned *at that time* exclusively to missionary labor among the Jewish Diaspora, so that, as Oscar Cullman notes, 'he, just like Paul and Barnabas, interrupted his missionary travels to go to Jerusalem for the so-called Apostolic Council [of Acts 15],'[43] at which council James was clearly presiding. Paul's description of affairs in the Jerusalem church at the time of his

---

43. Oscar Cullmann, *Peter: Disciple – Apostle – Martyr*, translated by Floyd V. Filson (Philadelphia: Westminster, 1953), 42.

Galatians 2 visit, however, suggests that Peter was still residing in Jerusalem at that time as one of the 'pillars' of the church there. And Peter's subsequent dissembling at Antioch immediately after Paul's Galatians 2 visit out of fear of the circumcision party 'from James' suggests that Peter still saw himself as immediately related to and answerable, as one of its leaders, to the Jerusalem church leadership shared by James and John.

10. According to Paul's description of the meeting in Galatians 2:1-10, the Jerusalem apostles 'added nothing to my gospel' (2:6), requesting only that 'we should go on remembering the poor, the very thing I had been eager to do' (2:10)[44]; whereas the Jerusalem Conference 'added' the so-called 'Apostolic Decree' (15:23-29) to Paul's message, which in turn would have been a valuable weapon to employ against his adversaries if he had had it at his disposal at the time of his writing his letter to the Galatians.

11. The two issues discussed in the meeting described by Paul in Galatians 2:1-10, namely, the character of Paul's gospel and the demarcation of spheres of missionary activity, are not the same as the issue discussed at the Conference in Acts 15, namely, whether Gentile believers had to be circumcised and keep the law of Moses in order to be saved. Bruce observes: 'Circumcision receives only marginal mention [in Gal 2:1-10],'[45] and even then in terms which could be construed to mean that it was not discussed at the Conference at all.

This reason takes seriously the suggestion of T. W. Manson,[46] followed by Bruce and others, that the anacoluthon in Galatians 2:4-5 (the syntax is fractured here; these two verses lack a principal clause) is a parenthetical allusion to the later incident Luke records in Acts 15:1-2a which Paul mentions here simply because he had alluded in Galatians 2:3 to the Jerusalem apostles' attitude of acceptance toward Titus in spite of his uncircumcised state,[47] and is not to be construed

---

44. Bruce in *New Testament History*, 270, comments here: 'This request, which Paul records at the end of his account of the conference, makes the famine-relief visit the more appropriate as a setting for it, the more so as he adds immediately, "And in fact I had made a special point of doing this very thing." '

45. Bruce, *Acts*, 283.

46. T. W. Manson, *Studies in the Gospels and Epistles*, edited by M. Black (Manchester: University Press, 1962), 175-76. Fung, *Galatians*, agrees that Galatians 2:3-5 refers to a subsequent development (13).

47. Paul expressly states: 'Yet not even Titus, who was with me, was compelled to be circumcised, even though he was Greek' (Gal 2:3). F. C. Burkitt, *Christian Beginnings* (London: University of London, 1924), and others have argued that the Greek phrase

as evidence that the issue of Gentile circumcision was a major topic of discussion at this particular meeting between the Jerusalem apostles and Paul.[48] In other words, some such main clause as 'This matter did arise later' should be supplied at the beginning of Galatians 2:4. This necessitates the conclusion that Paul wrote Galatians during or after the controversy referred to in Acts 15:1-2a but before the Jerusalem Conference itself, in other words, during the time period of Acts 15:2.

12. It is more likely that Paul would have felt that he had to make the lengthy defense of his apostleship which he does to the Galatians (1:6–2:21) prior to the Jerusalem Conference rather than after it, since it would have been publicly evident to all but the most stubborn and perverse mind after the Conference of Acts 15 that the Jerusalem apostles recognized Paul's apostolic authority and commission to the Gentiles (see their term of endearment and description of him – 'our dear friends [τοῖς ἀγαπητοῖς ἡμῶν] Barnabas and Paul, men who have risked their lives for the name of our Lord Jesus Christ' – in the 'Apostolic Decree', Acts 15:25-26).

13. In the particular defense of his apostleship which he mounts in Galatians 1–2, Paul would have felt a certain necessity to refer to all of his visits to Jerusalem up to the moment of his writing the letter. To have omitted all reference to any one visit (in this case, on the North Galatian view, the 'famine relief visit') at which time he could have consulted with (some of) the apostles (which visit his opponents could readily have known about) would have exposed him to the charge of dishonesty and suppression of facts and thus would have seriously damaged his whole argument. He could not afford to have his opposition say: 'Yes, but Paul purposely neglected to inform you Galatians about his famine-relief visit to Jerusalem. Since he omitted reference to it, he may well have omitted to tell you about other visits as well, at any one of which he could have received his commission

---

οὐδὲ...ἠναγκάσθη ('was not compelled') means that Titus was indeed circumcised but was simply not compelled to be, that Paul, making a concession to the 'false brothers' who 'had infiltrated our ranks to spy on the freedom we have in Christ Jesus and to make us slaves', allowed Titus to be circumcised: 'Who can doubt [Burkitt writes] that it was the knife which really did circumcise Titus that has cut the syntax of Gal. 2:3-5 to pieces' (118). But Dunn has rightly observed in his *Jesus, Paul, and the Law*: 'How Paul could have "preserved the truth of the gospel" preached to the Galatians by allowing Titus to be circumcised, when it was precisely the demand for circumcision which threatened the Galatians' freedom (in Paul's view), is an unresolved mystery on Burkitt's interpretation' (125).

48. See Bruce's discussions in his *Paul*, 158-59, and *Acts*, 283.

from the Jerusalem apostles.' Thus both Paul's argument for his apostolic commission directly from Christ could have been rebutted and his moral integrity called into question by this one objection.

14. It is difficult to see how the 'certain men from James' (Gal 2:12) could have advocated *in Antioch* the Judaizers' view of salvation immediately after the Jerusalem Conference's deliverance of its 'Apostolic Decree' (Acts 15:23-29).

Of course, if Paul's 'certain men from James' are Luke's 'some men from Judea' who came to Antioch before the Jerusalem Conference (Acts 15:1), and it is very likely that they are, they 'exceeded the terms of their commission'.[49] That is to say, they were not representing James' soteriology when they taught what they did, although in light of James' thought and manner of expression as exhibited in James 2:14-26 it is understandable why they may have thought—wrongly, of course—that they were representing James' view accurately.

15. It is equally difficult to see how Barnabas (Gal 2:13) could have become confused immediately after the Conference's 'Decree'.

16. It is even more difficult to see how Peter (Gal 2:11-13) could have dissembled the way he did in Antioch if the Antioch incident occurred immediately after the major role he played at the Conference and in light of the Conference's 'Decree'. Tenney quite rightly observes:

> The episode of Peter's defection (Gal. 2:11ff.) can be much more easily explained if it preceded the council, for the confusion and discussion which it precipitated could hardly have taken place in Antioch after the decision had been rendered, and after the letters had been sent to the Gentile churches.[50]

While the confrontation between Paul and Peter could just possibly have occurred shortly after Paul's return to Antioch from the 'famine relief visit', it is more likely that it occurred in conjunction with the controversy which precipitated the Jerusalem Conference (Acts 15:1-2). Therefore, I will treat the confrontation at that point.

17. Paul assumes that the Galatians whom he addresses know Barnabas (2:1, 9, 13), but Barnabas accompanied Paul only on his first missionary journey. I grant that this argument is somewhat

---

49. Bruce, *Acts*, 286; see Acts 15:24.
50. Tenney, *New Testament Survey*, 267.

weakened by the fact that Paul appears to assume that the Corinthians also know Barnabas (1 Cor 9:6) in spite of the fact that there is no evidence that Barnabas was ever in Corinth. But this objection is based upon silence. We simply do not know whether Barnabas made his way at some time to Corinth or not—he may (or may not) have— since he disappears from the Acts narrative after Acts 15:39. But we do know that he was with Paul in South Galatia and *was* known to the churches in that region. Therefore, I feel my point still carries weight.

18. As Paul began his third missionary journey in the summer of A.D. 52, Luke reports that Paul 'traveled from place to place [Luke refers here doubtless to Derbe, Lystra, Iconium, and Pisidian Antioch, to name just a few cities] throughout the region of Galatia and Phrygia, strengthening all the disciples' (Acts 18:23). Luke's account says nothing about Paul having to contend with Judaizers in the churches of Galatia at that time.

Then three years later, in the spring of A.D. 55 (we will give our reasons for the dates in this argument in Chapter Nine), Paul apparently wrote 1 Corinthians from Ephesus toward the end of his ministry there (he states in 1 Corinthians 16:5 that he was anticipating passing through Macedonia and then moving on to Achaia, indeed, perhaps even spending the winter in Achaia with the Corinthians). So three years into his third missionary journey Paul writes 1 Corinthians. Now in 1 Corinthians 16:1, concerning the collection for the Jewish saints, he refers the Corinthians to the directions he had given to the churches of Galatia, doubtless as he passed through the Roman province on his way to Ephesus. There is not even a whisper of any conflict between Paul and the Galatian churches at this time. And one must wonder, if during that three-year period the Galatian churches were working through a conflict between Paul on the one hand and the Judaizers on the other, whether Paul would have used those particular churches as his prime exemplars regarding the collection for the Jewish saints at Jerusalem.

Once Paul left Ephesus he was constantly on the move, his missionary focus, according to both Acts and Romans, quite apparently then directed toward the West and not toward any trouble that may have risen back in the East. Indeed, in the spring of A.D. 57 at the very end of his third journey, Paul informs the Romans that from Jerusalem and as far round as Illyricum he had fully proclaimed the good news of Christ (Rom 15:19) which was his stated reason for wanting to move westward first to Rome and then to Spain. One must wonder, if during the period between the spring of A.D. 55 and the spring of A.D. 57 Paul had had to deal with 'another gospel' in the Galatian churches, how he could have been so certain that the good news of the gospel had taken root in Galatia and how, not having returned to Galatia to see for himself the effect of his purported letter to them, he could have exhibited the eagerness he does in Romans 15 to move on toward the West.

When all the facts are taken into consideration, there is not one hint in anything that Acts says or in anything that Paul wrote that would suggest that during his third missionary journey he ever had to address the serious departure from the gospel on the part of the Galatian churches that he addresses in his letter to the Galatians. But we know from Acts 15 that around A.D. 49 or 50 he did have to address the Judaizing heresy both at Antioch and then at the Jerusalem Council where the issue was formally settled, which suggests that the Judaizers—in their heyday during this earlier period—would most likely have done their Judaizing work in Galatia during this earlier period, prior to the Jerusalem Council, and not some years later.

This interpretation of Galatians 2:1-10 requires, of course, that Paul's reference to 'fourteen years' in 2:1 be construed to mean 'fourteen years after my conversion [in A.D. 32]', that is, about A.D. 46, and not 'fourteen years after my first visit to Jerusalem', that is, 'seventeen years after my conversion'. Admittedly, the expression can be understood either way. Bruce writes: 'The construction of the phrase "after fourteen years" [διὰ δεκατεσσάρων ἐτῶν] is different from that of the phrase "after three years" [μετὰ ἔτη τρία], but it is not clear what significance, if any, lies in the difference of construction.' Bruce translates the former preposition, 'in the course of,' and the latter preposition, 'after'.[51]

Regardless of how one reckons this matter of dating, it is plain that the Jerusalem leaders recognized during Paul's Galatians 2 visit (which, I would note again, I think was the famine-relief visit) not only his law-free gospel as the authentic gospel but also that his vocation, unlike theirs, was to preach to the Gentiles his doctrine of justification by faith alone apart from law-keeping. Paul's mission to the Gentiles would now go forward, not with the Jerusalem church's authorization but clearly with its approving endorsement.

---

51. Bruce, *Paul*, 151, fn. 13.

CHAPTER SIX

PAUL'S FIRST MISSIONARY JOURNEY, PETER'S LATER HYPOCRISY, AND PAUL'S LETTER TO THE GALATIANS

> Runs not the Word of Truth through every land?
> A sword to sever, and a fire to burn?
>   If blessed Paul had stayed
>   In cot or learned shade,
>   With the priests' white attire,
>   And the saints' tuneful choir,
> Men had not gnashed their teeth, nor risen to slay,
> But thou hadst been a heathen in thy day.
>   – John Henry Newman

Paul's First Missionary Journey (c. A.D. 47 to A.D. 48) (Acts 13:1-14:28)

In this first section we will simply 'walk' ('run' might be the more appropriate term) with Paul through his first missionary journey, noting as we do so at the appropriate place what some Paul scholars consider to be an *often overlooked yet very significant advance* in Paul's missionary strategy concerning the preaching of the gospel. But to see this, the reader must remember that Paul was now laboring under the broad general constraints of the admittedly not-too-clear terms (perhaps only to us) of the agreement that he and the Jerusalem leaders had reached in Jerusalem during his 'famine relief visit' to Jerusalem.[1]

To aid the reader in this overview of Paul's first journey and of his other four journeys, I will underline the first significant occurrence of all important place names. I have also provided the Greek word or

---

1. For the historical and geographical details of Paul's first missionary journey, see F. F. Bruce, *The Book of the Acts* (The New International Commentary on the New Testament; revised edition; Grand Rapids: Eerdmans, 1988) and Richard N. Longenecker, *The Acts of the Apostles* (Expositors Bible Commentary 9; Grand Rapids: Zondervan, 1981). Bruce's *New Testament History* (London: Nelson, 1969) also provides rich historical and geographical background to Paul's travels.

phrase Luke employs to describe Paul's preaching activity. It is my earnest prayer, as we follow Paul through his journeys, that the Holy Spirit will call some readers to become cross-cultural church planters.

Called specifically by the Holy Spirit to the work of Gentile missions, and 'commended [by the church at Antioch,[2] 13:2-3] to the grace of God for the work' to which the Spirit had called them (14:26), Barnabas and Saul traveled to Seleucia, Antioch's port city, and sailed the approximately one hundred and fifty miles from there to Cyprus, Barnabas' home country (Acts 4:36), taking John Mark with them. There they labored first in Salamis, their port of entry. Then they traveled, probably taking the southern coastal route, 'through the whole island until they came to Paphos,' the capital.

In the former city, that is, in Salamis, they *preached* (κατήγγελλον) in the 'synagogues of the Jews' (see excursus, 118-19). In the latter city, that is, in Paphos, three to four days travel southwest of Salamis, they contended against Elymas (an example of the 'signs of an apostle' [2 Cor 12:12] is given in 13:11), a Jewish sorcerer and false prophet, and as a result brought to faith in Christ the Roman proconsul (ἀνθύπατος), Sergius Paulus, who had 'wanted to hear the word of God' (13:4-12).

It is Sergius Paulus' conversion that provided the occasion for the 'significant advance' in Saul's gospel proclamation to Gentiles to which I referred earlier.[3] This Roman official, Luke informs us, summoned Barnabas and Saul to him because he 'wanted to hear the word of God' (13:7). What is unique to this man's conversion is the fact that he seemed to have no relation to the synagogue. Here was a Roman to whom Saul preached directly with no intervening 'synagogue connection' and who believed as a result, just as Greeks had done earlier at Antioch! Though Saul had earlier informed the leaders of the Jerusalem church of his apostleship to the Gentiles when they had discussed together the 'division of labor' during his 'famine relief visit', very possibly at that time both he and they had in mind an outreach to the Gentiles that would be conducted through the synagogues of the dispersion, for it was still the conviction of the

---

2. See Bruce, *Paul: Apostle of the Heart Set Free* (Grand Rapids: Eerdmans, 1996 reprint of the 1977 edition), 148-50, for his discussion of the leadership of the church at Antioch.

3. I am indebted to Richard N. Longenecker, *The Ministry and Message of Paul* (Grand Rapids: Zondervan, 1971), 43, 47, for the origin though not the development of this intriguing insight.

Excursus on travel in Paul's day

In the first century A.D. the Mediterranean Sea was busy with merchant ships plying their trade from one port of call to another. Shipwrecks were, of course, not uncommon: Paul himself experienced shipwreck four times that we know of (2 Cor 11:25; Acts 27). The winter months were quite dangerous for sailing; in fact, from mid-November through February all sailing stopped, with a couple of months on either side of this period of time considered somewhat risky.

As for land travel, because the Romans had deliberately built good roads to tie the Empire together and to provide for the movement of troops and for imperial postal service, Paul's travels over land were relatively easy. These Roman roads included some fifty thousand miles of primary roads and about four times that much of secondary roads. A primary road was built on a foundation of layers of sand and gravel, up to a depth of three feet or more. A bed of concrete (invented by the Romans) might then be laid. Where some roads, in other words, had a gravel surface, the most important ones, especially near the big cities, were paved with large blocks of stone bound together by mortar. Such roads might be twenty feet wide although those in mountainous terrain (or lesser roads) might be as narrow as five or six feet. Using the Roman arch as the basic construction form, stone bridges were built across many small rivers and streams. Stone posts six to eight feet tall marked each 'mile' (1620 yards), as measured from the golden milestone in the forum in Rome. It was no exaggeration then that 'all roads led to Rome'.[4]

R. F. Hock has estimated that Paul traveled nearly 10,000 miles in the course of his missionary endeavors.[5] Barry J. Beitzel raises that number to around 13,400 air miles, with the actual distance Paul traveled, due to the circuitous roads he necessarily had to use at times, exceeding that figure by a sizeable margin. Beitzel arrives at that figure by adding the following conservative number of miles per trip that we know about: Damascus to Jerusalem (Gal 1:17-18), 140 miles; Jerusalem to Tarsus (Acts 9:30), 375 miles; Tarsus to Antioch (Acts 11:25-26), 90 miles; his 'famine-relief visit' to Jerusalem and back (Acts 11:30-12:25; Gal 2:1-10), 560 miles; his first missionary journey (Acts 13:4-14:28), 1400 miles; his trip to Jerusalem for the Jerusalem Conference and back (Acts 15), 560 miles; his second missionary journey (Acts 15:39-18:22), 2800 miles; his third missionary journey (Acts 18:23-21:17), 2700 miles; his trip to Caesarea (Acts 23:31-32), 60 miles; his trip to Rome (Acts 27:1-28:16), 2250 miles; his known travels, following the shortest possible itinerary, after his first Roman imprisonment, 2350 miles.[6]

---

4. Robert E. Picirilli, *Paul the Apostle* (Chicago: Moody, 1986), 66-67.
5. Robert F. Hock, *The Social Context of Paul's Ministry: Tentmaking and Apostleship* (Philadelphia: Fortress, 1980), 27.
6. Barry J. Beitzel, *The Moody Atlas of Bible Lands* (Chicago: Moody, 1985), 177.

Excursus on the Jewish synagogue

Christians tend to think of the Jewish synagogues which arose during the Babylonian exile as being something like our churches today, but there are differences. For the Diaspora Jews themselves, the local synagogue was much more than a Sabbath-day meeting place. Requiring at least ten men to start one, it was something of a Jewish 'university' for the Jewish community in exile, in which not only worship was conducted on the Sabbath day but also the education of the Jewish youth was carried out and serious discussions of everything and anything involving the Jewish community were conducted by and for the men. Each synagogue elected elders who not only governed all the functions of the synagogue but who also wielded a measure of authority (as a local 'Sanhedrin'; see Matt 10:17; Mark 13:9) in the Jewish community. This local 'Sanhedrin' (סַנְהֶדְרִין in the Mishna, meaning 'high council', which came over into Greek as συνέδριον) also administered discipline, among which options were flogging and excommunication, either temporary or permanent. The names of those who had been excommunicated were posted for display on a board. Paul informs us that he experienced such synagogue disciplines in abundance: 'Five times I received from the Jews the forty lashes minus one. Three times I was beaten with rods' (2 Cor 11:24). He probably received these disciplinary punishments mainly during the so-called 'silent years' of his ministry in Tarsus and its vicinity which began after his first visit to Jerusalem.

On the Sabbath day itself men and women sat apart, sometimes separated by a screen. In the earlier times the order of service was quite simple, having three main parts: first came a worship part consisting mainly of prayers, second came readings from the Law and the Prophets, third came a 'word of exhortation' delivered by someone sitting down. Later, the service included the recitation of the Shema ('Hear, O Israel...', Deut 6:4-9; 11:13-21; Num 15:37-41), prayer (often fixed and framed by the local rabbi), reading from the law, reading from the prophets, translations for the benefit of the Gentile God-fearers who were present, all followed by a homily. No one fixed person was designated to bring the exhortation, as in our churches; any competent male Israelite could officiate, read Scripture, or preach, although the last item tended to become more and more the duty of the rabbi. Because visitors were welcome, anyone who seemed capable might be asked to speak, even to bring the sermon (see Luke 4:16-21). It was in this last feature of the Sabbath day service that the opportunity resided for Paul to speak both to the Diaspora Jews and to the Gentile God-fearers everywhere he went (Acts 13:14-16ff). Machen asserts:

> It is hard to exaggerate the service which was rendered to the Pauline mission by the Jewish synagogue. One of the most important problems for every missionary is the problem of gaining a hearing. The problem

may be solved in various ways. Sometimes the missionary may hire a place of meeting and advertise; sometimes he may talk on the street corner to passers-by. But for Paul the problem was solved. All that he needed to do was to enter the synagogue and exercise the privilege of speaking, which was accorded with remarkable liberality to visiting teachers. In the synagogue, moreover, Paul found an audience not only of Jews but also of Gentiles; everywhere the 'God-fearers' were to be found.[7]

Unlike 'proselytes' who were Gentile converts to Judaism and who accordingly had (1) received circumcision (in the case of males, of course), (2) undergone a ceremonial bath ('proselyte baptism'), (3) offered the prescribed sacrifice, and (4) vowed to keep the law of Moses, the 'God-fearers' of the Roman world (οἱ σεβόμενοι, from σέβειν, 'to worship'; see Acts 13:43-50; 16:14; 17:4, 17; 18:7) were Gentiles who (1) were attracted by and accepted Judaism's monotheistic doctrine of the one true God, (2) 'had already, through the lofty ethical teaching of the Old Testament, come to connect religion with morality in a way which is to us matter-of-course but was very exceptional in the ancient world',[8] and (3) attended the synagogue services but did not submit to circumcision or follow all the details of the Jewish way of life. Concerning Paul's ministry to the God-fearers Bruce declares:

> Paul looked on the God-fearers who were in the habit of attending synagogue services as a providentially prepared bridgehead into the wider Gentile world. By listening to the reading and exposition of the scriptures those Gentiles learned to worship the 'living and true God' and became familiar in some sense with the hope of Israel. But they were told that they could not participate in this hope, or share the privileges of the people of God, unless they were prepared to become proselytes to Judaism—an issue to which, no doubt, their Jewish friends confidently looked forward. Now, however, these Gentiles were assured by Paul that the hope of Israel had been fulfilled by Jesus, and that through faith in him they could receive the saving grace of God on equal terms with Jewish believers, and become members of the messianic fellowship of the people of God in which the religious distinction between Jew and Gentile was obliterated. It was as natural for God-fearing Gentiles to embrace the blessings of the gospel on these terms as it was for Jews to decline them on these terms. Only by visiting the synagogue could Paul establish contact with the God-fearers, but the almost inevitable result of his policy was a breach with the synagogue.[9]

---

7. J. Gresham Machen, *The Origin of Paul's Religion* (Reprint of 1925 edition: Grand Rapids: Eerdmans, 1965), 10.
8. Machen, *Origin*, 10-11.
9. Bruce, *Paul*, 167-68.

whole of Judaism—and likely also at that time of the leaders of the Jerusalem church and Saul as well—that God intended Israel's ministrations to be his appointed means for the administration of and advance of the Abrahamic blessing to the Gentiles.

Moreover, probably neither the leaders of the Jerusalem church nor Saul foresaw the degree of hostility which the synagogues of the empire would incite within Diaspora Judaism against him. But Saul, ever sensitive to the theological meaning in what for others would have been simply an ordinary turn of events, apparently realized immediately that, if God, in the salvation of Sergius Paulus, had in fact and in some sense reached a Roman with Abrahamic blessing directly through the ministrations of 'Israel' but that the 'Israel' he employed was not an established institution of *ethnic* and *religious* Israel but rather himself – a *Christian* apostle – and his missionary team, then there had to be a 'spiritual Israel' (of which he was a member) within ethnic Israel (Rom 9:6). And that 'spiritual Israel' within ethnic Israel —the remnant about which Isaiah had spoken (שָׂרִיד, Isa 1:9; שְׁאָר, 10:22; see ὑπόλειμμα, Rom 9:27-29)—it was clear to Paul had come to expression in terms of the New Testament ἐκκλησία (Gal 6:16)!

Moreover, ever strategizing, Saul apparently saw more clearly in this incident what the church's mission to Gentiles logically involved. In it he saw God explicating, just as he had done in the salvation of Cornelius directly through Peter's ministrations, what was entailed both in the church's and in his own mission calling to Gentiles: without neglecting to evangelize Jews, the church may and ought to go directly to Gentiles with the gospel. Thus Saul's mission policy and his typical pattern of Gentile mission labor began to crystallize: in a city he would make his initial proclamation of the gospel to Jews and to any Gentile 'God-fearers' who were present *within the context of a dispersion synagogue* in the hope that the synagogue would acknowledge Jesus as the Jewish Messiah and place their trust in his death-work, become then a 'Christian synagogue' such as James mentions in James 2:2, and assume the responsibility to evangelize other Jews and Gentiles in its area. But if a synagogue began to speak evil of the Way and refused his mission team further audience in the synagogue, he would 'shake the dust of the synagogue off his feet' and turn directly, as a representative of 'spiritual Israel', to the Gentiles in that city and begin a ministry among them (see Acts 13:46 and Paul's later expression, 'to the Jews first and also to the Greeks', Rom 1:16; 2:9-10).

This strategy helps us understand two features in Luke's narrative. Firstly, it provides the reason at this point in his record why Luke begins to address Saul (Σαούλ or its Grecized form Σαῦλος) by his Roman surname of 'Paul' (Παῦλος, the Greek equivalent of the Latin Paullus) (Acts 13:9),[10] with Saul's name from this time forward always appearing first in connection with Barnabas with two understandable exceptions in Acts 14:12 and 15:12 (but see 15:25 where the Jerusalem church also follows the older order), which practice we too shall observe. Apparently, when Saul began to do missionary work in the Greco-Roman world, specifically at the point when he approached the Roman proconsul Sergius Paulus, he assumed his Roman cognomen which was also Paullus. Ben Witherington III notes too that there was a very good reason behind Saul's abandoning at this time his Hebrew name as he moved about in the Empire – 'In Greek *saulos* was used for someone who walked in a sexually suggestive manner like a prostitute!'[11] It seems that from this time forward Saul was prepared to approach Gentiles as Gentiles, directly if necessary, completely apart from the common ground supplied by a synagogue, and form his Gentile converts into Christian assemblies.

Secondly, if Saul's determination to conduct a direct ministry to Gentiles apart from the ministrations of the synagogue (if and when a synagogue rejected his message) became a topic of debate among the three missionaries themselves on their way to Perga, this might suggest the reason why John Mark may have left the group and returned to Jerusalem. He may have become very concerned about the effect which such a direct Christian ministry to Gentiles would have upon the Jerusalem church and its efforts to evangelize Jews in Palestine, and he may have no longer wanted any part in this ministry. This may account too for Paul's obstinate opposition toward Mark recorded in Acts 15:37-39, which suggests that Mark's departure at Perga involved more than merely personal reasons but may have grown out of strong disagreement on his part with Paul's mission strategy to Gentiles.

A related issue is the Jerusalem church's response to Paul's mission

---

10. As a Roman citizen Paul would have had three Latin names – his *cognomen* or family name which was probably *Paullus*, his *nomen* or name of the founding member of his gens or tribe, and his *praenomen* or given name, about the last two of which we know nothing. 'Saul' was his Hebrew name, the name also of the first king of Israel who was from the tribe of Benjamin as was Paul.

11. Ben Witherington III, *The Paul Quest* (Downers Grove, Ill.: InterVarsity, 1998), 72. See T. J. Leary, 'Paul's Improper Name' in *New Testament Studies* 38 (1992), 467-69.

practice. It was all very well and good for Paul and Barnabas to forge ahead with direct Gentile evangelization throughout the empire totally apart from any synagogue connection, but on both religious and political grounds such a Pauline practice could only pose problems back home for the mother church in Jerusalem even though its leadership would have been delighted that so many Gentiles were acknowledging Jesus as Messiah and Lord. For the Jerusalem church still had the responsibility to commend the gospel to Jews in Jerusalem and Judea. And the discharge of its responsibility in this regard would not be made any easier when reports reached the Sanhedrin, as they most certainly would and did, that the Jerusalem church's 'Gentile mission' under Paul was bringing large numbers of Gentiles into the Christian church completely apart from any connection with Israel's Diaspora synagogues. The mother church in Jerusalem as well as its leaders could quite quickly lose much of any public goodwill they still may have enjoyed in Jerusalem.

Some members of the Jerusalem church doubtless had a very simple solution: Paul's policy must be stopped in its tracks: all male Gentile converts should be required to be circumcised and agree to keep the law of Moses if they would be saved. Even the Zealots would have no valid argument against the admission of Gentiles into the church on these terms. Even with all of the terrible implications it would have for the teachings of salvation by grace alone and justification by faith alone, this approach doubtless commended itself to many Jewish Christians and some would have been disposed to insist upon it. Herein lies the reason, after Paul's first journey, that 'some men came down from Judea' to Antioch[12] and were teaching the brothers: 'Unless you are circumcised, according to the custom taught by Moses,[13] you cannot be saved' (Acts 15:1). The stage was thus set for the events of the Jerusalem Conference which Luke recounts in Acts 15, which we will consider in the next chapter.

'Paul and his party' (note here Luke's change of wording from his former 'Barnabas and Saul') now sailed the approximately one

---

12. These men were very probably the 'certain men from James' whom Paul mentions in Galatians 2:12, who in their Judaizing efforts went beyond their commission from James (see Acts 15:24). Luke suggests in Acts 15:5 that they were 'believers who belonged to the party of the Pharisees'.

13. Never did Moses teach that circumcision was essential to salvation. Related as circumcision was to the Abrahamic Covenant (Gen 17:10-14), it was the sign and seal of 'the righteousness that [Abraham] had by faith while he was still uncircumcised' (Rom 4:11). Moses understood this (see Rom 10:6-9); the Judaizers did not.

hundred and seventy miles from Paphos to Perga, a port city six miles inland on the southern coast of Asia Minor in the district of Pamphylia. There John Mark, as we just said, left them (Acts 13:13; Luke does not give us Mark's reason for going home; some suggest fear of what lay ahead, others suggest jealousy for Barnabas[14]; Longenecker urges the view I mentioned above) and returned to Jerusalem.[15] Luke does not tell us whether the missionaries preached in Perga at this time, but he does indicate in Acts 14:25 that they did so on their return trip.[16]

Paul and Barnabas then traveled from Perga to Pisidian Antioch, one hundred plus miles north, where Paul preached his first recorded 'word of exhortation' (see here Heb 13:22) in the synagogue on the Sabbath day (13:15-41). Special note should be taken here in Paul's application of the κήρυγμα of his distinctly 'Pauline representation' of the 'good news' of the gospel in terms of divine acquittal from sins through faith in the glorified Jesus: 'Therefore, my brothers, I want you to know that through Jesus the forgiveness of sins *is proclaimed* [καταγγέλλεται] to you. Everyone who believes in him *is justified* [δικαιοῦται] from everything *you could not be justified from* [οὐκ ἠδυνήθητε δικαιωθῆναι] by the law of Moses' (13:38-39). As far as the Acts record is concerned, no one before Paul had preached so explicitly that men could be justified individually before God solely on the ground of their faith in Christ. Other preachers in Acts, true enough, had proclaimed that forgiveness of sins is available through Jesus (Acts 2:38; 10:43), but Paul included in his preaching of the gospel not only the blessing of forgiveness but also his teaching of divine acquittal which, as we have already suggested, he saw as a significant eschatological aspect of redemptive history. C. H. Dodd comments:

> ...if we recall the close general similarity of the *kerygma* as derived from the Pauline epistles to the *kerygma* as derived from Acts, as well as Paul's emphatic assertion of the identity of his Gospel with the general

---

14. So Bruce, *Paul*, 163.
15. See Acts 15:37-39 for Paul's penultimate expression of disapproval of Mark's departure from them, but see Colossians 4:10, Philemon 24, and 2 Timothy 4:11 for Paul's ultimate words of approval of Mark.
16. From Galatians 4:13-15 we learn that Paul became ill (acute chronic ophthalmia, malaria?) during this time (his 'thorn in the flesh' of 2 Cor 12:7?), and that throughout this first journey he conducted his ministry under this very trying condition. This may account for his by-passing Perga in order to reach Pisidian Antioch with its higher altitudes and cleaner air (so Bruce, *Paul*, 135-36).

Christian tradition [1 Cor 15:11], we shall not find it altogether incredible that the speech at Pisidian Antioch may represent in a general way one form of Paul's preaching, that form, perhaps, which he adopted in synagogues when he had the opportunity of speaking there.[17]

The response to Paul's sermon was truly amazing (13:42-43): 'Many of the hearers..., both Jews by birth and proselytes,...showed themselves favorably disposed to the message, with its proclamation of forgiveness and justification through faith in Jesus.'[18] The following Sabbath almost the whole city came together to hear the Word of God (13:44). When synagogue opposition solidified against them (13:45), Paul and Barnabas announced that they were turning to the Gentiles (13:46-47), much to the joy of the Gentiles who heard their announcement. Luke's summary of the results of the Pisidian Antioch mission at this point is worthy of quotation: 'And as many as had been ordained to eternal life [ὅσοι ἦσαν τεταγμένοι εἰς ζωὴν αἰώνιον] believed. And the word of the Lord was being spread throughout all the region' (13:48b-49).

Wherever the Lord Jesus—'a sign that is spoken against' (Luke 2:34)—is preached, however, there is always ferment, disturbance, upheaval, and persecution mounted against both his message and his messenger: 'The Jews incited the God-fearing women of high rank, and the principal men of the city, and stirred up persecution against Paul and Barnabas. The authorities expelled them from the district' (13:50).

Shaking the dust from their feet against their Pisidian Antiochene persecutors, Paul and Barnabas traveled to <u>Iconium</u>, about ninety miles east by southeast from Pisidian Antioch. Again Luke's comment at this point is worthy of quotation: 'The disciples, meanwhile, were filled with joy and the Holy Spirit' (13:51-52). In Iconium they went as usual to the synagogue and 'spoke so effectively that a great number of Jews and Greeks believed' (14:1). Jewish opposition immediately began to arise which stirred up Gentile sentiment against the missionaries, who in spite of this opposition 'stayed there a considerable time, *speaking boldly* [παρρησιαζόμενοι] in reliance upon the Lord [Jesus], who was bearing witness to the word of his grace by granting signs and wonders to be done through their hands' (14:3; see Acts 15:12; Gal 3:5). Finally, at the instigation of the synagogue and city

---

17. Dodd, *Apostolic Preaching and Its Developments*, 30.
18. Bruce, *Commentary on the Book of the Acts*, 264.

rulers, a riot broke out in which the scheme was hatched to stone Paul and Barnabas. Hearing of this plan, the missionaries departed (14:4-6).

Fleeing Iconium, they journeyed to the Lycaonian city of Lystra, about eighteen miles south by southwest of Iconium, and there they began to *preach the gospel* (εὐαγγελιζόμενοι ἦσαν) directly to the Gentiles since apparently there was no synagogue there (14:6-7). There Paul healed a certain man, a cripple from birth (14:8-10). When the people saw what he had done, they concluded that the gods had come down to them in the likeness of men, Hermes as Paul and Zeus as Barnabas. Efforts were made to sacrifice to them, but Barnabas and Paul only with much difficulty constrained them to stop (14:11-18).[19] 'Then Jews from Antioch and Iconium came there; and having persuaded the multitudes, they stoned Paul [see 2 Cor 11:25; Gal 6:17] and dragged him out of the city, supposing him to be dead. However, when the disciples [note: *some* had apparently believed] gathered around him, he rose up and went back into the city. The next day he departed with Barnabas to Derbe' (14:19-20). In spite of seemingly little positive results at Lystra, apparently one positive result at this time was the conversion of Timothy (see Acts 16:1).

Leaving Lystra, Paul and Barnabas came to Derbe, about sixty miles southeast of Lystra, where they '*preached the gospel* [εὐαγγελισάμενοί] and made many disciples' (14:20b-21a).

After their ministry in Derbe, Paul and Barnabas 'returned to Lystra, Iconium, and Antioch,[20] strengthening the souls of the disciples, *exhorting* [παρακαλοῦντες] them to continue in the faith, and saying: "We must through many tribulations enter the kingdom of God." So *when they had appointed* [χειροτονήσαντες, i.e., 'when they had arranged by a show of hands the election of'] elders in every

---

19. Bruce, *Acts*, 276, writes: 'The summary which Luke [gives] of their expostulation [14:15-17] provides us with one of the two examples in Acts of the preaching of the gospel to purely pagan audiences—to people who, unlike the Gentiles who attended synagogue worship, had no acquaintance with the God of Israel or with the Hebrew prophets. The other, and fuller, example is the speech delivered by Paul to the Athenian Court of the Areopagus (17:22-31). Preachers to such audiences should not be expected to insist on the fulfilment of Old Testament prophecy, as they did in addressing synagogue congregations; instead, an appeal to the natural revelation of God the Creator is put in the forefront. Yet this appeal is couched in language largely drawn from the Old Testament. Martin Dibelius points out that... "The proclamation about God...is preached completely in Old Testament style; the gods are described as 'vain ones' or 'vanities'."'

20. This return trip through the regions of Lycaonia and Pisidia explains how Paul in Galatians 4:13 could speak of 'preaching the gospel to you the first time' (τὸ πρότερον).

church,[21] and prayed with fasting, they commended them to the Lord in whom they had believed' (14:21b-23).

Then Paul and Barnabas, having passed through the region of Pisidia, returned to Pamphylia and particularly to Perga where they *'preached the word* [λαλήσαντες τὸν λόγον]' (14:24-25).

Traveling on to the port city Attalia, they booked passage for home and sailed back to Antioch. There they 'gathered the church together, and reported all that God had done with them, and *how he had opened the door of faith to the Gentiles*' (14:26-27). The Antioch church was now a 'mother church' with several thriving 'daughter churches' comprised mainly, though not entirely, of Gentiles. May her tribe increase! It should not go unnoticed that the team's success among Gentiles would cause the Jerusalem church no little trouble, as we shall see in a moment.

Peter's Hypocrisy at Antioch (Galatians 2:11-14ff.)

Their mission completed (14:26), Paul and Barnabas stayed 'not a little time [χρόνον οὐκ ὀλίγον]' with the disciples in Antioch (14:28). Their first missionary journey, now over, probably took a year or more to accomplish and was a resounding success. Their stay in Antioch may also have been as much as a year in length. Most likely it was during this year's stay that Peter visited Antioch[22] and enjoyed table fellowship with the Gentile church there as he had in connection with the Cornelius incident (see Acts 10:48) until 'certain men from James' arrived. At this time, and in spite of his 'Cornelius experience', Peter separated himself from the Gentile Christians in the Antioch church and would not eat with them (see Gal. 2:11-21), which was a serious schismatic act, to say the least, since the common meal and the celebration of the Lord's Supper were closely connected in the early church.

I believe Paul's 'men from James' (Gal 2:12) are Luke's 'men who came down from Judea' who attempted to Judaize the church in

---

21. Some New Testament authorities have contended that the formal appointment of elders here reflects the later situation of the Pastoral Letters rather than this early stage in apostolic history. But Paul arranged for elders to govern the churches he founded from the very beginning of his missionary labors.

22. Herod's search for Peter after his supernatural deliverance from prison (Acts 12:19) may well have been a second reason, after his calling as the 'apostle to the circumcision', that prompted him to leave Jerusalem and to visit other churches such as the church at Antioch.

Antioch (Acts 15:1) since Paul also refers to them as 'those of the circumcision' (τοὺς ἐκ περιτομῆς) (2:12).[23] Although Luke describes them as 'believers who belonged to the party of the Pharisees' (Acts 15:5), which descriptive 'clue' suggests, but with some ambiguity, that they were true Christians, if T. W. Manson's insights are correct,[24] as I think they are, they were, according to Paul, actually *'false brothers'* (ψευδαδέλφους) (Gal 2:4).[25] This connection of persons, if accurate, is exceedingly solemn in its implications for any *professing* Christian who believes that he must do something beyond what Christ has already done in order to be saved, for it means that he is not a real Christian at all but is in fact a 'false brother'. If it should be the case that his problem is merely one of spiritual immaturity or lack of teaching, it must still be insisted upon that such a person must not be given a place of leadership or a teaching position in the church until he clearly sees that justification before God is by grace alone through faith alone in Jesus Christ to the glory of God alone.

In addition to their legalistic teaching, Bruce suggests that these 'certain men from James' brought a message to Peter in Antioch that

> news of his free and easy intercourse with Gentiles at Antioch had come to Jerusalem and was causing a scandal to many good brethren there, besides hampering the mission in which James and others were engaged among their Jewish neighbors. [His] reported conduct was being exploited by unsympathetic scribes and Pharisees to the detriment of the Christian cause in Judaea, and might even provoke violent reprisals from those militants who condemned fraternization with non-Jews as treasonable.[26]

In somewhat the same vein Longenecker opines that

> one should probably view the messengers 'from James' as bringing, not an ultimatum from a faction of extremists, but an urgent warning that increasing rumors of Jewish Christian fraternizing with uncircumcised Gentiles in Antioch and southern Asia Minor were putting all the churches in Judea in considerable danger. In such a situation Peter might have thought it expedient to modify his practice for a while until the danger abated.[27]

---

23. It is possible that by his 'those of the circumcision' Paul intended not only those in the Jerusalem church 'who belonged to the party of the Pharisees' (Acts 15:5) but also the non-Christian Jews of Jerusalem.
24. See Bruce, *Paul*, 158-59.
25. See Bruce, *Paul*, 175.
26. Bruce, *Paul*, 176-77.
27. Longenecker, *Paul*, 50-51.

Accordingly, Peter 'began to draw back and separate himself from the Gentiles because he was afraid of those who belonged to the circumcision group. The other Jews[28] joined him in his hypocrisy, so that by their hypocrisy even Barnabas was led astray' (Gal 2:12-13). Bruce, quite insightfully, remarks:

> ...it is not difficult to appreciate Peter's dilemma, or to see how he could defend his change of course. ...[he could say that] though he could not emulate Paul's versatility, he too [like Paul] was [just] endeavouring to be 'all things to all men' for the gospel's sake. [So since his] practice in Antioch was a stumbling-block to members of the Jerusalem church whose consciences were scrupulous and unemancipated, he might well think it right to discontinue it for their sakes.
>
> ...Whatever Peter's motives were, Paul would have regarded them as negligible in comparison with the progress of the Gentile mission and the wellbeing of Gentile Christians. Even worse, if possible, than Peter's actions in itself was the effect of his example on other Jewish Christians, and when even Barnabas—the last man of whom it might have been expected—was persuaded to join in withdrawing from table-fellowship with Gentiles, what must the Gentile Christians have thought? They could draw only one conclusion: *so long as they remained uncircumcised, they were at best second-class citizens in the new community.* In that case they might either repudiate the message which (despite what Paul said) consigned them to second-class status in comparison with their fellow-believers of Jewish birth, or they might decide that (despite what Paul said) their best policy was to go the whole way of the proselyte and accept circumcision, since only so could they become first-class citizens. Either way...*the truth of the gospel*[29] *would be hopelessly compromised.* In Christ, Paul believed and affirmed, there was 'neither Jew nor Greek' (Galatians 3:28), whatever distinctions might persist in the world at large. The middle wall of partition between them had been demolished by the

---

28. Paul's 'the other Jews' (οἱ λοιποὶ Ἰουδαῖοι) refer to the Christian Jews of the Antioch church.

29. Bruce's phrase here, 'the truth of the gospel,' was first Paul's: 'When I saw that they [Cephas, Barnabas, and the other Jews at Antioch] were not acting in line [οὐκ ὀρθοποδοῦσιν] with the truth of the gospel [ἡ ἀλήθεια τοῦ εὐαγγελίου], I said to Peter in front of them all...' (Gal 2:14; see also 2:5). What Peter was doing, according to Paul, 'was not in line with' and thus jeopardized the truth of the one saving gospel of God, for his actions implied that the gospel demanded of Gentiles Jewish eating practices. Paul saw more clearly than anyone in Christendom at that moment that the 'truth of the gospel' is preserved only when Jewish ritual laws such as circumcision and Jewish food laws are regarded as extraneous to the gospel and not mandatory for Gentiles. In sum, the good news of the gospel is that men may be justified before God by faith alone in the work of Jesus Christ alone completely apart from law-keeping on their part. The gospel of God is indeed a law-free gospel!

work of Christ; Paul would not stand idly by and see it rebuilt, whether as a religious or as a social barrier. *The only logical reason for preserving it as a social barrier would be its continuing validity as a religious barrier, and to recognize such a continuing validity...would be to nullify the grace of God.* If God's redeeming grace was to be received by faith, and not by conformity with the law of Moses, then it was available on equal terms to Jew and Gentile, and *to make a distinction in practice between Jewish and Gentile believers, as Peter and the others were doing, was in practice to deny the gospel.*[30]

So Paul, clearly understanding, if the Judaizers were right, that Christianity offered very little, if any, gain over Judaism, and perceiving more clearly at that moment than any other man in Christendom the dire consequences of Peter's action for the future of the gospel and of the church, rebuked Peter to his face with the words that we find in Galatians 2:14b-21, which then provided him his lead-in to his sustained argument in 3:1-5:12 for the doctrine of justification by faith alone:

If you, though a Jew, live like a Gentile and not like a Jew, how can you compel the Gentiles *to live like Jews* [Ἰουδαΐζειν, lit. 'to Judaize', occurs only here in the New Testament and means 'to live according to Jewish customs and commandments']? We are Jews by birth and not sinners of Gentiles; yet we know that a man is justified not by works of law but through faith in Jesus Christ. And we believed in Christ Jesus in order that we might be justified by faith in Christ and not by works of law, because by works of law no flesh shall be justified.... For through law to law I died, in order that to God I might live. With Christ I have been crucified. And *I* no longer live, but Christ in me lives. And the life I now live in the flesh I live by faith in the Son of God who loved me and gave himself for me. I do not *nullify* [or 'set aside', ἀθετῶ] the grace of God; for if through [works of] law justification comes, then Christ *for nothing* [δωρεάν, 'in vain', 'to no purpose'] died. (author's translation)

Paul set before Peter here an either/or – either attempt to achieve righteousness 'through the law' and in doing so negate the value of Christ's cross-work or die to the law through union with Christ in his death and live to God through his life (Gal 2:19-20).

Given Peter's later words and actions at the Jerusalem Council in Acts 15, we can justifiably glean that Peter saw the error of his way,

---

30. Bruce, *Paul*, 177-78, emphasis supplied.

acknowledged his wrong, and did not persist in his 'separate table' policy which would have divided the church by 'another gospel'.

Paul's Letter to the Galatians (written c. A.D. 49 or 50)
The Magna Carta of Christian Liberty

The Letter's Place of Origin

Paul wrote Galatians from somewhere in the environs of Syrian Antioch after his first missionary journey and just prior to or actually on his trip up to Jerusalem to take part in the Jerusalem Conference of Acts 15 (most likely during the period of time covered by Acts 15:2). I stated my reasons for this conclusion toward the end of Chapter Five. The reader may want to review the eighteen arguments I gave there.

The Date of the Letter

Paul received word of the destructive activity of the Judaizers and of their success among the Galatian churches while he was in Antioch. (Quite possibly this news came out in connection with his debate with the men who had come down from Judea that precipitated the Jerusalem Conference.) Since he was about to go up to Jerusalem to thrash out the question raised by these 'men from Judea' with the apostles and elders there, he could not go to Galatia – which he would have liked to do (Gal 4:20) – to respond personally to the Judaizers' false doctrine and insidious attack against his apostolic commission from Christ. He therefore determined to write them this letter, to be dated about A.D. 49. Thus was born the group of letters which we now know and revere as the 'Pauline literature'.

The Occasion of the Letter

Apparently organized in Galatia under a single leader since Paul seems to refer to one personality as particularly responsible for the harm that had been done to the Galatian Christians (Gal 5:10), the Judaizers had come to the churches which Paul and Barnabas had established in South Galatia on their first missionary journey and had brought 'a different gospel' which was not the gospel of Christ.

A. What they did not deny: 'To judge from Paul's polemic against them, they did not in so many words deny any positive teaching that Paul had brought to the Galatians; they acknowledged and proclaimed Jesus as the Messiah, the Son of God, the risen and exalted Lord, the Giver of the Spirit, in whose name is salvation; they did not deny that He would soon return in glory to consummate God's work in grace and judgment.'

B. What they taught about salvation: By their own profession, they had come to complete Paul's work (Gal 3:3). 'The coming of the Christ [in their proclamation] did not free men from the Law; the Christ confirmed the teaching of the Law and deepened the obedience which it demanded. Salvation by the mediation of the Christ therefore most assuredly included the performance of the works of the Law. A Christian estate based on faith alone, without circumcision and without the Law, was a very rudimentary and unfinished state; perfection lay in circumcision and in keeping the Law to which it committed a man. [In this way] a man became a true son of Abraham and the inheritor of the blessing promised to Abraham.'[31]

---

31. Reflection on points A. and B. will lead anyone who knows the teachings of Roman Catholicism on justification to conclude that the Judaizers were Rome's forerunners. Rome, as did the Judaizers earlier, confesses Jesus of Nazareth to be the Messiah, the divine Son of God, the risen and exalted Lord, the Giver of the Spirit, in whose name is salvation. Rome also confesses that he sits today on his Father's throne in heaven and that he will return someday in great power and glory to raise the dead and to judge the world. But Rome, as did the Judaizers also, contends that faith in the perfect obedience and finished work of Jesus Christ accomplished in the sinner's behalf is not sufficient for his justification. In addition to trusting in Christ's saving work the sinner must himself perform good works, which infused works of righteousness, though initiated by grace, are meritorious and contribute to his justification. Canons 9, 11, 12, 17, 23, 24, and 32 following the sixteen chapters on the subject of justification of the Sixth Session of the Council of Trent (January, 1547) declare respectively:

9. If anyone says that the sinner is justified by faith alone, meaning that nothing else is required to cooperate in order to obtain the grace of justification, and that it is not in any way necessary that he be prepared and disposed by the action of his own will, let him be anathema.

11. If anyone says that men are justified either by the sole imputation of the justice of Christ or by the sole remission of sins, to the exclusion of the grace and the charity which is poured forth in their hearts by the Holy Ghost, and remains in them, or also that the grace by which we are justified is only the good will of God, let him be anathema.

12. If anyone says that justifying faith is nothing else than confidence in divine mercy, which remits sins for Christ's sake, or that it is this confidence alone that justifies us, let him be anathema.

17. If anyone says that the grace of justification is shared by those only who are predestined to life..., let him be anathema.

C. What they taught about Paul: 'Paul, these men insinuated, had not told them all that was necessary for their full salvation. He was, after all, not an apostle of the first rank, not on a par with the original Jerusalem apostles, through whom he had received his apostolate. His failure to insist on the keeping of the Law was a piece of regrettable weakness on his part, due no doubt to his missionary zeal, but regrettable nonetheless; he had sought to gain converts by softening the rigor of the genuine Gospel of God – he had, in other words, sought to "please men." They, the Judaizers, were now come to complete what Paul had left unfinished, to lead them to that Christian perfection which Paul's Gospel could never give them.'[32]

---

23. If anyone says that a man once justified can sin no more, nor lose grace, and that therefore he that falls and sins was never truly justified...let him be anathema.

24. If anyone says that the justice received is not preserved and also not increased before God through good works, but that those works are merely the fruits and signs of justification obtained, but not the cause of its increase, let him be anathema.

32. If anyone says that the good works of the one justified are in such manner the gifts of God that they are not also the good merits of him justified; or that the one justified by the good works that he performs by the grace of God and the merit of Jesus Christ, whose living member he is, does not truly merit an increase of grace, eternal life, and in case he dies in grace, the attainment of eternal life itself and also an increase in glory, let him be anathema.

Such unevangelical, anti-Pauline nomism Rome has never repudiated. Indeed, Rome continues to this day to urge upon the world the teachings of Trent, thus evidencing its own apostate condition. Paul condemned the Judaizers' teaching in his day, and were he living today he would denounce in equally condemnatory terms the teachings of Rome as well.

32. These insights are extracted from Franzmann, *The Word of the Lord Grows*, 53-54. For additional insights into the situation in the Galatian churches which provoked Paul's letter to them, see also F. F. Bruce, *The Epistle to the Galatians* (The New International Greek Testament Commentary; Grand Rapids: Eerdmans, 1982); E. DeW. Burton, *A Critical and Exegetical Commentary on the Epistle to the Galatians* (International Critical Commentary; Edinburgh: T. & T. Clark, 1921); Ronald Y. K. Fung, *The Epistle to the Galatians* (New International Commentary on the New Testament; Grand Rapids: Eerdmans, 1988); Donald Guthrie, *Galatians* (New Century Bible; London: Marshall, Morgan & Scott, 1973); G. Walter Hansen, *Galatians* (InterVarsity Press New Testament Commentary; Downers Grove, Ill.: InterVarsity, 1994) and 'Galatians, Letter to the' in *Dictionary of Paul and His Letters* (Downers Grove, Ill.: InterVarsity, 1993); G. Howard, *Paul: Crisis in Galatia: A Study in Early Christian Theology* (Society for New Testament Studies Monograph Series 35; Cambridge: University Press, 1979); Richard N. Longenecker, *Galatians* (Word Biblical Commentary 41; Dallas: Word, 1990); H. N. Ridderbos, *The Epistle of Paul to the Churches of Galatia* (New International Commentary on the New Testament; Grand Rapids: Eerdmans, 1953).

The Content of the Letter[33]

SALUTATION, 1:1-5.

A. Paul's benediction, 'Grace and peace be to you from God our Father and the Lord Jesus Christ' (1:3), appears in the salutation section of all of his epistles except Hebrews.

B. No commendation of any kind appears in the salutation section of Galatians; rather, after his benediction Paul moves immediately and directly to his letter's concern, namely, the Galatians' departure from him who called them by the grace of Christ (1:6).

I. PAUL'S DEFENSE OF HIS APOSTOLATE, 1:6–2:21.

A. Not a 'men pleaser', 1:6-10. To demonstrate that he was not a 'men pleaser' as the Judaizers accused him of being with his 'law-free gospel,' Paul twice calls down God's 'anathema' on the Judaizers and their law-ridden 'gospel, which is really no gospel at all'.

The word 'anathema' (ἀνάθεμα) is derived from the preposition ἀνά ('up'), the verb τίθημι ('to place or set'), and the -μα noun ending conveying passive voice significance.[34] Hence it refers to 'something set or placed up [before God]' and is the New Testament synonym of the Old Testament חֵרֶם ('devoted') principle of handing something or someone over to God for destruction. The implication of Paul's usage here is clear: irrespective of whatever else they may believe, they who would teach others that in order to be justified before God and go to heaven when they die they, in addition to casting themselves upon Christ's saving work at Calvary, must 'keep the law', that is, perform good works, are 'false brothers' and stand under God's condemnation. And the sad truth is that from the post-apostolic age to the present time many church fathers as well as many church communions, including the Roman Catholic Church, have proclaimed 'another gospel' and thus stand under Paul's apostolic anathema.

---

33. I have adapted Martin Franzmann's very helpful outline of Galatians, to be found in his *The Word of the Lord Grows*, with certain minor alterations which I felt were necessary for my purpose. See also Merrill C. Tenney, *New Testament Survey* (Grand Rapids: Eerdmans, 1961), 270, for a very helpful outline of the letter.
34. See BAGD, *A Greek-English Lexicon of the New Testament and Other Early Christian Literature*, 54, no. 2.

B. Reception of his apostolate directly from Christ, 1:11-24. As we have already noted (pp. 66-72), Paul demonstrates that he did not get his gospel and the authority to proclaim it from any other source than Jesus Christ.

C. Acceptance of his apostolate by the Jerusalem apostles, 2:1-10.

D. Rebuke even of Peter when Peter's conduct betrayed the truth of the gospel that righteousness is by grace alone through faith alone in Christ, 2:11-21.

II. PAUL'S DEFENSE OF THE GOSPEL OF FREE GRACE, APART FROM THE WORKS OF THE LAW, 3:1-4:31.

A. Three witnesses to the shortcomings of legalism, 3:1-14.

1. The Galatians' experience, 3:1-5. They did not receive the Spirit through obedience to the law but through believing the gospel Paul proclaimed to them.

2. Abraham's example, 3:6-9. Abraham was justified by faith alone and not by circumcision.

3. The Law's expectation, 3:10-14. If one is going to follow the way of the law for righteousness, then he must keep it perfectly; because no one can do so, all men stand under its curse.

B. Three characteristics of the relationship between the promise of God and the law, 3:15-29.

1. The permanency of the promise, 3:15-18. The law, even though it was given hundreds of years later, did not supersede God's promise to Abraham.

2. The purpose of the law, 3:19-24. The law was given to Moses, not to lay out the way of salvation, but to show men their need for and to drive them to Christ.

3. The Christian's position under the promise, 3:25-29. By faith in Christ, the Christian becomes a son of God, Abraham's seed, and an heir according to the promise.

C. Three aspects of gospel sonship which confirm the truth of the gospel of free grace, 4:1-31.

1. Majority sonship under the gospel, 4:1-11. The Old Testament dispensation of law was a time of 'minority' for the people of God; majority sonship and full rights as sons of God come through Christ and God's Spirit of adoption.

2. Paul's paternal concern for his children in the gospel, 4:12-20. He warns his 'children' in the faith that the Judaizers' purpose was to win over their allegiance to them, not to Christ.

3. Gospel sonship related to Isaac, not Ishmael, 4:21-31. It is not enough to claim that one is a son of Abraham. One must recall that Abraham had two sons, the first of whom was Ishmael, the son of the slave Hagar, who was set aside in deference to Isaac who was the son of the free woman. Only those, like Isaac, who are children of the 'free woman' through faith are heirs with Isaac. All the others are Ishmaelites.

III. PAUL'S DEFENSE OF THE GOSPEL'S FREEDOM IN ITS PRACTICAL RESULTS, 5:1-6:10.

A. What freedom under the gospel means principially, 5:1-24.

1. Incompatibility between gospel freedom and the Law, 5:1-12.

2. Gospel freedom, not the path to license, but the path to the service of others in love, 5:13-15.

3. Gospel freedom the path to life in the Spirit, 5:16-24.

B. What freedom under the Spirit means practically, 5:25–6:6.

1. The end of all self-centered pride, self-assertion, and envy, 5:25-26.

2. A life of meek and gentle ministry to the erring, 6:1-5.

3. Loving generosity toward those who teach in the church, 6:6.

C. What freedom under grace means in terms of the Christian's hope, that is, eschatologically, 6:7-10.

CONCLUSION, 6:11-18.

The Dominant Themes in the Letter

A. Paul's apostolic authority was given directly by Christ Himself.

B. Justification, or right standing before God, comes through faith in Jesus Christ completely apart from law-keeping.

C. Justification by faith leads to a life of freedom lived in the Spirit.

We may be sure that the Galatians who had remained faithful to Paul and to his teachings would have doubtless been overjoyed to hear from him and would have been delighted that he had written in defense of his apostolic authority and of his gospel; those who had 'Judaized', who may have been in the majority in the churches of Galatia, probably received his letter, at least at first, with a certain disdain and distrust. We have every reason to believe, however, that Paul's letter did its 'perfect work', for on his later missionary journeys he returned to these churches and apparently was received by them as an apostle of Christ. Moreover, we hear no more from Paul in the way of rebuke regarding the Galatians. To the contrary, he suggests in 1 Corinthians 16:1 that these churches had joined him in his effort to gather a collection for the Jewish Christians in Jerusalem.

The soteric principles reiterated in this letter guaranteed that Christianity would continue on its march toward becoming a world religion that meets the needs of all men. Had Paul not enunciated and fought for them, this march would have been stopped dead in its tracks and Christianity would have become what many perceived at that time it already was, namely, a sect of Judaism. As such it would have become subject at any and every moment to the same fortunes that Judaism would experience, and any advance it would enjoy would have come by the good graces of, that is, by the whim of, the world's acceptance of that religious faith. Because Paul insisted that right standing before God is by faith completely apart from the works of the law, his letter to the Galatians has rightly been called the 'Magna Carta of Christian Liberty'.

The Results of Paul's First Missionary Journey

Posturing themselves against Paul's law-free gospel, the Judaizing party among the Jewish Christians (actually they were 'false brothers,' according to Paul) believed that the growth of the Gentile church must mean the inevitable end of the Jewish church as such. To insure its perpetuity, these people concluded that in addition to faith in Christ adherence to the law, the Jew's distinctive, must be mandated for all – for Paul's Gentile Christians as well as for themselves. Hence their concern to bring Gentile Christians under the dictates of the law.

Paul, however, clearly saw three things: firstly, that if law-keeping was the way of justification, then the Age of the Messiah had not yet dawned and Jesus could not be the Messiah; secondly, that for Gentiles to accept such bondage to the law meant the end of salvation by grace for everyone, including Jews; and thirdly, that for him to tolerate the teaching of these Judaizing Christians, since he knew that he would not and could not alter his message, would mean nothing less finally than the emergence of two churches advocating two plans of salvation – one essentially Jewish, advocating the Judaizing heresy addressed in Galatians, and the other essentially Gentile, committed to salvation by grace alone and justification by faith alone. So at the same time that he labored tirelessly for a law-free gospel of pure grace, he urged the Judaizers to lay aside their advocacy of legalism that would pollute the pure river of grace that makes glad the city of God and to enter into free fellowship with Gentiles. At the same time, he (and after the Jerusalem Conference presumably, the entire church) also urged Gentiles, for the sake of church unity (but not for salvation), to abstain from things that would offend Jewish Christians with certain Jewish scruples. But central to his κήρυγμα was his doctrine of eschatological 'acquittal' (the doctrine of justification)—here and now before the Great Day—by grace alone through faith alone in Jesus Christ.

It was the doctrine of justification through faith alone in Christ's saving work, apart from all 'works of law', for which Paul contended mightily both at Antioch and in his churches in Galatia, for he clearly saw that without this doctrine there is no saving gospel at all! Accordingly, to quote first Tenney and then Franzmann, concerning his letter to the Galatians:

> the tone of the book is warlike. It fairly crackles with indignation though it is not the anger of personal pique but of spiritual principle. 'Though we, or an angel from heaven, should preach unto you any gospel other than that which we preached unto you, let him be anathema' (1:8), cried Paul as he reproved the Galatians for their acceptance of the legalistic error.[35]

---

35. Tenney, *New Testament Survey*, 271.

Scarcely another epistle so emphasizes the 'alone' of 'by grace alone, through faith alone' as does this fighting exposition of the Gospel according to Paul, with its embattled stress on the fact that Law and Gospel confront man with an inescapable, not-to-be-compromised either-or. Paul's Letter to the Romans expounds the same theme more calmly and more fully and has a value of its own; *but there is no presentation of the Gospel that can equal this letter in the force with which it presents the inexorable claim of the pure grace of God.* Luther, who had to fight Paul's battle over again, said of the Letter to the Galatians: 'The Epistle to the Galatians is my own little epistle. I have betrothed myself to it; it is my Catherine of Bora.'

It should be remembered that the letter addresses itself to a very earnest, very pious, and very Christian sort of heresy and crushes it with an unqualified anathema. Our easy age, which discusses heresy with ecumenical calm over tea cups, can learn of this letter the terrible seriousness with which the all-inclusive Gospel of grace excludes all movements and all men who seek to qualify its grace.[36]

---

36. Franzmann, *The Word of the Lord Grows*, 61-62, emphasis supplied.

CHAPTER SEVEN

THE JERUSALEM CONFERENCE, c. A.D. 49 or 50 (Paul's Third Post-Conversion Trip to Jerusalem) (Acts 15)

> Christ! I am Christ's! and let the name suffice you,
> Ay, for me too He greatly hath sufficed:
> Lo with no winning words I would entice you,
> Paul has no honour and no friend but Christ.
> – From 'Saint Paul,' Frederic W. H. Myers

The Conference's Occasion

As we noted in the previous chapter, but it will bear repeating, during Paul's and Barnabas's stay at Syrian Antioch after their first missionary journey, 'some men came down from [the hill country of] Judea to Antioch and were teaching the brothers: "Unless you are circumcised, according to the custom taught by Moses,[1] you cannot be saved"' (Acts 15:1). If these are the 'certain men from James' (Gal 2:12), as they most likely are, and if these Judaizers at Antioch are those to whom Paul refers when he declares that 'some *false* brothers [ψευδαδέλφους] had infiltrated our ranks [in Antioch] to spy on the freedom we have in Christ Jesus and to make us slaves' (Gal 2:4), then it is clear, I would stress again, that they had gone beyond their commission in what they were teaching (see Acts 15:24: 'with words which we did not authorize').

We also suggested earlier that the coming of these 'certain men from James' is quite likely the same occasion when Peter, having come to Antioch before these Judaizers 'from James' arrived and having enjoyed table fellowship for a time with the Gentile Christians in the Antioch church as he had enjoyed table fellowship with Cornelius

---

[1]. As we have already said, never did Moses teach that circumcision was essential to salvation. Related as circumcision was to the Abrahamic Covenant (Gen 17:10-14), it was the sign and seal of 'the righteousness that [Abraham] had by faith while he was still uncircumcised' (Rom 4:11). Moses understood this (Rom 10:5-8); the Judaizers did not.

and his household earlier at Caesarea (Acts 10:48), in an act which Paul describes by the strong word ὑπόκρισις ('hypocrisy, insincerity') and also as 'not acting in line with the truth of the gospel [οὐκ ὀρθοποδοῦσιν πρὸς τὴν ἀλήθειαν τοῦ εὐαγγελίου]', 'drew back and separated himself' from their fellowship when the Judaizers arrived 'because he was fearing those who belonged to the circumcision party'. By his example he led other Jews, even Barnabas, also astray (Gal 2:11-13).[2]

It should not go unnoticed that Paul employs the phrase, 'the truth of the gospel' (ἡ ἀλήθεια τοῦ εὐαγγελίου) twice in the Galatians 2 passage, the first time in connection with his confrontation with the 'false brothers' ('We did not give in to them for a moment, so that *the truth of the gospel* might remain with you [Galatians],' 2:5), the second time in connection with his confrontation with Cephas ('When I saw that they [Cephas, Barnabas, and the other Jews] were not acting in line with *the truth of the gospel*, I said to Peter in front of them all...', 2:14). This connection suggests that Cephas and those under his influence were acting in this situation as if they were 'false brothers'. We know, of course, that Cephas believed better than he acted, which is the reason Paul described his actions as 'hypocritical' or 'insincere' and not as an apostate act, out of deference to Peter's apostolicity.

Because of the intense debate that arose between the Judaizers and Paul and Barnabas, the Antioch church decided to send their missionaries up to Jerusalem to confer with the apostles and elders there and officially to settle this matter, if possible, once and for all. On their way south and up to Jerusalem, as they traveled through Phoenicia and Samaria—never a pair to fail to seize an opportunity that presented itself—they told the brotherhood along the way how God had been converting the Gentiles, which made the brotherhood very glad (Acts 15:3).

The issue that the Judaizers were raising by their teaching at Antioch was not whether Gentiles could be saved or not. The Old Testament prophets had foretold the salvation of the nations, and all parties to the dispute agreed that they could be (see the church's judgment in Acts 11:18). The issue was, *what did Gentiles have to do in order to be saved*. Three clearly distinguishable theological positions were present at the council:

---

2. Refer again to Bruce's analysis of the issue that was at stake as Paul saw it (*Paul*, 177-78).

(1) the Antioch group, represented by Paul and Barnabas—and not without some wavering on the latter's part (see Gal 2:13: 'even Barnabas was *led astray* [συναπήχθη]')—was insisting *on biblical and experiential grounds*[3] that Gentiles were being justified by grace alone through faith alone in Christ completely apart from circumcision and the other works of law (see Acts 13:39);

(2) the Judaizing group (consisting of 'believers who belonged to the party of the Pharisees', Acts 15:5) was insisting *on what it mistakenly believed was biblical grounds* (see their reference to 'the custom taught by Moses')[4] that Gentiles had to be circumcised and obey the law of Moses (that is, had in effect to become Jews) in order to be saved; and

(3) the Jerusalem church leadership, basing its position *on expediency*, was apparently urging—I think inappropriately—that Jewish Christians might not want to fraternize with uncircumcised Gentile Christians because of the difficulties such fraternization created for their mission efforts among their Jewish kinsmen.

The Conference's Proceedings

Arriving in Jerusalem for what Raymond E. Brown describes as 'the most important meeting ever held in the history of Christianity',[5] Paul and Barnabas 'were welcomed by the church and the apostles and elders, to whom they reported everything God had done through them' (Acts 15:4). Immediately the Judaizers stood and raised their objection to Paul's mission theology (15:5). Apparently the meeting went into recess at that time, for Luke informs us that the apostles and elders later 'convened [Συνήχθησάν] to consider the matter' (15:6) under the moderatorship of James, half-brother of Jesus.

---

3. I say 'and experiential grounds' because Barnabas and Paul would later argue at the Conference that God himself had borne witness to the Gentiles' salvation through faith in Christ apart from works of law by 'the miraculous signs and wonders [he] had done among the Gentiles through them' (Acts 15:12).

4. I infer from the fact that the Judaizers were so overt with their teaching before the leaders of the Jerusalem church that they apparently believed that the Jewish Christian leadership in Jerusalem supported their view as well. All the more likely may this have been their thinking if the Judaizers were interpreting in their own way such Jacobean teaching as may be found, for example, in James 2:14-26.

5. Raymond E. Brown, *An Introduction to the New Testament* (Anchor Bible Reference Library; New York: Doubleday, 1997), 306. Devoting as much space and detail to this meeting as he did in his short 'history' of Christianity, apparently Luke also regarded this meeting as extremely significant to the progress of Paul's law-free gospel.

Excursus on James

James ['Ιάκωβος], 'the Lord's brother' (Gal 1:19), was one of the three 'pillars' (the other two were Peter and John) of the church of the circumcision (Gal 2:9, 12). He presided over the mother church of Christendom in Jerusalem (Acts 12:17; 15:13; 21:18).

Hegesippus (c. A.D. 170), the Jewish Christian historian cited by Eusebius, *Ecclesiastical History*, 2.23, states that James was a Nazarite from birth, but of this we cannot be certain.[6] As the oldest of Jesus' four half-brothers (Joseph, Judas, and Simon being the other three, Matt 13:55; Mark 6:3; John 2:12; 7:3, 10), he was not a believer in his brother's messianic claims before Christ's resurrection (John 7:5). In fact, with his entire household, he seems to have believed that his older half-brother was—if not completely out of touch with reality—at least suffering delusions of grandeur with his claims to the Old Testament messiahship and hence delivered the taunting and disrespectful challenge to Jesus to 'manifest yourself to the world' if he was really the Messiah (John 7:5). Accordingly, he was not one of the original apostles. However, Jesus appeared to James after his resurrection (1 Cor 15:7), bringing him to repentance and faith in him as the Shekinah 'Glory' of God (James 2:1), and thus he appears, along with his other brothers, among the one hundred and twenty believers who gathered in the upper room to await the Spirit's coming (Acts 1:14). From an incidental remark of Paul, we may infer that he was married (1 Cor 9:5).

James wrote the New Testament letter bearing his name around A.D. 45-48, and from its contents one discerns that he was obviously a man keenly observant of nature, life, and human character; a man of deep moral and religious convictions; a devout Jew who had not ceased to be a Jew when he became a Christian. Because of his special relation to Jesus and his legendary piety (tradition distinguishes him as 'James the Just [הַצַדִּיק or ὁ δίκαιος]'), he came to enjoy an authority in the early church virtually equivalent to the original Eleven. In fact, Paul refers to him as an apostle in Galatians 1:19, some scholars explaining this title by the speculation that he was given the place of the martyred son of Zebedee and brother of John (Acts 12:2).

From Acts 12:17 we may perceive something of his prominence in the fact that it is specifically James that Peter, himself an

---

6. See Philip Schaff, *History of the Christian Church*, I, 276-77.

undisputed apostle, singles out by name when he requested that news be communicated to the church of his miraculous escape from Herod's prison. From Acts 15:13 we learn that James presided over the Jerusalem Conference in A.D. 49 or 50, summarized the apostles' arguments with a speech beginning with ἀδελφοί, ἀκούσατέ μου ('Brothers, hear me'), a formula resembling one in the epistle bearing his name (see Acts 15:13 and James 2:5), issued its judgment, and probably prepared the 'Apostolic Decree' which has the same greeting formula peculiar to his letter ('Greetings', χαίρειν [see Acts 15:23 and James 1:1] instead of the specific Christian greeting, 'Grace and peace' [χάρις καὶ εἰρήνη]). Finally, from Acts 21:18ff we learn that he was among those in the Jerusalem church who, entertaining the hope that the Jews would accept Paul if he would give evidence of his 'Jewishness' to them, suggested that Paul join in a rite of purification at the temple. (Subsequent events proved their hope to be a vain one, for the Jews seized Paul and attempted to kill him.) Schaff states that

> the mission of James was evidently to stand in the breach between the synagogue and the church, and to lead the disciples of Moses gently to Christ. He was the only man [in Jerusalem] that could do it in that critical time of the approaching judgment of the holy city. As long as there was any hope of a conversion of the Jews as a nation, he prayed for it and made the transition as easy as possible. When that hope vanished his mission was fulfilled.[7]

Josephus tells us that, at the instigation of Ananus the high priest of the sect of the Sadducees and son of the Annas mentioned in John 18:13, James was stoned to death with some others, as 'breakers of the law', that is, as Christians, in the interval between the procuratorship of Festus and of Albinus (A.D. 62 or 63). Josephus also adds that this act of injustice created such great indignation among the Pharisees that they induced Albinus and King Agrippa to depose Ananus.[8] This Jewish historian thus furnishes an impartial testimony to the high standing of James even among many unbelieving Jewish leaders in the capital city of the Jewish nation itself. Hegesippus places his death a few years later, shortly before the destruction of Jerusalem (c. A.D. 69).

---

7. Schaff, *History*, I, 267. The interested student would enjoy reading Schaff's brief descriptive history of James the man, *History*, I, 265-77.
8. Josephus, *Antiquities*, XX, 9, 1.

After 'much discussion', Peter, also having returned to Jerusalem and apparently having been convinced by Paul of the error of his actions in Antioch, stood up and addressed the assembly. Expressing what had been his real theological convictions all along, he described the soteric significance of his mission to Cornelius in these words:

> Brothers, you know that some time ago [it had actually been about ten to twelve years before] God made a choice among you that the Gentiles might hear from my lips the message of the gospel and believe.[9] God, who knows the heart, showed that he accepted them by giving the Holy Spirit to them, just as he did to us. *He made no distinction between us and them*, for he purified their hearts by faith [I think I could add the word 'alone' here in light of Peter's next sentence.]. Now then, why do you try to test God by putting on the necks of the disciples a yoke that neither we nor our fathers have been able to bear? No! We believe [here is the *original* 'Apostles' Creed'] it is through the grace of our Lord Jesus that we are saved, just as they are [an interesting inversion, this 'we...as they' rather than 'they...as we', but the reader should recall that he is trying to persuade the Judaizers who were present and thus is addressing this statement primarily to them]. (Acts 15:7-11)

Barnabas and Paul[10] then told the assembly about the miraculous signs and wonders God did among the Gentiles through them (15:12), which divine wonders would have attested to God's approval of their message of the law-free gospel among the Gentiles.

With his authoritative 'Brothers, hear me', James then began to speak, declaring that the words of the prophets 'are in agreement with [συμφωνοῦσιν]' the missionary activities conducted by Peter, Paul, and Barnabas among the Gentiles. He cited Amos 9:11-12 as a summary description of what God had declared in Old Testament times that he would do in behalf of the Gentiles in this present age. He concluded by issuing the judgment that 'we should not make it difficult for the Gentiles who are turning to God', requesting only that Gentiles be told, not for their salvation's sake but for the sake of church unity, that they should abstain from 'food polluted by idols, from sexual immorality, from the meat of strangled animals [which would have

---

9. An unbiased observer will have to admit, however, that the Jerusalem church leadership had done very little with this major advance of the Great Commission to Gentiles through Peter's ministry beyond its later endorsement of Paul's apostolic ministry to the Gentiles.

10. Note Luke's name order here. In the Jerusalem context where he had been known and loved from the beginning, Barnabas' name is given the priority over Paul's.

The Jerusalem Conference

been a specific example of 'blood'] and from blood' (15:13-21).

James cites a version of Amos 9 which reflected more closely the Septuagint version than the present-day Masoretic Text. The latter can and should be emended to conform to the Hebrew text which doubtless underlay the cited Septuagint translation. In verse 12,

A. The verb יִירְשׁוּ ('possess') should be emended to יִדְרְשׁוּ ('seek') —the change of the י to the ד;

B. The sign of the accusative אֶת —clearly suspect as an indicator that 'remnant of Edom and all the Gentiles...' are direct objects inasmuch as a single אֶת never introduces two direct objects— should be emended to אֹתִי (either 'me' or 'the Lord' [construing the י as a hypocoristic abbreviation for (יְה(וה)]);

C. The proper noun אֱדוֹם ('Edom') should be emended to אָדָם ('men'), a mere repointing of the word;

D. The result of these slight alterations? Instead of reading, 'that they may possess the remnant of Edom and all the Gentiles who bear my name,' the text now reads, 'that the remnant of men, even all the Gentiles who bear my name, may seek the Lord'—precisely the words Luke quotes James as saying!

Because some dispensational scholars, such as C. I. Scofield, have maintained that 'dispensationally, [James's summary speech] is the most important passage in the N.T.', describing, they say, 'the final regathering of Israel' after this present age,[11] these scholars have insisted that the verb συμφωνοῦσιν in Acts 15:15 has the connotation, 'are in agreement with', not 'speak about', and simply indicates that the missionary policies being observed in connection with Gentile evangelism in the present age are harmonious with the policies to be followed in the future Jewish kingdom age – the real referent of Amos' prophecy.[12] But aside from the fact that such an interpretation imposes an inanity on the text since the Jerusalem assembly hardly needed to be informed that God's prescribed missionary policies throughout history are consistent with each other from age to age, this is a classic example of 'theological reaching' in order to avoid the obvious. If

---

11. See *Scofield Reference Bible* (New York: Oxford University, 1917), 1169-70, note 1 on Acts 15:13-17.

12. See *New Scofield Reference Bible*, 1185, note 1; 1186, note 1.

there is no connection between the cited 'words of the [Old Testament] prophets' and the missionary activity of this present age beyond the mere fact that the (according to dispensationalists, unpredicted) character of the church's present missionary activity among the Gentiles 'fits in with' the (according to dispensationalists, predicted) character of Jewish missionary activity among the Gentiles in the reputed future millennial age, one is left with no acceptable explanation for James' citation of the Amos prophecy in this context. In fact, by this line of reasoning James is made to introduce, by dispensational reckoning, an irrelevancy that has no bearing on the issue before the assembly. I will explain.

According to the classic dispensational interpretation, James cited Amos in order to justify, in light of what was going to be done in the future kingdom age, the propriety of the character of Gentile evangelism in this present age. But then he must acknowledge, if this is so, that James violated one of the cardinal canons of dispensational hermeneutics since, according to dispensational thought, one must never attempt to justify a truth or activity for one age by arguing from the normativeness of that truth or activity in another age. To do so is to 'confuse the ages'—a cardinal sin in dispensational hermeneutics. Furthermore, if James did utilize, as dispensationalists allege, a kingdom age practice in order to demonstrate that Gentiles should not be required to be circumcised now, it is not apparent how his conclusion follows from what dispensationalists allege elsewhere will be the practice in the kingdom age, since they argue on the basis of Ezekiel 44:9 that Gentile believers must be circumcised in the kingdom age! If James were really attempting to justify a church age practice from a future kingdom age practice, as dispensationalists allege, and if he had held the dispensational interpretation of Ezekiel 44:9, he should have drawn the opposite conclusion from the one which he drew: he should have concluded that circumcision was essential to Gentile salvation in this present age! One can only conclude that the dispensational interpretation does justice neither to James' statement in 15:15 nor to his supporting citation, Amos 9:11-12.

Employing Amos 9:11-12 as he did in Acts 15:16-17, James designates the church to which the 'remnant of men', even 'all the Gentiles who bear my name', was being drawn through the missionary activity of Peter and Paul as Amos' 'fallen tabernacle of David' which God was even then in process of 'rebuilding' precisely by means of drawing from the Gentiles a people for himself and making them members of the church of Jesus Christ. But for James to represent the church of Jesus Christ as the 'fallen tabernacle of David' which Amos predicted was to be 'rebuilt' means that James (1) believed that the prophets did speak of this age and the church of this age, (2) that Gentiles were being drawn into 'David's fallen tabernacle'— Amos' picturesque term for Israel, and (3) that an unbroken continuity exists between God's people in the Old Testament and Christians in the New Testament.

The Conference's 'Conciliar Decree'

The decision reached by the Jerusalem Conference was no doubt gratifying to Paul. The Conference, under the influence of James' summary judgment, not only upheld the essential soteric principle for which he had earlier argued at Antioch against the Judaizers and Cephas but it also endorsed him *personally* and *publicly* (see 'our beloved [ἀγαπητοῖς] Barnabus and Paul' in the Conference's decree). Richard Longenecker notes:

> When one considers the situation of the Jerusalem church in A.D. 49, the decision reached by the Jerusalem Christians must be considered one of the boldest and most magnanimous in the annals of church history. While still attempting to minister exclusively to the [Jewish] nation, they refused to impede the progress of that other branch of the Christian mission whose every success meant further oppression for them.[13]

The Conference's 'decree' (15:24-29, described in Acts 16:4 as τὰ δόγματα, 'the decisions', 'the decrees') sent to 'the Gentile believers in Antioch, Syria, and Cilicia' by the two Jerusalem church leaders, Judas and Silas, is a model of 'walking the razor's edge' between truth and error, and is worth citing in full, with some concluding comments:

> The apostles and elders, your brothers. To the Gentile believers in Antioch, Syria and Cilicia: Greetings.
> Since we heard that certain ones, going out from us, troubled you with words, unsettling your minds, with [words, we say,][14] which we did

---

13. Richard Longenecker, *The Ministry and Message of Paul* (Grand Rapids: Zondervan, 1971), 56.
14. I have provided my own translation of the first part of this 'decree' because I believe the NIV misleads when it suggests by its translation that it was the very going out of these Judaizers and not what they said which was not authorized. But Paul distinctly

not authorize, we all agreed to choose some men and send them to you with our dear friends [τοῖς ἀγαπητοῖς ἡμῶν] Barnabas and Paul – men who have risked their lives for the name of our Lord Jesus Christ. Therefore we are sending Judas and Silas[15] to confirm by word of mouth what we are writing. The Holy Spirit has made it abundantly clear to us[16] that we should not burden you with anything beyond *these following requirements* [πλὴν τούτων τῶν ἐπάναγκες]: You are to abstain from food sacrificed to idols, from blood, from the meat of strangled animals, and from sexual immorality. You will do well to avoid these things. Farewell.[17]

By its decree the Jerusalem Conference, setting the standards for Gentile participation in the Christian community, manifestly upheld God's demand for truth and for love for the brotherhood: the Judaizers

---

states that these men were 'from James', and therefore we must acknowledge that James had commissioned them to go to Antioch.

15. This Silas is the 'Silvanus' (his Roman cognomen) of 1 Thessalonians 1:1, 2 Thessalonians 1:1, 2 Corinthians 1:19, and 1 Peter 5:12, who accompanied Paul on his second missionary journey. Luke informs us in Acts 15:22 that Silas was one of the 'leaders' (ἄνδρας ἡγουμένους) among the Christian brotherhood in Jerusalem and in Acts 15:32 that he was a 'prophet [προφήτης]'. It appears from the account of their later adventures in Philippi (see the plural nouns in Acts 16:37: ἀνθρώπους ʽΡωμαίους and 16:38: ʽΡωμαῖοι) that Silas, like Paul himself, was a Roman citizen.

16. The Greek literally is 'For *it seemed good* [ἔδοξεν] to the Holy Spirit and to us.' Why do I translate as I do? Because the speeches at the Conference had 'made it abundantly clear' to those at the Conference that the Holy Spirit had placed his divine *imprimatur* upon the conclusion they had reached. The Spirit's endorsement of their conclusion may be seen in his threefold, collectively incontrovertible, objective involvement in

(1) the conversion of the uncircumcised Cornelius and all the other Gentiles who had heard Peter's sermon on that occasion (see Acts 10:19, 44-47), to which Peter referred later both in Jerusalem and at the Conference (11:12, 15-17; 15:8);

(2) the Spirit-mandated (13:1) and Spirit-validated ministry of Barnabas and Paul (13:9 [see Gal 3:5]; 14:27; 15:3) and their later description at the Conference of his validation of their ministry by the signs and wonders (σημεῖα καὶ τέρατα) he empowered them to perform among the Gentiles (15:12); and

(3) James' citation of the Spirit-inspired Scripture of Amos 9:11-12 which prophetically endorsed the mission activities of Peter and Barnabas and Paul among the Gentiles (15:13-19).

In light of this incontrovertible data, because the expression 'it *seemed* good' conveys to the English ear (though apparently not to the Greek ear since it was a formula widely used in imperial and governmental decrees) the notion of perhaps some doubt on the part of the apostles and elders regarding their decision, I would urge that the verb would be better translated 'the Holy Spirit has made it abundantly clear to us that we should not burden you...'.

17. See Bruce M. Metzger, *A Textual Commentary on the Greek New Testament* (New York: United Bible Societies, 1971), 429-34, for full discussion of the debate over whether the decree entailed a twofold or threefold stipulation (Western text) or a fourfold stipulation (Alexandrian text). All things considered, it appears best to settle for the fourfold stipulation as reflected in the above account, but it should be recognized that the three dietary regulations may be reduced to two inasmuch as 'strangled meat' would have been a specific type of meat which had not been drained of its blood.

must accept the truth of God's law-free gospel; the Gentiles must in love avoid offending the Jewish Christian who might still hold certain Jewish dietary and ceremonial scruples. Moreover, the Jerusalem Conference stands as a great testimony to the truth that good things *can* come out of church controversy. Ministers of the gospel must contend for the truth as they understand it, even if it means some loss of tranquility for a time among them. If they are truly desirous of knowing the truth, the Spirit of God in the church will guide them to it (see John 7:17; 1 Cor 11:19).

What should be made of the 'requirements' which it stipulated? And required for what? R. H. Stein writes with rich insight:

> Many scholars see these requirements as compromising the Pauline teaching of justification by faith alone and have denied that Paul could ever have accepted such a decree.... As a result some scholars deny the historicity of the Jerusalem decree altogether; some argue that the decree took place at a later time...; and a great many scholars argue that Paul would never have accepted such a decree for it conflicts with his teachings and practice (1 Cor 8:1-13; 10:25-33). Paul saw all such things as lawful (1 Cor 6:12; 10:23). To have accepted the decree would have compromised his gospel. It would have placed the Gentiles under the Law.
>
> It must be admitted that if the Jerusalem decree taught that salvation for the Gentiles demanded that they keep certain food restrictions, then Paul in principle lost at the Jerusalem Council. Salvation is either free and through faith alone or it is not free. It cannot be "mostly" free. Yet it is questionable whether the Jerusalem decree should be interpreted in this manner. Luke explains the cause for the establishment of the decree as being due to the the fact that 'Moses has been preached for generations in every city and has been read each Sabbath in the synagogues' (Acts 15:21). The issue at stake, according to Luke, is not justification but rather social intercourse between Jews and Gentiles. The decree does not add a requirement for Gentiles who are seeking salvation. Rather they are directions given by the Spirit (Acts 15:28) which seek to promote sensitivity on the part of Gentile Christians with respect to issues that were especially offensive to Jews.
>
> If we observe Paul's own practice concerning the scruples of "weaker" brethren, it is quite clear that he always accommodated his personal liberty and practice in order not to offend the sensitive among his congregations. On several occasions a similar problem arose in his churches. At times it involved eating food dedicated to idols (1 Cor 8:1-13; 10:23-33); at times it involved those who objected to eating meat (Rom 14:1-15). In such instances, whereas Paul agreed with those

advocating freedom, he always surrendered his own freedom in order not to offend the "weak", and he urged those who had a similar understanding of the freedom of the gospel to do the same. For Paul circumcision was an irrelevant issue in itself, for it only involved the presence or absence of a piece of skin unless one argued that the removal of this piece of skin was a requirement for salvation. Thus when a theological issue was at stake, he refused to have Titus circumcised (Gal 2:1-3); but in the case of Timothy, when it did not involve a theological issue but permitted greater freedom in ministering among the Jews, he was willing to have him circumcised (Acts 16:1-3).

To understand Paul's view of freedom, we must recognize that he was so free that, unless a theological issue was at stake, he could willingly surrender his freedom in order to facilitate the spread of the gospel. This is seen most clearly in 1 Corinthians 9:19-23. Although free, Paul voluntarily became a slave to the weaknesses of others...[He] would have no problem urging Gentile believers that they should keep the decree when they were in the presence of Jews, for truly free persons are only free when they can surrender their freedom out of love for the weak. For Paul this could even involve taking a Jewish vow, if it helped in his ministry among the Jews (Acts 18:18; 21:26).[18]

Longenecker observes that the Conference's decree was

the type of decision consistent with the character and commitments of James and the Jerusalem apostles as portrayed elsewhere in Acts and Galatians. They could hardly have officially commended the Pauline policies.... But neither could they be found resisting the general teaching of Scripture or the evident acceptance of the Gentiles by God expressed in miraculous and providential fashion. On the other hand, they could not overlook the practical demands involved in a ministry to Israel. Therefore, while they could not clasp the Gentile mission to their bosom or condone certain excesses which were rumored among the Jews to be prevalent in the Gentile world, they did disassociate themselves from the disruptive preaching of the Judaizers. And that was of immense importance to Paul and the furtherance of the Gentile mission.[19]

Franzmann quite correctly observes, then:

The "necessary things" requested of the Gentiles are not marked as necessary to salvation and are therefore not a reimposing of the Law

---

18. R. H. Stein, 'Jerusalem,' *Dictionary of Paul and His Letters* (Downers Grove, Ill.: InterVarsity, 1993), 471.
19. Richard Longenecker, *The Ministry and Message of Paul*, 56.

upon them; this is [a prudent – RLR] *request* [for the sake of peace and unity – RLR] addressed to the Gentiles, a request which asked them to abstain from foods and practices abominable to Jewish feelings, foods and practices which their pagan past and their pagan surroundings made natural and easy for them. It is understandable that abstention from "unchastity" should be included also in the request when we remember how closely connected unchastity was with pagan worship, pagan festivals, and pagan life generally. The so-called Apostolic Decree is therefore anything but a triumph of Judaic legalism. If a burden of love was laid upon the Gentile brethren by it, the Judaic brethren also assumed no light burden in not expecting and asking more. The reception of the letter at Antioch (Acts 15:31), and later on in the province of Galatia (Acts 16:4,5), shows that the Gentile churches did not view it as a defeat for Gentile freedom: "They rejoiced at the exhortation [παρακλήσει – 'encouraging message']" (15:31) and [the churches] "were strengthened in the faith, and they increased in numbers daily" (Acts 16:5).

The men of the church learned [thereby] not to use their freedom as an opportunity for the flesh, but through love to "be servants of one another" (Gal. 5:13). Thus Christianity was safeguarded against a reimposition of the Law; the very real danger that Christianity might degenerate into a Judaic sect (and so perish with Judaism) was averted. And the unity of the church was preserved; the new Gentile church was kept in contact with the Judaic church, to which it owed the Gospel and was thus kept firmly rooted in the Old Testament Scriptures—a great blessing, for the history of the church has shown how readily alien and corrosive influences beset the Gospel, once contact with the Old Testament is lost. To surrender the Old Testament is the first step toward misunderstanding, perverting, and so losing the Gospel of the New Testament.[20]

Their position having been completely endorsed by the conciliar decree drawn up by the Jerusalem Conference, Paul and Barnabas, accompanied by Judas and Silas, two leaders of the Christian brotherhood in Jerusalem whose assigned task was to 'confirm by word of mouth' what the Conference had written in its decree, returned to Antioch, the pure gospel of grace having been once again defended and reaffirmed!

Judas and Silas, being prophets, 'spent a period of time' (ποιήσαντες χρόνον) in Antioch encouraging and strengthening the Antioch brotherhood. Then they returned to Jerusalem. Paul and Barnabas remained in Antioch 'some days' (see Acts 15:36: Μετὰ

---

20. Martin Franzmann, *The Word of the Lord Grows* (St. Louis: Concordia, 1961), 52.

τινας ἡμέρας) where they *continued to teach* (διδάσκοντες) and *to preach* (εὐαγγελιζόμενοι) the word of the Lord (Acts 15:32-36). No doubt it was Paul's observance of Silas' manly and congenial leadership qualities during the latter's visit to Antioch that commended him to Paul later as a colleague for the second missionary journey.

CHAPTER EIGHT

PAUL'S SECOND MISSIONARY JOURNEY, HIS FOURTH POST-CONVERSION (UNEVENTFUL) TRIP TO JERUSALEM, AND HIS THESSALONIAN CORRESPONDENCE

> Only like souls I see the folk thereunder,
>   Bound who should conquer, slaves who should be kings,–
> Hearing their one hope with an empty wonder,
>   Sadly contented in a show of things;–
>
> Then with a rush the intolerable craving
>   Shivers throughout me like a trumpet call, –
> Oh, to save these! to perish for their saving,
>   Die for their life, be offered for them all!
>   – From 'Saint Paul,' Frederic W. H. Myers

Paul's Second Missionary Journey (from c. early spring, A.D. 50, to spring, A.D. 52) (Acts 15:36–18:22)

When the reader thinks of Paul's first missionary journey with Barnabas accompanying him, he should think immediately of *South Galatia* – the primary area evangelized by the missionary pair.

When he thinks of Paul's second missionary journey accompanied by Silas (who is first mentioned in Acts 15:22, 32f.), Timothy (from Lystra), and Luke (from Troas to Philippi), the student should think immediately of *Corinth* since the heart of the apostle's second missionary journey was his eighteen-month ministry in that great commercial center of Greece (Acts18:1-18).

Paul's ministry in Corinth was, of course, preceded by, first, a revisitation of the churches of Syria and Cilicia (which he had founded during the nine or ten 'silent years' of his missionary labors there before Barnabas came to Tarsus to find him; see Gal 1:21) (Acts 15:41) and of the South Galatia churches which he founded on his first missionary journey (16:1-6); second, the Macedonian vision

(16:8-10); third, his missionary labors in the European cities of Philippi (16:12-40), Thessalonica (17:1-9), and Berea (17:10-14); and fourth, his visit to Athens, the great cultural center of Greece, and his *Areopagitica* before the Areopagus there (17:16-34). It was followed, first, by a brief visit to Ephesus which prepared for his long ministry there on the third journey (18:19-21), and second, by a brief visit to Jerusalem (18:22) before he returned to his home city and sending church in Antioch.

I will now flesh out these general observations in some detail, again underlining the first occurrence of all significant place names and providing the Greek words Luke employs to describe Paul's gospel proclamation.

Paul began his second missionary journey accompanied by Silas[1] after he and Barnabas could not agree on whether John Mark should accompany the original missionary pair again (Acts 15:36-40). Apparently, the Antioch church approved of this new arrangement since Luke informs us that Paul and Silas were 'commended by the brothers to the grace of God' before they left (v. 40), as it had done earlier for Barnabas and Paul (Acts 13:3). Barnabas, taking Mark, sailed to Cyprus, his home country (Acts 4:36), no doubt to encourage the churches which he and Paul had founded on their first missionary journey. Barnabas disappears from the Acts narrative here, but there is some indication that he eventually traveled to Corinth since Paul intimates that he was known by the Christians there (1 Cor 9:6). Apparently, Barnabas, ever the 'encourager', helped Mark greatly because years later Paul instructed Timothy to 'get Mark and bring him with you, because he is helpful to me in my ministry' (2 Tim 4:11; see also Col 4:10; Phil 24).

Believing that evangelization and the planting of new churches must be followed by consolidation, Paul and Silas traveled first north around the northeast corner of the Mediterranean Sea and then west through the combined Roman province of Syria/Cilicia '*strengthening*

---

1. Paul had to fetch Silas back to Antioch from Jerusalem to which he had just recently returned after his brief time of ministry in Antioch. As we noted in the last chapter, Silas is the 'Silvanus' (his Roman cognomen) of 1 Thessalonians 1:1, 2 Thessalonians 1:1, 2 Corinthians 1:19, and 1 Peter 5:12. Luke refers to Judas and Silas in Acts 15:22 as 'leaders [ἄνδρας ἡγουμένους]' among the Jerusalem Christian brotherhood, and in Acts 15:32 he calls Judas and Silas 'prophets [προφῆται]'.

From the account of their later adventures in Philippi (see the plural nouns in Acts 16:37: ἀνθρώπους ʹΡωμαίους and 16:38:ʹΡωμαῖοι) it would appear that Silas, like Paul himself, was a Roman citizen.

[ἐπιστηρίζων] the churches' there (Acts 15:41). Then they traveled through the mountain pass in the Taurus Range called the Cilician Gates into the province of Galatia to the <u>Lycaonian cities of Derbe and Lystra</u>, 'delivering the decisions reached by the apostles and elders in Jerusalem for the people to obey' (Acts 16:4). The 'decisions' obviously had their desired effect on the churches that were comprised of Jews and Gentiles, since Luke offers his fourth progress report in Acts on the success of the gospel at this juncture: 'So the churches were strengthened in the faith and grew daily in numbers' (16:5). In the latter city, Timothy, who very likely had come to faith on Paul's first visit,[2] joined the missionary effort, being circumcised first—since he was half Jewish by birth but wholly Jewish by training (Acts 16:1; 2 Tim 1:5; 3:14-15—in order that he might be acceptable to the Jews of the Diaspora along the way (Acts 16:3).[3]

The missionary trio then continued west through <u>the region of Phrygia and Galatia</u> (which included <u>Iconium</u> and <u>Pisidian Antioch</u>). Then having been kept by 'the Spirit of Jesus' from preaching the Word in the provinces of Asia or Bithynia,[4] they moved in a diagonal southeasterly to northwesterly direction across Asia Minor and came to <u>Troas on the Aegean coast</u>. Here Paul received what missionaries for many generations have called his 'Macedonian vision'. For in spite of all their philosophy, culture, and success toward political democratization, Macedonia and Greece still had a great need—a *spiritual* need! Accordingly, the man from Macedonia in Paul's vision begged him: 'Come over to Macedonia and *help* [βοήθησον] us' (Acts 16:9). It is no different in the West today! In spite of the great advances in learning and technology in the 'first world', there is still great spiritual need which only the truth of the gospel will meet!

Luke having now joined the missionary trio (Paul, Silas, and Timothy) as indicated by the 'we' in 16:10, the missionary group,

---

2. If Paul was God's instrument to bring Timothy to the Faith, he had only 'watered' and 'reaped' where someone else had planted, for Timothy had 'from infancy...known the holy Scriptures, which are able to make...wise for salvation through faith in Christ Jesus' (2 Tim 3:15), having been instructed by his godly Jewish grandmother Lois and his mother Eunice (2 Tim 1:5).

3. For F. F. Bruce's discussion of Timothy's circumcision, see *Paul, Apostle of the Heart Set Free* (Grand Rapids: Eerdmans, 1996 reprint), 214-16; see also T. R. Schreiner, 'Circumcision' in *Dictionary of Paul and His Letters* (edited by G. F. Hawthorne, R. P. Martin, D G. Reid; Downers Grove, Ill.: InterVarsity, 1993), 137-39.

4. With this divine direction the gospel moved west to Europe. If Paul had not been so directed, perhaps the gospel would have gone to the Orient and the West would still be in darkness! Truly, Christians of the West are trophies of grace!

now a quartet, immediately booked passage and sailed for Europe.[5]

Landing at Neapolis, the seaport of Philippi, they traveled the Via Egnatia about ten miles to Philippi where they stayed 'several days'.

Excursus on Philippi

Named for its founder, Philip II of Macedonia, who established it in 356 B.C. on the earlier site of Krenides (Κρηνῖδης) which was situated on the Gangites River, Philippi, Luke informs us, was a 'leading city' of the district of Macedonia and 'a Roman colony' (Acts 16:12, NIV, NRSV).[6] Luke's word μερίδος ('a district') reflects Macedonia's earlier division in 167 B.C. into four districts by Lucius Aemilius Paullus. His word κολωνία ('a colony'), occurring only here in the New Testament, English translators have rightly interpreted as 'a Roman colony' (see Acts 16:21). The city became a colony of Rome in 42 B.C. after the battle of Philippi in which Antony and Octavian (later Augustus) defeated the party led by Julius Caesar's assassins, Brutus and Cassius. The victors settled some veteran soldiers there and called the new colony Colonia Victrix Philippensium. Twelve years later, after Octavian had disposed of his subsequent rival Antony, he renamed the colony after himself.

When one observes that Luke's first 'we' section ends in Philippi (Acts 16:17) and his second begins there (20:6), it seems apparent that Luke remained in Philippi when Paul, Silas, and Timothy continued on to Thessalonica.

During their stay at Philippi two significant recorded conversions occurred (there were, of course, others), contributing to the establishment of a vibrant church there. First, Lydia, 'a dealer in purple woolen cloth' (πορφυρόπωλις) from the city of Thyatira and a 'worshiper of God' (σεβομένη τὸν θεόν)[7] responded to Paul's message ('the Lord opened her heart,' Luke writes), and both she and the members of her household were baptized (16:13-15). She then persuaded the

---

5. Three 'we' passages are found in Acts, each largely concerned with a journey by sea (16:10-17; 20:5–21:18; 27:1–28:16). Bruce insightfully observes that 'each of the three ends with a statement in which Paul is distinguished from the narrator and the rest of his companions' (*Paul*, 218).

6. This translation follows the majority reading which has πρώτη (nominative case) and thereby connects 'leading' to 'city'; πρώτης (genitive case), which would connect 'leading' to 'district', is supported only by a few Latin codices and some medieval versions based on the Latin. See BAGD, μερίς, 505.1, for the problems with either translation.

7. Bruce, *Paul*, 219-20, opines, because apparently there was no synagogue in Philippi since there was no Jewish community there to speak of, that Lydia had probably become a God-fearer at Thyatira where a Jewish colony did exist.

missionaries to stay in her home during their stay in Philippi.

Second, after Paul had cast a demonic spirit out of a slave girl whom Luke represents as a 'pythoness', that is, one who had a 'spirit of Python' (16:16: πνεῦμα πύθωνα),[8] whose deliverance moved her owners, when they realized that their hope of making any more money from her fortunetelling was gone, to accuse the missionaries before the city magistrates (στρατηγοί) of throwing the city into an uproar, Paul and Silas were beaten with rods, thrown into jail, and placed in the stocks. About midnight as they were praying and singing hymns a great earthquake occurred; all the jail doors were opened and all the prisoners' chains were unfastened. The Philippian jailer, awaking and seeing all the doors open and thinking that all the prisoners had escaped, was about to kill himself but Paul stopped him. Moved with fear, he fell down before Paul and Silas and asked them the now-famous question: 'Sirs, what must I do to be saved?' Receiving the simple response, 'Believe in the Lord Jesus, and you will be saved – you and your house' (16:31), he believed in Christ and he and his household were baptized that very night (16:25-34).[9]

In the morning Paul informed the city magistrates through their 'officers' (ῥαβδοῦχοι, lit. 'rod-bearers', a reference probably to the bundle of sticks carried by the Roman lictor) that, though he and Silas were Roman citizens (see the plural nouns in 16:37: ἀνθρώπους Ῥωμαίους and 16:38: Ῥωμαῖοι), they had been beaten without a trial and thrown into jail. Therefore, he demanded that the magistrates

---

8. Python was a Greek designation for the god Delphi or Apollo, the god associated with the giving of oracles at the oracular shrine of Delphi in central Greece.

9. At least twice in Acts (16:15, 33, 34; but see 11:14; 16:31) and once in 1 Corinthians (1:16) reference is made to what has come to be termed 'household baptisms' where the adult who came to faith presumably had his family baptized with him. Luke reports that after Lydia responded to Paul's message, 'she *and the members of her household* were baptized' (16:15). While Luke declares that the Lord opened *her* heart to receive the things spoken by Paul, he says nothing of her household's faith, and yet they were baptized as well.

In the case of the Philippian jailer, there is a sustained emphasis throughout the Acts pericope (16:31-34) upon the jailer's faith alone. Luke informs us that, after Paul and Silas had instructed him, 'Believe [Πίστευσον – first aorist active imperative *second masculine singular*] in the Lord Jesus, and you will be saved – you and your household', they spoke the word of the Lord *to him* (αὐτῷ), with all who were in his house being present at that time (vs 32). Then after he had washed the prisoners' wounds, '...immediately he *and all his family* were baptized, and bringing them up into his house, he set a meal before them and he greatly rejoiced with all his house because *he* had believed [πεπιστευκὼς – perfect active participle nominative *singular* used causally] in God.' While it is virtually certain that the jailer's entire family heard the gospel, Luke says nothing at all about his family's believing (they may have; we simply do not know). Rather, he pointedly highlights only the jailer's faith, and yet his entire household was baptized as well.

personally come to the jail and escort them out. The magistrates, alarmed upon hearing that they had beaten Roman citizens without a trial, came to the jail and apologized, brought them out, and requested that they leave the city. But they returned first to Lydia's house where they 'encouraged the brothers' and then they departed.

From Luke's expression, 'Then *they* left [Philippi]' (16:40), we may infer that he remained behind in Philippi, perhaps to serve as the church's pastor or to continue the evangelization of Macedonia. Bruce draws what he calls 'a simple-minded inference' that Luke was left there to oversee the Philippian Christians' contribution to the relief fund for the Jerusalem church.[10] He also suggests that Luke was the unnamed 'true yokefellow' whom Paul will later ask in his letter to the Philippians to help Euodia and Syntyche who had contended at his side in the cause of the gospel (4:3).

Passing through Amphipolis and Apollonia along the Egnatian Highway, the missionary team, now apparently back to three in number, soon arrived at the port city of Thessalonica on the Thermaic Gulf, about ninety miles west by southwest of Philippi.

Excursus on Thessalonica

The largest city of Macedonia, Thessalonica was founded around 315 B.C. by Cassander, king of Macedonia, who named it after his wife Thessalonica, daughter of Philip II of Macedonia and half-sister of Alexander the Great. He forcibly settled citizens there from other towns and villages in the area as its first inhabitants. When Lucius Aemilius Paullus divided Macedonia into four districts in 167 B.C. Thessalonica became the capital of the second district, and when Macedonia was made a Roman province in 146 B.C. the city became the seat of provincial government. In 42 B.C. it became a 'free city' governed by its own 'city magistrates' (πολιτάρχας, Acts 17:6, 8).

The missionary team resided in Thessalonica for three weeks, and 'as his custom was', Paul went to the synagogue each Sabbath, and '*reasoned* [διελέξατο] with them from the [Old Testament] Scriptures, *explaining and proving* [διανοίγων καὶ παρατιθέμενος] that the Christ had to suffer and rise from the dead: "This Jesus *I am proclaiming* [καταγγέλλω] to you is the Christ," he said' (17:2-3). Apparently, he was also representing Jesus, because he is the Messiah,

---
10. Bruce, *Paul*, 219, fn. 28.

as mankind's 'king' (17:7). The results of this brief ministry were quite encouraging. 'Some of the Jews were persuaded and joined Paul and Silas, as did a large number of God-fearing Greeks and not a few prominent women' (17:4; see 1 Thess 1:9-10; 2:13)—again, core families for the founding of a thriving young church. Because of mob hostility and the charge of sedition (incited by Jewish animosity) toward Jason, who had provided shelter for the trio, they had to slip away from Thessalonica by night (17:5-10a), but not before Paul had instructed them concerning some of the features of the Eschaton (see 1 and 2 Thessalonians).[11]

Their next mission effort came in Berea (17:10b-14), sixty miles west by southwest of Thessalonica, where again Paul taught in the synagogue. Again the results were quite striking. After *examining* (ἀνακρίνοντες) the Scriptures every day, presumably with Paul, to see if what he said was so (17:11), 'many of the Jews believed, as did also a number of prominent Greek women and many Greek men' (17:12). But when the Jewish leaders in Thessalonica learned that Paul was making disciples in neighboring Berea, they came to Berea and stirred up the crowds against him. Once again, his converts thought it best, for his safety's sake, that Paul should leave. So leaving Silas and Timothy at Berea to complete the work, Paul was escorted alone by some of his Berean friends to Athens, where they left him, but not before Paul had intructed them to send Silas and Timothy to join him as soon as possible (17:13-15).

Excursus on Athens

'No city in the Hellenic world could match Athens for those qualities which Greeks counted most glorious.'[12] The cradle of democracy and 'the eye of Greece, Mother of Arts and Eloquence',[13] Athens, located in the southeastern part of the country with its harbor outpost town of Piraeus, attained the place of prominence among the city-states of Greece early in the fifth century B.C. because of the leading role it played in resisting the Persian invasions. Defeated by the Spartans in the Peloponnesian War (431-404 B.C.), the city quickly regained much of its earlier influence. Even though Athens took the lead in resisting Macedonian aggression in the fourth century B.C. and suffered defeat

---

11. For Paul's own moving description of his ministry among the Thessalonians, see 1 Thessalonians 2:3-12.
12. Bruce, *Paul*, 237.
13. From John Milton's 'Paradise Regained'.

by Philip of Macedon at Chaeronea (338 B.C.), Philip treated the city with kindness and permitted it to retain much of its liberties which it enjoyed until Rome conquered Greece in 146 B.C. Even then, because of the city's past glory, Rome permitted it to continue with its own institutions as a free, allied state in the Empire. 'The sculpture, literature and oratory of Athens in the fifth and fourth centuries B.C. have never been surpassed.'[14] Being the native city of Socrates and Plato (the latter of whom established the Academy in the northwest sector of the city near the Cephisus River) and the adopted home of Aristotle (who established the Lyceum in the east sector near the Ilissus River), Epicurus and Zeno, Athens occupied the chief place among the cities of the ancient world for great philosophers.

The Attic dialect of Greek, spoken over a very restricted area as compared to Ionic or Doric Greek, became the main basis of the Koine ('common') Greek, which was spoken throughout the Empire and which is the Greek dialect in which the New Testament is written.

If Paul entered the city from the south through the Piraeic gate leading to the harbor, he would have been confronted immediately with the sculpture of Neptune seated on a horse and hurling his trident. Nearby was the Temple of Ceres within which stood the sculptured forms of Minerva, Jupiter and Apollo, with statues of Mercury and the Muses near a sanctuary to Bacchus. Entering the Agora, the center of the city's public life where citizens gathered to exchange the latest news and to debate with strangers (see Acts 17:21), which contained statues dedicated to Apollo, the patron deity of the city, and the Altar of the Twelve Gods (Zeus, Hera, Poseidon, Hades, Apollo, Artemis, Hephaestus, Athena, Ares, Aphrodite, Hermes, Hestia; Demetrius and Dionysus were sometimes substituted for Hades and Hestia), which was for the Athenians what the Golden Milestone was to the Romans, Paul would have seen the craggy promontory of the Areopagus to the north on which rested the Temple to Mars, and looking toward the east he would have seen the Acropolis on the rising ledges of which were shrines to Bacchus, Aesculapius, Venus, Earth, and Ceres, ending with the beautiful Temple of Unwinged Victory. Observation would have revealed to him that every public building in the Agora was a sanctuary to some god or goddess: the Record House was a temple of the Mother of the Gods, and the Council House enshrined statues of Apollo and Jupiter and an altar to Vesta. The theater was consecrated to Bacchus, and altars erected to the abstract ideas of Fame, Modesty, Energy, Persuasion, and Pity, along with altars 'to unknown gods' (Pausanius 1.1.4; 5.14.8; Philostratus, Vit. Ap. 6.3). While the Athenians perceived these many altars to be expressions of religious *devotion*, Paul correctly perceived them to be acts of religious *ignorance* (Acts 17:23) dotting the streets and by-ways. On the Acropolis itself, the whole of which was one vast composition of architecture and sculpture dedicated to the nation's glory and the worship of its gods, stood the Temple of Victory which contained statues of Venus and the Graces. It also housed an edifice dedicated to Minerva, the goddess of health, and a shrine to Diana. Also sculptures of Theseus, Hercules, Earth and Minerva could be found there. The most magnificent edifice of all on the Acropolis was the Parthenon (the 'Virgin's House') dedicated to Minerva. A colossal statue of this goddess in ivory and gold stood within the columns of the Parthenon. Two other statues of Minerva also stood in the temple precincts – the most venerated of the three was called the *Erectheium*, and the third, the *Minerva Promachus* with spear and shield, rose in gigantic proportions above all the buildings of the Acropolis as the tutelary divinity of Athens and Attica.

With just this much of a description of ancient Athens, one can understand why Luke tells us that Paul's spirit 'was stirred within him when he saw the city was full of idols' (Acts 17:16). Indeed, it was so full of statues to gods that one ancient writer said there were more statues in Athen than in all the rest of Greece put together, while another said that in Athens it was easier to meet a statue than to meet a man.[15]

Alone in Athens, Paul was 'greatly distressed to see that the city was full of idols. So he *reasoned* [διελέγετο] in the synagogue with the Jews and God-fearing Greeks, as well as in the marketplace day by day with those who happened to be there' (17:16-17). We are not left to conjecture concerning what he 'dialogued' about, Luke informing us that Paul '*was preaching the good news* [εὐηγγελίζετο] about Jesus and the resurrection' (17:18).

Paul's 'dialoguing' in the Agora brought him to the attention of a group of Epicurean and Stoic philosophers,[16] some of whom thought

---

14. Bruce, *Paul*, 237.

15. See the first 168 pages of the Loeb edition of Pausanias' *Description of Greece* for a good tourist's guide to the antiquities of Athens. For W. J. Conybeare and J. S. Howson's description of Athens, see their *The Life and Epistles of St. Paul* (Grand Rapids: Eerdmans, 1971 reprint), 268-88.

16. The Epicurean school, founded by Epicurus (341-270 B.C.), taught that pleasure, the highest of such being a life of tranquility (ἀταραξία) free from pain, disturbing passions, and superstitious fears, including the fear of death, is the chief end of life. It did not deny the existence of the gods, believing in them as 'blessed and immortal beings'; it simply maintained that the gods took no interest in the affairs of men. Accordingly, it upheld the validity of free will over against fatalism.

The Stoic school, founded by the Cypriot Zeno (340-265 B.C.) and taking its name from

he was just a 'spermologos' (σπερμολόγος, translated by the NIV as 'babbler', but literally, 'seed-picker', that is, a 'gutter-sparrow', or 'one who "picks up and retails" scraps of information for money') while others thought he was advocating 'foreign demons (Ξένων δαιμονίων)' (17:18; note the plural here) because he preached to them about 'Jesus and the resurrection [ἀνάστασιν]'. They may have thought the term ἀνάστασις, since it is a feminine noun, referred to Jesus' paramour or consort.[17] So they brought him to a meeting of the Areopagus, the town council which owed its name to the fact that in antiquity it had convened on 'Mars' Hill' but which in Roman times met mainly in the Royal Portico in the Agora. The council requested that he tell them more about this 'new teaching' and these 'strange ideas' (17:18-21), for as Luke states: 'All the Athenians and the foreigners who lived there spent their time doing nothing but talking about and listening to the latest ideas' (17:21). So Paul delivered his famous address (known as the *Areopagitica*) before the Areopagus, doing it in terms that could be understood by the Epicurean and Stoic philosophers gathered there but without any accommodation of his message to what they were prepared to believe. In a masterful theological summary presented with evangelistic and apologetic sensitivity, Paul carefully contextualized the great truths of revelation concerning the self-sufficient Creator, man created in his image, and man's need to come to God through the Judge he had appointed and raised from the dead for that end. And while the results were not as externally apparent as in previous cities, a few did become followers of Paul and believed, among them Dionysius, a member of the Areopagus, and a woman named Damaris.

Some well-intending (but I think incorrect) expositors of Paul

---

the 'painted Stoa' (portico) where he taught in Athens, taught a pantheistic religious materialism: all that was real, including God, was material. It aimed at living consistently with nature, its over-arching question being: 'How can the wise man live in harmony with nature?' The life lived in harmony with nature is a life lived rationally, it contended, which life also included accepting one's fate from God which was inevitable anyway. It believed that the virtuous life was the only absolute 'good'. All else, including health, wealth, beauty, even life and death, was termed 'indifferent' because such things made no difference to virtue or happiness. It laid great emphasis on the primacy of man's rational faculty and on individual, self-centered pursuit of 'virtue' which emphasis, though it was marked by great moral earnestness and a high sense of duty, marked it also by great spiritual pride.

17. If these Greeks associated the name ᾿Ιησοῦς ('Jesus') with ἴασις ('healing') and ᾿Ιησώ, the Ionic form of the name of the goddess of health, and the feminine noun ἀνάστασις with physical restoration, they may have viewed 'Jesus and the resurrection' as denoting the personified and deified powers of 'healing' and 'restoration'. See F. C. Chase, *The Credibility of Acts* (London, Macmillan, 1902), 205ff.

have suggested from the resolution which he made on his way to Corinth (see 1 Cor 2:2) that he had concluded from the 'poor results' of his *Areopagitica*, expressing as it does (so they say) a *theologia gloriae* devoid of a *theologia crucis*, that his sermonic strategy had been unwise if not downright compromising in its content.[18] But Bruce, with deeper insight, writes:

> At Athens, as formerly at Lystra, the Paul of Acts does not expressly quote Old Testament prophecies which would be quite unknown to his audience: such direct quotations as his speech contains are from Greek poets. But he does not argue from 'first principles' of the kind that formed the basis of various systems of Greek philosophy; his exposition and defence of his message are founded on the biblical revelation and they echo the thought, and at times the very language, of the Old Testament writings. Like the biblical revelation itself, his speech begins with God the creator of all [no mention of any Demiurge], continues with God the sustainer of all [citing Epimenides of Crete whom he quotes also in Titus 1:12, and Aratus of Cilicia], and concludes with God the judge of all [all three of which concepts were terribly offensive to the Greek mind—RLR].[19]

When one considers too that Paul's address was interrupted by the council when he mentioned the resurrection of Jesus (what Luke reports, in other words, was little more than his introduction), and bears in mind at the same time that Paul 'by this time was no novice in Gentile evangelization, experimenting with this approach and that to discover which was most effective',[20] Paul will have been sufficiently absolved of missiological wrongdoing in the minds of all but his most antagonistic and hostile interpreters.

After his speech, Paul left Athens, still without the company of Silas or Timothy. We do not know whether Timothy, having been left at Berea, had rejoined Paul in Athens and had been sent back to Thessalonica from there, or whether, alone at Athens, Paul had directed Timothy by letter to revisit Thessalonica before joining him

---

18. See Merrill C. Tenney's comment, *New Testament Survey* (Grand Rapids: Eerdmans, 1961), 287: '...the unusual dismissal which Athens gave him unnerved him and caused him to rethink his whole procedure in apologetics.' Bruce, *Commentary on the Book of the Acts* (Grand Rapids: Eerdmans, 1954), 365, however, declares: 'The popular idea that his determination, when he arrived in Corinth, to know nothing there "save Jesus Christ, and him crucified", was the result of disillusionment with the line of approach he had attempted at Athens, has little to commend it.'
19. Bruce, *Paul*, 239.
20. Bruce, *Paul*, 246.

at Corinth. It would seem from 1 Thessalonians 3:1-2 that one or the other of these possibilities occurred. But whatever happened, Paul went on to Corinth alone, arriving there in the late summer or fall of A.D. 50.

As we said at the beginning of this chapter, Paul's eighteen-month ministry at Corinth (and it may have been even longer, see 18:11, 18) became the focal point of his second journey (18:1-18a).

It was in Corinth that Paul first met Aquila and Priscilla, Jewish Christians who had themselves 'recently come from Italy...because Claudius had ordered all the Jews to leave Rome' (Acts 18:2),[21] who were to become life-long supporters of Paul. Because he was a tentmaker as they were, he stayed with them (18:3).[22] Every Sabbath he *reasoned* (διελέγετο) in the synagogue (18:4). It was at this juncture on the journey that Silas and Timothy arrived in Corinth from Thessalonica, bringing possibly a gift from but certainly good news about Paul's converts there.

Immediately, in addition to writing 1 Thessalonians (and 2 Thessalonians a few weeks or months later), Paul *devoted himself exclusively to the Word* (συνείχετο τῷ λόγῳ), '*testifying* [διαμαρτυρόμενος] to the Jews that Jesus was the Christ' (18:5). In so doing, he was simply fulfilling his own mission resolve to 'know nothing among them but Jesus Christ and him crucified' (1 Cor 2:2). When the Jews opposed him, he pronounced a judgment against them, set up headquarters next door at the house of Titius Justus (likely the Gaius of 1 Cor 1:14 and Rom 16:23), and continued to preach. In due course, the household of Stephanas ('the first converts [ἀπαρχὴ] in Achaia,' 1 Cor 16:15), Crispus, the synagogue ruler, and his whole household, and many other Corinthians came to faith, were baptized, and became the nucleus of the church there. Crispus, Gaius (Titius Justus?), and the household of Stephanas were the only converts personally baptized by Paul (1 Cor 1:14-16), this duty probably being carried out primarily by Silas and Timothy.

Even with the triumphs which he witnessed, apparently Paul went through times of discouragement, because the Lord in a vision commanded him not to fear and to keep on speaking. So Paul

---

21. Luke's words in Acts 18:2 are corroborated by the Roman historian Suetonius in his *Twelve Caesars*, Claudius 25.4: 'Because the Jews at Rome caused continuous disturbances at the instigation of Chrestus [probably a misspelling of "Christ"], [Claudius] expelled them from the city.'

22. For Bruce's brief description of this godly pair of Christians, see *Paul*, 250-51.

Excursus on Corinth

Geographically, the city of Corinth, known as 'the City of Two Seas', was strategically located at the western end of the Isthmus of Corinth (the occurrence of the Greek word, ἰσθμός, 'neck [of land]', in this context has given to every similar neck of land in the world this name), thus controlling the trade routes between mainland Greece to the north and Peloponnesian Greece to the south. Lechaeum, one and a half miles northwest of the city on the Corinthian Gulf, was its western port; Cenchrea, five and a tenth miles east on the Saronic Gulf, was its eastern port. To avoid sailing around Cape Malea, the extreme southern tip of Greece, a journey regarded as so dangerous that two famous Greek proverbs stated, 'Let him who sails around Malea forget his home', and 'Let him who thinks of sailing around Malea make his will', smaller vessels would actually be hauled overland at the narrowest part of the Isthmus on a sort of railroad of wooden logs called a *diolkos* (δίολκος) about three and a half miles in length from one port to the other, and the cargoes of larger vessels would likewise be carried across this distance on a paved road built in the sixth century B.C. and deposited on ships on the other side.

Just to the south of the city was the Acrocorinth, a steep, flat-topped rock rising 1886 feet above the plain on top of which was a temple of Aphrodite, goddess of love (whose service gave rise to the city's proverbial immorality), which served the city as its citadel. Thanks to its geographic situation, the city experienced great commercial prosperity and luxury over the years; and its name became synonymous with sexual laxity: Plato used the term 'Corinthian girl' as a synonym for a prostitute, and 'to play the Corinthian' (κορινθιάζεσθαι) was current from the fifth century B.C. for the practice of fornication.

Originally a Greek city-state whose name first appears in Homer's *Iliad* ii 570 and xiii 664, Corinth was destroyed by the Romans in 146 B.C. by way of reprisal for the leading role it played in the revolt of the Achaian League against the overlordship of Rome. For a hundred years it remained unbuilt, and little of the Greek city remains visible today with the exception of the temple to Apollo. Recognizing its strategic location and in order also to relax the crowded conditions of Rome, in 44 B.C. Julius Caesar established a Roman colony on the old site and the city began to flourish again. Although most Roman colonies were founded for veterans, Corinth's 'colonists' were poor but freed slaves. This means that the first settlers were not in fact Romans but persons from the eastern Mediterranean Basin, probably for the most part Syrians, Egyptians and Jews. No doubt the Jewish population swelled in the first century A.D.

due to the imperial edicts of A.D. 19 and 41 that expelled Jews from Rome. In Paul's time, then, the population—doubtless in the tens of thousands—was very heterogeneous, representing Greeks, Romans, and eastern peoples. Latin was the official language, but Greek was the language of the streets, marketplaces, and homes.

A forum—an open marketplace and the administrative center—lay at the heart of the city just south of the old city's most prominent temple (either to Apollo or Athena). The city boasted also of many public buildings including a judgment-seat, porches for public gatherings, a great number of temples dedicated to various gods and goddesses, public baths, gymnasiums, and an amphitheater capable of seating fourteen thousand people.

Local government was conducted by a city council presided over by two magistrates elected annually. From 27 B.C. onwards Corinth was the capital of Achaia and thus was the residence of the governing proconsul of the Roman Senate.

One important feature of life in Corinth was the Isthmian Games, second only to the Olympic Games in importance, staged every other year under the city's sponsorship and dedicated to Poseidon, god of the sea. Living as long as he did in Corinth, Paul very likely attended some of the events of the Isthmian Games, seeing the Games doubtless as an evangelistic opportunity to spread the gospel of Christ, from which he drew some metaphors for the Christian life. For example, he knew about the boxer's sparring habit (1 Cor 9:26), the herald who summoned the runners to the starting line (1 Cor 9:27), the course along which the athletes pressed on toward their goal (Phil 3:14), the judge's awarding the prize at the end of the race (2 Tim 4:8), the prize of the laurel crown for the victor (1 Cor 9:24), the joy and exultation of the victor (Phil 4:1), the strict discipline of training under which the athlete placed himself (1 Tim 4:7-8), and the strict regulations which the athlete had to observe (2 Tim 2:5). In addition to the featured athletic contests competitions were held in music, speech, and drama.

Many religions were practiced in Corinth including, first, the worship of the deities and cults of Greece such as the cults to Apollo, Athena, Aphrodite (whose temple on the Acrocorinth was staffed by a thousand slave-prostitutes who for the profit of their goddess descended to the streets of Corinth each evening and plied their immoral trade), Aesculapius, Demeter, Kore, Neptune, and Venus; second, the Roman imperial cult represented by a temple built probably during Claudius's reign; and third, Judaism. Paul doubtless had Corinth's 'many gods and many lords' in mind when he penned these words in 1 Corinthians 8:5.[23]

---

23. For Bruce's description of Corinth, see *Paul*, 249-50; for Conybeare and Howson's description, see their *The Life and Epistles of St. Paul*, 321-26.

'*continued teaching* [διδάσκων] them the word of God' (18:11) for (at least) eighteen months, even in the face of mounting Jewish opposition which at one point took the form of bringing him before Lucius Junius Gallio, a brother of Seneca the Stoic philosopher, who was appointed the proconsul of Achaia in A.D. 51 (less probably A.D. 52),[24] and charging him with propagating an illicit religion. Gallio rejected the Jewish charges against Paul, however, and ejected his accusers from the court. This judgment sheltered Paul's ministry under the legality of Judaism. When Paul felt his ministry was sufficiently discharged, he left to return to Syria, accompanied by Aquila and Priscilla.

Luke's record of Paul's return trip to Antioch is quite brief (18:18b-22). Probably in the early spring of A.D. 52, as soon as the seas were navigable, Paul left Corinth. Crossing the Aegean, he stopped in Ephesus where his tentmaking partners left him. He himself stayed long enough to go to the synagogue where he '*reasoned* [διελέξατο] with the Jews. When they asked him to spend more time with them, he declined in order to fulfil a vow he had made to visit the temple in Jerusalem. But as he left, he promised, "I will come back if it is God's will." ' Then sailing to Caesarea, he went up to Jerusalem – his fourth and uneventful visit (commonly known as the 'quick visit') to that city recorded in Acts – and visited the brotherhood there, and then went down once again to Antioch, and to his 'home [and the "sending"] church'.

It must be noted again that Antioch was now the 'mother church' of thriving 'daughter churches' not simply in Asia Minor but also in Macedonia and Greece.

This is the appropriate place to discuss Paul's Thessalonian correspondence, written on his second missionary journey from Corinth to the church which he had founded only weeks or months before its composition.

---

24. See Bruce, *Paul*, 253, fn. 20.

Paul's Letters to the Thessalonians

1 Thessalonians[25]

A. The Letter's Place of Origin
That Paul wrote 1 Thessalonians from Corinth on his second missionary journey is evident from the following facts:

1. He includes Silas with him in his salutation as he dictates (1:1); the second journey is the only one of the five in Acts on which Silas accompanied Paul.

2. His visit to Athens seems to be represented as already behind him (3:1).

3. Finally, Timothy has already returned to Paul from Thessalonica (3:6); Acts 18:5 makes it clear that Paul was at Corinth when Timothy came to him.

B. The Date of the Letter
Late in A.D. 50 or early A.D. 51.

C. The Occasion of the Letter
1. In Corinth Paul was filled with anxiety for the church in Thessalonica (2:17; 3:1, 5). Would the brethren stand fast under the persecution which had come upon them? Would they begin to question the trustworthiness of either the gospel (3:5) or him (3:6)? Would they misunderstand his continued absence from them (2:17-18)?

2. Humanly speaking, he could well be worried. 'Paul and his companions were not the only propagandists and pleaders for a cause that traveled the Roman roads in those days; they were part of a numerous and motley troup [sic] of philosophers, rhetoricians, propagandists for various foreign and domestic cults, missionaries,

---

25. Some expositors have urged that our 1 Thessalonians may be 2 Thessalonians and our 2 Thessalonians may be 1 Thessalonians since the recipients of 2 Thessalonians are described (1:4f.) as actually enduring persecution for their faith whereas in 1 Thessalonians (1:6, 2:14) such persecution is treated in the past tense. This is a tenuous basis for the temporal reversal of the letters.

charlatans, and quacks who went from town to town, all intent on getting a hearing, all eager for money or fame or both. These usually came and went, never to be heard from again. Paul would in the popular mind be classified with them. And Paul in Thessalonica, A.D. 51, was not yet the apostle Paul as the church has learned to see him since; he was simply a hitherto unknown little Jew who had come and gone, like hundreds of brilliant and persuasive men before him. The church of Thessalonica would of itself not be minded to classify Paul thus; but his enemies would, and they would thus undermine his apostolic authority and, with it, the faith in the Gospel with which he was identified as apostle.'[26]

3. When Timothy joined Paul at Corinth (Acts 18:5), he reported the good news that the church was continuing both in the faith and in its love for Paul (3:6). But he also reported that
   a. The Thessalonian Christians were having difficulty in maintaining that chastity which a life of faith demands;
   b. Their past made it difficult for them to shed the unscrupulous craftiness which they had heretofore regarded as normal and prudent;
   c. Their fervent anticipation of the return of Christ easily degenerated into an irresponsible enthusiasm which led them to neglect the tasks and duties of daily life;
   d. Their imperfect understanding of the circumstances surrounding the return of Christ made them despondent regarding their relatives and fellow believers who had died (perhaps under the persecution they had experienced) before his return;
   e. They were not content to leave the times and seasons of the eschatological fulfillment in God's hands but were seeking to calculate and predict when the Eschaton would appear;
   f. They were, in spite of their bond to one another in faith and love, not without their frictions and difficulties.[27]

---

26. Martin Franzmann, *The Word of the Lord Grows* (St. Louis: Concordia, 1961), 67.
27. For additional insights into the situation behind the Thessalonian correspondence, see F. F. Bruce, *1 and 2 Thessalonians* (Word Biblical Commentary; Waco: Word, 1982); J. E. Frame, *A Critical and Exegetical Commentary on 1 and 2 Thessalonians* (International Critical Commentary; Edinburgh: T. and T. Clark, 1912); William Hendriksen, *New Testament Commentary: I and II Thessalonians* (Grand Rapids: Baker, 1955); I. Howard Marshall, *1 and 2 Thessalonians* (NCBC; Grand Rapids: Eerdmans, 1983); L. Morris, *The First and Second Epistles to the Thessalonians* (The New International Commentary on the New Testament; Grand Rapids: Eerdmans, 1959).

D. The Content of the Letter[28]

I. THANKSGIVING FOR THE WORD OF GOD IN THESSALONICA; A GRATEFUL SURVEY OF THE HISTORY OF THE CHURCH, 1:1-3:13.

A. Looking back to the time of the founding of the church, 1:1-2:12.
   1. The coming of the gospel to the Thessalonians and their exemplary reception of it, 1:1-10.
   2. Paul's behavior as a missionary, courageous, pure in motive, unselfish, and gentle, 2:1-8.
   3. Paul's pastoral behavior toward the church, his selfless devotion in supporting himself by the toil of his hands while he tended them with a father's care, 2:9-12. The verses behind this and the preceding point are so important for missionary candidates who may wonder what will be expected of them in their missionary labor that they deserve to be quoted in full inasmuch as they provide a window into the missionary heart and labors of Paul:

   2:1-12: You know, brothers, that our visit to you was not a failure. We had previously suffered and been insulted in Philippi, as you know, but with the help of our God we dared to tell you his gospel in spite of strong opposition. For the appeal we make does not spring from error or impure motives, nor are we trying to trick you. On the contrary, we speak as men approved by God to be entrusted with the gospel. We are not trying to please men but God, who tests our hearts. You know we never used flattery, nor did we put on a mask to cover up greed—God is our witness. We were not looking for praise from men, not from you or anyone else.

   As apostles of Christ we could have been a burden to you, but we were gentle among you, like a mother caring for her little children. We loved you so much that we were delighted to share with you not only the gospel of God but our lives as well, because you had become so dear to us. Surely you remember, brothers, our toil and hardship; we worked night and day in order not to be a burden to anyone while we preached the gospel of God to you.

   You are witnesses, and so is God, of how holy, righteous, and blameless we were among you who believe. For you know that we

---

28. I have adapted this outline, with minor alterations, from Franzmann, *The Word of the Lord Grows*, 68-70.

dealt with each of you as a father deals with his own children, encouraging, comforting and urging you to live lives worthy of God, who calls you into his kingdom and glory.

B. Looking back to the time of persecution, when they experienced persecutions comparable to those endured by the churches in Judea, 2:13-16.

C. Looking back to the time of Paul's separation from the church, 2:17-3:5.
    1. Paul's longing to see them again, 2:17.
    2. Paul's attempts to return to them, 2:18-20.
    3. Paul's dispatch of Timothy to them, 3:1-5.

D. Looking to the church's present state according to Timothy's report, Paul's joy at their steadfastness in the faith and their loyalty to him, 3:6-10.

E. Looking forward in intercessory prayer to when God may direct Paul's way back to them and to their faith being established in perfect love and sure hope, 3:11-13.

II. EXHORTATIONS (designed to 'supply what is lacking in their faith'), 4:1-5:28.

A. Moral exhortations for individuals, 4:1-12.
    1. To sexual purity, 4:1-8.
    2. To ever-increasing brotherly love, 4:9-10.
    3. To lives of quiet industry, 4:11-12.

B. Two exhortations concerning last things, 4:13-5:11.
    1. To assurance concerning those who have died in faith, 4:13-18.
    2. To vigilance and sobriety in view of the coming of the day of the Lord, 5:1-11.

C. Exhortations for congregational life, 5:12-22.
    1. To a due recognition of Christian leaders, 5:12-13.
    2. To a life of loving and patient service to one another, 5:14-15.
    3. To a worship life of unbroken joy, prayer, and thanksgiving, 5:16-18.
    4. To a full but discerning use of the gifts of the Spirit, 5:19-22.

D. Conclusions, 5:23-28.
   1. Paul's intercessory prayer for the church, 5:23-24.
   2. Paul's request for the church's intercessions, greetings, instructions for the public reading of the letter (Note here the beginning of the liturgical use of the apostolic word), 5:25-27.
   3. Closing benediction, 5:28.

E. Dominant Themes of the Letter
1. Sanctification (see 4:3).
2. Eschatological matters. Every major section of the letter closes with a reference to the return of Christ (1:10; 2:12; 2:16; 2:19; 3:13; 4:13-18; 5:1-11; 5:23).

F. Conclusion
This letter provides a particularly poignant and vivid picture of Paul the missionary pastor at work in a young Gentile mission church. Aspiring pastors and missionaries would do well to study carefully and then to emulate Paul's ministerial heart and skills as we find them exhibited in 1 Thessalonians 2:1-12.

* * * * *

Second Thessalonians

A. The Letter's Place of Origin
That Paul also wrote 2 Thessalonians from Corinth is evident from the following data:

1. He again includes Silas with him in the salutation of the letter (1:1).

2. There is hardly another place after Corinth (where he ministered for eighteen months) from which he might have written, for once he left Corinth, his second missionary journey was as good as over.

B. The Date of the Letter
Late in A.D. 50 or early A.D 51, some few weeks or months after the first letter.

C. The Occasion of the Letter

Somehow—we do not know how it reached him; perhaps the Thessalonians themselves wrote to him—the report had come to Paul in Corinth that, while the church was still standing firm under persecution (1:4), someone had been teaching, by virtue of an alleged prophetic utterance and/or 'a letter supposed to have come from us [Paul, Silas, and Timothy]' (2:2), that the Day of the Lord had already come. As a result,

1. Some had begun to entertain false ideas about 'the coming of our Lord Jesus Christ and our assembling to meet him' (2:1). The result was that these Christians had abandoned their regular occupations and were leading idle and disorderly lives in dependence upon the charity of the church (3:6-12).

2. Still others, perhaps from the apostle's high demands that they live righteously in spite of all opposition, had apparently grown despondent at the thought of Christ's return. For them his coming would mean judgment for their sins and not salvation. So Paul addresses these two situations in this letter.

D. The Content of the Letter[29]

I. THANKSGIVING AND PRAYER, 1:1-12.

A. Thanksgiving for the faith and love of the church and for their steadfastness amid persecutions, 1:3-10.

B. Prayer that God in his power and grace may sustain and perfect them, 1:11-12.

II. INSTRUCTION CONCERNING THE COMING OF THE LORD, 2:1-17.

A. His coming to be preceded by the great apostasy and the coming of the man of lawlessness, 2:1-12.

B. His coming to mean salvation for God's elect, 2:13-15.

C. The church to be preserved until his coming, 2:16-17.

---

29. I have adapted this outline, with minor alterations, from Franzmann, *The Word of the Lord Grows*, 72-3.

III. EXHORTATIONS, 3:1-14.
A. To pray for the success of the word and Paul's preservation, 3:1-5.
B. To correct and to discipline the idle and disorderly, 3:6-15.

IV. CONCLUSION, 3:16-18.
A. Benediction, 3:16.
B. Autograph conclusion as authentication of the letter, 3:17.
C. Second benediction, 3:18.

D. The Dominant Themes of the Letter
1. Sanctification (see 2:17; 3:13).
2. Eschatology (see 2:1-11).

E. Conclusion
1. For those who were idle, Paul indicates that certain events, which had not taken place to that moment, must come to pass before the Day of the Lord comes. These people, 'not busy but busybodies', must get back to work or go hungry (3:11-12).

2. For the despondent and fearful, Paul reassures them of God's certain judgment, not of them but of their persecutors (1:4-10), and also of their election (2:13-15).

The Results of Paul's Misionary Journey

Even farther away from herself than before, as the result of the labors of her missionary team, the Antioch church, as the sending church, enlarged her borders as Paul and Silas planted new 'daughter churches' around the Aegean Basin. It is indeed thrilling to review the advance of the word of the living Christ away from Antioch into the New Testament world of the Roman Empire. Martin Franzmann summarizes the history of the second missionary journey this way:

> The word of the Lord sped on and triumphed (2 Thess. 3:1) in Europe, but in its peculiarly divine way. It sped on surely but not without opposition; it triumphed with the inevitable triumph of a work of God, but its history is not the history of an easy and effortless triumph – it is a history marked, rather, by the persecution, suffering, and internal difficulties of the human bearers and the human recipients of the word.[30]

---

30. Franzmann, *The Word of the Lord Grows*, 63.

Men and women who respond to Christ's call to a life of missionary service should not demand or expect that it will be different in their ministries today. God's Word will surely triumph today as then through his church messengers (Isa 55:11), but they should not expect things necessarily to go more smoothly and evenly for them than they did for Paul. Paul himself, they should recall, had taught the South Galatians earlier that 'we must through many tribulations enter the Kingdom of God' (Acts 14:22), and that he would later counsel Timothy that 'everyone who wants to live a godly life in Christ Jesus will be persecuted' (2 Tim 3:12).

CHAPTER NINE

PAUL'S THIRD MISSIONARY JOURNEY, HIS FIFTH POST-CONVERSION (VERY EVENTFUL) TRIP TO JERUSALEM, HIS CORINTHIAN CORRESPONDENCE, AND HIS LETTER TO THE ROMANS

> Ay, for this Paul, a scorn and a reviling,
>   Weak as you know him and the wretch you see, –
> Even in these eyes shall ye behold Him rising,
>   Strength in infirmities and Christ in me.
>   – From 'Saint Paul,' Frederic W. H. Myers

Paul's Third Missionary Journey (from summer, A.D. 52, to early summer, A.D. 57) (Acts 18:23-21:16)

Just as the Bible student, when he thinks of Paul's first missionary journey, should think immediately of *South Galatia*; just as he, when he thinks of Paul's second missionary journey, should think immediately of *Corinth*; so also, when he thinks of Paul's third missionary journey, he should think immediately of *Ephesus* where Paul spent the better part of three years (20:31)[1] evangelizing so effectively that 'all who dwelt in Asia heard the word of the Lord Jesus, both Jews and Greeks' (19:10) – a notation, though quite brief, which suggests that it was during this period that the churches in Colossae,[2] Hierapolis, Smyrna, Pergamos, Thyatira, Sardis, Philadelphia, and Laodicea were founded.[3] Preceding that period of

---

   1. Bruce calculates this three-year period from the fall of A.D. 52 to the summer of A.D. 55 in his *Commentary on the Book of the Acts* (Revised edition; Grand Rapids: Eerdmans, 1988), 366, fn. 23.

   2. Colossae was situated one hundred miles east of Ephesus in Phrygia on the Lycus River. In Paul's day it was a 'small town' (Strabo, *Geography*, 12.8.13).

   3. None of these churches was necessarily established by Paul personally and immediately. More than likely they were established by his converts 'for him' (Col 1:7), which is obviously the case with the churches at Colossae, Hierapolis, and Laodicea in the Lycus valley which were founded through the evangelistic efforts of Epaphras (see Col 1:7; 4:12-13), a native of Colossae and one of Paul's colaborers who may have become a Christian during a visit to

ministry in Ephesus Paul had revisited the churches he had founded on his first missionary journey; following his time of ministry in Ephesus he revisited the Macedonian and Achaian churches he had founded on his second missionary journey.

To Paul's third missionary journey our interest now turns. The reader should be forewarned at the outset, as we begin our overview of this period of Paul's ministry, that the biblical material relating to the Ephesian period of Paul's ministry confronts the student of Scripture with some of the most baffling historical, textual, and interpretative problems in the New Testament. In the course of our overview I will present these problems and what I think are their best solutions as clearly and with as much brevity as I can. Once again I will underline for quick location the first occurrence of all significant place names, and again I will provide the Greek terms Luke employs to describe Paul's gospel proclamation.

Luke gives us no information regarding either Paul's activities in Antioch after his return from his second journey or how long he stayed there. He simply declares: 'After spending some time in Antioch, Paul set out from there [for the last time (though he did not know it), probably accompanied only by Timothy (see 19:22), Silas apparently having left his company earlier at Jerusalem where prior to the second journey he had been a church leader] and traveled from place to place [he refers here doubtless to Derbe, Lystra, Iconium, and Pisidian Antioch, among others] throughout the region of [South] Galatia and Phrygia, strengthening all the disciples' (18:23). It was probably at this time that he instructed the South Galatia churches to gather a contribution together for the aid of the poor in Jerusalem (see 1 Cor 16:1-2).

I. Luke's Depiction in Acts of Paul's Ministry at Ephesus

Luke's account of Paul's third journey quickly brings Paul to Ephesus in the province of Asia where Paul almost certainly lived and worked again with Aquila and Priscilla whom he had left at Ephesus some months previously (18:19).

Ephesus. Paul wrote a letter to the Colossians during his first Roman imprisonment. John's Revelation was written to the last six churches in the list (Rev 2–3).

Excursus on Ephesus

Ephesus, situated on the west coast of Asia Minor at the mouth of the Caÿster River, was the chief city of the Roman province of Asia. Leading up to (and through) the city from the harbor in Paul's day was a magnificent road seventy feet wide and lined with marble columns. The streets of the main part of the city were themselves paved with marble.

The Greek city was founded by Ionian colonists around 1100 B.C. It came under Persian rule during the heyday of the Persian Empire, but in 334 B.C. Alexander gained control of the city (as well as the rest of Asia Minor) on his eastward imperialistic march. After Alexander's death, Lysimachus, his successor, relocated the population away from the Artemis temple and nearer to the harbor. In 133 B.C. Attalus III bequeathed the city to Rome, and because of the ensuing stability the city began to prosper and thrive and became a great commercial center. Estimates place the population of the city in Paul's day at around a quarter of a million people.

Ephesus had a theater which could seat around twenty-four thousand people (see Acts 19:30-41), a number of baths and gymnasiums, and a stadium. The town hall (known as the *prytaneion*) was used not only for the conducting of the city's political business but also for various religious functions in honor of the goddess Hestia Boulaia (the building's principal deity), Artemis, Demeter and Kore. The commercial agora was located in the center of the city, measured one hundred and ten meters square, and was surrounded on all four sides with stoas for commercial purposes. The state agora, in which the law courts convened, was situated in the southeast sector of the city across from the town hall. The city was also the site of a medical school.

Numerous gods and goddesses were worshiped in Ephesus. Beautiful temples were erected for Sarapis and Isis of Egypt, and there is evidence that Aphrodite, Apollo, Aesculapius, Athena, Concord, Cybele the mother goddess, Dionysus, Enedra, Hecate, Hephaestus, Heracles, Nemesis, Pan, Pluto, Poseidon, and Zeus were also venerated there. Finally, it sponsored two important festivals each year, the first in the early spring and the second in May, to honor the patroness deity of the city, Artemis Ephesia. The festival in May, called the *Artemision*, sponsored the Pan-Ionian games, attended by virtually everyone in Ionia, and public spirit ran so high then that men counted it a great honor to have the task of planning the arrangements and bearing the expenses. These men were given the title *Asiarchs* ('Chiefs of Asia') **and are referred to in Acts 19:31.**

In addition to these 'claims to fame', doubtless the city's greatest such claim was that it was the site of the great temple of Diana (who was actually the Greek goddess Artemis), which building was regarded by the ancients as one of the seven wonders of the ancient world until its destruction by the Goths in A.D. 260. Thereafter its site gradually sank thirty feet beneath the surface of a swamp, making its discovery in the nineteenth century so difficult that it took six years to locate it. Surpassing in magnificence and fame all the other buildings in Ephesus, no religious building in the world every knew a greater concentration of admiration, enthusiasm, and superstition. Four times larger than the Parthenon atop the Athenian Acropolis and made entirely of marble, it was four hundred and twenty-five feet long and two hundred and twenty feet wide. Its one hundred and twenty-seven columns—each cut from Parian marble and each the gift of a king, with thirty-six of them enriched with ornament and color—were sixty feet high. Horizontal entablatures rested atop the columns which were done in Ionic style, with the enclosed temple area itself—like most of the temples of the ancient world and unlike our church buildings— unroofed for the most part and open to the sky. Its tall folding doors were made of cypress wood, and the one enclosed area that was not open to the sky was roofed over with cedar. In its role as the treasury where a large portion of the wealth of Western Asia was stored in an inner shrine behind the image of Diana it has been compared to the Bank of England in the modern world. Little wonder that the city saw itself as the esteemed '*neokoros* of the great Artemis and her image which fell from heaven' (Acts 19:35).[4] Ephesian pride in the sanctuary was so great that when Alexander the Great offered to give the city of Ephesus the entirety of the spoils of his eastern campaign if it would only allow him to inscribe his name on the building, the city declined him this 'honor', saying that none but the name of Ephesus itself might appear on the temple.

But if the temple proper was magnificent, the image enshrined in the *cella* within the temple enclosure behind velvet curtains was at the other extreme in appearance, being primitive and crude. The female figure, a squat, black, ugly, even hideous thing made of cyprus or cedar wood or of stone, was endowed with twenty-four breast-like protuberances on her chest, signifying her fertility, and she held a trident in one hand and a club in the other. Her dress was covered with mystic devices. There was no beauty here, only repulsive ugliness. Yet because it was thought that this image had fallen from the sky, it was one of the most sacred images in all the ancient world and the object of the greatest imaginable devotion and admiration. A hierarchy of eunuch priests called *Megabyzi* under a high priest called an *essen* (ἐσσήν, 'king bee') and thousands of virgin priestesses called *melissae* (μέλισσα, 'bee'), with the aid of multitudes of slaves (the original *neokoroi* who swept the temple precincts), maintained order and conducted the worship ceremonies at the Temple.

An extensive and very lucrative trade grew up in Ephesus from the manufacture and sale of little models of the goddess and her shrine, made of wood, gold, or silver (Acts 19:23-41), which would be carried in the city's spring processions, on journeys, and on military campaigns. Accordingly, with the wide circulation of these works of art as cult objects around the Mediterranean Basin, it could be said with no exaggeration that her worship was recognized 'throughout the whole province of Asia and the [inhabited] world [οἰκουμένη]' (Acts 19:27).

But in spite of the temple's presence – indeed, it could be argued, precisely because of the temple's presence – Ephesus was a very wicked city. The Greeks used to say that every single person in Ephesus deserved to be choked to death one by one. Legend has it that the famous Greek philosopher, Heraclitus, known as the weeping philosopher, when he was asked why he wept and never smiled, replied: 'What else can I do when I look at Ephesus?' One of the main reasons for the wickedness of the city has to be traced to the fact that the temple of Diana possessed the right of asylum, that is to say, if a person who committed a crime could reach the temple precincts, the law could not touch him. The legend behind this right of asylum maintained that Mithridates, king of Pontus (120-63 B.C.), stood atop the temple and declared that the right of asylum should extend all around it as far as he could shoot an arrow. And his arrow carried two hundred and twenty yards! So all around the temple the scum of Asia Minor gathered until the place that was supposed to be sacred became the center of a cesspool of iniquity.

It should be noted in passing that according to Irenaeus and Eusebius, Ephesus became the adopted home of the apostle John and thus, according to one tradition, the last home also of Mary, Jesus' mother, whom Jesus had placed in John's care. A long line of Eastern bishops made the city their bishop's seat, and the Third Ecumenical Council convened there in A.D. 431 and condemned Nestorian Christology by reconfirming the worship of Mary as θεοτόκος, 'God-bearer'.[5]

---

4. The Greek νεωκόρος originally denoted a humble 'temple sweeper', which term in time came to be a term of honor denoting a city as a 'temple guardian'.

5. For Bruce's description of Ephesus, see *Paul, Apostle of the Heart Set Free* (Grand Rapids: Eerdmans, 1996 reprint), 287-88; for W. J. Conybeare and J. S. Howson's description, see *The Life and Epistles of St. Paul* (Grand Rapids: Eerdmans, 1971 reprint), 419-28.

Luke presents Paul's ministry in Ephesus 'schematically, as a series of...conflicts'.[6] The first such conflict was with *inadequate knowledge of the gospel* (19:1-7). Even as Paul was making his way to Ephesus, a Jew named Apollos[7] from Alexandria had already arrived in Ephesus, and though he was 'a learned man, with a thorough knowledge of the Scriptures, who had been instructed in the way of the Lord, and spoke with great fervor and taught about Jesus accurately' (18:24-25), he nonetheless knew 'only the baptism of John', that is, strange as it may seem, he had no awareness of the Acts 2 Pentecost event which attended the church of Jerusalem.

Priscilla and Aquila,[8] hearing him speaking boldly in the synagogue in Ephesus and detecting a gap in his knowledge, invited him to their home and 'explained the way of God more adequately' (18:26). Desiring to go to Achaia, he was sent on his way with a letter of recommendation (from them?) and eventually came to Corinth (19:1). He proved to be 'a great help to those who by grace had believed' (18:27), for he '*vigorously refuted* [εὐτόνως διακατηλέγχετο] the Jews in public debate, *proving* [ἐπιδεικνὺς] from the Scriptures that Jesus was the Christ' (18:28). So effective did Apollos minister in Corinth that eventually an 'Apollos party' formed in the church (1 Cor 1:12; 3:4). Doubtless, this was a great embarrassment to Apollos, for he left Corinth and returned to Ephesus where equally apparently he and Paul got along famously.[9]

Now the twelve men to whom Paul ministered when he first arrived in Ephesus were most likely men whom Apollos had instructed during his period of inadequate knowledge of the Way. It is not entirely clear from Luke's report precisely what the full situation was with them, but Paul, detecting the same lack in them that Priscilla and Aquila had earlier detected in Apollos, asked them 'if they had

---

6. Martin Franzmann, *The Word of the Lord Grows* (St. Louis: Concordia, 1961), 76.

7. For Bruce's discussion of Apollos and his 'school', see *Paul*, 255-58.

8. God had providentially arranged for Priscilla and Aquila, Jews originally from Rome, to be in Corinth when Paul arrived there on his second journey to assist him in his work (Acts 18:2-3), to be in Ephesus during his third journey to assist him there (18:19), and then very likely to be back in Rome to assist him during his first Roman imprisonment (Rom 16:3). It is possible, however, that they had already departed from Rome before Paul arrived there, for from 2 Timothy 4:19 we learn that they had returned to Ephesus at some point after Paul wrote his letter to the Roman church.

9. For indicators of the character of their relationship see 1 Corinthians 16:12 where Apollos is plainly with Paul at Ephesus, and also where Paul refers to him as 'our brother Apollos' and declares that he had urged him to return to Corinth with their messengers presumably to continue his ministry there, and Titus 3:13 where Paul urges Titus to assist Apollos on his way and to see that he has everything he needs.

received the Holy Spirit when they believed'. They replied that they had not heard 'whether the Holy Spirit is [εἰ πνεῦμα ἅγιον ἔστιν]' (19:2), which expression does not mean that they had no knowledge at all of the Holy Spirit's existence but that they had not heard that the Holy Spirit had been given.[10] They, like Apollos before them, knew of John's baptism and had become disciples of John, but their faith had stopped short of faith in Christ. So Paul told them that John himself had urged his followers to look beyond him to the one coming after him, even to Jesus (Acts 19:4). Hearing this, they put their faith in Christ, were baptized 'in the name of the Lord Jesus' and received the Holy Spirit, spoke in unstudied foreign languages and prophesied. These twelve men, then, became the beginning nucleus of the Christian church in Ephesus. Epenetus may have been one of these twelve men (Rom 16:5).

What does all this mean? Why does Luke report in such detail Apollos' prior defective ministry at Ephesus and Paul's bringing these twelve disciples of John to faith in Christ? It would seem that the last remaining 'holdouts' to the Christian 'Way' who could have claimed any legitimacy for their cause whatever (inasmuch as John the Baptist had been a true prophet) were disciples of John the Baptist who knew of John's teaching that the Messiah was coming and that he would baptize with the Holy Spirit, but who either had not heard that the Messiah had actually come (which is doubtful) and/or that the Age of the Spirit had begun (which is more likely) or who had refused, out of inappropriate loyalty to their own 'master', to believe that Jesus was the Messiah and accordingly were still following the Forerunner of the Lord (which, in my opinion, is a distinct possibility). It was important apparently to Luke to report in this concrete way that this last remaining group which might feel that it still had grounds to remain isolated from the church should 'cease and desist' and should join the ranks of the church. Hence occurred the event of the Ephesian 'Pentecost', and Luke's report of it was for the benefit and instruction of those remaining disciples of John the Baptist who still maintained their loyalty to him.

The second conflict at Ephesus was with the synagogue (19:8-10). Paul, as was his custom, went to the synagogue where he had 'dialogued' only some few months earlier at the end of his second

---

10. For a parallel construction see the Greek of John 7:39, οὔπω γὰρ ἦν πνεῦμα, which does not mean that the Holy Spirit 'was not yet [in existence]' but rather that the Holy Spirit had not yet been given.

missionary journey (see 18:19-21) and *'spoke boldly* [ἐπαρρησιάζετο] there for three months [longer than at any previous city], *arguing persuasively* [διαλεγόμενος καὶ πείθων] about the kingdom of God' (19:8). When the Jews could tolerate his witness no longer and began to malign the 'Way', Paul left the synagogue, taking the disciples with him, and set up headquarters in the lecture hall of Tyrannus,[11] daily *'discussing with* [διαλεγόμενος]' (19:9) and *'preaching* [κηρύσσει] Jesus to' (19:13) all who would listen to him. This he did for two years, 'so that all the Jews and Greeks who lived in the province of Asia heard the word of the Lord' (19:10). Luke later records Paul's own description of his ministry in Ephesus when to the Ephesian elders he declared:

> You know how I lived the whole time I was with you, from the first day I came into the the province of Asia. I served the Lord with great humility and with tears, although I was severely tested by the plots of the Jews. You know that I have not hesitated to *preach* [ἀναγγεῖλαι] anything that would be helpful to you but have *taught* [διδάξαι] you publicly and from house to house. I *have declared* [διαμαρτυρόμενος] to both Jews and Greeks that they must turn to God in repentance and have faith in our Lord Jesus. (Acts 20:18-21)

Then he summarized his ministry this way: 'I went about among you *preaching* [κηρύσσων] the kingdom' (20:25), and he concluded his descriptive summary two verses later by saying, 'I have not hesitated *to proclaim* [ἀναγγεῖλαι] to you the whole will of God' (20:27).

The third conflict was with the prevailing practice of pagan magic (19:11-20). When God through Paul did 'wonders not of an ordinary kind' [δυνάμεις οὐ τὰς τυχούσας] by healing the sick and exorcizing demons through the application of his 'sweat bands and work aprons' (not gentlemen's pocket handkerchiefs!), seven Jewish exorcists tried to drive out spirits by using the name of Jesus. But their demoniac patient, saying 'Jesus I know, and I know about Paul, but who are you?,' leaped upon them and beat them so badly that they ran from the building naked and bleeding. As a result, the Jews and Greeks living in Ephesus held 'the name of the Lord Jesus in high honor' and many abandoned their sorcery. Luke pauses at this point in his narrative to make his fifth progress report: 'So the word of the Lord spread widely and grew in power' (19:20).

---

11. Bruce playfully wonders whether his parents or his students (or his tenants, RLR) gave him this name which means 'Tyrant' (*Paul*, 290).

After this, Paul determined to go to Rome (Acts 19:21) as his next major destination. Bruce notes: 'From this point on...we follow Paul to Rome until, at the end of Acts, he reaches the imperial city by an unforeseen route and is busily preaching the gospel there when the readers take their leave of him.'[12] But he determined upon a circuitous route which would take him first through Macedonia and Achaia, the regions he had visited on his second journey, and then to Jerusalem in order 'to hand over to the leaders of the Jerusalem church the proceeds of the fund...for the relief of the poor'.[13] So he dispatched Timothy and Erastus to Macedonia to prepare for his coming while he remained for an unspecified amount of time still in Ephesus (19:21-22).[14] Aquila and Priscilla probably left Ephesus around this same time also and returned to Rome where they had lived originally (Acts 18:2), because in his letter to the Roman church written several months later Paul extended greetings to them there from Corinth (16:3).

During this stay Paul was confronted by the fourth conflict – *conflict with the commercialized state religion of Ephesus* (19:23-41). The guild of silversmiths, who made their living making replicas of the goddess Diana and her shrine for the many tourists visiting the city, aroused a city mob against Paul which embroiled the whole city of Ephesus in an uproar and threatened Paul's life. But the riot was finally quelled by the town clerk, and Paul bid farewell to the Ephesian Christians and left for Macedonia.

II. Paul's Additional Details About His Activities in Ephesus Drawn From His Corinthian Correspondence

The above description of Paul's ministry in Ephesus is based upon Luke's depiction of it in Acts. But more can and must be said about his activities in Ephesus on the basis of his letters to the Corinthian church.

First, it is quite clear from Paul's Corinthian correspondence that sometime after Paul had left Corinth on his second missionary journey he had written them a letter, now lost,[15] in which he had counseled

---

12. Bruce, *Acts*, 371.
13. Bruce, *Acts*, 372.
14. If one adds the three months of Acts 19:8, the two years of Acts 19:10, and the unspecified 'time' of Acts 19:22, he will have an amount of time approximating Paul's 'three years' in Acts 20:31.
15. Some scholars postulate that fragments of this 'lost letter' are found in 1 Corinthians 6:12-20 and 2 Corinthians 6:14, but this is sheer conjecture since there is no external supporting evidence that this is so.

his children in the faith 'not to associate with sexually immoral people' (see 1 Cor 5:9). Bruce designates this lost letter 'Corinthians A'.

Secondly, some time later, after Paul had begun his ministry at Ephesus, 'Chloe's people'—members of the church at Corinth—came to Ephesus and visited Paul, and informed him that major factions existed among the Corinthian believers (1 Cor 1:11)[16] and that the church had other problems as well. Paul had also received a letter from the church at Corinth, brought to him by Stephanas, Fortunatus, and Achaicus (1 Cor 7:1; 16:17), in which the church assured him that they were observing all the 'traditions' he had delivered to them (1 Cor 11:2). The Corinthian church then proceeded to ask him a series of questions. A third source of information about the Corinthian church was Apollos who in the meantime had also returned to Ephesus from Corinth (1 Cor 16:12); he doubtless told Paul what he knew about the problems existing in the church. So Paul wrote our canonical '1 Corinthians'—Bruce designates this letter 'Corinthians B'—during the latter part of his ministry in Ephesus, probably in the early spring of A.D. 55,[17] to address these problems and to answer the church's questions, sending it by Timothy (1 Cor 4:17; 16:10). Before he concluded his letter (16:5-6), he promised to visit them *after* he had visited Macedonia (here is his *first* statement of his plans relative to visiting Corinth).[18]

Thirdly, sometime after that, a segment of 'Pauline travel history' occurred which Luke's Acts passes over in silence. Through some means—perhaps Timothy had returned from Corinth and informed him—Paul learned that certain leaders in the church there, apparently one in particular, in spite of his letter (1 Corinthians) to them calling for an end to the divisions among them, continued to stir up so much opposition against him and with so much success[19] that Paul felt it necessary to interrupt his ministry at Ephesus to make a quick trip across the Aegean Sea to Corinth to address the problem personally

---

16. Though factions existed within the Corinthian church, it should be noted, as Johannes Munck reminds us in his *Paulus und die Heilsgeschichte*, Aarsskrift for Aarhus Universitet XXVI, I, Teologisk Serie 6 (Aarhus-Copenhagen, 1954), 162-66, that, as Paul wrote 1 Corinthians, the church was still outwardly united: the factions were not so radical in their separateness as to prevent the church from meeting in one place and Paul could address all the members of the church with his comprehensive 'you' and expect them all to read or hear what he had to say.

17. This time datum is apparent from the fact that Paul indicates that he had already made plans to leave Asia and to make an extended visit to Macedonia and Asia.

18. See my later treatment of the occasion and outline of 1 Corinthians, pp. 192-200.

19. See my later discussion, p. 201.

(see 2 Cor 12:14; 13:1-2). This is the 'painful visit' to which he alludes in 2 Corinthians 2:1—painful both to the Corinthians (2:2; 13:2) and to him—'for the opposition to him, under the leadership of the men who claimed to be Christ's, proved strong. They must have been bold, intellectually vigorous, and capable...able to face Paul and to keep a sizable part of the congregation with them.'[20] It would appear that he made little headway in stemming the opposition against him. Certain comments in 2 Corinthians imply that he was grossly insulted and his counsel rejected. So he left Corinth – humiliated and heavy-hearted – and returned to Ephesus, but not before he promised them that he would return to Corinth when his work in Ephesus was done, indeed, that he would visit and 'benefit them twice' (2 Cor 1:15), *both before and after* his trip to Macedonia. The reader should note that *this was a change from the travel plans which he had originally announced in 1 Corinthians 16:5-6.*

Fourthly, once back in Ephesus, Paul decided that to return directly to Corinth after his ministry in Ephesus was concluded would only subject both the Corinthian church and him to another futile and 'painful' visit as long as the Christians there refused to give him any reason to assume that their attitude toward him had improved. So *changing his plans for a second time*, he wrote, 'with many tears', a letter instead, generally referred to as his 'stern letter' (2 Cor 2:4, 9), now lost[21]—Bruce designates this letter 'Corinthians C'—in which he severely reprimanded the church for their foolishness in following these false apostles and for their sinful attitude toward him. He doubtless informed them in it that he would not be coming directly to them as he had promised earlier on his 'painful visit' but was reverting back to his original plan to go to Macedonia first and then to visit them. He dispatched this letter to Corinth by Titus with instructions to his assistant to meet him in Troas. Paul shortly thereafter bade farewell to the church at Ephesus and departed *directly* for Macedonia via Troas.

Fifthly, on his way to Macedonia (and this is a *second* piece of 'Pauline travel history' which Luke's Acts passes over in silence), Paul stopped in Troas, as he had arranged with Titus, 'with a view to [preaching] the gospel of Christ [εἰς τὸ εὐαγγέλιον τοῦ Χριστοῦ]' (2 Cor 2:12), and probably spent the late summer of A.D. 55 there.

---

20. Franzmann, *The Word of the Lord Grows*, 96.
21. Some scholars conjecture that this letter is 2 Corinthians 10–13.

But when Titus did not appear, oppressed with worry over how the Corinthian church had responded to his 'stern letter', Paul left Troas for Macedonia and there met Titus returning from Corinth with the good news that his letter had done its intended work of conviction in the hearts of the majority of the believers who had opposed him (2 Cor 2:3-11) and that the church had disciplined the leader who had opposed and offended him (2 Cor 2:5-8; 7:5-16). But Titus also informed Paul that the same old hostility still continued toward him on the part of a few influential 'hold outs' and that these leaders were using the very fact that he had changed his announced travel plans twice as evidence that he was wishy-washy and fearful of confronting them face to face. So in late A.D. 55 or early 56, somewhere in Macedonia, he paused long enough to write our canonical (and conciliatory) '2 Corinthians, chapters one through nine' to the reconciled majority (Bruce terms this portion of 2 Corinthians 'Corinthians D'). But before Paul dispatched this portion of our canonical 2 Corinthians, he subsequently added our canonical (and vindicatory) '2 Corinthians, chapters ten through thirteen' directed toward the still rebelling minority (Bruce designates this portion of 2 Corinthians 'Corinthians E'), which longer or shorter lapse of time between writing sessions and the shift in the intended recipients are sufficient to explain the undisputed change in tone between chapters 1–9 and chapters 10–13.[22]

When Paul had completed this portion of his travels throughout Macedonia, including quite likely his visit to Illyricum,[23] during which travels he encouraged the Christian churches (Acts 20:1-3; note that here we are once again relying on the history recorded in Acts), he finally arrived in Greece (Achaia) where he stayed three months (from late A.D. 56 to early A.D. 57), probably for the most part in Corinth with his friend Gaius. No doubt at this time he disciplined the church leaders who had continued in their opposition to him, as he had warned in 2 Corinthians 13:2. It was probably during this three-month stay

---

22. See Donald A. Carson, *From Triumphalism to Maturity: An Exposition of 2 Corinthians 10–13* (Grand Rapids: Baker, 1984), 14-16, for his discussion of a lapse of time between the writing of 1–9 and the writing of 10–13 during which time Paul received additional news about the situation in the Corinthian church.

23. In Romans 15:19 Paul gives us his own evaluation of the extent of his missionary labors to that point in his life: 'From Jerusalem all the way around to Illyricum, I have *fully proclaimed* [πεπληρωκέναι] the gospel of Christ.' Bruce writes: 'How long Paul spent in Macedonia we are not told; it seems to have been a rather prolonged period. It was probably at this time that he went as far as Illyricum (Rom. 15:19)' (*Acts*, 381). He calculates that this

that he also wrote his magnificent theological treatise to the Roman Christians ('The Gospel According to Paul') from Corinth,[24] preparing them for the visit which he was planning to make as soon as he had discharged his responsibilities in Jerusalem (see Rom 1:9-15; 15:22-29). He sent this 'doctrinal treasure' to Rome by 'our sister Phoebe' (Rom 16:1).

As he was about to board a ship bound directly from Corinth (really, from Cenchrea, Corinth's eastern port city) to Syria, accompanied by several representative delegates from his Gentile churches who were overseeing their respective church's gift to the Jerusalem poor, Paul learned of a Jewish plot against him. So instead of sailing directly to Syria, he went alone back through Macedonia to Philippi, while Sopater from Berea, Aristarchus and Secundus from Thessalonica, Gaius from Derbe, Timothy, and Tychicus and Trophimus from Asia (Acts 20:3b-4) sailed on ahead of him to Troas (20:5).[25] At Philippi Paul met Luke once again (see the 'we' in 20:6), where the two of them remained until the Feast of Unleavened Bread had passed, and then they sailed to Troas where they were united again with the Gentile church delegates.

Paul and his companions spent a week at Troas where Paul preached on the Lord's Day, probably to the very church he had founded almost two years previously. He preached so long into the night that a young man named Eutychus fell asleep, tumbled from the third storey window, and apparently died from the fall. Paul went down, quickly restored him to life and continued to preach until daylight (20:7-12). Leaving Troas alone the next day on foot, Paul met the others who had gone ahead by ship at Assos. From there Paul and his companions together sailed, in turn, to Mitylene, Kios, Samos, and Miletus (20:13-16).

Because he had decided not to revisit Ephesus because of his desire to reach Jerusalem by Pentecost (20:16), at Miletus Paul sent for the elders of the church at Ephesus, and delivered his famous farewell address to them (20:17-38). The minister of the gospel should

---

period may well have covered about a year and a half, from the summer of A.D. 55 to the late part of A.D. 56.

24. See pp. 205-7 below for the argument.

25. This rather large group of Christian men fulfilled a two-fold purpose: to assist Paul in guarding what was doubtless the sizeable Gentile offering which he was carrying to Jerusalem and to vouch that the amount Paul turned over to the church was in fact the amount he had collected.

thoroughly familiarize himself with this great address and expound its teaching to his people.

Leaving Miletus, Paul and his companions sailed to Cos, then on to the island of Rhodes and from there to Patara on the southern coast of Asia. From there they booked passage on a ship going to Syria. So sailing past Cyprus on their port side, they landed at Tyre (21:1-3).

They stayed a week at Tyre, where the disciples warned Paul not to go to Jerusalem (21:4). But 'compelled by the Spirit' (20:22), Paul boarded ship again and sailed to Ptolemais, stayed with the Christians there for one day, then sailed on to Caesarea (21:8a).

At Caesarea Paul and company stayed with Philip the evangelist and his four prophetess daughters for 'a number of days' (21:8b-9).[26] There Agabus the prophet, coming down from Judea, informed Paul that in Jerusalem he would be bound by the Jews and handed over to the Gentiles, but Paul could not be dissuaded from going. So Paul and his companions, accompanied by some disciples from Caesarea, continued on up to Jerusalem—his fifth and last visit to Jerusalem recorded in the book of Acts—arriving in the early summer of A.D. 57. They stayed at the home of Mnason, a Cypriot and an early disciple, perhaps even a disciple from the beginning (21:10-16).

Here Paul's third missionary journey comes to an end, for if Paul had any intentions – as he undoubtedly did – to continue on to Antioch after his visit in Jerusalem those intentions were never to be realized, for in Jerusalem (as we shall see in greater detail in Chapter Ten) he was seized by the Jewish and Roman authorities and was eventually sent to Rome. Merrill C. Tenney summarizes the accomplishments of Paul's ministry to this point in this way:

> With this visit to Jerusalem closed the most active part of Paul's missionary activity. In a little less than a decade he had won the freedom of the Gentile believers from the yoke of legalism. He had built a strong chain of churches from Antioch of Syria and Tarsus of Cilicia straight across southern Asia Minor to Ephesus and Troas, and thence through Macedonia and Achaia to Illyricum. He had chosen and trained companions like Luke, Timothy, Silas, Aristarchus, Titus, and others who were well qualified to maintain the work with him or without him.

---

26. It was probably at this time that Luke obtained firsthand information from Philip about the ministry which he had conducted around twenty-five years before, which Luke later reported in Acts 8.

He had commenced an epistolary literature which already was regarded as a standard for faith and practice. In his preaching he had laid the groundwork for future Christian theology and apologetics, and by his plans he pursued a statesmanlike campaign of missionary evangelism. His plans for a trip to Rome and Spain showed that he wanted to match the imperial commonwealth with an imperial faith. Notwithstanding his bitter and active enemies, he had established the Gentile church upon a firm foundation and had already formulated the essence of Christian theology as the Spirit of God revealed it to him.[27]

Before we leave Paul at this point in Jerusalem we should point out that Luke's second 'we' passage ends at Acts 21:18. With Luke also now in Jerusalem, he may have decided to seize the opportunity to stay a while and interview Mary, the mother of Jesus (if she was still alive and lived there) about our Lord's birth, early life, and public ministry. He may also have interviewed many early disciples, such as Mnason himself, who could have furnished him with firsthand information about both Jesus' public ministry, death, resurrection, and ascension, information which would eventually find its way into the Third Gospel, and Peter's early ministry in Jerusalem which he reports in Acts 1–12.

Paul's Corinthian and Roman Correspondence

First Corinthians

A. The Letter's Place of Origin

That Paul wrote 1 Corinthians from Ephesus during his missionary labors there is established by several facts:

1. According to 1 Corinthians 16:5, as he writes, Paul is anticipating a trip to Macedonia and possibly a stay with the Corinthian believers during the approaching winter months; this fits Luke's statement in Acts 19:21.

2. According to 16:10, Paul suggests that Timothy may be on his way to visit the church in Corinth; this fits Luke's statement in Acts 19:22a.

---

27. Merrill C. Tenney, *New Testament Survey* (Grand Rapids: Eerdmans, 1961), 308.

3. In 16:8 Paul seems to suggest from his statement that he will stay on at Ephesus until Pentecost, that he is writing from that city; this fits Luke's statement in Acts 19:22b admirably.

4. Finally, the fact that Paul says that, along with the churches in the province of Asia in general, Aquila and Priscilla in particular sent their greetings to the church at Corinth (16:19) indicates that Paul's writing locale is Ephesus, for we know that Ephesus was the site where these two helpers had settled earlier (Acts 18:19).

B. The Date of the Letter
Spring, A.D. 55.

C. The Occasion of the Letter

Even as Paul was writing 1 Corinthians four identifiable factions were vying for the ascendancy in the church: a faction committed to Paul who had founded the church; a faction following Peter, the leaders of which faction had probably come to Corinth from some eastern churches which Peter had evangelized, maybe even from the church in Jerusalem and perhaps even with letters of recommendation from the Jerusalem leadership;[28] a faction enamored with Apollos'

---

28. Many commentators from early times to the present have believed that Paul's opponents at Corinth were Jewish 'outsiders' (2 Cor. 11:22) who had come to Corinth professing to be 'ministers of Christ' (11:23a) whom Paul sarcastically describes as 'super apostles (οἱ ὑπερπλίαν ἀπόστολοι, 2 Cor. 11:5; 12:11) but who were actually 'false apostles' (ψευδαπόστολοι, 11:13) because of what they taught. It is just possible that after Paul had departed from Corinth for Jerusalem Peter, carrying out his apostolic responsibilities to evangelize the circumcision (Gal 2:7-9), had come in person to Corinth and, without making circumcision a saving aspect of his κήρυγμα, had nonetheless preached and taught there a Judaic form of the Christian life. If so, without intending to do so, Peter would have contributed to the rise of the 'Cephas faction'. These Corinthian believers may have even viewed him as the 'more original' apostle, as the 'rock' upon which the church should be built (see 1 Cor 3:10-11). Paul's comments in 2 Corinthians 10:12-18 intimate that he believed that it was he who was in his designated and agreed-upon territory of labor (see again Gal 2:7-9) when he founded the church in Corinth and that the original apostles should avoid working 'in another man's territory' because of the potential for factions which such overlapping of apostolic labors could create. C. K. Barrett in his 'Cephas and Corinth' in *Essays on Paul* (Philadelphia: Westminster, 1982), 28-39, actually argues that Cephas had indeed visited Corinth, that the 'man' who was building on Paul's foundation in 1 Corinthians 3:10-17 was either Peter or someone acting in his name, and that a Jewish-Christian 'Cephas party', without Peter's endorsement, existed in Corinth in opposition to Paul.

If Barrett's scenario is close to what in fact occurred, then Paul's reference to 'the super-apostles' (οἱ ὑπερπλίαν ἀπόστολοι) in 2 Corinthians 11:5 and 12:11 may not be referring to the 'false apostles' of 2 Corinthians 11:13 (since Paul would not have claimed to be on a par with men whom he regarded as servants of Satan) but his ironic employment of their own overblown description of the original apostles which members of either the Peter faction or

eloquence and knowledge of the Scriptures; and a faction claiming to be 'Christ's people'.[29]

It would appear that Paul had no particular theological quarrel with the views of the Paul faction, the Peter faction, or the Apollos faction beyond the divisiveness which the party spirit within the factions bred.[30] It was the fourth faction—the Christ party—that apparently caused Paul the greatest concern. Its leaders are not named, but whoever they were, Paul clearly distinguishes them and their followers from the factions professing loyalty to himself, to Peter, and to Apollos. At least these three men were preaching the same Christ and the same gospel (see 1 Cor 15:11), but not so the leaders of this fourth group, even though it is they who claimed to be 'Christ's people'. (Sadly, this is often the case.) From Paul's description of

---

the Christ faction had coined (in comparison with whom, he states, he was not 'in the least inferior') in order to destroy completely or to reduce to second-class status his apostolic standing. By using such a term he was not putting down the Jerusalem leadership but only his opponents' inflated or exaggerated view of them. Bruce too suggests that the term 'super-apostles' may be either '[the Jerusalem messengers'] own designation of the Jerusalem apostles or Paul's ironical summing-up of their portrayal of those leaders' (*Paul*, 277). All this would mean that, though these 'Jerusalem men' may have been themselves 'apostles' in the sense that the Jerusalem leaders had sent them, in opposing Paul these messengers had clearly exceeded their commission as the Judaizers had done earlier at Antioch (see Acts 15:24) and had become 'false apostles [ψευδαπόστολοι], deceitful workmen [ἐργάται δόλιοι], masquerading as apostles of Christ [μετασχηματιζόμενοι εἰς ἀποστόλους Χριστοῦ]', and 'servants of Satan [οἱ διάκονοι τοῦ Σατανᾶς]' (2 Cor 11:13, 15), terms which Paul would have never used against the original Jerusalem apostles themselves. If Paul's term 'super-apostles' is in fact an oblique reference to the Jerusalem apostles, such a description is paralleled by his earlier reference to them as 'those who seemed to be leaders', 'those who seemed to be important – whatever they were makes no difference to me', and 'those reputed to be pillars' (Gal 2:2, 6, 9).

These words constitute as acrid an attack as Paul ever made against any of his adversaries (unless Gal 5:12 and Phil 3:2 exceed it). What would these 'Jerusalem men' as 'false apostles' have been proclaiming? While it is true, as has been often noted, that Paul says nothing in his Corinthian correspondence, including any mention of circumcision, that would imply that these men were Judaizers, it is still possible, if these men – holding such high regard for the original apostles and so little regard for Paul – were from Jerusalem, that they were in fact Judaizers and had launched their attack against Paul's law-free gospel by attacking first his apostolic authority, keeping back their conviction about the necessity of circumcision and obedience to the law of Moses until they had both destroyed Paul's authority and any and all allegiance to him. Only after they had accomplished that task would they have then revealed their Judaizing teachings. Of course this last is only a conjecture.

29. See C. K. Barrett, 'Christianity at Corinth' and 'Paul's Opponents in 2 Corinthians' in *Essays on Paul*, 1-27, for discussions of the condition of the Corinthian church in the mid-fifties of the first century. In the latter essay Barrett argues that Paul's opponents at Corinth were in the main Judaizers from Jerusalem.

30. Since Paul opposed even the Paul faction in Corinth as disruptive to church unity, we may be certain that he surely would have opposed the later dogmatic assertion of the Roman Catholic Church concerning the 'primacy' of Peter over Paul, Apollos and the universal church.

these men, we know that they were 'Hebrews' and 'Israelites', 'Abraham's descendents' and in some sense even 'servants of Christ'[31] (2 Cor 11:22-23) who had come into the Corinthian church from outside with letters of recommendation from some unnamed churches, possibly even from Jerusalem (2 Cor 3:1). They were apparently haughty and domineering (2 Cor 11:19-20), but were not willing to do pioneering work or to suffer for Christ as Paul was (2 Cor 11:23f.). Moreover, and most tragic of all, they preached 'a different Jesus', a 'different Spirit', and a 'different gospel' from what he, Peter, and Apollos had been preaching (2 Cor 11:4-5). In sum, they were actually 'servants of Christ' in name only and not true brothers at all but instead were really 'false apostles [ψευδαπόστολοι],[32] deceitful workmen, masquerading as apostles of Christ', and 'servants of Satan' (2 Cor 11:13, 15; see 'false brothers' in 11:26).

What was their 'Jesus' and their 'Christ' like? It seems rather clear from Paul's remarks that their 'Jesus' had given them a special 'knowledge' (γνῶσις, 1 Cor 3:18-20; 8:1-3, 10, 11; 13:9) which had 'liberated' them from all previous revelatory authority—both Old Testament authority and apostolic authority. For these 'Christ people', all previous standards were now null and void, all former moral obligations now inoperative, and all the 'old taboos' now meaningless: 'Everything is permissible for me' (1 Cor 6:12; 10:23) was their proud boast. Bruce appears to be on target when he identifies their doctrine as 'incipient Gnosticism'.[33]

How did their new 'knowledge' manifest itself in the life of the church? Apparently one Christian was using his newly learned liberty to live with his father's wife (1 Cor 5). Others were using their newly gained freedom to associate with prostitutes, arguing that the law demanding sexual purity was on the same level as the divinely rescinded law concerning clean and unclean food. 'Food is for the stomach and the stomach is for food; so sex is for the body and the body is for sex,' seemed to be their argument (1 Cor 6:12-20). For these 'Christ people', marriage was an impediment to the religious life: the unmarried could refrain from marriage, even though it

---

31. Paul can call these opponents 'servants of Christ' just as Luke can call the Judaizing 'false brothers' of Galatians 2:4 'believers [τῶν...πεπιστευκότες]' though they apparently still belonged to the party of the Pharisees (Acts 15:1, 5).

32. See C. K. Barrett, 'ΨΕΥΔΑΠΟΣΤΟΛΟΙ (2 Cor. 11:13)' in *Essays on Paul*, 87-107, particularly 103, for his argument that the 'false apostles' were Judaizers.

33. Bruce, *Paul*, 261.

resulted in what had been viewed before as illicit sexual behavior, and the married could free themselves of their spouses, especially pagan spouses, in order to be 'free for the Lord' (1 Cor 7). Most disheartening to Paul was the fact that the church, for the most part, not only tolerated this gross display of immorality (Paul's description of the church's attitude here, as rendered in the King James Version, is classic: 'Ye suffer fools gladly,' 2 Cor 11:19), but also their spirit of toleration toward evil and hostility toward him exhibited at the same time a real arrogance toward any who would insist it be any way otherwise (1 Cor 5:2).[34]

There were other manifestations of this new-found freedom in the Corinthian church. Church members were no longer seeking to arbitrate their differences themselves but were going to the pagan courts. And in the worship life of the church, the women were asserting their freedom by appearing at worship without a 'head covering',[35] the badge of their 'womanness' and their position of submission which God had assigned them both in creation and in the community of the redeemed (1 Cor 11:2-16). These women were also assuming a teaching authority which neither Jesus nor the apostles had given them (1 Cor 14:33-36). This faction's antinomian attitude had also turned the Lord's Supper into a scene of feasting and carousing. Those infected by this 'new knowledge' received from 'their Christ' were exercising their spiritual gifts to elevate *themselves*, not to edify the church (1 Cor 12–14). Finally, these 'people of knowledge', who disregarded and degraded the body, had no use for the resurrection of the body as such (1 Cor 15), for they were (Paul sarcastically declares) 'already reigning' (1 Cor 4:8). And their single slogan seemed always to be, as a sufficient answer to anyone with an opposing point of view, 'You follow Paul [or Cephas, or Apollos],

---

34. Should the reader be thinking to himself, 'How could anyone ever think that such teaching was acceptable in the Christian life? Surely, the above representation is highly overdrawn,' he should recall that Corinthian society as such was morally loose and licentious. Even in Greek thinking, to live licentiously or to practice whoredom was to 'Corinthianize' (κορινθιάζεσθαι, 'to play the Corinthian' in the sense of practising fornication). The believers at Corinth could well have been drawn back into former associations and habits.

As modern exhibitions of the same spirit that fostered these Corinthian 'Christ people', I would submit that one needs to look no further than some contemporary preachers and television evangelists who, while claiming to be 'Christ's people' because of some purported 'special knowledge' they have of him, think they have special license to 'do their own thing' religiously and morally.

35. Does Paul mean by περιβόλαιον long hair or a veil – which? I personally think he refers to the woman's long hair.

but we belong to Christ!' Such arrogant self-exaltation necessarily involved a break with Paul's apostolic authority.[36]

Paul's letter (our canonical '1 Corinthians') addressed this situation, and offered, for all its variety, a single unified answer to the various sins in the church. That single answer was the cross of Christ, viewed in the light of his resurrection. 1 Corinthians is a brilliant demonstration of how apostolic authority made itself felt.[37]

D. The Content of the Letter[38]

I. PAUL'S RESPONSE TO THE REPORT OF CHLOE'S HOUSEHOLD, CHAPS 1-6.

A. *Factions in the Church, 1-4.* Paul's response: The cross of Christ, the absolute opposite of that wisdom of the world which fosters human greatness and accordingly which makes men boast of men and creates cliques clustered around men, 'pronounces judgment on all human greatness and on all human pretenses to wisdom, cuts off all boasting of man, and marks as monstrous and unnatural any clustering about great men in schools and factions that give loyalty to men.'[39]

In 4:8-13 Paul provides us with one of his personal vignettes describing his mission ministry. It is worthy of citation for the realistic depiction it provides of the apostle's ministry among Christians who rashly believed that they did not need apostolic doctrine and were already reigning without him:

> Already you have all you want! Already you have become rich! You have become kings – and that without us! How I wish that you really had become kings so that we might be kings with you! For it seems to me that God has put us apostles on display at the end of the procession, like men condemned to die in the arena. We have been made a spectacle to the whole universe, to angels as well as to men. We are fools for Christ, but you are so wise in Christ! We are weak, but you are strong!

---

36. See Bruce, *Paul*, 259-62, for his discussion of this faction.

37. For additional insights into the situation in Corinth which provoked Paul to write 1 Corinthians, see C. K. Barrett, *The First Epistle to the Corinthians* (Harper's New Testament Commentaries; New York: Harper & Row, 1968); F. F. Bruce, *1 and 2 Corinthians* (New Century Bible; Grand Rapids: Eerdmans, 1971); Gordon D. Fee, *The First Epistle to the Corinthians* (The New International Commentary on the New Testament; Grand Rapids: Eerdmans, 1987).

38. I have adapted the following outline with minor alterations from Martin Franzmann, *The Word of the Lord Grows*, 89-92.

39. Franzmann, *The Word of the Lord Grows*, 87.

You are honored, and we are dishonored! To this very hour we go hungry and thirsty, we are in rags, we are brutally treated, we are homeless. We work hard with our own hands. When we are cursed, we bless; when we are persecuted, we endure it; when we are slandered, we answer kindly. Up to this moment we have become the scum of the earth, the refuse of the world.

B. *Moral Problems, 5-6.*
1. Incest, 5:1-13. Paul's response: 'The church, liberated from bondage [to sin] by the Passover sacrifice of the Lamb of God, cannot tolerate the leaven of impurity, but must keep the new feast of unleavened bread in sincerity and truth.'[40]

2. Litigation, 6:1-11. Paul's response: The church which has been washed, sanctified, and justified in the name of the Lord Jesus and by the Spirit of God (6:11) 'must take seriously its freedom [from the world], by disciplining itself and thus retaining its character as the pure people of God. The church cannot commit its task of dealing with brothers at variance with one another to the powers of this judged and dying world.'[41]

3. Immorality, 6:12-20. Paul's response: 'If the church dare not tolerate impurity [see comment on incest, above], much less may the members of the church, whose bodies are members of Christ, practice impurity with harlots. "You are not your own; you were bought with a price. So glorify God in your body." '[42]

II. REPLY TO THE CHURCH'S WRITTEN QUESTIONS, CHAPS 7-16 (see 7:1, 25; 8:1; 11:2; 12:1; 15:1; 16:1).

A. *Celibacy and Marriage*, 7. Paul's response: Because the cross of Christ has bought them (7:23), members of his church 'dare not attempt a self-chosen course of celibate devotion to their Lord which will plunge them into sin, 7:2-5, 9, 36, 38', nor may they 'in blind enthusiasm, set out blithely and boldly to free themselves of the marriage bond which the word of their redeeming Lord has hallowed, 7:10'.[43]

---

40. Franzmann, *The Word of the Lord Grows*, 89.
41. Franzmann, *The Word of the Lord Grows*, 89.
42. Franzmann, *The Word of the Lord Grows*, 89.
43. Franzmann, *The Word of the Lord Grows*, 90.

B. *Eating of Meat Offered to Idols*, 8:1-11:1.

1. Paul's first response: 'The cross has put men under the sole Lordship of Christ, 8:6; they are free men – no idol has a claim upon them or power over them. But a man's weaker brother, the brother for whom Christ died, 8:11, has a claim upon him which calls for a self-sacrificing love, such as marked the ministry of Paul himself, chap 9.'[44]

2. Paul's second response: Since demonic powers stand behind idolatry, the church must be aware that she is no more automatically secure than ancient Israel was (10:1-13), that there is an essential incompatibility between idol feasts and the Lord's Supper (10:14-22), and that there are limitations on the believer's freedom: whatever he does, he is to do all to the glory of God, which means in turn that he will endeavor not to cause anyone to stumble, whether Jews, Greeks, or the church of God (10:23-11:1).

C. *Disorders in the Worship Life of the Church*, 11:2–14:40.
1. Women in the church, 11:2-16 (see also 14:33-36). Paul's response: 'God's act of redemption in the cross has not abrogated the order which He established in creation, 11:7-10; rather, the cross has affirmed and hallowed that primal order, 11:3.'[45]

2. The Lord's Supper, 11:17-34. Paul's response: 'The Lord's Supper is the Lord's; it is the gift of His cross effectually present in the church to enrich and to unify the church. To make of it man's supper...is to invite the judgment of God upon the church.'[46]

3. Use of the spiritual gifts, 12-14. Paul's response: 'The Holy Spirit puts men under the Lordship of the Crucified.'[47] Accordingly, the Spirit's gifts are to be used for the nurturing of the body of Christ, 12; believers should seek the Spirit's gift of love, his most valuable gift, which sets them free to minister to others, 13; and finally, the Spirit's gifts are not to be used to foster individualism in worship and to create confusion in worship which cannot edify, 14.

---

44. Franzmann, *The Word of the Lord Grows*, 90.
45. Franzmann, *The Word of the Lord Grows*, 90.
46. Franzmann, *The Word of the Lord Grows*, 91.
47. Franzmann, *The Word of the Lord Grows*, 91.

D. *The Denial of the Resurrection of the Dead*, 15.

1. Paul's first response, underscoring the significance of Christ's resurrection, 15:1-34: 'So firmly established is the link between...the resurrection of the Christ and the resurrection of those who are His, that...the resurrection of the Christ stands or falls with the resurrection of the dead. And if the resurrection of the Christ falls, all is lost; the cross is "emptied of its power", for no mere martyr's death can assure the forgiveness of sins; what the apostles proclaim [becomes] a lie; what the church believes is nothing; and the church's hope is nothing. Christian suffering and martyrdom have lost all point and purpose.'[48]

2. Paul's second response, treating the manner of the resurrection of the dead, 15:35-58: '[Those, boasting in human wisdom, who accordingly foolishly ask, How are the dead raised?] reveal their ignorance of the creative possibilities of God...who can...certainly create a spiritual body for His new creature, the man in Christ, as He created a physical body for man in Adam. The Corinthians [were casting to the wind] the victory over death which God has given them through the Lord Jesus Christ, that triumphant certainty of life which makes men..."steadfast, immovable, always abounding in the work of the Lord." '[49]

E. *Practical and Personal Matters*, 16.
   1. Collection for the poor saints in Jerusalem, 16:1-4.
   2. Paul's travel plans, 16:5-9.
   3. Timothy's coming visit, Apollos' plans, 16:10-12.
   4. Commendation and greetings, 16:15-20.
   5. Autograph conclusion: Paul pronounces an anathema on all who have no love for the Lord Jesus, and prays for his coming, 16:21-24.

E. The Dominant Theme of the Letter
The significance of the cross for the believer's sanctification.

---

48. Franzmann, *The Word of the Lord Grows*, 91-2.
49. Franzmann, *The Word of the Lord Grows*, 92.

F. Conclusion
This letter 'drives home the centrality of the cross in a peculiarly vital way; it proclaims the cross not as a tenet to be held or as an article to be believed, but as a power which makes possible, and demands, a life lived to God in all its parts and all its functions, a human life judged by the righteousness of God and a new life created and endowed by His grace. [It] draws the line between the church and the world, between human wisdom and the Gospel.... [It reminds] the church that she must dare to be "other" if she is to be the apostolic church of God, that she must dare to cut athwart the axioms and standards of this world if she is to do her divine work in the world'; it makes manifestly clear that 'the Gospel is not ideas and principles about which man may theorize and speculate; the Gospel is news of that culminating act of God which has transformed the relationship between God and man and will transfigure all creation.'[50]

* * * * *

Second Corinthians

A. The Letter's Place of Origin
That Paul wrote 2 Corinthians somewhere in Macedonia (we cannot be more definite) on his third missionary journey is established by the following internal data:
1. His ministry in the province of Asia is behind him (1:8).
2. His journey to and his stay in Troas is behind him (2:12-13).
3. His journey to Macedonia is behind him (2:13; 7:5).
4. As he writes, Macedonia seems to be as far as he has proceeded on his journey (8:1).
5. As he writes, he is boasting (καυχῶμαι; note the Greek present tense) to the Macedonians about the Corinthian church's readiness to contribute to the fund for the Jerusalem poor (9:2); and
6. He intends to visit the Corinthian church shortly (12:14; 13:1).

B. The Date of the Letter
Late A.D. 55 or early 56.

---

50. Franzmann, *The Word of the Lord Grows*, 93, 94.

C. The Occasion of the Letter

As we have already noted, Paul had learned from Titus, 'somewhere in Macedonia', that his 'stern letter' had produced its desired fruit in the hearts of most of the church members at Corinth. They had repented of their moral carelessness and unkind attitude toward him personally and had punished the chief offender. But he had also learned, perhaps also from Titus, that neither his 2 Corinthians (which actually is our 1 Corinthians), nor his 'painful visit', nor his 'stern letter' (his 3 Corinthians, now lost) had silenced all of the opposition against him. A few 'different Christ' teachers were still maliciously misinterpreting his every word and action. For example, they said that he was plainly wishy-washy, incapable of making up his mind concerning even such a small thing as travel plans (2 Cor 1:17). They said that he was a coward, for he wrote letters that sounded like thunder but in actual presence he was about as authoritative as a mouse (10:1, 10). They said that he did not maintain his dignity when he refused to take support from the churches but demeaned himself by working (11:7). They claimed that since he was not one of the original apostles, he was not qualified to teach, and that he had no credentials, *as did they*, that he could show (3:1). They attacked his personal character by saying that he 'lived by the standards of the world' (10:2), that he was boastful (10:8), deceitful (12:16), and that he embezzled the funds for the poor that were being entrusted to him (8:20-23).[51] This last insinuation, in fact, had brought to a standstill the collection among them for the poor at Jerusalem, a concern which was very near and dear to the apostle's heart. So Paul wrote his 4 Corinthians (our 2 Corinthians), determined to answer once and for all the charges against his apostolic authority, not only for the benefit of the Corinthian church but also for the benefit of 'all the saints throughout Achaia' (1:1), and to get the collection for the poor back on track.[52]

---

51. See Merrill C. Tenney, *New Testament Survey*, 301.
52. For additional insights into the situation in Corinth which provoked Paul to write 2 Corinthians, see C. K. Barrett, *The Second Epistle to the Corinthians* (Harper's New Testament Commentaries; New York: Harper & Row, 1973); Philip E. Hughes, *Paul's Second Epistle to the Corinthians* (The New International Commentary on the New Testament; Grand Rapids: Eerdmans, 1962); Simon J. Kistemaker, *New Testament Commentary: Exposition of the Second Epistle to the Corinthians* (Grand Rapids: Baker, 1997); Ralph P. Martin, *2 Corinthians* (Word Biblical Commentary 40; Waco: Word, 1986); Alfred Plummer, *A Critical and Exegetical Commentary on the Second Epistle of St. Paul to the Corinthians* (International Critical Commentary; Edinburgh: T. & T. Clark, 1925).

D. The Content of the Letter[53]

I. RETROSPECT: PAUL'S APOSTOLIC AUTHORITY WITH SPECIAL REFERENCE TO HIS MINISTRY IN CORINTH (a survey of the ministry which God had assigned to him), 1-7.

A. His ministry was one carried out and sustained by pure grace, 1:1-11.

B. His ministry was accordingly one full of agonizing stress, 1:12-2:17.

C. His letter of commendation was the church itself, 3:1-3.

D. His ministry was not of the letter but of the Spirit, was not of transient and fading glory but of surpassing and enduring glory, was not a matter of proclaiming himself but Christ, 3:4-4:6. Because of the significance of this last point for pastors, Paul's statement should be cited for the instruction it gives to them: 'For we do not preach ourselves, but Jesus Christ as Lord, and ourselves as your servants for Jesus' sake' (4:5).

E. Because the glory of this apostolic ministry is solely God's, not man's, his suffering and frailty were

1. Not to be perceived as detracting from its glory but as enhancements of its glory, 4:7-12. Because of the importance of Paul's comments here for the pastoral ministry, I will again cite this passage in full:

> But we have this treasure in jars of clay to show that this all-surpassing power is from God and not from us. We are hard pressed on every side, but not crushed; perplexed, but not in despair; persecuted, but not abandoned; struck down, but not destroyed. We always carry around in our body the death of Jesus, so that the life of Jesus may also be revealed in our body. For we who are alive are always being given over to death for Jesus' sake, so that his life may be revealed in our mortal body. So then, death is at work in us, but life is at work in you.

2. Not discouraging to Paul who labored with the confidence that God will raise him from the dead and will give him a new and eternal bodily life, 4:13-5:5, and with the strong and courageous desire to please Christ, before whose judgment seat all must stand, 5:6-10.

---

53. I have adapted the following outline with minor variations from Franzmann's *The Word of the Lord Grows*, 98-106.

Paul's confidence here is worthy of citation for the encouagement it is to pastors and pastoral candidates:

4:16-18: 'Therefore we do not lose heart. Though outwardly we are wasting away, yet inwardly we are being renewed day by day. For our light and momentary troubles are achieving for us an eternal glory that far outweighs them all. So we fix our eyes not on what is seen, but on what is unseen. For what is seen is temporary, but what is unseen is eternal.'

F. His ministry of reconciliation, conducted with high independence with regard to the praise or blame of men, was motivated by Christ's love for him, 5:11-15, and executed as an ambassadorial investiture, 5:16-21.

G. Ambassadorial plea to the church not to accept the grace of God in vain, 6:1-2, then a summary of the glory of his apostolic ministry, 6:3-10, then a call for a radical break with all that opposes God, 6:11-7:1, and finally an appeal to accept his apostolic authority, 7:2-4.

H. Account of Titus' report of their genuine repentance and of their mutual joy and encouragement because of it, 7:5-16.

II. THE PRESENT: THE COLLECTION FOR THE POOR SAINTS IN JERUSALEM, 8–9.

A. The example of the Macedonian churches, 8:1-7.

B. Reminder of the grace of Christ and of what they have already done, 8:8-15.

C. Titus and two other brothers to come and aid in the collection task lest he and they be ashamed when he comes with representatives from the Macedonian churches and finds their collection still uncollected, 8:16-9:5.

D. Reminder that a generous gift will reap a great harvest, 9:6-15.

III. PROSPECT: PERSONAL VINDICATION IN THE FACE OF CHARGES BROUGHT AGAINST HIM BY HIS OPPONENTS; PAUL'S COMING VISIT TO CORINTH, 10–13.

A. Defense against the charges of his opponents, 10:1-18.
   1. The charges, with Paul's comments, 10:1-12.
   2. Paul's authority as an apostle, 10:13-18.

B. Paul's reluctant 'foolish boasting', 11:1-12:21.
   1. Of knowledge, 11:1-6.
   2. Of the fact that he worked without pay, 11:7-15.
   3. Of all that his opponents boast of – and more, even of his weaknesses, 11:16-33.
   4. Of visions and revelations, 12:1-10.
   5. Of the signs of the apostle, 12:11-18.
   6. To spare him and them the grief of another 'painful' visit, 12:19-21.

C. Paul's impending visit, 13:1-10.

D. Concluding remarks (admonition, greetings, benediction), 13:11-14.

E. The Dominant Themes of the Letter
   1. Paul's defense of his apostolic commission and authority.
   2. The collection for the poor of Jerusalem.

F. Conclusion.
Concluding his analysis of 2 Corinthians, Franzmann writes:

> The battle which Paul wages in this letter reveals him down to the very roots and bases of his apostolic existence. We learn from this revelation that battle must be, and why it must be, within the church of the God and the Prince of Peace, that lines must be drawn and where they must be drawn.... We learn that battle is necessary in the life of the church and can be salutary for the life of the church.
>
> We learn also that the necessity of the battle need not harden the battler; the church that fights for truth need not lose the love it had at first...the first seven chapters of this letter are a witness to the fact that the love which 'does not rejoice at wrong but rejoices in the right' (1 Cor. 13:6) is the only genuine love....
>
> As an apostle, Paul is a 'man in Christ', a man whose whole existence and activity is shaped and formed by the single fact of Him in whom God reconciled the world to Himself. There is hardly a more vivid documentation of this lived Christianity than the Second Letter to the Corinthians....
>
> As apostle, Paul is a man in whom Christ speaks; he is the earthen vessel that conveys the treasure of the Christ. Paul is here fighting for

his apostolate; that means, he is fighting for the Christ, for the apostolate is nothing less than the power and the presence of Christ among men. Men will find the treasure in this earthen vessel or they will not find it at all; they will behold the light of the knowledge of the glory of God in the face of Christ in the apostolate or they will not behold it at all. There is nothing like this letter to bind the church to the apostolic word of the New Testament. The Reformation's embattled emphasis on *Sola Scriptura* finds powerful justification in this embattled epistle.

As we conclude, perhaps we should note that the New Testament does not say anything regarding this last letter's effect on the church. But there is reason to believe that, while it doubtless moved the elect of God to new levels of piety, it did not correct everyone. Accordingly, we may be sure that when Paul arrived in Corinth, he doubtless did as he had warned the church he would do: he did not spare those who continued to resist him, but with powerful signs of the apostle excommunicated these leaders and their people from the church (13:2). But even with these excommunications, apparently the leaven of old ideas and habits remained. For in his letter to the Corinthians in A.D. 95, Clement of Rome, while he commended the church for the 'ripeness and soundness of their knowledge' and the 'purity and blameless lives of their women', rebuked them for their 'envy, strive, and party spirit', accusing them of being devoted to 'the cause of their party leaders rather than to the cause of God', and declaring that their divisions were 'rending asunder the body of Christ' and 'casting a stumbling block in the way of many' (see 1 Clement, chps 1, 2, 3, 14, 46, 54). This is the last word we have from the Apostolic age about the Corinthian church, and so the curtain of information falls in Corinth upon a scene of unchristian strife.[54]

* * * * *

Romans

A. The Letter's Place of Origin

There is little doubt that Paul wrote Romans from Corinth probably during his three month visit to Achaia on his third missionary journey (Acts 20:2-3). This is established by the following considerations:

1. From Romans 15:25-26 we are told that the provinces of Macedonia and Achaia had finished collecting funds for the poor of Jerusalem and that Paul was about to go to Jerusalem; this fits what we know of Paul's movements in Acts 20:2-3.

---

54. Franzmann, *The Word of the Lord Grows*, 108-10.

2. In Romans 16:1 Paul commends to the Roman church Phoebe, a servant in the church of Cenchrea, the eastern harbor town of Corinth.

3. In Romans 16:21 a 'Sosipater' sends his greetings to the Roman Christians; from Acts 20:4 we learn that a 'Sopater', a shorter form of the same name, is with Paul in Achaia (which term almost certainly intends to include Corinth).

4. At the time of writing he is the guest of Gaius (16:23a), who was a member of the church at Corinth (1 Cor 1:14).

5. Then in 16:23b, Paul extends greetings to the Roman Christians from Erastus, the city's director of public works. This Erastus is associated with Corinth in 2 Timothy 4:20. Moreover, in April 1929 archaeologists based at the American School at Athens uncovered in Old Corinth a marble paving-block dating to the first century that bears a Latin inscription which reads: 'Erastus, in consideration of his aedileship [directorship of public works], laid this pavement at his own expense.'

B. The Date of the Letter
Early spring (since, according to Acts 20:6, Paul's departure from Philippi only days after he had left Corinth, where he had written Romans, occurred immediately after the days of unleavened bread in late March or early April), A.D. 57.

C. The Occasion of the Letter
Paul wrote to the church at Rome apparently for two reasons: first, to prepare it to assume the responsibility of providing the base for his mission operations – what the church at Syrian Antioch had been for him in the East – as he turned his attention to the farthest reaches of the West (15:24). In order that he and the church which he hoped to make his missionary base had a full and complete common understanding of the gospel, he wrote this extensive exposition of his theology, carefully rehearsing his understanding of the gospel and its implicates. Apparently Paul felt it necessary to disabuse the church of any false misinterpretations of his preaching and teaching which it may have heard (see 3:8). He wrote, second, to resolve

tensions he had learned (perhaps from Aquila and Priscilla) existed in the church there which quite probably had to do with the 'weak' Jewish Christians' continuing adherence to the law and the 'strong' Gentile Christians' scorn of anything Jewish (see 14:1–15:13).[55]

---

55. John W. Drane, 'Why Did Paul Write Romans?,' *Pauline Studies: Essays presented to Professor F. F. Bruce on his 70th Birthday*, edited by Donald A. Hagner and Murray J. Harris (Grand Rapids: Eerdmans, 1980), 208-27, has argued that the *Sitz im Leben* behind Paul's writing Romans was not in the church at Rome at all but was, first,—and here he follows G. Bornkamm, *Paul* (New York: Harper & Row, 1971), 88-96,—in his need to work out exactly what he would say in Jerusalem in support of his law-free gospel to those who disagreed with him there, and second, but *more important*, in the events of Paul's *past* ministry at Corinth. According to Drane, having just 'come through one of the most difficult periods of his whole ministry' in dealing with the complex problems in the church at Corinth, Paul had to face the fact that 'his emphasis on the freedom of the Christian man from the law had led to precisely that kind of antinomianism that the Judaizers had always said it would' (223). Drane suggests that doubt had seized Paul as to whether 'he had any kind of workable theology at all'. He concludes that 'what we have in this, his *magnum opus*, is therefore a conscious effort to *convince himself* as well as his opponents that it is possible to articulate a theology which is at once antilegalistic without also being intrinsically antinomian' (223-24; second emphasis supplied).

I find Drane's argument wanting for several reasons.

(1) It is highly doubtful whether Paul was wondering at this late stage in his missionary ministry whether his theology was workable or not.

(2) He had already written by his letter to the Galatians what J. B. Lightfoot delightfully describes in his *St. Paul's Epistle to the Galatians* (Reprint; Grand Rapids: Zondervan, 1957) as 'the rough model to the finished statue' of Romans (49), in which he argued essentially the same point of theology: his gospel was a law-free gospel that does not give licence to sin.

(3) As an apostle of Christ he would have been convinced that what he had taught the Corinthian church was the truth of God; never doubting that, he fought valiantly for the truth of his gospel in spite of the Corinthians' moral laxity.

Accordingly, he did not write Romans to convince himself that his law-free gospel was not antinomian. Therefore, as I have already stated, hoping that the church at Rome would become his sending base of operations for his westward push into Spain, he wrote Romans to prepare the church at Rome to receive him and his law-free gospel and to feel a kinship with it and with him.

For more discussions on the situation in Rome that led Paul to write Romans, see C. K. Barrett, *The Epistle to the Romans* (Harper's New Testament Commentaries; New York: Harper & Row, 1957); C. E. B. Cranfield, *Romans* (2 vols; International Critical Commentary; Edinburgh: T. & T. Clark, 1975, 1979); James D. G. Dunn, 'Romans, Letter to the' in *Dictionary of Paul and His Letters*, edited by Gerald F. Hawthorne, Ralph P. Martin, Daniel G. Reid (Downers Grove, Ill.: InterVarsity, 1993), 838-50; Douglas Moo, *The Epistle to the Romans* (The New International Commentary on the New Testament; Grand Rapids: Eerdmans, 1996); John Murray, *The Epistle to the Romans* (The New International Commentary on the New Testament; Grand Rapids: Eerdmans, 1968); William Sanday and Arthur C. Headlam, *A Critical and Exegetical Commentary on the Epistle to the Romans* (International Critical Commentary; Edinburgh: T. & T. Clark, 1902); Thomas R. Schreiner, *Romans* (Baker Exegetical Commentary on the New Testament; Grand Rapids: Baker, 1998).

D. The Content of the Letter

I. INTRODUCTION AND THEME, 1:1-17.
   A. Salutation, 1:1-7.
   B. Thanksgiving, 1:8-15.
   C. Theme: Justification by faith, 1:16-17.

II. THE NEED OF THE GOSPEL OF JUSTIFICATION BY FAITH ALONE, 1:18-3:20.
   A. Condemnation of the unrighteous Gentile, 1:18-32.
   B. Condemnation of the self-righteous man, Gentile or Jew, 2:1-16.
   C. Condemnation of the 'religious' Jew, 2:17-3:8.
   D. Summary conclusion, 3:9-20.

III. THE STATEMENT OF THE DOCTRINE OF JUSTIFICATION BY FAITH ALONE (the heart of the letter), 3:21-31.
   A. Gospel explained, 3:21-23.
   B. God vindicated, 3:24-26.
   C. Boasting excluded, 3:27-28.
   D. Ethnic distinctions abolished, 3:29-30.
   E. Law established, 3:31.

IV. OLD TESTAMENT CONFIRMATION OF JUSTIFICATION BY FAITH ALONE: ABRAHAM AND DAVID, 4:1-25.
   A. Justification of Abraham and David by faith, 4:1-8.
   B. This justification before and apart from circumcision, 4:9-12.
   C. This justification before and apart from the law, 4:13-17.
   D. Abraham's faith the instrumentality through which he was justified, 4:18-25.

V. THE CERTAIN AND FINAL END OF THOSE JUSTIFIED BY FAITH ALONE: GLORIFICATION, 5:1–11:36 (Note: 6:1–7:25 is an inserted extended excursus; see below), 8:1-39 (Note: 9:1–11:36 is a second inserted extended excursus; see below). It should be noted that, according to this outline, this is the longest section of the letter, extending from the beginning of chapter 5 to the end of chapter 11 (seven chapters in all).

A. Their absolute security (or, because it is God's doing), 5:1-11.
B. Their union with Christ (or, because of the way he does it), 5:12-21.

FIRST EXCURSUS: Reply to first objection: 'The teaching of justification by faith alone promotes sin,' 6:1-7:25.
1. Union with Christ produces holiness, 6:1-7:6.
2. The Law is powerless to produce holiness, 7:7-25.[56]

C. The Christian, having been delivered from the law's condemnation, has been justified and is thus assured that there is 'no condemnation' in his future. Thus his final glorification is guaranteed, 8:1-4.

D. The Holy Spirit, dwelling within the Christian and doing his mighty work of producing a new mind within him which is 'set on what the Spirit desires', a mind which is 'controlled not by the sinful nature but by the Spirit', brings 'life and peace'. By the indwelling Spirit who performs these works the Father 'will also give life to your mortal bodies'. Thus the Christian's resurrection to glorification is guaranteed, 8:5-11.

E. The indwelling Spirit of adoption, doing his mighty work within the Christian of 'leading' him to 'put to death the misdeeds of the body' and enabling him to cry to God, '[You are] *Abba*, Father,' testifies to the Christian's spirit that he is a child of God, thereby giving him the assurance and guarantee of his sonship and heirship to God and his joint-heirship with Christ, 8:12-17a.

F. The Christian's present joint-sufferings with Christ, which are 'not worth comparing with the glory that will be revealed in us', assure him that he will 'share in Christ's glory'. Moreover, since the *absolutely certain* future glorification of the entire cosmos, itself also now 'suffering', cannot occur apart from or before the Christian's future glorification as a son, which 'adoption' occurs with the resurrection of his body to imperishability, glory, power, and spirituality, his final glorification is guaranteed, 8:17b-25.

---

56. For my argument that the man in Romans 7:14-25 is the convicted but yet unconverted Saul of Tarsus, see my *A New Systematic Theology of the Christian Faith* (Nashville: Thomas Nelson, 1998), Appendix F, 1127-32.

G. The Spirit's all-wise intercessory prayer work—whose prayers are always 'in accordance with God's will' and thus honored by him 'who searches hearts'—in behalf of the Christian, who prays in ignorance in the midst of this world's problems and difficulties, guarantees the Christian perpetual divine aid and thus his final glorification, 8:26-27.

H. The eternal divine decree, consisting in God's covenantal forelove and predestination of the elect to glorification, as the ultimate ground of the Christian's salvation, guarantees the Christian's final glorification. This is to say, from God's eternal perspective those whom he calls and justifies are also already viewed as 'glorified'. Thus the Christian's future is secure, 8:28-30.

I. Grand summary statement of their final glorification, 8:31-39. The specific labors of the Father, 31-33, and of the Son, 34, and the inseparable love of the Godhead (35, 39), in spite of the seventeen items which are encompassed by the 'all things' of 8:28 (see 8:35, 38-39), guarantees the Christian's final glorification. Thus Romans 8 begins with 'no condemnation' and ends with 'no separation' from God's love for the Christian.

SECOND EXCURSUS: Reply to second objection: 'Since the teaching of justification by faith annuls God's ancient promises to Israel, there can be no certainty of final glorification for Christians either,' 9:1–11:36.
 1. God's sovereign election of grace, 9:1-33.
 2. Israel's misguided zeal for God, 10:1-21.
 3. Israel's glorious future, 11:1-36.

VI. THE ETHICAL OUTWORKING OF JUSTIFICATION BY FAITH ALONE, 12:1–15:13.
 A. Service in the church and other duties, 12:1-21.
 B. Citizen responsibilities, 13:1-7.
 C. Personal responsibilities, including specifically Christian unity, 13:8–15:13.

VII. PAUL'S MISSIONARY AMBITION AND PLANS TO SPREAD THE GOSPEL OF JUSTIFICATION BY FAITH ALONE, 15:14-33.

VIII. SOCIAL GRACES FLOWING FROM JUSTIFICATION BY FAITH ALONE, 16:1-27. These social graces show themselves in Paul's extending greetings to 26 (!) people.

E. The Dominant Theme of the Letter
Justification by faith and its implications for the justified man's (1) final glorification and (2) manner of life in this world.

F. Conclusion

1. The Letter's Effect

No Scripture assertion states in so many words how the church at Rome received Paul's letter. But we have reason to believe that the church there had taken his letter to heart and had determined to stand with him in the furtherance of the gospel. This we infer from Luke's statement that when Paul finally reached Rome over three years later, 'the brothers there had heard that we were coming, and they traveled as far as the Forum of Appius and the Three Taverns to meet us' (Acts 28:15a).[57] When Paul saw these men, he 'thanked God and was encouraged' (28:15b). 'Whatever Rome might hold for Paul, whatever the future might bring – death or work in Rome and beyond Rome – Paul knew that the church of Rome was one with him in the Gospel; and for that he thanked God.'[58] If Aquila and Priscilla were still there (see Rom 16:3), they would certainly have been a comfort to Paul, and would have doubtless been at least partially instrumental in preparing the hearts of the brotherhood to receive Paul. But it is possible that they had departed from Rome before Paul arrived, for from 2 Timothy 4:19 we learn that they returned to Ephesus at some point in time after Paul wrote Romans.

2. The Letter's Value

How can one adequately describe the natural glories of the Grand Canyon or Niagara Falls? To put in words the value of this letter is just as impossible. For myself, I think it is unquestionably the most important theological treatise ever written. It is an understatement to say that Paul's letter to the Romans has played an important role

---

57. The Forum of Appius was at a distance of some forty-three miles, the Three Taverns some thirty-three miles, south of Rome on the Via Appia.
58. Franzmann, *The Word of the Lord Grows*, 115.

within Christendom. Chrysostom had the letter read aloud to him twice a week. Romans 13:13-14 was instrumental in the conversion of Augustine and played a major role in his subsequent theological labors. It was primarily this letter that drew Martin Luther to salvation, spiritual peace, and to the doctrine of justification by faith alone. In the *Preface to his Commentary on the Epistle to the Romans*, Luther writes:

> This epistle is the very heart and center of the New Testament and the purest and clearest Gospel. It well deserves to be memorized word for word by every Christian man; and not only that: A man ought to live with it day by day, for it is the daily bread of souls. One cannot read it too often or too thoroughly or consider it too often or too well; and the more one deals with it, the dearer it becomes and the sweeter it grows upon the tongue...we find in the epistle all that a Christian ought to know, and that in great abundance, namely, what the Law is, what the Gospel is, what sin and punishment are, what grace, faith, righteousness, Christ, God, good works, love, hope, and the cross are, and what our attitude toward all men ought to be, toward saints and sinners, the strong and the weak, friend and foe, and toward ourselves. And all this excellently supported [by Scripture and argument] so that there is nothing left to be desired here. Wherefore it would seem that Paul intended this epistle to give a kind of summary of the whole Christian Gospel, and to open up for us the Old Testament. For there is no doubt that if a man has well learned this epistle by heart, he has the light and the power of the Old Testament for his own. Therefore every Christian should be familiar with this epistle and practice its teachings constantly.

John Calvin wrote: 'When anyone understands this epistle, he has a passage[way] opened to him to the understanding of the whole Scriptures.'

Through hearing Martin Luther's *Preface* to his commentary on Romans read in a Moravian society meeting one evening in Aldersgate Street, London, John Wesley was brought to faith: 'While [Luther] was describing the change which God works in the heart through faith in Christ, I felt my heart strangely warmed. I felt I did trust in Christ, Christ alone for salvation; and an assurance was given me, that he had taken away my sins, even mine, and saved me from the law of sin and death.'

I could call upon almost an endless list of witnesses on the theological continuum between orthodoxy and heterodoxy who would testify to the influence of Paul's letter to the Romans on Christianity and the world. But men's poor powers to laud, and no number of superlatives, can gild this lily of God. What one must finally do to appreciate it and learn to love it is to take up the letter and to read it and in faith assimilate its truths for oneself.

The Results of Paul's First Three Missionary Journeys

Roland Allen helpfully summarizes for us the results of Paul's first three missionary journeys in the following words:

> In little more than ten years St. Paul established the Church in four provinces of the Empire, Galatia, Macedonia, Achaia, and Asia. Before A.D. 47 there were no Churches in these provinces; in A.D. 57 St. Paul could speak as if his work there was done, and could plan extensive tours in the far West without anxiety lest the Churches which he had founded might perish in his absence for want of his guidance and support.[59]

---

59. Roland Allen, *Missionary Methods: St. Paul's or Ours? A Study of the Church in the Four Provinces* (London: World Dominion, 1912), 3.

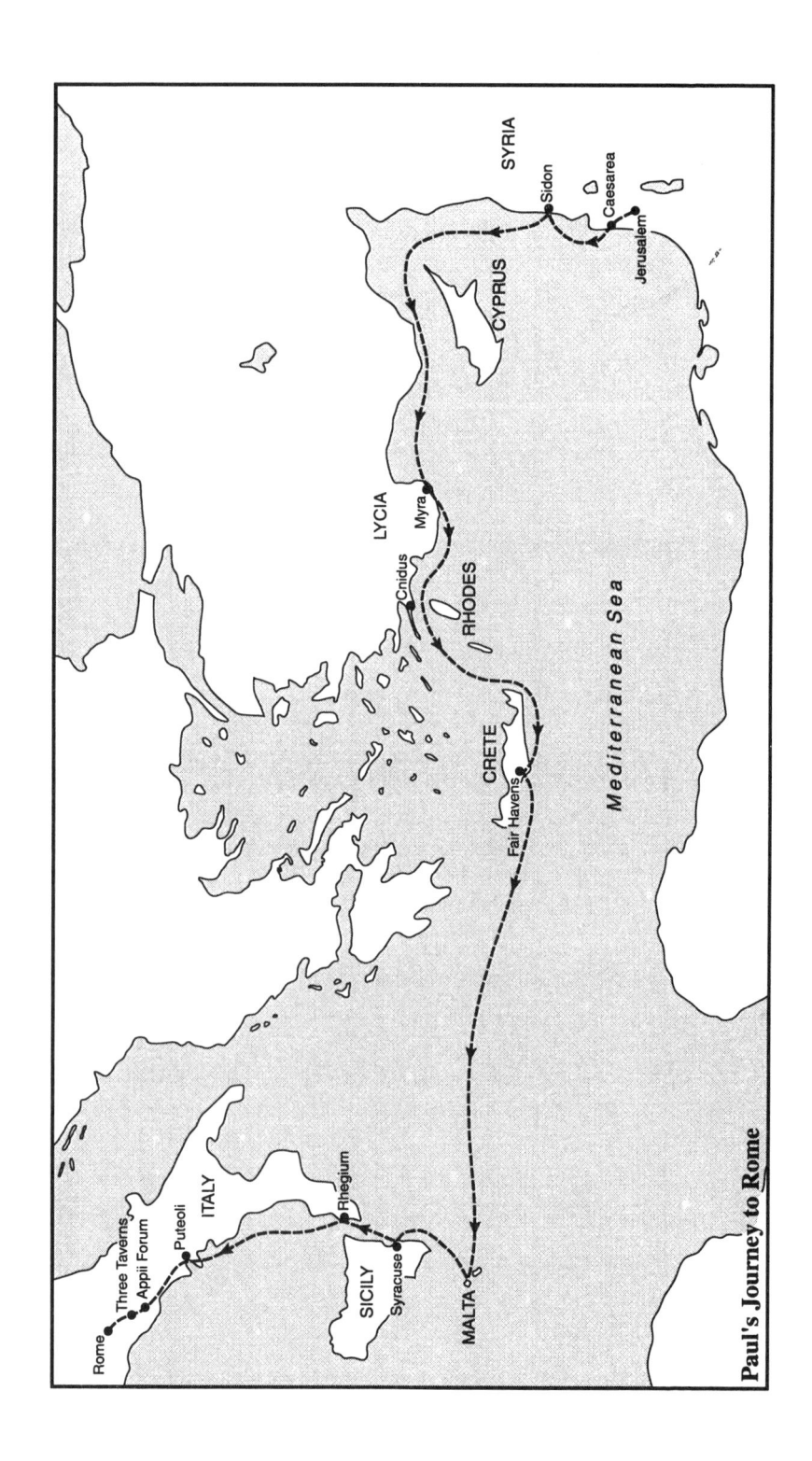

Paul's Journey to Rome

CHAPTER TEN

PAUL'S JOURNEY TO CAESAREA AND TO ROME, HIS FIRST ROMAN IMPRISONMENT, AND HIS PRISON LETTERS FROM ROME

> O comrade bold of toil and pain!
>   Thy trial how severe,
> When severed first by prisoner's chains
>   From thy loved labour-sphere.
>
> Say, did impatience first impel
>   The heaven-sent bond to break?
> Or couldst thou bear its hindrance well
>   Loitering for Jesu's sake?
>   – John Henry Newman

>   But patience, to prevent
> That murmur, soon replies, 'God doth not need
> Either man's work or his own gifts. Who best
> Bear his mild yoke, they serve him best. His state
> Is kingly; thousands at his bidding speed,
> And post o'er land and ocean without rest;
> They also serve who only stand and wait.'
>   – From 'On His Blindness,' John Milton

Paul's Journey to Caesarea and to Rome, A.D. 57-60 (Acts 21:17-28:16)

Just as the reader should immediately think of *South Galatia* when he thinks of Paul's first journey, of *Corinth* when he thinks of his second, and of *Ephesus* when he thinks of his third, so he should think of *Caesarea*, the journey by ship and the shipwreck at *Malta*, and *Rome* when he thinks of Paul's fourth recorded journey. As we follow Paul's footsteps in this chapter, again we will underline the first occurrence of the significant place names and once again provide the Greek words Luke employs to describe Paul's proclamation of the gospel.

We noted in the last chapter that Paul had come to Jerusalem after his third journey to 'bring to his nation alms and offerings' from the Gentile churches (Acts 24:17). Franzmann notes that Paul 'knew how much his unbelieving fellow countrymen hated him and how desperately they wanted him out of the way; he had been in "danger from his own people" more than once before (2 Cor. 11:26; see 11:24).'[1] Evidently Paul was hoping that the gift from the Gentiles to his nation would speak unmistakably to his brethren after the flesh of the universal grace of God and open their eyes to the 'inexpressible gift' of God in Christ.

Excursus on Paul's relationship with the Jerusalem church

Here seems to be an appropriate place to review Paul's relationship with the Jerusalem church as it is reflected in the five visits Paul paid to Jerusalem over his career as an apostle of Christ.

On his *first* visit three years after his conversion (c. A.D. 35 or 36), with Barnabas serving as his sponsoring advocate, he met only Peter and James and spent fifteen days with them (Acts 9:26-30; Gal 1:18-19). In their conversations together Paul no doubt learned from these two men many things about his Lord's earthly life and ministry. But clearly these two men did not give him his gospel or authorize him to preach it, for this he had already been doing for some three years. During this two-week period he also moved about freely in Jerusalem, speaking boldly in Jesus' behalf. But when he spoke to and argued with the Hellenistic Jews, they attempted to kill him. So the Jerusalem brotherhood determined that he should return to Syria/Cilicia. It should be noted that Peter appears to be regarded as the leader of the Jerusalem church at this time, with the support of John, son of Zebedee (Acts 1:13, 15ff.; 2:14ff.; 3:1ff.; 4:8ff., 19ff.; 5:3ff., 29ff.; 10:9ff.).

On his *second* visit (the 'famine-relief visit') fourteen years after his conversion (c. A.D. 46 or 47), accompanied by Barnabas and uncircumcised Titus, Paul with some apprehension 'set before [James, Cephas, and John] the gospel which I preach among the Gentiles', but he 'did this *privately* to those who seemed to be leaders, for fear that I was running, or had run, my race in vain' (Acts 11:27-30, 12:25; Gal 2:1-10).[2] The Jerusalem leadership, not requiring Titus to be

---

1. Martin Franzmann, *The Word of the Lord Grows* (St. Louis: Concordia, 1961), 119.
2. See pp. 102-04 for my discussion of Paul's 'for fear that I was running...my race in vain' remark in Galatians 2:2.

circumcised, approved of his law-free gospel and his apostleship to the Gentiles. It should be noted that by this time James, not Peter, seems to have assumed the leadership role of the Jerusalem church (Gal 2:9; Acts 15:13-22). It should also be noted that Paul strongly suggests his independence at this time from the Jerusalem leadership by referring to them four times as 'the ones who seemed [to be important]' (Gal 2:2), 'the ones who seemed to be something' (Gal 2:6), and 'the ones who seemed to be pillars' (Gal 2:9), even stating in Galatians 2:6: 'Whatever they were makes no difference to me; God shows no partiality,' underscoring that 'the ones who seemed [to be something] added nothing to me'.

On his *third* visit (the Jerusalem Conference visit of Acts 15) which came after his first missionary journey (around A.D. 49 or 50)—and also in the wake of Peter's recent 'hypocritical' activity at Antioch when 'certain men from James' (Gal 2:12), who were 'believers who belonged to the party of the Pharisees' (Acts 15:5), came to Antioch and, overstepping their commission (Acts 15:24), declared to the Gentile Christians: 'Unless you are circumcised according to the custom of Moses, you cannot be saved' (Acts 15:1) – Paul's apostleship and his law-free gospel were again vindicated, but *publicly* now, and in the presence of the Judaizing believers, first, by Peter's speech, second, by Barnabas' and Paul's own recounting of God's attestation to their ministry among the Gentiles by the 'signs and wonders' which he did through them, third, by James' summation, and fourth, by the Council's written deliverance.

On his *fourth* visit (known as the 'quick visit') at the termination of his second missionary journey (c. the spring of A.D. 52), he did little more than 'greet the church' there and then depart for Antioch (Acts 18:22). Luke's complete silence about this visit beyond stating the simple fact itself may mean little or nothing; it may mean much, about the Jerusalem church's deepening unease about Paul's mission to the Jewish Diaspora.

On his *fifth* and last visit five years later at the termination of his third missionary journey (in early summer, A.D. 57), 'the brothers [this term probably refers to the household of Mnason and the Hellenist remnant in the Jerusalem church, not to James and the church eldership; Paul met *them* the next day] received us warmly,' Luke writes (Acts 21:17). He makes no mention of any apostles at the meeting the next day with James. Apparently Peter had departed Jerusalem for parts unknown, winding up eventually, according to tradition, in Rome, and apparently John by this time had also departed Jerusalem, winding up eventually, according to tradition, in Ephesus. Only the Jerusalem elders are present, with James clearly their leader. P. W. Barnett notes:

James had been a member of the Jerusalem church from its beginning until his death in A.D. 62, a period of about thirty years....
Over this thirty-year period the Jerusalem church became more conservatively Jewish.... First, the Hellenists emigrated in the thirties [Acts 8:2; 11:19-21], and by the late forties they were followed by Peter (and John?) and possibly the other apostles. The final glimpse of the Jerusalem church given by Acts at the time of Paul's final visit is a thoroughly Jewish enclave.[3]

Barnett makes this last comment because, despite the good face Luke gives to the meeting—James and the elders, he writes in Acts 21:20, 'glorified God' upon hearing from Paul concerning what God had done through his ministry among the *Gentiles* (note Luke's restrictive word 'Gentiles' in 21:19), it is quite apparent that the Jerusalem elders were distrustful of Paul's manner of ministry among the Jews of the Diaspora. Luke makes no mention of any expression of gratitude on their part for the collection of money from the Gentile churches even though we know Luke knew of the collection's existence (Acts 24:17) and even though it would no doubt have been a very sizeable amount of money.[4] Rather, he reports that the elders pointedly and singularly remarked on the size and thorough Jewishness of the believing community in Jerusalem whose widely held conviction it was that Paul had betrayed the cause of Judaism in the Diaspora. It was their understanding that Paul had taught Jews to abandon Moses and not to circumcise their children. They were wrong, of course; he continued to live the scrupulous life of a Jew when among Jews during his missionary travels in order to win as many as possible (1 Cor 9:19-20). Their precise words were:

> You see, brother, how many thousands of Jews have believed, and all [πάντες] of them are zealous for the law [ζηλωταὶ τοῦ νόμου, lit., 'zealots for the law']. They have been informed that you teach

---

3. P. W. Barnett, 'Opponents of Paul,' *Dictionary of Paul and His Letters* (Downers Grove, Ill.: InterVarsity, 1993), 650.

4. I am assuming here that the Jerusalem leaders accepted the Gentile church's money gift but this is by no means certain. It is entirely possible that Jewish prejudice against Paul's Gentile mission may have become so strong by this time in the Jerusalem church that its leaders may have rejected it. That even Paul had been uncertain whether the Gentile church's gift would be received is evident from Romans 15:31 where he asked the Roman church to pray that his 'service for Jerusalem may be acceptable to the saints there'. His implied uncertainty here had to be based on something, and it is highly unlikely that it was simply his awareness of the normal human sensibilities about receiving charity (Cranfield). Much more likely it was his awareness of the Jerusalem church's distrust of him and his law-free gospel among the Jewish Diaspora.

all the Jews who live among the Gentiles to turn away from Moses, telling them not to circumcise their children or live according to our customs. (Acts 21:20-21)

And their reminder to him that the Jerusalem Conference had made certain ritual requests of Gentile Christians (Acts 21:25) suggests that they were not entirely convinced that he had been faithfully carrying out the edict of the 'Apostolic Decree' of the Conference.

These Lucan statements suggest that by this time a strongly held theological viewpoint within the messianic community in Jerusalem —no doubt partly due simply to the church's Jewish environs and its proximity to the Temple and its ritual, perhaps also partly due to the turning of many (Essene?) priests to the faith (Acts 6:7), and no doubt partly due to the influence of the party of the Pharisees who had believed (15:5)—was promoting a nationalistic and therefore a 'Mosaic version' of the Christian faith and which therefore regarded Paul's mission to the Jewish Diaspora with profound suspicion.

I do not intend to suggest that James was personally apprehensive about Paul since the complaints appear to have come from the mouths of the elders and not from James (21:18-25). But there can be little doubt either that for James, as the leader of the Jewish church in Jerusalem, Paul's missionary labors had raised acute difficulties for relationships between the messianic Jewish community and the wider Jewish community in Jerusalem and Judea at a time of rapidly increasing religious nationalism. And he apparently approved of—he certainly raised no objection to—the elders' suggestion that Paul participate in and bear the expense of the rite of purification which four Jewish Christians had undertaken in order that, in their words, 'everyone will know there is no truth in these reports about you, but that you yourself are living in obedience to the law' (21:24). Because Paul was willing to 'become all things to all men that [he] may by all means save some' (1 Cor 9:22), he submitted himself to the advice of the Jerusalem leadership and entered into a week-long ceremonial rite of purification which necessarily required his presence at the Temple.

Biblical information about the Jerusalem church terminates at this point in Luke's narrative. But it has to be said that it is not the most complimentary ending that one might have devoutly wished for. For after a riot broke out when some Jews from the province of Asia saw Paul at the Temple and stirred up the assembled crowd against him (21:27), even though he was there at the church leadership's request and even though they knew that the charges leveled against Paul were false, Luke makes no mention of the church leaders doing anything to save him from the accusations which he was falsely accused of. Rather, it was the Roman battalion stationed at the fortress of Antonia adjacent to the Temple that saved him from certain death at the hands of the Jewish mob that was already beating him at the time when Claudius Lysias (see Acts 23:26 for his name), the Roman commander, rescued him. And no church leaders appeared on his behalf the next day when he was taken by Claudius Lysias before the Sanhedrin to find out more about the accusations which the Jews had brought against him. In fact, it was Paul's nephew, learning later of some Jews' plot to kill Paul, to which the Sanhedrin was privy, who informed first Paul and then the Roman commander, the latter of whom then spirited Paul away by night to Caesarea to insure his physical safety.

In sum, from this brief overview it is clear that one cannot and should not deny that at times suspicion and tension did exist between Paul and the Jerusalem church—on Paul's part because he had to wonder at times whether the Jerusalem church truly accepted his Gentile converts as first class Christians because he did not insist that those converts should live like Jews; on the Jerusalem church's part because it wondered at times whether Paul had not betrayed Moses and the cause of Judaism among the Jews of the Diaspora. While the Jerusalem apostolate itself had accepted Paul's apostleship and his law-free gospel for Gentiles and had supported—indeed, had vindicated—him when it had been called upon to do so (see Gal 2:1-10; Acts 15), nevertheless, it seems rather clear that the leaders of the Jerusalem church in the late 50s were not indoctrinating their Jewish converts in Paul's doctrine of Christian liberty from the ceremonial and dietary regulations of the Old Testament. In sum, given its geographic location in the very world center of ethnic and religious Judaism, there can be no question that Paul's entire Gentile mission created serious problems for the Jerusalem church.

Questions which the Jerusalem church had to face squarely include:

First, is it permissible for Jewish Christians who are living as Jews to have 'table fellowship' (and thus celebrate the Lord's Supper) with Christian Gentiles who are not living as Jews? The Cornelius incident of Acts 10, Paul's later rebuke of Peter at Antioch as recorded in Galatians 2, and the Jerusalem Conference of Acts 15 should have settled this issue. It was indeed permissible, but whether the 'zealots for the law', who seem to have been in the ascendency in the Jerusalem church, would have done so is an open question. Most likely not, and if they did indeed refuse to do so they were guilty of the same schismatic spirit for which Paul had to rebuke Peter at Antioch and placed themselves thereby, at best, in the category of what Paul terms 'weak brothers' of 'weak faith' (Rom 14:1-2; 15:1) and of 'weak conscience' (1 Cor 8:9-11); at worst, in the category of what Paul terms 'false brothers' (Gal 2:4; 2 Cor 11:26) and 'false apostles' (2 Cor 11:13). Of course, Gentile Christians needed always to be reminded not to offend a sensitive Jewish conscience which had scruples concerning the law's ceremonial and dietary regulations before it had received instruction that these regulations were for the church's training only in its Old Testament 'minority' years (Gal 4:1-6).

Secondly, should Jews of the Diaspora who became Christians be instructed to continue to live as Jews or should they be informed that they could live as 'Gentile Christians' if they so desired? It is highly doubtful that the 'zealots for the law' in the Jerusalem church would have agreed with Paul that the Jewish Christian of the Diaspora was free in Christ to continue to live as a Jew or was free to live as a Gentile Christian, having been freed in Christ from Old Testament ritual laws such as circumcision and the dietary laws. Of course, it should be recalled that Paul also taught that whatever the Christian, whether Jew or Gentile, determined to do, the 'strong' believer was not to insist upon the exercise of his freedom in Christ if it offended his 'weak' brother who had scruples unless that 'weak' brother believed that such religious observances were necessary for salvation. Then the 'strong' brother, while still doing what he could to avoid offending the 'weak' brother, was obliged to make it clear that his observance of such things was only being done to avoid giving offence to, and in order to maintain Christian unity with, the 'weak' brother, but in no sense was it being done in order to either earn salvation or maintain covenant status because God required it to be done. Paul was himself quite sensitive to heed his own instructions in this regard too (1 Cor 8:13; 10:31–11:1).

Thirdly, how were Christian Jews in Jerusalem and Judea to live, surrounded as they were with ethnic and religious Jews? If we apply these same principles to their situation, we must conclude that the Christian community in Jerusalem was acting properly when it continued to observe Old Testament ritual and dietary laws as long as it did not continue to involve itself in the Temple's sacrificial system, did not forsake first-day Lord's Day worship, did not forsake Christian baptism and the Lord's Supper in lieu of circumcision and the Passover, and as long as it made clear to its Jewish neighbors that its observance of Old Testament ritual legislation was not being done in order to be either saved or maintain covenant status but simply in order not to offend the Jew's sensitive conscience. All this – given the time and circumstances – was admittedly no little burden to bear! And it is not at all clear that the membership of the Jerusalem church in the late 50s understood (or, if they did, accepted) the liberating principles enunciated by Paul and managed accordingly to live consistently as law-free Christians. Paul's letter to the Hebrews suggests that they in fact did not. Indeed, scholars have debated whether the Jerusalem church ever knew and lived out the freedom in Christ in the full sense which Paul knew it, and whether therefore it was as careful to draw the distinctions in these matters of human relationship which Paul drew. But I think that it must be said, not only because of the death of James in A.D. 62 and then the destruction of Jerusalem itself in A.D. 70 but also *because of its continuing (and continually intensifying) commitment to a 'Jewish form of Christianity'*, that the Jerusalem church after A.D. 70, even though it was the mother church of Christianity, quickly lost its position of leadership in the empire-wide communion of saints whose members were even then far and away mainly Gentile in number primarily because of Paul's missionary efforts, with the geographic centers of influence shifting to such major cities as Antioch, Alexandria, Ephesus, Rome, and later Constantinople.[5]

We turn now to Luke's account of Paul's journey to Rome.[6] While Paul was in the Temple in connection with the rite of purification mentioned above,[7] Jews from the province of Asia saw him and immediately began to charge him (falsely on both accounts), first, with anti-Jewish propaganda,[8] and second, with bringing Trophimus, an Ephesian convert who had accompanied him to Jerusalem (see Acts 20:4), into the Temple, which act was regarded by the Jews as a capital crime. Word spread about Paul's presence among them, and with the entire city in an uproar, the Jews seized Paul, began to beat him, and would have killed him on the spot if he had not been rescued by Claudius Lysias and the Roman guards stationed in the fortress of Antonia. Paul then requested that he might address the mob, which he did in Aramaic (see Acts 21:17-40).

---

5. What I am about to say I say, if I know my heart, with no rancor at all, but I believe I must issue the following warning: my dear Christian Jewish friends who regard themselves as 'completed' or 'Messianic Jews' and accordingly who worship together on Saturdays, use ancient Jewish synagogue liturgies, and refrain from intermingling on the Lord's Day with Gentile Christians must carefully examine what they are doing to insure that they are not creating again the very barrier between Jewish Christians and Gentile Christians that Paul labored all his life as a Christian apostle to tear down.

6. From Acts 20:5 on it is likely that Luke was with Paul to the end (note carefully Luke's employment of 'we' after Acts 20:5). Luke was clearly with Paul in Rome during both of his imprisonments there (Col 4:14; 2 Tim 4:11).

7. See Bruce, *Paul, Apostle of the Heart Set Free* (Grand Rapids: Eerdmans, 1996 reprint), 348, for his discussion of this rite of purification.

8. It would seem that Paul pleased neither the Jewish church nor the Jews of Jerusalem. Both thought he had betrayed Moses.

He proceeded to recount his conversion encounter with Jesus Christ on the Damascus Road. When he informed them that Jesus, in a vision in the very Temple where he had just been accosted by the Jews, had later instructed him to go specifically to the Gentiles, the Jewish crowd could take it no longer and began to cry for his immediate execution. So Claudius Lysias took him into the Antonia and started to have him flogged to find out why the people were so enraged at him. But Paul informed him that he was a Roman citizen and thus avoided Claudius Lysias' torture (22:1-29).[9]

The next day Claudius Lysias took him to the Sanhedrin to find out exactly why Paul was being accused by the Jews (22:30). By appealing to the fact that he, in concert with the Pharisees in the Sanhedrin,[10] believed in the hope in the resurrection of the dead, Paul caused the Pharisees and Sadducees to divide. Indeed, the Pharisees even came to Paul's defense (23:1-9). Fearing that Paul would be torn to pieces in the violent uproar that ensued in the Sanhedrin, Claudius Lysias took him back to the Antonia. The following night Jesus appeared to Paul and told him that, as he had testified about him in Jerusalem, so he would testify about him in Rome (23:11). Learning from Paul's nephew of a Jewish plot to kill Paul, to which the Sanhedrin was privy, Claudius Lysias sent him away by night via Antipatris to Caesarea (23:12-35).[11]

Five days after he had arrived at Caesarea, several members of the Sanhedrin came to Caesarea and charged Paul before the Roman procurator, Marcus Antonius (or Claudius) Felix, with being a 'troublemaker, stirring up riots among the Jews all over the world. He is a ringleader of the Nazarene sect and even tried to desecrate the temple' (24:5-6). Paul responded that the charges were totally untrue and pointed out that his accusers had produced no evidence to support their charges (24:10-21). Sadly, it must be noted that the Jerusalem church sent no one to side with Paul in his defense. So Felix adjourned the meeting and ordered the Roman guard to keep Paul in their custody but to give him some freedom and permit his friends to take care of his needs (24:22-23). Because Felix was hoping that Paul would offer him a bribe, he kept Paul in custody at Caesarea for the next two years (A.D. 57-59), frequently sending for him and

---

9. See Bruce, *Paul*, 348-52, for his account of Paul's arrest.
10. See his cry: 'I am a Pharisee, the son of a Pharisee. I stand on trial because of my hope in the resurrection of the dead' (Acts 23:6).
11. See Bruce, *Paul*, 352-53.

talking with him (24:26-27). Luke tells us that Paul spoke to him about faith in Jesus Christ, *discoursing* (διαλεγομένου) on righteousness, self-control, and the judgment to come (24:24-25).

Porcius Festus succeeded Felix as procurator of Judea in A.D. 59. Three days after arriving in the province he made a trip to Jerusalem where the Sanhedrin – evidently long on memory – presented their charges against Paul to him. He demanded that the Jewish leadership return to Caesarea with him and press charges against Paul there. This they did, but they could not prove any of their charges. Again, no help for Paul was forthcoming from the Jerusalem church. When Festus asked Paul if he was willing to return to Jerusalem and stand trial before him there, Paul appealed to Caesar's court because he was confident that he would not receive a fair trial in Jerusalem. 'You have appealed to Caesar. To Caesar you shall go!' declared Festus (25:1-12).[12]

Before he released Paul for his journey to Rome, however, Festus arranged for Herod Agrippa II (or Marcus Julius Agrippa, as he calls himself on his coins), king of the former tetrarchies of Philip and Lysanias, the regions of Tiberias and Tarichaea, and Julias and fourteen neighboring villages, at his request, to hear Paul (25:13-26:1). Paul happily obliged them and spoke again of his conversion on the Damascus Road (26:2-23). Neither Festus (26:24-27) nor Agrippa (26:28-29) were persuaded of the truth of the gospel, but they agreed privately that Paul had done nothing that deserved death or imprisonment and that he could have been set free if he had not already appealed to Caesar (26:31-32).[13]

By this time Luke had come to Paul at Caesarea (see the 'we' in 27:1; doubtless Luke had used the two years Paul was at Caesarea collecting material for his Gospel and the earlier parts of Acts). Aristarchus from Thessalonica (see 20:4) had also come to him (27:2). (Where were any elders from the Jerusalem church?) In the custody of Julius, a centurion of the Imperial Regiment, Paul with his two friends boarded a grain ship and sailed for Sidon where some friends provided for the trio's needs. Then sailing past Cyprus they landed at Myra in Lycia.[14] There they changed ships, and sailed along the leeward (southern) side of Crete, coming to a harbor named Fair

---

12. Bruce, *Paul*, 362-63.
13. Apparently the 'paper work' had already been dispatched to Rome concerning the case. See Bruce, *Paul*, 365.
14. Bruce, *Paul*, 370-72.

Havens near Lasea sometime after October 5, A.D. 59. The pilot and the owner of the ship, against Paul's better advice, decided to sail for Phoenix, another harbor in Crete, in order to winter there (this would have been the winter of A.D. 59). But before the ship could make it to Phoenix, it was caught by a violent wind of hurricane force (Acts 27:14: Εὐρακύλων, that is, 'Northeaster') and for two weeks was driven at the wind's mercy across the Sea of Hadria, that is, the central Mediterranean. In the midst of this frightening ordeal, an angel of the Lord appeared to Paul and informed him that the entire crew would survive the storm though the ship would be destroyed. On the fourteenth night of the storm, the ship approached land, and at dawn the next day the crew decided to try to run the ship aground. The ship struck a mudbar and was broken into pieces by the pounding waves. But all the crew members, swimming and clinging to planks, pieces of the ship, and perhaps to one another, reached land safely as Paul had predicted (27:3-44).

Once on shore the crew discovered that they had landed on the small island of Malta.[15] There Paul was bitten by a venomous snake that had inadvertently been trapped in a pile of brushwood he had gathered. But when Paul suffered no ill effects, the people of Malta concluded that he was a god. Paul also healed both the father of Publius, the chief official of Malta, and the rest of the sick on the island. As a result, the missionary trio were honored in many ways by the people who furnished the three with the supplies they needed for their journey on to Rome (28:1-10).

After three months on Malta, Paul, still under the care of the courteous and kindly Roman guard Julius, sailed to Syracuse on the east coast of Sicily, then to Rhegium in the toe of Italy, and finally landed at Puteoli in the Bay of Naples. There they stayed with Christian friends for a week, and then started up the Appian Way to Rome. They were met by Christian friends who had come from Rome to meet them at the Forum of Appius and the Three Taverns. This gesture on the part of these Roman Christians was a great encouragement to Paul (28:11-15). 'And so,' writes Luke with literary art and remarkable constraint, '[in the company of these friends] we came to Rome' (28:14).[16]

---

15. Bruce, *Paul*, 372-73.
16. Bruce, *Paul*, 374.

Excursus on Rome

Founded, according to tradition, in 753 B.C. on its seven hills (Quirinal Hill, Viminal Hill, Esquiline Hill, Caelian Hill, Capitoline Hill, Palatine Hill, and Aventine Hill; see Rev 17:9), Rome in Paul's day was 'in the full flush of her growth', a city approximately six square miles in area and surrounded by thirteen miles of walls with a population of one to two million people which extended beyond the the city walls.

The Roman Forum was the center of the Imperial government in which stood the Senate House, an assembly hall, and temples for Mars and Saturn. Here also was the golden milestone from which all road distances throughout the empire were measured. Surrounding the Forum were four of Rome's seven hills: on the Capitoline Hill were several temples including one to Jupiter, the head of the Roman pantheon; on the Palatine Hill were the palaces of the emperors and of other noblemen; on the Caelian Hill was a temple to the deified Emperor Claudius; and on the Quirinal Hill were forums constructed by Julius and Augustus.

Words cannot begin to describe the splendor of the city's public buildings; everywhere the city displayed temples, triumphal arches, basilicas, fountains, palaces, and mausoleums. (In A.D. 28 alone Augustus received the Senate's approval to rebuild and/or to restore eighty-two temples.) The dwellings of the majority of city dwellers (from one half to a full million people), however, stood in stark contrast: tenement houses a block long and up to six stories high containing one-room flats were flimsy (and often collapsed) and in constant danger of fires. Most of the city's inhabitants worked hard for meager incomes, and to keep the poor of Rome happy the city provided them with free wheat and water. Grain fleets from Africa and Egypt supplied Rome with its bread needs (vegetables were scarce and meat was served only on the tables of the very rich), and aqueducts brought water from great distances to supply the city with two to three million gallons of water a day for its thousand plus free public baths. While the city itself was essentially a great slum, the citizens were among the cleanest in the world.

To keep its restless population in check, the city sponsored athletic events, chariot racing and gladiatorial games (involving man against man and man against beast in mortal combat) free of charge at the Circus Maximus which accommodated one hundred and fifty thousand spectators. Bloodthirsty crowds could call for the death or the sparing of the life of the defeated combatant. Gambling on the outcome was, of course, quite popular and riots were not uncommon. By Claudius' time (A.D. 41-54), there were one hundred and fifty-nine holidays per year with ninety-three of these devoted specifically to the games.

Of course, when Paul came to Rome, it should be recalled, Nero was the emperor of Rome (A.D. 54-68). Because his mother Agrappina had been banished as a political danger when he was only three, Nero had been reared by two slaves, a barber and a dancer. When her uncle Claudius became emperor in A.D. 41, she returned home and received once again her honor and her position. She then persuaded Claudius to marry her. Claudius already had two children, a son named Britannicus and a daughter named Octavia. Agrappina procured Octavia's betrothal to Nero after having a brilliant young Roman named Lucius Julius Silanus, to whom she was already betrothed, accused of a crime he never committed (which drove him to suicide). Then by sheer persistence she persuaded the weak-minded Claudius to adopt Nero as his son. Nero, being three years older than Britannicus, was placed then in direct line for the throne. Agrappina then had Claudius poisoned, and after Nero became emperor he had Britannicus poisoned, Agrappina executed in a second attempt on her life (his first [unsuccessful] attempt was by drowning, his second by stabbing was successful), and Octavia murdered. He kicked his second wife Poppaea to death when she was expecting a child. He set fire to Rome and the city burned for a week, and then he blamed the fire on the Christians of Rome and had them tortured by rolling them in pitch, setting them ablaze and using them as living torches in his garden, and by sewing them in the skins of wild animals and setting his hunting dogs on them to tear them to pieces. There is scarcely a crime on the books which Nero did not commit. And while it is true that some of his crimes were yet future when Paul reached Rome, nonetheless it must be noted that it was this emperor of Rome who was destined to try Paul's case.[17]

Three years had passed since Paul had written the Roman Christians from Corinth, in which letter he had expressed his desire to visit them and had promised to come to them shortly. God had finally answered his prayer and fulfilled his longing to bear witness to his Lord in Rome, but little did he realize when he wrote Romans the extent of the hardships that lay between him as he wrote and his arrival three years later in Rome, the 'Eternal City' and capital of the Empire.

---

17. For Bruce's description of Rome, see *Paul*, 22-25, 379-384; for W. J. Conybeare and J. S. Howson's, see *The Life and Epistles of St. Paul* (Grand Rapids: Eerdmans, 1971 reprint), 673-79.

Paul's First Roman Imprisonment, A.D. 60-62 (Acts 28:16-31)

In Rome Paul was allowed to live by himself, in his own rented house, with only a soldier to guard him (28:16, 30). He immediately called the Jewish leaders in Rome to him and explained to them that he had 'done nothing against our people or against the customs of our ancestors', that though he had been arrested in Jerusalem and turned over to the Roman authorities, they had examined him and concluded that he had done nothing deserving death, and that he had brought no counter charges against his people even though the Jewish leaders had objected to his release, which objection had made his appeal to Caesar necessary (28:17-20).

The Jewish leaders informed Paul that they had received no letters from the Jerusalem Sanhedrin concerning him, and that no one who had recently come to Rome from Jerusalem had reported anything bad about him. They then requested that Paul explain to them his views about 'this sect' (28:21-22).

On the agreed-upon day a large number of Jews assembled in Paul's rented house, and 'from morning till evening he *explained and declared* [ἐξετίθετο διαμαρτυρόμενος] to them the kingdom of God and *tried to convince* [πείθων] them about Jesus from the Law of Moses and from the Prophets' (28:23). Some believed, but others refused to believe. These Jews then began to disagree among themselves, and began to leave after Paul applied the words of Isaiah 6:9-10 to those who refused to believe. He then declared to them: 'I want you to know that God's salvation has been sent to the Gentiles, and they will listen!' (28:24-28).

Paul remained under house arrest for two years (A.D. 60-62), the reason for the delay in his case going to trial probably due either to tardiness on the part of his accusers to come from Jerusalem or to the backlog of cases before the Roman court. (It could be that two years was the legal time limit for charges to be brought against him, but this is by no means certain.) In any case, during this time Paul 'welcomed all who came to see him. Boldly and *without hindrance* [ἀκωλύτως][18] he preached [κηρύσσων] the kingdom of God and

---

18. This word is Luke's last word in Acts. Bruce points out that this word, meaning 'without hindrance' (ἀκωλύτως), is a strictly legal term, and has the apologetic value of implying that 'if the gospel were illegal and subversive propaganda, it could [not] have been proclaimed for two years at the heart of the empire by a Roman citizen who had appealed to Caesar...the authorities must have known what he was doing at the time, yet no obstacle was

taught [διδάσκων] about the Lord Jesus Christ' (28:30b-31).[19]

Paul's Roman imprisonment was anything but an interruption of his apostolic ministry. Rather, it was a fruitful extension of it. Consider, for instance, not only the converts he made during this time but the prison letters he wrote to his churches while there. He referred to himself during this time, not as a prisoner of Rome, but as 'the prisoner of Christ Jesus for the sake of you Gentiles' (Eph 3:1), a 'prisoner for the Lord' (Eph 4:1; Phlm 9; Phil 1:13), and an 'ambassador in chains' for the gospel (Eph 6:19-20). And he regarded his imprisonment as a confirmation and advance of the gospel (Phil 1:7), for he himself wrote:

> ... what has happened to me has really served to advance the gospel. As a result, it has become clear throughout the whole palace guard and to everyone else that I am in chains for Christ. Because of my chains, most of the brothers in the Lord have been encouraged to speak the word of God more fearlessly and boldly. (Phil 1:12-14)

Thus Luke brought his inspired account of the exalted Christ's continuing acts and words ('the treasure') through mortal men ('the earthen vessels') to a close. The gospel in victorious conquest had advanced upon the world and had penetrated Rome, indeed, even into Caesar's very household (Phil 4:22).

Now you the reader must decide whether you will become a part of the continuing conquest of the gospel. Will you seriously face the demands of the Great Commission and your responsibility to it? Will you make yourself available to the Lord Jesus Christ for cross-cultural ministry? Before you decide to stay at home and involve yourself in some work here, you must first be able to give yourself good reasons why you may stay at home. Cross-cultural ministry, I would submit, should be given first priority in your thinking. Only when the Lord has made it clear that he does *not* want you to involve yourselves cross-culturally should you then decide to stay at home.

---

put in his way' (*Paul*, 511). So Luke's account in Acts ends on this triumphant note: the gospel, the only legitimate message from heaven, was being freely and without fetters proclaimed at Rome.

19. For a description of what likely occurred if Paul's case did in fact go to trial, see Conybeare and Howson, *The Life and Epistles of St. Paul*, 741-45.

Paul's Prison Letters

Colossians

A. The Letter's Place of Origin
I will deal with the place of origin of the Colossian letter in connection with the larger issue of the place of origin of Colossians, Philemon, and Ephesians, taken together, moving toward my conclusion by a series of steps.

1. That Colossians, Philemon, and Ephesians are 'prison letters' is clear from Colossians 4:3, 10, 18; Philemon 1, 9, 13, 23; and Ephesians 3:1, 4:1. But where is Paul imprisoned – in Caesarea, Ephesus, or Rome? Each of these places has been suggested as the site of one or more of these letters.

2. Colossians, Philemon, and Ephesians seem rather definitely to be linked together to the same place of origin. Colossians and Philemon are linked together, first, by the fact that Onesimus, who is carrying Paul's letter to Philemon, is identified as a Colossian and is represented as being in the company of Tychicus, who is carrying Paul's letter to the Colossians (Col 4:7-10); secondly, by the fact that both Colossians (4:17) and Philemon (Philemon 2) address Archippus, possibly Philemon's son; and thirdly, by the fact that in both Colossians (4:10-14) and Philemon (23-24) the same 'greeters' – Epaphras, Mark, Aristarchus, Demas, and Luke – send greetings to the recipients of the two letters. Clearly, Colossians and Philemon were written at approximately the same time and from the same place.

3. Colossians and Ephesians are linked together by the remarkable similarity of content[20] and by the fact that both were placed in the custody of Tychicus, their mutual bearer (Col 4:7-10; Eph 6:21-22), suggesting that they were written around the same time and from the same place. We may conclude at this juncture that Colossians, Philemon, and Ephesians were written from the same place. But what place?

---

20. See William Hendriksen, *Exposition of Ephesians* (Grand Rapids: Baker, 1979), 5-26.

4. It is highly unlikely that Onesimus, as a runaway slave, would have made his way to Caesarea, where he could have hardly escaped detection, rather than to Rome, or that Paul, if he was at Caesarea at the time he wrote these three letters, being determined as he was to visit Rome, would have told Philemon that he was planning, on his release, to visit Philemon in Colossae. So Caesarea, in my opinion, is not a very likely site for the prison letters, although, as we noted in our overview of Paul's journey to Rome, he did spend two years in prison there.

5. There is a possibility that these three letters could have originated from Ephesus during an imprisonment Paul experienced while there on his third missionary journey.[21] Onesimus could have come in contact with Paul there, Ephesus being only about 125 miles from Colossae. But there are several weaknesses in the view that Ephesus is the city of origin for these letters. First, there is only a tradition (the so-called Monarchian Prologues dating from the third or fourth centuries) but no biblical evidence that Paul was ever imprisoned in Ephesus. If, however, he did experience an imprisonment in Ephesus that was desperate to the point of being 'life-threatening' (2 Cor 1:8-10), that condition does not comport well with the relatively relaxed outlook of these three letters and the ministries of Paul's associates which are mentioned therein. Secondly, 'it is as likely that the fugitive slave...made for Rome because it was distant, as that he went to Ephesus because it was near' (Dodd).

6. Three things can be said in favor of Paul's first Roman imprisonment as the provenance of the letters.

First, Paul's situation as Luke describes it in Acts 28:30-31 certainly provides the time and atmosphere for him to say the things that he does in these letters.

Secondly, it is clear that Luke was with Paul during the imprisonment when he wrote these letters (Col 4:14; Phlm 24), which was true of his Roman imprisonment (see the 'we' of Acts 28:16) but which would not have been true of the conjectured Ephesian imprisonment. Luke, the reader may recall, remained at Philippi on the second journey (16:40), had rejoined Paul when the latter passed through Philippi on his way to Jerusalem at the end of his

---

21. See Franzmann, *The Word of the Lord Grows*, 145-48.

third journey (20:6), and had then accompanied Paul from Caesarea to Rome (27:1). But he had not been with Paul at Ephesus.

Finally, from Philippians 1:20 it appears that Paul was at least willing to face the prospect of an adverse verdict in his trial, and the sentence of death as a consequence. But such a verdict could only be handed down in Rome since in any provincial court such as the one at Ephesus Paul could have always appealed such a decision to the emperor as he did before Festus in Acts 25:11-12. Therefore, we conclude that until it can be demonstrated that the Ephesian hypothesis explains all the known facts about Paul's imprisonment better than the Roman hypothesis, we are on safer ground in assigning these three so-called 'prison letters' to the known and verifiable first Roman imprisonment.

B. The Date of the Letter
Sometime during A.D. 60-62.

C. The Occasion of the Letter
One of Paul's visitors during his Roman imprisonment was Epaphras who probably had founded the church in Colossae under Paul's direction during Paul's great Asian ministry originating from Ephesus during his third missionary journey. He brought the good news to Paul of the Colossian Christians' faith and love (1:4-8). But apparently he also informed Paul that the church was being threatened by a new teaching which, while it resembled the Christian message in some ways, was actually undermining it. Apparently both proclaimed a transnational, universal religion, both recognized the great gulf between God and natural man, and both offered a redemption which would bridge that gulf. Apparently Epaphras, while he sensed the difference between the true gospel and this distortion of it, could not analyze and define it well enough to oppose it vigorously and effectively. He therefore came to Rome and appealed to Paul, wise in the ways of Jew and pagan alike and keen in spiritual insight, to help him.

It is extremely difficult to get a clear picture of the Colossian heresy since all we know about it is what we read in the Colossian letter itself (and it is not always easy, as Picirilli rightly observes, to diagnose the disease from the prescribed medicine[22]). It appears to

---

22. Robert E. Picirilli, *Paul the Apostle* (Chicago: Moody, 1986), 197.

have been an amalgam of Judaic folk beliefs, Phrygian folk beliefs, and some basic Christian ideas urging 'the philosophy' (ἡ φιλοσοφία, Col 2:8) of a religious syncretism,[23] for Paul modifies this term with the phrases, 'according to the tradition of men, according to the elemental powers [τὰ στοιχεῖα] of the world.' Whatever these modifying phrases mean, Paul makes it clear that they were 'not according to Christ' (Col 2:8). These phrases would suggest that 'the philosophy' was

(1) *theosophic*, laying claim to the possession of, and the power to impart to others, an occult, profound knowledge (γνῶσις) or wisdom derived from God (see 1:9, 28; 2:3, 8, 23; 3:16; 4:5),

(2) *ritualistic*, stressing circumcision (2:11; 3:11), dietary laws, and the keeping of special seasons (2:16-17),

(3) *ascetic*, prescribing abstinence (2:21) and severe treatment of the body (2:23), and

(4) *magic*, for referring as he does to (a) 'thrones or powers or rulers or authorities' (1:16; see 2:10, 15), (b) 'the elemental powers of the world [τὰ στοιχεῖα τοῦ κόσμου, probably hostile angelic powers[24]]' (2:8, 20; Gal 4:3, 9[25]; see also Heb 5:12 for a fifth Pauline usage of τὰ στοιχεῖα where it has an altogether different meaning, namely, 'the elementary principles of the oracles of God'), and (c) the 'worship [or conjuration] of angels' (θρησκεία τῶν ἀγγέλων, construing the genitive as an objective genitive, 2:18), Paul intimates that the Colossians were magically invoking good personal angelic 'powers' in addition to the Christ as mediators between God and man for protection against the evil στοιχεῖα, with their ritualistic and ascetic practices being the means of placating or of obtaining

---

23. For a defense of this suggestion, see Clinton E. Arnold, *The Colossian Syncretism: The Interface Between Christianity and Folk Belief at Colossae* (Grand Rapids: Baker, 1996), Second Part.

24. See Arnold, *The Colossian Syncretism*, 158-94, for the argument. For variations on this theme, see R. P. Martin, *Colossians and Philemon* (New Century Bible; Grand Rapids: Eerdmans, 1981); P. T. O'Brien, *Colossians, Philemon* (Word Biblical Commentary 44; Waco: Word, 1982); N. T. Wright, *Colossians and Philemon* (Tyndale New Testament Commentary; Grand Rapids: Eerdmans, 1986); Richard N. Longenecker, *Galatians* (Word Biblical Commentary 41; Dallas: Word, 1990); P. T. O'Brien, 'Colossians, Letter to the,' and D. G. Reid, 'Elements/Elemental Spirits of the World,' both articles appearing in *Dictionary of Paul and His Letters*, 147-53, 229-33 respectively; and M. D. Hooker, 'Were There False Teachers in Colossae?' in *Christ and Spirit in the New Testament: Studies in honour of Charles Francis Digby Moule*, edited by B. Lindars and S. S. Smalley (Cambridge: University Press, 1973), 315-31.

25. See Chapter Twenty-Four, 'The Pauline Eschatology,' 541, fn. 12, for my discussion of τὰ στοιχεῖα τοῦ κόσμου in Galatians 4:3, 9.

contact with these 'power' intermediaries.

What Epaphras sensed, surely, and what Paul clearly saw was this: the new teaching called into question the unique and final greatness of Jesus Christ and the sufficiency of his atoning work. What made this syncretistic 'philosophy' all the more dangerous was the fact that it did not claim to supplant the gospel but to supplement it, to carry the Colossian Christians beyond their rudimentary Christianity to fulness and perfection. Franzmann declares that Paul does not so much oppose it by moving logically from plank to plank in the opposition's religious platform with a Christian counter-proposal, that is, by taking up 'the philosophy' and answering it point by point, as by simply overwhelming it with the vaster riches and the surpassing greatness of the lordship of the cosmic Christ of the true gospel over 'the elemental things of the world'.[26] O'Brien adds that 'in his handling of the Colossian false teaching Paul places his emphasis on realized eschatology (see especially Col 2:12; 3:1-4). Within the "already-not yet" tension the stress is on the former,' that is to say, the Colossians have

> already been delivered from a tyranny of darkness and transferred into the kingdom of God's beloved Son (Col 1:13)...they were already raised with him (Col 2:12; 3:1; cf. 3:3). ...the "already" needed to be asserted again and again over against those who were interested in "fullness" and the heavenly realm, but who had false notions about them, believing they could be reached by legalistic observances, a special knowledge, visionary experiences and the like. Christ has [already] done all that was necessary for the Colossians' salvation.[27]

D. The Content of the Letter[28]

INTRODUCTION: GREETINGS, THANKSGIVING, AND PRAYER, 1:1-14.

I. THE COMPLETENESS AND ALL-SUFFICIENCY OF CHRIST AND HIS GOSPEL, 1:15-2:23.

---

26. Franzmann, *The Word of the Lord Grows*, 123.
27. O' Brien, 'Colossians, Letter to the' in *Dictionary of Paul and His Letters*, 150.
28. I have adapted the following outline, with minor variations, from Franzmann, *The Word of the Lord Grows*, 124-26.

Paul's Journey to Caesarea and to Rome

A. The full glory of the Christ, the Son of God, 1:15-23.
   1. His person, 1:15-18.
   2. His work, 1:19-23.

B. The full glory of the gospel which proclaims the Christ, 1:24-2:5.
   1. Precious, 1:24-25.
   2. Universal, 1:26-27.
   3. Complete and sufficient, 2:1-5.

C. The refutation of the Colossian heresy, 2:6-23.
   1. Introductory admonition: 'In this Christ and in this gospel, walk, rooted and confirmed in faith,' 2:6-7.

   2. Second admonition: 'Do not let "the philosophy" [folk belief] or tradition lead you astray,' 2:8, because
      a. 'In Christ you are complete, for in Him is the fullness of deity,' 2:9-10.
      b. 'In Christ you have the true circumcision – even baptism, and with it new life, forgiveness of sins, and victory over all evil powers,' 2:11-15.
      c. 'In Christ the ritual shadows of the Old Testament have found their substance and fulfillment, so that they can have no real meaning for you now,' 2:16-19.
      d. 'In Christ you have died to the elemental spirits of the universe and to asceticism; and those who promote such teaching are expressing mere human wisdom whose value is nil in restraining sensual indulgence,' 2:20-23.

II. LIFE IN THE ALL-SUFFICIENT CHRIST, 3:1-4:6.

A. To be lived out as one whose life is hidden with Christ in God, 3:1-17.
   1. Exhibiting a life of purity and morality, 3:1-11.
   2. Exhibiting a life of love and peace, 3:12-17.

B. To be expressed in all social relationships – between husband and wife, between parents and children, between servants and masters, 3:18-4:1.

C. To be characterized by constant prayer and thanksgiving, and by wisdom toward outsiders, 4:2-6.

CONCLUSION: Personal matters, the sending of Tychicus and the coming of Onesimus, greetings, directions for an exchange of letters with Laodicea, and autographic conclusion, 4:7-18.

E. The Dominant Theme of the Letter: The sole lordship of Christ is alone sufficient for the Christian's spiritual health and protection.

* * * * *

Philemon

A. The Letter's Place of Origin
Rome, during Paul's detention under house arrest while awaiting trial (see discussion above).

B. The Date of the Letter
Sometime during A.D. 60-62.

C. The Occasion of the Letter
Epaphras was not Paul's only visitor from Colossae. Onesimus, a runaway slave belonging to Philemon, a wealthy Colossian who had come to faith through Paul's ministry, had come to Rome. Somehow, he came in contact with Paul who led him to Christ. Though he would have liked to retain Onesimus's services for himself, Paul sent him back to Colossae along with Tychicus, the bearer of his letter to the Colossians (Col 4:7-9), and he wrote this letter—his shortest and most personal letter—in which he intercedes on behalf of his new convert before Philemon.[29]

---

29. See F. F. Bruce, *The Epistles to the Colossians, to Philemon, and to the Ephesians* (New International Commentary on the New Testament; Grand Rapids: Eerdmans, 1984); R. P. Martin, *Colossians and Philemon* (New Century Bible; Grand Rapids: Eerdmans, 1981); P. T. O'Brien, *Colossians, Philemon* (Word Biblical Commentary 44; Waco: Word, 1982); N. T. Wright, *Colossians and Philemon* (Tyndale New Testament Commentary; Grand Rapids: Eerdmans, 1986); Arthur G. Patzia, *Ephesians, Colossians, Philemon* (Peabody, Massachusetts: Hendrickson, 1991) and 'Philemon, Letter to' in *Dictionary of Paul and His Letters*, 703-07, for excellent discussions of issues related to the letter.

Paul's Journey to Caesarea and to Rome

D. The Content of the Letter

I. GREETINGS TO PHILEMON, HIS WIFE APPHIA, AND ARCHIPPUS, PROBABLY HIS SON, AND THE CHURCH IN PHILEMON'S HOUSE, 1-3.

II. THANKSGIVING FOR PHILEMON'S FAITH AND LOVE, AND A PRAYER FOR THEIR CONTINUED EFFECTUAL WORKING, 4-7.

III. PAUL'S PLEA FOR ONESIMUS, HIS CHILD IN CHRIST, 8-21.

The reader should note the beautiful illustrative depiction of the doctrine of justification which is present in Paul's plea for Onesimus:

1. Verse 17: 'So if you consider me a partner, welcome him as you would welcome me.' That is to say, 'If in your eyes I have merit, reckon to him my merit and receive him for it.'

2. Verse 18: 'If he has done you any wrong or owes you anything, charge it to me. I, Paul,...I will pay it back.' That is to say, 'Any demerit he has in your eyes, reckon to me that demerit; I will bear it.'

IV. PAUL'S ANNOUNCEMENT THAT HE WILL SOON VISIT PHILEMON, HIS GREETINGS FROM FELLOW WORKERS, AND A BENEDICTION, 22-25.

E. The Dominant Theme of the Letter: Paul's statesman-like, Christ-like intercession for Onesimus before Philemon.

* * * * *

Ephesians

A. The Letter's Place of Origin
Rome, during Paul's detention under house arrest while awaiting trial (see discussion above).

B. The Date of the Letter
Sometime during A.D. 60-62.

C. The Occasion of the Letter
There seems to be no particular heresy troubling the letter's recipients in the Ephesian church such as that which was troubling the Colossian church. But Paul apparently seized the opportunity afforded him—since he was unable to return to the province of Asia himself and since Tychicus and Onesimus were going to be passing through the province on their way to Colossae anyway—to 'strengthen the churches' once more by writing a letter to them (Acts 15:41). So he wrote possibly two letters—a letter to the Laodicean church in particular since it was very close to Colossae and thus was in danger of being infected by the same heresy afflicting the Colossian church (Col 4:16; see also Rev 3:14-22) and a circular letter to the churches throughout the province of Asia (unless Paul's letter to the Laodiceans is the letter we now speak of as his letter to the Ephesians,[30] in which case he wrote only one). If he did write two letters, we must acknowledge that we know nothing about his letter to the Laodicean church beyond the mere fact of its existence. As we suggested earlier, it possibly addressed the same heresy troubling the Colossian church. In the circular letter (the one we now speak of as Paul's letter to the Ephesians, but I say again, our letter to the Ephesians may be Paul's letter to the Laodiceans since it is very strange, to say the least, that Paul would extend no final greetings to friends in a church with which he had spent three years), believing that 'an ounce of prevention is worth a pound of cure', he elaborated upon the spiritual wealth which the Christian has in Christ and upon the only walk which comports with that spiritual wealth.[31]

D. The Content of the Letter

I. THE CHRISTIAN'S WEALTH IN CHRIST (see 'riches': 1:7, 18; 2:4, 7; 3:8, 16) (OR, THE CHURCH GOD'S WORKMANSHIP), 1-3.

---

30. The words 'in Ephesus' (ἐν ᾿Εφέσῳ) in Ephesians 1:1 are missing in P[46], A*, B*, and several other early witnesses.

31. For additional insights into the situation behind Paul's letter to the Ephesians, see F. F. Bruce, *The Epistles to the Colossians, to Philemon, and to the Ephesians* (New International Commentary on the New Testament; Grand Rapids: Eerdmans, 1984); A. T. Lincoln,

A. Salutation, 1:1-2.

B. Doxology to God the Father which surveys the whole range of his redemptive blessing, 1:3-14.

C. First prayer to God the Father that Paul's readers may be enabled to comprehend better all that God has done for them: the hope to which he has called them, the riches of the inheritance which he has bestowed upon them, and his power which is at work in them, 1:15-23.

D. Explication of what God the Father has done for them, 2:1-22.
1. Individually, redemptively, vertically, 2:1-10.
   a. What they were, 2:1-3.
   b. What the Father did, 2:4-6.
   c. Why he did it, 2:7.
   d. What they are now, 2:8-10.

2. Corporately, covenantally, horizontally, 2:11-22.
   a. What they were, 2:11-12.
   b. What Christ did, 2:13-18.
   c. What they are now, 2:19-22.

E. Second prayer to God the Father, 3:1-19.
1. An excursus on his apostolic mission to the Gentiles and the great grace exhibited toward him which lay behind his call, which transfigures the suffering which the apostolic task entails, 3:2-13.

2. The prayer that his readers may be enabled to comprehend better the Father's blessing bestowed upon them: the incomprehensible love of Christ for them, the fullness of God who has blessed them, 3:14-19.

II. THE CHRISTIAN'S WALK IN CHRIST (see 'walk': 2:10; 4:1, 17; 5:2, 8, 15) (OR, THE CHURCH CREATED FOR GOOD WORKS), 4-6.

Ephesians (Word Biblical Commentary 42; Dallas: Word, 1990); R. P. Martin, *Ephesians, Colossians, and Philemon* (Interpretation Commentaries; Louisville: John Knox, 1992); Clinton E. Arnold, 'Ephesians, Letter to the,' *Dictionary of Paul and His Letters*, 238-49.

A. A walk in unity—the utilization of the church's diversity of gifts to be used to enhance that unity, that the church may be the mature, functioning body of Christ, its Head, 4:1-16.

B. A new walk—a radical break with their pagan past and the putting on of the 'new self created to be like God in true righteousness and holiness', 4:17-24.

C. A walk in charity—lying, thievery, anger, bitterness, brawling, slander, and malice must be replaced in their lives by kindness, compassion, forgiveness, and love, 4:25-5:2.

D. An illumined walk—all sexual immorality, impurity, obscenity, and foolish or coarse joking must be replaced by moral purity, goodness, righteousness, and truth, and further that the former fruits of darkness must be avoided and exposed for what they are, 5:3-14.

E. A wise walk—the former life of foolishness and wasteful debauchery must be replaced by a Spirit-filled life of mutual encouragement and thanksgiving to God (5:15-20).

F. A walk in which their reverence for Christ will govern their conduct in the relationships of this age, 5:21-6:9.
   1. In the relationship between wife and husband, 5:22-33.
   2. In the relationship between children and parents, 6:1-4.
   3. In the relationship between slave and master, 6:5-9.

G. A walk in the 'armor of God' against the powers of Satan, 6:10-18.

H. Conclusion (Paul's need of their intercession, word of Tychicus' coming, benediction), 6:19-24.

E. The Dominant Themes of the Letter
It has been often observed that, if the letter to the Colossians is his letter about Christ the Head of the church, Paul's circular letter to the 'Ephesians' (possibly to the Laodiceans, see Col. 4:16) is his letter about the church the Body of Christ. Paul elaborates upon the great wealth which members of the body of Christ possess and upon the only walk which will please God and commend the gospel to the world.

Philippians

A. The Letter's Place of Origin

That Paul was in prison at the time of writing is clear from Philippians 1:7, 13, 16. That this imprisonment was his Roman imprisonment seems virtually certain from his references in 1:13 to 'the whole palace guard' (ὅλῳ τῷ πραιτωρίῳ) and in 4:22 to 'Caesar's household' (τῆς Καίσαρος οἰκίας).

B. The Date of the Letter

Probably toward the end of his Roman imprisonment, around A.D. 62, since sufficient time would have had to elapse

(1) for the Philippian church to learn that Paul was in Rome and to gather a gift to send to him by Epaphroditus (2:25; 4:14, 18),

(2) for Epaphroditus to have labored for Paul so untiringly while in Rome that he became seriously ill (2:27, 29),

(3) for news of his serious illness to get back to the Philippian church (2:26), and

(4) for news of their concern for him to get back to Epaphroditus (2:26).

Furthermore, as we noted earlier, Paul seems to be willing to entertain the idea that he might not be acquitted in his trial (Phil 1:20). This suggests that the trial was in progress and nearing the moment of resolution one way or the other, which in turn suggests that the letter was written toward the end of this imprisonment period.

C. The Occasion of the Letter

Since Paul felt it necessary to send Epaphroditus back to Philippi and thus a trusted courier was ready at hand who could carry a letter for him, Paul took the opportunity to write the Philippian Christians (1) to thank them for their gifts to him (4:10-18), (2) to reassure them concerning his circumstances in prison (1:12-26), (3) to encourage them to remain steadfast in the face of opposition (1:27-30), (4) to give general instructions about Christian living (2:1-18), (5) to warn them once again about the Judaizers (3:1-21), (6) to urge reconciliation between Euodia and Syntyche (4:2-3), and (7) to encourage the church to rejoice with him in all things (4:4).[32]

D. The Content of the Letter[33]

I. INTRODUCTION, 1:1-11.

A. Salutation, 1:1-2.

B. Thanksgiving for the Philippians' 'partnership in the gospel', 1:3-8.

C. Prayer that their love, demonstrated by their gift, may increase, 1:9-11.

II. GOOD NEWS FROM PRISON, 1:12-26.

A. His trial—vindication of his contention that he is not what his accusers have charged, a disturber of the Roman peace, but what he himself has always maintained, merely a 'prisoner for Christ', 1:12-13.

B. The outcome of his trial—the emboldening of his brethren to speak the word of Christ more fearlessly, and in this Paul rejoices, even though some of them are motivated by selfish and partisan zeal, 1:14-18.

C. His chief concern—that whatever should befall him, Christ will be exalted, whether by his life or by his death, 1:19-26. (His own desire is to depart and to be with Christ forever. But he will gladly remain in the service of his Lord on earth, so he looks forward to his release and reunion with the church in Philippi.)

---

32. For additional insights into the situation behind Paul's letter to the Philippians, see Gordon D. Fee, *Paul's Letter to the Philippians* (The New International Commentary on the New Testament; Grand Rapids: Eerdmans, 1995); Gerald F. Hawthorne, *Philippians* (Word Biblical Commentary 43; Waco: Word, 1983) and 'Philippians, Letter to the,' *Dictionary of Paul and His Letters*, 707-13; R. P. Martin, *The Epistle of Paul to the Philippians* (Tyndale New Testament Commentary; Grand Rapids: Eerdmans, 1959), *Philippians* (New Century Bible; Grand Rapids: Eerdmans, 1976), and *Carmen Christi: Philippians 2. 5-11 in Recent Interpretation and in the Setting of Early Christian Worship* (Grand Rapids: Eerdmans, 1983); P. T. O'Brien, *The Epistle to the Philippians* (Grand Rapids: Eerdmans, 1991); and N. T. Wright, 'Harpagmos and the Meaning of Philippians ii.5-11' in *Journal of Theological Studies* 37 (Oct 1986), 321-52.

33. I have adapted the following outline, with minor variations, from Franzmann, *The Word of the Lord Grows*, 139-44.

Paul's Journey to Caesarea and to Rome

III. ADMONITION, 1:27-2:18. ('Let your manner of life be worthy of the gospel of Christ.')

A. In unity of spirit, 1:27-2:2.

B. In the humility and self-abasement that make true unity possible, even such humility and self-abasement as characterized 'Christ Jesus' himself, 2:3-11.

C. In their attitude as obedient children of God 'shining like stars in the universe and holding out [or, onto] the word of life', 2:12-18.

IV. PAUL'S PLANS ON THE PHILIPPIANS' BEHALF, 2:19-30.

A. His plan to send Timothy to bring back word from them, 2:19-23.

B. His hope to come himself to them soon, 2:24.

C. His plan to send Epaphroditus, no longer ill, back to them, 2:25-30.

V. APOSTOLIC WARNINGS TO 'STAND FIRM IN THE LORD', 3:1-4:1.

A. Against his old and persistent enemies, the Judaizers, who boast in the flesh, 3:1-11.

B. To follow his example and press on toward maturity and perfection, 3:12-17.

C. Against the enemies of the cross of Christ who would make this world their home (their own citizenship is in heaven, from whence they await the Savior who will transform them to his likeness), 3:18-4:1.

VI. CONCLUDING ADMONITIONS, 4:2-9.

A. Settle your quarrels, 4:2-3.

B. Rejoice in the Lord, whose advent is near; and carry all of your burdens to God in prayer, 4:4-7.

C. Fill your hearts and minds only with that which is true, honorable, just, pure, lovely, admirable, excellent and praiseworthy; emulate Paul's life, 4:8-9.

VII. THANKS FOR THEIR GIFT, 4:10-20.

A. His joy over their concern for him, 4:10.

B. His contentment in whatever situation he finds himself, 4:11-13.

C. His deep appreciation for their gift, 4:14-18.

D. His promise of God's provision for them, 4:19-20.

VIII. FINAL GREETINGS AND BENEDICTION, 4:21-23.

E. The Dominant Theme of the Letter

Joy in the Lord under all circumstances (see 1:4, 18 [twice], 25; 2:2, 17 [twice], 18 [twice], 28, 29; 3:1; 4:1, 4 [twice], 10. The idea of 'exulting' in the Lord also occurs in 1:26; 2:16; 3:3.

The Outcome of Paul's First Imprisonment

During Paul's time of enforced retirement he doubtless spent large periods of time in prayer and reflection, from which came his so-called Prison Letters. The very fact that he did have such an opportunity may help explain their more tempered style and orderliness. Moreover, as Merrill Tenney observes:

> [Paul's] appeal to Caesar brought Christianity directly to the attention of the Roman government and compelled the civil authorities to pass upon its legality. If it was to be allowed as a *religio licita*, a permitted cult, the persecution of it would be illegal, and its security would be assured. If, on the other hand, it were adjudged to be a *religio illicita*, a forbidden cult, then the ensuing persecution would only advertise it and offer an opportunity for a demonstration of its power...[Either way, the church] was now ready for even greater advances in missionary expansion.[34]

---

34. Merrill C. Tenney, *New Testament Survey* (Grand Rapids: Eerdmans, 1961), 328.

CHAPTER ELEVEN

PAUL'S RELEASE FROM PRISON, HIS 'FIFTH MISSIONARY JOURNEY', HIS SECOND ROMAN IMPRISONMENT, THE LETTER TO THE HEBREWS, THE PASTORAL LETTERS, AND HIS MARTYRDOM

> Yea, thro' life, death, thro' sorrow and thro' sinning
> He shall suffice me, for He hath sufficed:
> Christ is the end, for Christ was the beginning,
> Christ the beginning, for the end is Christ!
> – From 'Saint Paul,' Frederic W. H. Myers

> Servant of God, well done! Well has thou fought
> The better fight, who single hast maintained
> Against revolted multitudes the cause
> Of truth – in word mightier than they in arms.
> – John Milton

Historical Background (A.D. 62-65, possibly as late as A.D. 67)

Paul's three Pastoral Letters and his Letter to the Hebrews fall outside the historical province of Acts. Therefore we will have to reconstruct Paul's history from the end of Acts to his martyrdom entirely from hints in these letters themselves which represent him as traveling freely with Timothy to Ephesus (1 Tim 1:3), with Titus to and in Crete (Tit 1:5), apparently by himself in Macedonia (1 Tim 1:3), by himself at Troas (2 Tim 4:13), with Trophimus at Miletus (2 Tim 4:20), with Erastus, the city official, at Corinth (2 Tim 4:20), by himself at Nicopolis (Tit 3:12), and again in Rome with Onesiphorus and Luke (Heb 13:24; 2 Tim 1:16-17). The following representation is a possible reconstruction, but only that, of what transpired after the conclusion of Luke's Acts.

After two years of imprisonment, either Paul's accusers failed to appear or he was exonerated in his trial from any and all wrongdoing against Caesar. In either case, it is virtually certain that Paul was released from prison around A.D. 62, since there is no evidence that Paul's Acts 28 imprisonment terminated in his martyrdom. Bruce notes: '...if Paul's two years' detention was followed immediately by his conviction and execution, Luke's failure to mention it is very strange.'[1] It is therefore almost certain that very soon after his release from house arrest he left Rome on what we may regard as his fifth missionary journey.

Whether Paul traveled to Spain after his release is uncertain. While he clearly expressed such an intention in Romans 15:28,[2] it is a fact that in neither his Prison Letters nor his Pastoral Letters does he say anything about having accomplished such an undertaking. Moreover, the Spanish church has no tradition that traces its origin to Paul's missionary labors. On the other hand, Clement's letter to the Romans (5:1-7) written around A.D. 96, seems to suggest such a trip:

> Paul, on account of jealousy and strife, showed the way to the prize of endurance; seven times he wore fetters, he was exiled, he was stoned, he was a herald both in the east and in the west, he gained the noble renown of his faith, he taught righteousness through the whole world and, *having reached the limits* [τέρμα, 'farthest limits'] *of the west*, he bore testimony before the rulers, and so departed from the world and was taken up into the holy place – the greatest example of endurance (emphasis supplied).[3]

The Muratorian Canon written around A.D. 175, speaks of 'Paul's journey when he set out from Rome for Spain'. And the apocryphal *Acts of Peter* written around A.D. 180-200 speaks of Paul's departure from Italy by sea for Spain. No ancient source positively states that he did not go. If he did go, quite likely he went to Spain shortly after his release from prison, did some mission work there, and then returned to strengthen the churches in Asia.

---

1. F. F. Bruce, *Paul, Apostle of the Heart Set Free* (Grand Rapids: Eerdmans, 1996 reprint), 376.
2. While it is true that as far as we know for certain Paul's missionary efforts covered only the northeastern arc of the Mediterranean world, J. Knox argues in his article, 'Romans 15:14-33 and Paul's Conception of His Apostolic Ministry' in *Journal of Biblical Literature* 83 (1964), that Paul's choice of words in surveying his mission in Romans 15:19 (see his κύκλῳ, 'in a circle', 'circularly') hints that his plan at that time was much larger, namely, to proceed after missionarizing Spain in circuit right around the entire Roman Empire which included North Africa and Egypt. The lexical hint here is rather slim at best.
3. See Bruce's discussion of Clement's statement in *Paul*, 446-48.

In Philemon 22 and Philippians 2:24 Paul had indicated that he intended to visit the churches in Asia and Macedonia. The Pastoral Letters suggest that he may have done this, traveling first to the island of Crete where he with Titus carried on some missionary activities for a time. He then traveled farther east, leaving Titus in Crete to consolidate and to organize the church there (Titus 1:5). In his later letter to Titus Paul instructed Titus to join him in Nicopolis (probably the Nicopolis in Epirus) for the winter (Titus 3:12). Paul's only visit in the book of Acts to Crete was when, under Roman arrest, he was being transferred from Caesarea to Rome (Acts 27:7-8). Titus was not with him on that occasion. And Nicopolis is not mentioned in Acts at all. It seems best then to place this visit to Crete sometime after his first imprisonment in Rome.

According to Paul's statement in 1 Timothy 1:3, he seems to have returned with Timothy to Ephesus for a time (where he left Timothy) and journeyed on to Macedonia where he apparently writes 1 Timothy. On only one occasion in the book of Acts (Acts 20:1) did Paul go from Ephesus to Macedonia, but on that occasion he had sent Timothy ahead of him (Acts 19:22); he did not leave him there. So again it seems best to place this visit to Ephesus after his first imprisonment.

Apparently Aquila and Priscilla had also returned to Ephesus, for Paul later requested Timothy there in Ephesus to greet his two friends for him (2 Tim 4:19). He also wrote Titus either from Macedonia or while he was en route from Macedonia to Nicopolis (in Epirus?), at which time he instructed Titus to join him there (3:12).

Then sometime between the writing of Titus and 2 Timothy, Paul visited Troas alone, Corinth (staying with Erastus), and Miletus (with Trophimus) (2 Tim 4:13, 20). Such movements are hard to fit into Paul's movements in Acts since, while it is true that he visited Corinth, Troas and Miletus in that order on the last leg of his third journey (Acts 20:2-3, 5, 15), his comments in 2 Timothy suggest that the visits mentioned there were in the recent past, not some four or five years before, that is, the period of time encompassing his last visit to Jerusalem, his two year imprisonment at Caesarea, and his two year imprisonment in Rome. And he did not stop at these places on his trip to Rome.

Paul apparently was then at some unknown place arrested again and sent back to Rome for a second period of incarceration, the conditions of this second period of imprisonment being so different from the former period that Onesiphorus who had come from Ephesus had to search hard to find him in Rome (2 Tim 1:16-17), Luke alone being with Paul (4:11).

We can only speculate about the specific charges brought against him, but most likely they included the two charges of propagating a new and illicit religion (*religio nova et illicita*) and of conspiring with the Roman Christians before he had departed from Rome after his release from house arrest and inciting them to their falsely alleged act of torching Rome in A.D. 64.[4] Though Paul suggests that he had successfully defended himself against the first charge, whatever it was (2 Tim 4:16-17), he himself saw little hope of full and final acquittal (2 Tim 4:6). From his Roman prison cell he wrote the Letter to the Hebrews to the Jewish church in Jerusalem, warning these Jewish Christians not to forsake their freedom from the law and the righteousness they had in Christ and return to the legalism of Judaism (see Acts 21:20-24), and 2 Timothy to his son in the faith in Ephesus. He requested Timothy to come to him quickly before winter (4:9, 21), urging him to pick up his cloak and his scrolls (Were these copies of his correspondence? Did they include the certificate proving his Roman citizenship?) which he had left with Carpus in Troas (4:13). Hebrews 13:23 suggests that Timothy did indeed arrive in Rome in time to visit and encourage the aged Paul before his trial and was himself temporarily detained but then released. This time Paul's trial concluded with the passing of a sentence of capital punishment against him, which punishment was doubtless speedily carried out.

Paul's martyrdom was accomplished by decapitation. Like his Savior he was executed 'outside the city walls' at Tre Fontane near the third milestone on the Ostian Way.[5] There the executioner's sword ended his long course of sufferings and released his heroic spirit from his tired enfeebled body and into the heavenly presence of the Savior whom he had served so faithfully and for so long a time. Some friends took his scarred and decapitated corpse and head and buried them.

Having traced Paul's life and travels for several chapters now, I hope that the reader feels with me that the church lost that day its greatest apostolic advocate for the uniqueness of the Christian faith

---

4. So W. J. Conybeare and J. S. Howson, *The Life and Epistles of St. Paul* (Grand Rapids: Eerdmans, 1971 reprint), 767-70, 81.

5. Bruce, *Paul*, 450-51.

with its liberating, law-free gospel, and that we lost a genuine personal friend that day on the Ostian Way. I suspect that we feel a real sense of sadness that it had to end this way. But we could have almost predicted Paul's end, given the conditions of the Empire and the growing hatred of Christians generally in Rome and of Paul personally. Nor must we second-guess divine Providence which is always good and wise. Paul, of course, would remind us that that day was his coronation day, for that day he entered into a state which was 'better by far' than this present one, one that was only positive 'gain' (Phil 1:21, 23), where he was 'made perfect in holiness' (*Westminster Shorter Catechism*, Question 37), and where he responded for the very first time to his Savior's sinless love for him with a sinless love of his own.

Before the end of the second century a monument was erected where he was said to have been buried, about a mile nearer the city on the same route. About A.D. 324 Emperor Constantine built a small basilica there which was replaced by a larger one near the end of the fourth century. That one burned in 1823 but was rebuilt and consecrated by Pope Pius IX in 1854 as the Basilica of St. Paul-Without-the-Walls.

During the excavations necessary for the erection of the present basilica two slabs were discovered bearing together the inscription *PAULO APOSTOLO MART* ('To Paul, apostle and martyr') and dating to the fourth century A.D. Paul would probably have approved of that simple epitaph if he would have been permitted to add: 'But to Christ alone be the glory forever and ever. Amen.'

Since it is difficult to believe that Paul would have urged Timothy to come to him during the great Neronian persecution in A.D. 64, it is likely that he was martyred either before it, around A.D. 63, or more likely after it, around A.D. 65 (perhaps even as late as A.D. 67, the last year of Nero's reign).

Paul's First Two Pastoral Letters

The name 'Pastoral' has been applied to these letters since the eighteenth century (Thomas Aquinas applied the term to 1 Timothy alone as early as the thirteen century), intending to underscore the truth that they were directed to 'pastors' or shepherds of the church, and dealt with the office of the pastor. These letters present Christ as the Administrator of his church, demanding through his apostle that his orders and the traditions established by his apostles be obeyed and passed on. Franzmann writes:

> [The designation, 'Pastoral',] is more properly applied to the First Letter to Timothy and the Letter to Titus than to the Second Letter to Timothy. The Second Letter to Timothy has pastoral elements in it, but is basically a personal letter and in a class by itself. The First Letter to Timothy and the Letter to Titus are official letters, covering the whole range of church life: offices in the church, the worship life of the church, the care of souls, and especially the combating of error which threatens the health of the church. The official character of the letters is seen in their form; the usual Pauline thanksgiving at the beginning is replaced by words which indicate that the content of the letter is a repetition in writing of oral instructions already given – a common feature in official letters (1 Tim. 1:3; Titus 1:5). The personal communications usually found at the close of Pauline letters are either absent entirely, as in the Letter to Timothy, or kept extremely brief, as in the Letter to Titus. The style of the letters likewise reflects this "official" character: We have here terse and pointed directions delivered with apostolic authority; the doctrinal background and basis of the directions are given in pointed and pregnant formulations, designed to be readily grasped and remembered; some of them are 'sure sayings,' probably already familiar to the churches [1 Tim. 1:15; 3:1; 4:9; Titus 3:8].[6]

First Timothy

A. The Letter's Place of Origin
Probably somewhere in Macedonia.

B. The Date of the Letter
Sometime after Paul's arrival in Macedonia and before his second arrest, probably A.D. 62 or 63.

C. The Occasion of the Letter
Before we consider the situation which led to the writing of this letter, a summary word of reminder is in order about Timothy, the recipient of this and Paul's last letter. Timothy, as we noted in a previous chapter, was half Jew and half Greek by birth (Acts 16:1) but wholly Jewish by rearing. He had been taught the Old Testament from childhood (2 Tim 3:15; see 1:5). New Testament prophetic voices

---

6. Martin Franzmann, *The Word of the Lord Grows* (St. Louis: Concordia, 1961), 151.

had assigned him the 'good warfare' in which he was engaged (1 Tim 1:18), and God had given him the requisite gift to wage it (4:14). He had been Paul's almost constant companion for about a dozen years, from the very beginning of Paul's second missionary journey in A.D. 50. The apostolic 'pattern of sound words' (2 Tim 1:13) had become part of his personal make-up, and the example of the apostle had been constantly before him for many years (2 Tim 3:10-14). Paul, moreover, had entrusted him as his emissary on several early occasions, though never for so extended and difficult a mission as the one he was executing in Ephesus at the time of the writing of 1 Timothy: when Paul was prevented from returning to Thessalonica from Athens on his second journey, he dispatched Timothy to the church there to strengthen and encourage the believers in their faith (1 Thess 3:1-2); when the Corinthians were succumbing to the heady Gnosticism of the 'Christ party', Paul sent Timothy to Corinth to remind them of the apostle's 'way of life in Christ Jesus' (1 Cor 4:17; 16:10); when Paul could not visit the Philippians during his first Roman imprisonment, he sent Timothy there as the bearer of his letter to them, paying him in that letter this high compliment: 'I have no one like him, who takes a genuine interest in your welfare. For everyone looks out for his own interests, not those of Jesus Christ. But you know that Timothy has proven himself, because as a son with a father he has served with me in the work of the gospel' (Phil 2:20-22). Surely Timothy is a man we should seek to emulate!

Now a word about the situation which occasioned and made necessary the letter itself. It seems rather clear that Timothy was facing an early stage of that Gnosticism which was to become more fully developed in the second century. The gnostic teaching at Ephesus apparently held

(1) that what is nonmaterial is of itself good and what is material is of itself evil,

(2) that the world accordingly is not to be viewed as God's good creation but rather as alien matter hostile to God,

(3) that man's plight is not moral rebellion against God but the entanglement of his soul within the world of matter,

(4) that redemption consists in being liberated from the material world in which he dwells, this liberation to be achieved through the acquisition of an esoteric knowledge and bodily asceticism (abstinence from such things as foods and marriage),

(5) that the Old Testament must be interpreted through the use of allegorizing 'myths and endless genealogies' (1:4) and

(6) that there can be no such thing as a real incarnation of the Son of God, for how can the divine, which is spiritual, enter into union with matter, which is in and of itself evil?

What was the remedy for all this? Franzmann insightfully summarizes Paul's instructions to Timothy this way:

(1) to the demonic denial of God the Creator and the rejection of his good gifts Timothy must oppose the glorious gospel of the blessed God who 'gives life to all things' (6:13) and who 'richly provides us with everything for our enjoyment' (6:17), and whose creation is 'good, and nothing is to be rejected if it is received with thanksgiving, because it is consecrated by the word of God and prayer' (4:4);

(2) to 'godless myths and old wives' tales' he must oppose the grateful adoration of the Creator (4:7);

(3) to the gnostic misuse of the law he must oppose its right and lawful use and let the sinner hear the fearful verdict of God in order that he may also hear the divine acquittal in the gospel (1:8-11);

(4) to the rarefied and unreal Christ of gnostic speculation he must oppose 'the man Christ Jesus' (2:5), who really entered human history in the flesh (3:16) under Pontius Pilate (6:13), and who died a real substitutionary death for others (2:6);

(5) to gnostic self-redemption by means of an esoteric knowledge and ascetic self-manipulation he must oppose a real redemption from sin as the sole act of Christ who came into the world, not to impart a higher 'knowledge' to the 'initiate', but to save sinners (1:15);

(6) to the narrow sectarian pride of Gnosticism he must oppose the gospel of God's all-embracing grace (2:1, 4); and finally,

(7) to the imposing picture of the brilliant, speculative, disputatious and mercenary gnostic teachers he must oppose the picture of the true teacher. Indeed, he himself must be that picture, holding faith and a good conscience (1:19), being nourished on 'the words of faith and of the good doctrine' which he has been following (6:3-12). He must train himself, like an athlete, in godliness (4:6-7). And he must train faithful men to do the same, and to meet the qualifications of true leadership (3:1-13).[7]

Accordingly, Paul wrote Timothy this letter in which he sums up one more time the oral instructions which he had already given him

---

7. Franzmann, *The Word of the Lord Grows*, 154.

(1:3). By this letter he would also give to Timothy's work the authoritative sanction of the apostle himself. Paul in effect here tells the church at Ephesus what he had once told the Corinthians: 'He is doing the work of the Lord, as I am. So let no one despise him' (1 Cor 16:10-11).[8]

D. The Content of the Letter[9]

I. SALUTATION, 1:1-2.

II. FIRST ATTACK: THE 'GNOSTIC' HERESY CORRUPTS THE TEACHING OF THE CHURCH, BOTH LAW [1:7] AND GOSPEL [1:4-5, 11], 1:3-3:16.

A. Timothy is to oppose this corrupting influence, 1:3-7.
   1. By recognizing the true function of the Law, 1:8-11.

   2. By seeing in the gospel of pure grace the only power that can recreate rebellious man and make him a doer of the will of God, as Paul's own example has demonstrated, 1:12-17.

   3. By waging this good warfare in the conviction that God himself has called him to this task through the utterance of certain New Testament prophets, 1:18-20.

B. Timothy is to oppose this corrupting influence
   1. By so ordering the church's prayers that they are a recognition of government as a good and wholesome ordinance of God and an expression of the all-embracing grace of God, 2:1-7.

   2. By so ordering the church's worship (1) that its prayers may be said in the peaceable and forgiving spirit of the Fifth Petition

---

8. For additional insight into the situation behind Paul's first letter to Timothy, see Gordon D. Fee, *The Pastoral Epistles* (Peabody, Massachusetts: Hendricksen, 1988); Donald Guthrie, *The Pastoral Epistles* (Tyndale New Testament Commentary; 2nd edition; Grand Rapids: Eerdmans, 1990); J. N. D. Kelly, *The Pastoral Epistles* (London: Black, 1963); George W. Knight III, *The Pastoral Epistles* (The New International Greek Testament Commentary; Grand Rapids: Eerdmans, 1992); Walter Lock, *A Critical and Exegetical Commentary on the Pastoral Letters* (International Critical Commentary; Edinburgh: T. & T. Clark, 1924).

9. I have adapted the following outline, with minor variations, from Franzmann, *The Word of the Lord Grows*, 156-59.

of the Lord's Prayer, 2:8, and (2) that the conduct of the worshipers may be a recognition of the sanctity of the position which God the Creator has assigned to women, 2:9-15.

3. By providing for the church elders and deacons whose conduct, example, and influence shall be the living embodiment of the fact that the church is the 'pillar and ground of the truth'—the truth, namely, of the gospel which proclaims the Christ as the Savior of men by a real incarnation which united him to flesh, to the nations, to the world, 3:1-16.

III. SECOND ATTACK: THE 'GNOSTIC' HERESY CORRUPTS THE DAILY LIFE OF THE CHURCH, 4:1-6:2. Timothy is to oppose this corrupting influence

A. By a sober, scrupulous, and strenuous performance of his duties: by avoiding the godless and silly myths which obscure the good doctrine of the gospel, by training himself in godliness, by fixing his hope in the living God who is the only Savior of men, by using to the full the gift which God has given him—thus setting an 'example in speech and conduct, in love, in faith, in purity', 4:6-16.

B. By his treatment of the various groups and classes in the church, 5:1-6:2.

1. Elderly and the young as his own 'kin', 5:1-2.

2. Widows with respect and realism, 5:3-16.

3. Elders with honor, and those who fail in their duties with soberness, impartiality, and conscientiousness, 5:17-25.

4. Christian slaves to be instructed that their relationship with their masters is not abrogated by their freedom in Christ, but is rather hallowed by that freedom so that they are to serve all the better for serving freely, 6:1-2.

IV. THIRD ATTACK: 'GNOSTIC' FALSE TEACHING CORRUPTS ITS TEACHERS, WHO HAVE BROKEN WITH 'SOUND

Paul's Release, Fifth Journey, and Second Imprisonment

WORDS' AND HAVE BECOME CONCEITED, CONTENTIOUS, AND MERCINARY, 6:3-10. Timothy is to oppose their influence, 6:11-21,

A. By being a true 'man of God', pursuing true virtues and fighting the good fight of faith, laying hold on eternal life, 6:11-12.

B. By keeping pure the 'commandment' he received at his baptism (or, at his ordination) until the Lord's return, 6:13-16.

C. By admonishing the rich to find their true riches in God, in good works, and in the life to come, 6:17-19.

D. By faithfully guarding the truth which had been entrusted to him, remembering that the key to the Christian life is not 'knowledge' but faith, 6:20-21.

E. The Dominant Themes of the Letter.
I. Opposition to false teaching;
II. The administration of the affairs of the church;
III. Timothy's personal conduct in his life and ministry.

* * * * *

Titus

A. The Letter's Place of Origin
Somewhere in Macedonia or en route to Nicopolis.

B. The Date of the Letter
Sometime after Paul's arrival in Macedonia and before his second arrest, probably around A.D. 63.

C. The Occasion of the Letter
Titus, the reader will recall, was the uncircumcised Greek Christian who had accompanied Paul and Barnabas on their 'famine relief visit' to Jerusalem (Gal 2:1, 3), and who later had rendered Paul invaluable service on his third journey when the relationship between Paul and the Corinthian church was strained to the breaking point (2 Cor 2:13;

7:6ff., 8:6, 17-18; 12:18), serving as the courier of both the 'stern letter' and our 2 Corinthians. As we noted above, at his departure from Crete Paul left Titus there to consolidate and organize the church in the face of a pronouncedly Judaizing kind of gnostic thought (Tit 1:14; 3:9). He wrote Titus this letter (1) to encourage him, (2) to aid him in combating the false teaching which threatened the health of the church, (3) to advise him in his task of organizing and edifying the church, and (4) to give Titus' presence and work in Crete the full sanction of his own apostolic authority (see Paul's salutation in 1:1-4 and his closing greeting in 3:15 ('Grace be with all of you [πάντων ὑμῶν].') which shows that the letter was intended for the ears of the whole church.[10]

D. The Content of the Letter[11]

I. SALUTATION, 1:1-4.

Titus' tasks in Crete were:

II. TO APPOINT ELDERS (Men of unimpeachable character, firmly grounded in sound doctrine, able to instruct the faithful and to confute the contradictor), 1:5-9.

III. TO EXPOSE THE PERNICIOUS TEACHING OF THOSE WHO PROFESS TO 'KNOW' GOD ('GNOSTIC' JUDAIZERS) BUT WHO DENY HIM BY THEIR DEEDS, 1:10-16.

IV. TO EDIFY THE CHURCH, 2:1–3:8.

A. By instructing men of all ages and classes, by word and by example, in that high conduct of life which the grace of God, manifested to all men in Christ, has made possible, 2:1-15.

B. By reminding believers to be obedient to governmental authority and to show all men that persuasive Christian courtesy which has been engendered in them by the 'goodness and lovingkindness of God our Savior', 3:1-7.

---

10. For additional insight into the situation behind Paul's letter to Titus, see the commentaries listed on p. 253, ft. 8.
11. I have adapted the following outline, with minor variations, from Franzmann, *The Word of the Lord Grows*, 160-61.

C. By impressing upon all who have come to faith that they have but one profession which they must pursue, namely, good works, 3:8.

V. TO EXCLUDE FROM THE CHURCH THOSE WHO PERSIST IN FALSE TEACHING AFTER THE SECOND ADMONITION, 3:9-11.

VI. PERSONAL INSTRUCTIONS AND GREETINGS, 3:12-15.

E. The Dominant Themes of the Letter.
I. Opposition to false teaching;
II. the administration of the affairs of the church;
III. Titus' personal conduct in his life and ministry.

* * * * *

Paul's Last Pastoral Letters: Hebrews and 2 Timothy

Hebrews

I. The theology of the letter

In order better to ascertain the possible author of this letter and to see if there is anything in it that Paul could *not* have written, I think it will be helpful if we begin by taking a look at the author's theology. I grant that for the Paul we have already surveyed we will see a rather 'original' characterization of Christ being developed here—Christ's cross work represented as the work of the high priest—but 'original' does not necessarily mean 'another' author. Stephen Neill has noted the originality that is present *throughout* Paul's writings:

> A great thinker, Paul can be and often is abominably difficult. But he is not intentionally difficult. *Again and again he is trying to say things that had never been said before* and for which he has no vocabulary to hand.... It often happens that when Paul is most difficult, he is also *most original*.[12]

We should bear in mind then that simply because something may be 'new' in something Paul writes, it must not on that account be adjudged as non-Pauline. Paul had to be original simply because there was little or no theological vocabulary ready at hand to frame some theological constructs which had never been framed before.

---

12. Stephen C. Neill, *Jesus Through Many Eyes: Introduction to the Theology of the New Testament* (Philadelphia: Fortress, 1976), 42.

A. The author's doctrine of God

There can be no question that the author's God, the 'Father of spirits' (12:9), is the God of the Old Testament. His God is the Creator of the world (1:2; 3:4; 4:3-4; 11:3) and of men (2:7). He executed his creative work through the agency of his Son (thus we may speak of the author's *Christological* cosmogony). Angels, whose function it is to worship and to serve God (1:6-7), belong to his God. His God spoke to the forefathers through the prophets (1:1), and has also spoken to us in 'these last days' (ἐσχάτου τῶν ἡμερῶν τούτων) in his Son (1:2). Thus there is continuity between the Old Testament and New Testament ages. The same God is the God of both ages: he speaks in both; he acts in both. He providentially sustains and governs all things (1:3; 6:3). He made a promise to Abraham and backed it with an oath (6:13); he came down on Mount Sinai (12:18-21); he was approached through the Aaronic priesthood and the Levitical ceremonies; he spoke through the prophets; he blessed the Old Testament saints (ch. 11); he has now sent his Son; and he is the Judge of all (12:23) (observe the sweep here of history). The author's God is thus the God of both general human history, creating and governing all things, and the God of 'holy history' (see again 1:1-2; 11).

The author's God being the God of both ages, it is not surprising to find him ascribing attributes to God which we learn about from the Old Testament. His God is 'the most high God' (7:1), 'the living God' (3:12; 9:14; 10:31), and a 'consuming fire' (12:29; see Deut 4:24; 9:3) into whose hands it is a fearsome thing to fall (10:31). His God cannot lie (6:18).

His God is the God of redemption and revelation (taught throughout the letter). As such, he is the God of the Abrahamic covenant and thus the God of promise (the author uses the word 'promise' fourteen times, more than any other New Testament writer, and in each instance refers to what *God* has promised). The salvation which we now have through Christ is the result of his gracious will to bless. He made salvific promises and and has fulfilled them in Christ.

The author is, of course, a 'principial trinitarian', making references to God the Father (*passim*), to Jesus as the divine Son (1:8, 10; 10:29), and to the Holy Spirit (10:15). The 'stuff' of trinitarianism is quite evident when God speaks to his Son and calls him God.

B. The author's doctrine of man

For the author of Hebrews, man is God's creature, made only a little lower than the angels, indeed, the crowning act of God's creative activity (2:7). But men have become sinful (12:3), live in a state of weakness in which they are incapable of saving themselves (4:15; 7:28), are *appointed* (ἀπόκειται) to die and then to face divine judgment (9:27), and are in need of 'great salvation' without which only condemnation awaits them (2:2-3).

The author devotes considerable attention to man's need. But as Donald Guthrie states: 'It is against the background of the levitical sacrificial system [which presupposes sin and guilt] that the superiority of Christ as high priest is seen, and therefore the Old Testament recognition of sin is taken over without discussion.'[13]

C. The author's doctrine of Christ

The Christ of Hebrews is arguably as fully and truly human as everywhere else in Scripture, including Paul: he shared our humanity (2:14), was made like his brothers in every way (2:17), was a descendant of Judah (7:14), who could sympathize with human weakness, having been tempted in every way like we are (2:18; 4:15), and who 'in the days of his flesh' offered up prayers and petitions with loud crying and tears (a reference to Gethsemane?) (5:7) as he 'learned obedience from the things which he suffered' (5:8). And he was finally put to death outside Jerusalem (13:12). All this points to a genuinely human life and death.

But the Christ of Hebrews is indisputably divine as well. While the usual New Testament designations of Christ may be found scattered throughout the letter—the simple 'Jesus' (2:9; 3:1; 6:20; 7:22; 10:19; 12:2, 24; 13:12), '[the] Christ' (3:6, 14; 5:5; 6:1; 9:11, 14, 24, 28; 11:26), 'Jesus Christ' (10:10; 13:8, 21), '[the] Lord' (1:10; 2:3; 7:14; perhaps 12:14; the first two occurrences of which clearly intended in the Yahwistic sense), 'Lord Jesus' (13:20), 'Jesus, the Son of God' (4:14)—the author's favorite title for Jesus, above all others, is '[the] Son' (1:2, 5 [twice], 8; 3:6; 5:5, 8; 7:28) or its fuller form '[the] Son of God' (4:14; 6:6; 7:3; 10:29). Indeed, it is as God's Son in the preeminent (divine) sense of that title that the author first introduces Jesus to his readers (1:2).

---

13. Donald Guthrie, *New Testament Theology* (Downers Grove, Ill.: InterVarsity, 1981), 213.

As God's 'Son' he is the highest and final form of revelation to men, and as God's 'Son' he is higher than the greatest representatives of God on earth, that is, the prophets of the Old Testament (1:1-2), higher even than Moses who in comparison was only a servant in God's house (3:5-6). Finally, his name as 'Son', the Bearer of which is represented as (1) the heir of all things, (2) God's cooperating Agent in the creation of the world, (3) the Radiance of God's glory, (4) the very Image of his nature, (5) the Sustainer of all things, (6) the Purifier from sin, and (7) the Lord (of Psalm 110:1) sitting at the right hand of the Majesty on high (1:2-3), is 'more excellent' even than that of the highest of creatures, that of 'angel' (1:4), whose bearers are only 'ministering spirits' (1:14), and whose duty it is to worship him (1:6).

As explications of the content of that superangelic 'more excellent name' of 'Son', and *not simply new titles or names* adduced in addition to that of 'Son', he is the 'God' (θεός) of Psalm 45:6-7 and 'the Lord' (κύριος), that is, the Yahweh, of Psalm 102:25-27. That is to say, when the author designates Christ as the 'Son', he intends to include within that title these other appellations.

When he wrote, 'To the Son, on the other hand, [God says], "Your throne, O God, will last for ever and ever" ' (1:8), the author of Hebrews, as did Thomas, Paul, Peter, and John, uses θεός as a Christological title. The controversy surrounding this verse is over whether ὁ θεός is to be construed as a nominative (if so, it may be a subject nominative: 'God is your throne for ever and ever', or a predicate nominative: 'Your throne is God for ever and ever') or a vocative, which would yield the translation given above. With the 'overwhelming majority of grammarians, commentators, authors of general studies, and English translations',[14] I believe that the author applies Psalm 45:6 to Jesus in such a way that he is addressed directly as God in the ontological sense of the word. This position requires (1) that ὁ θεός be interpreted as a vocative, and (2) that the theotic character ascribed to Jesus be understood in ontological and not functional terms.

That ὁ θεός is vocatival and not nominatival is apparent for the following reasons: first, the fact that the noun appears to be nominative in its inflected form means nothing. The so-called articular nominative

---

14. Murray J. Harris, 'The Translation and Significance of ὁ θεός in Hebrews 1:8-9,' *Tyndale Bulletin* 36 (1985): 146-48.

with vocative force is a well-established idiom in classical Greek, the Septuagint, and New Testament Greek.[15] The case of the noun in Hebrews 1:8 must be established then on other grounds than its case form.

Second, the word order in Hebrews 1:8 most naturally suggests that ὁ θεός is vocatival. A vocative immediately after 'Your throne' would be perfectly natural. But if ὁ θεός were intended as the subject nominative ('God is your throne'), which Nigel Turner regards as a 'grotesque interpretation',[16] it is more likely that ὁ θεός would have appeared before 'your throne'. If it were intended as a predicate nominative ('Your throne is God'), which Turner regards as 'only just conceivable',[17] it is more likely that ὁ θεός would have been written anarthrously, appearing either before 'your throne' or after 'for ever and ever'.

Third, in the LXX of Psalm 45, which the author is citing, the king is addressed by the vocative δυνατέ ('O Mighty One') in 45:4 and 45:6. This dual vocative heightens the probability, given the wordorder, that in the next verse ὁ θεός should be rendered 'O God'.

Fourth, although 'about' or 'concerning' is probably the more accurate translation of the preposition πρὸς in Hebrews 1:7 (given the cast of the following quotation), it is more likely that πρὸς introducing the quotation in verse 8 should be translated 'to' in light of the second-person character of the quotation itself and on the analogy of the formula (a verb of speaking followed by πρός) in Hebrews 1:13, 5:5, and 7:21. This would suggest that ὁ θεός is vocatival.

Fifth, the following quotation in Hebrews 1:10-12 (from Psalm 102:25-27) is connected by the simple καί to the quotation under discussion in verses 8-9, indicating that it too stands under the regimen of the words introducing verses 8-9. In the latter verses the Son is clearly addressed as κύριε ('O Lord'). These five textual and syntactical features clearly indicate that ὁ θεός should be construed

---

15. H. E. Dana and J. R. Mantey, *A Manual Grammar of the Greek New Testament* (New York: Macmillan, 1954 reprint of 1927 edition), 71, write: '...we agree with Robertson that the true situation...is not one case used for another, but one case ending serving for two cases. Wherever the idea of address is present, the case is vocative, regardless of the inflectional form (cf. R. 461).'
16. Nigel Turner, *Grammatical Insights Into the New Testament* (Edinburgh: T. & T. Clark, 1965), 461.
17. Nigel Turner, *A Grammar of New Testament Greek* (Edinburgh: T. & T. Clark, 1963), III, 34.

vocativally, meaning that the Son is addressed as 'God'. But what did he means by this address? Opinions run the gamut from Vincent Taylor's question-begging comment that 'nothing can be built upon this reference, for the author shares the same reluctance of the New Testament writers to speak explicitly of Christ as "God",'[18] to Oscar Cullmann's comment that 'the psalm is quoted here precisely for the sake of this address',[19] the chapter in which it occurs leading him to declare that 'Jesus' deity is more powerfully asserted in Hebrews than in any other New Testament writing, with the exception of the Gospel of John'.[20] What should we conclude? I would urge from the context of Hebrews 1 itself that the Son is addressed as God in the ontological sense. This may be seen from the fact that, as a 'Son-revelation', as the final and supreme speech of God to man (vs 2), he is the heir of all things and the Father's Agent in creating the universe. He *abides* (see the timeless ὤν in verse 3) as the 'perfect Radiance of God's glory' and the 'very Image of his nature' (vs 3). As God's Son, he is superior to the angels, such that it is appropriate that they be commanded to worship him (vs 6). He is the Yahweh and the Elohim of Psalm 102, who eternally existed before he created the heavens and earth (vs 10), and who remains eternally the same though the creation itself should perish (vss 11-12; see Heb 13:8). Because he is all these things, it is really adding nothing to what the author has said to understand him as describing the Son as God in the ontological sense in 1:8.

E. C. Wickham and others have suggested that if ὁ θεός is really ascribing ontological deity to the Son, the climax of the author's argument would come at verse 8 since nothing higher could be said about him. But, it is urged, since in fact the author goes on in verse 10 to describe the Son as κύριος (Lord), this further development of the Son's character becomes the climax, indicating that the former description cannot be construed ontologically. But this objection fails to apprehend the significance of the two terms. While θεός is indeed a term of exalted significance when used ascriptively of the true God, it speaks only of his divine essence. It is κύριος, coming to us out of the Old Testament citation here, that is God's personal name. In the

---

18. Vincent Taylor, *The Person of Christ in New Testament Teaching* (London: Macmillan, 1959), 96.
19. Oscar Cullmann, *The Christology of the New Testament*, translated by Shirley C. Guthrie and Charles A. M. Hall (London: SCM, 1959), 310.
20. Cullman, *Christology*, 305.

covenantal sense, it is the more sacred of the two! So actually, the author's argument, even though it ascribes ontological deity to the Son in 1:8, does not reach its climax until it ascribes the character of Yahweh himself to the Son, indicating by this ascriptive title that the Son is not only the Creator but the covenant God as well. The author truly can say nothing higher than this.

Two of the descriptive phrases above deserve further comment. In addition to ascribing to him the divine work in eternity of creating the world, and the divine work in time of sustaining the universe, the author describes the Son as 'the Radiance [ἀπαύγασμα] of God's glory [δόξα]' and 'the very Image [χαρακτήρ] of his nature [ὑπόστασις]'. In the former expression, with God's δόξα denoting his nature under the imagery of its splendor, as his ἀπαύγασμα (from ἀπαυγάσειν, 'to emit brightness'), one has to do in Jesus with the personal 'outshining' of God's divine glory as the radiance shining forth from the source of light. In the latter expression, with God's ὑπόστασις denoting his 'whole nature, with all its attributes' (Warfield), his 'real essence' (F. F. Bruce), or his 'very essence' (P.E. Hughes), as his χαρακτήρ (from χαράσσειν, 'to engrave, to inscribe, to stamp'), one has to do in Jesus with God's 'very image' by which is meant 'a correspondence as close as that which an impression gives back to a seal' (Warfield), his 'exact representation and embodiment' (Bruce), or the 'very stamp' (Hughes) of God. Clearly, such exalted descriptions intend the ascription of divine status to the Son. Accordingly, it is altogether likely, inasmuch as the Son is the Yahweh of Psalm 102:25-27 who remains forever the same (1:11-12) and who in the person of Jesus Christ is 'the same yesterday, today, and forever' (13:8), that he is the subject of the doxology in 13:21, to whom eternal glory is ascribed. Certainly, the collocation of the relative pronoun and the title 'Jesus Christ' in 13:21 favors such an interpretation.

Whatever the case may be with regard to the rather minor matter of the subject of the concluding doxology of the letter, there can be no doubt in view of the content of his first chapter that for the author of Hebrews all that God is as God, that Jesus is, as the Son, from, to, and throughout eternity.

This conclusion has not gone unchallenged. J. A. T. Robinson, for example, has urged that all of these exalted descriptions are true of Jesus as 'God's Man', with only his functional relationship to

God as God's 'son' being 'decisively different' from the relationship that obtains between God and other men.[21] He adduces in support of his view (1) the supposed derivation of the descriptions of 1:3 from Philo and Wisdom 7:26 and (2) what he terms 'adoptionist' terminology in 1:2, 4, 9, 13; 2:9, 10, 12f, 16; 3:2f; 5:1-6, 8, 10; 7:28 (pp. 156-61). James D. G. Dunn also insists (1) that 'there is more "adoptionist" language in Hebrews than in any other New Testament document',[22] and (2) that 'the element of Hebrews' christology which we think of as ascribing pre-existence to the Son of God has to be set within the context of his indebtedness to Platonic idealism and interpreted with cross-reference to the way in which Philo treats the Logos', that is to say, 'what we may have to accept is that the author of Hebrews ultimately has in mind an *ideal* pre-existence [of the Son], the existence of an idea [of the Son] in the mind of God,'[23] and this within a strict monotheism in which the concept of pre-existent Sonship is 'perhaps more of an idea and purpose in the mind of God than of a personal divine being'.[24] In sum, for Dunn, the Christology of Hebrews views Jesus in terms of Wisdom language, so that 'the thought of pre-existence is present, but in terms of Wisdom Christology it is the act and power of God which properly speaking is what pre-exists; Christ is not so much the pre-existent act and power of God as its eschatological embodiment'.[25]

I concur with I. Howard Marshall's assessment that this impersonal construction of the author's doctrine of divine Sonship is 'very alien to the biblical understanding of God as personal, quite apart from imposing a very artificial interpretation upon the biblical text'.[26] For while it is true that the Son 'was *appointed*' heir of all things (1:2), and 'sat down on the right hand of the Majesty on high, having *become* by so much better than the angels, as he has *inherited* a more excellent name than they' (1:4), this need not be 'adoptionist' language, but rather, language that envisions the glory which became his following upon the conclusion of his humiliation in his role as Messiah and Mediator (see Heb 2:9; Ps 2:8). Philip Edgecombe Hughes concurs

---

21. J. A. T. Robinson, *The Human Face of God* (London: SCM, 1973), 156.
22. James D. G. Dunn, *Christology in the Making: A New Testament Inquiry into the Origins of the Doctrine of the Incarnation* (London: SCM, 1980), 52.
23. Dunn, *Christology*, 54.
24. Dunn, *Christology*, 56.
25. Dunn, *Christology*, 209.
26. I. Howard Marshall, 'Incarnational Christology in the New Testament,' *Christ the Lord*, edited by Harold H. Rowdon (Leicester: Inter-Varsity, 1982), 11.

that this is how the so-called 'adoptionist' language should be construed, writing on 1:4:

> It is true, of course, that by virtue of his eternal Sonship he has an eternal inheritance and possesses a name which is eternally supreme – *the name* signifying, particularly for the Hebrew mind, the essential character of a person in himself and in his work. But our author at this point is speaking of something other than this: the Son who for our redemption humbled himself for a little while to a position lower than the angels has by his ensuing exaltation *become* superior to the angels (2:9 below), and in doing so has achieved and retains the inheritance of a name which is *more excellent than theirs*.[27]

And if he is said to have 'inherited' the name of 'Son', as Bruce declares,

> this does not mean that the name was not his before his exaltation. It was clearly his in the days of his humiliation: 'Son though he was, he learned obedience by the things which he suffered' (Ch. 5:8). It was his, indeed, ages before his incarnation: this is the plain indication of the statement in Ch. 1:2 that God has spoken to us 'in his Son, – through whom also he made the worlds'.[28]

---

27. Phillip Edgecumbe Hughes, *A Commentary on the Epistle to the Hebrews* (Grand Rapids: Eerdmans, 1977), 50.
28. F. F. Bruce, *Commentary on the Epistle to the Hebrews* (Grand Rapids: Eerdmans, 1964), 8. I have pointed out in my *A New Systematic Theology of the Christian Faith* (Nashville: Thomas Nelson, 1998), 580-81, that for Paul it was 'the Lord of Glory' (ὁ κύριος τῆς δόξης), this expression meaning 'the Lord to whom glory belongs as his native right', who was also just both 'God over all' (Rom 9:5) and 'our great God' (Tit 2:13), who was crucified for us (1 Cor 2:8). As God's Son, then, Jesus continued, as he always had done, to uphold all things by the word of his power (Heb 1:3) and to exercise the powers and lordly rights which were intrinsically his as the Second Person of the Godhead (see John Calvin, *Institutes of the Christian Religion*, II.13.4). Consequently, when the apostles tell us that Jesus was 'appointed' Lord or was 'exalted' and 'given' authority and the title of 'Lord' at his ascension, or as here that he 'inherited' the name of 'Son', it is necessary that we understand that these things were said of him in his *mediatorial* role as the divine-human Messiah.
It is appropriate to say these things about him but only because he, 'the Son', who is intrinsically and essentially 'rich', who is 'Lord' by right of nature, had *first* deigned to take into union with himself our 'flesh', becoming thereby 'poor' (2 Cor 8:9). It was as the divine-human Messiah, then, that he 'acquired' or 'was given' at his ascension *de facto* authority to exercise mediatorial dominion. It was not then the exaltation but the prior humiliation which was the 'strange experience' (Warfield) for the Son as God. Conversely, it was not the humiliation but the exaltation which was the 'strange experience' to the Son *as the divine-human Messiah*. If we are to take history seriously as the New Testament does we must say this. We must be willing to say that in a certain sense his exaltation entailed for the Son an experience which had not been his before. This 'new experience' was universal dominion, not as God, of course, but as the divine-human Messiah and as the divine-human Mediator

All of the so-called 'adoptionist' language of Robinson and Dunn can be similarly explained; none of it requires that the Son's personal preexistence has to be forfeited in deference to an ideal, impersonal preexistence in the mind of God. And even if the author's language is that of Philo and the Book of Wisdom, again as Bruce affirms,

> his meaning goes beyond theirs. For them the Logos or Wisdom is the personification of a divine attribute; for him the language is descriptive of a man who had lived and died in Palestine a few decades previously, but who nonetheless was the eternal Son and supreme revelation of God.[29]

Viewed, then, from the Scriptural perspective of the *humiliatio-exaltatio* paradigm, as they rightly should be, the supposed 'adoptionist' passages in Hebrews are not 'adoptionist' at all. Accordingly, the full unabridged deity of the Son is secure and intact throughout the letter to the Hebrews.

D. The author's doctrine of salvation

The author develops his original vision of our 'so great salvation' (2:3) around his portrayal of Christ as our priest or high priest – a unique and illuminating way to consider the saving work of Christ. Morris points out that the author of Hebrews employs the term 'priest' fourteen times (no other New Testament author has it more often than Luke's five) and the term 'high priest' seventeen times (a term found elsewhere only in the Gospels and Acts – and there in reference to the contemporary Jewish holders of the office) for Christ, putting no great difference of meaning between the two.[30] The author's salvific vision, in a word, is that we need a representative priest before God and Christ is that representative priest.

He has a rich treatment of Christ's high priestly role 'after the order of Melchizedek' (see 5:6, 10; 6:20; 7:1-8:6). Unlike the

---

between God and man. We even learn elsewhere that this mediatorial dominion is a temporarily-delegated authority. When he and his Father have subjugated finally all his and our enemies, then he will yield up not his sonship but his delegated authority as the Messiah to God, even the Father, and his special mediatorial dominion will be reabsorbed into the universal and eternal dominion of the triune God (1 Cor 15:24-28).

In sum, his ascension meant for the Son, as the divine-human Messiah, the assumption of the prerogatives of the Messianic investiture on a universal scale, rights which were already his by right of nature as God the Son but which he 'won' or was 'awarded' as the incarnate Son for fulfilling the obligations pertaining to the estate of humiliation intrinsic to the Messianic investiture.

29. Bruce, *Hebrews*, 5.
30. Leon Morris, *New Testament Theology* (Grand Rapids: Zondervan, 1986), 304.

Melchizedekian order of priests, the priests serving in the Levitical order served the 'old covenant' (8:6), 'without benefit of an irrevocable divine oath' which ordained them to their service (7:20), 'at a sanctuary which was [only] a copy and shadow of what is in heaven' (8:5) and which actually served to keep men away from God (9:8). And they had to offer sacrifices for their own sins before they could offer sacrifices for the people (7:27; 9:7), then *stand* daily and offer again and again the same 'weak and useless' (7:18) sacrifices which in themselves could never purify the conscience (9:9) or take away sins (10:4, 11). Indeed the very repetition of the sacrifices only reminded the offerers of their sins (10:2-4). Finally, the Levitical priests themselves died (7:23). Because of these imperfections in the Levitical system (see 7:11, 19; 9:9; 10:1ff), according to the author of Hebrews (following David's prophetic insight in Psalm 110:1-4), Melchizedek provides the priestly order in which Christ serves.

Melchizedek (Gen 14:18-20; Ps 110:4), whose name means 'King of righteousness' and whose title means 'King of peace', typically 'remains a priest forever' (7:3) because he had 'neither father nor mother' (that is, nothing is recorded in Genesis of his ancestry), and he was 'without genealogy, without beginning of days or end of life' (that is, he simply appears in the Genesis record with nothing said about him as to his parentage, his length of life or his death, or progeny). And because he blessed Abraham who had received the covenant promises ('and without doubt the lesser person is blessed by the greater' – 7:7) who then paid him a tithe, the author argues that his priestly order is to be viewed as greater than the Levitical order because 'Levi being still in the loins of his ancestor' when Abraham gave the tithe to Melchizedek 'paid the tenth' to him as well.

In contrast to the Levitical priests, like Melchizedek, Christ
• came from a 'different tribe' (the 'royal' tribe of Judah, 7:13-14),
• appeared *once for all* (ἅπαξ) at the end of the ages to put away sin by the sacrifice of himself (9:26),
• was ordained by an *irrevocable* (οὐ μεταμεληθήσεται) divine oath (7:20-21) to a *permanent* (ἀπαράβατον) priesthood which can save those *completely and forever* (εἰς τὸ παντελὲς) who come to God through him because he *ever lives* (πάντοτε ζῶν) to intercede for them (7:24), thus mediating a 'new covenant' (9:15) and better promises (8:6),

- served the heavenly sanctuary (4:14; 9:11, 24),
- did not have to offer a sacrifice first for his own sins (7:27), but made *one* offering of himself *once for* all (that is, decisively and finally; ἐφάπαξ – 7:27; 9:12; 10:10) for others,
- has been offered *once for all* (ἅπαξ) to bear the sins of many (9:28),
- offered one sacrifice for sin (10:12),
- and by one offering has perfected those who are sanctified (10:14).
- He has accordingly taken his seat at the right hand of God on his throne, always living to intercede for his own (7:25) and waiting for his enemies to be made his footstool (10:12-13).

From these notices we learn that Christ's high priestly work achieved three things that the Levitical system could never achieve: first, Christ's work *purifies* the conscience from dead works to serve the living God (9:14; see 10:2-4, 16-18, 22); second, his work *sanctifies*, that is, sets apart for God's service, the redeemed (9:13; 10:10; 13:12); and third, his work *perfects* those who have been sanctified with a perfection unattainable under the old covenant (7:11; 10:14).

First excursus on the author's alleged Philonic Platonism

A matter pertaining to the author's representation of our Lord's high priestly ministry requires comment. In some passages he appears to teach that the Old Testament sanctuary service did not embody ultimate realities, that the Levitical priests served at a sanctuary which was only 'a copy and a shadow [ὑποδείγματι καὶ σκιᾷ] of the heavenly sanctuary' (8:5), and that Christ at his ascension entered into the 'true' Most Holy Place in heaven, taking his own blood (9:12, 24), and *there* purified the heavenly realities with better sacrifices than the animal sacrifices of the Old Testament system, that is, with his blood (9:23). Some scholars have suggested that this representation reflects a Philonic Platonism. F. D. V. Narborough, for example, writes:

Whereas Jewish and Christian Apocalyptists envisaged the difference between imperfection and perfection primarily under the categories of *time*, distinguishing between this age and the age to come, the language of Hebrews suggests categories of *space*, distinguishing between this world and the heavenly world of spiritual realities.[31]

J. Héring concurs:

> Like Philo, our author accepts a kind of philosophical and cosmological framework which is more Platonic than biblical. Two successive aeons are replaced by two co-existent, superimposed planes—the suprasensible world and the phenomenal world. The former contains the eternal ideas, which the second one attempts to embody materially. The former is 'heaven' for Philo, as it is in our epistle.[32]

Bruce Demarest also declares:

> The writer utilizes Plato's distinction between the ideal form in heaven and the imperfect copy on earth to argue that the levitical sanctuary and sacrifices are mere shadows of the heavenly realities.[33]

And Donald Guthrie states that 'there may be here...a trace of the background of the Platonic theory of ideas'.[34]

Accordingly, it has often been suggested that the author of Hebrews has discarded the apocalyptic dualism of the 'already' and the 'not yet' found everywhere else in the New Testament and has substituted in its place a Platonic dualism.

What should we say about this interpretation? The first thing that must be underscored is that the author, completely apart from the question of whether or not he employs a Platonic grid in his argument, has not abandoned the dualism of a 'realized' present eschatology (the 'already') and an unrealized future eschatology (the 'not yet'), as we shall see in a moment in section F. Second, as for his alleged 'Platonism', I concur with Franzmann that the author's

> view and use of the Old Testament never degenerates into mere allegory; that is, the Old Testament figures are never merely symbols of eternal truths, as in the allegorizing interpretation of the Jewish philosopher Philo; rather, the Old Testament history is always taken seriously as history. As such, as history, it points beyond itself to the last days [ushered in at Christ's incarnation].[35]

---

31. F. D. V. Narborough, *The Epistle to the Hebrews* (Oxford: Clarendon, 1930), 43.
32. J. Héring, *The Epistle to the Hebrews* (London: Epworth, 1970), xii.
33. Bruce A. Demarest, 'Hebrews, Letter to the', *Baker Encyclopedia of the Bible* (Grand Rapids: Baker, 1988), 1, 947.
34. Donald Guthrie, *New Testament Introduction* (Downers Grove, Ill.: Inter-Varsity, 1970), 719.
35. Martin Franzmann, *The Word of the Lord Grows*, 244-45.

I think then that we should insist with Ladd that

> it is not accurate to say that Hebrews, like Philo, contrasts the phenomenal world with the noumenal, regarding the former as unreal and ephemeral. Hebrews applies the idea of two worlds primarily to the Old Testament cult. The tabernacle with its priests was a copy and shadow of the heavenly sanctuary. *The real has come to men in the historical life and death of Jesus of Nazareth.* History has become the medium of the eternal. There is nothing ephemeral or transitory about Jesus' life and work. The Christ-event was history with an eternal significance. What Jesus did, he did once for all (ἐφάπαξ, 7:27; 9:12; 10:10)....
>
> It is difficult to think that the author of Hebrews conceived of Jesus after his ascension realistically entering a literal Holy Place in heaven. To be sure, he does say, 'Thus it was necessary for the copies of the heavenly things to be purified with these [animal] rites, but the heavenly things themselves with better sacrifices than these' (9:23). [But] it is self-evident that the heavenly things experience no defilement or sin and therefore require no cleansing.... A statement like this should make it clear that Hebrews is describing heavenly things in earthly, symbolic language. What Christ did on the cross, although an event in space and time, was itself an event in the spiritual world. Eternity at this points intersects time; the heavenly is embodied in the earthly; the transcendental occurs in the historical. Christ's entrance into the Holy Place and [his] sprinkling of his blood to effect cleansing and an eternal salvation occurred when 'he...appeared once for all at the end of the age to put away sin by the sacrifice of himself' (9:26)...Hebrews uses the liturgical language of the Old Testament cult to depict the spiritual meaning of what Jesus accomplished by his death on the cross. Here in history on earth is no shadow, but the very reality itself.[36]

In other words, Christ's 'entrance into the heavenly sanctuary' occurred when he assumed his high priestly role as Mediator of the new covenant at the incarnation, and the Most Holy Place was his cross! What these scholars perceive in the author to be the noumenal category of a Platonic world view in actuality is the historical 'already' of his 'realized eschatology' and not Philonic Platonism at all! In sum, his eschatological vision accords with what we know from the undoubted sources regarding Paul's eschatology. *End of first excursus.*

---

36. George Eldon Ladd, *A Theology of the New Testament*, 574-75.

Second excursus on the author's doctrine of apostasy

Throughout his letter the author issues exhortation after exhortation, all intended to encourage the Jewish believer to stand fast in his new faith. These exhortations have essentially one theme, although stated in appropriately different words—they all warn the Christian about the real danger of apostasy. Consider his following words:

2:1-4: 'We must pay more careful attention, therefore, to what we have heard, so that we do not *drift away* [παραρυῶμεν]. For if the message spoken by angels was binding and every violation and disobedience received its just punishment, how shall we escape if we *ignore* [ἀμελήσαντες] such a great salvation' (2:1-3a).

3:7-19: 'See to it...that none of you has a sinful, unbelieving heart that *turns away* [ἐν τῷ ἀποστῆναι] from the living God' (3:12).

4:11-16: '...make every effort to enter that rest, so that no one *will fall* [πέσῃ] by following their example of disobedience' (4:11).

5:11-6:20: '...*have fallen away* [παραπεσόντας]...' (6:6).

10:19-39: 'But we are not *of those who shrink back unto destruction* [ὑποστολῆς εἰς ἀπώλειαν], but of those who believe and are saved' (10:39).

12:12-29: 'See to it that no one *misses* [ὑστερῶν ἀπὸ] the grace of God and that no bitter root grows up to cause trouble and defile many. See that no one...is godless like Esau, who for a single meal sold his inheritance rights as the oldest son' (12:15-16).

These warnings against apostasy (others may be found elsewhere in the New Testament, for example, in Matthew 13:12, 21; 10:33; 25:26-30; 2 Timothy 2:12) address those who have embraced the gospel and who have entered the Christian life and the fellowship of the church, but who are becoming disillusioned under suffering and persecution. The author's warnings underscore the foundational truth for every believer that for those professing Christians who *deliberately* turn their back on Christ and deny the profession they have made, 'there can remain no way of salvation, for there can be no salvation except in Christ'[37] – '*If we deliberately keep on sinning* ['Εκουσίως ἁμαρτανόντων ἡμῶν] after we have received the knowledge of the

---

37. Ladd, *A Theology of the New Testament*, 586.

truth, no sacrifice for sins is left, but only a fearful expectation of judgment and of raging fire that will consume the enemies of God' (10:26). But I would urge that such appeals to perseverance prove effectual in those who have genuine faith – 'Even though we speak this way, dear friends, we are confident of better things in your case – things that accompany salvation' (6:9). But to superficial or surface faith ('temporary faith'), the 'falling away' of which these verses speak is descriptive of what actually can and does occur, and demonstrates how close one can come to salvation and not be genuinely saved (see Matt 12:21; 1 John 2:19).[38] *End of second excursus.*

E. The author's doctrine of the church

For the author of Hebrews the church is the 'house of God' (3:6), the 'wandering people of God' (see the 'wilderness' theme in 3:7-4:13; 11:9, 13; 13:14), and 'brethren' of the great High Priest (2:17). Metaphorically, the church, as the 'church of the firstborn', is Mount Zion, the heavenly Jerusalem, the city of the living God (12:22). Entrance into the church follows upon repentance from dead works and faith in God and entails ritual baptism (6:1; see 10:22-23 which also appears to be an allusion to Christian baptism).

While he says little about formal worship in the church, he does exhort Christians not to forsake the assembling of themselves together. When they do come together, they should do so for the purpose of mutual encouragement (10:25). Nothing is said about the government of the church beyond the fact that the church does have 'leaders' (ἡγούμενοι) who speak the word of God to and who are to set a godly example of faith before the gathered assemblies, who are to watch over the souls under their care as those who must give account, and who in return are to be obeyed (13:7, 17).

F. The author's doctrine of last things

With the other New Testament authors, and in particular Paul, the author of Hebrews rather clearly endorses the New Testament's 'apocalyptic dualism' of the 'already' and the 'not yet'. He believed that he and his readers were in the 'last days' (ἐσχάτου τῶν ἡμερῶν τούτων) (1:2). Christ has come 'at the end of the ages [ἐπὶ συντελείᾳ τῶν αἰώνων] to do away with sin by the sacrifice of himself' (9:26), and

---

38. For a careful exegetical treatment of these warning passages, especially Hebrews 6:4-8, I would recommend Philip E. Hughes, *A Commentary on the Epistle to the Hebrews*.

he has already been crowned with glory and honor (2:9). His messianic reign has already begun in that he has already been seated at the right hand of the throne of the Majesty in heaven, waiting for his enemies to be made the footstool of his feet (1:3, 8, 13; 8:1; 10:12-13). The day of God's 'great salvation' had dawned, the rejection of which leads to just punishment (2:2-3). Christians have already 'tasted the powers of the age to come' (6:5), and have already been purified (9:14), sanctified (9:13; 10:10; 13:12), and perfected (7:11; 10:14). Yet he speaks of 'the world to come [τὴν οἰκουμένην τὴν μέλλουσαν]' (2:5) and of the 'coming age [μέλλοντος αἰῶνος]' (6:5), to be ushered in when Christ '*will appear a second time* [ἐκ δευτέρου...ὀφθήσεται], not to bear sin, but to bring salvation to those who are waiting for him' (9:28; see also 10:37). He insists that 'there remains a Sabbath rest for the people of God' (4:9) which we must 'strive to enter' by obedience (4:11). And he envisions a future cataclysmic cosmic 'shaking' of everything which can be shaken down in order that the one thing which cannot be shaken down— even the eschatological Kingdom of God—might remain (12:26-28; see also 1:11-12). Clearly, while Christians already enjoy the benefits of salvation, Christ's *parousia* will consummate their salvation. Christians are to continue to meet together for mutual encouragement, and all the more so, as they see '*the Day [of judgment] approaching* [ἐγγίζουσαν τὴν ἡμέραν]' (10:25). Those who experience the divine judgment, both after death (9:27) and at Christ's coming, will face God as a 'consuming fire' (10:27; 12:29; see Deut 4:24; 9:3), a God into whose hands it is a fearsome thing to fall (10:31). The author of Hebrews makes no reference or allusion to a millennium.

From this overview of the letter's theology I think we can safely conclude that there is nothing in it that the apostle Paul could not have written (this conclusion, of course, does not prove that he did write the letter). We will now turn directly to a consideration of the letter's authorship.

II. The question of authorship
The letter, as we have seen, is a rich, compelling, sustained argument for Christianity's finality as the New Covenant substance of the Old Testament shadow and as the fulfilment of the Old Testament promise. Who is the author of this magnificent homily on the high priestly work of Jesus Christ? This is an *extremely* difficult question to answer,

with Paul, Barnabas, Luke, Sylvanus, Apollos, Aquila and Priscilla, Priscilla alone,[39] Philip, and even Clement of Rome all having been advanced as the author by some authority at one time or another.[40] Donald Guthrie's conclusion—'an open verdict is clearly the safest course and in this the opinion of Origen can hardly be improved upon'[41]—reflects the most common course followed today. But it is regrettable that about the only thing one hears popularly expressed about this question today is this referred-to opinion of Origen (c. 185-c. 254) to the effect that 'in truth God [alone] knows [τὸ μὲν ἀληθὲς θεὸς οἶδεν]' the real truth of the matter. It is not so commonly recognized that the immediately preceding context of this remark suggests that in Origen's opinion the letter was Pauline—certainly in content if not by the actual pen of Paul. He writes:

> ...that the thoughts of the epistle are admirable, and not inferior to the acknowledged writings of the apostle, to this...everyone will consent as true who has given attention to reading the apostle.... But as for myself, if I were to state my own opinion, I should say that *the thoughts are the apostle's*, but that the style and composition belong to one who called to mind the apostle's teachings and, as it were, made short notes of what his master said. If any church, therefore, holds this epistle as Paul's, *let it be commended* [εὐδοκιμείτο]. For *not without reason* have the ancients [from only about a century and half earlier] handed it down as Paul's. (cited by Eusebius, *Ecclesiastical History*, 6.25.12-13; emphasis supplied).

The letter, admittedly, is anonymous. But whoever the author was, it is clear that the letter's original recipients knew who it was who was speaking to them, for he calls upon them to pray that he would be restored to them shortly (13:18-24). Could Paul be the author, as I am suggesting? In Egypt and North Africa Paul's authorship seems never to have been a matter of serious dispute.[42] Primarily in Italy and particularly in Rome it was later disputed for a time.

As evidence of this Eastern tradition, while it is true that Paul in

---

39. The participle διηγούμενον in 11:32, with its masculine ending, will not allow the ascription of authorship to a woman. We must refer to the author as a 'he'.
40. See Donald Guthrie, *New Testament Introduction*, 685-98, for his carefully nuanced discussion of the authorship question.
41. Guthrie, *New Testament Introduction*, 698.
42. R. Laird Harris, *Inspiration and Canonicity of the Bible* (Grand Rapids: Zondervan, 1957), writes: '...Hebrews was always received in the East and received as Pauline – though with a translator of some kind often mentioned' (268).

every other instance that we know of indicated authorship by name, Eusebius informs us that Clement of Alexandria (A.D. 155-215) declared (1) that Paul wrote the letter to Hebrew Christians in Hebrew and that Luke had carefully translated it into Greek and had it published for Greek-speaking Christians, and (2) that Paul had omitted his name in the letter both out of deference to his Lord whom he looked upon as the real apostle to the Hebrews (3:1; see Rom 15:8) and to avoid Jewish prejudice against the letter which would have surely come were they to know that he had authored it. Eusebius's exact words (*Ecclesiastical History*, 6.14.2f.), summarizing a passage in Clement of Alexandria's *Hypotyposeis*, are as follows:

...as for the Epistle to the Hebrews, [Clement] says indeed that it is Paul's, but that it was written for Hebrews in the Hebrew tongue, and that Luke, having carefully translated it, published it for the Greeks; hence, as a result of this translation, the same complexion of style is found in this Epistle and in the Acts: but that the [words] 'Paul an apostle' were naturally not affixed. For, says he, 'in writing to Hebrews who had conceived a prejudice against him, he very wisely did not repel them at the beginning by putting his name.'

If Clement is right (admittedly, he may not be)—that what we have in Hebrews is a Lukan rendering in Greek of Paul's letter composed originally in Hebrew—this could account for all the much discussed differences in style and vocabulary with the known letters of Paul. Eusebius (*Ecclesiastical History*, 6.14.4) then quotes Clement as having written:

But now, as the blessed elder [Pantaenus (d. c. A. D. 200), first catechist of the catechetical school at Alexandria] used to say, since the Lord, being the apostle of the Almighty, was sent to the Hebrews, Paul, through modesty, since he had been sent to the Gentiles, does not inscribe himself as an apostle to the Hebrews, both to give due deference to the Lord and because he wrote to the Hebrews also out of his abundance, being a preacher and apostle of the Gentiles.

Moreover, Hebrews was accepted from the very first both in the Eastern and the Western church, being both known and quoted. Paul's authorship of Hebrews, as we have noted, was apparently never a matter of serious dispute in Egypt and North Africa. In the West the letter to the Hebrews asserted its intrinsic authority in *1 Clement*, written in Rome c. A. D. 95-97, and the *Shepherd of Hermas*, written in Rome between A. D. 120 and 140. Only later in the Western church – primarily in Italy, particularly in Rome, and *on dogmatic grounds* – did the dispute arise over the acceptance of the letter. The Western church's dispute over Hebrews, while it placed the question of its authorship in the foreground, was certainly connected with the particular way the Montanists attached themselves to Hebrews 6:1-8 which treats the problem of the lapsed or those who had denied the faith under persecution. But the recently discovered *The Gospel of Truth* (Codex I, known as the Jung Codex), possibly authored by the gnostic teacher Valentinus himself, near Nag Hammadi shows that around A. D. 150 the letter to the Hebrews did not have lesser authority in Rome than Paul's other letters. And although the letter is omitted from the Muratorian Canon (due perhaps to the corrupt state of the text of that Canon), Eusebius himself grouped it with the 'fourteen' epistles of Paul (*Ecclesiastical History*, 3.3.5), this striking notice no doubt reflecting an earlier opinion such as is found (1) in the Chester Beatty papyrus P[46] (c. A. D. 200) which places Hebrews between Romans and 1 Corinthians, (2) in the ancestor of Vaticanus which places it between Galatians and Ephesians, and (3) in the majority of ancient Greek copies which place it after 2 Thessalonians, all three positions implying Pauline authorship. Both Jerome in Jerusalem (*Vir.* 5; *Ep.* 53.8; 129.3) and Augustine in North Africa (*Doctr. Christi.* 2.8; *Civ. D.* 16.22) cite it as Paul's, and Theodore of Mopsuestia (c. A.D. 350-428) tells us that believers 'accept the epistle as having been written by Paul, like the others. If this were not so, what is written [in it] would not be profitable to them'.

Internal evidence also supports the legitimacy of holding that Paul could have been the author. It is consistently Pauline to call upon his readers to pray for him (1 Thess 5:25; Rom 15:30-31; Eph 6:19-20). Moreover, the author's reference to 'our brother Timothy' (13:23) surely has a 'Pauline ring' about it (see 1 Thess 3:2; 2 Cor 1:1; Col 1:1; Philemon 1). Furthermore, there is a definite affinity of language and thought between the letter and the recognized Pauline letters (compare Heb 1:4 and Phil 2:9; Heb 2:2 and Gal 3:19; Heb 2:10 and Rom 11:36; Heb 7:18 and Rom 8:3; Heb 7:27 and Eph 5:2; Heb 8:13 and 2 Cor 3:11; Heb 10:1 and Col 2:17; Heb 10:33 and 1 Cor 4:9; Heb 11:13 and Eph 2:19; Heb 12:22 and Gal 4:25, 26).

As a sampling of these, first, the statement in Hebrews that the

Son obtained his 'more excellent name' (1:4) has an affinity with Paul's statement that the Father gave Jesus 'the name which is above every name' (Phil 2:9);

secondly, the author's treatment of the new covenant[43] has some parallels in 2 Corinthians 3;

thirdly, his assessment of the law as 'a shadow of good things to come' (10:1) is paralleled by Paul's statement that the ritual law was 'a shadow of things to come' (Col 2:17);

fourthly, although the author's treatment of Christ's high priesthood is undeveloped in the acknowledged letters of Paul, the person and work of Christ in general are undeniably central in Hebrews as in the acknowledged epistles and Christ's high priesthood in particular has at least 'a foothold in Paul...at Romans 8:34'[44];

fifthly, the Old Testament quotation in Hebrews 10:30 departs from the Septuagint text in the same way that the same quotation does in Romans 12:19.

In my opinion, far too much weight in settling this issue has been given to the statement in Hebrews 2:3 ('...so great salvation, which having first been spoken by the Lord, was confirmed to us by the ones who heard [him]') as being 'the most significant point' *against* Pauline authorship.[45] The statement, by this construction, supposedly

---

43. I think it noteworthy that Geerhardus Vos, *Biblical Theology* (Grand Rapids: Eerdmans, 1948), after declaring that 'Paul is in the N. T. the great exponent of the fundamental bisection in the history of redemption and of revelation' because 'with him we find the formal distinction between the "New Diatheke" and the "Old Diatheke" (2 Cor. 3:6, 14),' immediately goes on to state:

The Epistle to the Hebrews gives us the clearest information [but if Paul is "the great exponent" how can the author of Hebrews be clearer than Paul?] in regard to the structure of redemptive procedure, and that particularly, as based on and determined by structure of revelation. It is not necessary to quote single passages, the whole Epistle is full of it. We read here of the "New Diatheke" (9:15). The phrase "Old Diatheke" does not occur, although other phrases practically equivalent do. How intimately to the writer the unfolding from the Old into the New is bound up with the unfolding of Revelation, may be seen from the opening words of the Epistle. "God having spoken [to our ancestors by the prophets]—spake [in these last days to us]—in a Son...." The participle aorist "having spoken" and the finite verb "spake" link the old and the new together, representing the former as preparatory to the latter. (323)

But to say this about the author's understanding of the relation of the old covenant to the new is to describe Paul's understanding as well.

44. James D. G. Dunn, 'Pauline Legacy and School' in *Dictionary of the Later New Testament and Its Developments*, edited by Ralph P. Martin and Peter H. Davids (Downers Grove, Ill.: InterVarsity, 1997), 891.

45. So Simon J. Kistemaker, *Exposition of the Epistle to the Hebrews* (Grand Rapids: Baker, 1984), 7. Paul Ellingworth, *The Epistle to the Hebrews: A Commentary on the Greek*

teaches that the author was a 'second-generation' Christian who had heard the gospel from the apostles and who was converted as a result of their preaching, thus precluding Paul as the author because he claims in Galatians 1:1, 12 that he received his gospel directly from Christ (see Acts 9:1-9). But Hebrews 2:3 *does not say* what this construction contends that it says. While the author of Hebrews certainly acknowledges here that he was not among the original Twelve (nor was Paul) he does not categorically state that he had first *heard* the gospel from the apostles and was *converted* by their words to him. Rather, he says that the message which began with Jesus was *confirmed* (ἐβεβαιώθη) to him by those who had heard the Lord, implying thereby that he was already in possession of the message at the time of its confirmation to him, an activity which the apostles plainly could have done for Paul either on the occasion of his first visit to Jerusalem when he met Peter and James (Gal 1:18-19) or during his second visit to Jerusalem when he met with the 'pillars' of the Jerusalem church (Gal 2:1-10). Certainly the action of the apostles, as described by Paul in Galatians 2:9 ('...recognizing the grace that had been given to me, James and Cephas and John...gave to me and Barnabas the right hand of fellowship') has the appearance of being a 'confirming' activity.

As for its style, vocabulary, grammar, and doctrinal content, as I have already intimated, I grant that these matters are markedly different in some respects from Paul's other letters to specific churches and individuals. But it must be observed that, first, the letter's specific recipients, namely, the Jerusalem church, which dictated to a large degree its subject matter, namely, the superiority of the Melchizedekian high priestly ministry of Christ over the Aaronic priesthood; secondly, its purpose, namely, to warn the mother church of Christendom against apostasy back into Judaistic legalism; and thirdly, Paul's likely use of an amanuensis (Luke perhaps, who, according to 2 Timothy 4:11, was with him during his second Roman imprisonment) could have had much to do with regard to the variation in style and vocabulary of this letter away from Paul's undisputed letters. And who else living in the New Testament world at that time

---

New Testament (The New International Greek Testament Commentary; Grand Rapids: Eerdmans, 1993), 7, says virtually the same things when he describes the author's statement in 2:3 as the 'single most striking piece of *internal* evidence against Pauline authorship. This [statement]...is in sharp contrast with Paul's claim (Gal. 1:1, 12) that he received his commission directly from the risen Lord'.

besides Paul could have spoken, particularly 'from Italy' (Heb 13:24), to Judaic Christianity not only with such originality but also *with the massive authority* that is reflected in this letter? Only a little reflection on what we know of the other proposed authors should convince us that Paul alone possessed both the originality and the apostolic authority to speak to Jewish Christianity in this way and to make the broad urgent appeal to it that we find in the letter.

Finally, to William L. Lane who, after stating categorically that 'the author clearly was not Paul', declares:

> We are left to conclude that Hebrews was composed by a creative theologian, one well trained in the art of expounding the Greek Scriptures, whose thought world was shaped by, and whose vocabulary, traditions, and theological conceptions were indebted to Hellenistic Judaism and the early Hellenistic church,[46]

I would rejoin that precisely these – *all of these* – are among my reasons for ascribing Pauline authorship to the letter (perhaps originally in Hebrew), with Luke likely serving as Paul's amanuensis (or later translator into Greek). For it is widely acknowledged today by students of the New Testament world that there was *no region* of the Roman Empire that was not a 'Hellenized region', including the region of Judea. Paul, trained as a youth in Jerusalem as he was, could have and very likely would have received, *even in Jerusalem*, instruction in Greek rhetoric, Greek literature and Greek philosophy (evidence of all three of which are present in his letters) so that he might be able to communicate well with Diaspora Jews coming to Jerusalem.[47]

While admittedly there are differences between Hebrews and Paul's acknowledged letters (for example, as I have already noted, the absence of his name in the salutation), I conclude that there is nothing in the content of the letter that Paul could not have written and that the Pauline authorship of Hebrews best explains, humanly speaking, the letter's place in the canon.[48]

---

46. William L. Lane, 'Hebrews' in *Dictionary of the Later New Testament & Its Development*, edited by Ralph P. Martin and Peter H. Davids (Downers Grove, Ill.: InterVarsity, 1997), 444.

47. See the section on 'Paul's Education' in Ben Witherington III, The Paul Quest: The Renewed Search for the Jew of Tarsus (Downers Grove: Ill.: InterVarsity, 1998), 94-98.

48. I would recommend that the reader consult R. Laird Harris, *Inspiration and Canonicity of the Bible*, 263-70, who neatly surveys the patristic evidence and concludes that Hebrews is 'a genuine Epistle of Paul' who used Barnabas as his secretary (269), though he concedes

III. The letter's place of origin

The author's statement to his readers that 'those [Jewish Christians] from Italy send you their greetings' (13:24) suggests Italy, possibly and likely Rome, as the letter's place of origin. This would fit with a Pauline authorship, since we know that he was imprisoned there twice. It could also explain the author's statement that 'our brother Timothy has been released' (13:23), since it is entirely possible that Timothy had come to Rome as Paul had urged him (2 Tim 4:9) and had been detained, but being judged an unimportant figure in the case, had then been released.

It should be pointed out in the interest of thoroughness, however, that many scholars contend that the preposition ἀπό (from) in 13:24 should be interpreted to mean 'away from', and hold that the phrase 'those from Italy' refers to a group of Italian Christians *away from* or *outside* of Italy with whom the author found himself. These scholars then urge that the author addresses Christians in Italy, probably Christians in Rome, perhaps even *from* Jerusalem. Admittedly, the preposition is ambiguous,[49] but Philip Schaff remarks that 'in Italy' seems 'more natural, and is defended by Theodoret, who knew Greek as his mother tongue'.[50]

For my part, I believe that Paul wrote Hebrews from Rome to the Jewish Christians living in Jerusalem and the environs of Judea, perhaps after James' martyrdom in A.D. 62 (or 63) (Hebrews 13:7 suggests that some of the recipients' leaders were no longer with them, having been taken away from them by death).

IV. The date of the letter

The letter had to be written before A.D. 95 since Clement of Rome in A.D. 96 made use of it in his letter to the Corinthians. Most likely it was written in the late sixth or early seventh decade of the first century and almost certainly before the destruction of Jerusalem in A.D. 70

---

that another person may have served Paul as an amanuensis (Luke is a strong possibility here). Some scholars, as Donald Guthrie notes (*New Testament Introduction*, 690-93), think that Barnabas could have been the *original* author, for as a Levite (Acts 4:36) he would have been intimately acquainted with the temple ritual, and as 'a son of consolation' (Acts 4:36) he might have written just such a 'word of consolation' (13:22). But Guthrie is right when he concludes that any solid data for Barnabas' authorship is 'practically non-existent' (691).

49. BAGD, ἀπό, *A Greek-English Lexicon of the New Testament and Other Early Christian Literature* (Chicago: Chicago University Press, 1979) states that the 'Italians' in Hebrews 13:24 'could be inside as well as outside Italy' (87, IV.b).

50. Philip Schaff, *A History of the Christian Church* (New York: Charles Scribner's Sons, 1910), I, 817, fn. 1.

since no reference is made to that event which would have been telling historical confirmation of his argument and since the temple service appears to be represented as still continuing in Jerusalem (see the present tenses in Hebrews 8:4, 13; 10:1, 8, 11; 13:10, 11). Moreover, no reference is made to such important events as the outbreak of the Jewish War (A.D. 66) or the Neronian persecution (A.D. 64). If Paul wrote it, Hebrews would have had to be written, of course, before his martyrdom in Rome around A.D. 65, but possibly as late as A.D. 67, most likely during his second imprisonment.

V. The occasion of the letter

The title 'To the Hebrews' is not part of the original text but was probably added in the second century when the New Testament letters were gathered into a collection. Although this traditional conclusion has not gone unchallenged,[51] it is still most probably the case that Paul wrote the letter to Jewish Christians in Judea in danger of lapsing back into Judaism.[52] This conclusion, I believe, will be borne out from a careful analysis of the letter's content. Paul had witnessed first-hand how narrowly 'Mosaic' the church in Jerusalem had increasingly become during his last visit there (see again Acts 21:20-25). He would understandably have become very concerned about the direction in which the leadership there appeared to be allowing the church to go. Philip Schaff makes the following interesting comments about the situation which evoked the composition of this letter:

> Strange that but thirty years after the resurrection and the pentecostal effusion of the Spirit, there should have been such a danger of apostasy in the very mother church of Christendom. And yet not strange, if we realize the condition of things between 60 and 70. The Christians in Jerusalem were the most conservative of all believers, and adhered as closely as possible to the tradition of their fathers. They were contented with the elementary doctrines, and needed to be pressed on 'unto perfection' (5:12; 6:1-14).... The strange advice which [James] gave to his brother Paul, on his last visit, reflects their timidity and narrowness. Although numbered by 'myriads', they made no attempt in that critical

---

51. Many modern scholars urge that the author penned this exhortation to Gentile Christians in danger of lapsing into irreligion, the main argument here being that the original recipients are represented as in danger of 'falling away from the living God' (3:12) which suggests in turn lapsing not into Judaism but into paganism. See Martin Franzmann, *The Word of the Lord Grows*, 238, and George E. Ladd, *Theology of the New Testament*, 571 and fn. 2, for further description of this view.

52. See Guthrie, *New Testament Introduction*, 704-5.

moment to rescue the great apostle from the hands of the fanatical Jews; they were 'all zealous for the law', and afraid of the radicalism of Paul on hearing that he was teaching the Jews of the Dispersion 'to forsake Moses, telling them not to circumcise their children, neither to walk after the customs' (Acts 21:20, 21).

They hoped against hope for the conversion of their people. When that hope vanished more and more, when some of their teachers had suffered martyrdom (13:7), when James, their revered leader, was stoned by the Jews (62), and when the patriotic movement for the deliverance of Palestine from the hated yoke of the heathen Romans rose higher and higher, until it burst out at last in open rebellion (66), it was very natural that those timid Christians should feel strongly tempted to apostatize from the poor, persecuted sect to the national religion, which they at heart still believed to be the best part of Christianity. The solemn service of the Temple, the ritual pomp and splendor of the Aaronic priesthood, the daily sacrifices, and all the sacred associations of the past had still a great charm for them, and allured them to their embrace. The danger was very strong, and the warning of the Epistle fearfully solemn.[53]

Guthrie makes the following similar comment:

The hankering after the old must have been very real [for the Jewish Christians in Jerusalem], for the new camp [that is, Christianity] had no prestige comparable to that which Judaism derived from Moses, and the danger of apostasy was correspondingly great. In place of the grandeur of the ritual of the old order was substituted a spiritual conception centred entirely in a Person and no longer in a splendid temple. It must have caused much perplexity in the minds of the recently converted Jews.[54]

Reflecting upon the deteriorating condition of the Jerusalem church later in his Roman cell, Paul was moved by the Spirit of God, I would suggest, to write this letter to the Christians living in the shadow and pull of the Temple and its ceremonies.[55]

---

53. Philip Schaff, *History of the Christian Church* (New York: Charles Scribner's Sons, 1910), I, 814-15.
54. Guthrie, *New Testament Introduction*, 705.
55. For other opinions concerning the author and the occasion behind the Letter to the Hebrews, see F. F. Bruce, *The Epistle to the Hebrews* (revised edition; The New International Commentary on the New Testament; Grand Rapids: Eerdmans, 1990); Paul Ellingworth, *The Epistle to the Hebrews: A Commentary on the Greek New Testament* (The New International Greek Testament Commentary; Grand Rapids: Eerdmans, 1993); Donald A. Hagner, *Hebrews* (The New International Biblical Commentary; Peabody, Massachusetts: Hendricksen, 1990); Simon J. Kistemaker, *New Testament Commentary: Exposition of the Epistle to the Hebrews* (Grand Rapids: Baker, 1984); William L. Lane, *Hebrews 1-8, 9-13* (2 vols.: Word Biblical Commentary 47a, b; Dallas: Word, 1991); James Moffatt, *A Critical and Exegetical*

VI. The content of the letter[56]

Though it begins like an essay and ends like a letter, Hebrews is actually a sustained homily (see 'time would fail me to tell,' 11:32; 'my word of exhortation,' 13:22). The author (Paul) writes to warn his readers against apostasy (see 2:1-4; 3:7–4:11; 5:11–6:12; 10:19-39), founding his Christ-centered message on the Old Testament and admonishing them to faithfulness in light of the fact that the 'last days' have come (1:2; 6:5; 9:26; 10:25). He develops his argument by a series of contrasts or comparisons which give substance to and are the basis for his several admonitions. His contrasts or comparisons are between Christ and Christianity on the one hand and Old Testament religious ceremonialism on the other, and his evaluation is that Christ is superior to all that that ceremonialism offered. His admonitions are to the effect that his readers should not abandon Christianity, the 'substance', and return to the lower and now obsolete things, the 'shadows' (see 10:1). In the course of his presentation, he urges

A. that Christ's revelational mediation is 'better' (κρείττων) than that of angels (1:4);
B. that he is 'worthy of greater honor than Moses' (3:3-6);
C. that the rest he provides, unlike that which Joshua provided, is God's own rest (4:1-11);
D. that his priesthood is 'better' than the Levitical priesthood (7:7);
E. that the covenant of which he is the surety and mediator is 'better' than the old (7:22; 8:6);
F. that Christ's are 'better' sacrifices than the animal rites of the old economy (9:23); and
G. that we have 'better' things accompanying our salvation than before (6:9): a 'better' hope (7:19), 'better' promises (8:6), a 'better' possession in heaven (10:34), a 'better' country (11:16), a 'better' resurrection (11:35), the 'better' provisions from God (11:40), and a blood sacrifice that speaks of something 'better' than that of Abel (12:24).

Commentary on the Epistle to the Hebrews (International Critical Commentary; Edinburgh: T. & T. Clark, 1924); Leon Morris, *Hebrews* (Bible Study Commentary; Grand Rapids: Eerdmans, 1983); B. F. Westcott, *The Epistle to the Hebrews* (1892 reprint; Grand Rapids: Eerdmans, 1970).
    56. I have adapted the following outline, with minor variations, from Franzmann, *The Word of the Lord Grows*, 239-41.

Paul develops the same idea by employing the word 'more excellent' (διαφορώτερον): Jesus has a 'more excellent' name than angels (1:4) and a 'more excellent' ministry than the Levitical priests (8:6).

I. INTRODUCTORY SECTION: GOD HAS SPOKEN HIS ULTIMATE WORD IN HIS SON, WHO SURPASSES ALL PREVIOUS MEDIATORS OF DIVINE REVELATION; THEREFORE, GIVE HEED TO HIS WORD, 1:1-4:13.

A. 1. Instruction, 1:1-3.
God's revelation to men in his Son is superior to all previous revelation. Christ is God's *final* word because of who he is and what he did (this passage has always been considered crucial for the concept of the finality of the revelation we have in the complete Scriptures, that is, the closed canon).

In this section Paul introduces Christ as the Son (actually 'a Son', but because his Sonship is unique, the indefinition of quality is as significant as the definition of the definite article). God's Son was and is the Creator (1:2), in his essence is the mirror or exact image of God (1:3), who providentially upholds all things (1:3), who has dealt with sins (1:3) and sits in victory with God at his right hand as the appointed heir who bears the name, Son of God (1:4). Christ reveals in his redemptive work, the reality of which all else before was only the foreshadowing, and in his person the 'radiance of God's glory and the exact representation of his nature'. And in this we have received the fulness of God's revelation to man. (Only the revelation associated with Christ's work at his return is lacking, and that will be added then and not before. The implication of this passage is that in Christ and his apostles God has spoken his full and ultimate Word until Christ returns.)

2. Admonition (implicit), 1:2.
'God has spoken to us by his Son for the *last* time.' Therefore, the reader must not return to or look back to an earlier and less full and definitive stage of revelation.

B. 1. Instruction, 1:4-14.
Jesus is superior to the angels who mediated the message of the Law (see 2:2). Through a series of Old Testament quotations corroborated

with a reasoned argument, Paul demonstrates his point that Christ is much better than the angels (1:4). He does so by appealing to the superiority of who Christ is and also of what he has done.

2. Admonition, 2:1-4.
'Therefore we must pay the closer attention to what we have heard, lest we drift away from it... how shall we escape if we neglect so great a salvation.'

C. 1. Instruction, 2:5-18.
Since man (Adam) to whom the task was given to act for God failed (2:6ff, Ps 8), it was necessary for the Son to become a man and in that humanity represent the seed of Abraham and render powerless the devil who holds the power of death. So he became a 'faithful and merciful high priest' in order to 'make propitiation for the sins of the people'. The humiliation of Jesus does not call into question his unique greatness; his humiliation is necessary to his priesthood.

2. Admonition, 3:1.
'Therefore...consider Jesus, the Apostle and High Priest of our confession.'

D. 1. Instruction, 3:2-6.
Jesus is superior to ('worthy of greater honor than') Moses, the mediator of the Law. Christ is the Son over the house in which Moses served as servant (3:5-6).

2. Admonition, 3:7-19.
'...if we hold on to our courage and the hope of which we boast.... See to it, brothers, that none of you has a sinful, unbelieving heart that turns away from the living God' (3:6, 12).

E. 1. Instruction, 4:1-13.
Christ is superior to Joshua. Although Joshua led Israel into the promised land, the land of rest, he did not give the people rest (4:8), implying that a better Joshua/Jesus (see 4:14) will bring us into that ultimate Sabbath-rest for the people of God, a rest which God himself has entered (4:9-10). Because Jesus has passed through the heavens (4:14), and entered that land of rest, he can bring us in also.

2. Admonition, 4:1.
Therefore, 'since the promise of entering his rest still stands, let us be careful that none of you be found to have fallen short of it.' Give heed, lest you, like the ancient people of God in the wilderness, forfeit the promised rest by unbelief and lose your portion in the promises given to the people of God.

II. MAIN THEME: THE SUPERIORITY OF JESUS, THE NEW TESTAMENT HIGH PRIEST, AND THE NEED OF UNWAVERING FAITH IN HIM, 4:14-12-29.

A. 1. Instruction, 4:14-5:10.
Jesus is marked as a true high priest by the fact that he is one with man and therefore capable of sympathy with man's frailty, and is appointed by God.

2. Admonition, 5:11-6:20.
Go on to maturity in knowledge of your great high priest, lest you stagnate, fall away, and come under the judgment of God, 5:11-6:20. Your godly past has in it the promise that you *will* overcome your present torpor and go on to realize the full assurance of hope, 6:9-12, a hope based on the certainty given by the promise and oath of God and by the work of Jesus as the high priest after the order of Melchizedek, 6:13-20.

B. 1. Instruction, 7:1-10:19.
Jesus is a high priest of a higher order, not of Aaron but of Melchizedek, and accordingly is both priest and king forever; his priesthood antiquates and supercedes the old Levitical priesthood, chap 7. He performs his priestly ministry in a better sanctuary, the heavens, and by it he mediates the promised new and better covenant, chap. 8. He offers the final and perfect sacrifice for sin, 9:1-10:18.

2. Admonitions, 10:19-12:29.
Having such a way into the holy place, let us not forsake our own assembling together and fall away. Draw near to God in word and work by the 'new and living way' which the great high priest has consecrated, 10:19-25. Beware of apostasy, that deliberate rejection of the proffered redemption which will deliver you up to the judgment of God, 10:26-31. Recall the believing steadfastness of your former

days; for your encouragement remember that you stand in the succession of the ancient men of faith, and look to Jesus, the greatest example, the pioneer and perfecter of your faith, 10:32-12:3. Remember that your present suffering is proof of God's fatherly love for you; he is the Lord who chastens every child whom he receives, 12:4-11. Repent and grow strong again before the time of repentance is past; do not refuse the God who has spoken his supremely gracious word for the last time, before his last judgment comes, 12:29.

III. CONCLUDING ADMONITIONS, 13:1-19.

A. Continue in brotherly love, in charity toward the stranger and the prisoner, in sexual purity, in contentment based on a confident trust in God, 13:1-6.

B. Remember your past teachers and imitate their faith in the abiding and unchanging Christ, their resistance to false teaching, their resolute break with Judaism, their pure worship, their sacrifice of praise and well-doing. To the same end, obey your present leaders and pray for us, 13:7-19.

Conclusion: Intercessory prayer, appeal to receive the admonitions of the letter, news, greetings, and benediction (note in this great benediction the reference to Christ's eternal sacrifice and to our good works which result from that sacrifice and which are pleasing to God), 13:20-25.

The Dominant Theme of the Letter. Hebrews offers a sustained warning not to fall away from the unique, final, and 'better' high priestly work of Christ and to lapse again into Judaism.

* * * * *

Second Timothy

A. The Letter's Place of Origin
From Paul's prison cell in Rome.

B. The Date of the Letter
Just prior to his martyrdom sometime around A.D. 65 but possibly as late as A.D. 67.

C. The Occasion of the Letter

Franzmann sensitively describes the occasion of the writing of 2 Timothy in the following way: Paul writes from prison in Rome. He has been a prisoner for some time: Onesiphorus, a Christian of Ephesus, has already sought him out and visited him in Rome (2 Tim. 1:16, 17). There has already been one hearing, at which Paul was deserted by all men and yet, with the Lord's help, so successfully defended himself that he was 'rescued from the lion's mouth' (2 Tim. 4:16, 17). But Paul has no hope of ultimate acquittal; he is at the end of his course. And he is virtually alone; only Luke is with him. He longs to see 'his beloved child' Timothy once more and bids him come to Rome before the winter makes travel by sea impossible (2 Tim. 1:4; 4:9, 21). But he must reckon with the possibility that Timothy may not reach Rome in time; and so he must put in writing all that he hopes to tell Timothy in person if and when he arrives. The letter is thus Paul's last written word, in which he bids Timothy to preserve the apostolic gospel pure and unchanged, to guard it against the increasingly vicious attacks of false teachers, to train men to transmit it faithfully, and to be ready to endure his own share of suffering in the propagation and defense of it. This very personal letter is therefore in a sense 'official' too; for Paul cannot separate his person from his office. The man who had been 'set apart for the gospel of God' (Rom. 1:1) remained one with that gospel both in life and in death.[57]

D. The Content of the Letter[58]

SALUTATION, 1:1-2, AND THANKSGIVING, 1:3-5. Paul (1) gives thanks for the bond of affection which has united him and Timothy, (2) expresses his strong desire to see Timothy again, and (3) gratefully recalls the sincere faith that dwells in Timothy. This introduces

I. PAUL'S APPEAL TO TIMOTHY TO REKINDLE THE GIFT OF GOD THAT WAS WITHIN HIM, TO MAKE FULL PROOF OF THAT 'SPIRIT OF POWER AND LOVE AND SELF-

---

57. Franzmann, *The Word of the Lord Grows*, 161. For additional insights into the situation behind Paul's second letter to Timothy, see the commentaries in footnote 8.
58. I have adapted the following outline, with minor variations, from Franzmann, *The Word of the Lord Grows*, 161-64.

CONTROL' WITHIN HIM (1:6-7) WHO WOULD ENABLE HIM, 1:6-18,

A. To remain loyal to the imprisoned apostle and to be ready to assume his share of suffering for the gospel, 1:8-12.

B. To hold fast to and to guard the truth which Paul has communicated to him, by the power of the Spirit that dwells in him as it dwells in Paul, 1:13-14.

C. To recall (as a warning example) that 'all those in Asia' had deserted him, and (as an encouraging example) that Onesiphorus, who had already ministered to him in Ephesus, had courageously found him in Rome and had ministered to his needs there, 1:15-18.

II. PAUL'S CHARGE TO TIMOTHY, 2:1-4:5.

A. To entrust the truth he had learned from Paul to faithful men who would teach others, 2:1-13.

1. He can do this only if he himself is faithful, ready to endure hardness and to toil with a soldier's loyalty, an athlete's self-discipline, and a farmer's industry, 2:1-7.

2. He can do this only by the strength to be found in the risen Christ (2:8-10), and with the faith that union with Christ in his suffering is the promise of union with him in life and glory, 2:11-13.

B. To train these faithful men in the defense of the truth against the attacks of false teachers, 2:14-26. Hence,

1. Timothy must warn them against sinking to the level of their opponents with their disputes about words – the teacher of the church is not to be a noxious debater, 2:14. Timothy can do this only if

   a. He, unlike Hymenaeus and Philetus, is a teacher who rightly handles the word of truth, 2:15-18.
   b. He does his work with the confidence that God's truth cannot be overcome, 2:19.

c. He seeks to be holy and pure, and to avoid foolish and ignorant disputes that generate strife, 2:20-23.

2. Timothy must train servants of the Lord who will overcome error with apt teaching, with kindly, forbearing, and gentle correction, in the faith and hope that God will grant their opponents repentance and deliverance from Satan, 2:24-26.

C. To do his work with the *sobering* conviction that both the times and men will grow worse and that opposition to the truth will increase, 3:1-8.

D. To do his work with the *encouraging* conviction, 3:9-17,

1. That the folly of those who oppose the truth will expose itself, 3:9.

2. That he has sufficient equipment for his difficult and dangerous task in the apostolic example he has witnessed (3:10-13), in the apostolic teaching he has received (3:14), and in the 'God-breathed' Scripture which he has known from childhood, 3:15-17.

E. To fulfill his ministry strenuously, insistently, courageously in the face of men's indifference to sound teaching and in spite of their desire for false teaching, 4:1-5.

III. PAUL'S REQUEST TO TIMOTHY – 'COME TO ME QUICKLY (AND BRING MARK)' (4:9), 'COME BEFORE WINTER' (4:21), 4:9-18. (Alone in prison [except for Luke], Paul longs to see his beloved son in the faith, but is still confident that the Lord would preserve him for his heavenly kingdom.)

GREETINGS AND BENEDICTION, 4:19-22.

E. The Dominant Themes of the Letter. (1) Encouragement of Timothy to steadfastness in the face of Paul's imminent martyrdom; (2) a reminder to Timothy about the need to resist false doctrine.

* * * * * * * * *

With his final benediction, 'The Lord be with your [sing.] spirit. Grace be with you [pl.]' (2 Tim 4:22), Paul, pioneer missionary to the nations, laid down his pen, thus closing the literary chapter of his life's work, and shortly thereafter he laid down his very life for the sake of Christ, for whom he had been willing to 'suffer the loss of all things, considering them rubbish' compared to the surpassing greatness of knowing his Lord and being found in him, not having his own righteousness that comes from the law but that righteousness which comes through faith in Christ and from God (Phil 3:7-9).

Such willing sacrifice on his part should not surprise us when we recall that he had said to the Ephesian elders: 'I consider my life worth nothing to me, if only I may finish the race and complete the task the Lord Jesus has given me – the task of testifying to the gospel of God's grace' (Acts 20:24). And finish the race he did, joyously, freely, contentedly, as he himself wrote: '...the time has come for my departure. I have fought the good fight, I have finished the race, I have kept the faith. Now there is in store for me the crown of righteousness which the Lord, the righteous Judge, will award to me on that day – and not only to me, but also to all who have longed for his appearing' (2 Tim 4:6-8).

Who now will 'follow in his train'?

CHAPTER TWELVE

THE DIVINE AUTHORITY AND CANONICITY OF THE PAULINE CORRESPONDENCE

'...we also thank God continually because, when you received the word of God, which you heard from us, you accepted it not as the word of men, but as it actually is, the word of God, which is at work in you who believe' (1 Thess 2:15).

'...hold to the teachings we passed on to you, whether by word of mouth or by letter' (2 Thess 2:15).

'We have not received the spirit of the world but the Spirit who is from God, that we may understand what God has freely given us. This is what we speak, not in words taught us by human wisdom but in words taught by the Spirit, expressing Spirit-revealed truths in Spirit-taught words' (1 Cor 2:12-13).

'All Scripture is God-breathed and is useful for teaching, rebuking, correcting and training in righteousness, so that the man of God may be thoroughly equipped for every good work' (2 Tim 3:16).

'...just as our dear brother Paul also wrote you with the wisdom God gave him. He writes the same way in all his letters, speaking in them of these matters. His letters contain some things that are hard to understand, which ignorant and unstable people distort, as they do the other Scriptures, to their own destruction' (2 Peter 3:15-16).

'I charge you before the Lord to have this letter read to all the brothers' (1 Thess 5:17).

'After this letter has been read to you, see that it is also read in the church of the Laodiceans and that you in turn read the letter from Laodicea' (Col 4:16).

The letters of Paul reflect both great unity and great diversity. The person and work of Christ, salvation in Christ, and the godliness of life necessarily flowing from salvation are always present, but the particular way in which these doctrines are expressed varies from letter to letter. For example, justification by faith alone is prominent in Galatians and Romans. Eschatological themes are prominent in the Thessalonian correspondence. The high priestly ministry of Christ is underscored in his letter to the Hebrews. And the themes of godliness, holiness, and obedience to God's law are prominent in them all, far more so than those students of Paul suggest who subsume all of Paul's teachings under the rubric of justification. Underlying them all is Paul's redemptive-historical vision that the Eschaton appeared in grace with the first coming of Jesus the Messiah (the 'already' of eschatology) and that Christ's kingdom will appear in power and glory in the final judgment at the second coming of Christ (the 'not yet' of eschatology). This much is clear: regardless of their emphases or themes, the letters of Paul, because he was an inspired apostle of Christ, were accepted by the true people of God from the beginning as possessing divine authority (1 Thess 2:13; 2 Thess 2:15; 1 Cor 2:6-13; Gal 1:1, 11-12; 2 Tim 3:16; 2 Pet 3:15-16). And they were publicly read in the congregations to whom they were written and were circularized in and collected by congregations apparently through the normal process of exchange and circulation (1 Thess 5:27; Col 4:16; see here Rev 1:3). Indeed, after the first century, as evidenced by Marcion's *Apostolicon* (c. A.D. 140), the Muratorian Fragment (c. A.D. 175), and the Chester Beatty Codex P^{46} (c. A.D. 200), Paul's letters circulated as collections, including at times seven, ten, thirteen, or fourteen of his letters. More specifically, with respect to the issue of their canonicity, it appears that there was never a question in the early church from the first about Paul's fourteen letters and by the middle of the third century the content of the *Corpus Paulinum* had been pretty well fixed.[1] Paul clearly endorsing with his Lord before him the Old Testament canon of first-century

---

1. As noted in the last chapter, Paul's letter to the Hebrews was accepted from the first in both the Eastern and the Western church, his authorship of Hebrews seemingly never having been a matter of serious dispute in Egypt and North Africa. It was in the Western church – primarily in Italy, particularly in Rome, and on *dogmatic grounds* – that dispute over the authorship of Hebrews arose later. The Western church's setting Hebrews aside later, while it placed the question of its apostolicity in the foreground, was certainly connected with the way the Montanists attached themselves to Hebrews 6:1-8. But the recently discovered *The Gospel of Truth* (Codex I), possibly authored by Valentinus, near Nag Hammadi shows that

Palestinian Judaism and treating that ancient canon in its entirety as the oracles of God (Rom. 3:2), added to that canon his own letters which the apostolic church, as did he, immediately regarded as the Word of God. This much is borne out by Scripture and early church history and is indisputable.

But the church's coming to an understanding of which books were to comprise what eventually came to be the *entire* New Testament canon for this age and to the realization that the canon was complete was a slow, almost imperceptible, process. Franzmann notes that before 170 A.D. none of the Apostolic Fathers

> explicitly asks or answers the question, 'Which books are to be included in the list of those which are normative for the church?' What we do find in the writings of the so-called Apostolic Fathers (Clement of Rome, the Epistle of Barnabas, Ignatius, Polycarp, Hermas, the Teaching of the Twelve Apostles) is, first, a witness to the fact that the books destined to become the New Testament canon are *there*, at work in the church from the first. The books are quoted and alluded to, more often without mention of author or title than by way of formal quotation.
>
> Secondly, we find a witness to the fact that the thought and life of the church were being shaped by the content of the New Testament writings from the first, and moreover by the content of all types of New Testament writings. The influence of [all these types] (Synoptic Gospels, Johannine works, Pauline Letters, the Catholic Letters) is clearly discernible. *To judge by the evidence of this period, the four Gospels and the letters of Paul were everywhere the basic units in the emerging canon of the New Testament.*
>
> And, thirdly, there is some specific witness in these writings to the fact that the New Testament writings assumed a position of authority in the church which they share with no other writings. 'The Lord' and 'the apostles' appear as authoritative voices besides the Old Testament Scriptures....
>
> Further evidence for the authority exercised by the New Testament writings is found in the fact, recorded by Justin Martyr, that the New Testament writings...were read in the worship services of the church, interchangeably with the Old Testament. This is perhaps the most significant bit of evidence for this period.[2]

---

around A.D. 150 the letter to the Hebrews did not have lesser authority in Rome than Paul's other letters.

2. Martin H. Franzmann, *The Word of the Lord Grows*, 287-88 (emphasis supplied).

Herman N. Ridderbos concurs with Franzmann's opinion:

> There was never any discussion of the 'canonicity' of the majority [and at first of none] of the New Testament writings. The church never regarded those writings as being anything but the authoritative witness to the great time of redemption.... Uncertainty about *some* of [its] writings...only arose later, as a result of certain actions that occurred within or against the church.[3]

By his last comment Ridderbos is alluding to the time around 140 A.D. when Marcion, the gnostic heretic, repudiated the entire Old Testament and accepted only a mutilated version of Luke and ten 'edited' epistles of Paul, altogether excluding Hebrews, 1 and 2 Timothy and Titus (which 'rewrite' of Paul he called the *Apostolicon*), as his canon. Thus the question of the New Testament canon became a matter of concern in some regions of the church. And it seems that this later regional uncertainty 'damaged the authority a document had from the beginning and destroyed the original certainty of the church' about some New Testament books.[4] Even so, according to the Muratorian Canon or Muratorian Fragment (so named from the librarian of the Ambrosian Library in Milan, Cardinal Lodovico Muratori, who discovered the document and published it in 1740), which was written by an unknown author (Muratori ascribed it to Caius, an elder in Rome) around 175 A.D., there seems never to have been any doubt on the part of the church at large concerning the canonical status of twenty New Testament books, namely, the four Gospels, Acts, thirteen letters of Paul, 1 Peter, and 1 John. The canonical status of the remaining seven New Testament books, namely, James, Hebrews, 2 Peter, 2 John, 3 John, Jude, and Revelation (as well as the canonical status of some other books, such as the Acts

---

3. Herman N. Ridderbos, *Redemptive History and the New Testament Scriptures* (Second revised edition; Phillipsburg, N. J.: Presbyterian and Reformed, 1988), 40. See also Ridderbos, 'The Canon of the New Testament' in *Revelation and the Bible*, edited by Carl F. H. Henry (Grand Rapids: Baker, 1958), 189-201; F. F. Bruce, *The Canon of Scripture* (Downers Grove, Ill.: InterVarsity, 1988), 255, agrees with Franzmann and Ridderbos, writing:

> The earliest Christians did not trouble themselves about criteria of canonicity; they would not have readily understood the expression. They accepted the Old Testament scriptures as they had received them: the authority of those scriptures was sufficiently ratified by the teaching and example of the Lord and his apostles. The teaching and example of the Lord and his apostles, whether conveyed by word of mouth or in writing, had axiomatic authority for them.

4. Ridderbos, *Redemptive History*, 44.

The Divine Authority and Canonicity of Paul's Letters 297

of Paul, the Shepherd of Hermas, the Revelation of Peter, and the Epistle of Barnabas, which were finally rejected), continued to be a matter of concern in some regions for about two centuries before they eventually found a fixed place in the church's New Testament canon. But as the several regions of the church grew in their ecumenical ties with one another it became increasingly evident that the doubts concerning these writings were only regional and that these regional doubts contradicted what the larger church had for a long time believed about these matters.

Therefore, during the third century, along with the ever-widening rejection of all the other literary claimants to canonical status, the seven disputed books continued slowly to gain ground in the churches. Yet no commission of theologians or church council met to define or impose a canon on the church. In the fourth century (325 A.D.), since Eusebius of Caesarea could appeal then to nothing 'official'—no conciliar decree, no definitive pronouncement that had church authority behind it—he surveyed in his *Ecclesiastical History*, book 3, chapter 25, the status of the various books in the church. And this is what he reports: twenty-seven books then occupied a place of authority in the life of the church. But because there was still some controversy, Eusebius, desiring to be scrupulously accurate, divided the twenty-seven books into the *homologoumena* (the 'agreed upon' books) and the *antilegomena* (the 'spoken against' books). Among the former he listed twenty-two books: the four Gospels, Acts, fourteen letters of Paul (including Hebrews among the Pauline letters!), 1 Peter, 1 John, and the Revelation of John (with the notation, 'if it really seem proper'). Among the *antilegomena* ('which are nevertheless recognized by many') he listed five books: James, Jude, 2 Peter, 2 John, and 3 John. Somewhat curiously, if his second placement of John's Revelation was not an unwitting error on his part, he lists John's Revelation again, not among the *antilegomena* but among a third group, the *nothoi* (the 'rejected' books), with the notation, 'if it seem proper, which some, as I said, reject, but which others class among the accepted books.' A little over forty years later, in 367 A.D., Athanasius, in his *Thirty-Ninth Paschal Letter* (often referred to as his 'Easter' letter because it announced the official date of Easter to the churches), drawing no distinction as Eusebius had done between *homologoumena* and *antilegomena*, felt the liberty to list the twenty-seven books of Eusebius' canon as 'the wellsprings of salvation, from which he who thirsts may take his fill of sacred words'. From this date onward the canon of the church was practically determined, and before the end of the fourth century, under the influence of Jerome and Augustine, the church had resolved all the canonical questions to its satisfaction. Accordingly, in 397 A.D. the Third Council of Carthage demanded that nothing be read in the church under the title of divine Scripture except the 'canonical' books, and then it affirmed precisely the current collection of twenty-seven New Testament books as the New Testament canon. And because of the near-universal Christian conviction which has prevailed ever since then[5] that the Lord of the church had given these specific books and only these books to his people as the New Testament canon, the church for the last sixteen hundred years has restricted the New Testament canon to the twenty-seven commonly received New Testament books. In sum, from that point on the New Testament canon has been 'a literary, historical and theological datum'.[6]

Long have Christian scholars, after the fact, debated about what criteria the church employed during the third and fourth centuries to determine a given book's canonicity. It has been urged that the early church applied such criteria as

(1) apostolicity (Was a given book written by an apostle or by one so closely associated to an apostle that it received his apostolic endorsement?),

(2) antiquity (Since only documents from the apostolic age should be considered as candidates for canonicity, was a given document written in that age?),

(3) orthodoxy (Was a given book doctrinally correct, that is, in accord with the 'apostolic faith', particularly concerning the person and work of Christ?),

(4) catholicity (Was a given book universally or virtually universally accepted throughout the church?),

(5) lection (Was a given book being widely read and used in the churches?), and

(6) inspiration (Was a given book inspired?),

to judge whether any given book was to be viewed as 'canonical' or not.[7]

---

5. The Ethiopian church is the 'holdout' here, having both the twenty-seven-book New Testament canon and a longer New Testament canon with seven extra books. This latter canonical tradition must be regarded as aberrant in this respect.

6. Bruce, *The Canon of Scripture*, 250.

Richard B. Gaffin, Jr., has convincingly argued, however, and I think correctly, given the peculiar mix of books that make up the New Testament, that scholarship has not been able to establish a set of criteria for canonicity which does not at the same time threaten to undermine the New Testament canon as it has come down to us. According to Gaffin, the problems with the several suggested criteria are as follows:

(1) The criterion of *apostolicity* does not account for Mark, Luke-Acts, Hebrews,[8] Jude, and most likely James being included. To say that Mark and Luke/Acts are apostolic because the former is 'Peter's Gospel' (so Papias) and the latter is 'Paul's Gospel', is not sufficient, since we are given no reason to think that apostles could impart their apostolicity to others. Nor does this criterion explain why some of Paul's other letters (see 1 Cor 5:9; 2 Cor 2:4, 9; Col 4:16) were not included.

(2) The criterion of *antiquity* is really a variation on apostolicity and fails to explain why Paul's 'previous' letter (1 Cor 5:9) which was earlier than Hebrews was not included while Hebrews was included.

(3) The criterion of *inspiration*, while certainly necessary to canonicity, cannot explain why Paul's letter to the Laodiceans (Col 4:16), also apostolic and also inspired, was not included. This criterion also faces the insuperable difficulty of demonstrating the inspiration of such books as Mark and Jude.

And (4) the criterion of *lection* cannot explain why documents such as the *Shepherd of Hermas* and the *Didache*, which were used and occasionally read in public worship, were finally rejected, while there is little to no evidence that such works as 2 Peter, 2 John, 3 John, and Jude were so used.

While not denying that criteria such as apostolic authorship and conformity to apostolic orthodoxy were made use of in the early church as it moved toward a consensus on the New Testament canon, Gaffin contends that even the early church's employment of its

---

7. Warfield, 'The Westminster Doctrine of Holy Scripture,' *Selected Shorter Writings of Benjamin B. Warfield*, edited by John E. Meeter (Nutley, N. J.: Presbyterian and Reformed, 1973), II, 565, declares: 'The order of procedure in ascertaining Scripture is to settle first the canon, then its inspiration, and then, as a corollary, its authority.' For a contrary view, see R. Laird Harris, *Inspiration and Canonicity of the Bible* (Grand Rapids, Mich.: Zondervan, 1957), 219-80, particularly 280: 'The principle of canonicity was inspiration and...the test of inspiration was authorship by...apostles.'

8. I obviously disagree with Gaffin here.

criteria, whatever they were, were at times defectively applied in reaching what eventually turned out to be right decisions. He has in mind here the book of Hebrews whose authorship the early church (he thinks incorrectly but I think correctly) ascribed to Paul. Furthermore, Gaffin contends, all attempts to demonstrate these criteria subject the absolute authority of the canon to the relativity of historical study and fallible human insight.[9] Regarding this last point Ridderbos also observes:

> no matter how strong the evidence for apostolicity (and therefore for canonicity) may be in many instances and no matter how forceful the arguments in favor of the apostolicity of certain other writings may be, historical judgments cannot be the final and sole ground for the church's accepting the New Testament as canonical. To accept the New Testament on that ground would mean that the church would ultimately be basing its faith on the results of historical investigation.[10]

I concur with Ridderbos. What the evidentialist apparently does not realize when he attempts to establish the grounds and extent of the New Testament canon by his (often very elaborate) list of criteria and historical judgments is that, however much he may claim infallibility for the individual books of the New Testament, by his methodology he can neither establish their infallibility with certainty nor can he place them in an 'infallible' canon. The New Testament, for him, is a compilation of 'books with possible infallibility in a fallible canon'. But a fallible canon cannot support the church's need for and claim of divine authority for the New Testament since the

---

9. Richard B. Gaffin, Jr., 'The New Testament as Canon,' *Inerrancy and Hermeneutics*, edited by Harvey M. Conn (Grand Rapids, Mich.: Baker, 1988), 168-70.
10. Ridderbos, *Redemptive History*, 32-33. R. C. Sproul, *Essential Truths of the Christian Faith* (Wheaton, Ill.: Tyndale, 1992), declares, precisely because of the reason stated by Ridderbos, that our New Testament is 'a fallible collection of infallible books' (22). Of course, given his reasons for asserting that the Bible is a 'fallible collection', he ought to assert that it is a fallible collection of 'fallible books' as well, for he employs the same basic procedure to establish the authority of the individual books of the Bible. Suffice it to say, *I disagree with him. I believe that he is wrong and that the New Testament is an infallible collection of infallible books but for reasons he does not share with me*. Of course, he is only being consistent as an evidentialist when he asserts this (I regret that more evidentialists do not see as clearly as he that his opinion is the only consistent conclusion that evidentialists may hold). But if our New Testament is, at best, 'a fallible collection' of infallible books, as he suggests, then it follows that perhaps our New Testament collection failed to include some 'infallible' book that it should have included or may have included an 'infallible' book that God did not intend should become a part of the church's witness to redemption and a part of its rule for faith and life throughout this age. I sincerely and deeply regret that Sproul holds this view, for it casts a shadow over the infallible authority of the New Testament.

evidentialist, by his method, can never know for certain whether God intended a particular 'possibly infallible' book in the fallible New Testament canon to bear authoritative witness to the great objective central events of redemptive history throughout the Christian era and specifically to bear that witness to him.

Of course, if Ridderbos, Gaffin, and I are right about this, one may then ask, if the church is not to rely on historical investigation and human judgments as the final and sole grounds for the church's accepting the New Testament as canonical, how can it be certain, without a direct statement from God on the matter, that it was only these particular books that he intended should be canonical? How can one be certain that the New Testament does not include a book that should not have been included or that it fails to include a book that should have been included? Specifically, how can one be certain that Paul's 'fourteenth' letter—the letter to the Hebrews—should have been included as indeed it was? How can one be certain that the New Testament canon is even closed? And would not the position espoused by Ridderbos, Gaffin, and me, if endorsed, involve the church at the very foundation of its faith in a sort of mindless 'fideism'?

To such questions no answers can be given that will fully satisfy the mind that desires to think autonomously, that is, independently from Scripture. For regardless of whether or not the Christian scholar thinks he possesses the one right criterion or the one right list of criteria for a given book's canonicity, at some point—and if at no other point, at least at the point of the established number, namely, twenty-seven New Testament books, not twenty-six or twenty-eight —the Christian must accept by faith that the church, under the providential guidance of God's Spirit, got both the number and the 'list' right since God did not provide the church with a specific list of names of books which should be included in the New Testament canon. All that we know for certain about the history of the first four centuries of the church would suggest (1) that God's Spirit providentially led his church—imperceptively yet inexorably—when it asked its questions, whatever they were, to adopt the twenty-seven documents—Paul's fourteen letters among them—that the Godhead had determined would serve as the foundation of the church's doctrinal teaching and thus bear infallible witness throughout the Christian era to the great objective central events of redemptive history, and (2) that *this* 'apostolic tradition' *authenticated and established itself* over time in the mind of the church as just this infallible foundation and witness.

As for the question concerning canon closure, the sixteen hundred years that have passed since the church resolved all questions regarding the issue of canonicity to its satisfaction, during which period of time no serious attempt has been made anywhere to add an additional document to or to take one away from the New Testament canon, is a strong circumstantial argument for its closure. Even as significant a figure in Reformation times as Martin Luther got nowhere when he raised the question of the canonicity of James, which he termed 'an epistle full of straw' because it seemed to focus more on the law than on Christ and the gospel.[11] Moreover, the possibility that a document ever will be presented for inclusion in the canon that, given the fragmented state of the church for the last thousand years, could or would receive the full church's acceptance, is so infinitesimally small that, for all practical purposes, it is non-existent.

In sum, the formation of the twenty-seven-book New Testament canon, after all is said and done, appears ultimately to have been the work, not of men, not even of the church, but of God's Spirit alone. If this be not the case, then we have to conclude that the New Testament is a fallible collection of possibly infallible letters. F. F. Bruce notes in this regard:

> Certainly, as one looks back on the process of canonization in early Christian centuries, and remembers some of the ideas of which certain church writers of that period were capable, it is easy to conclude that in reaching a conclusion on the limits of the canon they were directed by a wisdom higher than their own. It may be that those whose minds have been largely formed by scripture as canonized find it natural to make a judgment of this kind. But it is not mere hindsight to say, with William Barclay, that 'the New Testament books became canonical because no

---

11. See Luther's *Preface to the New Testament* ('In comparison with [the gospel and first epistle of St. John, St. Paul's epistles, especially those to the Romans, Galatians, and Ephesians, and St. Peter's first epistle], the epistle of St. James is an epistle full of straw, because it contains nothing evangelical.') and his *Preface to the Epistle of St. James* in which he rejects its apostolic authorship and provenance and refuses it 'a place among the writers of the true canon' (1) 'because, in direct opposition to St. Paul and all the rest of the Bible, it ascribes justification to works,' (2) 'because, in the whole length of its teaching, not once does it give Christians any instruction or reminder of the passion, resurrection, or spirit of Christ,' and (3) because it appeared to him to be written 'far later than St. Peter or St. Paul'.

one could stop them doing so' or even, in the exaggerated language of Oscar Cullmann, that 'the books which were to form the future canon *forced themselves on the Church by their intrinsic apostolic authority*, as they do still, because the Kyrios Christ speaks in them'.[12]

D. A. Carson, Douglas J. Moo, and Leon Morris agree:

...it is important to observe that although there was no ecclesiastical machinery like the medieval papacy to enforce decisions, nevertheless the worldwide church almost universally came to accept the same twenty-seven books. It was not so much that the church selected the canon as that the canon selected itself. This point has frequently been made, and deserves repeating.

The fact that substantially the whole church came to recognize the same twenty-seven books as canonical is remarkable when it is remembered that the result was not contrived. All that the several churches throughout the Empire could do was to witness to their own experience with the documents and share whatever knowledge they might have about their origin and character. When consideration is given to the diversity in cultural backgrounds and in orientation to the essentials of the Christian faith within the churches, their common agreement about which books belonged to the New Testament serves to suggest that this final decision did not originate solely at the human level.[13]

Concluding his own review of the history of canon formation, Franzmann appears to agree with this judgment:

the New Testament as a collection has a curiously informal and almost casual sort of history. The book that was destined to remain the sacred book for millions of Christians for century upon century came into the church without fanfare, in a quiet, shuffling sort of way. Its history is not at all what *we* should expect the history of a sacred book to be. The story of the Book of Mormon is a good example of how man thinks a sacred book should come to man—miraculously, guaranteed by its miraculousness. The canon is a miracle indeed, but a miracle of another

---

12. Bruce, *The Canon of Scripture*, 282. I do not think that Cullmann's language is 'exaggerated' at all.
13. D. A. Carson, Douglas J. Moo, and Leon Morris, *An Introduction to the New Testament* (Grand Rapids: Zondervan, 1992), 494. The citation in their quotation is from Glenn W. Barker, William L. Lane, and J. Ramsey Michaels, *The New Testament Speaks* (San Francisco: Harper & Row, 1969), 29.

sort, a miracle like the incarnation of our Lord, a miracle in servant's form. Only a God who is really Lord of all history could risk bringing his written word into history in the way the New Testament was actually brought in. Only the God who by his Spirit rules sovereignly over his people could lead his weak, embattled, and persecuted churches to ask the right questions concerning the books that made their claim upon God's people and to find the right answers; to fix with Spirit-guided instinct on that which was genuinely apostolic (whether written directly by an apostle or not) and therefore genuinely authoritative. Only God himself could make men see that public reading in the churches was a sure clue to canonicity; only the Spirit of God could make men see that a word which commands the obedience of God's people thereby established itself as God's word and must inevitably remove all other claimants from the scene.

This the 27-book canon did. It established itself in the early centuries of the church and maintained itself in the continued life of the church.... And it will maintain itself henceforth. The question of the limits of the canon may be theoretically open; but the history of the church indicates that it is for practical purposes closed. The 27 books are there in the church, at work in the church. They are what Athanasius called them, 'the wellsprings of salvation' for all Christendom. And in the last analysis, the church of God can become convinced and remain assured that they are indeed the wellsprings of salvation only by drinking of them.[14]

In response then to the 'bottom-line' question, why did the current twenty-seven books of the New Testament, including Paul's fourteen pieces, and only these twenty-seven, finally become the self-authenticating New Testament canon, we must be content finally to say, with Gaffin:

> just these twenty-seven books are what God has chosen to preserve, and he has not told us why....
>
> In the matter of the New Testament as canon, too, until Jesus comes 'we walk by faith, not by sight' (2 Cor. 5:7 RSV). But that faith, grounded in the apostolic tradition of the New Testament, is neither arbitrary nor blind. It has its reasons, its good reasons; it is in conflict only with the autonomy of reason.[15]

---

14. Franzmann, *The Word of the Lord Grows*, 294-95.
15. Gaffin, 'The New Testament as Canon,' 181.

PART TWO

PAUL'S MISSIONARY THEOLOGY

Presenting Paul's Missionary Theology

In my presentation of Paul's missionary theology, I do not intend to involve myself directly in the debate presently being conducted by Paul scholars concerning the central organizing principle in Paul's theology. Not only is the discussion of interest primarily to scholars and at times the conclusions highly tendentious and subjective but also the number and variety of suggestions that can be found here are simply bewildering. For example, in the last century Adolf Deissmann made central to Paul what he termed Paul's 'mysticism' of the 'in Christ' relation.[1] More recently, the most narrow suggestions for the center are simply 'Jesus Christ' or 'the lordship of Christ',[2] 'Jesus as the Son of God',[3] and 'Christological soteriology'.[4] Another rather narrow suggestion that has been challenged by several scholars[5] is Ernst Käsemann's view, held by Martin Luther himself, that the classic Lutheran view of justification by faith is the core of Paul's thought at all times.[6] At the other extreme, J. Plevnik contends that

> any center of Pauline theology must...include all those components of the apostle's gospel: his understanding of Christ and of God, his understanding of God's salvific action through Christ, involving the

---

1. Adolf Deissmann, *Die neutestamentliche Formel 'in Christo Jesu,'* (Marburg: Elwert, 1892); so also Wilhelm Bousset in his *Kyrios Christos* and Albert Schweitzer who in his *The Mysticism of Paul the Apostle* (London: Black, 1931) urges that Paul's doctrine of justification by faith is 'a subsidiary crater, which has formed within the rim of the main crater—the mystical doctrine of redemption through being-in-Christ' (225).
2. See J. G. Gibbs, *Creation and Redemption* (Leiden: E. J. Brill, 1971) and James D. G. Dunn, *Unity and Diversity of the New Testament* (Philadelphia: Westminster, 1977), 369-72, and *The Theology of Paul the Apostle* (Grand Rapids: Eerdmans, 1998), 729-30.
3. L. Cerfaux, *Christ in the Theology of St. Paul* (New York: Herder & Herder, 1959), 4.
4. J. A. Fitzmyer, *Pauline Theology: A Brief Sketch* (Englewood Cliffs, N.J.: Prentice-Hall, 1967), 16.
5. See J. Plevnik, 'The Center of Paul's Theology' in *Catholic Biblical Quarterly* 51 (1989), 461-62.
6. Ernst Käsemann, *New Testament Questions of Today* (London: SCM, 1979), 168-69. See here also P. Stuhlmacher, *Biblische Theologie des Neuen Testaments*, Bd. 1: Grundlegung. Von Jesus zu Paulus (Göttingen: Vandenhoeck & Ruprecht, 1992), 311-48.

Easter event and its implications, the present Lordship, the future coming of Christ, and the appropriation of salvation. Accordingly, for him 'the center is thus not any single aspect of Christ...but the whole Christ'.[7] E. P. Sanders suggests that two convictions 'governed Paul's Christian life: (1) that Jesus Christ is Lord, that in him God provided for the salvation of all who believe...; (2) that he, Paul, was called to be the apostle to the Gentiles.'[8] C. J. A. Hickling, accepting Sander's suggestions, adds a third conviction to the Pauline center, that 'God has already brought about in Christ a decisive and final transformation of time'.[9] Jürgen Christiaan Beker combines three of Paul's principal concepts, namely, Paul's theology of election, his theology of the cross, and his doctrine of justification, and urges that the second—his theology of the cross—is the real center which is the defining 'canon' of his theology of election and which is itself clothed in the language of his doctrine of justification. This means then for Beker that 'apocalyptic is the indispensable means for [understanding Paul's] interpretation of the Christ-event'.[10] Ralph P. Martin submits that reconciliation between God and man is the central theme of Paul's thought.[11] Finally, Heikki Räisänen even expresses skepticism concerning the existence of *any* central organizing principle in Paul's thought.[12]

If I were to hazard a suggestion I would urge that central to Paul's thought is the primacy of God's sovereign divine grace as his grace comes to expression in the cross-work of the incarnate Christ in behalf of sinners, which instrument is God's eschatological saving event both for elect sinners now (the eschatological 'already') and for the

---

7. Plevnik, 'The Center of Paul's Theology,' 477-78.
8. E. P. Sanders, *Paul and Palestinian Judaism* (Philadelphia: Fortress, 1977), 441-42. In his *Paul* (Past Masters; Oxford: University Press, 1991), Sanders seems to suggest that the center of Paul's thought was his 'in Christ' experience, conceived either as an expression of his 'participationist eschatology' or as a kind of Jewish 'apocalyptic mysticism'. In agreement with this last suggestion is Alan F. Segal, *Paul the Convert: The Apostolate and Apostasy of Saul the Pharisee* (New Haven: Yale University Press, 1990), 34-71.
9. C. J. A. Hickling, 'Centre and Periphery in Paul's Thought' in *Studia Biblica III. Papers on Paul and Other NT Authors*, edited by E. A. Livingstone (Sheffield: Academic Press, 1978), 199-214.
10. Jürgen Christiaan Beker, *Paul the Apostle: The Triumph of God in Life and Thought* (Philadelphia: Fortress, 1980).
11. R. P. Martin, *Reconciliation: A Study of Paul's Theology* (Grand Rapids: Zondervan, 1990); see also his 'Center of Paul's Theology', *Dictionary of Paul and His Letters*, edited by Gerald F. Hawthorne, Ralph P. Martin, Daniel G. Reid (Downers Grove, Ill.: InterVarsity, 1993), 94.
12. Heikki Räisänen, *Paul and the Law* (Philadelphia: Fortress, 1983), 264-69.

recovery of the entire cosmos in the Eschaton (the eschatological 'not yet'). Accordingly, I intend to present Paul's theology in the form of a 'mini' systematic theology which takes into account Paul's perception of the triune God's gracious work of saving the elect and restoring the cosmos to its paradisaical state by the cross-work of Christ. I see no real profit in trying to capture his thought by a 'biblical theology' method of presentation for the following two reasons:

A. The literary period of Paul's missionary ministry (about fourteen years long, from around A.D. 49 to 63) would have hardly provided sufficient time for his thought to develop in any discernible way accessible to analysis beyond what it already had become as a result of his conversion and ministry as evangelist and teacher during his pre-literary period (about sixteen years long, from around A.D. 33 to 49). The Christ of his last letter is the same Christ that we find in his first one. His sermon statement in Acts 13:38-39 (A.D. 48) and his very first letter, Galatians, written in A.D. 49, evince a carefully inflected, precise doctrine of justification consistent in every way with his later exposition of justification written to the Romans some eight years later, c. A.D. 57. And his doctrines of sanctification and eschatology evidence no substantive change from the first to his last letter.

B. Paul's letters are so *ad hoc*, that is, so situation-specific—written for vastly varying reasons and directed to very different problems— that one could never be sure that what he thought was a development in the apostle's thought was not simply the result of Paul's thought (encapsulated by the words expressing it) assuming the shape essential to addressing a specific *ad hoc* problem, but flowing nonetheless from the same theological vision throughout.

The Sources of Paul's Missionary Theology

The sources of Paul's theological responses to the time-specific and occasion-specific situations invoking his letters are four in number:

(1) God's providential preparation of Saul to become the Paul that we see in Acts and in his letters (such as his racial and religious background, his social and political setting as a Jew of the Diaspora and as a Roman citizen, his early training under Gamaliel, etc.);

(2) the Old Testament Scriptures,[13] citing those Scriptures one hundred and forty-one times in his letters: sixty times in Romans, thirty-eight of these essentially Masoretic with the remaining twenty-two following the Septuagint; seventeen times in 1 Corinthians, thirteen of these essentially Masoretic with the remaining four following the Septuagint; ten times in 2 Corinthians, nine of these essentially Masoretic with the one remaining following the Septuagint; ten times in Galatians, nine of these essentially Masoretic with the one remaining following the Septuagint; five times in Ephesians, four of these essentially Masoretic with the one remaining following the Septuagint; one time in 1 Timothy, essentially Masoretic; one time in 2 Timothy, essentially Masoretic; and thirty-seven times in Hebrews, twenty-four of these essentially Masoretic with the remaining thirteen following the Septuagint;[14]

(3) direct revelation as an apostle of Christ as he travelled and wrote his letters, and

(4) the wider tradition of the apostolic church (see, for example,

---

13. Perhaps it should be also noted here that Paul does not ground his apostolic assignment to the Gentiles solely in his life-transforming experience on the Damascus Road (Gal. 1:1; 15-16) but sees it as also having been predicted in the Old Testament Scriptures. Against his Jewish opponents at Pisidian Antioch Paul, after first telling them, 'We had to speak the word of God to you first. Since you rejected it and do not consider yourselves worthy of eternal life, we now turn to the Gentiles', then cites that portion of Isaiah 49:6 which immediately follows Yahweh's declaration concerning the Messiah that 'it is too small a thing for you to be my servant to restore the tribes of Jacob and bring back those of Israel I have kept', and declares: 'For this is what the Lord has commanded us: "I have made you a light to the Gentiles, that you may bring salvation to the ends of the earth"' (Acts 13:46-47). In Romans 10:11-15 Paul cites Isaiah 52:7 as a description of his gospel proclamation to all men, including the Gentile world (see also here Rom. 15:8-12). Then, in his final Acts speech, delivered before the Jews who has assembled in Rome 'to hear what his views are' (Acts 28:22), after citing Isaiah 6:9-10 which foretold Israel's hardness of heart, Paul said, 'Let it be known to you then that this salvation of God has been sent to the Gentiles; they will listen' (Acts 28:28). Clearly, Paul saw his labors as a missionary to the Gentile world as grounded squarely in the Old Testament vision of the salvation of the nations in accordance with the promises of the Abrahamic covenant.

14. See 'Index of Quotations', The Greek New Testament (UBS fourth edition; Stuttgart: Deutsche Bibelgesellschaft, 1993), 889-90. Moisés Silva, 'Old Testament in Paul' in Dictionary of Paul and His Letters, 630-42, especially 631, ignoring the citations in Hebrews, categorizes his one hundred and seven Old Testament citations in Paul as follows: forty-two are in essential agreement with both the Masoretic Text and the Septuagint; seven more are in essential agreement with the Masoretic Text over against the Septuagint; seventeen more are in essential agreement with the Septuagint over against the Masoretic Text; thirty-one more are uniquely Paul's renderings, differing from both the Masoretic Text and the Septuagint; and ten more are debatable either because the source of the citation is debated or because scholars disagree as to whether the citation is an actual citation or simply an allusion to an Old Testament text.

[a] his possible citations of early Christian creeds[15] in Romans 1:3-4, 10:9; 1 Corinthians 12:3, 15:3-5 [b] his allusions to the tradition he heard from the other apostles in Galatians 1:18-19, 2:8-9; 1 Corinthians 9:5, 15:11]; [c] his possible citations of early Christians hymns in Philippians 2:6-11, Colossians 1:15-20, and 1 Timothy 3:16, and [d] his five citations of 'faithful sayings' in the Pastoral Letters [1 Tim 1:15, 3:1; 4:7-9; 2 Tim 2:11-13; Titus 3:4-8]).

The God of Paul's Missionary Theology

That Paul regarded himself as an orthodox Jew, worshiping in his monotheism the one living and true God of Israel's ancient patriarchs, is clear in everything he wrote:

Romans 3:30: '...*there is only one God* [εἷς ὁ θεός], who will justify the circumcised by faith and the uncircumcised through that same faith.'

Romans 16:27: '*to the only wise God* [μόνῳ σοφῷ θεῷ] be glory forever through Jesus Christ. Amen.'

1 Corinthians 8:4, 6: 'We know that an idol is nothing at all in the world and that *there is no God but one* [οὐδεὶς θεὸς εἰ μὴ εἷς]...for us *there is but one God* [εἷς θεός], the Father, from whom all things came and for whom we live; and *there is but one Lord* [εἷς κύριος], Jesus Christ, through whom all things came and through whom we live.'

Galatians 3:20: '...God is one [θεὸς εἷς ἐστιν].'

1 Timothy 1:17: 'Now to the King eternal, immortal, invisible, *the only God* [μόνῳ θεῷ], be honor and glory for ever and ever. Amen.'

1 Timothy 2:5: '*For there is one God* [εἷς γὰρ θεός], and one mediator between God and men, the man Christ Jesus.'

1 Timothy 6:15-16: 'God, the blessed and *only Ruler* [μόνος δυνάστης], the King of kings and Lord of lords, who *alone* [μόνος]

---

15. See J. N. D. Kelly, 'Creedal Elements in the New Testament,' *Early Christian Creeds* (London: Longmans, Green, 1950).

is immortal and who lives in unapproachable light, whom no man has seen or can see. To him be honor and might forever. Amen.'

Further evidence of Paul's orthodox – even radical – monotheism may be seen in the contrast he draws between his theology as a Jew and the former theology of his Gentile converts. Of the latter he would write that his converts 'turned to God from idols to serve the living and true God' (1 Thess 1:9), that they had formerly worshiped 'beings that by nature are not gods' (Gal 4:8, NRSV) and 'mute idols' (1 Cor 12:2). And though he believed that 'no idol in the world really exists' (1 Cor 8:4, NRSV), with deep perception into the true character of the spiritual world, he would also declare that the sacrifices that the pagans offered to their 'so-called gods' (1 Cor 8:5) were in reality being 'offered, not to God, but to demons' (δαιμονίοις; 1 Cor 10:20) behind whom stands Satan who disguises himself as an angel of light (2 Cor 11:14) and who, under God, is the 'god of this age' (2 Cor 4:4), the 'ruler of the kingdom of the air' (Eph 2:2).

In accord with Old Testament teaching Paul believed and taught that the one living and true God (Heb 3:12; 9:14; 10:31) created the universe (Acts 17:24; Rom 1:20-25; 11:36; 1 Cor 8:6; 11:12; Col 1:16; Eph 3:9; Heb 1:2; 3:4; 4:3-4; 11:3) and mankind (Acts 17:29; Heb 2:7), but not out of an ontological need to complement himself (Acts 17:25). After creating the universe, unlike the god of Deism, the God of Paul's theology sovereignly continues to preserve the universe (Acts 14:17) and to govern all his creatures and all their actions (Acts 17:25; Rom 11:36; Heb 1:3; 6:3). All that he does and all that occurs in heaven and on earth are determined by his eternal decree (Rom 9:11-23; Eph 1:3-14).

The one living and true God, for Paul, is also God the Father: in every letter he writes he calls God 'Father' (Gal 1:3; 1 Thess 1:1; 2 Thess 1:2; 1 Cor 1:3; 2 Cor 1:2; Rom 1:7; Col 1:2; Phil 1:2; Eph 1:2; Philem 3; 1 Tim 1:2; Tit 1:4; Heb 1:2-8; 12:9; 2 Tim 1:2 (Paul generally reserves 'Lord' to refer to Christ to avoid the impression of believing in two Gods; see his epistolary salutations and 1 Corinthians 8:6 for examples of this pattern of speech). And the attributes of Paul's God are unquestionably orthodox. He is the 'most high God' (Heb 7:1), the Father of glory (Eph 1:17), of spirits (Heb 12:9), of mercies (2 Cor 1:3), and of humankind (Eph 3:14-15). He is eternal, immortal, invisible, the king and judge of the world (1 Tim

1:17; Rom 3:4-6; Heb 12:23). He is wise and all-knowing (Rom 11:33-34; 16:26), holy and just (Rom 2:11; 3:26), and as the covenant God of Israel (Rom 9–11) is gracious, loving and faithful toward sinners (Rom 3:24; 5:8, 15; 1 Cor 1:9; 10:13; 2 Cor 1:18-20; Eph 2:4-10).

In only three of his letters does Paul use θεός as a Christological title (Rom 9:5; Tit 2:13; Heb 1:8, but see his expressions in Phil 2:6; Col 1:15-20; 2:9), but in eight of his letters Paul refers to Jesus as God's 'Son' in the divine sense of that title (Gal 1:16; 2:20; 4:4, 6; 1 Thess 1:10; 1 Cor 1:9; 15:28; 2 Cor 1:19; Rom 1:3, 4, 9; 5:10; 8:3, 29, 32; Col 1:13; Eph 4:13; Heb 1:2, 5 [twice], 8; 3:6; 4:14; 5:5, 8; 6:6; 7:3, 28; 10:29). And in Hebrews 1:4-14 in particular, as ontological explications of Jesus' 'more excellent name' of 'Son' and not simply as new names adduced in addition to that of 'Son', Paul speaks of the 'Son' as the God of Psalm 45:6-7 and the Yahweh of Psalm 102:25-27. In Galatians 4:4, Romans 8:3, 32 and Colossians 1:13, 16-17 he assumes and teaches the Son's eternal preexistence.

But as we have already intimated, if Paul is a monotheist, just as certainly did he accept the new factor introduced into redemptive history with the twin historical events of the Incarnation and Pentecost and the emergence of the Christian gospel, namely, the fully divine nature of Jesus Christ and the distinct personhood of the Holy Spirit. Accordingly, we find evidence in his letters of this 'Trinitarian' adjustment to his monotheism. In the following verses Paul refers to all three persons of the Godhead:

1 Corinthians 12:3-6: '...no one who is speaking by the Spirit of God says, "Jesus be cursed," and no one can say, "Jesus is Lord," except by the Holy Spirit. There are different kinds of gifts, but the same Spirit. There are different kinds of service, but the same Lord. But the same God works all of them in all men.'

2 Corinthians 13:14: 'May the grace of the Lord Jesus Christ, and the love of God, and the fellowship of the Holy Spirit be with you all.'

Ephesians 1:3-14: 'Praise be to the God and Father of our Lord Jesus Christ, who...chose us in him before the creation of the world.... Having believed, you were marked in him with a seal, the promised Holy Spirit.'

Ephesians 2:18: '...through him [Christ] we both [Jew and Gentile] have access to the Father by one Spirit.'

Ephesians 4:4-6: 'There is one body and one Spirit – just as you were called to one hope when you were called – one Lord, one faith, one baptism, one God and Father of all, who is over all through all and in all.'

2 Thessalonians 2:13-14: 'But we ought always to thank God for you, brothers loved by the Lord, because from the beginning God chose you to be saved through the sanctifying work of the Spirit and through belief in the truth. He called you to this through our gospel, that you might share in the glory of our Lord Jesus Christ.'

Titus 3:4-6: 'But when the kindness and love of God our Savior appeared, he saved us, not because of righteous things we had done, but because of his mercy. He saved us through the washing of rebirth and renewal by the Holy Spirit, whom he poured out on us generously through Jesus Christ our Savior.'

Since virtually none of this is denied by most Paul scholars, I see no need in the following pages to provide a separate discussion of Paul's monotheistic 'Trinitarianism' *per se*,[16] but we shall in due course consider Paul's perception of the role each person of the Godhead plays in the accomplishment and application of redemption.

---

16. See my *A New Systematic Theology of the Christian Faith* (Nashville, Tenn.: Thomas Nelson, 1998), Chapter Nine, esp. 324-41, for my discussion of the doctrine of the Trinity in which I maintain that the doctrine is sufficiently captured in the following three simple propositions: (1) there is only one God; (2) the Father, the Son, and the Holy Spirit are each fully God; and (3) God the Father, God the Son, and God the Holy Spirit are distinct persons within the Godhead. I maintain further that the Nicene doctrine of the Father's eternal generation of the Son (A. D. 325) and the Niceno-Constantinopolitan doctrine of the Spirit's procession from the Father ('and the Son' was added later) are not propositions essential to the orthodox doctrine, indeed, that these propositions deny to the Son and the Spirit their autotheotic nature.

CHAPTER THIRTEEN

SIN AND 'MAN IN ADAM'

> All our knowledge, sense, and sight
> Lie in deepest darkness shrouded,
> Till your Spirit breaks our night
> With the beams of truth unclouded,
> Christ alone to God can win us;
> Christ must work all good within us.
> — T. Clausnitzer, 1663

Some Paul scholars would say that to begin an exposition of Paul's theology with an overview of his doctrine of sin and the natural human condition is to skew the emphasis in the theological thought of the great Apostle on the cross, his law-free gospel, and salvation by divine grace alone through faith alone in Jesus Christ. Their concern reveals how little they understand Paul's theology as a whole. For no other human condition, if it is not human sin, provides the background against which the need for the law-free gospel and salvation by divine grace alone through faith alone in Jesus Christ makes sense. No other human condition, if it is not human depravity, moral inability, and real guilt before God justifies the need for the cross and the doctrines of grace.

In this connection it is important to note where Paul himself begins when he lays out in his letter to the Roman church the most systematic exposition of his thought to be found anywhere: even a brief perusal of Romans 1:18–3:20 will show that he begins with the declaration that 'the wrath of God is being revealed from heaven against all godlessness and wickedness of men who suppress the truth [of their knowledge of him] by their wickedness' (Rom 1:18). He continues in this vein throughout the rest of Romans 1, 2, and 3:1-20, underscoring both the universal sin of mankind and (as sin's resultant comcomitant) God's universal wrath toward and condemnation of the human race. Three times in Romans 1:24-28 he declares, because man prefers his thankless, idolatrous ways to the worship and praise of the one living and true God, that God has abandoned the race (see his 'God gave them over unto', παρέδωκεν αὐτοὺς ὁ θεὸς εἰς, in 1:24, 26, 28): he has abandoned it to sexual impurity, shameful lusts, and depraved thinking. In Romans 2:1-3:8 he demonstrates that even the religious man, whether Gentile or Jew, is guilty before God, and in Romans 3:9-18 he sets forth his fourteen-point indictment against the entire human race, concluding that all men are lawbreakers before God (Rom 3:19-20). The race's universal transgression of God's holy law silences every mouth and the whole world stands guilty before God.

Only after Paul declares and argues all this, and not before, does he turn to an exposition of his gospel which he explicates in terms of his doctrine of justification by faith in Christ apart from works of law (Rom 3:21-4:25). After explicating his gospel, Paul then returns to the subject of human sin in Romans 5:12-21, now that he has placed the two representative heads of the race before his reader, and traces the origin of the race's sin to the original sin of Adam who stood as the race's first covenantal representative. In sum, the biblical gospel 'fits hand in glove' with the fallen human condition and meets all of the exigencies of that human condition. And it can be said, without fear of refutation, that the Bible knows no other reason for Christ's Incarnation and his cross-work at Calvary than the fallenness and lostness of mankind. As Paul himself declares: 'Here is a trustworthy saying that deserves full acceptance: Christ Jesus came into the world to save sinners' (1 Tim 1:15).[1]

So to address at the outset the only condition which makes necessary the cross-work of Christ is to be *quite* Pauline and to be *quite* sensitive to the great Apostle's theological vision. Accordingly, we will begin our exposition of Paul's theology with his description

---

1. Paul's doctrine of sin stands in opposition to E. P. Sanders's portrayal of it who argues in his *Paul* (Oxford: University Press, 1991), 36-39, that Paul, not coming to Christianity with 'a pre-formed conception of humanity's sinful plight', began with a universal soteric solution as a fixed view and went looking for a problem big enough for the solution to address. He declares that Paul's anthropology did not include a notion of inherited sin (37) and that his arguments in Romans 1-2 and 5 are 'weak as reasoned arguments', 'efforts at rationalization' (38), and 'the reflex of his soteriology' (39). But Paul, as a student of the Old Testament, was fully aware of Israel's moral failings as reported therein, and he knew what the Old Testament declared about the sinfulness of the race: his fourteen-point indictment of the whole human race for its sin in Romans 3:10-18 is nothing more than a compilation of statements from the Old Testament. Such great exegetical commentaries on Paul's letter to the Romans as those by Charles Hodge, Robert Haldane, John Murray, Leon Morris, and Douglas Moo show how shallow Sanders' insights are.

of the fallen human condition. Moreover, rather than to deal first with sin in its cosmic[2] (world, age) or representative (Adam, flesh) sense, as do Ridderbos and Ladd, with many brilliant insights I might add, I would propose that we follow Paul's example in his letter to the Romans and deal with sin first as moral depravity and inability and the cause of mankind's state of being morally guilty before God as well as man's *personal* responsibility and response to God in the religious and moral spheres. After this, with Paul, we will speak of sin in terms of Adam's representation.[3]

Paul's Vocabulary

Paul's vocabulary characterizing the present human condition is quite full, including the following words: ἀδικία, 'wickedness, unrighteousness' (around twelve times), ἁμαρτία, 'sin, missing the mark' (over sixty times), ἀνομία, 'lawlessness' (eight times), ἀσέβεια, 'ungodliness, impiety' (four times), παράβασις, 'transgression' (six times), παρακοή, 'disobedience' (three times), and παράπτωμα, 'trespass' (fourteen times). To these must be added the word-cluster from the πιστ- root—ἀπιστέω, 'disbelieve, be unfaithful' (two times),

---

2. Paul did not believe that evil originally entered the world through Adam's sin. While he believed that God was the sole sovereign of the universe he created, he also believed that Satan (Σατανᾶς; Rom 16:20; 1 Cor 5:5; 7:5; 2 Cor 2:11; 11:14; 12:7; 1 Thess 2:18; 2 Thess 2:9; 1 Tim 1:20; 5:15) or the devil (διάβολος; Eph 4:27; 6:11; 1 Tim 3:6, 7; 2 Tim 2:26), once a mighty archangel, though under God's ultimate control, was the tempter behind the fall of Adam (2 Cor 11:3, 12-15). Paul also calls him Belial (2 Cor 6:15), the evil one (Eph 6:16; 2 Thess 3:3), the ruler of the kingdom of the air (Eph 2:2), and the tempter (1 Thess 3:5). And while Satan, as we have already noted, does not exercise totally free rein over men because of divinely-imposed limitations and restraints, Paul still declares that Satan works in the sons of disobedience (Eph 2:2), blinds the minds of unbelievers so that they cannot see the light of the gospel of the glory of Christ (2 Cor 4:4), turns men away from God to serve him (1 Tim 5:15), takes men captive to do his will (2 Tim 2:26), obstructs world missions (1 Thess 2:18), masquerades as an angel of light (2 Cor 11:14), holds (under God) the power of death (Heb 2:14), and tormented Paul with a thorn in the flesh (2 Cor 12:7).
According to Paul there are definite 'power-aspects' of Satan's kingdom of darkness (Col 1:13) under the control of principalities and powers (Eph 6:12; Col 2:15), powers of this dark world (Eph 6:12), and spiritual forces of evil in the heavenly realm against which the man who lacks the whole armor of God cannot possibly stand (Eph 6:12-13). He also teaches that Satan devises schemes (Eph 6:11) and traps (2 Tim 2:26) and inspires false religions (1 Cor 10:20).
See Daniel G. Reid, 'Satan, Devil,' *Dictionary of Paul and His Letters*, edited by Gerald F. Hawthorne, Ralph P. Martin, Daniel G. Reid (Downers Grove, Ill.: InterVarsity, 1993), 862-67.
3. In dealing with sin in others, especially in missionary evangelism, I would urge that it is normally best to follow Paul's approach and to deal with sin in a person's *actual* experience (Rom 1–3) and only after that to trace his sin to its ultimate source in 'original [or race] sin' (Rom 5:12-19).

ἀπιστία, 'unfaithfulness, unbelief' (seven times), and ἄπιστος, 'faithless, unbelieving' (fourteen times), and the occurrences of ἀπειθέω, 'disobey' (six times) and ἀπείθεια 'disobedience' (seven times).

Man's Moral Depravity and Inability to Please God

The following verses will suffice to illustrate Paul's teaching that mankind, in their natural state, is morally depraved:

Romans 1:29-32 (see also 1:18-28): Men, Paul asserts, 'have become filled with every kind of wickedness, evil, greed and depravity. They *are full* [μεστούς] of envy, murder, strife, deceit and malice. They are gossips, slanderers, God-haters, insolent, arrogant and boastful; they invent ways of doing evil; they disobey their parents; they are senseless, faithless, heartless, ruthless. Although they know God's righteous decree that those who do such things deserve death, they not only continue to do these very things but also approve of those who practice them.'

Romans 3:9-23: 'Jews and Gentiles alike are all *under [the mastery of] sin* [ὑφ᾽ ἁμαρτίαν]. As it is written [and now follows his fourteen-point indictment against the entire human race – all drawn from the Psalms with one exception]:

> "There is no one righteous, not even one;
> there is no one who understands,
> no one who seeks God.
> All have turned away,
> they have together become worthless;
> there is no one who does good,
> not even one. [Ps 14:1-3]
> Their throats are open graves;
> their tongues practice deceit. [Ps 5:9]
> The poison of vipers is on their lips. [Ps 140:3]
> Their mouths are full of cursing and bitterness. [Ps 10:7]
> Their feet are swift to shed blood;
> ruin and misery mark their ways,
> and the way of peace they do not know. [Isa 59:7-8]
> There is no fear of God before their eyes" [Ps 36:1].'

'...for *all sinned* [πάντες ἥμαρτον] and *are continually falling short* [ὑστεροῦνται] of the glory [righteousness] of God.'

Galatians 3:22: '...the Scripture "shuts up in prison" under sin the whole world [συνέκλεισεν ἡ γραφὴ τὰ πάντα ὑπὸ ἁμαρτίαν].' (Here we see that the one who disputes the universality of sin's dominion is not arguing with the Christian who asserts such but with the Scripture, the very Word of God.)

Ephesians 2:1-3: 'As for you, you were dead in your trespasses and sins, in which you used to live when you followed the ways of this world and of the ruler of the kingdom of the air, of the spirit which is now at work in those who are disobedient. All of us also lived among them at one time, gratifying the cravings of our sinful nature and following its desires and thoughts. Like the rest, we were by nature objects of wrath.'

Ephesians 4:17-19: The Gentiles live 'in the futility of their thinking. They are darkened in their understanding and separated from the life of God because of the ignorance that is in them due to the hardness of their hearts. Having lost all sensitivity, they have given themselves over to sensuality so as to indulge in every kind of impurity, with a continual lust for more.'

The following two verses will suffice to illustrate Paul's teaching on man's moral inability to please God or to save himself:

Romans 8:7-8: '...the sinful mind...does not submit to God's law, nor can it do so. Those controlled by the sinful nature cannot please God.'

1 Corinthians 2:14: 'The man without the Spirit does not accept the things that come from the Spirit of God, for they are foolishness to him, and he cannot understand them, because they are spiritually discerned.'

From the teaching of these verses it is apparent that Paul regarded every person in his raw, natural state as he comes from the womb *as morally and spiritually corrupt in disposition and character.* Every part of his being – his mind, his will, his emotions, his affections, his conscience, his body – has been affected by sin. His understanding is darkened, his mind is at enmity with God, his will to act is slave to his darkened understanding and rebellious mind, his heart is corrupt, his emotions are perverted, his affections naturally gravitate to that which is evil and ungodly, his conscience is untrustworthy, and his body is subject to mortality.

Theologians have termed this teaching of Paul the doctrine of *total or pervasive depravity*. By this they do not mean that people actually *act* as bad as they really are by nature since they are prevented from doing so by the manifestations of God's common restraining grace, such as their innate awareness of God and his judgments (*sensus deitatis*) (Rom 1:21, 32), the works of the law written on their hearts and consciences (Rom 2:15) and civil government (Rom 13:1-5). They mean rather that every person is corrupt throughout the *totality* of his being, with every part, power, and faculty of his nature – mind, intellect, emotions, will, conscience, body—being affected by the fall.[4]

With respect specifically to the noetic effects of sin, none of the above is intended to say or to imply that Adam's fall brought him and his progeny to a state of brutish non-reason, that is, to the inability to think and to reason correctly. But the reason that every man can still reason correctly, at least to some degree, is because the divine Son of God, the Logos or Reason of God, noetically illumines every man who comes into the world (John 1:9), and not, as Roman Catholicism teaches, because Adam's sin did not affect his progeny's ability to reason. In sum, Scripture teaches that it is only because of God's common grace[5] extended to them in Christ, to whom the Father has given authority over *all* men (common grace) in order that he might give eternal life to those whom the Father has given to him (special grace) (John 17:2), that fallen men are able at all to mount and to follow a logical argument. Otherwise, I would submit, the fall

---

4. See Louis Berkhof, *Systematic Theology* (Grand Rapids: Eerdmans, 1941), 246-47.
5. The Bible clearly affirms that God has shown and continues to show a measure of favor or undeserved kindness to his creatures in general. He provides the sustenance they need for their physical well-being. He restrains the effects of sin in both individuals and society and enables the unregenerate to perform civic good, that is, to accomplish things that promote the welfare of others. Not the least evidence by any means of his common goodness to them is his sustaining of men in their scientific enterprises and their search for truth about themselves and the physical universe, enabling them to make many very fruitful discoveries about this world and the universe. Of course, the knowledgeable Christian will recognize that the efforts of the unregenerate scientist are only successful because he is unwittingly 'borrowing capital' from a Christian-theistic universe in which uniformity in nature and the orderly meaning of facts are guaranteed by God and his plan.

would have had the effect of bringing man to brutish non-reason, indeed, to physical non-being.[6] But because of sin's effects on them men now must face the fact, as they construct their sciences, that, in spite of God's common grace, falsehood, unintentional mistakes, lapses in logical reasoning, self-delusion and self-deception, the intrusion of fantasy into the imagination, intentional negative influences of other men's minds upon their's, physical weaknesses influencing the total human psyche, the disorganized relationships of life, the effect of misinformation and inaccuracies learned from one realm of science upon ideas in other realms, sinful self-interest, the weakening of mental energies, the internal disorganization of life-harmonies, and most importantly, their detachment from the ποῦ στῶ[7] found only in the revealed knowledge of God which alone justifies human knowledge and from which alone true human predication may be launched – *now*, I say, men must face the fact that any and all of these effects of sin can and do bring them in their search for knowledge to unrecognized and thus unacknowledged ignorance.

Man's Accountability

Paul regards sin as the disobedience of a man (1) created by God in his image, (2) living in relation to him, and (3) therefore *accountable* to him. He looks upon sin as both an attitude and an action on the part of the rational creature, which attitude and action always have a degree of self-consciousness and rebellion in them (Rom 1:18, 20, 21, 25, 32). The sinner's conscience may become seared with respect to his sin (1 Tim 4:2) but it does not begin that way.

For Paul sin is a turning away from God in the areas of worship and morality, that is to say, sin is any want of conformity unto or transgression of the law of God (see especially Rom 1:18ff.; also Rom 2).

---

6. These assertions are simply applying in the area of epistemology Paul's declaration that in Christ all things (including human reason) consist or hold together (Col 1:17).

7. When Archimedes, the Greek mathematician, working with the simple machine of the lever, said, '*Give to me [a place] where I may stand* (Δός μοι ποῦ στῶ) and I will move the world,' he was asking for a base for his lever's fulcrum necessarily *outside of* the cosmos. Accordingly, as I employ the phrase ποῦ στῶ in this context I intend the ultimate heart commitment of whatever kind from which a person launches all his argumentation and predication. Without a transcendental epistemological ποῦ στῶ man has no epistemological base for launching his first predication. For all men, and especially for Christians, it should be the revealed transcendental knowledge of God revealed in the Bible which provides the extra-cosmic epistemological base for human knowledge, meaning and predication.

Consequences of Sin

The consequence of this moral depravity is death in terms of relationship to God and appropriate spiritual responses and attitudes toward him (Eph 2:1, 5; see also 2:12-13). This death is not only physical but also the dissolution of the proper spiritual relationship with God in this life which results finally in the continuation of that dissolution through all eternity (Rom 5:21; 6:23).

Sin also brings bondage or enslavement with it, in which bondage the sinner serves his evil lusts and desires as well as the Evil One, and he is not free to do the good (Rom 3; Rom 6:6, 14, 17, 18, 19, 20; 7:14-25; Eph 2:2-3).

This condition *deserves* the wrath and condemnation of God as its just punishment (Rom 1:18, 32; 2:5; 5:9; 1 Thess 1:10). (Even the redeemed man can experience temporal punishments for his sin; see 1 Thess 4:6; 1 Cor 11:30-32; 2 Cor 2:6; 10:6; 1 Tim 5:20; Heb 12:6-8.)

Paul uses two Greek words in particular to denote God's anger against sin, θυμός and ὀργή, the former occurring one time (Rom 2:8); the latter occurring fifteen times (Rom 1:18; 2:5 (twice), 8; 3:5; 4:15; 5:9; 9:22; 12:19; Eph 2:3; 5:6; Col 3:6; 1 Thess 1:10; 2:16; 5:9). Some New Testament scholars have opposed placing any construction on these words that would suggest God is wrathful and angry with the race; they have insisted that wrath is an attitude inappropriate to God. They contend that the concept of 'wrath' is appropriate only to pagan gods and to men who have lost control of themselves. They urge that Paul uses this term only as a personification of the law of consequences, and that God's 'wrath' simply refers to the *impersonal*, natural consequences of sin and disobedience in the moral universe he created in the same way that the 'impersonal' law of gravity in the physical universe brings injury to one who falls from a height. But there is no reason why these terms should not refer to God's *personal* and settled attitude toward sin without the odious overtones seen in pagan gods and men. In fact, apart from such a construction, a salvation grounded in the necessity of Christ's death is incomprehensible. Moreover, these scholars have not been able to show how an *impersonal* cause and effect relationship has any meaning in a universe upheld and pervaded by a *personal* God.

Flesh

Sin is so much a part of the *being* of the sinner that Paul may speak of it under the terminology of 'flesh' (σάρξ). By this he does not mean to describe sin simply in terms of the external or material side of man, but in terms of that *state* which most characterizes *the sinner's existence now* and *in which he expresses his sinfulness* (see, for example, Rom 7:18; 8:3ff; 13:14; Gal 5:13; Eph 2:3; Col 2:23). The term is most often used in this sense in contrast with God's Spirit (Rom 8; Gal 5; note: in these contexts the terms 'flesh' and 'spirit' are *not* to be construed as intending an *anthropological* dualism in man [body/spirit] but rather as a valuative appraisal of man's state in sin *vis-à-vis* the nature and character of God).

The Representative Act of the First Man

While each human being commits his own sins as he appears on the stage of history and thereby render himself culpable before God, Paul sees the ultimate root of the sinner's sinful condition as residing in the representative act of the first man Adam by which all his descendents (except one) have been made sinners (Rom 5:12-19; see 1 Cor 15:21-22). It was through Adam's act that sin and death entered the world and mankind and accordingly that sin and death have spread to all men descending from him by ordinary generation.[8]

From his analysis of Romans 5:12-19—the classic passage germane to this whole discussion which we ourselves will consider in a moment—John Murray rightly concludes that it clearly envisions some kind of solidarity existing between the 'one' (Adam) and the 'all' (the race) with the result that the sin contemplated can be regarded at the same time and with equal relevance as the sin of the 'one' or as the sin of 'all'.[9] But what is the nature of this 'solidarity'? Is it the *natural* union between Adam and his posterity? Or is it the *representative* union between Adam as the federal head of the race and the race itself? This is the issue which is now before us.

---

8. Clark H. Pinnock (ed.), *Grace Unlimited* (Minneapolis: Bethany, 1975), denies that Adam's sin affected his descendants in any biological or legal sense (104). The universal and 'cumulative degeneration' following upon Adam's sin Pinnock explains as the result of the 'warped social situation' which now confronts every man with the temptation to misuse his freedom (104-05) and which invariably perverts all men. According to Pinnock, this is the only construction of the doctrine of original sin which the Bible will tolerate (104). He is wrong, of course.

9. John Murray, *The Imputation of Adam's Sin* (Grand Rapids: Eerdmans, 1959) 21.

We begin our exposition at verse 12 with the ὥσπερ ('just as'), simply pointing out that the preceding διὰ τοῦτο ('because of this') commencing the verse refers back to the expression 'in his life' (ἐν τῇ ζωῇ αὐτοῦ) in verse 10. Now it is plain that the ὥσπερ introduces a protasis. Where is its apodosis? Some expositors have urged that the apodosis is also to be found in verse 12, commencing with the καὶ οὕτως ('and so'). But when Paul introduces his apodoses after ὡς or ὥσπερ, he regularly does so, not with the καὶ οὕτως but with the οὕτως καὶ ('so also') as in verses 5:15, 18, 19, 21; 6:4; and 11:30. Where then is the apodasis after the ὥσπερ if it does not occur in verse 12? It is the οὕτως καὶ of verse 18 with the original ὥσπερ clause of verse 12 introduced again in different language by the ὡς. The thought would then be, when worked out, something on the order of the following:

Verse 12: Because of this [being in Christ], *just as* by one man sin came into the world and death by that sin, and so death came upon all men in that all sinned –

(Verses 13-17: An excursus commences [verses 13-14] on the 'all sinned' phrase at the end of verse 12 in which Paul makes it clear that he means by the phrase 'all sinned [πάντες ἥμαρτον]' that 'all sinned in Adam's transgression'; then a second excursus [verses 15-17] follows on the first excursus, in which he shows that while Adam is indeed a 'type' of Christ [end of verse 14], Christ and God's gift of grace through him achieve far more than Adam's failure by reversing the operation of divine judgment not only against Adam's sin but also against 'many trespasses' [verse 16]) –

Verse 18: So then [having disposed of certain questions by the excurses], *as* through one transgression [judgment came] unto all men unto condemnation [note: this is the rephrasing of the 'just as' clause of verse 12 which I referred to above], *so also* through one act of righteousness, [the free gift came] unto all men unto justification of life.

Verse 19: [Having worked his total concept out in some detail in 12-18, Paul now summarizes the whole] For *just as* through the disobedience of the one man [Adam] the many were made sinners,

Sin and 'Man in Adam' 325

so also through the obedience of the one Man [Christ] the many were constituted righteous.

With the 'flow' of the passage now before us, it is important to observe its main point which turns upon the recurring (twelve times) term 'one' (εἷς). Note in these verses the reiterated point that 'in Adam's fall we sinned all', that is to say, for some reason the one sin of the one man Adam God regards as the sin of all:

Verse 12: 'through *one* man sin into the world entered and through that [demonstrative use of τῆς] sin [came] death, and so unto all men death came, in that all sinned [in Adam]' (this last bracketed phrase is argued in the excursus of verses 13-14);

Verse 15: 'by the trespass of the *one* the many died';

Verse 16: 'judgment [arose] out of *one* [trespass] unto condemnation [unto all men]' (the last bracket of words is drawn from verse 18);

Verse 17: 'by the trespass of the *one* death reigned through the one [Adam]';

Verse 18: 'through *one* trespass [judgment came] unto all men unto condemnation'; and finally,

Verse 19: 'through the disobedience of the *one* man, the many were appointed sinners.'

Could Paul have made himself any clearer respecting the solidarity of the 'one man' and 'the many' other men? And could he have been plainer in his insistence that Adam's sin is in some sense the sin of all? Some theologians, it is true, reject the idea of Adam's sin being also the sin of the race and therefore the ground on which the race's condemnation is based. But every effort to force any other meaning on Paul's words shatters on the rock of rigorous exegesis. Tragically, these efforts also destroy the ground on which man's salvation is based, even the alien righteousness of Jesus Christ. For consider the corresponding side of the Apostle's analogy:

Verse 14: '...Adam, who is a type [with respect to his federal headship] of the Coming One.'

Verse 15: '...grace...and the gift by grace abounded unto the many which [grace] is of the *one* Man Jesus Christ.'

Verse 16: 'The ones receiving the abundance of grace and the gift of righteousness shall reign in life through the one Jesus Christ.'

Verse 18: 'through *one* righteous act [the free gift came] unto all men unto justification of life.'

Verse 19: 'through the obedience of the *one* [Man] the many shall be constituted righteous.'

Verse 21: 'grace reigns through righteousness...through Jesus Christ our Lord.'

Clearly for Paul there is a connection between Adam's sin and the sin and condemnation of the race. How is that connection to be explicated? Warfield classifies the more recent proposals under four headings:[10]

1. The *agnostic view*, held by R. W. Landis, accepts the fact of the transmission of Adam's guilt and depravity to the race but refrains from framing a theory of the mode of transmission or the relation of guilt to corruption;

2. The *realist view*, postulated for example by W. G. T. Shedd and James Henley Thornwell, rejects the idea of the imputation of Adam's sin and contends that 'human nature' must be viewed generically and numerically as a *single* unit. The proponents of this view urge that Adam possessed the entire human nature and that all mankind, being present in Adam as generic humanity, corrupted itself by its own apostatizing act in Adam. Individual men are not separate substances but manifestations of the same generic substance. They are numerically one in nature. The reason that all men are accountable for Adam's sin, then, is because they *really* sinned in Adam before the individualizing of human nature began.

This view, however, cannot explain why Adam's descendants today are held responsible for his *first* sin only (see 'that sin' in verse 12; the 'one trespass' in verses 16 and 18) and not for all of his subsequent sins as well, not to mention the sins of all the generations of forefathers that followed Adam and that precede any particular

---

10. Benjamin B. Warfield, 'Imputation' in *New Schaff-Herzog Encyclopaedia of Religious Knowledge* (Reprint: Grand Rapids: Baker, 1977), V, 465-467.

man today. Moreover, it neglects the parallel which Paul draws between Adam and Christ (see his 'just as...so also'). Men are not righteous because they themselves *actually* do righteousness in Christ. They are constituted righteous because Christ's righteousness is forensically imputed (reckoned) to them. Paul's parallel would require the correlative conclusion that men are not ultimately unrighteousness because they *actually did* unrighteousness in Adam but because Adam's unrighteousness is imputed to them. Not to affirm this destroys the parallel which Paul draws between Adam and Christ. John Murray writes in this regard:

> ...since the analogy instituted between Adam and Christ [in Rom 5] is so conspicuous, it is surely necessary to assume that the kind of relationship which Adam sustains to men is after the pattern of the relationship which Christ sustains to men. To put the case conversely, surely the kind of relationship that Christ sustains to men is after the pattern which Adam sustains to men (see Rom. 5:14).[11]

Murray goes on to argue, and I think correctly, that since *natural* or seminal headship is not and can never be descriptive of Christ's relationship to men, and since the relationship between Christ and the justified, therefore, must be one of vicarious representation, we must assume that the relationship between Adam and his posterity, on the basis of which *his one* [first] sin is imputed, is also one of *vicarious representation*.[12]

3. The *federal (immediate imputation) view*, held by Charles Hodge and John Murray, urges that the *representative* principle is Paul's point in Romans 5:12-19, with the natural union between Adam and his posterity only determining the 'direction of application' which the imputation of Adam's sin with its corruption would take.

Determined to do justice to the representative principle which alone governs the relationship between Christ and the justified, this view regards the relation between Adam's first sin and the sin of the race as also grounded in *federal representation*. In other words, because Adam was the federal representative of the human race in the covenant of works, in God's righteous judgment he imputed Adam's first transgression to the race that was federally related to him.

---

11. John Murray, *The Imputation of Adam's Sin*, 39.
12. Murray, *Imputation*, 40.

Charles Hodge, an *immediate* imputationist, in the interest of infant salvation believed, however, that what God imputed was only *reatus poenae*, the liability to punishment, and not *reatus culpae*, true guilt. But it would surely be a violation of strict justice were God to hold a person liable for punishment whom he did not at the same time justly regard as guilty of the sin being punished. John Murray, more consistently in my opinion, insists that Romans 5 intends that we understand that both *reatus culpae* and *reatus poenae* and not just the latter were imputed to the race. Indeed, he insists that God imputed to the race, as an implicate of the race's representational solidarity with Adam, both Adam's guilt and Adam's corruption (that is, his disposition to sin). After all, he notes, Paul does not say that God imputed only Adam's liability to punishment but rather that he imputed Adam's sin itself to the race, which necessarily entails both guilt and corruption.

4. *The 'new school' (mediate imputation) view* denies that Adam's first sin was immediately or directly imputed to his descendants, and urges instead that Adam's descendants derive their corruption from him because of their racial solidarity with him and only then does God, on the basis of this antecedent corruption (or through the *medium* of this corruption), impute to them the guilt of Adam's apostasy. In other words, this view contends that men are not born corrupt because God imputed Adam's sin to them; rather, God imputed Adam's sin to them because they are corrupt. That is to say, 'Their condition is not based on their legal status, but their legal status on their condition.'[13]

The *immediate imputationist* insists, however, if one follows Berkhof,[14] that God immediately, that is, directly, imputed Adam's sin to his descendants, and that, *as a result*, God then willed that Adam's corruption would be transmitted to the race by natural generation, or, if one follows Murray, that God immediately imputed, as an implicate of the race's representative solidarity with Adam, both Adam's guilt and his corruption to the race.

On the basis of the Pauline analogy in Romans 5, of these four imputation views the 'immediate imputation' view seems to me to be the correct one, for men are not regarded as righteous in Christ

---

13. Berkhof, *Systematic Theology*, 243.
14. Berkhof, *Systematic Theology*, 242.

because in some sense they are antecedently righteous. Rather, they are regarded as righteous on the basis of Christ's immediately imputed righteousness, and it is this punctiliar justification which leads to their progressive sanctification. I would urge, in conclusion, that the Adam/Christ parallel in Romans 5 teaches that under the terms of the covenant of works Adam's first sin, along with the true guilt of that sin, was imputed to the human race solely on the basis of Adam's *federal representation* of the race. Consequently, mankind's state today is one of total depravity, natural inability, and real guilt before God.

Paul also urges, following Genesis 3, that Adam's sin brought the earth under the dominion of the Evil One (Eph 2:2) and the slavery of corruption (Rom 8:20-22).

The Law's Function in Regard to Sin

In the life of sin, the law of God, because it is a summary revelation of God's standards and demands, can serve no other function than that of condemnation. It does so both for those who seek to break it (Rom 1) and for those who seek to keep it (Rom 2:17ff). Indeed, for those who would use it as a defense of self-righteousness, it becomes only a curse (Rom 4:15; Gal 3:10ff), while for those who are convicted of their transgression against God's law but who would seek to continue to follow the path of law-keeping to achieve right standing before God, it becomes indwelling sin's instrument to provoke to even further sin (Rom 5:20; 7:5, 7-13).

Present Deliverance

Paul views deliverance from sin as a transformation from spiritual death to spiritual life (Rom 6:2-7), as a transition from bondage to freedom, but a freedom to *serve* God only (Rom 8:2-4), and from being God's enemies and under his wrath to being under the blessing and power of God as Father and sovereign Lord (Eph 2:1-10). He views this transformation and this transition as radical and absolute, as indeed a new creation (2 Cor 5:17), as the making of the sinner anew (Eph 4:22-24; Col 3:9-10).

Continuing Effects of Sin on the Body (Sickness and Death)

As with the earth, so with our human bodies. Their full transformation will not be accomplished until the resurrection. In other words, there is no realized eschatology for the body in this present evil age (1 Corinthians 4:8 and Philippians 3:14 even oppose a *completely* realized eschatology for our spiritual status in this age). Thus even for the believer there is still physical sickness, pain, and death, and the earth still has its thorns. It is this perspective, that 'our outer man is decaying, yet our inner man is being renewed day by day' (2 Cor 4:16), that leads the believer on to his hope in that glorious day of resurrection alluded to in 2 Corinthians 5 with its truth about the resurrection of the body.

* * * * *

It is the state of affairs discussed in this chapter—man originally created good but now fallen through disobedience—which is the Bible's context for the active and passive obedience of Christ. There is no other background that will do justice to his work. To deny either man's original state of integrity or his self-willed fall from that estate into the state of corruption and misery is to rob Christ's cross of the only context in which it has any meaning. For this reason, as unpopular as Paul's teaching on sin is today in many quarters, it is imperative that the Christian missionary continue to proclaim and to teach Paul's doctrine of man's total sinfulness, total inability, and real guilt before God. For if men are not corrupt, they have no need of the saving benefits of the cross! If men are not sinners who are incapable of saving themselves, they have no need of the Savior! If men are not lost, they have no need of the Lord's mercies! It is *only* when men by God's enabling grace see themselves as they truly are—as sinful, incapable of saving themselves, and guilty before God—that they will see their need of Christ's saving work.

CHAPTER FOURTEEN

THE SOVEREIGNTY OF GOD IN SALVATION

> Lord, my weak thought in vain would climb
>   To search the starry vault profound,
> In vain would wing her flight sublime
>   To find creation's utmost bound.
>
> But weaker yet that thought must prove
>   To search thy great eternal plan,
> Thy sovereign counsels, born of love
>   Long ages ere the world began.
>
> When my dim reason would demand
>   Why that, or this, thou dost ordain,
> By some vast deep I seem to stand,
>   Whose secrets I must ask in vain.
>
> When doubts disturb my troubled breast,
>   And all is dark as night to me,
> Here, as on solid rock, I rest –
>   That so it seemeth good to thee.
>
> Be this my joy, that evermore
>   Thou rulest all things at thy will;
> Thy sovereign wisdom I adore,
>   And calmly, sweetly, trust in thee.
>   – Ray Palmer, 1858

The Pauline Terminology

Paul employs a variety of 'predestinarian' terms to explicate his views on God's sovereignty over men, particularly in the sphere of salvation.

To show the elect subject's *state*, six times he employs ἐκλεκτός, meaning 'chosen' (Rom 8:33; 16:13; Col. 3:12; 1 Tim 5:21 (angels here); Tit 1:1; 2 Tim 2:10). To highlight the fact that men are elect by virtue of *God's action*, five times he uses ἐκλογή, meaning 'selection, election, [a] choosing' (1 Thess 1:4; Rom 9:11; 11:5, 7, 28). Then he grounds all of this in God's eternal purpose by employing five times πρόθεσις ('purpose') (Rom 8:28; 9:11; Eph 1:11; 3:11; 2 Tim 1:9), three times εὐδοκία ('good pleasure') (Eph 1:5, 9; see Phil 2:13), and one time βουλὴ τοῦ θελήματος αὐτοῦ ('counsel of his will') (Eph 1:11). To underscore God's *precreational* love for and *precreational* determination of the elect he employs two times the verb προγινώσκω, meaning 'foreknow', that is, 'forelove' (Rom 8:29; 11:2), five times the verb προορίζω, meaning 'predestine' (Rom 8:29, 30; 1 Cor 2:7; Eph 1:5, 11), two times the verb προετοιμάζω, meaning 'prepare beforehand' (Rom 9:23; Eph 2:10), and one time the verb προτίθημι, meaning 'purpose' (Eph 1:9).

Exposition of the Pertinent Passages

An exposition of several pertinent passages will make clear Paul's thought on these matters. With regard to the fact itself of an eternal plan in which God loved and determined the salvation of an elect group of mankind that he designates the 'elect', Paul's statements should remove all doubt for any mind who would be informed by Scripture. Consider the following Pauline assertions:

I. God's 'eternal purpose' (Eph 3:11; 1:9; Rom 8:28; Eph 1:11; 2 Tim 1:9; Rom 9:11-13).

We will begin by considering simply the term for 'purpose' as it is found in Ephesians 3:11. Here Paul speaks of God's 'eternal *purpose* [πρόθεσιν] which he accomplished in the Christ, Jesus our Lord.' Five brief comments are in order here.

A. The Greek word πρόθεσις translated quite properly here as 'purpose', which may also be translated 'plan' or 'resolve',[1] is in the singular: God has *one* overarching purpose or plan (of course, with many different parts as we shall see).

---

1. See BAGD, *A Greek-English Lexicon of the New Testament and Other Early Christian Literature* (Second edition; Chicago: Chicago University Press, 1979), 713, 2.

B. Paul describes God's purpose or plan as his *eternal* purpose' (πρόθεσιν τῶν αἰώνων[2]; lit. "purpose of the ages"), intending by this genitive case noun that there was never a moment when God's plan with all of its parts was not fully determined by him, that is to say, that God has *always* had the plan, and that within the plan itself there is no time factor *per se*. The several parts of the plan must be viewed, accordingly, as standing in a (teleo)logical rather than a chronological relationship one to the other.

C. The person and work of Jesus Christ are clearly central to God's 'eternal plan' because Paul says that God 'accomplished' or 'effected' (ἐποίησεν) it 'in the Christ, Jesus our Lord'. The closely related earlier statement in Ephesians 1:9 echoes the same truth: Paul states there that 'the mystery of [God's] *will* [θελήματος], according to his *good pleasure* [εὐδοκίαν]' he *purposed* (προέθετο) to put into effect in Christ (ἐν αὐτῷ) – that 'purposed good pleasure' being 'to bring *all things* in heaven and on earth under one head *in Christ*' (ἐν τῷ Χριστῷ). Here we learn that God's eternal plan, which governs all his ways and works in heaven and on earth, he *purposed* to fulfill in and by Christ. Clearly, Christ is at the beginning, the center, and the end of God's eternal purpose.

D. This eternal purpose or plan, directly and centrally concerned as it is with Jesus Christ, is accordingly directly and centrally concerned with *soteric* issues as well. In the verses immediately preceding this reference to God's 'eternal purpose which he accomplished in the Christ' Paul declares that God 'created all things in order that *through the church*, the manifold wisdom of God should be made known to the rulers and authorities in the heavenly realms' (Eph. 3:9-10), and then he follows this statement with the words of 3:11 to the effect that the indicated activity in 3:9-10 was '*according to* [κατὰ] *his eternal purpose* which he accomplished in the Christ, Jesus our Lord'. The church of Jesus Christ – the redeemed community – then also clearly stands with Jesus Christ at the beginning, the center, and the end of God's eternal purpose.

This soteric feature of the divine purpose receives support from the other passages where Paul refers to God's purpose. In Romans

---

2. The related αἰώνιος means literally 'pertaining to an age'. Theoretically, the age could be any age, but in usage it has come to refer to the 'age to come'. Since that age is endless, the word has come to mean 'eternal'.

8:28 Paul writes that Christians were 'called [to salvation] *according to* [κατά][*his*] *purpose*'. In Ephesians 1:11 he says that Christians 'were made heirs [of God], having been predestined *according to* [κατά] *the purpose* of him who works all things *according to* [κατά] *the purpose* [βουλὴν] of his will'. And in 2 Timothy 1:9 Paul affirms that 'God saved us and called us with a holy calling, not according to our works but *according to* [κατά] *his own* [ἰδίαν] *purpose* and grace which was given to us in Christ Jesus before the beginning of time'.

E. The last occurrence of the noun 'purpose' is found in Romans 9. In this great chapter, in view of Israel's high privileges as the Old Testament people of God and the lengths to which God had gone to prepare them for the coming of the Messiah, Paul addresses the naked anomaly of Israel's official rejection of Christ. He addresses this issue at this point for two reasons: first, if justification is by faith alone (as he had argued earlier), the racial connection of a man accordingly being irrelevant to his justification, he is aware that one could ask: 'What then becomes of all of the promises which God made to Israel as a nation? Haven't they proven to be ineffectual?' He knows that, unless he can answer this inquiry, the integrity of the Word of God would be in doubt, at least in the minds of some. This in turn raises the second possible question: 'If the promises of God proved ineffectual for Israel, what assurance does the Christian have that those divine promises implicit in the great theology of Romans 3–8 will not also prove to be finally ineffectual for him?' Accordingly, he addresses the issue of Israel's unbelief. His explanation in one sentence is this: *God's promises to Israel have not failed, simply because God never promised to save every Israelite; rather, God promised to save the elect (true) 'Israel' within Israel* (9:6). He proves this by underscoring the fact that from the beginning not all the natural seed of Abraham were accounted by God as 'children of Abraham' – Ishmael was excluded from being a child of promise by sovereign elective divine arrangement (9:7-9).

Now it is likely that few Jews of Paul's day would have had much difficulty with the exclusion of Ishmael from God's gracious covenant. But someone might have argued that Ishmael's rejection as a 'son' of Abraham was due both to the fact that, though he was Abraham's seed, he was also the son of Hagar the servant woman and not the son of Sarah, and to the fact that God knew that he would

The Sovereignty of God in Salvation

'persecute him that was born after the Spirit' (see Gen 21:9; Ps 83:5-6; Gal 4:29). In other words, it could be argued, God drew the distinction between Isaac and Ishmael not because of a sovereign divine election of the former, but because they had two different earthly mothers and because of Ishmael's foreknown subsequent hostility to Isaac. The fact of two mothers is true enough, and indeed this fact is not without *figurative* significance, as Paul himself argues in Galatians 4:21-31.[3] But Paul sees clearly that the principle which is operative in Isaac's selection over Ishmael is one of sovereign divine discrimination and not one grounded in human circumstances. Lest this elective principle (which serves in turn the grace principle) which governed the choice of Isaac (and all the rest of the saved) be lost on his reader, Paul moves to a consideration of Jacob and Esau. In their case there were not two mothers. In their case there was one father (Isaac) and one mother (Rebekah) and, in fact, the two boys were twins, Esau – as Ishmael before him – even being the older and thus the one who should have been shown the preferential treatment normally reserved for the firstborn son. Moreover, the divine discrimination was made, *prior* to their birth, *before* either had done anything good or bad. Listen to Paul: 'Before the twins were born or had done anything good or bad – in order that God's purpose according to election might stand: not by works but by him who calls – she was told, "The older will serve the younger." Just as it is written: "Jacob I loved, but Esau I hated" ' (9:11-13). Clearly, for Paul both election ('Jacob I loved') and reprobation ('Esau I hated') are to be traced to God's sovereign discrimination among men.

The Arminian contends, because Romans 9:13 is a quotation of Malachi 1:2-3 which was written at the end of Old Testament canonical history, that God's election of Jacob and his rejection of Esau are to be traced to God's prescience of Edom's sinful existence and despicable historical treatment of Israel (Ezek 35:5). But this interpretation intrudes an element that is foreign to Paul's entire argument in Romans 9 and totally distorts his point. This is evident for at least three reasons:

1. The Malachi context is against it. The very point the prophet is concerned to make is that God continued to love Jacob, in spite of Jacob's (Israel's) similar history to that of Esau (Edom) as far as his

---

3. See my discussion of this passage in Chapter 20, p. 459.

covenant faithfulness is concerned, and to reject Esau because of his wickedness.

2. To inject into Paul's thought here to the slightest degree the notion of human merit or demerit as the ground for God's dealings with the twins is to ignore the plain statement of Paul: '*before the twins were born or had done anything good or bad* – in order that God's purpose according to election might stand: not by works but by him who calls – she was told....'

3. Finally, to inject into Paul's thought here the notion of human merit or demerit as the ground for God's dealings with the twins is also to make superfluous and irrelevant the following objection to his position which Paul anticipates and captures in the questions: 'What then shall we say? Is God unjust?' No one would even think of accusing God of injustice if he had related himself to Esau purely on the basis of human merit or demerit for clearly Esau was undeserving of God's favor. But it is precisely because Paul had declared that God related himself to the twins, not on the basis of human merit but solely in accordance with his own elective purpose, that he anticipates the question: 'Why does this not make God arbitrarily authoritarian and unjust?' It is doubtful whether any Arminian will ever be faced with the question that Paul anticipates here simply because the Arminian doctrine of election is grounded in God's prescience of men's faith and good works. It is only the Calvinist who insists that God relates himself to the elect 'out of his mere free grace and love, without any foresight of faith or good works, or perseverance in either of them, or any other thing in the creature, as conditions, or causes moving him thereunto; and all to the praise of his glorious grace' (*Westminster Confession of Faith* III/v) who will face this specific charge that God is unjust.

The Arminian also has to struggle with Paul's response to this question concerning God's justice, for using Moses as the type of the elect man and Pharaoh as the type of the non-elect man, Paul declares: '[Salvation] does not depend on man's will or effort, but on God who shows mercy.... Therefore, God has mercy on whom he wants to have mercy, and he hardens whom he wants to harden' (9:16, 18). By these remarks Paul makes it abundantly clear again that God's dealings with men are grounded in decretive, elective considerations

The Sovereignty of God in Salvation

which brook no recourse to human willing or human working. This is placed beyond all legitimate controversy by Paul's second anticipated question: 'One of you will say to me: "Then why does God still blame us? For who resists his will?" ' To this Paul simply rejoins: 'Who are you, O man, to talk back to God? Shall what is formed say to him who formed it, "Why did you make me like this?" Does not the potter have the right to make out of the same lump of clay some vessels for honor and some for dishonor? [Surely God has the right, does he not], if, determining to show his wrath and to make his power known [see same verbs in 9:17], he endured with much long-suffering vessels of wrath prepared for destruction [as he did with Pharaoh throughout the period of the plagues], even in order to make the riches of his glory [grace] known to vessels of mercy prepared in advance for glory?'

God's Word has not failed regarding Israel, Paul argues in sum here, because God's dealings with men are not ultimately determined by anything they do but rather are determined by his own sovereign elective purpose. Therefore, Christians too may be assured that, God having set his love upon them from all eternity by his sovereign purposing arrangement, nothing will be able to separate them from the love of God which is in Christ Jesus their Lord (Rom 8:28-39).

There is one more great truth that we should learn from Romans 9:11-13. It is that the *elective* principle in God's eternal purpose serves and alone comports with the *grace* principle which governs all true salvation. Paul writes: 'Yet, before the twins were born or had done anything good or bad—in order that *God's purpose according to election* might stand: *not according to works but according to him who calls*—she was told, "The older will serve the younger." Just as it is written: "Jacob I loved, but Esau I hated." ' Here we see the connection between God's grace and his elective purpose dramatically exhibited in God's discrimination between Jacob and Esau, which discrimination, Paul points out, occurred '*before* [μήπω] the twins were born, before either had done anything good or bad' (see Gen 25:22-23). Paul elucidates the reason standing behind and governing the divine discrimination signalized in the phrase, 'in order that God's "according to [κατά] election purpose" might stand [that is, might remain immutable],' in terms of the following phrase, 'not *according to* [ἐκ, 'on the strength of'] works but *according to* [ἐκ, 'on the strength of '] him who calls [unto salvation],'[4] which is equivalent to saying 'not according to works but according to grace'. Paul teaches here that God's elective purpose is not, as in paganism, 'a blind unreadable fate' which 'hangs, an impersonal mystery, even above the gods', but rather that it serves the intelligible purpose of 'bringing out the *gratuitous* character of grace.'[5] In fact, Paul refers later to 'the election of grace' (Rom 11:5).

From just this much data we can conclude that God has a single eternal purpose or plan at the center of which is Jesus Christ and his church, and which entails accordingly also at its center such soteric issues as God's election, predestination, and effectual call of men to himself for salvation in order to create through them the church, which in turn serves as the vehicle for showing forth, not the glory of man (see Rom 9:12; 2 Tim 1:9), but the many sides (πολυποίκιλος) of his own infinite grace and *wisdom* (Eph 3:10) – the latter a synonym for the plan itself.

II. God's foreknowledge and predestination of the elect in the plan

From Romans 8:29-30 we learn of other aspects of God's eternal purpose or plan. Paul tells the Christian that '[the ones] whom he [the Father] *foreknew* [προέγνω—that is, set his heart upon in covenantal love], he also *predestined* [προώρισεν] to be conformed to the image of his Son..., and whom he *predestined* [προώρισεν], those he *called* [ἐκάλεσεν – that is, in history], etc.' Two things are clear from this:

A. We learn that in his eternal plan (note the προ-prefixes ['before'] attached to the first two verbs) God 'set his heart upon' certain people in covenantal love and 'predestined' their conformity to his Son's likeness. And in this very context (Rom 8:33) Paul designates those whom God has always so loved as 'God's elect' (ἐκλεκτῶν θεοῦ).

Why have we interpreted the first verb (προέγνω) as we have? Reformed theologians have uniformly recognized that the Hebrew verb יָדַע ('to know') (see its occurrences in Gen 4:1, 18:19; Exod 2:25; Pss 1:6, 144:3; Jer 1:5; Hos 13:5; Amos 3:2) and the Greek verb γινώσκω ('to know') (see its occurrences in Matt 7:22-23, 1 Cor 8:3, and 2 Tim 2:19) can mean something on the order of 'to

---

4. See BAGD, *A Greek-English Lexicon of the New Testament*, 235, 3, i, for this rendering of ἐκ.

5. Geerhardus Vos, *Biblical Theology* (Grand Rapids: Eerdmans, 1948), 108, 110.

know intimately', 'to set one's affections upon', or 'to have special loving regard for', and that the latter verb (with the προ- prefix) intends something approaching these meanings rather than the sense of mere prescience in Romans 8:29.[6]

Reformed theologians also interpret Paul to mean here that God did not set his love upon the elect from all eternity because of *foreseen* faith or good works or perseverance in either of them or any other condition or cause in them moving him thereunto. To assert that he did, they insist, not only intrudes circumstances and conditions into the context which are absent from it, but also flies in the face of (1) the teaching of Romans 9:11-13 that election is according to grace and not according to works; (2) the teaching of Ephesians 1:4 that God chose us before the creation of the world 'that we *should be* holy', *not* because he saw that we *would be* holy; and (3) the teaching of 2 Timothy 1:9 that he saved us and called us to a holy life, not because of anything we have done but because of *his own* (ἰδίαν) purpose and grace.

Excursus on the anticipated charge of arbitrariness

This particular teaching raises a major question for many Christians— is there arbitrariness in God? Vos, commenting on Romans 9:11-13, speaks of 'the risk of exposing the divine sovereignty to the charge of arbitrariness'[7] which Paul was willing to run in order to underscore the fact that the *gracious* election of Jacob (and the corresponding reprobation of Esau) was decided before (indeed, eternally before) the birth of the brothers, before either had done good or bad. Arminian theologians would, of course, spare their readers the words 'risk of' and simply charge that the Reformed understanding of election does in fact expose God to the charge of arbitrariness in his dealings with men.

What may be said in response to this charge? Does the Reformed understanding of election (which we would insist is the Pauline understanding of election as well), when it affirms that God discriminated between one man and another man before they were born (is this not what Paul says?), completely apart from a consideration of any conditions or causes or the absence of these in either of them (is this again not what Paul means by his 'not by works' and his 'before either had done good or bad'?), impute arbitrariness to God?

---

6. For an excellent discussion of the meaning of 'foreknew' in Romans 8:29, see David N. Steele and Curtis C. Thomas, *Romans: An Interpretive Outline* (Philadelphia: Presbyterian and Reformed, 1963), Appendix C, 131-137.

7. Vos, *Biblical Theology*, 109.

Our response can and will be brief at this point. With Paul (9:14), we respond simply and tersely: 'Not at all!' Here we will highlight one reason for our response. It involves the meaning of the word 'arbitrariness'. If Arminians mean by the word to choose or to act this way at one time and that way at another, that is to say, willy-nilly or inconsistently, or to choose or to act without regard to any norm or reason, in other words, capriciously, such choosing or acting Reformed thinkers steadfastly deny that they impute to God. They insist that God always acts in a fashion consistent with his prior, settled discrimination, and that his prior, settled discrimination among men, as Paul informs us, was wisely determined *in the interests of* the grace principle (see Rom 9:11-12; 11:5). As Vos says, because Paul recognized that the degree, however small, to which an individual is allowed to be the decisive factor in receiving and working out the subjective benefits of grace for his transformation 'detract(s) in the same proportion from the monergism of the divine grace and from the glory of God,'[8] he (Paul) calls attention to God's 'sovereign discrimination between man and man, to place the proper emphasis upon the truth, that *his grace alone* is the source of all spiritual good to be found in man'.[9] Which is just to say that if God chose the way he did, out of the infinite depth of the *riches of his wisdom and knowledge* (11:33) in order to be able to manifest his *grace* (9:11), *then he did not choose arbitrarily or capriciously.* In other words, the condition governing the reason for his choosing the way he did does not need to lie in the creature. (Indeed, from the very nature of the case the condition could not lie in the creature. If it did, the creature would be God.) If there was a wise reason in himself for choosing the way he did (and there was—that he might make room for the exhibition of his grace as alone the source of all spiritual good in men) then he did not choose capriciously. Of course, 'there may be many other grounds [that is, reasons for] election, unknown and unknowable to us,' it is true. But, as Vos reminds us, 'this one reason we *do* know, and in knowing it we at the same time know that, whatever other reasons exist, they can have nothing to do with any meritorious ethical condition of the objects of God's choice.'[10]

B. We learn too from the tight grammatical construction between the verbs 'predestined' and 'called' in Romans 8:29-30 that what God planned before the creation of the world, he executes *in* the world. So there is a clear connection between his plan and his execution of his plan. He is the Author of both. The former is the 'blueprint' of the latter. The latter is the 'historical construction' of the former.

---

8. Vos, *Biblical Theology*, 108
9. Vos, *Biblical Theology*, 110, emphasis supplied. 10. Vos, *Biblical Theology*, 110.

III. The election of men in the plan (Eph 1:4-5; 2 Thess 2:13)

A. In Ephesians 1:4-5 Paul tells us that God the Father '*chose* [ἐξελέξατο] us in him [Christ] *before* [πρὸ] the creation of the world, that we should be holy and without blame before him, in love *having predestinated* [προορίσας] us unto sonship by adoption through Jesus Christ unto himself, according to the good pleasure of his will'. Here in this great doxology to God the Father Paul enunciates in no uncertain terms that from all eternity God has chosen the Christian to holiness and predestinated him to sonship. And he did so, Paul writes, 'according to the good pleasure of his will' (see also in this same regard Eph 1:9, 11). And 'it is to trifle with the plain import of the terms, and with the repeated emphasis' here, writes Murray,

'to impose upon the terms any determining factor arising from the will of man. If we say or suppose that the differentiation which predestination involves proceeds from or is determined by some sovereign decision on the part of men themselves, then we contradict what the apostle by eloquent reiteration was jealous to affirm. If he meant to say anything in these expressions in verses 5, 9, and 11, it is that God's predestination, and his will to salvation, proceeds from the pure sovereignty and absolute determination of his counsel. It is the unconditioned and unconditional election of God's grace.[11]

B. In 2 Thessalonians 2:13 Paul informs his readers, whom he describes as 'brothers who have been loved by the Lord', that 'God *chose* [εἵλατο] you *from the beginning* [ἀπαρχὴν] unto salvation'. This verse, in addition to the previous verses cited, underscores the truth that from all eternity God had determined upon a course of salvific activity for himself which would result in the salvation of his elect.

My expositions of Paul's statements in this chapter have made it abundantly clear that he believed that God is the absolute Sovereign of his world and that his sovereignty extends in minutest detail not only to the governance of all his creatures and all their thoughts and actions in accord with his most wise and holy purpose but also to the issues of salvation. It is God who determines who will be saved,

---

11. John Murray, 'The Plan of Salvation', in *Collected Writings of John Murray* (Edinburgh: Banner of Truth, 1977), 2, 127.

when they will be saved, and the circumstances and conditions leading to their salvation.

When the Council of Trent, in Canon 17 of its Sixth Session on Justification, states: 'If anyone says that the grace of justification is shared by those only who are predestined to life, but that all others who are called are called indeed but receive not grace, as if they are by divine power predestined to evil, let him be anathema,' we are confronted with yet further evidence of how far the Roman Church, in the interest of its insistence upon man's free will, has departed from Pauline doctrine.

CHAPTER FIFTEEN

GOD THE FATHER'S SALVIFIC WORK

> O Father, you are sovereign
> In all affairs of man;
> No pow'rs of death or darkness
> Can thwart your perfect plan.
> All chance and change transcending,
> Supreme in time and space,
> You hold your trusting children
> Secure in your embrace.
>
> O Father, you are sovereign!
> We see you dimly now,
> But soon before your triumph
> Earth's every knee shall bow.
> With this glad hope before us
> Our faith springs up anew:
> Our sovereign Lord and Savior,
> We trust and worship you!
> — Margaret Clarkson, 1982

Salvation in its Entirety Ultimately God the Father's Plan and Work

For Paul, salvation in its entirety begins and ends with God the Father. It begins with the Father's foreknowledge and predestination of the elect, is carried on by his calling, justification, and adoption of them, and terminates with his glorification of them in the Eschaton (Rom 8:28-30):

> And we know that with reference to those who love God [the Father] all things are working together for good, with reference to those who are *called* according to his [the Father's] purpose; because those whom he *foreknew*, he *predestinated* to be conformed to the image of his

[the Father's] Son, that he might be the Firstborn among many brethren. And those whom he predestinated, those he *called*; and those whom he called, those he *justified*; and those whom he justified, those he *glorified*.

God the Father is also the subject of nearly all the verbs in Paul's great doxology in Ephesians 1:3-14:

> Blessed be the God and Father of our Lord Jesus Christ, who has *blessed* us in the heavenly realms with every spiritual blessing in Christ. For he *chose* us in him before the creation of the world to be holy and blameless in his sight. In love he *predestined* us to be adopted as his sons through Jesus Christ, in accordance with his pleasure and will – to the praise of his glorious grace, which he has *freely given* us in the one he loves. In him we have redemption ... in accordance with the riches of God's grace that he *lavished* upon us with all wisdom and understanding. And he *made known* to us the mystery of his will according to his good pleasure, which he *purposed* in Christ.... In him we were also *chosen* [by the Father], *having been predestined* according to the plan of him who *works out everything* in conformity with the purpose of his will [that is, according to the plan of the Father].

In fact, there is a sustained emphasis throughout the first three chapters of Ephesians on the role that the Father fulfills in our salvation (see 1:17-23; 2:4-10; 3:14-21).

Having treated already the doctrine of election, I will say no more about it here, except to underscore again the fact that for Paul it is the Father who foreloves and predestines the elect and thus who initiates the entire salvific work of the Godhead. Which is just to say that if the Father had not loved us, the Son would not have died for us.

The Father's Summons

The person of the triune Godhead to whom Paul regularly attributes the effectual summoning of men to faith in Christ, as we have already suggested, is God the Father (Rom 8:30, 1 Cor 1:9, Gal 1:15, Eph 1:17-18; 1 Thess 5:23-24; 2 Thess 2:13-14; 2 Tim 1:9). There is perhaps one instance where he says Christ issues the call (1 Cor 7:22; but see also Matt 9:13; Mark 2:17; Luke 5:32; 2 Pet 1:3).

Paul teaches that the Father's effectual call of the elect, carried

God the Father's Salvific Work

out in accordance with his eternal purpose (Rom 8:28-29; 2 Tim 1:9), is holy in character (κλήσει ἁγίᾳ— 2 Tim 1:9), heavenward in its destination (τῆς ἄνω κλήσεως—Phil 3:14), and irrevocable once issued (ἀμεταμέλητα—Rom 11:29; see also 1 Cor 1:8-9; 1 Thess 5:23-24). By it the Father summons the elect sinner (see 1 Cor 1:26-30) into fellowship with Christ (1 Cor 1:9), calls him into his kingdom and glory (1 Thess 2:12; 2 Thess 2:14) and to eternal life (1 Tim 6:12). By it he summons the Christian to freedom from the law (Gal 5:13), to one hope (Eph 4:4), to holiness (1 Thes 4:7; see Rom 1:7; 1 Cor 1:2), and to follow Christ in peaceful human social relations (1 Cor 7:15; Col 3:15). Accordingly, Paul exhorts Christians 'to walk in a manner suited [ἀξίως] to the [Father's] calling by which you were called' (Eph 4:1).

The Father's Quickening Work and Gift of Faith

We commonly (and correctly, according to John 3:8) attribute the quickening or regenerating aspect of our salvation to the Holy Spirit. Yet in accord with Jesus who expressly taught the Father's part in regeneration when he declared: 'No one can come to me, unless the Father who sent me *draws* [ἑλκύσῃ] him' (John 6:44), and 'Everyone who has heard and *learned* from the Father comes to me'(John 6:45; see Matt 16:17), Paul also attributes to the Father our quickening: 'Because of his great love for us, God *made us alive with* [συνεζωοποίησεν] Christ' (Eph 2:4-5). Accordingly, to the Ephesians Paul also writes: '...by grace you have been saved *through faith* [διὰ πίστεως] – and *this* [τοῦτο] not of yourselves, it is the *gift of God* [θεοῦ τὸ δῶρον] – not of works, lest any man should boast.' Here he teaches that our very faith in Christ is the Father's gift to us.

The Father's Justifying Act

Justification refers to that wholly objective forensic judgment concerning the sinner's standing before the law that God the Father issues regarding him (to this doctrine, because it is so central to Paul's preaching, I have devoted an entire chapter—Chapter Twenty).

Because the Father imputes the sinner's sin to Christ who dies for him (on which ground the sinner is pardoned) and Christ's obedience and satisfaction to the sinner (constituting the sinner thereby righteous), he judges the sinner to be righteous in his sight. In other words, as Paul writes: '*For the one who does not work* [τῷ μὴ ἐργαζομένῳ], but *believes* [πιστεύοντι] in *him who justifies the ungodly* [τὸν δικαιοῦντα τὸν ἀσεβῆ]' (Rom 4:5), the Father (1) *pardons* him of all his sins (see Romans 4:6-7: 'David also speaks of the blessedness upon the man to whom God *reckons righteousness apart from works*: "Blessed are those whose lawless deeds *have been forgiven* [ἀφέθησαν] and whose sins *have been covered* [ἐπεκαλύφθησαν]*"*. '), and (2) *constitutes* him righteous in his sight by imputing or reckoning the righteousness of Christ to him (see Romans 5:1: '*having been justified* [δικαιωθέντες] by faith,' and 5:19: 'so also through the obedience of the one man the many *shall be constituted* [κατασταθήσονται] righteous'). On the basis of his *constituting* the ungodly man righteous, the Father *declares* the ungodly man righteous in his sight.

In its declarative character justification possesses an *eschatological* dimension for it amounts to the divine verdict of the Eschaton being brought forward into history and rendered here and now concerning the sinner. By the Father's act of justifying him, the sinner, as it were, has been brought, before the time, to the Final Assize and has already passed successfully through it, having been acquitted of any and all charges brought against him! The Father declares him to be righteous in the law's sight!

I will say no more at this time about this central doctrine of the Christian faith inasmuch as I will deal with it at much greater length in Chapter Twenty.

The Father's Adopting Act

The terminology with which we are concerned here are the following nouns:

(1) υἱοθεσία, the act itself of 'adoption'—found five times in the New Testament, all in Paul: Romans 8:15, 23; 9:4 (here Paul speaks of Israel's national 'adoption'); Galatians 4:5; Ephesians 1:5;

(2) υἱός, 'son'—found forty times in Paul, for example, in Romans 8:14, 19; 2 Corinthians 6:18; Galatians 3:26; 4:6-7;

(3) (τὰ) τέκνα (τοῦ) θεοῦ, 'children of God'—Rom 8:16, 17, 21; 9:8b, c; Eph 5:1; Phil 2:15—indicating the filial relationship which the Christian sustains to God the Father by virtue of the Father's adoptive act; and

God the Father's Salvific Work

(4) κληρονόμος, 'heir' – found eight times in Paul, in Romans 4:13, 14; 8:17 (twice); Galatians 3:29; 4:1, 7; Titus 3:7 (see also the related noun κληρονομία and the verb κληρονομέω). As can be seen from this data, the terms tend to cluster together in those places where Paul is announcing our sonship in Christ (Rom 8; Gal 3–4), although they do occur elsewhere. Let us now consider each of them in turn.

I. Of the Christian's υἱοθεσία, 'adoption', arranged in the biblical-theological order in which the divine actions occur of which the relevant verses speak, Paul writes:

> Ephesians 1:4-5: 'In love he [the Father] predestinated us to *adoption* through Jesus Christ unto himself.'

Here it should be noted, in light of the fact that Paul (1) sounds this 'adoption' note at the very beginning of Ephesians, (2) refers to 'the Father' at critical junctures in Ephesians (1:2, 3, 17; 2:18; 3:14; 4:6; 5:20; 6:23), (3) represents him as the subject of most of the verbs that speak of the divine activity, and (4) develops the Christian's walk in Ephesians 4-6 in terms of the walk of a 'child' before the Father (5:1, 8), that just as Romans is Paul's treatise on justification so also Ephesians in a special sense is Paul's treatise on adoption.

> Galatians 4:4-5: 'But when the fulness of time came, God sent forth his Son, born of a woman, born under law, in order that he might redeem those under law, that we might receive the *adoption*. And because you are sons [by adoption], God has sent forth the Spirit of his Son [by his very nature] into our hearts, crying, "Abba, Father."'

> Romans 8:15-16: 'For you have not received a Spirit of slavery again to fear, but you have received the Spirit of *adoption*, by whom we cry, "Abba, Father." The Spirit himself testifies with our spirit that we are God's children.'

> Romans 8:23: '... we ourselves, having the firstfruits of the Spirit, even we ourselves groan within ourselves, waiting for the *adoption*, even the redemption of our body.'

From these four Pauline texts, so arranged, we have from Paul the following biblical theology of adoption:

(1) In love the Father predestinated the believer's adoption in Christ before the foundation of the world.

(2) The Father sent his Son into the world to do the objective redemptive work necessary both to save his people from the law's condemnation and to adopt them into the status of full, mature sonship from the tutelary discipline of the Mosaic economy (Gal 4:1-2) under which his adopted children in the Old Testament had lived.

(3) The Father sent forth the Spirit of his Son, even the Spirit of adoption, into the heart of the believer, subjectively assuring him that he is the Father's child and enabling him to cry 'Abba, Father'.

(4) The child of God, having received the firstfruits of the Spirit of adoption, awaits the final stage of his adoption in the Eschaton when finally even his fallen body will be redeemed from corruption.

This biblical theology of adoption, then, encompasses (1) the Father's love from all eternity, (2) redemption from sin and past enslavement, (3) a status and way of life in the present, and (4) a future expectation.

II. By υἱός, 'son', Paul speaks of that sonship rooted in God's choice and calling (Rom 9:25, 26).

Sonship becomes our status through faith in Christ, and thus we become sons of Abraham (Gal 3:7, 26). Sons of God are led by the Spirit of God (8:14) and cry 'Abba, Father' (Gal 4:6), being conformed to the image of God's Son (Rom 8:29). It is for the purpose of being conformed to the image of God's Son as the Firstborn among many brothers that we are made sons.

Adoption and sonship are privileges conferred and realities realized in the here and now which manifest themselves in a life of filial praise and obedience. There is also an expectation and desire for the culmination of our sonship just as heirs may look forward to the fulness of their inheritance.

Sonship in Galatians 3–4 is presented as our gift status over against the immaturity of Old Testament covenantal existence and the attempt on the part of the Judaizers to earn one's status before God. In Romans 8 it is also employed of our gift status, but there it is used of people who by God's Spirit are actively obedient and who are willing to suffer for Christ.

One final word. The masculine term 'sons', as often in the Bible and in literature in general, is used to designate men and women alike. Although its maleness is perceived as a disadvantage in our polarized generation, it still has the advantage of correlating our status with the Jesus who is none other than *the* Son of God (ὁ υἱὸς τοῦ θεοῦ). The fact that Paul can and does use τέκνον which has no gender aspect and applies υἱός to men and women alike shows that no prejudice or bias is in view or intended. We should continue to be open to this Pauline usage ourselves and not deny its appropriateness simply because of a misperception of our day.

III. By (τὰ) τέκνα (τοῦ) θεοῦ, 'children of God', Paul describes those who are adopted and who know of their adoption by means of God's Spirit witnessing with their spirits that the objective promise of salvation has been subjectively realized (Rom. 8:16). These children also know themselves to be heirs (8:17) and they look to the freedom of the glory which will be theirs in the resurrection (8:21). They are encompassed by and do themselves embrace the promise given to Abraham (Rom 9:8; see also Gal 3:14, 29).

IV. By κληρονόμος, 'heir', Paul describes both what we are now in Christ (designated heirs) (Gal 3:29; see Rom 4:13, 14) and what we shall be (heirs in full possession of the inheritance) (Rom 8:17; Tit 3:7).

This complex of concepts describes our *present status* (adopted), our *present existence and reality* (sons led by the Spirit), and our *future status* (heirs who are to enter into the fullness of our adoption at the resurrection).

The Father's Glorifying Act

According to Paul it is the Father who will finally glorify the elect (Rom 8:30). Paul speaks of salvation in all three temporal tenses:

I. The *past tense* – the Christian has been saved from the guilt and condemnation of sin (Luke 19:9—'Today salvation *has come* [ἐγένετο] to this house'; Eph 2:8—'For by grace you *have been saved* [ἐστε σεσῳσμένοι] through faith'; 2 Tim 1:9—[God] *has saved* [σώσαντος] us'; Tit 3:5—'according to his mercy he *saved* [ἔσωσεν] us');

II. The *present tense* – the Christian is being saved from the power of sin (1 Cor 1:18 – '...to us who *are being saved* [σῳζομένοις] [the cross] is the power of God'; 1 Cor 15:2 – 'by which you *are being saved* [σῴζεσθε]'; 2 Cor 2:15 – 'because we are a fragrance of Christ to God among those who *are being saved* [σῳζομένοις]'); and

III. The *future tense* – the Christian will be completely saved someday from the very presence of sin (see Rom 5:9, 10 – 'we *shall be saved* [σωθησόμεθα] through him from the Wrath'; 13:11 – '...for our salvation is nearer than when we first believed'; 1 Cor 3:15 – 'he *shall be saved* [σωθήσεται], but as through fire'; 1 Thess 5:18 – '...having put on...as a helmet, the *hope* of salvation'; 1 Pet 1:5 – '...kept by the power of God through faith for the salvation ready to be revealed in the last time').

It is this future tense of our salvation that we address when we consider our glorification (Rom 8:30).

The Nature of the Christian's Glorification

It must be stressed at the outset that individual salvation encompasses not only all three tenses of time, as we have just said, but also the whole man – body and soul. God the Father will not be satisfied with his salvific work in our behalf until we stand before him as saved people in Christ, redeemed in spirit and in body; nor will our 'so great salvation' be consummated until he has brought our full and final glorification to reality. Consequently, while there is a sense in which death itself now serves the Christian (see 1 Cor 3:22 – 'death...belongs to you') in that 'the souls of believers are at their death made perfect in holiness, and do immediately pass into glory' (*Shorter Catechism*, Ques 37a; see 2 Cor 5:8; Phil 1:21-23; Heb 12:23), it is nonetheless true that 'their bodies, being still united to Christ, do rest in their graves till the resurrection' (*Shorter Catechism*, Question 37b). In other words, while the intermediate state of believers in heaven, brought to pass in his will when God calls his children to himself through death, is a more blessed state than their present one, it is not the best and most glorious state. Accordingly, death is not the ultimate experience to which Christians should longingly look. Rather, according to Paul, their blessed hope is the glorious appearing (or the appearing of the glory) of their great God and Savior Jesus

Christ (Tit 2:13), at whose coming those who have died in the faith and those who are alive at the time of his coming

> will all be changed – in a flash, in the twinkling of an eye, at the last trumpet. For the trumpet will sound, the dead will be raised imperishable, and we will be changed. For the perishable must clothe itself with the imperishable, and the mortal with immortality. When the perishable has been clothed with the imperishable, and the mortal with immortality, then the saying that is written will come true: 'Death has been swallowed up in victory.' Where, O death, is your victory? Where, O death, is your sting? The sting of death is sin, and the power of sin is the law. But thanks be to God! He gives us the victory through our Lord Jesus Christ (1 Cor 15:51-57).

'At the resurrection, believers, being raised up in glory, shall be openly acknowledged, and acquitted in the day of judgment, and made perfectly blessed in the full enjoying of God to all eternity' (*Shorter Catechism*, Question 38). All the more will their state of blessedness, as the consequence of their full and open acquittal in the judgment, be evident by its contrast to the state of those 'vessels of wrath fitted for destruction, even in order that [God] might make known the riches of his glory [grace] upon the vessels of mercy, which he prepared beforehand unto glory' (Rom 9:22-23). For whereas they will enter into everlasting life and receive that fullness of joy and refreshing which shall come from the presence of the Lord, the wicked who know not God and who obey not the gospel of our Lord Jesus will pay the penalty of eternal destruction away from the approving presence of the Lord and from the glory of his power.

At this point Christians together will enter upon their glorified state, the goal toward which the triune Godhead, in all of their salvific exercises, have been relentlessly driving from the moment of creation, and that ultimate end which was the first of the decrees in the eternal plan of salvation.

I. The significance of Christians' glorification for creation

With the arrival of their full 'adoption as sons' through the redemption of their bodies at the resurrection (Rom 8:23), Paul teaches that the renewal of creation itself will also occur (Rom 8:19-21). Creation will be 'liberated from its bondage to decay and brought into the glorious freedom of the children of God'. Biblical scholars have ardently debated whether 'the new heaven and the new earth' condition which Paul envisions will involve simply the renewal or a complete destruction of the present universe followed by a re-creation *ex nihilo*. The preponderance of biblical evidence suggests the former – a renewal, but the transformation of the universe will be so complete that, for all intents and purposes, it will introduce a radically new order of existence.

II. The significance of their glorification for Christians themselves

In their glorified state believers, having received the fullness of their adoption by the resurrection of their bodies from the dead (Rom 8:23), will be fully conformed to the likeness of the Son of God. For at his coming, the Lord Jesus Christ, 'by the power that enables him to bring everything under his control, will transform our lowly bodies so that they will be like his glorious body' (Phil 3:21). Moreover, believers will then reflect the holy character of their Savior (Rom 8:29), their wills being 'made perfectly and immutably free to do good alone, in the state of glory' (*Westminster Confession of Faith*, IX/v). 'This is the highest end conceivable for created beings, the highest end conceivable not only by men but also by God himself. God himself could not contemplate or determine a higher destiny for his creatures.'[1] John Murray with trenchant insight observes that, though Christ will be the 'Firstborn' at that time, a term referring to priority and supereminence, his will be a

> supereminence among brethren, and therefore the supereminence involved has no meaning except in that relation. Hence, though there can be no underestimation of the pre-eminence belonging to the Son as the firstbegotten, yet the interdependence is just as necessary. The glory bestowed upon the redeemed is derived from the relation they sustain to the 'firstborn'. But the specific character involved in being the 'firstborn' is derived from the relation he sustains to the redeemed in that capacity. Hence they must be glorified together.[2]

Little wonder then that Paul can inform Christians, who were originally called '*with the view of obtaining the glory* [εἰς περιποίησιν δόξης] of our Lord Jesus Christ' (2 Thess 2:14) and who will '*be glorified together with* [συνδοξασθῶμεν]' Christ (Rom 8:17), that

---

1. John Murray, 'The Goal of Sanctification', in *The Collected Writings of John Murray* (Edinburgh: Banner of Truth, 1977), 2, 316.
2. Murray, 'The Goal of Sanctification', 2, 315.

'our present sufferings are not worth comparing with the *glory* [δόξαν] that will be revealed in us' (8:18), indeed, that 'our light and momentary troubles are achieving for us an *eternal glory that far outweighs* [αἰώνιον βάρος δόξης] them all' (2 Cor 4:17).

III. The significance of the church's glorification for his Son

Even when understood in terms of its arrival at its *summum bonum*—its conformity to Christ's glorious likeness—the church's glorification is not the *terminus ad quem* of the Father's purpose. For the Father's determination to conform 'a great multitude that no one can count, from every nation, tribe, people and language' (Rev 7:9) to the likeness of his well-beloved Son was only designed as a means to effect a still higher end—the final phase of his glorification of his well-beloved Son, the church's Savior and Messianic King. Paul teaches this when he declares that the church's final conformity to Christ is 'in order that his Son might become the Firstborn [πρωτότοκος] among many brothers' (Rom 8:29). Again, Murray assists us in our appreciation of this truth:

> There is a final end that is more ultimate than the glorification of the people of God. It is the pre-eminence of Christ, and that pre-eminence vindicated and exemplified in the final phase of his glorification. 'Firstborn' reflects on the *priority* and *supremacy* of Christ (cf. Col. 1:15, 18; Heb. 1:6; Rev. 1:5). The glory of God is always supreme and ultimate. And the supreme glory of God is manifested in the glorifying of the Son.... But the glory for the people of God is only enhanced by the emphasis placed upon the pre-eminence of Christ. For it is *among many brethren* that Christ is the firstborn. That they should be classified as brethren brings to the thought of glorification with Christ the deepest mystery of community. The fraternal relationship is subsumed under the ultimate aim of the predestinating decree. This means that the *pre-eminence* of the Son as the firstborn carries with it the correlative *eminence* of the children of God. The unique dignity of the Son enhances the dignity bestowed upon the many sons who are to be brought to glory....
> We thus see how, in the final realization of the goal of sanctification, there is exemplified and vindicated to the fullest extent, an extent that staggers our thought by reason of its stupendous reality, the truth inscribed upon the whole process of redemption, from its inception in the electing grace of the Father (see Eph. 1:4; Rom 8:29) to its consummation in the adoption (Rom 8:23; Eph. 1:5), that Christ in all his offices as Redeemer

is never to be conceived of apart from the church, and the church is not to be conceived of apart from Christ. There is correlativity in election, there is correlativity in redemption once for all accomplished, there is correlativity in the mediatorial ministry which Christ continues to exercise at the right hand of the Father, and there is correlativity in the consummation, when Christ will come the second time without sin for those that look for him unto salvation.[3]

So with the church's glorification and the accompanying yet more ultimate and preeminent glorification of Christ himself, the Father's eternal decree respecting the salvation of men will reach that moment toward which the execution of his work through all of human history has been irresistibly moving. The Father will not be finally satisfied until Christ and his church are fully and finally glorified, to the praise of his Son and his own most holy name (Phil 2:11), and that to all eternity.

---

3. Murray, 'The Goal of Sanctification', 2, 316-17.

CHAPTER SIXTEEN

THE PERSON OF CHRIST

> Mighty God, while angels bless you,
> > May a mortal sing your name?
> Lord of men as well as angels,
> > You are every creature's theme.
>
> Lord of every land and nation,
> > Ancient of eternal days,
> Sounded through the wise creation
> > Be your just and lawful praise.
>
> For the grandeur of your nature,
> > Grand beyond a seraph's thought,
> For created works of power,
> > Works with skill and kindness wrought.
>
> Brightness of the Father's glory,
> > Shall your praise unuttered lie?
> Fly, my tongue, such guilty silence,
> > Sing the Lord who came to die.
>
> From the highest throne in glory,
> > To the cross of deepest woe,
> All to ransom guilty captives,
> > Flow my praise, forever flow.
> > > — Robert Robinson, 1774

As we have already noted, as a strict Jew, the apostle Paul was a monotheist. He declares: 'There is only one God' (Rom 3:30); again, 'We know that an idol is nothing at all in the world and that there is no God but one' (1 Cor 8:4); finally, 'There is one God and one mediator between God and men, the man Christ Jesus' (1 Tim 2:5). And yet about that 'one mediator, the *man* [ἄνθρωπος] Christ Jesus', Paul says enough to place beyond all legitimate doubt that he regarded

Jesus Christ as also the Son of God and as such *very God* as well as very man.

When we consider Paul's Christology, we are addressing what for him was essential to everything else in his thought. And he is by no means silent with regard to who Christ is.[1]

The Son's Preexistence

A first line of evidence suggesting that Jesus Christ, for Paul, was divine is the catena of verses in his letters that imply his preexistence as God's Son (see 2 Cor 8:9; Rom 1:3; 5:10; 8:3, 29, 32; Gal 4:4, 6; Phil 2:6-7; Col 1:13-16; Eph 4:8-9).[2] It has been suggested that such statements need reflect no more than an 'ideal' preexistence, and do not require Christ's personal preexistence. But such a contention will fail to persuade any but the gullible once the passages have been carefully examined. Consider: The apostle will appeal for Christian generosity on the ground that Christ, the Christian's example, 'though he was [ὤν, lit. 'is continually'] rich, yet for your sakes...[he] became poor [ἐπτώχευσεν]' (2 Cor 8:9). He urges Christians to live as sons of God because 'God sent forth [ἐξαπέστειλεν] his Son' to make us his sons (Gal 4:4). He grounds his argument for Christian self-effacement in the fact that 'though [Christ] was in the form of God [that is, was divine in nature],...he poured himself out, having taken [λαβών] the form of a servant' (Phil 2:6-7).[3] He insists that the

---

1. Working as he does with a low view of Paul's letters as inspired Scripture, E. P. Sanders, *Paul* (Oxford: University Press, 1991), asserts that 'it is impossible to derive from Paul's letters anything approaching one single doctrine of the person of Jesus Christ' (82). He urges that 'the two most substantial passages in which he commented on who Jesus was are Romans 1:1-6 and Philippians 2:5-11' (81). Failing to provide any real exegesis of either passage, Sanders contends that in the former passage Paul sets forth what was to be termed later as 'an "adoptionist" Christology. Jesus was adopted by God as Son, not born that way' (81) while in the latter passage Paul 'states that Jesus Christ was pre-existent and was in some sense divine, but that he became human before being exalted even higher than he had originally been, to the status "Lord"' (81-82). These statements completely misrepresent the facts, as my expositions of these two passages demonstrate in my *A New Systematic Theology of the Christian Faith* (Nashville, Tenn.: Thomas Nelson, 1998), 238-45, 253-64. It is difficult to retain confidence in the scholarship of one who so totally distorts the plain words of the apostle.
2. Herman Ridderbos in his *Paul: An Outline of His Theology*, translated by John R. DeWitt (Grand Rapids: Eerdmans, 1975), 68-69, argues that it is Paul's teaching on Christ's ontological preexistence that negates Oscar Cullmann's functional Christology urged in his *The Christology of the New Testament*, translated by Shirley C. Guthrie and Charles A. M. Hall (London: SCM, 1959), 293, 325-26, and undergirds and informs Paul's intended ascription of full deity to the Christ when he calls Christ 'God' and the 'Son of God'.
3. See my treatment of Philippians 2:6-11 in my *Jesus, Divine Messiah: The New Testament Witness* (Phillipsburg, N. J.: Presbyterian and Reformed, 1990), 251-66.

Colossians must not find in the pagan πλήρωμα (fullness) their fullness because it is Christ, God's Son (see verse 13), who is 'before all things' and 'by whom and for whom all things were created' (Col 1:16-17). To bring about such practical ends as are here envisioned by the apostle Paul, it is highly doubtful that he would have grounded his pastoral appeals in a mere speculative 'ideal' preexistence. Much more likely is it that such appeals were based upon a familiar, treasured, foundational truth central to the Christian faith – namely, that Christ as God's Son had personally preexisted with the Father from eternity and had come to earth on a mission of mercy.

Jesus as 'the Christ'

Beyond all doubt, Jesus was, for Paul, the promised Messiah. Not only does 'Christ' become a proper name for Jesus in Paul's writings, indeed, even his favorite designation for him, occurring (more often with than without the article, that is, 'the Christ') around two hundred and fifteen times by itself in this sense and many more times in conjunction with other designations (three hundred and eighty-four times out of five hundred and twenty-nine times in the New Testament, or 72% of the occurrences), but also Paul affirms that it was of Jesus that the Old Testament Scriptures spoke (see, for example, Acts 13:27-36; 17:2-3; 26:22-23; Rom 1:1-3; 1 Cor 15:3-4). And precisely because he employs 'Christ' in conjunction with the term 'Lord' ('the Lord Christ' in Rom 16:18; Col 3:24; 'the [or, 'our'] Lord Jesus Christ'; 'Christ Jesus, the [or 'our', or 'my'] Lord'; 'Jesus Christ, our Lord'), it is clear that for Paul 'Christ' was a title of great dignity, compatible in every way with the implicates of deity which are often suggested by the title combinations in which it is found and the predicative statements surrounding it (see, for example, the statements in Colossians 3:24: 'The Lord Christ you are serving', and Romans 9:5: 'Christ...who is over all, God blessed forever').

Jesus as 'Lord'

In Paul the simple designation 'Jesus' occurs only some twenty-five times while the simple 'Lord' occurs some one hundred and forty-seven to one hundred and forty-nine times, to which should be added ninety-six to ninety-seven more instances when it occurs in conjunction with the proper name 'Jesus' (the total occurrences of

'Lord' moving from a low of two hundred and forty-three times to a high of two hundred and forty-seven times). It is in his description of Jesus as 'the [or 'our' or 'my'] Lord' (κύριος), that Paul brings out most clearly his assessment of Jesus as divine. From the five distinct facts that Paul

(1) prayed to Christ as 'the Lord' (2 Cor 12:8-9);

(2) declared 'the name of our Lord Jesus Christ' to be the name to be 'called upon' in the church (1 Cor 1:2; Rom 10:9-13; see Joel 2:32a);

(3) coupled 'the Lord Jesus Christ' with 'God the Father' as the co-source of those spiritual blessings (grace, mercy, and peace) which God alone has the power to grant (Gal 1:3; 1 Thess 1:1; 2 Thess 1:1-2; Rom 1:7; 16:20; 1 Cor 1:3; 2 Cor 1:2; Eph 1:2; Phil 1:2; Col. 1:2; Phile. 3; 1 Tim 1:2; 2 Tim 1:2; Tit 1:4; see 1 Thess 3:11; 2 Thess 1:12; Eph 6:23);

(4) applied to Christ the very term (κύριος) that in the Septuagint is employed to translate the sacred name of Yahweh; and

(5) more specifically, applied directly to Jesus Old Testament passages in which God (Yahweh) is the subject (see Isa 8:14 and Rom 9:32, 33; Joel 2:32 and Rom 10:12-13; Isa 40:13 and 1 Cor 2:16; Ps 24:1 [LXX, 23:1] and 1 Cor 10:26 [see 10:21-22]; Ps 68:18 and Eph 4:8-10; Isa 45:23 and Phil 2:10; Ps 102:25-27 and Heb 1:10-12),

there can be no legitimate doubt that as 'the Lord', Jesus was, for Paul, divine and rightly to be regarded by others as such. When it is further noted that it is as 'the Lord' that Paul speaks of Jesus in his 'Trinitarian' passages (Rom 15:30; 1 Cor 12:4-6; 2 Cor 13:14; Eph 4:4-6), it is not too much to say that the title 'Lord' was for Paul the Christological title which both equates and distinguishes him from the Father and the Spirit, and that it is the heavenly triad that is his presupposition when he speaks of Jesus as 'Lord'.[4]

Magnificently does Warfield capture the essence of the meaning of 'Lord' as a Christological title in Paul's writings when he writes:

> 'Lord' to [Paul] is not a general term of respect which he naturally applies to Jesus because he recognized Jesus as supreme, and was glad to acknowledge him as his Master (Eph 6:9, Col 4:1), or even in the great

---

4. See Herman Ridderbos' treatment of Christ's lordship in his *Paul: An Outline of His Theology*, 86-90.

The Person of Christ

words of Col 2:19 as the 'head' of the body which is his Church (see Eph 4:15). It is to him the specific title of divinity by which he indicates to himself the relation in which Jesus stands to Deity. Jesus is not 'Lord' to him because he has been given dominion over all creation; he has been given this universal dominion because he is 'Lord,' who with the Father and the Spirit is to be served and worshipped, and from whom all that the Christian longs for is to be expected.[5]

The foregoing material makes it abundantly clear, then, that for Paul, the One who apprehended him on the Damascus Road was indeed God the Son in his own right and the proper recipient of man's worship and service. Consequently, Paul can move 'easily into a complete linguistic identification of Christ with Yahweh':

> If Yahweh is our sanctifier (Ex. 31:13), is omnipresent (Ps. 139:7-10), is our peace (Judg. 6:24), is our righteousness (Jer. 23:6), is our victory (Ex. 17:8-16), and is our healer (Ex. 15:26), then so is Christ all of these things (1 Cor. 1:30; Col. 1:27; Eph. 2:14). If the gospel is God's (1 Thess. 2:2, 6-9; Gal. 3:8), then that same gospel is also Christ's (1 Thess. 3:2; Gal. 1:7). If the church is God's (Gal. 1:13; 1 Cor. 15:9), then that same church is also Christ's (Rom 16:16). God's Kingdom (1 Thess. 2:12) is Christ's (Eph. 5:5); God's love (Eph. 1:3-5) is Christ's (Rom. 8:35); God's Word (Col. 1:25; 1 Thess. 2:13) is Christ's (1 Thess. 1:8; 4:15); God's Spirit (1 Thess. 4:8) is Christ's (Phil. 1:19); God's peace (Gal. 5:22; Phil. 4:9) is Christ's (Col. 3:15; cf. Col. 1:2; Phil. 1:2; 4:7); God's 'Day' of judgment (Isa. 13:6) is Christ's 'Day' of judgment (Phil. 1:6, 10; 2:16; 1 Cor. 1:8); God's grace (Eph. 2:8, 9; Col. 1:6; Gal. 1:15) is Christ's grace (1 Thess. 5:28; Gal. 1:6; 6:18); God's salvation (Col. 1:13) is Christ's salvation (1 Thess. 1:10); and God's will (Eph. 1:11; 1 Thess. 4:3; Gal. 1:4) is Christ's will (Eph. 5:17; cf. 1 Thess. 5:18). So it is no surprise to hear Paul say that he is both God's slave (Rom. 1:9) and Christ's (Rom. 1:1; Gal. 1:10), that he lives for that glory which is both God's (Rom 5:2; Gal. 1:24) and Christ's (2 Cor. 8:19, 23; cf. 2 Cor. 4:6), that his faith is in God (1 Thess. 1:8, 9; Rom. 4:1-5) and in Christ Jesus (Gal. 3:22), and that to know God, which is salvation (Gal. 4:8; 1 Thess. 4:5), is to know Christ (2 Cor. 4:6).[6]

Such linguistic identification is pervasive throughout Paul's writings and may be observed by ranging freely through the Pauline corpus.

---

5. Benjamin B. Warfield, *The Lord of Glory* (Reprint; Grand Rapids: Baker, 1974), 231.
6. David F. Wells, *The Person of Christ* (Westchester, Ill.: Crossway, 1984), 64-65.

Jesus as 'Savior'

'Savior' (σωτήρ) is found twelve times in Paul, with ten of the occurrences in the Pastoral Letters (1 Timothy, 3 times; Titus, 6 times; 2 Timothy, 1 time). The references in the Pastorals are divided between God the Father (1 Tim 1:1; 2:3; 4:10; Tit 1:3; 2:10; 3:4) and Jesus Christ our Lord (Tit 1:4; 2:13: 3:6; 2 Tim 1:10). The two remaining occurrences (Eph 5:23; Phil 3:20) refer the title to Jesus.

The Seven Great Christological Passages and Hymns and the Three Pauline Occurrences of Θεός as a Christological Title

Finally, the great Christological passages and 'hymns' in Romans 1:3-4, Colossians 1:15-20, 2:9, Philippians 2:6-11, Ephesians 4:9-10, 1 Timothy 1:15, and 3:16,[7] and the three occurrences of θεός as a Christological title in Romans 9:5, Titus 2:13, and Hebrew 1:8 round out the major Christological material in the Pauline corpus. The three θεός passages and their closely related fellow in Colossians 2:9 deserve some comment.

Romans 9:5

'Theirs are the patriarchs, and from them came the Messiah according to the flesh, who is over all, God blessed forever. Amen.' The debate surrounding this verse arises not from a divergence of opinion over textual variants or the meaning of words. The debate is rather over the question of punctuation. The most natural way to punctuate the verse is to place commas after both 'flesh' and 'all' and a period after 'forever' as above. This punctuation is supported by both the context and the grammatical and implicatory demands of the verse itself.

No one expresses the significance of the context for the meaning of Romans 9:5 with greater depth of insight that E. H. Gifford:

> St. Paul is expressing the anguish of his heart at the fall of his brethren: that anguish is deepened by the memory of their privileges, most of all, by the thought that their race gave birth to the Divine Saviour, whom they have rejected. In this, the usual interpretation, all is most natural: the last and greatest cause of sorrow is the climax of glory [namely, the divine Messiah's work which brought to full fruition the covenantal

---

7. For treatment of these Christological passages see my *Jesus, Divine Messiah, The New Testament Witness* (Phillipsburg: Presbyterian and Reformed, 1990), 199-210; 243-72.

history which constituted Israel's distinctiveness – RLR] from which the chosen race has fallen.⁸

As for the grammatical demand of the verse, it can hardly be denied that the most natural way to handle ὁ ὤν (the definite article and present participle) is to view the phrase as introducing a relative clause and to attach it to the immediately preceding ὁ Χριστὸς. The implicatory demand of the verse flows from the presence of the words τὸ κατὰ σάρκα ('insofar as the flesh is concerned'). This expression naturally raises the question: in what sense is the Messiah *not* from the patriarchs? The second half of the implied antithesis is supplied in the words which follow: 'who is over all, God blessed forever.' This treatment of the verse, of course, ascribes full, unqualified deity to the Messiah.

This natural, straightforward rendering of Romans 9:5—'which every Greek scholar would adopt without hesitation, if no question of doctrine were involved' (Gifford) – has enjoyed not only the support of a not inconsiderable number of early fathers and the large majority of commentators but also the primacy of choice in the AV (1611), RV (1881), ASV (1901), NASV (1971), NIV (1978), and the NKJV (1982).

Because some opposing scholars have judged it to be an un-Pauline locution to refer to Christ as 'God', they (see RSV [1946] and NEB [1970]) have proposed two alternative punctuations: the first detaching the last expression, θεὸς εὐλογητὸς εἰς τοὺς αἰῶνας, construing it as a doxology, from the preceding; the second detaching the entire expression after σάρκα from the preceding, again construing the clause as a doxology.

As for the objection itself, it is a clear case of 'begging the question' to declare it 'un-Pauline' for Paul to refer to Christ as 'God' in a Pauline letter where all the syntactical evidence indicates that this may well be the very time that he has done so. Can a writer never express a theological *hapax legomenon* ('said one time')? And to assert that Paul does so nowhere else requires the additional judgment (which these scholars, of course, have made) that Titus 2:13 is at best 'deutero-Pauline', that is, non-Pauline in authorship though 'Pauline-like' in style and essential substance. Furthermore, it is to ignore the words of Colossians 2:9, not to mention the profusion of

---

8. E. H. Gifford, *The Epistle of St. Paul to the Romans* (London: John Murray, 1886), 168-69.

exalted terminology throughout Paul's writings which ascribe deity to Jesus.

But what about the two alternative proposals? Can their sponsors justify them? The first, as we indicated, suggests that the last words of the verse should be construed as a disconnected doxology ('May God be blessed before!'). But Bruce M. Metzger appears to be correct when he writes: 'Both logically and emotionally such a doxology would interrupt the train of thought as well as be inconsistent with the mood of sadness that pervades the preceding verses.'[9]

Furthermore, if this detached clause is a doxology to God, it reverses the word order of the subject and the predicate present in every other such doxology in the Bible (over thirty times in the Old Testament and twelve times in the New) where the verbal adjective always *precedes* the noun for God and never follows it as it is reputed, by this counter-proposal, to do in Roman 9:5. It is difficult to believe that the apostle, whose ear for proper Hebraic and Hellenistic linguistic and syntactical formulae was finely tuned, would violate the established form for expressing praise to God which even he himself observes elsewhere (Eph 1:3; 2 Cor 1:3).

Finally, if this clause is an ascription of praise to God, it differs in another respect from every other occurrence of such in Paul's writings. Invariably, when Paul would ascribe blessedness to God, he connects the expression either by some grammatical device or by direct juxtaposition to a word which precedes it. There is, in other words, an antecedent reference to God in the immediately preceding context. For example, he employs ὅ ἐστιν (Rom 1:25), ὁ ὢν (2 Cor 11:31), ᾧ (Gal 1:5; 2 Tim 4:18), αὐτῷ (Rom 11:36; Eph 3:21), and τῷ δὲ θεῷ (Phil 4:20; 1 Tim 1:17) to introduce ascriptions of praise to God. In the cases of Ephesians 1:3 and 2 Corinthians 1:3, even here there is an antecedent reference to God in the immediately preceding contexts. Thus all of Paul's doxologies to God are connected either grammatically or juxtapositionally to an immediately preceding antecedent reference to God. Never is there an abrupt change from one subject (in this case, the Messiah in 9:5a) to another (God the Father in 9:5b) as suggested by the counter-proposal. Consequently, this proposal has nothing to commend it and much to oppose it.

The second proposal – the one preferred by most of the scholars

---

9. Bruce M. Metzger, 'The Punctuation of Romans 9:5,' *Christ and Spirit in the New Testament* (Cambridge: Cambridge University Press, 1973), 108.

who reject the natural view and which is also commended by the *Greek New Testament* (UBS), the RSV, and the NEB – has even less to commend it, for not only do the objections against the former proposal tell equally against it as well, but an additional objection may be registered. By disconnecting everything after σάρκα and construing the disconnected portion as an independent ascription of praise, it denies to the participle ὤν any real significance. Metzger highlights this failing:

> If...the clause [beginning with ὁ ὤν] is taken as an asyndetic [disconnected] doxology to God,...the word ὤν becomes superfluous, for 'he who is God over all' is most simply represented in Greek by ὁ ἐπὶ πάντων θεός [and 'he who is over all' is most simply represented by ὁ επὶ πάντων – RLR]. The presence of the participle suggests that the clause functions as a relative clause (not 'he who is...' but 'who is...'), and thus describes ὁ Χριστός as being 'God over all'.[10]

Nigel Turner also points out that detaching the words beginning with ὁ ὤν from the preceding clause 'introduces asyndeton and there is no grammatical reason why a participle agreeing with "Messiah" should first be divorced from it and then be given the force of a wish, receiving a different person as its subject'.[11] One must surely wonder at the strange facility of some scholars to recognize the presence and natural force of the ὁ ὤν in 2 Corinthians 11:31 where we find precisely the same syntactical construction ('God..., who is blessed forever') as the construction here in Romans 9:5 and to fail to recognize its presence and force in Romans 9:5.

I would conclude that there can be no justifiable doubt that Paul in Romans 9:5, by his use of θεός – surrounding it with the particular descriptive phrases that he does – ascribes full deity to Jesus Christ who *is and abides as* (the force of the present participle) Lord over the universe and who deserves eternal praise from all.

Titus 2:13

The debate surrounding this verse relative to our present interest is whether the apostle Paul intended to refer to one person (Christ) or

---

10. Metzger, 'The Punctuation of Romans 9:5,' 105-6. The best brief treatment of Romans 9:5 that I am aware of is Metzger's discussion in his *A Textual Commentary on the Greek New Testament* (New York: United Bible Societies, 1971), 520-23.
11. Nigel Turner, *Grammatical Insights Into the New Testament* (Edinburgh: T. & T. Clark, 1965), 15.

to two persons (the Father and Christ) when he wrote: '...while we wait for the blessed hope, even the appearing of the glory [or, glorious appearing] of the great God and Savior of us, Jesus Christ.' The issue, more pointedly put, is this: Are the two words 'God' and 'Savior' to be construed as referring to one person or are they to be divorced from one another, because of the demands of exegesis, and referred to two persons? In my opinion, there are five compelling reasons for understanding Paul to be referring to Christ alone throughout the verse and to translate the relevant phrase: 'the appearing of our great God and Savior, Jesus Christ.'

First, it is the most natural way to render the Greek sentence as numerous commentators and grammarians have observed. Indeed, more than one grammarian has noted that there would never have been a question as to whether 'God' and 'Savior' referred to one person if the sentence had simply ended with 'our Savior'.

Second, the two nouns both stand under the regimen of the single definite article preceding 'God', indicating that they are to be construed together, not separately, that is to say, that they have a single referent.[12] If Paul had intended to speak of two persons, he could have expressed this unambiguously by inserting an article before 'Savior' or by writing 'our Savior' after 'Jesus Christ'.

Third, inasmuch as 'appearing' is never referred to the Father but is consistently employed to refer to Christ's return in glory, the *prima facie* conclusion is that the 'appearing of the glory of our great God' refers to Christ's appearing and not to the Father's appearing.

Fourth, note has often been made of the fact that the terms θεὸς καὶ σωτήρ ('god and savior') were employed in combination together in the second and first century B.C. secular literature to refer to single recipients of heathen worship. James H. Moulton, for example, writes:

> A curious echo [of Titus 2:13] is found in the Ptolemaic formula applied to the deified kings: thus GH 15 (ii/B.C.), τοῦ μεγάλου θεοῦ...καὶ σωτῆρος.... The phrase here is, of course, applied to one person.[13]

---

12. According to the Granville Sharp rule, when two singular nouns of the same case of personal description are connected by καί with the article preceding only the first noun, the second noun denotes a farther description of the first-named noun, whereas the repetition of the article with both nouns denotes particularity.

13. James Hope Moulton, *A Grammar of New Testament Greek* (Third edition; Edinburgh: Clark, 1930), I, 84.

and Walter Lock writes in the same vein:

> The combination σωτήρ καὶ θεός had been applied to Ptolemy I, θεὸς ἐπιφανής to Antiochus Epiphanes, θεὸν ἐπιφανῆ καὶ...σωτῆρα to Julius Caesar [Ephesus, 48 B. C.]....[14]

It is very likely in light of this data that one impulse behind Paul's description here of Christ was his desire to counteract the extravagant titular endowment that had been accorded to human rulers.

Fifth, contrary to the oft-repeated assertion that the use of θεός as a Christological title is an 'un-Pauline locution' and thus the noun cannot refer to Christ here, I would simply say that our exposition of Romans 9:5 has already demonstrated that this simply is not so. Grammatically and biblically, the evidence would indicate that Paul intended in Titus 2:13 to describe Christ as 'our great God and Savior'.

Hebrews 1:8

As explications of the content of Christ's superangelic 'more excellent name' of 'Son' (Heb 1:4) and *not* simply new names adduced in addition to that of 'Son', he is the 'God' (θεός) of Psalm 45:6-7 and 'the Lord' (κύριος), that is, the Yahweh, of Psalm 102:25-27.

When Paul wrote, 'To the Son, on the other hand, [God says], "Your throne, O God, will last for ever and ever" ' (1:8), Paul uses for a third time θεός as a Christological title. The controversy surrounding this verse is over whether ὁ θεός is to be construed as a nominative (if so, it may be a subject nominative: 'God is your throne for ever and ever', or a predicate nominative: 'Your throne is God for ever and ever') or a vocative, which would yield the translation given above. With the 'overwhelming majority of grammarians, commentators, authors of general studies, and English translations',[15] I believe that Paul applies Psalm 45:6 to Jesus in such a way that he is addressed directly as God in the ontological sense of the word. This position requires (1) that ὁ θεός be interpreted as a vocative,

---

14. Walter Lock, *A Critical and Exegetical Commentary on The Pastoral Epistles* (International Critical Commentary; Edinburgh: T. & T. Clark, 1936), 145; see W. Dittenberger, *Sylloge Inscriptionum Graecarum* (Third edition; Hildesheim: Georg Olms, 1960), 760.6 (=second edition, 347.6).

15. See Murray J. Harris, 'The Translation and Significance of ὁ θεός in Hebrews 1:8-9,' *Tyndale Bulletin* 36 (1985), 146-48; see footnotes 56, 57, 58, 59. To the sources Harris cites should be added his own definitive article and the one that appeared antecedent to it: 'The Translation of אלהים in Psalm 45:7-8,' *Tyndale Bulletin* 35 (1984), 65-89.

and (2) that the theotic character ascribed to Jesus be understood in ontological and not functional terms.

That ὁ θεός is vocatival is apparent for the following reasons:

First, the fact that the noun is nominative in its inflected form means nothing since the use of the nominative with vocative force is a well-established idiom in classical Greek, the Septuagint, and New Testament Greek. The case of the noun in Hebrews 1:8 must be established then on other grounds than its case form.

Second, the word order in Hebrews 1:8 most naturally suggests that ὁ θεός is vocatival. A vocative immediately after 'Your throne' would be perfectly natural. But if ὁ θεός were intended as the subject nominative ('God is your throne'), which Nigel Turner regards as a 'grotesque interpretation',[16] it is more likely that ὁ θεός would have appeared before 'Your throne'. If it were intended as a predicate nominative ('Your throne is God'), which Turner regards as 'only just conceivable',[17] it is more likely that ὁ θεός would have been written anarthrously, appearing either before 'Your throne' or after 'for ever and ever'.

Third, in the Septuagint, in Psalm 45 which Paul is citing here, the king is addressed by the vocative Δύνατε ('O Mighty One') in verses 4 and 6. This double use of the vocative heightens the probability, given the word-order, that in the next verse ὁ θεός should be rendered 'O God'.

Fourth, although 'about' or 'concerning' is probably the more accurate translation of the preposition πρός in Hebrews 1:7 (given the cast of the following quotation), it is more likely that πρός introducing the quotation in verse 8 should be translated 'to' in light of the second-person character of the quotation itself and on the analogy of the formula (a verb of speaking followed by πρός) in Hebrews 1:13, 5:5, and 7:21. This would suggest that ὁ θεός is vocatival.

Fifth, the following quotation in Hebrews 1:10-12 from Psalm 102:25-27 is connected by the simple καί to the quotation under discussion in verses 8-9, indicating that it too stands under the regimen of the words introducing verses 8-9. In the latter verses the Son is clearly addressed as κύριε ('O Lord').

These five textual and syntactical features clearly indicate that ὁ θεός should be construed vocatively, meaning that Paul intended to

---

16. Nigel Turner, *Grammatical Insights into the New Testament*, 461.
17. Nigel Turner, *A Grammar of New Testament Greek* (Edinburgh: T. & T. Clark, 1965), 3.34.

represent God (the Father) as addressing the Son as 'God'. But what did Paul intend by this ascription? Opinions run the gamut from Vincent Taylor's question-begging comment that 'nothing can be built upon this reference, for the author shares the same reluctance of the New Testament writers to speak explicitly of Christ as "God",'[18] to Oscar Cullmann's comment that 'the psalm is quoted here precisely for the sake of this address',[19] the chapter in which it occurs leading him to declare that 'Jesus' deity is more powerfully asserted in Hebrews than in any other New Testament writing, with the exception of the Gospel of John'.[20] What should we conclude?

I would urge from the context of Hebrews 1 itself that the Son is addressed as God in the ontological sense. This may be seen from the fact that, as a 'Son-revelation' and the final and supreme Word of God to man (1:2), he is the heir of all things and the Father's agent in creating the universe. He *abides* as (see the ὤν in 1:3) the 'perfect Radiance of God's glory' and the 'very Image of his nature' (1:3). As God's Son, he is superior to the angels, such that it is appropriate that they be commanded to worship him (1:6). He is the Yahweh and the Elohim of Psalm 102, who eternally existed before he created the heavens and earth (1:10), and who remains eternally the same though the creation itself should perish (1:11-12; see Heb 13:8). Because he is all these things, it is really adding nothing to what Paul has said to understand him in Hebrews 1:8 as describing the Son as God in the ontological sense.

---

18. Vincent Taylor, *The Person of Christ in New Testament Teaching* (London: Macmillan, 1958), 96. Raymond E. Brown's comment is quite to the point: 'We cannot suppose that the author did not notice that his citation had this effect' of addressing the Son of God ('Does the New Testament Call Jesus God?' in *Theological Studies* 26/4 [1965], 563).

19. Oscar Cullman, *The Christology of the New Testament* (London, SCM, 1980), 310.

20. Cullman, Christology, 305. I must register one caveat here. Cullmann, of course, must say these things as an honest exegete. But one must not forget that Cullmann is a 'functional christologist'. He writes: 'We must agree with Melanchthon when he insists that the knowledge of Christ is understood only as a knowledge of his work in redemptive history.... All speculation concerning his natures is...unBiblical as soon as it ceases to take place in the light of the great historical deeds of redemption' (*Christ and Time*, translated by Floyd V. Filson [Philadelphia: Westminster, 1950], 128). He says again: 'We come to the conclusion that in the few New Testament passages in which Jesus receives the title "God", this occurs on the one hand in connection with his exaltation to lordship...and on the other hand in connection with the idea that he is himself the divine revelation' (*Christology*, 325). In other words, after all is said and done, in spite of his splendid exegetical work in Chapter 11 on 'the designation of Jesus as "God",' for Cullman Jesus is not God in himself but only God in *Heilsgeschichte* ('holy-' or 'salvation-history').

Colossians 2:9

In Colossians 1:19, Paul had written: 'In [Christ] [God] willed all the fullness to dwell.' In Colossians 2:9 Paul says virtually the same thing, only here he gives specificity to the nature of the 'fullness' and the manner in which the 'fullness' dwells in Jesus. I propose that we follow his thought. In Colossians 2:2 Paul declares that God's 'mystery' is Christ 'in whom all the treasures of wisdom and knowledge are deposited' (2:3). This is striking enough in that it highlights the uniqueness of Christ as the sole true repository and integrating point of all knowledge. But in 2:9 Paul excels even himself in his exaltation of Christ. For while he does not in so many words, as in Romans 9:5, Titus 2:13 and Hebrews 1:8, describe Christ directly as 'God' (θεός), his statement comes as close to it without doing so as is humanly imaginable and gives the reason why his readers are to 'walk' in Christ and to 'be on guard' that no one should take them captive through the pursuit of knowledge which springs from human philosophy and tradition. Translated literally, Colossians 2:9 reads as follows: 'because in [Christ] dwells all the fullness of deity bodily.'

To assess Paul's intention here, it will be necessary to give some attention to three of his words. By 'the fullness' (τὸ πλήρωμα), which is perhaps his employment of his opponents' terminology, Paul means plainly and simply 'the completeness', 'the totality', or 'the sum-total'. To insure that no one would miss his intention, Paul qualifies this noun with 'all' (πᾶν), that is, '*all* [not just some of] the fullness.'

If it is an allusion to his opponents' language, this phrase already carries overtones of 'fullness of deity', but Paul clarifies his intention by the following defining genitive 'of deity' (τῆς θεότητος). The word for 'deity' here is θεότης, the abstract noun from θεός, meaning 'the being as God', or 'the being of the very essence of deity'. Putting these two words together, Paul is speaking of the 'totality of all that is essential to the divine nature'. Concerning this 'totality of divine essence' Paul affirms that it 'dwells [permanently]' – for this is the force of the preposition κατά prefixed to the verb and the present tense of the verb κατοικέω – in Jesus.

Precisely how it is that this 'totality of the very essence of deity' permanently 'dwells' in him, Paul specifies by the Greek adverb σωματικῶς. Some scholars suggest that the word means 'essentially' or 'really' (as over against 'symbolically'; see the contrast in 2:17 between 'shadow' [σκιά] and 'reality' [σῶμα]). Much more likely the adverb means 'bodily', that is, 'in bodily form', indicating that the mode or manner in which the permanent abode of the full plenitude of deity in Jesus is to be understood is in incarnational terms. In short, Paul intends to say that in Jesus we have to do with the very 'embodiment' or incarnation of deity. Christ is God 'manifest in the flesh' (1 Tim 3:16). Here we have the Pauline equivalent to the Johannine ὁ λόγος σάρξ ἐγένετο ('the Word became flesh').

Finally, to underscore Jesus' uniqueness as such, Paul throws the 'in him' forward in the sentence to the position of emphasis, implying by this, against his opponents' claim that 'fullness' could be found elsewhere, that 'in him [and nowhere else]' permanently resides in bodily form the very essence of deity!

To interpret Paul so is clearly in keeping with his earlier 'hymn' to Christ in Colossians 1:15-20, as virtually every commentator acknowledges. This view alone coincides with the rich language of the hymn where Christ is described as the 'image of the invisible God', who was 'before all things' and 'by, through, and for whom God created all things', and in whom all things 'hold together'.

A fair reading of these four texts will conclude that Paul's was a Christology of the highest kind. The one who had identified himself on the Damascus Road as 'Jesus of Nazareth' (Acts 22:8), who as Paul's Lord had called him to himself and whom Paul now served as Lord, was 'over all things, the ever-blessed God' (Rom 9:5), God the Son (Heb 1:8), his 'great God and Savior' (Tit 2:13), and the one in whom permanently resided in bodily form the plenitude of Godness (Col 2:9). And if this was Paul's Christological vision, considering the extensiveness of his missionary travels and the significance of the churches (Rome, Jerusalem, and Colossae) and the man (Titus) to whom he wrote these letters, we may assume that this same high Christology would have become widely revered and regarded as precious by those for whom Paul's apostolic authority was not a matter of debate. In sum, for Paul and his churches, theirs would have been a high, ontological, incarnational Christology.

What we find in Paul, then, is essentially what we find everywhere else in the New Testament: Jesus is preexistent God incarnate, Christ, Lord, and Savior. There can be no legitimate questioning of the fact that for Paul Christ was the divine Messiah promised by the Old Testament. Nor will it satisfy all of the data which we have considered to acknowledge on the one hand that Jesus was for Paul both *vere deus* and *vere homo*, but to assert on the other that his Christology was an anomaly in the thinking of the first-century church. What Warfield wrote over three quarters of a century ago is still true today:

> Paul is not writing a generation or two [after the generation of those who had companied with Jesus in His life], when the faith of the first disciples was a matter only of memory, perhaps of fading memory; and when it was possible for him to represent it as other than it was. He is writing out of the very bosom of this primitive community and under its very eye. His witness to the kind of Jesus this community believed in is just as valid and just as compelling, therefore, as his testimony that it believed in Jesus at all. In and through him the voice of the primitive community itself speaks, proclaiming its assured faith in its divine Lord.[21]

If anything has changed since Warfield wrote these words, it is that there seems to be even more evidence today than there was in his time that his insight accords with the actual situation then existing. For there is a general consensus today among both critical and evangelical scholars that in Colossians 1:15-20, Philippians 2:6-11, and 1 Timothy 3:16 we have, in *non-Pauline* hymnic form, reflections of the primitive Christology of the early church that may very well antedate the letters of Paul in which they appear respectively. Then in 1 Corinthians 15:3-5 and Romans 1:3-4 we have what may well be reflections of *non-Pauline* primitive church confessions, while in 1 Timothy 1:15 we have, beyond doubt, an early church confession in the form of a *non-Pauline* 'faithful saying' which Paul endorsed when he declared it to be 'worthy of acceptance'. When taken at face value – and there is no compelling reason why they should not be – all of these pericopes reflect the highest kind of Christology in which Jesus is regarded as the divine, pre-existent Son of God who through 'descent' (κατάβασις) became 'flesh' for us men and for our salvation and who through 'ascent' (ἀνάβασις) assumed mediatorial headship over the universe and the church. And in the case of 1 Timothy 1:15 it is significant that here we have the spokesman of the so-called 'Pauline community' commending what is now commonly recognized as a piece of teaching framed in the wording of the 'Johannine community'. So instead of there being *competing* communities in the early church, each headed up by one of the original

---

21. Warfield, *The Lord of Glory*, 257.

The Person of Christ

apostles and each vying with one another for the minds of the masses, here is indication that the primitive church—at least that majority portion of it which followed the lead of the apostles and for whom the apostles were authoritative teachers of doctrine in the church—was united in its essential understanding of Christ. When one also takes into account that the Jerusalem apostles approved Paul's gospel (which surely would have included an account of who Jesus was for Paul) when he informed them of it on his second visit to Jerusalem (Gal 2:2, 6-9), plus the fact that for both the Palestinian Aramaic-speaking and Hellenistic Greek-speaking Christians in the primitive church Jesus was 'Lord' (see the occurrence of both κύριος, 'Lord', and Μαράνα θά [Greek transliteration of the Aramaic, מָרַנָא תָא], meaning 'Our Lord, come!' in 1 Cor 16:22), we must conclude that such strict distinctions as have been drawn by some modern scholars between an early Christology of the Jewish Palestinian church, a later Christology of the Jewish Hellenistic church (or mission), and a still later Christology of the Hellenistic Gentile church (or mission) (all stages of development before Paul) exist more in the minds of those who espouse the view than in the actual first-century church itself. Paul's testimony, reflected throughout his letters, gives evidence of the fact that for Christians generally who lived at that time, Jesus was, as Warfield writes:

> a man indeed and the chosen Messiah who had come to redeem God's people, but in His essential Being just the great God Himself. In the light of [Paul's] testimony it is impossible to believe there ever was a different conception of Jesus prevalent in the Church: the mark of Christians from the beginning was obviously that they looked to Jesus as their 'Lord' and 'called upon His name' in their worship.[22]

But because of the fuller scope of Paul's letters and their highly theological character, the perspective on Jesus in Paul's thought is deepened and extended but not altered from that of the uniform testimony of the New Testament. Jesus' self-testimony is carried on faithfully by Paul, but his significance as the second Adam, the Wisdom of God, and as Lord (in the twofold sense of his exaltation as the second person of the Godhead and as the incarnate Messiah) becomes quite pronounced.

---

22. Warfield, *The Lord of Glory*, 255-256.

CHAPTER SEVENTEEN

THE OLD TESTAMENT ROOTS OF THE PAULINE GOSPEL

> In the cross of Christ I glory,
> Towering o'er the wrecks of time;
> All the light of sacred story
> Gathers round its head sublime.
> — John Bowring

A discerning reader will have already observed that Paul derives his doctrines of sin, divine election, and adoption primarily from the Old Testament. Before we consider Paul's depiction of God the Son's salvific work, it is important now that we consider the ground of his 'gospel concerning [God's] Son' in the covenantal theology of the Old Testament.

It is quite apparent from his writings that Paul clearly felt the urgent need to root his gospel proclamation about Christ to the nations solidly in the soil of the Old Testament. Apart from such rootage not only would his gospel have 'hung in mid-air' as a novel invention but also his Gentile churches would have felt no kinship with, nor be sensitive to the scruples of, nor respond to his own appeal to come to the aid of the Jerusalem church with its financial needs. Conversely, apart from such an Old Testament base the more original Jerusalem church would never have viewed the law-free Gentiles churches he was founding as one with it. The risk would have been great that two churches over time would have resulted—a Jewish church and a Gentile church—each maintaining its authenticity over against the other and each charging the other with serious theological error. Indeed, two churches would have inevitably emerged unless the case could be made that the Old Testament had envisaged the gospel spreading to the Gentiles *as Gentiles* in precisely the way the apostle was carrying out his mission. Accordingly, in his writings, clearly perceiving that the task naturally and uniquely fell to him as the apostle to the Gentiles to make such a case, Paul in several striking ways rooted his Gentile churches in the Old Testament as the age of covenant promise. And in providing Old Testament legitimacy to his Gentile churches, he addressed at the same time the criticisms that the Judaizers habitually leveled against him. We shall consider here four such ways in which he related his churches to the theology of the Old Testament scriptures.[1]

The Significance of the Abrahamic Covenant for the Nations

With God's call of Abraham in Genesis 12:1-3, redemptive history underwent a remarkable advance, definitive for all time to come. The instrument of that advance is the covenant which God made with Abraham which guaranteed and secured soteric blessing for 'all the families of the earth'. So significant are the promises of grace in the Abrahamic covenant, found in Genesis 12:1-3; 13:14-16; 15:18-21; 17:1-16; 22:16-18, that it is not an overstatement to declare these verses, from the covenantal perspective, as the most important verses in the Bible. The fact that the Bible sweeps across the thousands of years between the creation of man and Abraham's time in only eleven chapters, with the call of Abraham coming as early in Scripture as Genesis 12, suggests that the information given in the first eleven chapters of the Bible was intended as preparatory 'background' to the revelation of the Abrahamic covenant. And revelation subsequent to it discloses that all that God has done savingly in grace since the revelation of the Abrahamic covenant is the result and product of it. In other words, once redemptive history had come to covenantal expression in terms of the salvific promises of the Abrahamic covenant – that God would be the God of Abraham and his descendants (17:7) and that in Abraham all the nations of the earth would be blessed (12:3; see Rom 4:13) – everything that God has done since then to the present moment he has done in order to fulfill his covenant with Abraham (and thus his eternal plan of redemption). This is just to suggest that God's execution of his soteric program from Genesis 12 onward, should be viewed in terms of the salvific promises contained in the Abrahamic covenant. This line of evidence demonstrates the unity of biblical covenantalism from Genesis 3 to the farthest reaches of the future.

From his understanding of the salvific significance of the Abrahamic covenant for all ages to come thereafter, Paul developed the followings arguments for his mission to the Gentiles as Gentiles:

---

[1]. For a full treatment of this topic see my *A New Systematic Theology of the Christian Faith* (Nashville, Tenn.: Thomas Nelson, 1998), 503-44.

I. After noting that Abraham 'believed God, and it was credited to him as righteousness' (Gal 3:6)[2] and concluding from this that 'those who believe are children of Abraham' (Gal 3:7), in Galatians 3:8 Paul cites Genesis 12:3: 'The Scripture[3] foresaw that God would justify the Gentiles by faith, and *announced the gospel in advance to* [προευηγγελίσατο; lit. 'preevangelized'] Abraham: "All nations[4] will be blessed through you."' Accordingly, he concludes: 'So those who have faith are blessed along with Abraham' (Gal 3:9).

How should one explain to himself this striking Pauline insight that, when God promised Abraham that 'all the nations will be blessed through you', he was (1) announcing the gospel in advance to Abraham and (2) intending by this preannounced gospel proclamation precisely his declarative justification of the Gentiles by faith? In other words, how does one get from the divine statement in Genesis 12:3 to the conclusions that Paul draws in Galatians 3:8?

It would appear, since Abraham could not personally bless all the nations who were not his physical seed and since the nations of the world would not and could not literally be Abraham's physical seed

---

2. Paul will note later in Romans 4:10-11 that Abraham, *after* being justified—indeed, some *fourteen years* after—'received the sign of circumcision, a seal of the righteousness that he had by faith while he was still uncircumcised.' Obviously, Paul was able to reason, circumcision is not indispensable to one's right standing before God (see also here Rom 2:25-29).

3. In his analysis of this statement in his article, '"It Says," "Scripture Says," "God Says,"' in *The Inspiration and Authority of the Bible* (Philadelphia: Presbyterian and Reformed, 1948), Benjamin B. Warfield notes that Paul's unusual personification of the text in Genesis 12:3 ('The Scripture foresaw') shows the absolute identification that he drew in his mind of the Scriptures in his hands with the living voice of God, for he speaks here as if the Scriptures are God himself. The reader should reflect carefully and thoughtfully on Warfield's exposition (299-300):

'The Scripture, foreseeing that God would justify the heathen through faith, preached before the gospel unto Abraham, saying, In thee shall all the nations be blessed' (Gen. xii. 1-3) [see also Rom 9:17 for another example of this personification of 'Scripture' as a stand-in for 'God' – RLR]... It was not, however, the Scripture (which did not exist at the time) that, foreseeing God's purposes of grace in the future, spoke these precious words to Abraham, but God Himself in His own person...[This divine speech] could be attributed to 'Scripture' only as the result of such a habitual identification, in the mind of the writer, of the text of Scripture with God as speaking, that it became natural to use the term 'Scripture says', when what was really intended was 'God, as recorded in Scripture, said'.

4. Paul cites here a conflation of Genesis 12:3c and 22:18a in the Septuagint in order to bring into the discussion τὰ ἔθνη ('the nations') instead of 'all the families', because of the current use of τὰ ἔθνη for 'Gentiles'.

and thus be blessed through such a physical connection, that Paul legitimately inferred that the promised blessing of the nations would have to come to them in some other way. Perhaps then, if not immediately and directly by Abraham himself, they could be blessed through his physical seed. In fact, this is precisely what Genesis 22:18 states: 'through your seed [בְזַרְעֲךָ] all nations on earth will be blessed.' But who is this 'seed', his entire natural progeny or some one person in particular from his loins? Because of Abraham's physical seed's own problems with sin, Paul rightly concludes that the nations can be blessed along with Abraham only through faith in Jesus Christ who, in addition to Abraham himself, was *the* (messianic) seed of Abraham (τῷ σπέρματί σου) to whom the promises were spoken (Gal 3:16; see Gen 13:15; 17:8). And only by belonging through faith to Christ, *the* seed of Abraham, can anyone – Jew or Gentile – regard himself as Abraham's seed and an heir according to the promise (Gal 3:29). Hence, Paul concludes that when God promised what he did to Abraham in Genesis 12:3, the source of the blessing God had in mind was his Messiah as the one through whom all the nations would be blessed. And that blessing (right standing before God) must come through faith.

II. Paul also declares that 'Christ became a servant of the circumcision ... *in order that* he might confirm the promises made to the patriarchs [Abraham, Isaac, and Jacob], and *in order that* the Gentiles might glorify God for his mercy' (Rom 15:8-9).

Here Paul states that one purpose behind Christ's mission to the circumcision was to enable the Gentiles to glorify God for his mercy shown to them in Christ. So once again we see Paul making the connection between the Messiah's ministrations in behalf of the Jews and God's mercy to Paul's Gentile churches. Douglas Moo notes here that the passage describes

> the benefit that both Jews and Gentiles derive from Christ's mission – promises made to the Jewish patriarchs are confirmed and Gentiles are enabled to glorify God for his mercy to them...Matching God's purpose in confirming his promises made to the Jews is God's purpose in causing the Gentiles to glorify God 'for the sake of his mercy', that is, because of the mercy that he has shown to them [in the Abrahamic promises].[5]

---

5. Douglas Moo, *The Epistle to the Romans* (The New International Commentary on the New Testament; Grand Rapids: Eerdmans, 1996), 876, 878,

III. Paul further declares in Galatians 3:13-14 that Christ redeemed us by dying on the cross and bearing in himself the law's curse, '*in order that* [ἵνα] the blessing given to Abraham might come to the Gentiles in Christ Jesus' in fulfillment of Genesis 12:3, '*in order that* [ἵνα] we [that is, Jews and Gentiles] might receive the promise of the Spirit through faith.'

The two ἵνα clauses here are coordinate, the latter an explanatory expansion of the former. God, having delivered his covenant people among the Jews from the curse of the law through Christ's cross work, by that same cross work is free to deal likewise in grace with elect Gentiles, with both Jew and Gentile receiving the promised Spirit through faith.

IV. Paul expressly declares also that the Mosaic law, introduced several centuries after God gave his covenant promises to Abraham and to his seed (who is Christ, the only Abrahamic seed who now counts because of who he is, even the sinless Son of God), 'does not set aside the covenant previously established by God [with Abraham] and thus do away with the promise' (Gal 3:16-17).

Clearly then the Abrahamic promise made to Abraham's seed (Christ) is still normative, and those who trust in him, whether they be Jews or Gentiles, become 'Abraham's seed, and heirs according to the promise' (Gal 3:29).

V. Paul also declares that Abraham is the 'father of *all who believe*' among both Jews and Gentiles (Rom 4:11-12), and he interprets the divine promise that in Abraham all the nations of the world would be blessed to mean that Abraham through his seed would be 'the heir of the world' (Rom 4:13). Moo rightly observes that the 'heir of the world' expression

> does not exactly match any promise to Abraham found in the OT but succinctly summarizes the three key provisions of the promise as it unfolds in Genesis: that Abraham would have an immense number of descendants, embracing many nations..., that he would possess the land..., and that he would be medium of blessing to 'all the peoples of the earth'.... Particularly noteworthy is the promise in Gen. 22:17b that Abraham's seed would 'possess [LXX κληρονομήσει] the gate of their enemies.' Later in the OT, there are indications that the promise of the land had come to embrace the entire world (cf. Isa. 55:3-5), and many Jewish texts speak of Israel's inheritance in similar terms.[6]

In sum, according to the general teaching of the Old Testament, the Abrahamic promise encompassed the Gentile world as well, and by highlighting this fact Paul grounded the legitimacy of his law-free Gentile churches in the most significant covenant of the Old Testament in a way that the Judaizer could not legitimately controvert them.

The Old Testament Prophets' References to the Death and Resurrection of Christ

In addition to the many well-known Old Testament citations in his sermons and letters, too numerous to list here, which endorsed his views of Christ and his death and resurrection and his own teaching on justification by faith (see Rom 4:3-8), all of which would have been of vital interest both to his Jewish as well as to his Gentile readers, Paul on his missionary journeys regularly 'reasoned with [the Jews] *from the Scriptures*, explaining and proving that the Messiah had to *suffer* and rise from the dead' (Acts 17:2-3). For example, in the synagogue at Pisidian Antioch he taught that 'the people of Jerusalem and their rulers...*fulfilled the words of the prophets that are read every Sabbath when they condemned him.... When they had carried out all that had been written about him*, they took him down from the tree and laid him in a tomb. But God raised him from the dead' (Acts 13:27-30). Beyond all doubt, Paul argued, the Old Testament prophets wrote about a suffering Messiah whose death is of vital salvific interest to Jews and Gentiles alike.

1. Paul also declared that 'the gospel concerning [God's] Son...Jesus Christ our Lord,' to which he had been set apart, 'God *promised beforehand* [προεπηγγείλατο[7]] *through his prophets in the Holy Scriptures*' (Rom 1:2-3).

Paul expressly declares here that the Old Testament prophets wrote about the gospel 'regarding [God's] Son...Jesus Christ our Lord'. On this clause Moo observes:

> It is doubtful whether Paul has any particular OT passages in mind here; his purpose is general and principial, to allay possible suspicion about 'his' gospel as new and innovative by asserting its organic relationship to the OT.[8]

---

6. Moo, *Romans*, 274.
7. Compare Paul's προεπηγγείλατο here with his προευηγγελίσατο in Galatians 3:8.
8. Moo, *Romans*, 44.

II. Explicating the content of the gospel he had preached to the Corinthians, Paul wrote that 'Christ died for our sins *according to the Scriptures*' and 'was raised the third day *according to the Scriptures*' (1 Cor 15:3-4). From this passage we learn that the Old Testament scriptures spoke about the death and resurrection of the Messiah, a topic which would be of vital interest to both Jews and Gentiles, and once again Paul grounds his gospel to the Gentile churches in the Old Testament.

III. On the solemn occasion of his defense before Herod Agrippa II Paul testified that he was standing trial only because of his teaching concerning 'the hope of the promise made by God to our fathers, to which our twelve tribes [themselves] hope to attain as they earnestly serve God day and night, concerning which hope I am being accused by the Jews' (26:6-7). In his defense which immediately followed he explicated what he meant by Israel's hope by declaring that throughout his long missionary ministry of some thirty years he had never said anything 'beyond what *the prophets and Moses said would happen – that the Messiah would suffer and, as the first to rise from the dead, would proclaim light to his own people and to the Gentiles*' (Acts 26:22-23).

From these verses it is clear beyond all legitimate doubt that Paul believed that the Old Testament hope to which Moses and the prophets witnessed was the Messiah's death, resurrection, and saving ministrations, which 'light' the Messiah himself would proclaim both directly and through his apostles both to the Jewish people and to the Gentiles (see Eph 2:17; 4:21).

IV. Under house arrest, Paul told the Jewish leaders at Rome: 'I am wearing this chain *because of the hope of Israel* [ἕνεκεν...τῆς ἐλπίδος τοῦ 'Ισραὴλ]' (Acts 28:20), which hope was fulfilled in the death, resurrection, and ministry of Messiah. Then Luke tells us that Paul from morning to evening 'explained and declared to them the Kingdom of God and tried to convince them about Jesus *from the Law of Moses and from the Prophets*' (28:23).

Can anyone really believe that this seasoned missionary of the cross – the author of Galatians, 1 and 2 Corinthians, and Romans – would have talked about Jesus from morning to evening with these Jewish leaders from the Old Testament scriptures and said nothing about Christ's sufferings and the glory that would follow (see Acts 13:27-30; 17:2-3; 26:22-23)? Once again, it is plain from this passage that Paul was concerned always to ground his gospel in the covenantal theology of the Old Testament.

The Church as the Present-Day Expression of the People of God Whose Roots Go Back to Abraham

Paul makes it clear, in precise conformity to the details of the 'new covenant' prophecy in Jeremiah 31:31-34, that, when he missionarized Gentiles and they became Christians in ever-increasing numbers, they were being brought into the fellowship of that covenant community designated by the 'new covenant' prophecy in Jeremiah 31:31 as 'the house of Israel and the house of Judah' (see Heb 8:8-13; 9:15).

Because of the great number of Gentiles in the church today, it is very difficult for Gentile Christians to think of the church of Jesus Christ of which they are privileged members (by 'church' here I refer to the *true* church, that is, the body of truly regenerate saints) as being God's chosen people, the true (*not* a new) spiritual 'Israel'. But Paul would clearly endorse this identification. And from the following passages it is also clear that he wanted his Gentile converts to understand that, when they believed in Christ, they entered into a relationship with the 'Israel of God' and became spiritual 'Israelites'.

I. To the Ephesian church, clearly a 'Gentile' Christian church, Paul wrote:

> ...remember that formerly you who are Gentiles by birth and called 'uncircumcised' by those who call themselves 'the circumcision' (that done in the body by the hands of men) – remember that at that time you were separate from Christ, excluded from citizenship in Israel [πολιτείας τοῦ 'Ισραὴλ] and foreigners [ξένοι] to the covenants of the promise, without hope and without God in the world. But now in Christ Jesus you who once were far away have been brought near through the blood of Christ (Eph 2:11-13).

Paul teaches here that the blessed state to which the Ephesian Gentiles (who formerly were 'far away') had now been 'brought near' includes *Christ*, from whom they had been separated, and *hope* and *God* which

The Old Testament Roots of the Pauline Gospel 381

had not been their possessions before (the first, fourth, and fifth items in Paul's list). Surely every Christian will happily acknowledge this. But between his first and fourth items Paul also says that they had been excluded from citizenship in Israel and that they had been foreigners to the covenants of the promise (the second and the third). I would submit, since Paul clearly suggests that the first, fourth, and fifth of their previous conditions have been reversed, that he also intends to teach that the second and third conditions have been reversed as well. On what authority may one eliminate these two from Paul's list of five conditions which he says God addressed in Christ in behalf of Gentiles? Accordingly, I would urge that Paul is teaching here that Gentile Christians are now citizens of the true Israel and beneficiaries of the covenants of the promise. And he seems to say this very thing in Ephesians 2:19 when, summing up, he writes: 'Therefore you are no longer *foreigners* [ξένοι] and *aliens* [πάροικοι] but *fellow citizens* [συμπολῖται] of the saints and *members of God's household* [οἰκεῖοι τοῦ θεοῦ].'

II. To the Gentile churches in Galatia, Paul describes those who repudiate Judaistic legalism and who 'never boast except in the cross of our Lord Jesus Christ' as 'the Israel of God' (6:12-16).

It is possible that Paul intended to refer exclusively to *Jewish* Christians by this expression, but it is more likely that he intended to refer to the church of Jesus Christ *per se*, made up of Jews *and* Gentiles. Ronald Fung helpfully comments on Paul's expression here:

> The specifying phrase 'of God' makes it unlikely that the reference is to Israel as such..., and Paul 'can hardly have meant to bless the whole of Israel..., irrespective of whether of not they held to the canon [6:16: τῷ κανόνι] of the cross of Christ'. The view that v. 16 refers to, respectively, 'the Gentiles who believe the gospel and the Jewish Christians who recognize the unimportance of circumcision' faces the objection that 'whoever'...would naturally include Jewish as well as Gentile Christians; moreover, particularly in the light of v. 15, it is improbable that Paul, with his concern for the unity of the church..., would here single out Jewish Christians as a separate group within his churches. Perhaps the least unsatisfactory view is to suppose that in the two parts of his benediction Paul is thinking first of those of his readers who qualify under the *hosoi* ['as many as'] and passes from there on to the new Israel, the new people of God – both Jews and Gentiles being included in each instance.[9]

III. To the Gentile church at Philippi, Paul describes those 'who worship by the Spirit of God, who glory in Christ Jesus, and who put no confidence in the flesh' as *'the [true] circumcision'* (3:3), an Old Testament term, as he notes in Ephesians 2:11, which the nation of Israel had come to use as a designation of itself.

IV. Paul's metaphor of the two olive trees (Rom 11:16-24) also reflects this same perception. Olive shoots from a *wild* olive tree, that is, the Gentiles, are by faith being grafted into the *cultivated* olive tree, that is, Israel. From the latter tree many natural branches (not all, for there was always a true 'remnant according to election', even the 'Israel' within Israel of 9:6), that is, many faithless Jews, had been broken off. This tree, Paul says, has a 'holy root' (the patriarchs, 11:28). Clearly, Paul envisions saved Gentile Christians as 'grafted shoots' in the cultivated olive tree of the true 'Israel of faith', and he wanted Gentiles Christians to know this and not to boast over the rejected branches: 'If you do, consider this: You do not support the root [the patriarchs], but the root supports you' (11:18). And just as clearly, it is into this same cultivated olive tree (which now includes multitudes of 'wild shoots') that the elect 'natural branches' of ethnic Israel (the 'all Israel' of 11:26) are being grafted in again through their coming to faith in Jesus Christ throughout this age.[10]

V. In the course of his description of the Christian life and the life of the church itself Paul draws heavily upon Old Testament citations, terminology, and concepts. For example, prior to their salvation, Paul writes, Christians had been 'slaves to sin', the very idea of slavery having its roots in the soil of Israel's slavery in Egypt (Rom 6:17-22). Again, Christ is the Christian's 'high priest' (Heb 9:11-14) and his 'Passover lamb' (1 Cor 5:7), Christian baptism is 'Christian circumcision' (Col 2:11-12), Christians offer up 'sacrifices' of praise and good works to God (Heb 13:15-16), and Christians live under the ancient rule of 'elders' (1 Tim 3:1-7; Tit 1:5-9; Heb 13:17). By such Old Testament allusions Paul clearly teaches that he saw no discontinuity between the true Israel of the Old Testament and the

---

9. Ronald Y. K. Fung, *The Epistle to the Galatians* (The New International Commentary on the New Testament; Grand Rapids: Eerdmans, 1988), 310-11.

10. For a fuller discussion of the 'all Israel' of Romans 11:26 see my *A New Systematic Theology of the Christian Faith*, 1024-30.

The Old Testament Roots of the Pauline Gospel

Gentile churches he was founding throughout the Roman world.

To sum up, for Paul there was clearly salvific continuity between the people of God in the Old Testament age of promise and the people of God in the New Testament age of fulfillment; he appears self-consciously to teach the unity of the covenant of grace and the oneness of the people of God in all ages.

The Identical Requisites for Salvation in Both Testaments

Some dispensational scholars maintain that *no* Old Testament saint could have been saved through faith in the Messiah's death work simply because knowledge of this event was 'as yet locked up in the secret counsels of God',[11] while the *Westminster Confession of Faith*, to the contrary, affirms that the Holy Spirit employed 'promises, prophecies, sacrifices, circumcision, the paschal lamb, and other types and ordinances..., *all* foresignifying Christ to come', in his Old Testament saving operations 'to instruct and build up the elect in *faith in the promised Messiah*, by whom they had full remission of sins, and eternal salvation' (VII/v, emphasis supplied). Both positions cannot be true; one has to be in error. The Scriptures alone should decide the issue. What is Paul's perception of the nature of salvation in both Testaments?

I. Paul wrote to Timothy that 'from infancy you have known the holy Scriptures [the Old Testament], which are able to make you wise for *salvation through faith in Christ Jesus*' (2 Tim 3:15).

Evidently, Paul believed that the Old Testament contained revelational information about 'salvation through faith in the Messiah'.

II. Paul argued his doctrine of justification by faith alone, apart from all human works, by citing in support of it David's words in Psalm 32:1-2 (Rom 4:6-7) and before him the example of Abraham who 'believed God, and it was credited to him for righteousness' (Gen 15:6; Rom 4:1-3). The last thing that Paul would have wanted anyone to believe is that his was a 'new doctrine'. In light of these Old Testament examples it would have never dawned on Paul to say: 'We know how the New Testament saint is saved – he is saved by

---

11. *Scofield Reference Bible* (Revised edition; Oxford: University Press, 1917), 996.

grace through faith in Christ, but how was the Old Testament saint saved?' To the contrary, were he to say anything of this kind, he would have reversed the order of the sentence: 'We know how the Old Testament saint was saved – he was saved by grace through faith in the suffering of the coming Messiah; we had better make sure that we are saved the same way that he was saved, for there is no other way to be saved.'

* * * * *

We have reviewed enough material from Paul's writings to say without fear of being controverted that Paul was solicitous to ground his law-free gospel to the Gentiles in the Scriptures of the Old Testament and to relate that gospel to Jew and Gentile alike. Unlike 'that strange second-century Christian Marcion,[12] whose devotion to Paul's teaching was not matched by his understanding of it' and hence who 'cut the gospel off from its past..., denying the Christian relevance of the Old Testament', Paul, for his part, writes F. F. Bruce,

> did not jettison the Old Testament (as we call it): for him its writings constituted the holy scriptures (Romans 1:2), the only holy scriptures he knew. He called them 'the law and the prophets' (Romans 3:21) and described them as 'the oracles of God' (Romans 3:2). They found their fulfilment and had their meaning made plain in Christ; when people read them without using this key to unlock their significance, 'a veil lies over their minds' (2 Corinthians 3:15). Paul attached the greater value to them because they bore witness to the message of justification by faith in Christ: the gospel which in them was 'preached beforehand to Abraham' (Galatians 3:8) was the gospel which Paul was commissioned to proclaim; it was no recent invention.[13]

---

12. Marcion, a second-century gnostic heretic, repudiated the entire Old Testament and accepted only a mutilated version of Luke and ten 'edited' epistles of Paul, altogether excluding Hebrews, 1 and 2 Timothy and Titus (which 'rewrite' of Paul he called the *Apostolicon*), as his canon.

13. F. F. Bruce, *Paul: Apostle of the Heart Set Free* (Reprint; Grand Rapids: Eerdmans, 1996), 19-20.

CHAPTER EIGHTEEN

GOD THE SON'S SALVIFIC WORK

> Not all the blood of beasts
> On Jewish altars slain,
> Could give the guilty conscience peace,
> Or wash away the stain.
>
> But Christ, the heav'nly Lamb,
> Takes all our sins away,
> A sacrifice of nobler name
> And richer blood than they.
> —Isaac Watts, 1709

For Paul Christ was the crucified and risen Savior. For him it was a given that the same person who was crucified for his sins (1 Cor 15:3) also rose bodily from the dead the third day after death for his justification (Rom 4:25; 6:4; Gal 1:1; 1 Cor 6:14; 15:4, 20; Eph 1:20; Col 2:12) and is alive forevermore (Heb 7:24-25). Without Christ's resurrection to vouchsafe God's approbation of Christ's cross-work, according to Paul, no warrant exists to believe that Christ's death availed before God in behalf of those for whom he died.

It is important to note here that Paul does not argue that if Christ did not rise from the dead, then there is no God or no such things as human sin or mankind's lost estate. To the contrary, he argues, if Christ did not rise from the dead, that God is still there and men are still sinners and are still under divine wrath. That is to say, if Christ did not rise from the dead, the net result is that men simply have no Savior. Without Christ's resurrection the following facts inevitably ensue that seal the fate of all mankind in eternal woe: (1) the apostles' preaching is useless (κενὸν), (2) the faith response of Christians to that preaching is useless (κενὴ) and futile (ματαία), (3) the apostles become false witnesses; (4) Christians are still in their sins, (5) Christians who have already died have perished [ἀπώλοντο], and (6) more than all men Christians are to be pitied for their vain and futile hope in Christ (1 Cor 15:14-19). In sum, these facts underscore the truth that the efficacy of Christ's cross-work can never be separated from his resurrection.

As we approach now the issue of Paul's understanding of what Christ did at the cross, I want to begin by considering a key passage in which he articulates the meaning and significance of Christ's work and especially his death. In 1 Corinthians 15:3 Paul writes: 'For I delivered to you as of first importance what I also received, that Christ died for our sins according to the Scriptures.' At least two things stand out in this statement. The first is that Christ's death had reference to our sins. His death in some way addresses the exigency created by our sins and makes provision for them. The second thing is that his death, the death of the one, has significance for the sins of the many (see Rom 5:12,18-19). These two aspects of his death are of course intertwined, but let us say something about each of them, addressing the second issue first.

Paul assumes in making this statement the propriety of the one, the Christ, acting for and on behalf of the many. He does so because this is a principle recognized in the Old Testament (see 'according to the Scriptures') and acknowledged by his audience as an assumed truth. So Paul does not often raise or discuss this question. But when he does, as he does later in 1 Corinthians 15:22, he states that Christ was acting as a representative and that he was doing so as Adam had done before him. So he may be regarded as the last Adam. He argues that since death came by a man, even so must resurrection and life also come through a man (15:21). This truism is related to the representative character of both Adam and Christ (15:22; see 15:44-49).

Paul develops this truth of the representative character of Christ in comparison with Adam in Romans 5:14ff. The precise point of comparison is that of their *representative* similarity. Comparison beyond this is that Christ's representation does much more than Adam's did (5:15). Romans 5:14ff. insists that Christ's action for those he represented brings both deliverance from sin and righteousness and life. But the question, how does it accomplish this result for sinners, is still before us. So we turn now to the first point of 1 Corinthians 15:3 and ask how does Christ's death affect forgiveness. What does his death have to do with our sins? This is stated in Romans 5:14ff., but Paul does not develop the idea there.

Paul speaks eloquently about our sin problem and Christ's

God the Son's Salvific Work

representative action as our substitute in our stead and for our sins in 2 Corinthians 5:21 and Galatians 3:13. In the former, we are told: '[God] made him who knew no sin to be sin on our behalf, that we might become the righteousness of God in him.' That sin which he was made was ours, not his. He representatively was made what we are on our behalf (ὑπὲρ ἡμῶν) to act in such a way with reference to that which we are that we might become the righteousness of God in him. Here is a representative transaction, he receiving our sins, we receiving his righteousness. And he does so by his death for the 'all' (5:15). Similarly Paul speaks in Galatians 3:13: 'Christ redeemed us from the curse of the law, having become a curse for us.' The curse is God's cursing judgment and punishment on disobedience to his law and its demands (3:10). In sum, Christ paid a debt he did not owe because we owed a debt we could not pay.

But again, we must ask the question, What does his representation or substitution accomplish, so that it delivers us from God's curse because of our sin? Paul speaks to this question in Romans 3:24ff. (especially 3:25-26). There we see that Paul affirms that the just God who justifies the sinner shows his justice by demonstrating it in Christ's death justly bearing God's just wrath on sinners and their sin (see Rom 5:8). Because Christ in his death was a representative of others, his death satisfies the just demands of God's justice and thus removes the curse of sin justly due the sinner. By such a removal of their sin and the wrath and punishment which it justly deserves, Christ provides the basis upon which God can forgive and, with Christ's righteousness representatively imputed to us, justify us. There can now be a reconciliation between God and those who were sinners (Rom 5:10; 2 Cor 5:5:18ff).

From this brief survey of Paul's teaching, we have come to realize that the ultimate answers to our earlier questions are indeed to be found in such technical language as substitution, propitiation, and reconciliation. Thus a closer examination of these Pauline terms will prove to be very helpful in understanding Christ's work. When we have done this, we shall see why, for Paul, the cross of Christ was 'the *power* of God and the *wisdom* of God' (θεοῦ δύναμιν καὶ θεοῦ σοφίαν) (1 Cor 1:24). We shall see that by it, Christ, the Lord of glory (1 Cor 2:8), atoned for the sins of the elect, satisfied divine justice, reconciled the world to God, redeemed his own, and destroyed the kingdom of evil.

Christ's Obedience

Paul teaches that Christ's entire work of salvation is grounded in and flows out of his obedience. The three times where the New Testament speaks explicitly of the obedience of Christ occur in the Pauline corpus: (1) 'Through the *obedience* of the one man the many will be made righteous' (Rom 5:19); (2) 'He humbled himself and became *obedient* to death' (Phil 2:8); and (3) 'Although he was a son, he learned obedience from what he suffered' (Heb 5:8). Paul alludes to Christ's obedience in other ways as well. For example, he refers to Christ as God's 'servant' (Phil 2:7) and to his sinless life (2 Cor 5:21).

Christ's Expiatory Sacrifice

There can be no doubt that for Paul Christ expiated our sins through the sacrifice of himself:

1 Corinthians 5:7: 'Our Passover lamb [τὸ πάσχα] has been sacrificed [ἐτύθη] even Christ.'

Ephesians 5:2: 'Christ loved us and gave himself up for us as a fragrant *offering* [προσφορὰν] and *sacrifice* [θυσίαν] to God.'

Because the evangelical ear is accustomed to such language, the assertion that Christ offered himself up to God on the cross as a sacrifice may not seem significant. But the assertion is replete with implications. Since the Old Testament sacrificial system is the obvious background to Paul's thought here, he was certainly presupposing

(1) the sinless *perfection* of Christ since the acceptable sacrifice had to be 'without blemish',

(2) the *imputation* or transfer of the sinner's sin to Christ on the analogy of the Levitical legislation (Lev 1:4; 3:2, 8, 13; 4:4, 15, 24, 29, 33; 16:21-22; Num 8:12; see Isa 53:4, 5, 6, 7, 8, 10, 11, 12),

(3) the resultant *substitution* of Christ *because of* (διά—1 Cor 8:11; 2 Cor 8:9), *for* (περί – Rom 8:3), and *in behalf of* (ὑπέρ— Rom 5:6, 8; 8:32; 14:15; 1 Cor 11:24; 15:3; 2 Cor 5:15, 21; Gal 1:4; 2:20; 3:13; Eph 5:2, 25; 1 Thess 5:10; 1 Tim 2:6; Tit 2:14) those sinners whose sins had been imputed to him, and

(4) the necessary *expiation* or cancellation of *their* sins. Geerhardus Vos notes: 'Wherever there is slaying and manipulation of blood there is expiation.'[1]

---

1. Geerhardus Vos, *Biblical Theology* (Grand Rapids: Eerdmans, 1948), 135. E. P.

Christ's Propitiatory Sacrifice

Paul declares that God 'publicly displayed [Christ Jesus] as a *sacrifice which would turn aside his wrath, taking away sin* [ἰλαστήριον]' (Rom 3:25) and that Jesus became 'a merciful and faithful high priest...*in order to turn aside God's wrath, taking away the sins* [ἰλάσκεσθαι τὰς ἁμαρτίας] of the people' (Heb 2:17). This basic understanding of the word—'a sacrifice which turns aside God's wrath, taking away sin'—has not gone unchallenged. It was primarily the Cambridge scholar, C. H. Dodd, who led this challenge.[2] Dodd argues that the meaning conveyed by the word group is that of *expiation* (the cancellation of sin), not that of *propitiation* (the turning away of the wrath of God). While he acknowledged that the word-group had the meaning of 'placating an angry person' in both classical and popular pagan Greek literature, he insisted that this meaning was absent in Hellenistic Judaism as represented by the Septuagint. He concluded that the four New Testament occurrences should be rendered in accordance with the understanding that prevailed within Hellenistic Judaism.

Several rigorous critiques of Dodd's argument have been registered. Both Leon Morris[3] and Roger R. Nicole[4] have insisted that Dodd

---

Sanders, *Paul* (Oxford: University Press, 1991), contends that while Paul accepted the prevalent Christian interpretation of that time that Christ's death was an atoning act, still

> the sacrificial interpretation of Jesus' death does not lie at the heart of Paul's thought. W. D. Davies put it this way: 'Although in labouring to do justice to the significance of the Death of Jesus he uses sacrificial terms, Paul does not develop these but leaves them inchoate.' This view is common to numerous scholars of diverse schools of interpretation, and here the scholarly consensus is correct. (78-79)

Nothing could be further from the truth. From the numerous references to the substitutionary character of Christ's death just cited in the paragraph, it should be evident that the sacrificial character of the cross-work of Christ lies at the very heart of Paul's understanding of his soteriology.

2. C. H. Dodd, "Ἱλάσκεσθαι, Its Cognates, Derivatives and Synonyms, in the Septuagint' in *Journal of Theological Studies* 32 (1931), 352-360, which was republished in his *The Bible and the Greeks* (London: Hodder & Stoughton, 1935). See also his Moffatt *New Testament Commentary on Romans* (London: Hodder & Stoughton, 1932) and his *The Johannine Epistles* (London: Hodder & Stoughton, 1946).

3. Leon Morris addressed Dodd's argument both in his article, 'The Use of ἱλάσκεσθαι etc. in Biblical Greek' in The *Expository Times*, LXII.8 (1951), 227-233, and in his article, 'The Meaning of HILASTERION in Rom III.25' in *New Testament Studies*, 2:33-43, as well as in his *The Apostolic Preaching of the Cross*.

4. Roger R. Nicole, 'C. H. Dodd and the Doctrine of Propitiation' in *Westminster Theological Journal* XVII.2 (May 1955), 117-157.

makes two basic errors: (1) his extra-biblical evidence is incomplete, and (2) he has not paid enough attention to the biblical teaching.

With respect to his first error, his assessment of data in the Septuagint ignores the books of the Maccabees which contain several passages which speak of 'the wrath of the Almighty' being averted, while the meaning of 'placate' for the word-group prevails in the writings of Josephus and Philo. Friedrich Büchsel, they also note, demonstrated that in *First Clement* and the *Shepherd of Hermas* the word-group plainly means to 'propitiate' God.[5] Morris concludes: 'Throughout Greek literature, biblical and non-biblical alike, ἱλασμός means "propitiation". We cannot now decide that we like another meaning better.'[6] And Nicole judges that if Dodd's theory regarding this word-group usage in the Septuagint and the New Testament is correct, it would mean that these sources 'form a sort of linguistic island with little precedent in former times, little confirmation from the contemporaries, and no following in after years!'[7]

With respect to Dodd's notion that 'the wrath of God' denotes only the inevitable process of cause and effect in a moral universe, both critics show that the idea of the wrath of God is 'stubbornly rooted in the Old Testament, where it is referred to 585 times'[8] by no less than twenty (!) different Hebrew words that underscore God's indignation against sin and evil.[9] They also show that there are numerous times when the verb roots כָּפַר and ἱλάσκεσθαι – the latter employed by the Septuagint to translate כָּפַר – refer to propitiating the wrath both of men (for example, Gen 32:20; Prov 16:14) and of God (for example, see Ex 32:10 with 32:30, Num 16:41-50; 25:11-13; see also LXX, Zech 7:2, 8:22, Mal 1:9).[10]

It can be demonstrated that the matter is no different in Paul's thought. In Romans 1:18-3:20, the section leading up to the pericope in which the word occurs (3:21-31), Paul argues not only the case for universal human sin but in the process of doing so also directly refers

---

5. F. Büchsel, 'ἱλάσκεσθαι' in the *Theological Dictionary of the New Testament* (Grand Rapids: Eerdmans, 1965), 3.300-323.
6. Leon Morris, *The Cross in the New Testament* (Leicester: Paternoster, 1965), 349.
7. Roger Nicole, 'C. H. Dodd and the Doctrine of Propitiation,' 132.
8. Leon Morris, 'Propitiation' in *Evangelical Dictionary of Theology*, edited by Walter A. Elwell (Grand Rapids: Baker, 1984), 888.
9. Morris, *The Apostolic Preaching of the Cross*, 149.
10. See also George Eldon Ladd's discussion in his *A Theology of the New Testament* (Grand Rapids: Eerdmans, 1974), 429-33.

to God's wrath in 1:18 (see 1:24, 26, 28, 32), 2:5 (see 2:16), and 3:5 (see also 1 Thess 1:10). Morris quite properly concludes: 'Wrath has occupied such an important place in the argument leading up to this section that we are justified in looking for some expression indicative of its cancellation in the process which brings about salvation.'[11] John Murray urges in this same connection:

> The essence of the judgment of God against sin is his wrath, his holy recoil against what is the contradiction of himself (see Rom. 1:18). If Christ vicariously bore God's judgment upon sin, and to deny this is to make nonsense of his suffering unto death and particularly of the abandonment on Calvary, then to eliminate from this judgment that which belongs to its essence is to undermine the idea of vicarious sin-bearing and its consequences. So the doctrine of propitiation is not to be denied or its sharpness in any way toned down.[12]

And James Denney observes:

> If the propitiatory death of Jesus is eliminated from the love of God, it might be unfair to say that the love of God is robbed of all meaning, but it is certainly robbed of its apostolic meaning.[13]

Moreover, if this word-group means *only* expiation, the question must still be answered, What would be the result for men if there is no expiation? When they die in their sin, would they not face the divine displeasure? Surely! But is this not just another way of saying that Christ by his death satisfies divine justice and removes God's displeasure, that is, propitiates God, for those for whom he died? It surely seems so!

We would conclude, then, that there is no warrant to depart from the traditional understanding of ἱλαστήριον in Romans 3:25 as denoting placation or propitiation. To the contrary, we believe that the evidence at every critical juncture supports the traditional understanding. Accordingly, we would insist that, although the basic idea in the ἱλάσκεσθαι word-group is a 'complex one', yet 'the averting of anger [by an offering] seems to represent a stubborn substratum of meaning from which all the usages can be naturally explained'.[14]

---

11. Morris, *The Apostolic Preaching of the Cross*, 169.
12. John Murray, 'The Atonement' in *Collected Writings of John Murray* (Edinburgh: Banner of Truth, 1977), 2.145.
13. James Denney, *The Death of Christ* (London: Hodder & Stoughton, 1900), 152.
14. Morris, *The Apostolic Preaching of the Cross*, 155.

As we noted above, Paul also develops the propitiatory character of Christ's sacrifice by representing him as our priest or high priest (Heb 2:17) – a unique and illuminating way to consider the saving work of Christ. Morris points out that Hebrews employs the term 'priest' fourteen times for Christ (no other New Testament author has it more often than Luke's five) and the term 'high priest' seventeen times (a term found elsewhere only in the Gospels and Acts – and there in reference to the contemporary Jewish holders of the office), putting no great difference of meaning between the two.[15] Paul's salvific vision, in a word, is that we need a representative priest before God and Christ is that representative priest.

Paul provides a rich treatment of Christ's high priestly role 'after the order of Melchizedek' (see 5:6, 10; 6:20; 7:1-8:6). Unlike the Melchizedekian order of priests, the priests serving in the Levitical order served the 'old covenant' (8:6), 'without benefit of an irrevocable divine oath' which ordained them to their service (7:20), 'at a sanctuary which was [only] a copy and shadow of what is in heaven' (8:5) and which actually served to keep men away from God (9:8). And they had to offer sacrifices for their own sins before they could offer sacrifices for the people (7:27; 9:7), then they had to *stand* daily and offer again and again the same 'weak and useless' (7:18) sacrifices which in themselves could never purify the conscience (9:9) or take away sins (10:4, 11). Indeed the very repetition of the sacrifices only reminded the offerers of their sins (10:2-4). Finally, the Levitical priests themselves died (7:23). Because of these imperfections in the Levitical system (see 7:11, 19; 9:9; 10:1ff), David's prophetic insight in Psalm 110:1-4 foretold that Melchizedek would provide the priestly order in which Christ serves.

Melchizedek (Gen 14:18-20; Ps 110:4), whose name means 'King of righteousness' and whose title means 'King of peace', typically 'remains a priest forever' (7:3) because he had 'neither father nor mother' (that is, nothing is recorded in Genesis of his ancestry), and he was 'without genealogy, without beginning of days or end of life' (that is, he simply appears in the Genesis record with nothing said about him as to his parentage, his length of life or his death, or progeny). And because Melchizedek blessed Abraham who had received the covenant promises ('and without doubt the lesser person is blessed by the greater' – 7:7), who then paid Melchizedek a tithe,

---

15. Leon Morris, *New Testament Theology* (Grand Rapids: Zondervan, 1986), 304.

Paul argues that Melchizedek's priestly order is to be viewed as greater than the Levitical order because 'Levi, being still in the loins of his ancestor' when Abraham gave the tithe to Melchizedek, 'paid the tenth' to him as well.

In contrast to the Levitical priests, like Melchizedek, Christ came from a 'different tribe' (the 'royal' tribe of Judah, 7:13-14), appeared *once for all* (ἅπαξ) at the end of the ages to put away sin by the sacrifice of himself (9:26), was ordained by an *irrevocable* (οὐ μεταμεληθήσεται) divine oath (7:20-21) to a *permanent* (ἀπαράβατον) priesthood which can save those *completely and forever* (εἰς τὸ παντελὲς) who come to God through him because he *ever lives* (πάντοτε ζῶν) to intercede for them, (7:24), thus mediating a 'new covenant' (9:15) and better promises (8:6), served the heavenly sanctuary (4:14; 9:11, 24), did not have to offer a sacrifice first for his own sins (7:27), but made *one* offering of himself *once for all* (that is, decisively and finally; ἐφάπαξ – 7:27; 9:12; 10:10) for others, was offered *once for all* (ἅπαξ) to bear the sins of many (9:28), offered one sacrifice for sin (10:12), and by one offering perfected those who are sanctified (10:14). He has accordingly taken his seat at the right hand of God on his throne, always living to intercede for his own (7:25) and waiting for his enemies to be made his footstool (10:12-13).

From these notices we learn that Christ's high priestly work achieved three things that the Levitical system could never achieve: first, Christ's work *purifies* the conscience from dead works to serve the living God (9:14; see 10:2-4, 16-18, 22); second, his work *sanctifies*, that is, sets apart for God's service, the redeemed (9:13; 10:10; 13:12); and third, his work *perfects* those who have been sanctified with a perfection unattainable under the old covenant (7:11; 10:14).

Before we leave the topic of propitiation, something should be said here about Paul's concept of God's wrath. He plainly teaches the doctrine of the *wrath of God* (Rom. 1:18; 2:5; 3:5). He teaches that God is angry with the sinner, and that his holy outrage against the sinner must be assuaged if the sinner is to escape his due punishment. But God's wrath is not to be construed in any measure as capricious, uncontrolled, or irrational fury. Nor is God himself malicious, vindictive, or spiteful. God's wrath is simply his instinctive holy indignation and recoil, that is, the settled opposition of his holiness, against sin which, because he is righteous, expresses itself in the judicial punishment of sin. It is his personal divine revulsion to evil and his personal vigorous opposition to it. It is his steady, unrelenting, unremitting, uncompromising antagonism to evil in all its forms and manifestations. In sum, God's instinctive and vehement revulsion to sin demands, if sinners are ever to be forgiven, that their sins be punished. Accordingly, above everything else, it was this demand in God himself—that his infinite offended holiness (which when confronted with sin must react against it in the wrathful outpouring of divine judgment) must be satisfied—that necessitated the cross-work of Christ. When Christ died, because of his own infinite worth as the Son of God before the Father who stands as the legal representative of the Godhead, he fully paid the penalty for the infinite disvalue of the elect's sin and thus fully discharged the debt which their sin had accrued before God. In sum, he 'did enough' to 'satisfy' (Lat. *satis* – enough, *facere* – to do) fully the demands of the glory of God's offended holiness and justice. Apart from Christ's death-work, God could only have continued in an 'unpropitiated' state, and sinners would have had to bear the penalty for their sins in themselves. But since they can never 'do enough' to satisfy divine justice, they would have had to bear the penalty for their sins *eternally* in themselves.

Not one word of the exposition above is intended to suggest, however, that it was Christ's death-work that rendered God gracious toward the sinner. P. T. Forsyth has expressed this point succinctly and well: 'The atonement did not procure grace, it flowed from grace.'[16] M. A. C. Warren states: '[In the cross] we are to see not an attempt to change God's mind but the very expression of that mind.'[17] And John Stott declares:

> It cannot be emphasized too strongly that God's love is the source, not the consequence, of the atonement.... God does not love us because Christ died for us; Christ died for us because God loved us. If it is God's wrath which needed to be propitiated, it is God's love which did the propitiating. If it may be said that the propitiation 'changed' God, or that by it he changed himself, let us be clear he did not change from wrath to love, or from enmity to grace, since his character is unchanging. What the propitiation changed was his dealings with us.[18]

---

16. P. T. Forsyth, *The Cruciality of the Cross* (London: Hodder & Stoughton, 1909), 78.
17. M. A. C. Warren, *The Gospel of Victory* (London: SCM, 1995), 21.
18. John Stott, *The Cross of Christ* (Downers Grove, Ill.: InterVarsity, 1986), 174.

What this all means is that it was the same God who demanded satisfaction for sin who in grace provided in his Son the 'sacrifice which would turn aside his wrath, by taking away sin'. Never should the atonement be so represented as to suggest that it was the Father who hated the sinner, that it was the Son who loved the sinner, and that his cross-work won the Father over to clemency or 'extorted' the Father's gracious attitude toward the sinner from him against his will. Not only does Paul trace the entire plan of salvation back to the Father's electing love (Eph 3:11; 1:3-14; Rom 8:29; 2 Tim 1:9), not only does he trace the execution of the Father's plan back to his love (Rom 5:8 – 'God demonstrated his own love for us in this: While we were still sinners, Christ died for us'), but also even in the very passage where Christ's death-work is represented as a propitiating sacrifice directed toward the demand of the Godhead that divine justice be satisfied, Paul stresses the Father's provision and the Father's love as the spring from which his propitiatory activity flowed: '[God] publicly displayed [Christ Jesus] as a sacrifice which would turn aside his wrath, taking away sin...to demonstrate his justice' (Rom 3:25).

Christ's Reconciling Sacrifice

It is particularly Paul to whom we are indebted for the conception of the nature of Christ's salvific work as that of reconciliation. The basic words are the noun καταλλαγή (four times in the New Testament, all in Paul – Rom 5:11; 11:15; 2 Cor 5:18, 19) and the verbs καταλλάσσω (six times in the New Testament, all in Paul – Rom 5:10 [twice], 1 Cor 7:11; 2 Cor 5:18, 19, 20) and ἀποκαταλλάσσω (three times in New Testament, all in Paul – Eph 2:16; Col 1:20, 22). The linguistic backdrop of reconciliation is estrangement or alienation This concept may be found in ἀπαλλατριόομαι (three times in the New Testament, all in Paul – Eph 2:12; 4:18; Col 1:21). Here are Paul's statements:

Romans 5:10-11: 'If, when we were enemies, we *were reconciled* [κατηλλάγημεν] to God through the death of his Son, how much more, *having been reconciled* [καταλλαγέντες], shall we be saved by his life. And not only this, but also we rejoice in God through our Lord Jesus Christ, through whom now we received the *reconciliation* [καταλλαγὴν].'

2 Corinthians 5:17-21: 'If anyone is in Christ, he is a new creation. The old has gone; behold, the new has come. All this is from God who *reconciled*

[καταλλάξαντος] us to himself through Christ, and gave to us the ministry of *reconciliation* [καταλλαγῆς]: that God was, in Christ, *reconciling* [καταλλάσσων] a world unto himself, not imputing to them their trespasses, and entrusted to us the message of *reconciliation* [καταλλαγῆς]. We are therefore ambassadors in Christ's stead, as though God were summoning [men] through us. We implore in Christ's stead: *Be reconciled* [καταλλάγητε] to God. God made him who knew no sin to be sin in our stead, in order that we might become the righteousness of God in him.'

Ephesians 2:14-17: '[Christ] is our peace, who made both [Jews and Gentiles] one and destroyed the enmity, the dividing wall of hostility, in his flesh, nullifying the law of commandments with its regulations, in order that the two he might create in himself into one new man, making peace [between them], and that he *might reconcile* [ἀποκαταλλάξῃ] both in one body to God *through the cross*, slaying the enmity [of God] by it. And having come he preached the good news of peace to you who were far off and of peace to those who were near.'

Colossians 1:19-22: 'God was pleased that in him all the fulness [of deity] should dwell, and through him *to reconcile* [ἀποκαταλλάξαι] all things unto him(self?), making peace through *the blood of his cross*, through him whether things on earth or things in heaven. And you were once alienated and enemies in your mind because of evil deeds, but now *he has reconciled* [ἀποκατήλλαξεν] you by the body of his flesh through *death*, to present you holy and unblemished and blameless in his sight.'

Because of the repeated references in these Pauline texts to Christ's cross-work as a reconciling event, this characterization of his death achievement is not disputed by believing scholars. They acknowledge that Christ's death-work, construed as a reconciling work, presupposed that a state of alienation existed between God and man because of human sin, and that his death removed that alienation or enmity. But what is debated among them is whose alienation or enmity was it that was addressed and removed by Christ's cross-work. Both God and man, it is true, were alienated each from the other – God's alienation from man being, of course, both holy and completely justified because of man's rebellion against him; man's alienation from God being both unholy and completely unjustified, the reflex of his rebellion against God in the area of his personal relationship to God. Does Christ's cross-work viewed as a reconciling act terminate upon God's alienation or upon man's? Does it denote a Godward reference of the atonement, viewed now simply from a different perspective from that of propitiation, or is this a characterization of the atonement that ascribes a manward reference to it? It has often been said in response that, while Christ's death propitiated God, it reconciled man. But did the death of God's Son itself, even the precious blood of the cross, remove man's enmity against God or alter or change man's attitude toward God? Admittedly, the manner in which this Greek word-group is rendered by the English would seem to suggest so, for never does the English translation say that God was reconciled to man but, just to the contrary, either (active voice) that God *reconciled* the world to himself or (passive voice) that men *have been reconciled* to God. Scripture, history, and Christian experience would suggest, however, that men have not terminated their unholy hostility toward God. The race, by and large, either detests the cross and all that it implies about man's moral/ethical condition with unrestrained vehemence or regards the cross with indifference. Paul said it this way: the cross to the Jew is a stumbling block, to the Gentile it is foolishness! It is hardly true then that men for the most part, because of Christ's cross-work, now love God and live to honor and to glorify him. To the contrary, most men have lived and died hating him, neither glorifying him nor giving thanks to him, preferring to exchange the glory of the immortal God for images made to look like mortal man and birds and animals and reptiles (see Rom 1:21-23).

A careful exegetical study of these passages will conclude, I would urge, that Paul was teaching that it is God who is reconciled by the objective work of the blood of the cross.[19] The pertinent passages indicate that Christ's death-work construed as a reconciling work addressed God's alienation toward us because of our sin, and that by Christ's paying the penalty due to us for sin God's desire to bless us was realized as it could not have been apart from that work. While Christ would not have died for us had not God loved us, it is equally true that God would not be to us what he is if Christ had not died. That is to say, God could not have been reconciled to us and could only have continued in his holy hostility toward us had Christ not died for us. Plainly, the cross-work of Christ in its reconciling character had primarily a Godward reference.

---

19. For my exposition of these passages, see my *A New Systematic Theology of the Christian Faith* (Nashville: Thomas Nelson, 1998), 646-50.

Is it pagan to insist that God required the cross-work of Christ in order that he might be not only propitious toward men but also favorably disposed toward them? Liberal theologians have always thought so. But in all other religions men attempt to propitiate their gods and to win them over to clemency through some activity on their part. Christianity, however, declares that '*God* was, in Christ, reconciling the world to himself' (2 Cor 5:19), that even at the time when he had just cause for his alienation from us, he 'demonstrated his love for us' by reconciling us to himself through the death of his Son. Accordingly, we have not earned reconciliation with God. We neither could nor do we need to do so since God has in grace freely bestowed it upon us. As Paul declares: 'We have *received* the reconciliation' (Rom 5:11). This is *not* paganism; it is the exact opposite of paganism. Whereas every other religion of the world represents men as seeking after their gods, Christianity represents God as seeking after men. Such divine dealing with men is unique among the world religions. It is simply the manner in which the one living and true God acted in grace toward us.

Christ's Redemptive Sacrifice

That Christ's cross-work is to be viewed as a work of deliverance by great power cannot be legitimately doubted. Paul calls Christ '*the Deliverer* [ὁ ῥυόμενος] out of Zion' (Rom 11:26). He also declares that Christ 'delivered' him from his body of death (Rom 7:24 – ῥύσεται) and 'delivered' Christians in general from the coming wrath (1 Thess 1:10 – τὸν ῥυόμενον). E. F. Harrison has perceptively observed, however, that while Paul 'can content himself with the use of ῥύεσθαι when setting forth the relation of Christ's saving work for us with respect to hostile angelic powers (Col 1:13), yet when he passes to a contemplation of the forgiveness of our sins he must change his terminology to that of redemption (Col 1:14)'.[20]

Some scholars construe this redemptive work of the Lord of Glory purely in terms of deliverance by power *apart from price*. In his day Warfield spoke of those who urged this interpretation upon the church as 'assisting at the death bed of a [worthy] word'.[21] Furthermore,

---

20. Everett F. Harrison, 'Redeemer, Redemption' in *Evangelical Dictionary of Theology*, 919.
21. Benjamin B. Warfield, 'Redeemer and Redemption' in *The Person and Work of Christ* (Philadelphia: Presbyterian and Reformed, 1950), 345.

Warfield painstakingly demonstrated, against the contrary opinions of Westcott, Oltramare, and Ritschl specifically, that the λυτρ- word-group always retains its native sense of *ransoming* as the mode of deliverance throughout the whole history of profane Greek literature, the Septuagint (where it is employed to translate the Hebrew word-groups גָּאַל, פָּדָה, and כָּפַר), the New Testament material, and the early Patristic literature.[22] John Murray concurs:

> The idea of redemption must not be reduced to the general notion of deliverance. The language of redemption is the language of purchase and more specifically of ransom. And ransom is the securing of a release by the payment of a price.[23]

As we shall now show, the relevant Pauline word-groups (λυτρόω, ἀγοράζω, and περιποιέω [once]) everywhere support this conclusion. Of all of the New Testament writers, it is Paul who gives us the largest development of the doctrine. He taught, in concert with his Savior (Mark 10:45), that Jesus 'gave himself as a *ransom for all* [ἀντίλυτρον ὑπὲρ πάντων]' (1 Tim 2:6; note his interesting employment by this *hapax* of both ἀντί and ὑπέρ – 'a ransom *in the stead of* [and] *for the sake of*'). And Jesus, he says, 'gave himself for us in order that *he might redeem* [λυτρώσηται] [ransom] us from all wickedness' (Tit 2:14). Accordingly, Paul refers to the 'redemption' (ἀπολύτρωσις) which we have through Christ's blood or death seven times (Rom 3:24; 8:23; 1 Cor 1:30; Eph 1:7, 14; 4:30; Col 1:14).

In Romans 3:24-27, he asks: 'Having been *justified* freely by his grace through the *redemption which is by Christ Jesus* (whom God displayed publicly as a sacrifice which would *turn aside his wrath*) through faith *in his blood*..., where then is boasting?' Here in a single context where 'redemption' is the governing idea for the whole, Paul speaks of that redemption as 'by Christ Jesus' and 'in his blood', as a *propitiating* redemption, and as a redemption which purchased our *justification through faith*.

In Ephesians 1:7 and Colossians 1:14 he states that in Christ 'we *have redemption through his blood* [*through his blood* is omitted in Colossians], the forgiveness of sins'. Note should be taken of the

---

22. Warfield, 'The New Testament Terminology of Redemption,' *The Person and Work of Christ*, 429-475.

23. John Murray, *Redemption Accomplished and Applied* (Grand Rapids: Eerdmans, 1955), 42.

interpermeation of redemption and forgiveness here, the latter accruing to the Christian through the procurement of the former.

In four contexts Paul speaks of our eschatological 'redemption'. In Romans 8:23 he refers to the future 'redemption of the body'. In Ephesians 1:14 and 4:30 he refers to our final redemption from all evil, as did Jesus in Luke 21:28, which will occur in the 'day of redemption'. Here Paul underscores the great truth that Christ's redemption, which procured the Spirit's sealing for all those for whom he died, *secures our final salvation*. Likewise, in 1 Corinthians 1:30, the word order of the three nouns in Paul's declaration that Christ Jesus is our 'wisdom from God, that is, our *righteousness, sanctification*, and *redemption*', almost certainly intends that the third noun be construed as referring to our redemption in the eschatological consummation. Here the apostle affirms that Christ's cross-work secured our justification, our sanctification, and our final redemption. Again, we must insist that this eschatological redemption is grounded in the redemption secured by Christ at Calvary as many features surrounding these three verses indicate (see Eph 1:7; 4:32; 5:2; 1 Cor 1:18-25).

Shifting to the ἀγοράζω word-group (three times in the Pauline corpus, but the occurrence in 1 Corinthians 7:30 is unrelated to Christ's work), in 1 Corinthians 6:19-20 Paul writes: 'You are not your own; for *you were bought with a price* [ἠγοράσθητε τιμῆς],' and since this is so, he declares in 7:23: '*With a price you were bought* [τιμῆς ἠγοράσθητε]; do not become slaves of men.'

The ἐξαγοράζω word-group occurs four times in the New Testament, all in Paul, but the occurrences in Ephesians 5:16 and Colossians 4:5 are unrelated to Christ's work. This word-group suggests by the addition of the preposition ἐκ that the Christian has been *bought* and taken *out of* the market place. He is no longer 'for sale'. In Galatians 3:13 Paul writes: 'Christ *purchased* [ἐξηγόρασεν] us from the curse of the law, by becoming a curse for us,' and in 4:4-5 he teaches that God 'sent his Son...*to purchase* [ἵνα...ἐξαγοράσῃ] those under the law'.

Finally, to the Ephesian elders Paul declared that God '*purchased* [περιεποιήσατο] the church through his own blood' or 'through the blood of his own [Son]' (Acts 20:28).

From this survey of the pertinent Pauline material, it is quite evident that Paul viewed Christ's cross-work as a redemptive act. In *every* instance, either in the immediate or near context, the ransom price which he paid (his blood or death), which is what made his work *redemptive in nature*, is indicated. And it is only theological perversity of a deep hue that leads men to deny this and to insist rather that redemption and ransom simply speak of deliverance through power.

Just as we found with Christ's cross-work construed as propitiation and reconciliation, so also with his cross-work construed as redemptive act: Paul represents Christ's redemptive work, in its objective character, as an *accomplished* fact. In *every* instance the aorist (punctiliar) tense is employed to describe his redemptive work at the cross ('gave' – 1 Tim 2:6; Tit 2:14; 'publicly displayed' – Rom 3:25; 'bought' or 'purchased' – 1 Cor 6:20; 7:23; Gal 3:13; 4:5; Acts 20:28). In short, Paul affirms that when Jesus died, his death actually *redeemed*, it actually *procured everything* essential to the deliverance or liberation of those for whom he died.

Ransom and redemption presuppose bondage and are directed to the bondage to which our sin has consigned us. What specifically then did his death procure?

With reference to the law of God, (1) Christ redeemed us from the *curse* of the law, that is, from its just *condemnation* of us, by becoming a curse for us, that is, by bearing its just condemnation of us vicariously (Gal 3:13) (this redemptive feature ensures that there is no longer any condemnation awaiting those who are in Christ Jesus, Rom 8:1, that is, it guarantees our justification before God);

(2) Christ delivered the people of God from any further need for the *pedagogical* bondage implicit in the ceremonialism of the Old Testament salvific economy (Gal 3:23; 4:2-5; 5:1);

(3) Christ redeemed the Christian from any necessity of obtaining on his own, in order to be saved, a righteousness before God; Christ is our righteousness (1 Cor 1:30), and he is the end of law-keeping for righteousness for every believer (Rom 10:4).

With reference to sin, a close corrolary of the former referent,

(1) Christ redeemed us from the *guilt* of sin (Eph 1:7; Col 1:14) by bearing our sin in our stead, that is, he procured for those whose guilt he bore their deliverance from the law's condemnation;

(2) Christ redeemed us from the *power and fruitlessness* of sin (Rom 6:21-22; 7:4-6; Tit 2:14). This deliverance from the power of sin **is** the triumphal aspect of redemption as it relates to Christian

men. By virtue of the real spiritual union that exists between Christ and all those for whom he died (Rom 6:1-10; 7:4-6; 2 Cor 5:14-15; Eph 2:1-7; Col 3:1-4), the Scriptures affirm of them that they died to the realm and power of sin and that they live to serve him who died for them. It is this union which secures for the Christian his definitive and progressive holiness.

There is a second exigency which this 'triumphal aspect' of Christ's redemptive activity bears upon – the destruction of Satan's kingdom of darkness. This brings us to the final category under which Christ's cross-work must be viewed.

Christ's Destructive Sacrifice

Paul took very seriously the reality of Satan and the kingdom of evil. He refers to our archfoe as Belial (2 Cor 6:15), the Evil One (Eph 6:16; 2 Thess 3:3), the Ruler of the kingdom of the air (Eph 2:2), Satan (Rom 16:20), and the Tempter (1 Thess 3:5). He works, Paul affirms, in the sons of disobedience (Eph 2:2), blinds the minds of unbelievers so that they cannot see the light of the gospel of the glory of Christ (2 Cor 4:4), turns men away from God to serve him (1 Tim 5:15), takes men captive to do his will (2 Tim 2:26), obstructs world missions (1 Thess 2:18), and masquerades as an angel of light (2 Cor 11:14). It was he who tormented Paul with a thorn in the flesh (2 Cor 12:7).

Paul speaks of definite 'power-aspects' of Satan's kingdom of darkness: the *'reign* of darkness' (Col 1:13), principalities and powers (Eph 6:12; Col 2:15), the powers of this dark world (Eph 6:12), and spiritual forces of evil in the heavenly realm against which the man who lacks the whole armor of God cannot possibly stand (Eph 6:12-13). Satan devises schemes (Eph 6:11), 'traps' men (2 Tim 2:26), and inspires false religions (1 Cor 10:20).

Accordingly, Paul taught that Christ's redemptive work addressed and triumphed over Satan's 'evil kingdom', nullifying and reversing its powers and effects: '[God] *graciously pardoned* [χαρισάμενος] you of all your trespasses, *having canceled* [ἐξαλείψας] the written code, with its regulations, that was against us and that stood opposed to us – he took it out of the way, *by nailing it fast* [προσηλώσας] to the cross. *Having disarmed* [ἀπεκδυσάμενος] [thereby] the powers and the authorities, he exposed them openly, *triumphing* [θριαμβεύσας] over them *by the cross*' (Col 2:13c-15). What Paul means by his remarks is this: When Christ publicly died on the cross for his own, he paid the penalty, endured the curse, and died the death which their sins deserved, meeting fully all the penal sanctions of the law ('the written code, with its regulations, that was against us and that stood opposed to us'). It is the fact that God's own are transgressors of his law that has ever been the sole ground of Satan's accusations against them. But when Christ paid the penalty for their sins, God 'disarmed' Satan of that ground (Paul graphically declaring that it had been 'nailed fast to the cross') with respect to all those for whom Christ died, and 'triumphed' over Satan's kingdom thereby.

This means that Christ's death and resurrection effected a cosmic change as well. In Colossians 1:20 Paul declares that Christ by his cross 'pacified' the spiritual rulers and authorities with respect to any claims to authority they may have had over men and the world because of man's sin. They are now powerless, having no foothold or claim. This pacification of thrones and power, rulers and authorities, in the invisible realm, by the very nature of the case, applies to them in a non-soteric sense. The ultimate ground for the hostility of these spiritual forces in the earthly and heavenly realms, as touching men, has been removed by Christ's death. His death once and for all removed any claims they may have had over those for whom Christ died, by once and for all breaking sin's power and dominion over them. Thus too the bondage to which the world has been subjected because of man's sin will in the great day of Christ's coming enter into the liberty of the redemption of the believers and their bodies (Rom 8:19-23).

Christ's cross-work was a redemptive work of destruction and conquest! Thereby he proved himself Satan's Victor and secured for his own their victory over Satan as well. Consequently, living out their Christian experience in union with Christ and protected by the 'full armor' of God (truth, righteousness, readiness, faith, the hope of salvation, and the Word of God) (Eph 6:10-17), Christians overcome the kingdom of darkness through their God, the Father of mercies and the God of all comfort, 'who *always* [πάντοτε] *leads [them] in triumphal procession* [θριαμβεύοντι] in Christ' (2 Cor 2:14). They do so by using 'the sword of the Spirit, which is the Word of God' (Eph 6:17).

Christ's Application of the Atonement

We must not leave the topic of Christ's salvific work without pointing out that, for Paul, the Spirit by whom the Father effectually calls the elect is not the Father's Spirit alone. Paul teaches that the Spirit who regenerates is *Christ's* Spirit as well (see Rom 8:9-10). There is, therefore, a concurrent activity on the part of the Son in the application of the atonement to the elect sinner. Accordingly, the *Westminster Confession of Faith* (VIII/viii) perceptively depicts the present enthronement work of Christ as including within its scope the application of redemption:

> To all those for whom Christ hath purchased redemption, he doth certainly and *effectually apply and communicate the same*; making intercession for them, and revealing unto them, in and by the Word, the mysteries of salvation; *effectually persuading them by his Spirit* to believe and obey, and governing their hearts *by his Word and Spirit*; overcoming all their enemies by his almighty power and wisdom, in such manner, and ways, as are most consonant to his wonderful and unsearchable dispensation. (emphasis supplied)

CHAPTER NINETEEN

THE HOLY SPIRIT'S PERSON AND SALVIFIC WORK

Come, O Creator Spirit blest,
   And in our hearts take up your rest;
Spirit of grace, with heavenly aid
   Come to the souls whom you have made.

You are the Comforter, we cry,
   Sent to the earth from God Most High,
Fountain of life and fire of love,
   And our anointing from above.

Far from our souls the foe repel,
   Grant us in peace henceforth to dwell;
Ill shall not come, nor harm betide,
   If only you will be our guide.

Show us the Father, Holy One,
   Help us to know th' eternal Son;
Spirit divine, forevermore
   You will we trust and you adore.
         —Latin, 10th century

Names and Titles of the Holy Spirit in the Pauline Literature

Paul refers to the third person of the Godhead in several striking ways: He is 'the Spirit of the living God' (2 Cor 3:3), 'the Spirit of him who raised Jesus from the dead' (Rom 8:11), 'the Spirit of [God's] Son' (Gal 4:6), 'the Spirit of Christ' (Rom 8:9), 'the Spirit of Jesus Christ' (Phil 1:19), 'the Holy Spirit of promise' (Eph 1:13), 'the Spirit of sonship [or adoption]' (Rom 8:15), 'the Spirit of wisdom and revelation' (Eph 1:17), 'the eternal Spirit' (Heb 9:14), and 'the Spirit of grace' (Heb 10:29).[1]

---

1. I have argued in my *A New Systematic Theology of the Christian Faith* (Nashville, Tenn.: Thomas Nelson, 1998), 242-43, that Paul's reference to the 'spirit of holiness' (πνεῦμα

The Deity and Distinct Personality of the Holy Spirit

In Paul's writings the Holy Spirit is clearly a divine person within the Godhead. The following data puts beyond all question the fact that for Paul the Holy Spirit is, like Christ, a divine Person. Thus we have to do in Paul's theology with three divine Persons in the unity of the Godhead – God the Father, God the Son, and God the Holy Spirit.

I. The Holy Spirit a distinct person

A. Personal properties are ascribed to him, such as understanding or wisdom (1 Cor 2:10-11), will (1 Cor 12:11), and power (Rom 15:13; Eph 3:16).

ἁγιωσύνης) in Romans 1:4 is not a reference to the Holy Spirit, the third person of the Trinity, but to Christ's divine nature, to what he is, as the Son of God, on his divine side. I urge this for the following two reasons: first, because it stands in contrast to 'flesh' in the former clause which refers to what Christ, as the Son of David, is on his human side; the implication is that 'spirit' in the latter clause must also refer to something intrinsically inherent in Christ. But standing as it does in such close correlation to the title 'the Son of God' in the same phrase which denotes Christ in terms of his Godness, it follows that its referent here is to what he is, as the Son of God, on his divine side, that is, to his deity. Second, in the same letter (Rom 9:5) Paul refers again to Christ as 'from the fathers, specifically according to the flesh', intimating that something more can and must be said about him. In the Romans 9:5 context, what this 'something more' is, Paul himself provides us in the phrase 'who is over all, God blessed forever'. In other words, in Romans 9:5 Paul declares that Christ is 'of the fathers according to the flesh', but in the sense that he is not 'of the fathers' and not 'flesh' he was and is 'over all, God blessed forever'. Similarly, I would urge, in Romans 1:3-4 Paul informs us that Christ is 'of David, according to the flesh', but in the sense that he is not 'of David' and not 'flesh', he was and is, as the Son of God, 'the spirit of holiness' (see 1 Cor 15:45), that is, divine spirit, intending by this phrase what he explicitly spells out in the later Romans 9:5 context. Benjamin B. Warfield, 'The Christ That Paul Preached' in *The Person and Work and Christ* (Philadelphia: Presbyterian and Reformed, 1950), explains:

> [Paul] is not speaking of an endowment of Christ either from or with the Holy Spirit.... He is speaking of that divine Spirit which is the complement in the constitution of Christ's person of the human nature according to which He was the Messiah, and by virtue of which He was not merely the Messiah, but also the very Son of God. This Spirit he calls distinguishingly the Spirit of holiness, the Spirit the very characteristic of which is holiness. He is speaking not of an acquired holiness but of an intrinsic holiness; not, then, of a holiness which had been conferred at the time of or attained by means of the resurrection from the dead; but of a holiness which had always been the very quality of Christ's being [see Luke 1:35; 5:8; John 6:69].... Evidently in Paul's thought of deity holiness held a prominent place. When he wishes to distinguish Spirit from spirit, it is enough for him that he may designate Spirit as divine, to define it as that Spirit the fundamental characteristic of which is that it is holy. (87-88)

B. Personal activities are ascribed to him. He speaks (Acts 13:2: 1 Tim 4:1), he warns (1 Tim 4:1), he appoints to office (Acts 13:2; 20:28), and he may be grieved (Eph 4:30).

II. The Holy Spirit the Yahweh of the Old Testament

What Isaiah reports that Yahweh said in Isaiah 6:9-10, Paul asserts that the Holy Spirit said (Acts 28:25-27); and where Leviticus 26:11-12 foretells Yahweh's 'dwelling with his people', Paul, citing the Leviticus passage, speaks of the church in 2 Corinthians 6:16 as the antitypical 'temple of the living God' with whom Yahweh dwells. And how does Yahweh dwell in his church? In the person of the Holy Spirit (Rom 8:9).

III. The Holy Spirit's relation to the Father and the Son

He is the Father's Spirit and the Son's Spirit (Rom 8:9-10).

IV. The Holy Spirit's co-equality with the Father and the Son

(1 Cor 12:4-6; 2 Cor 13:14; Eph 2:18; 4:4-6).

V. The Holy Spirit's divine attributes

He is omnipotent (Rom 15:19) and omniscient (1 Cor 2:10-11). The Word of God is the Spirit's sword (Eph 6:17).

VI. The Holy Spirit's divine works

According to Paul, the Holy Spirit regenerates sinners (Tit 3:5), builds the church (Eph 2:22), 'comes upon' and indwells believers as the 'seal', the 'down payment', and 'firstfruits' of their full inheritance (Rom 8:9-11, 23; 2 Cor 1:22; Eph 1:13-14; 4:30), induces believers to their perception of Jesus as Lord (1 Cor 12:3) and to their filial consciousness of God as their Father (Rom 8:15-16; Gal 4:6), speaks to men through Holy Scripture (Heb 3:7; 10:15, 17), empowers believers to boldness, love, and self-discipline (2 Tim 1:7), sanctifies them (1 Cor 6:11; Rom 15:16; Gal 5:16-18) and produces holy fruit in them (Gal 5:22-23), warns them (1 Tim 4:1), 'engifts' them with various gifts (1 Cor 12:1-11), intercedes for them in their ignorance (Rom 8:26-27), and raises them to glory from the dead (Rom 8:11). These works require the following explanatory comments.

Union with Christ by the Spirit

In expressing the work of Christ in salvation, Paul not only treats what Christ has accomplished *for* us—atonement, propitiation, reconciliation, redemption, and deliverance from the kingdom of evil, not only the *states* in which Christ has placed us—the justified and adoptive states; but he speaks also of what Christ has accomplished *in* us, that is to say, that Christ has brought about a new life in us in and by spiritual union with himself. This motif is just as important for Paul as is justification and is often mentioned simultaneously with or intertwined with his teaching on justification. For example, concluding Galatians 2 which treats justification, Paul speaks of our being crucified with Christ and as a result living a new life in him (2:20) even before he returns to justification in Galatians 3–4; in Romans 6 he speaks of our new life hard on the heels of Romans 5 where he has treated the results and ground of our justification.

The terminology Paul uses to express this concept of our new life in Christ is radical and dynamic. One finds numerous occurrences of the ἐν Χριστῷ ('in Christ') and ἐν Κυρίῳ ('in the Lord') phrases as well as the equivalent of these using the pronoun ('in whom' or 'in him') plus the εἰς Χριστόν ('into Christ') and διὰ Χριστοῦ ('through Christ') phrases in Paul's letters. Paul also uses over a dozen 'with' compounds (usually verbs) that underscore the Christian's spiritual union with Christ:

συμπάσχω, 'suffer with', Rom 8:17
συναποθνήσχω, 'die with', 2 Tim 2:11
συσταυρόομαι, 'be crucified with', Rom 6:6; Gal 2:19
συνθάπτομαι, 'be buried with', Rom 6:4; Col 2:12
συνεγείρω, 'be raised with', Eph 2:6; Col 2:12; 3:1
συζωοποιέω, 'be made alive with', Eph 2:5; Col 2:13
σύμφυτος, 'grow together with', Rom 6:5
συμμορφίζομαι, 'take on the same form as', Phil 3:10
σύμμορφος, 'having the same form as', Rom 8:29; Phil 3:20
συγκαθίζω, 'sit with', Eph 2:6
συμβασιλεύω, 'reign with', 2 Tim 2:12
συζάω, 'live with', Rom 6:8; 2 Tim 2:11
συγκληρονόμος, 'joint heir', Rom 8:17
συνδοξάζομαι, 'be glorified with', Rom 8:17[2]

---

2. See James D. G. Dunn, *The Theology of Paul the Apostle* (Grand Rapids: Eerdmans, 1998), 402-03, fn. 62.

Clearly, for Paul the reality of the Christian life is expressed in terms of moving from death to life, that is, moving in Christ from being both dead in sin and to God (Eph 2:1-3) to having died to sin (Rom 6:2) and being made alive in God with Christ (Eph 2:4-5). The negative motif of death is utilized from several perspectives to show the plight of our previous estate and the radical difference of our new estate.

This change of condition is almost invariably presented in terms of our union with Christ in his death and resurrection: we died to sin in Christ's death for sins and we became alive to God in the new resurrection life of Christ (Rom 6). *This union is a spiritual union because it is effected by the Spirit.* The perspective is that of the once-for-all work of Christ in which he acted as our representative. By our spiritual union with him by the Spirit, we too were present in him and his work was accomplished for us. Now therefore *by the Spirit* his work is accomplished in us. Similarly, the terminology of crucifixion of our old self or man (Rom 6:6) is used.

The bridge between that once-for-all-time objective and representative work of Christ, on the one hand, and the Christian's present and personal situation where he is subjectively changed from being dead in his sin to being now alive in Christ, on the other, is seen to be

(1) from the divine side, the mighty act of God which makes him alive in Christ by grace (Eph 2:5),

(2) from the human side, the connecting link of his Spirit-wrought faith which unites him to Christ and to the benefits of Christ's death and resurrection (Eph 2:8),

(3) from the perspective of the transforming life of obedience, the presence and power of God's Spirit within him versus the remnants of his sinful nature (Rom 8:2ff), and

(4) from the perspective of the Christian community, his public acknowledgement of this inner transformation in the visible rite of baptism that symbolizes the reality of his union with Christ and the new life force at work in him by God's Spirit (Rom 6:2ff).

The Christian a Spirit-Wrought New Creation

From the point of view of the center and direction of the Christian life Paul speaks of the Christian as being, *through the ministry of the Holy Spirit*, a new man (Col 3:9, 10), a new creation (2 Cor 5:17), with a new life in Christ (Gal 2:20). This is a radical and absolute perspective, so radical and absolute that the language of death and resurrection may be used (Rom 6:6; Gal 2:20). Nothing in our experience short of repudiating the faith and returning to and abiding in sin can or will let us forget this truth. Paul urges us to 'consider yourselves to be dead to sin, but alive to God in Christ Jesus' (Rom 6:11; 1 Cor 1:2; 6:11; Eph 5:26). Our new life depends on the work of Christ, through union with him in his death and resurrection, *being applied to us by God's Spirit*. In and by this Spirit-wrought union we personally experience and appropriate *in us* that representative work for us (a personal spiritual union symbolized by baptism, Tit 3:5, 6).

Putting on the Spirit-Wrought 'New Self'

The Pauline indicative concerning the core of our being must be manifested throughout our body and during our life through the self-conscious activity of being dependent upon the presence and power of the Father and the Son through the ministry of the Holy Spirit. Thus of us Paul says: 'By the Spirit you are putting to death the deeds of the body' (Rom 8:13). We are consistently urged to repudiate the practices characteristic of our old man because we have put him off in Christ and we are to put on the characteristics of godly living that are true of the new self (Eph 4:22-24; Col 3:9-10). This activity comes about by letting our minds be renewed or instructed from the perspective of God's Word (Eph 4:23; Col 3:16; see Rom 12:2) and by being filled with the Spirit (Eph 5:18). The correlation of the responsibility of the Christian and of his dependence upon God is perhaps best described in Philippians 2:12-13:

> So then, beloved, just as you have always obeyed, not as in my presence only, but now much more in my absence, work out your salvation with fear and trembling, for it is God who works in you, both to will and to work for [his] good pleasure.

The Spirit's Baptism, Sealing, Filling, Sanctifying, and Engifting

According to Paul the Holy Spirit performs a significant number of works in and for the Christian: he is the 'instrument' by whom Christ baptizes each believer into his spiritual body; he seals them, fills them, sanctifies them, and engifts them. These five works of the Spirit, because they have been employed so often in the interests of sectarian bias, have caused much confusion among God's people in our time. The following comments, though brief, faithfully represent, I believe, Paul's teaching concerning each of them.

I. The Baptism of the Spirit

Luke records four 'baptisms' (or 'comings') of the Spirit in Acts (Acts 2, Jews; 8, Samaritans; 10, Gentiles; 19, followers of John), marking by them the strategic steps in the extension of the church and teaching thereby that there is but *one* church into which all converts are baptized by the same Spirit – whether Jews, Samaritans, Gentiles, or followers of John. But while Luke documents the great truth of the oneness of the people of God by recording these 'Spirit-comings', he nowhere expounds their significance theologically. This theological exposition is provided by Paul who essentially does it in one sentence: 'For we were all baptized by one Spirit into one body —whether Jews or Greeks, slave or free—and we were all given the one Spirit to drink' (1 Cor 12:13). What Paul means here is that this baptism—the joint act of both the glorified Christ as the 'agent' and the Holy Spirit as the 'instrument'—which *every* Christian has experienced, joins together into a spiritual unity people of diverse racial extractions and diverse social backgrounds so that they form the body of Christ—the *ekklesia*. The fact of the oneness of the *ekklesia* is, according to Paul, the theological meaning of the several extensions of Pentecost in Acts, and the four 'Pentecosts' in Acts should be understood accordingly in the light of his statement. In other words, these 'Spirit-comings' had *revelatory* import in the non-repeatable salvation-history process. They were intended to teach that there is only '*one* body and *one* Spirit—just as you were called to *one* hope when you were called—*one* Lord, *one* faith, *one* baptism; *one* God and Father of all, who is *over all and through all and in all*' regardless of the human mix within it—and therefore are not to be viewed as continuing normative occurrences in the history of the church. That is to say, now that the glorified Christ has made it clear from these unique 'Spirit-comings' that men of all races and social backgrounds are 'heirs together, members together, and sharers together' in the one church (Eph 3:6), there is no further need for their continuance.

It is the Spirit's baptism, whereby we are regenerated, cleansed, and placed in the spiritual body of Christ, of which the sacrament of baptism is the sign and seal.

II. The Sealing of the Spirit

The key passages in Paul for his teaching on the sealing work of the Spirit are Ephesians 1:13-14, '*After having believed* [πιστεύσαντες], in him *you were marked with a seal* [ἐσφραγίσθητε] by the Holy Spirit of promise, who is *a deposit guaranteeing* [ἀρραβών] our inheritance,' and 2 Corinthians 1:21-22, 'God is the One who makes both us and you stand firm in Christ, having anointed us; and he has also *set his seal of ownership* [σφραγισάμενος] upon us, and has given *the deposit guaranteeing what is to come* [ἀρραβών] in our hearts.' From these virtually identical statements we learn that, contingent upon our faith in Christ, God not only justifies us, not only definitively sanctifies us, not only adopts us into his family, but he also seals us in Christ by the Spirit of God.

We are not talking here about chronologically related events. This sealing (as is true of justification, definitive sanctification, and adoption) does not follow upon trust chronologically. That is to say, one does not trust Christ one moment and the Holy Spirit seals him in Christ the next. Rather, we are speaking of a logical order. That is to say, the moment one trusts Christ, that same moment the Holy Spirit seals him in Christ, but the Spirit's sealing is contingent upon the trust.

What is this 'sealing' of which the Spirit himself appears to be the 'seal'? The idea seems to be that the Holy Spirit – being himself the indwelling '*first instalment* [ἀρραβών] of our inheritance' (Eph 1:14; 2 Cor 1:22; 5:5)—becomes, by his 'reassuring indwelling' of the indwelt Christian that he is God's child, the 'seal' marking both God's *ownership* of the Christian and the *authenticating down payment* guaranteeing the Christian's full inheritance in the Eschaton of every spiritual blessing in heaven in Christ.

III. The Filling of the Spirit

The key passages in Paul for his teaching on the filling of the Spirit are Ephesians 5:18-21 and Colossians 3:15-17. In the Ephesians passage Paul introduces his instructions with a command containing two imperatives: 'Do not get drunk on wine, which leads to debauchery. Instead, *be filled with the Spirit* [πληροῦσθε ἐν πνεύματι].' The first thing to underscore is the significance of the second imperative itself. It is an authoritative command (an imperative), it is addressed to the whole Christian community (the imperative is plural), the command is to be continually observed (the imperative is in the present tense), and it calls us, not to sectarian techniques learned or to sectarian formulas recited, but to a *believing openness to the Spirit's working* in us (it is in the passive voice, best rendered: 'Let the Spirit continually fill you'). When we place all this in the prior contrasting context, Paul commands that we must never come 'under the influence' of the 'intoxicating spirit' of wine, but rather we must ever live under the 'intoxicating influence' of the Spirit of Christ who, far from taking away from us our self-control (which alcohol as a depressant drug does), actually *stimulates* us for the first time in everything that makes a man behave at his best and highest – *including* self-control (Gal 5:22).

The Colossian parallel reads, not 'Let the Spirit fill you', but 'Let the word of Christ *dwell in* [ἐνοικείτω] you richly' (3:16), also a present imperative. These two ideas, both highlighting a divine, *subjective* influence, are practically identical. To be filled with the Spirit is to be indwelt by the word of Christ; to be indwelt by the word of Christ is to be filled with the Spirit. One must never separate the Spirit from Christ's word or Christ's word from the Spirit. The Spirit works by and with Christ's word. Christ's word works by and with the Spirit.

Paul articulates the outworking and evidence of this joint work of the Spirit's 'filling' and Christ's word 'indwelling' us by the five present participles that qualify the Spirit's filling in Ephesians 5:19-21:

speaking (λαλοῦντες) *to one another* in psalms and hymns and spiritual songs (this is Christian fellowship);

singing (ᾄδοντες) and *psalming* (ψάλλοντες) in your heart *to the Lord* (this is Christian worship in spirit and truth);

giving thanks (εὐχαριστοῦντες) always for all things in the name of our Lord Jesus Christ to God the Father (this is Christian gratitude);

and being submissive (ὑποτασσόμενοι) to one another in the fear of Christ (wives and husbands; children and parents; slaves and masters) (this is Christian display of the meekness and gentleness of Christ himself in personal relationships).

Paul teaches virtually the same thing in Colossians 3:15-17. After admonishing the Colossians to 'let the word of Christ dwell in you richly', he immediately follows his admonition, as he does in Ephesians, with a series of four present participles showing result (evidence):

teaching (διδάσκοντες) with all wisdom and counseling (νουθετοῦντες) *one another* (this is Christian fellowship);

singing (ᾄδοντες) with psalms, hymns, and spiritual songs, with grace in your hearts, to God (this is Christian worship in spirit and truth);

and *giving thanks* (εὐχαριστοῦντες) to God the Father through Christ as you do whatever you do in word or in deed in the name of the Lord Christ (this is Christian gratitude in all our service for God).

He then follows these participles, as he does in Ephesians 5:22- 6:9, with commands for wives and husbands, children and parents, and slaves and master to behave toward each other as Christians should and as their respective stations warrant.

The Christian who evidences these things in his life is 'being filled with the Spirit', or what is tantamount, is '*letting the* word of Christ dwell in him richly'. As I have said, he does not need to practice certain sectarian techniques or to recite certain sectarian incantations in order to receive the Spirit's filling. He needs only to cultivate these things the more by remaining humbly and believingly open to the Spirit who works by and with the word of Christ (and the other means of grace) in his heart.

IV. The Fruit of the Spirit

Indwelling and 'filling' believers as he does (Rom 8:9, 11; 1 Cor 3:16; 6:19; 2 Tim 1:14), the Holy Spirit progressively sanctifies them by creating the very character of Christ himself in them: 'The fruit of the Spirit is love, joy, peace, patience, kindness, goodness, faithfulness, gentleness, and self-control. Against such things there is no law' (Gal 5:22). The chief of these nine named fruit is, of course, love (the 'more excellent way' [ὑπερβολὴν ὁδὸν] of 1 Corinthians 12:31; the 'greater' [μείζων] virtue than faith and hope of 13:13), which manifests itself in human personal relationships as patience, kindness, goodness, fidelity, gentleness, and self-discipline (see 1 Cor 13:4-7). Coupled with love are joy and peace (Rom 14:17; 15:13): the former not to be construed as emotional happiness but as that religious sentiment that finds its deepest satisfaction in the Lord; the latter not to be construed simply as emotional tranquility but as the terminological description of the salvation state encompassing the whole man.

V. The Gifts of the Spirit

Paul itemizes (some of?) the Spirit's gifts (χαρίσματα) in Romans 12:6-8; 1 Corinthians 12:7-11, 28-30; and Ephesians 4:11. He mentions eighteen in all (apostles, prophets, evangelists, teachers, discernment of spirits, the word of wisdom or knowledge, exhortation, faith, miracles, healings, tongues, translation of tongues, ministry, administration, rulers, helpers, mercy, and giving), with the apostle and prophet being of primary importance because they were vehicles of revelation (Eph 3:5) and thereby provided the foundation for the church (Eph 2:20).

I have argued in my *A New Systematic Theology of the Christian Faith* that the glossolalist was also an organ of revelation and that when his oracle was translated the church received thereby a direct word from God. The revelatory nature of the apostolic, prophetic, and glossolalic utterances in the early church is my reason for urging that, with the conclusion of the inscripturation of the canon, these gifted persons passed out of the life of the church, and that the Scriptures are now both 'most necessary' if men are to know God's will for his church (Westminster Confession of Faith, I/i) and sufficient – either by his direct instruction or by good and necessary inference from his instruction – to reveal the 'whole counsel of God concerning all things necessary for his own glory, man's salvation, faith and life' (WCF, I/vi).

The Christian's Spirit-Wrought New Obedience

By the Christian's Spirit-wrought new obedience we mean that the man in Christ, according to Paul, has a Spirit-wrought new attitude and new inclination toward the triune God as the Lord of his life, the one to whom he owes thankful obedience. As God is holy so he who belongs to God must seek to be holy, that is, to be sanctified. Sanctification is both the demand of God and the internal direction of the believer's new life directed by God's Holy Spirit.

Obedience not only indicates whom one obeys but also *what* one obeys. What particular and specific ethical norms or standards is the

Christian to obey? Paul makes it clear that obedience is to be governed by God's will and that God's revealed will provides the specific norms or standards. In Paul, as in the case of the content of the gospel message itself, the norms or standards are sometimes presumed or assumed and not always specifically stated. At other times, however, the basis or standard is stated in very significant ways. In *those* places it becomes clear that the foundation of Paul's ethic is in fact God's revealed will or law.

To be more specific here, one may speak of three aspects of this new obedience which are prominent in Paul's apostolic outworking of God's will in the sphere of ethics: holiness or righteousness (sanctification), God's order, and love.

I. Holiness or righteousness

In two of Paul's earliest letters, 1 and 2 Thessalonians, holiness or righteousness (sanctification) is a key concept (see again 1 Thess 3:13; 4:3; 2 Thess 2:13). The teaching of Paul in Galatians, Ephesians and Colossians is also couched in this mode. In these letters the flesh with its passions is to be crucified and the fruit of the Spirit is to be exhibited (Gal 5:18); sins are to be put off and virtues are to be put on (see Col 3:5ff, esp. vss 8 and 10; Eph 4:17ff, esp. vss 22 and 24, and Eph 5).

II. God's order

A. The creation order is to govern marriage and headship in the church (Eph 5; 1 Cor 11, 14; 1 Tim 2).

B. The God-ordained order of parents and children is to govern their relationship (Eph 6:1ff) as well as one's responsibility to widows (1 Tim 5).

C. The order reflecting the character of God is to prevail in worship services (1 Cor 14:40; see vs 33).

D. The God-appointed order in civil government is to be upheld and heeded (Rom 13:1-7; Tit 3:1).

In this short list the concept of order is presented in different ways, its sanction more directly and sometimes less directly related to God. Sometimes the form of the order or arrangement is mandated by God (husbands and wives, parents and children, leadership in the church). Sometimes the *need* for order rather than the exact *form* is in view (guiding the freedom of the church's worship by certain indicated elements and by the general concept of order).

III. Love

The love about which Paul speaks is that which fulfills the law and which itself is an expression of God's love of righteousness.

A. The correlation of love with every facet of new obedience

1. Love is the dominant and overarching concept in Paul's ethic. Love is the way that faith appropriately expresses itself – faith working itself out in love (Gal 5:6; see 1 Cor 7:19). It is the ingredient necessary for any activity to be meaningful and acceptable to God (1 Cor 13). It is that out of which we grow (Eph 3:17). It is that to which we seek to build one another up (Eph 4:16). It is the goal and aim of the Christian ministry and the Christian life (1 Tim 1:5).

2. Love, following Jesus' own example, is Paul's way to summarize the law (Rom 13:9, 10; see Gal 5:14).

B. Love's religious base and basic quality

For the Christian love has a religious base. It is communicated through and out of a 'pure heart and a good conscience and a sincere faith' (1 Tim 1:5). It is described in terms of Christ's giving of himself for our good, and this model is held up for us to follow (Eph 5:25).

C. The directing or orienting and controlling factor

1. In marriage, love—the kind Christ has for his church—is the orienting factor in the proper functioning of the headship of the husband (Eph 5:25-29). It is God's order, in reference to the wife, and vice versa. It ameliorates the effects of sin and the propensity to misuse order, authority, and another's submission.

2. Love is the controlling factor in the question of the right to eat meat offered to idols. Love states the truth but it does not insist on its own way (see 1 Cor 8-10; Rom 14-15).

Love does not set aside holiness or order, nor is it in conflict with them. Love provides, especially for order, the dimension of concern which keeps order, truth and principle from being misused by sinful man in a hard and impersonal way. In sum, love produces an orderly loving obedience and holiness.

IV. Christ's redemption and Christ's Spirit the enabling power in the 'new obedience'

A. The Christian's source of power (Eph 2:10; Rom 6 and 8)
Christian ethics are fearlessly absolute and demanding. They must be because they are setting forth the standards of the holy God. They can be because the enablement in man is also from God.

Paul's great summary of redemption in Ephesians 2 states the matter forcefully in 2:10: 'For we are God's workmanship, created in Christ Jesus for good works which God prepared beforehand that we should walk in them.' God created us as Christians in order to accomplish in our daily lives the good works which he had long ago prepared for us to do. As surely as he has made us alive from the death of sin, so surely can and does he give us life and power as his new creation to do his will. This creation is in Christ Jesus through the power of the indwelling Spirit.

So Paul at length in Romans 6 reminds us that by our union with Christ we are alive and new. Therefore, we cannot continue in sin. We must live in newness of life. The members of our body are to be presented as instruments of righteousness to God (6:13). 'But now, having been freed from sin and enslaved to God, you derive your benefit, resulting in sanctification' (6:22).

However, it is not even the new man in Christ on his own who is able to fulfill God's law in his own life. Such a perspective will only and always leave him in the frustration of Romans 7. But the adopted son of God who is led by the Spirit of God will know the joy and satisfaction of Romans 8 in which the will of God is brought to fruition in the day by day life of obedience. This life in the Spirit is not something essentially different from union with Christ and the newness of life which that union brings. Rather, it is another perspective or statement of the same truth. If there is a slight difference, it is that Romans 8 gives more attention to the ever-present 'leading' aspect of the Spirit (see, for example, Rom 8:14). Romans 6 speaks of the transformation from the old to the new; Romans 8 continues that perspective with emphasis on the Spirit's power enabling the new man in his continuing battle with 'the deeds of the body' (Rom 8:13). It is in walking according to the Spirit (8:4) that the requirements of the law are fulfilled in us.

B. The enabled exhorted (Gal 5:16; Phil 2:12, 13)

The enabling of the Spirit does not, however, take away the need for effort and involvement on the part of the believer, but rather makes available that power through which God works. There are still the exhortations in the Pauline corpus even in connection with the Spirit's work (Gal 5:16: 'But I say, walk by the Spirit, and you will not carry out the desire of the flesh'). This perspective is also very evident in Philippians 2:12, 13: 'So then, my beloved, just as you have always obeyed...work out your salvation with fear and trembling; for it is God who is at work in you, both to will and to work for [his] good pleasure.' In sum, *Christians may be vigorously urged and commanded to obey God because God will enable them to obey*!

The New Testament in general and Paul in particular do not write an ethic which makes allowance for or which tailors its demands to the powerful hold of sin on the sinful heart. To do so would be to deny God's perfect righteous standard and the calling of the redeemed man. Sloth and weakness are dealt with but not as acceptable grounds for the allowance of sin. Rather, they too are treated as sins which God graciously forgives and from which he demands that we turn and put behind us by his enabling grace (see, for example, unbiblical divorce or separation in marriage; 1 Cor 7:11: 'But if she does leave, let her remain unmarried, or else be reconciled to her husband').

C. Some motivating factors for holiness

For Paul, Spirit-wrought gratitude for one's salvation and Spirit-wrought love for Christ as one's Lord and Savior are the prime motivating factors for holiness of life (see 1 Cor 6:20; Rom 12:1; Gal 6:2). He also holds forth rewards for holiness, and makes his apostolic appeal to responsible obedience an additional reason for Christian holiness (Rom 13:2, 3, 4, 11; 15:1; 1 Cor 3:12-15; 1 Cor 7:17ff; 11:1, 2; 2 Cor 5:9, 10, 14; Gal 6:7-10; Eph 4:1ff, 6:1ff; Col 1:10; Phil 1:27; 1 Thess 2:12).

* * * * *

From this overview of Paul's teaching on the Holy Spirit we must conclude that the Holy Spirit is necessarily, directly, and vitally involved as creator, life-giver, and motivator in every aspect of the Christian's life – from the Christian's spiritual regeneration through his entire life of sanctification to his physical resurrection. James Dunn is surely right when he notes:

> That the Spirit is thus to be seen as the defining mark of the Christian is put in blunt terms in [Romans] 8:9: 'You are not in the flesh but in the Spirit, assuming that the Spirit of God does indeed dwell in you; if anyone does not have the Spirit of Christ, that person does not belong to him.' In this verse, in fact, Paul provides the nearest thing to a definition of a Christian (someone who is 'of Christ'). And the definition is in terms of the Spirit. It is 'having the Spirit' which defines and determines someone as being 'of Christ'. A Spiritless Christian would have been a contradiction in terms for Paul.[3]

Note should be taken that Paul does not say in Romans 8:9 and 8:14: 'If you are Christ's, you have the Spirit' and 'If you are God's sons, you are led by the Spirit'. In both cases he puts it the other way around: 'If you have the Spirit, you are Christ's' and 'If you are led by the Spirit, you are God's sons'. Paul could not be more explicit concerning the Spirit's necessary and vital place and role in the Christian's entire existence and sanctification as a Christian.

---

3. Dunn, *The Theology of Paul the Apostle*, 423; see also 430.

CHAPTER TWENTY

THE DOCTRINE OF JUSTIFICATION

> My hope is in the Lord who gave himself for me,
> And paid the price of all my sin at Calvary.
>
> No merit of my own his anger to suppress,
> My only hope is found in Jesus' righteousness.
> — Norman J. Clayton, 1945
>
> Thy righteousness, O Christ, alone can cover me:
> No righteousness avails save that which is of thee.
> — Horatius Bonar, 1857
>
> Jesus, thy blood and righteousness,
> My beauty are, my glorious dress;
> 'Midst flaming worlds, in these arrayed,
> With joy shall I lift up my head.
>
> Bold shall I stand in thy great day;
> For who aught to my charge shall lay?
> Fully absolved through these I am
> From sin and fear, from guilt and shame.
> — Nikolaus Ludwig von Zinzendorf, 1739

When one begins to discuss Paul's doctrine of justification he should be aware that, according to the inspired Apostle himself, he has come to the heart and core of Paul's gospel. For Paul gives first place in his letter to the Romans – his most systematic exposition of the character of the gospel of God – to the 'good news' that God graciously justifies sinners through faith alone in Jesus Christ apart from the works of law.[1] The centrality of the doctrine of justification by faith alone in the Christian gospel may be seen in the fact that when Paul begins to elucidate the 'gospel of God' to which he had been set apart (Rom 1:1), of which he was not ashamed (Rom 1:16), and which he

---

1. Herman Ridderbos, *Paul: An Outline of His Theology*, translated by John R. DeWitt (Grand Rapids: Eerdmans, 1975), 160-61.

proclaimed early on at Pisidian Antioch (Acts 13:38-39), he does so precisely in terms of justification by faith. He declares that 'in the gospel a righteousness from God is revealed, a righteousness that is by faith, from first to last' (Rom 1:17).[2] Consequently, great care must be taken when elucidating this doctrine lest one end up declaring 'a different gospel – which is really no gospel at all' (Gal 1:6-7) and bring down upon himself the apostolic condemnation (Gal 1:8-9). To illustrate, one occasionally hears justification popularly defined as God 'looking at me "just if I'd" never sinned'. This is an example of a (very) partial truth becoming virtually an untruth since nothing is said in such a definition concerning the ground of justification or the instrumentality through which justification is obtained. Much more accurately, the *Westminster Shorter Catechism* defines justification as 'an act of God's free grace, wherein he pardoneth all our sins, and accepteth us as righteous in his sight, only for the righteousness of Christ, imputed to us, and received by faith alone' (Question 33).

The Instrumental Function of Faith in Jesus Christ

The first thing I wish to discuss is that which, according to Paul, is the necessary instrument for justification before God – faith in Jesus Christ.[3]

For Paul faith in Jesus Christ is nothing more or less than trustful repose in the finished work of Jesus Christ. Paul discovered faith's instrumental character relative to justification in the Old Testament, specifically in Abraham's justification (Gen 15:6; see Rom 4:2-3), David's teaching in Psalm 32:1-2 (see Rom 4:6-8), and Habakkuk 2:4 (see Rom 1:17; Gal 3:11; Heb 10:38). The Reformers, following Paul, quite properly saw that it is not faith *per se* that saves but Christ who saves through or by the instrumentality of the sinner's faith in him:

---

2. The word 'Gospels' (upper case) is used to designate the four inspired 'lives of Jesus' in the New Testament which serve (with Acts) as something of a 'historical prologue' for the New Testament viewed as a covenant document. These four New Testament books, however, primarily provide in their inspired portrayals of the life of Christ the *historical* basis for *something else* that the New Testament calls the 'gospel [lower case] of God', namely, the 'good news' to mankind regarding the *salvific significance* of Christ's life, death and resurrection.

3. Ridderbos's treatments of 'Faith as the Mode of Existence of the New Life' and 'The Nature of Faith' in his *Paul: An Outline of His Theology*, 231-36 and 237-52 respectively, are well worth the student's effort to digest.

...the *saving power* of faith resides...not in itself, but in the Almighty Saviour on whom it rests. It is never on account of its formal nature as a psychic act that faith is conceived in Scripture to be saving, – as if this frame of mind or attitude of heart were itself a virtue with claims on God for reward.... It is not faith that saves, but faith in Jesus Christ.... It is not, strictly speaking, even faith in Christ that saves, but Christ that saves through faith. The saving power resides exclusively, not in the act of faith or the attitude of faith or the nature of faith, but in the object of faith;...we could not more radically misconceive [the biblical representation of faith] than by transferring to faith even the smallest fraction of that saving energy which is attributed in the Scriptures solely to Christ himself.[4]

The Reformers' clarity of vision respecting the instrumental function of faith with the real repository of salvific power being Christ himself and Christ alone resulted from their recognition that Scripture everywhere represents saving faith as (1) the gift of grace, (2) the diametrical opposite of law-keeping with regard to its referent, and (3) the only human response to God's effectual summons which comports with grace.

I. Faith's 'gift character' as procured by Christ's cross work and effected by regeneration

As with repentance unto life which is depicted in Scripture as a gift of grace (Ps 80:3, 7, 19; Jer 31:18; Lam 5:21; Acts 5:31; 11:18; 2 Tim 2:25), faith in Jesus Christ is also represented in Scripture as a 'saving grace', that is, as a saving *gift*. Saving faith, as with repentance unto life and 'every [other] spiritual blessing in the heavenly realms', was divinely provided for in election (Eph 1:3-4), procured for the elect by Christ's cross work, and actually wrought in them, as an effect of his Spirit's regenerating activity, normally in conjunction with the ministry of the Word. The following Scripture verses put the 'gift character' of saving faith beyond doubt:

Acts 13:46-48: Paul declared to the Jews of Pisidian Antioch, after they had blasphemed the Word of God: '...since you repudiate it, and *judge yourselves unworthy* [οὐκ ἀξίους κρίνετε ἑαυτοὺς] of eternal life, behold, we are turning to the Gentiles.' Luke then reports that

---

4. Benjamin B. Warfield, 'Faith' in *Biblical and Theological Studies* (Philadelphia: Presbyterian and Reformed, 1952), 424-25.

the Gentiles to whom Paul turned 'began to rejoice and glorify the word of the Lord, and as many as *were appointed* [ἦσαν τεταγμένοι] unto eternal life *believed* [ἐπίστευσαν]'.

Luke teaches here that, unlike the blaspheming Jews who repudiated the Word of God and *judged themselves unworthy* of eternal life (reflexive action), the reception of the Word of God by the believing Gentiles was due to the fact that they *had been appointed* unto eternal life (passive voice). When this passive voice is interpreted actively, it is apparent that Luke traced the Gentiles' believing reception of the Word of God back to their divine election as the ultimate source from which their faith originated.

Acts 16:14: 'The Lord opened [Lydia's] heart to respond to the things spoken by Paul.'

Clearly, Lydia's heart response to Paul's word was a faith response, but it was prompted by the Lord's regenerating work of 'opening' or enlightening her heart to it.

Acts 18:27: Apollos 'helped greatly *those who had believed through grace* [τοῖς πεπιστευκόσιν διὰ τῆς χάριτος]'.

Ephesians 2:8-9: To the Ephesians Paul writes: '...by grace you have been saved *through faith* [διὰ πίστεως]– and *this* [τοῦτο] not of yourselves, it is *the gift of God* [θεοῦ τὸ δῶρον] – not of works, lest any man should boast.'

Even though 'faith' is a feminine noun in the Greek and 'this' is a neuter demonstrative pronoun, it is still entirely possible that Paul intended to teach that 'faith', the nearest possible antecedent, is the antecedent of the pronoun 'this', and accordingly that saving faith is the gift of God. It is permissible in Greek syntax for the neuter pronoun to refer antecedently to a feminine noun, particularly when it serves to render more prominent the matter previously referred to (see, for example, 'your salvation [σωτηρίας], and this [τοῦτο] from God' – Phil 1:28; see also 1 Cor 6:6, 8).[5] The only other possible antecedents to the τοῦτο are (1) the earlier feminine dative noun 'grace' (χάριτί) which hardly needs to be defined as a 'gift of God'; (2) the nominal

---

5. See Abraham Kuyper, *The Work of the Holy Spirit*, translated by H. de Vries (Grand Rapids: Eerdmans, 1946), chap. XXXIX, 407-14, for his argument supporting this handling of Ephesians 2:8-9.

idea of 'salvation' (σωτηρία) implied in the verbal idea 'you have been saved', which Paul has already implied is a gift by his use of χάριτί, and like 'grace' (χάριτί) and 'faith' (πίστεως) is also feminine in Greek; or (3) the entire preceding notion of 'salvation by grace through faith', which, of course, amounts to saying that faith, along with grace and salvation, is the gift of God.[6] In whatever way the text is exegeted, when all of its features are taken into account, the conclusion is still unavoidable that faith in Jesus Christ is a gift of God.

Philippians 1:29: To the Philippians Paul writes: '...to you *it has been given* [ἐχαρίσθη] on behalf of Christ...*to believe on him* [τὸ εἰς αὐτὸν πιστεύειν].'

II. Faith's character as the diametrical opposite of law-keeping

With a gloriously monotonous regularity Paul pits faith against all law-keeping, viewed as its diametrical opposite. Whereas the latter relies on the human effort of the law-keeper *looking to himself* to render satisfaction before God and to earn merit, the former repudiates and *looks entirely away from self and all human effort* to the work of Jesus Christ, who alone by his obedient life and sacrificial death rendered full satisfaction before God for men.

Romans 3:20-22: '...no one will be declared righteous in his sight by observing the law...But now a righteousness from God, apart from law, has been made known.... This righteousness from God comes through faith in Jesus Christ[7] to all who believe.'

Romans 3:28: 'For we maintain that a man is justified by faith apart from observing the law.'

Romans 4:3, 5: 'What does the Scripture say? "Abraham believed God, and it was credited to him as righteousness"... to the man who

---

6. A. T. Robertson, *A Grammar of the Greek New Testament in the Light of Historical Research* (Nashville: Broadman, 1934), 704, urges that the demonstrative pronoun refers to 'the idea of salvation' in the clause before it.

7. It has been often urged in recent times that the expression, 'faith in Jesus Christ', should be rendered 'faithfulness of Jesus Christ'. While it is true that Paul's πίστεως 'Ιησοῦ Χριστοῦ can be translated either way, I prefer the traditional rendering for two reasons: first, the close connection of Romans 4, in which Paul speaks of Abraham's personal faith by which he was declared righteous, with Romans 3 supports the traditional rendering; second, whereas Paul often teaches the need for personal faith in Christ for justification, there is not

does not work but trusts God who justifies the wicked, his faith is credited as righteousness.'

Romans 4:13-14: 'It was not through law that Abraham and his offspring received the promise that he would be heir of the world, but through the righteousness that comes by faith. For if those who live by law are heirs, faith has no value and the promise is worthless.'

Romans 10:4: 'Christ is the end of the law so that there may be righteousness for everyone who believes.'

Galatians 2:16: '...a man is not justified by observing the law but by faith in Jesus Christ. So we, too, have put our faith in Christ Jesus that we may be justified by faith in Christ and not by observing the law, because by observing the law no one will be justified.'

Galatians 3:11: 'Clearly no one is justified before God by the law, because "The righteous will live by faith." '

Philippians 3:9: '...not having a righteousness of my own that comes from the law but that [righteousness] which is through faith in Christ.' (See also Rom 3:20; 4:2; Gal 2:20-21; 5:4; Tit 3:5).

From such verses it is plain that Paul clearly taught that justification is by 'faith alone' (*sola fide*). Roman Catholic apologists, of course, have always objected to the use of this *sola* ('alone') attached to *fide*, contending that nowhere does Paul say 'alone' when speaking of the faith that justifies. And, Rome continues, precisely where the Bible does attach *sola* to *fide* when speaking of justification it declares: 'You see that a person is justified *by what he does* [ἐξ ἔργων] and *not by faith alone* [οὐκ ἐκ πίστεως μόνον]' (James 2:24). All this is true enough, but I would insist, as the above citations indicate, that when Paul declares (1) that a man is justified 'by faith *apart from* [χωρὶς] works of law'; (2) that the man 'who *works not* but believes in him who justifies the ungodly' is the man whom God regards as righteous; (3) that a man is '*not* justified by works of the law but through faith'; and (4) that 'by the law no man is justified before God...because "The righteous by faith shall live," ' he *is* asserting the 'aloneness' of faith as the 'alone' instrument of

---

a single text that speaks unambiguously of the 'faithfulness of Jesus Christ' as needful for one's justification.

justification as surely as if he had used the word 'alone', and he is asserting it even more vigorously than if he had simply employed μόνος ('alone') each time in these contexts. Martin Luther replied to the criticism that the word 'alone' does not appear in Romans:

> Note...whether Paul does not assert more vehemently that faith alone justifies than I do, although he does not use the word *alone* (*sola*), which I have used. For he who says: Works do not justify, but faith justifies, certainly affirms more strongly that faith justifies than does he who says: Faith alone justifies.... Since the apostle does not ascribe anything to [works], he without doubt ascribes all to faith alone.[8]

John Calvin too, while acknowledging that μόνος does not appear in Paul's exposition of justification, urges that the thought is nonetheless there:

> Now the reader sees how fairly the Sophists today cavil against our doctrine, when we say that man is justified by faith alone. They dare not deny that man is justified by faith because it recurs so often in Scripture. But since the word 'alone' is nowhere expressed, they do not allow this addition to be made. Is it so? But what will they reply to these words of Paul where he contends that righteousness cannot be of faith unless it be free? How will a free gift agree with works? ... Does not he who takes everything from works firmly enough ascribe everything to faith alone. What, I pray, do these expressions mean: 'His righteousness has been manifested apart from the law'; and, 'Man is freely justified'; and, 'Apart from the works of the law'?[9]

Clearly, since Paul never represents faith as a good work – indeed, since Paul always sets faith off over against works as the receiving and resting upon what God has done for us in Christ and freely offers to us in Christ – then it is by faith alone that sinners are justified.[10]

---

8. Martin Luther, *What Luther Says*, edited by Ewald M. Plass (St. Louis: Concordia, 1959), 2, 707-08.

9. John Calvin, *Institutes of the Christian Religion*, 3.11.19. As for James 2:24, we will explain it in our treatment of justification.

10. The programmatic statement, 'Evangelicals and Catholics Together: The Christian Mission in the Third Millennium,' which appeared in the May 1994 issue of *First Things*, marginalizes the many stark theological differences which exist between Protestant Christianity and Roman Catholicism when its authors affirm their agreement on the Apostles' Creed and on the proposition that 'we are justified by grace through faith because of Christ' (Section I) and then on this 'confessional' basis call for an end to proselytizing each other's communicants and for a missiological ecumenism which cooperates together in evangelism and spiritual nurture (Section V).

III. Faith's character as alone comporting with a salvation by grace that excludes all human boasting.

Paul is explicit that if salvation is to be effected by God's grace (his undeserved favor and mercy) and exclude thereby all human boasting, it can only be by faith whose nature as a psychic act looks away from all the native human resources of the one believing to the Savior's salvific work which rendered full and total satisfaction before God.

Romans 4:16: '[God's promise to Abraham] comes by faith, *in order that* [ἵνα] it may be by grace.'

Romans 11:6: 'And if [a saved Jewish remnant] is by grace, then it is no longer by works [which "works" for Paul is opposed to faith]; if it were, grace would no longer be grace.'

Galatians 5:4: 'You who are trying to be justified by law [which is the diametrical opposite of being justified by faith] have been alienated from Christ; you have fallen away from grace.'

I recall on one occasion how shocked I was to hear a well-known, highly regarded preacher of the gospel say: 'I don't know why salvation is by faith in Jesus Christ. God just declared that that is the way it is going to be, and we have to accept it because God said it.' I was shocked, I say, because this preacher should have known why salvation is by faith. He should have known because Paul expressly declared: '[Salvation] comes by faith, in order that it may be by grace' (Rom 4:16).

Furthermore, only a salvation by grace alone through faith alone in Jesus Christ excludes all human boasting:

The word 'alone' after the word 'faith' in the statement's proposition on justification is thundering by its absence. As written, the statement is a capitulation to Rome's unscriptural understanding of justification, for never in the debate between Rome and the first Protestant Reformers did anyone on either side deny that sinners must be justified by faith. The whole controversy in the sixteenth century in this area turned on whether sinners were justified by faith *alone* or by faith *and* good works which earned merit before God. The Protestant Reformers, following Paul's teaching on justification in Romans and Galatians, affirmed the former and denied the latter; Rome denied the former and affirmed the latter. And the Protestant Reformers, again following Paul (compare his entire argument in Galatians), maintained that Rome's understanding was 'a different gospel – which is no gospel at all' and that the path the sinner follows here leads either to heaven or to hell.

The Doctrine of Justification

Romans 3:27-28: 'Where, then, is boasting? It is excluded. On what principle? On that of observing the law? No, but on that of faith.'

1 Corinthians 1:28-31: 'He chose the lowly things of this world and the despised things – and the things that are not – to nullify the things that are, *so that* [ὅπως] no one may boast before him. It is because of him that you are in Christ Jesus.... Therefore, as it is written: "Let him who boasts boast in the Lord."'

If God permitted the fallen creature to intrude his human works into the acquisition of salvation to the slightest degree, salvation would not be by grace alone and man would have reason to boast before him. Salvation by grace and salvation by works are mutually and totally exclusive. In sum, because salvation is by grace, salvation, including justification, must be by faith alone in Jesus Christ, the nature of which faith is to turn totally and continually away from one's own works to the work of Christ in one's behalf.

The Nature of Justification

The Catechism of the Catholic Church (1994), citing the Council of Trent (Sixth Session, Chapter VII, 1547), declares: 'Justification is not only the remission of sins, but also *the sanctification and renewal of the interior man*' (para. 1989, emphasis supplied). It also states: 'Justification is conferred in Baptism' and by it God '*makes us inwardly just* by the power of his mercy' (para. 1992, emphasis supplied).

In his review of R. C. Sproul's *Faith Alone: The Evangelical Doctrine of Justification* Donald G. Bloesch takes issue with Sproul's conclusions concerning Rome's more recent understanding of justification because, Bloesch states, Sproul

> does not appear to have kept abreast of the noteworthy attempts in the ongoing ecumenical discussion to bridge the chasm between Trent and evangelical Protestantism.[11]

To illustrate this *rapprochement*, Bloesch notes that

---

11. Donald G. Bloesch, 'Betraying the Reformation? An Evangelical Response,' *Christianity Today* (October 7, 1996), 54.

an increasing number of Roman Catholic scholars, especially in biblical studies, are coming to acknowledge the forensic or legal thrust of the New Testament concept of justification while Protestant scholars are now recognizing that justification also has a mystical dimension and is therefore more than bare imputation.[12]

Then Bloesch faults Sproul for too narrowly conceiving the options which are possible in any Roman Catholic/Protestant dialogue. Sproul allows for only three ways forward in the discussion: (1) Evangelicals would abandon *sola fide*, (2) Rome would adopt *sola fide*, and (3) the two sides would agree that *sola fide* is not essential to the gospel. Bloesch responds:

Yet there may be another option: to restate the issues of the past in a new way that takes into account both God's sovereign grace and human responsibility in living a life of obedience in the power of this grace. (55)

In response to Bloesch's first criticism of Sproul I would point out that Sproul makes numerous references to the *Catechism of the Catholic Church* (1994) (see *his Faith Alone*, 122-3, 141, 142, 43, 149, 150), which contains the most recent *official* Roman Catholic statement on justification. So he has not ignored Rome's *official* modern statements. By Bloesch's own admission, what he is speaking about are 'noteworthy attempts in the ongoing ecumenical discussion to bridge the chasm' which as far as I know have still not received the Roman Magisterium's and the Pope's official *imprimatur*. As for the 1983 document, 'Justification by Faith', which Bloesch mentions,[13] it is misleading on Bloesch's part to suggest that this document shows 'new ways of stating the doctrine of justification without compromising the tenets of either Reformation or Catholic faith.'[14] The document fails, in my opinion, to resolve the tension that exists between the parties at precisely the point that biblical Protestantism insists must be settled: Is one justified by faith *alone* in Christ's work or is one justified by faith in Christ's work *plus* something that the 'being justified' man must do?

---

12. Bloesch, 'Betraying the Reformation? An Evangelical Response,' 54.
13. See *Justification by Faith: Lutherans and Catholics in Dialogue VII*, edited by H. George Anderson, T. Austin Murphy, and Joseph A. Burgess [Minneapolis: Augsburg, 1985], 15-74.
14. Bloesch, 'Betraying the Reformation? An Evangelical Response,' 54.

Because Bloesch touts the statements emerging from the dialogues between the Lutheran World Federation (LWF) and the Pontifical Council for Promoting Christian Unity (PCPCU) as evidence of the *rapprochement* and growing consensus between these two church bodies on the crucial doctrine of justification, a brief discussion of the more recent 'The Joint Declaration on the Doctrine of Justification' is in order. This was finalized in 1997 and submitted for adoption to the Roman Catholic Church and to all the Lutheran churches in the world. An overwhelming number of member churches of the LWF approved this eleven-page document by early 1998, and on June 16, 1998 the Council of the LWF approved it unanimously. The generally positive official Roman Catholic response came nine days later. It is extremely important to note, however, that the document does not claim to be a synthesis of two opposing doctrines of justification; rather, it attempts to be an effort at 'reconciled diversity', a 'differentiated consensus', of two different doctrines of justification. It defines its consensus in terms of a 'bidimensionality' in which it declares that on one level there is a fundamental commonality of the two doctrines of justification and on the other level there are remaining differences. But an orthodox Protestant can only gasp when he reads what the 'Declaration' hails in paragraph 15 as the 'fundamental commonality' of the two doctrines of justification:

> By grace alone, in faith in Christ's saving work and not because of any merit on our part, we are accepted by God and receive the Holy Spirit, who renews our hearts while equipping and calling us to good works.

This basic statement is then clarified in paragraphs 19, 22, 25, 28, 31, 34, and 37, allegedly developing the commonality on the basic truths of justification point by point.

No statement could illustrate more clearly than does this Declaration that Sproul's 'only three options' is correct. This definition of justification is not the biblical meaning of justification by any stretch of the imagination. Rather, it is a wholesale abandonment of the Reformation *sola fide* as the instrument of justification and essentially an adoption of Rome's view of justification in terms of the Spirit's inner work of sanctification (Sproul's first option). In this 'commonality' statement Rome has given up nothing; the Lutherans have abandoned Luther and the magisterial Reformation.

Little wonder that reaction among many orthodox Lutheran pastors has ranged from amazement to disappointment to anger.

With reference to Bloesch's second criticism, I would like to know what the 'mystical dimension' in justification is. And I wonder who the evangelical theologians are who would represent justification simply as 'bare imputation'. Certainly not I, and I do not think that Sproul so represents justification either. For justification includes the forgiveness of sin, all sin.

Finally, I would concur with Sproul *contra* Bloesch that Sproul's are the only three options. As soon as Bloesch attempts to suggest a fourth, he misrepresents what the issue dividing Protestantism and Rome really is and brings the doctrine of sanctification into the discussion of justification, which is to ask Protestantism to abandon its *sola fide* position and to adopt Rome's position.

Over against Rome's tragically defective representation of justification, justification *per se* says nothing about the subjective transformation that necessarily begins to occur within the inner life of the Christian through the progressive infusion of grace that commences with the new birth (which subjective transformation Scripture views as progressive sanctification). Rather, justification refers to God's *wholly* objective, *wholly* forensic judgment concerning the sinner's standing before the Law, by which forensic judgment God declares that the sinner is righteous in his sight because of both the imputation of his sin to Christ on which ground he is pardoned and the imputation of Christ's perfect obedience to him on which ground he is constituted righteous before God. In other words, '*for the one who does not work* [τῷ μὴ ἐργαζομένῳ], but *believes* [πιστεύοντι] *in him*[15] *who justifies the ungodly* [τὸν δικαιοῦντα τὸν ἀσεβῆ]' (Rom 4:5),[16] God *pardons* him of all his sins (Acts 10:43;

---

15. We would be wrong if we spoke of the object of justifying faith as being Christ alone. Both in Romans 4:5 and in Romans 4:24 Paul declares that the object of saving faith is also the Father – the one who justifies the ungodly and the one who raised Jesus from the dead. We may safely say that justifying faith is directed toward all the persons of the triune Godhead.

16. On the basis of Paul's statement in Romans 4:5 to the effect that God 'justifies the ungodly' – the same Greek phrase as is used in the LXX in Exodus 23:7 and Isaiah 5:23 of corrupt judgments on the part of human judges which God will not tolerate – J. I. Packer declares that Paul's doctrine of justification is a 'startling doctrine' ('Justification' in *Evangelical Dictionary of Theology* [Grand Rapids: Baker, 1984], 595). For not only does Paul declare that God does precisely what he commanded human judges not to do but also that he does it in a manner designed 'to demonstrate his justice' (Rom 3:25-26). Of course, Paul relieves what otherwise would be a problem of theodicy by teaching that God justifies

The Doctrine of Justification

Rom 4:6-7)[17] and *constitutes* him righteous by imputing or reckoning the righteousness of Christ to him (Rom 5:1, 19; 2 Cor 5:21).[18] And on the basis of his *constituting* the ungodly man righteous by his act of imputation, God simultaneously *declares* the ungodly man to be righteous in his sight. The now-justified ungodly man is then, to employ Luther's expression, *simul iustus et peccator* ('simultaneously a righteous man and a sinner').

The doctrine of justification means then that in God's sight the ungodly man, now 'in Christ', has perfectly kept the moral law of God, which also means in turn that 'in Christ' he has perfectly loved God with all his heart, soul, mind, and strength and his neighbor as himself. It means that saving faith is directed to the doing and dying of Christ alone (*solus Christus*) and not to the good works or inner experience of the believer. It means that the Christian's righteousness before God is *in heaven* at the right hand of God in Jesus Christ and *not on earth* within the believer. It means that the ground of our justification is the vicarious work of Christ *for* us, not the gracious work of the Spirit *in* us. It means that the faith-righteousness of justification is not personal but vicarious, not infused but imputed, not experiential but judicial, not psychological but legal, not our own but a righteousness alien to us and outside of us (*iustitia alienum et extra nos*), not earned but graciously given (*sola gratia*) through faith in Christ which is itself a gift of grace. It means also in its declarative character that justification possesses an eschatological dimension, for it amounts to the divine verdict of the Eschaton being brought forward from the Great Assize and rendered here and now with respect to the repentant, believing sinner. By God's act of justifying him through faith in Christ, the sinner, as it were, has been brought, 'before the time', to the Final Assize and has already passed successfully through it, having been acquitted of any and all charges of sin brought against him by Satan, the law, and his own conscience! Justification then, properly conceived, contributes in a decisive way to the

---

the ungodly on just grounds, namely, that the claims of God's law upon them have been fully satisfied by Jesus Christ's doing and dying in their stead.
17. See Acts 10:43 – '...everyone who believes *has received* [λαβεῖν] forgiveness of sins,' and Romans 4:6-7 – 'David also speaks of the blessedness upon the man to whom God *reckons righteousness apart from works*: "Blessed are those whose lawless deeds *have been forgiven* [ἀφέθησαν] and whose sins *have been covered* [ἐπεκαλύφθησαν]." '
18. See Romans 5:1 – '...*having been justified* [δικαιωθέντες] by faith,' and 5:19 – '...so also through the obedience of the one man the many *shall be constituted* [κατασταθήσονται] righteous.'

Calvinistic doctrine of the eternal security of the believer. Let us now look in greater detail at some of the specific features of justification.

I. Justification's character as a juridical or forensic determination, that is, as a legal judgment

The primary Old Testament word-group dealing with justification comes from the verb root צָדַק and the New Testament word-group comes from the verb δικαιόω. John Murray demonstrates that 'there is a pervasive use of the forensic signification of the root צָדַק in the Qal, Hiphil, and Piel stems and the one instance of the Hithpael...is not essentially different',[19] and that the same is true of δικαιόω in both the Septuagint and the New Testament.[20] Leon Morris points out that 'verbs ending in -όω and referring to moral qualities have a declarative sense [see ἀξιόω, "to deem worthy," not "to make worthy"; ὁμοιόω, "to declare to be like," not "to make like"]; they do not mean "to make".'[21] That justification is an objective forensic judgment, as opposed to a subjective transformation, is evidenced, first, by the meaning of the term itself in the following contexts:

Deuteronomy 25:1: 'When men have a dispute, they are to take it to court and the judges will decide the case, *justifying* [Hiphil] *the righteous* and condemning the guilty.'

In justifying the righteous man, the judges were not *making* that man righteous; rather, they were *declaring* him to be what the evidence presented in the case showed him already to be.

Job 32:2: According to Elihu, Job '*justified* [Piel] *himself* before God'. In Elihu's opinion, Job was arguing his innocence before God, that is, declaring himself righteous before God.

Proverbs 17:15: '*Justifying* [Hiphil] *the guilty* and *condemning* [מַצְדִּיק רָשָׁע] the innocent – the Lord detests them both' (see also Ex 23:7; Isa 5:23).

---

19. John Murray, 'Appendix A: Justification,' *The Epistle to the Romans* (Grand Rapids: Eerdmans, 1968), I, 336-62, especially 339. Murray's treatment of justification in this appendix is one of the finest treatments anywhere in English. I strongly recommend it to anyone desiring to understand Paul's teaching.
20. Murray, *Romans*, I, 339-40, 351.
21. Leon Morris, *New Testament Theology* (Grand Rapids: Zondervan, 1986), 70.

The Doctrine of Justification

This is obviously a proverb directed toward the judges of the land. That judge who for a bribe (see 17:23) declared the guilty man to be righteous or who declared the innocent man to be guilty in either case provoked the Lord to anger.

Luke 7:29: '... they [the people] justified God.'
These people declared or acknowledged God to be just; they quite obviously did not make him so (see also 10:29; 16:15).

Romans 3:4: 'As it is written: "So that you [God] may be justified when you speak...."'
God cannot be 'made righteous'; the expression obviously means 'shown to be righteous' or 'vindicated'.

That justification is an objective forensic judgment, as opposed to a subjective transformation, is evidenced, secondly, by the fact that the antithesis of justification is invariably condemnation which latter term is clearly a juridical or forensic determination; for example:

Deuteronomy 25:1: '...*justifying* the guilty and *condemning* the innocent.' (see also Prov 17:15)

1 Kings 8:32: 'Judge between your servants, *condemning* the guilty.... *Justify* the innocent....' (see also 2 Chr 6:23)

Matthew 12:37: 'For by your words you will be *justified*, and by your words you will be *condemned*.'

Romans 5:16: '...the judgment followed one transgression and brought *condemnation*, but the gift followed many transgressions and brought *justification*.'

Romans 8:33-34: 'It is God who *justifies*. Who is he that *condemns*?'

That justification is an objective forensic judgment, as opposed to a subjective transformation, is evidenced, thirdly, by contextual considerations which place the act of justifying in the context of legal judgments. For example:

Psalm 143:2: 'Do not bring your servant into judgment, for no one living is righteous [that is, is justified] before you.'

Romans 3:19-20: 'Now we know that whatever the law says, it says to those who are under the law, that every mouth may be silenced and the whole world held accountable to God. Therefore no one will be declared righteous in his sight by observing the law.'

Romans 8:33: 'Who will bring any charge against those whom God has chosen? It is God who justifies.'[22]

This biblical evidence makes it clear and places beyond all legitimate controversy that justification is a juridical or forensic determination made by a judge.

Finally, Paul makes it quite clear that he does *not* mean by justification that the justified man acquires right standing before God because of an *infused* righteousness. Rather, the respect in which Paul declares that a man acquires right standing before God is because of an *imputed* or credited righteousness, which fact is made clear throughout Romans 4 by Paul's sustained employment of the verb λογίζομαι ('count, reckon, credit, look upon as'):

Romans 4:3: 'What does the Scripture say? "Abraham believed God, and it *was credited* [ἐλογίσθη] to him as righteousness."'

Romans 4:4: '...when a man works, his wages are *not credited* [οὐ λογίζεται] to him as a gift, but as an obligation.'

Romans 4:5: '...to the man who does not work but trusts God who justifies the ungodly, his faith is *credited* [λογίζεται] as righteousness.'

Romans 4:6: '...the man to whom God credits [λογίζεται] righteousness apart from works.'

Romans 4:8: 'Blessed is the man whose sin the Lord will *never count* [οὐ μὴ λογίσηται] against him.'

Romans 4:9: 'We have been saying that Abraham's faith *was credited* [ἐλογίσθη] to him as righteousness.'

Romans 4:10: 'Under what circumstances was *it credited* [ἐλογίσθη]?'

---

22. See Louis Berkhof's discussion, *Systematic Theology* (Grand Rapids: Eerdmans, 1932), 510-11.

The Doctrine of Justification

Romans 4:11: '...[Abraham] is the father of all who believe but have not been circumcised, in order that righteousness *might be credited* [λογισθῆναι] to them.'

Romans 4:22: 'This is why "*it was credited* [ἐλογίσθη] to him as righteousness".'

Romans 4:23-24: 'The words "it was credited [ἐλογίσθη] to him" were written not for him alone, but also for us, to whom God *will credit* [λογίζεσθαι] righteousness – for us who believe in him who raised Jesus our Lord from the dead.'

It is clear that in God's declaring the guilty person righteous in his sight, he constitutes that person righteous by the act of imputing an alien righteous to him. But whose righteousness?

II. The righteousness of justification the alien righteousness of Jesus Christ

Three passages in particular in Paul's writings pinpoint the source of our righteousness in justification. It is the alien righteousness of Christ's active and passive obedience.

Romans 5:19: 'For just as through the disobedience of the one man [Adam] the many were made sinners, so through the obedience of the one man [Christ] the many will be made righteous.'

2 Corinthians 5:21: 'God made him who had no sin [Christ] to be sin for us, so that in him we might become the righteousness of God.'

Philippians 3:8-9: 'What is more, I consider everything a loss compared to the surpassing greatness of knowing Christ Jesus my Lord, for whose sake I have lost all things. I consider them rubbish, that I may gain Christ and be found in him, not having a righteousness of my own that comes from the law, but that which is through faith in Christ – the righteousness that comes from God and is by faith.'

Some have construed the righteousness contemplated in justification as the psychic act of faith itself in Christ and have insisted that Genesis 15:6 teaches this: 'Abram believed the Lord, and he credited it [that is, his faith] to him as righteousness' (see also Rom 4:3, 5, 9, 22, 23; Gal 3:6; Jas 2:23). Never is *our* faith-act, however, represented in the New Testament as the ground or the cause of our righteousness. If this were so, faith would become a meritorious work, an idea everywhere opposed by Paul who pits faith in Christ over against every human work. We are said to be justified 'by faith' (the simple dative – Rom 3:28, 5:2), 'by faith' (ἐκ with the genitive – Rom 1:17; 3:30; 4:16 (twice), 5:1; 9:30; 10:6; Gal 2:16; 3:8, 11, 24; Heb 10:38), 'through faith' (διά with the genitive – Rom 3:22, 25, 30; Gal 2:16; Phil 3:9), 'upon faith' (ἐπί with the genitive – Phil 3:9), and 'according to faith' (κατά with the accusative – Heb 11:7). But never are we said to be justified 'because of faith' or 'on account of faith' (διά with the accusative). In other words, the psychic act of faith is not the righteousness of justification. That distinction the Scriptures reserve for Christ's God-righteousness alone. Faith in Christ is simply the regenerated sinner's saving response to God's effectual summons by means of which the righteousness of Christ— the sole ground of justification—is imputed to him. John Murray observes in this connection:

> ...the consideration that appears more relevant than any other [when interpreting the Genesis 15:6 formula] is that the righteousness contemplated in justification is righteousness by faith in contrast with righteousness by works and the emphasis falls to such an extent upon this fact that although it is a God-righteousness yet it is also and with equal emphasis a faith-righteousness. In reality these two features are correlative: it is the righteousness of God brought to bear upon us because it is by faith, and it is by faith that we become the beneficiaries of this righteousness because it is a God-righteousness. So indispensable is this complementation in the justification of the ungodly that the righteousness may be called "the righteousness of God" or "the righteousness of faith" without in the least implying that faith sustains the same relation to this righteousness that God does. In like manner in the formula of Gen. 15:6 faith can be regarded as that which is reckoned for righteousness without thereby implying that it sustains the same relation to justification as does the righteousness of God. The righteousness is a God-righteousness and it is a faith-righteousness. But it is a God-righteousness because it is of divine property; it is a faith righteousness because it is brought to bear upon us by *faith*. When faith is said to be imputed for righteousness this variation of formula is warranted

by the correlativity of righteousness and faith, and it is in terms of this correlativity that the formula is to be interpreted rather than in terms of equation.[23]

Over against Rome's polemic that the righteousness of justification is to be construed in terms of 'sanctification and renewal of the inward man', that is, in terms of the Christian's 'being inwardly made increasingly righteous' through the impartation or infusion of sanctifying grace[24] stands the consentient biblical (and Protestant) insistence that the righteousness of justification is neither a righteousness which comes through any effort on our part nor a righteousness infused or generated in us by the Holy Spirit. Rather, the righteousness of justification, as we have already said, is the objective God-righteousness of Jesus Christ which God the Father, in the very act of justifying the ungodly man, *imputes* to him, thereby *constituting* him legally righteous in his sight (which 'constituting' act, of course, no human judge can do when a guilty party stands before him).

That the righteousness of justification is the God-righteousness of the divine Christ himself, which is imputed or reckoned to the penitent sinner *the moment* he places his confidence in him (see justification as a finished work in Rom 5:1 – '*having been* justified'), is amply testified to when the Scriptures teach that we are justified

(1) in Christ (Isa 45:24-25; Acts 13:39; Rom 8:1; 1 Cor 6:11; Gal 2:17; Phil 3:9),

(2) by Christ's death-work (Rom 3:24-25; 5:9; 8:33-34),

(3) not by our own but *by the righteousness of God* (Isa 61:10; Rom 1:17; 3:21-22; 10:3; 2 Cor 5:21; Phil 3:9; Titus 3:5),[25] and

---

23. Murray, *Collected Writings*, 2, 358-59.

24. See Council of Trent, Sixth Session: 'Decree Concerning Justification,' particularly Chapters VII-X and Canons 9-12. In accord with the medieval Schoolmen such as Thomas Aquinas, the *Catechism of the Catholic Church* (1994), citing Trent, defines justification as 'not only the remission of sins [by baptism] but also the sanctification and renewal of the interior man' (para 1989), and by justification, the reader is informed, God 'makes us inwardly just' (para 1992); indeed, justification 'entails the *sanctification* of [the inner man's] whole being' (para. 1995, emphasis in original).

John H. Gerstner ('Aquinas Was a Protestant,' *Tabletalk* [May 1994] 13-15, 52) has argued that Thomas Aquinas held to a Protestant view of justification. See my response, 'Dr. John H. Gerstner on Thomas Aquinas as a Protestant,' *Westminster Theological Journal* 59, no. 1 (Spring 1997), 113-21.

25. Basing his conclusions on his expositions of Philippians 3:9, 2 Corinthians 5:20-21, and Romans 3:21-26, 10:2-4, and 1:17 in that order, N. T. Wright, *What Saint Paul Really Said* (Grand Rapids: Eerdmans, 1997), 95-100, declares that Paul's phrase δικαιοσύνη θεοῦ

(4) by the righteousness and obedience of Christ (Rom 5:17-19). In sum, the only ground of justification is the perfect God-righteousness of Christ which God the Father imputes to every sinner who places his confidence in the obedience and satisfaction of his Son. Said another way, the moment the sinner, through faith in Jesus Christ, turns away from every human resource and rests in Christ's saving work alone, the Father imputes his well-beloved Son's preceptive (active) obedience to him and accepts him as righteous in his sight. And the sinner, now a Christian, may (and as far as his righteousness before God is concerned he must) sing thereafter, in the words of Horatius Bonar:

> Not what my hands have done can save my guilty soul;
>   Not what my toiling flesh has borne can make my spirit whole.
> Not what I feel or do can give me peace with God;
>   Not all my prayers and sighs and tears can bear my awful load.
>
> Thy work alone, O Christ, can ease this weight of sin;
>   Thy blood alone, O Lamb of God, can give me peace within.
> No other work, save thine, no other blood will do;
>   No strength, save that which is divine, can bear me safely through.

('righteousness of God') refers neither to an imputed or to an imparted righteousness. Rather, the phrase, he says, speaks of God's 'covenant faithfulness, which operates through the faithfulness of Jesus Christ for the benefit of all those who in turn are faithful' (109). He reached these conclusions by arguing (1) that 'God's righteousness' in the Septuagint, especially in Isaiah 40-55, is 'that aspect of God's character because of which he saves Israel, despite Israel's perversity and lostness...God's righteousness is thus cognate with his trustworthiness on the one hand, and Israel's salvation on the other' (96); (2) that it is this meaning which is essentially the meaning of Paul's phrase, and (3) that Paul's phrase πίστεως Ἰησοῦ Χριστοῦ in Romans 3:22 means the same thing, namely, 'the faithfulness of Jesus Christ' and not 'faith in Jesus Christ' (106).

It is true that God's 'righteousness' is employed at times in the Old Testament in a remunerative or saving sense (see my *A New Systematic Theology of the Christian Faith* [Nashville: Thomas Nelson, 1998], 197-99). But it is extremely doubtful whether the references to δικαιοσύνη θεοῦ in these Pauline passages refer generally to God's covenant faithfulness and not more specifically to the God-righteousness which he imputes to those who trust in Christ (see the arguments in the chapter). It is also doubtful whether πίστεως Ἰησοῦ Χριστοῦ in Romans 3:22 is to be translated 'faithfulness of Jesus Christ' and not the more traditional 'faith in Jesus Christ', construing Ἰησοῦ Χριστοῦ as an objective genitive (see fn 7 and such Pauline statements as ἡμεῖς εἰς Χριστὸν Ἰησοῦν ἐπιστεύσαμεν, 'we into Christ Jesus believed', Gal 2:16). Wright's conclusions, though well-intended, must be rejected.

Objections to The Protestant Representation of Paul's Doctrine

The following six objections have been raised against the Protestant teaching that by faith alone in Jesus Christ, completely apart from the works of law, God immediately pardons the ungodly of all his sins and constitutes him righteous in his sight by imputing Christ's righteousness to him:

(1) such teaching encourages licentious living and hinders the development of true ethical conduct;

(2) James' teaching on justification by faith and works contradicts it;

(3) the fact that the final judgment is according to works in which there is a corresponding distribution of rewards to the faithful contravenes it;

(4) the fact that the Christian needs to continue to seek God's forgiveness for his sins throughout his life opposes it;

(5) justification, so construed, grounds the Christian life in a 'legal fiction', a not-according-to-truth 'as if'; and

(6) the Protestant doctrine carries grave implications for millions of professing Christians within Christendom. We will consider each in turn.

I. The Protestant doctrine leads to license

With regard to the contention that the teaching of justification by faith alone apart from law-keeping leads to licence and lasciviousness, Paul himself had to respond to this objection (see Rom 3:8), which fact in itself implies that the Protestant understanding of justification accords with Paul's teaching (a good test of the correctness of one's theology is whether one meets the same objections to it that Paul met). Paul meets this objection head on with his doctrine of the Christian's union with Christ (Rom 6-7; 2 Cor 5:14-15; Gal 3:1-5). He understood better than any other man of his time that to ground his summons of the Christian to a holy walk in anything other than salvation by grace alone through faith alone would only lead to legalism, self-righteousness, and ultimate frustration on the part of those who would become aware through the law's convicting power, like he himself had become aware, of the fact that all their law-keeping efforts to satisfy God fall far short of his perfect standards of righteousness and holiness. He knew too that the Christian, united as he is to Christ in his death to sin and his resurrection to newness of life (Rom 6:1-14), will not want to sin, indeed, will in gratitude for his salvation immediately and necessarily desire to live, no longer for himself, but for him who died and rose again for him (2 Cor 5:15). Consequently, harboring no fear that his teaching, when properly perceived, encourages men to moral license, Paul proclaimed that men are justified by faith apart from all law-keeping, that is, are saved by grace alone through faith alone; and this not of themselves, it is the gift of God, not of works, lest any man should boast.

II. James's teaching opposes the Protestant doctrine

It has been urged by Roman Catholic apologists (see Council of Trent, Sixth Session, Chapters VII, X) that James 2:14-26 is a corrective to the Protestant (not the Pauline) teaching that justification is through faith alone completely apart from works, for James expressly declares: '...a man is justified by works, and not by faith alone [ἐξ ἔργων δικαιοῦται ἄνθρωπος καὶ οὐκ ἐκ πίστεως μόνον]' (2:24). But a careful analysis of James' teaching will disclose that 'in James the accent [falls] upon the probative character of good works, whereas in the Pauline polemic the accent falls without question upon the judicially constitutive and declarative [character of justification]'.[26] Paul and James clearly mean something different by 'justified', 'faith', and 'works', and they turn to different events in Abraham's life to support their respective applications of Genesis 15:6. Consider the following:

Whereas Paul intends by 'justified' the *actual* act on God's part whereby he pardons and imputes righteousness to the ungodly, James intends by 'justified' the verdict which God *declares* when the *actually* (previously) justified man has *demonstrated* his actual righteous state by obedience and good works.[27]

---

26. Murray, 'Appendix A: Justification,' *The Epistle to the Romans*, 1, 351.
27. That a distinction must be drawn between God's *actual* act of justification whereby he pardons and constitutes the sinner righteous and his subsequent *declaring* act of justification whereby he openly acquits the justified sinner before others is verified by our Lord's actions in connection with the woman who washed his feet in Luke 7:36-50. He openly declares to Simon the Pharisee and to the woman herself that her many sins were forgiven (vss 47-48) '*because* she loved much [ὅτι ἠγάπησεν πολύ]' (47). But it is apparent that she had already been *actually* forgiven on some previous occasion because her acts of devotion toward him – the fruit and evidence of a lively faith – were due, he states, to her having already had 'her debt canceled' (41-43). The chain of events then is as follows: On some previous occasion Jesus had forgiven her (her *actual* justification). This provoked in her both love for him and acts of devotion toward him. This outward evidence of her justified state evoked from Christ his open declaration that she was forgiven (her *declared* justification).

The Doctrine of Justification

Whereas Paul intends by 'faith' trustful repose in the merits of Christ alone for pardon and righteousness, James is addressing those whose 'faith' was tending toward, if not already, a cold, orthodox intellectualism in which bare assent is given to such propositions as 'God is one', which even the demons confess with seemingly greater appreciation (2:19) but which is devoid of love for the brethren.

Whereas Paul, when he repudiates 'works', intends 'works of law', that is, any and every work of *whatever* kind done for the sake of acquiring merit, James intends by 'works' acts of kindness toward those in need performed as the fruit and evidence of the actual justified state and a true and vital faith (2:14-17).

Whereas Paul is concerned with the question, how may a sinner achieve right standing before God, and turns to Genesis 15:6 to find his answer, James is concerned with the question, how is a Christian to *demonstrate* that he is *actually* justified before God and has *true* faith, and turns to Genesis 22:9-10, as the *probative* 'fulfillment' of Genesis 15:6 (see Gen 22:12), to find his answer (2:21; see also his δεῖξόν ['show'] and δείξω ['I will show'] in 2:18; and his βλέπεις ['you see'] in 2:22 and ὁρᾶτε ['you see'] in 2:24). In other words, whereas Paul is speaking to the sinner's desperation, James is speaking to the Christian's complacency.

And whereas Paul believed with all his heart that men are justified by *faith alone*, he, as forthrightly as James does (2:17, 26), insists that such faith, *if alone*, is not true but dead faith: 'For in Christ Jesus neither circumcision nor uncircumcision means anything. [What counts] is *faith working through love* [πίστις δι' ἀγάπης ἐνεργουμένη]' (Gal 5:6), which expression is hardly different in meaning from James's expression: 'faith was working together with [Abraham's] works, and by works his faith was perfected [ἡ πίστις συνήργει τοῖς ἔργοις αὐτοῦ καὶ ἐκ τῶν ἔργων ἡ πίστις ἐτελειώθη]' (2:22). Paul can also speak of the Christian's 'work of faith [τοῦ ἔργου τῆς πίστεως]' (1 Thess 1:3). And in the very context where he asserts that we are saved by grace through faith and '*not by works*', Paul can declare that we are 'created in Christ Jesus *for good works*, which God prepared beforehand that we *should walk in them*' (Eph 2:8-10). In sum, whereas for James 'faith without works is dead', for Paul 'faith working through love' is inevitable if it is true faith. Clearly, there is no contradiction between them (see *Westminster Confession of Faith*, XVI: 'Of Good Works').

III. The final judgment takes works into consideration

Rome also asserts that the fact that the final judgment is according to works, on the basis of which principle of judgment rewards are distributed to the faithful, is a further indication that a person does not achieve right standing before God by faith alone but by faith and works of satisfaction which are deserving of congruous merit.[28]

Now it cannot and should not be denied that the Scriptures uniformly represent the final judgment as a judgment of works (Ps 62:12; Eccl 12:14; Matt 16:27; 25:31-46; John 5:29; Rom 2:5-10; 1 Cor 3:13; 4:5; 2 Cor 5:10; Gal 6:7-9; 1 Pet 1:17; see also *WCF*, XXXIII/i), and that they hold forth the promise of rewards for faithful living (Ex 20:5-6; Prov 13:13; 25:21-22; Matt 5:12; 6:1, 2, 4, 16, 18, 20; 10:41; 19:29; Luke 6:37-38; Col 3:23-24; 2 Tim 4:7-8; Heb 11:26). But to assert, on the one hand, that men are justified by faith alone completely apart from works of law and, on the other, that the final judgment is according to works is to assert two entirely different things which in no way are contradictory to one another. As we have already insisted, the justified man, justified by faith alone, will produce good works 'in obedience to God's commandments [as] the fruits and evidence of a true and lively faith' (*WCF*, XVI/ii). These works, as John Murray carefully discerns,

> done in faith, from the motive of love to God, in obedience to the revealed will of God and to the end of his glory are intrinsically good and acceptable to God. As such they will be the criterion of reward in the life to come.... We must maintain...justification complete and irrevocable by grace through faith and apart from works, and at the same time, future reward according to works. In reference to these two doctrines it is important to observe the following: (i) *This future reward is not justification* and contributes nothing to that which constitutes justification. (ii) *This future reward is not salvation.* Salvation is by grace and it is not as a

---

28. Rome distinguishes between *condign* or full merit (*meritum de condigno*) which imposes an obligation upon God to reward it and *congruous* or a kind of 'half' or proportionate merit (*meritum de congruo*), which, while it does not obligate God, is meritorious enough that it is 'congruous' or 'fitting' that God should reward it. Aquinas argued that the Christian's works, if viewed only in terms of the Holy Spirit's work within him, could be viewed as entailing condign merit, but when viewed in terms of the individual himself, they should be viewed as entailing only congruous merit since no human act fully deserves the reward of salvation. The Reformers contended that all talk of merit, save for Christ's, is out of place within the context of the biblical doctrine of salvation by grace.

reward for works that we are saved. (iii) The reward has reference to the station a person is to occupy in glory and *does not have reference to the gift of glory itself*. While the reward is of grace yet the standard or criterion of judgment by which the degree of reward is to be determined is good works. (iv) This reward is not administered because good works earn or merit reward, but because God is graciously pleased to reward them. That is to say it is a reward of grace.[29]

Two conclusions are clearly in order. First, the reason why Scripture is willing to affirm a final judgment according to works is that good works being what they are—works (1) done by persons accepted by God through Christ, (2) which proceed from his Spirit, (3) and which are done in faith, (4) from the motive of love to God, (5) in obedience to God's revealed will, and (6) for his glory—*only Christians will manifest such works*. But their works, as 'the fruits and evidences of a true and lively faith', only serve to underscore the truth that their salvation is not ultimately grounded in *their* works at all but in the salvific work of the entire Godhead graciously conceived and executed in their behalf.

As for the works, on the other hand, of unregenerate men whose very 'breaking of ground' (נִר Keil: 'husbandry') is sin (Prov 21:4) and whose sacrifice is an abomination to the Lord (15:8),[30]

> although for the matter of them they may be things which God commands; and of good use both to themselves and others: yet, because they proceed not from an heart purified by faith; nor are done in a right manner, according to the Word of God; nor to a right end, the glory of God, they are therefore sinful, and cannot please God, or make a man meet to receive grace from God: and yet, their neglect of them is more sinful and displeasing to God. (*WCF*, XVI/vii)

Second, the reason why Scripture is willing to affirm the distribution of rewards to Christians as an outcome of the final judgment is because they flow, never from any sense of indebtedness on God's part toward Christians as though their labors merited them

---

29. John Murray, 'Justification,' *Collected Writings*, 2, 221, emphasis supplied.
30. I am not saying here that the non-Christian cannot perform acts of civil righteousness in this life, for indeed they can and such acts they ought to do; but such acts do not constitute those 'good works' which in the final judgment will be adjudged to be the fruit of a true and living faith in Christ.

or placed him in their debt, but always from his mercy and grace toward them. John Calvin sensitively speaks of how God shows his children mercy through the promise of rewards when he writes:

> ...Scripture leaves us no reason to be exalted in God's sight. Rather, its whole end is to restrain our pride, to humble us, cast us down, and utterly crush us. But our weakness, which would immediately collapse and fall if it did not sustain itself by this expectation and allay its own weariness by this comfort, is relieved in this way.
>
> First, let everyone consider with himself how hard it would be for him to leave and renounce not only all his possessions but himself as well. Still, it is with this first lesson that Christ initiates his pupils, that is, all the godly. Then he so trains them throughout life under the discipline of the cross that they may not set their hearts upon desire of, or reliance on, present benefits. In short, he usually so deals with them that wherever they turn their eyes, as far as this world extends, they are confronted solely with despair.... Lest they fail amidst these great tribulations, the Lord is with them, warning them to hold their heads higher, to direct their eyes farther so as to find in him that blessedness which they do not see in the world. *He calls this blessedness 'prize', 'reward', 'recompense', not weighing the merit of works, but signifying that it is a compensation for their miseries, tribulations, slanders, etc.* For this reason, nothing prevents us, with Scriptural precedent, from calling eternal life a 'recompense', because in it the Lord receives his own people from toil into repose, from affliction into a prosperous and desirable state, from sorrow into joy, from poverty into affluence, from disgrace into glory. To sum up, he changes into greater goods all the evil things that they have suffered. Thus also it will be nothing amiss if we regard holiness of life to be the way, not indeed that gives access to the glory of the Heavenly Kingdom, but by which those chosen by their God are led to its disclosure. For it is God's good pleasure to glorify those whom he has sanctified.
>
> How absurd is it, when God calls us to one end, for us to look in the other direction? Nothing is clearer than that a reward is promised for good works to relieve the weakness of our flesh by some comfort but not to puff up our hearts with vainglory. Whoever, then, deduces merit of works from this, or weighs works and reward together, wanders very far from God's own plan.[31]

That the saints of heaven recognize that all that they receive from the Lord's hand is out of sheer mercy and never as their just desert is

---

31. John Calvin, *Institutes of the Christian Religion*, III.xviii.4.

The Doctrine of Justification

borne out by the picture in Revelation 4:10-11 where we see the twenty-four elders 'casting the crowns' they have received from him before God's throne as they sing, 'You are worthy, our Lord and God, to receive glory and honor and power.' Their symbolic action suggests that all that we receive from God, even our rewards at the Final Judgment, comes to us by his grace. This is glorious to contemplate: Ultimately it is *he* who does the work in and through us and yet he rewards *us* for it as if the work originated with us (see Phil 2:12-13)!

IV. The Protestant doctrine eliminates the Christian's need and responsibility to pray daily for forgiveness.

Rome also declares that if in his act of justifying the ungodly, God instantly pardons every sin – past, present, and future – as the Protestant teaching avers (see Rom 4:6-8), then there would be no further need for the Christian daily to seek divine forgiveness for his sin, which he is required to do by such passages as Matthew 6:12 and Luke 11:4.

This objection arises from Rome's failure to distinguish between God's wrath from which the Christian's justified state delivers him and God's fatherly displeasure which the Christian may still elicit by his daily sins and for which he needs to seek forgiveness as he grows in grace. The Scriptures will not permit the Christian to choose between his justification whereby he has been juridically pardoned and delivered from the wrath to come and his on-going sanctification, one necessary aspect of which is seeking pardon for his daily transgressions which grieve the Holy Spirit of God and evoke his heavenly Father's displeasure. *The Christian must affirm both* – the fact that he has been fully pardoned juridically (his justification) and also the fact that his daily sins are an offense to his Father in heaven, whose daily forgiveness he needs if he is to grow in grace as he should (his sanctification). Beautifully does the *Westminster Confession of Faith*, XI/v, highlight this distinction:

> God doth continue to forgive the sins of those that are justified; and, although they can never fall from the state of justification, yet they may, by their sins, fall under God's fatherly displeasure, and not have the light of his countenance restored unto them, until they humble themselves, confess their sins, beg pardon, and renew their faith and repentance.

V. The Protestant doctrine makes the Christian life rest upon a legal fiction.

Rome urges that if justification is only forensic, the Christian life is made to have its beginning in a fiction. But this objection is due to Rome's failure to realize that God does not treat the justified sinner *as if* he were righteous before him when actually he is not. To the contrary, the justified sinner is *in fact* righteous in God's sight because of the 'in Christ' relationship in which he stands (2 Cor 5:21), in which relationship the righteousness of Christ is actually imputed to him.[32] It is Rome's insistence that the righteousness of justification is infused and not imputed that lies at the base of this objection. But Rome's error here is serious, for it makes the very gospel of God itself – the teaching of justification by faith alone – truly a fiction.

VI. The Protestant doctrine calls into question the salvation of millions of professing Christians throughout history.

This argument, made in our time by some Protestants against a rigid application of Protestantism's doctrine of justification by faith alone, contends that if God justifies only those who self-consciously renounce all reliance upon any and all works of righteousness which they have done or will ever do and trust in Christ's vicarious cross work alone, then one must conclude that the vast majority of professing Christians throughout history have not been justified and thus saved. This vast group would include, we are informed, such church fathers as Athanasius, Augustine, Anselm, and Aquinas who as sacerdotalists believed in baptismal regeneration and, because they confused justification and sanctification, believed also in the necessity of deeds of penance for salvation.[33] N. T. Wright declares in this connection that he found the following 'vital and liberating point...in the works of the great Anglican divine Richard Hooker', for which, he says, he will 'always be grateful':

> *One is not justified by faith by believing in justification by faith.* One is justified by faith by believing in Jesus. It follows quite clearly that a great many people are justified by faith who don't know they are justified by faith. The Galatian Christians were in fact justified by faith, though they didn't realize it and thought they had to be circumcised as well. As

---

32. See George E. Ladd's exposition of 2 Corinthians 5:21 in his *Theology of the New Testament* (Grand Rapids: Eerdmans, 1987), 466, on this issue.
33. Timothy George, 'Letters to the Editor,' *Christianity Today*, Vol. 40, No. 9 (August 12, 1996): 8.

The Doctrine of Justification

Hooker said, many pre-Reformation folk were in fact justified by faith, because they believed in Jesus, even though, not knowing about or believing in justification by faith, they lacked assurance, and then sought to fill this vacuum in other ways. Many Christians today may not be very clear about the niceties of doctrine; but, however inarticulately [!], they hold on to Jesus; and, according to Paul's teaching, they are therefore justified by faith.[34]

Wright's statements here bristle with theological ambiguity! First, who was Richard Hooker to whom Wright stands indebted for this 'liberating' insight? Hooker (1554-1600) was the most accomplished advocate for episcopacy and Erastianism that Anglicanism ever had. Rejecting the authority of Holy Scripture as the primary norm for faith, he stood opposed to Puritanism on the basis of what he regarded as the absolute fundamental of natural law. According to Hooker, while the authority of Scripture which was of paramount importance for Puritans and the authority of tradition which was of paramount importance for Roman Catholics must both give way to the mores of the changing ages, natural law never changes. Natural law is the 'voice of God' and the 'voice of the people'. I would urge then that Hooker, who also countenanced a somewhat subordinationist Christology, should not be regarded as a trustworthy theological guide, and certainly not in soteriology.

Then Wright's italicized sentence is misleading: no Protestant of whom I am aware ever taught that one is justified by believing in justification by faith. Such a statement clouds the issue, for if one thing is certain, Protestants have always taught that one is justified only by believing in the finished work of Jesus Christ. Then it is amazing that Wright would use the Galatians as the support for his thesis since it is specifically against these very people that Paul leveled his charge of having followed 'another gospel' which cannot save when, in addition to their faith in Christ, they were looking to circumcision for salvation. If salvation does regularly come to men who believe that, in order to be saved, they *must* believe in Christ plus Hooker's 'other ways' as well, why did Paul even bother to write Galatians? Why did he become so vexed at the Judaizers who were urging his converts that, in addition to their faith in Christ, they also had to be circumcised and obey the law of Moses in order to be

---

34. N. T. Wright, *What Saint Paul Really Said*, 159, emphasis in the original.

saved if they would be saved anyway? Paul would condemn Hooker's 'other ways' too as 'another gospel', as vitiations of the 'truth of the gospel', and as a making void the work of Christ. In short, what Wright finds so 'liberating' in Hooker's thought is actually the major heresy that Paul opposed in his Galatian letter!

George's and Wright's contention is aimed not so much against Protestantism's 'rigidity' as it is against Paul's insistence

(1) that there is only one gospel – justification by faith alone in Christ's cross-work (Rom 1:17; 3:28; 4:5; 10:4; Gal 2:16; 3:10-11, 26; Phil 3:8-9),

(2) that any addition to or alteration of the one gospel is another 'gospel' that is not a gospel at all (Gal 1:6-7),

(3) that those who teach any other 'gospel' stand under the anathema of God (Gal 1:8-9), and

(4) that those who rely to any degree on their own works or anything in addition to Christ to merit their salvation nullify the grace of God (Rom 11:5-6), make void the cross-work of Christ (Gal 2:21; 5:2), become debtors to keep the entire law (Gal 5:3), and in becoming such 'fall from grace' (Gal 5:4), that is, place themselves again under the curse of the law.

And as for the four church fathers named above – and many others like them[35] – it is not my place to assure the Christian world that God

---

35. It is one of the saddest facts of church history that from the post-apostolic age onward the church fell more and more into serious soteriological error, with grace and faith giving way to legalism and the doing of good works as the pronounced way of salvation. An unevangelical nomism runs virtually unabated through the writings of the church fathers. Only upon rare occasion, and not even fully in Augustine, was the voice of Paul clearly heard again before the sixteenth-century magisterial Reformation. Kenneth Escott Kirk, *The Vision of God: The Christian Doctrine of the Summum Bonum* (1928 Bampton Lectures; London: Longmans, Green, 1931), writes: 'St. Paul's indignant wonder was evoked by the reversion of a small province of the Christian Church to the legalistic spirit of the Jewish religion. Had he lived half a century or a century later, his cause for amazement would have been increased a hundredfold. The example of the Galatians might be thought to have infected the entire Christian Church; writer after writer seems to have little other interest than to express the genius of Christianity wholly in terms of law and obedience, reward and punishment' (111). J. L. Neve, *A History of Christian Thought* (Philadelphia: Muhlenberg, 1946), I. 37-9, carefully documents in the Apostolic Fathers how quickly after the age of Paul—doubtless due to Jewish and Hellenistic influences without and the tug of the Pelagian heart within—the emphasis in their preaching and writings on soteriology fell more and more upon human works and their merit and upon moralism. J. N. D. Kelly, *Early Christian Doctrine* (London: Adam & Charles Black, 1958), reaches similar conclusions (163-64, 165, 168-69, 177-78, 184). And Richard Lovelace in his 'A Call to Historic Roots and Continuity,' *The Orthodox Evangelicals*, edited by Robert Webber and Donald Bloesch (Nashville, Thomas Nelson, 1978), affirms: 'By the early second century it is clear that Christians had come to think of

justified them by faith alone even though they themselves may not have known about justification by faith alone in Christ's finished work. To judge an individual's personal salvation is God's province and his alone. Therefore, I will not speculate one way or the other about their salvation. But I will say that our attitude should, with Paul, ever be: 'Let God's truth be inviolate, though *every* man becomes thereby a liar' (Rom 3:4). What I mean by this in the present context is that the clear teaching of the Word of God should be upheld and we should not look for reasons to avoid it, even if the alternative would force us to conclude that *these* church fathers – and *all* others like them – were not saved.

---

themselves as being justified through being sanctified, accepted as righteous according to their actual obedience to the new Law of Christ' (49, emphasis supplied).

Thomas F. Torrance, *The Doctrine of Grace in the Apostolic Fathers* (Grand Rapids: Eerdmans, 1959) – whose entire work is an inquiry into the literature of the Apostolic Fathers, that is to say, into the Didache of the Twelve Apostles, the First Epistle of Clement, the Epistles of Ignatius, the Epistle of Polycarp, the Epistle of Barnabas, the Shepherd of Hermas, and the Second Epistle of Clement, in order to discern how and why such a great divergence away from the teaching of the New Testament occurred in their understanding of salvation – concludes his research by saying:

> In the Apostolic Fathers grace did not have [the] radical character [that it had in the New Testament]. The great presupposition of the Christian life, for them, was not a deed of decisive significance that cut across human life and set it on a wholly new basis grounded upon the self-giving of God. What took absolute precedence was God's call to a new life in obedience to revealed truth. Grace, as far as it was grasped, was subsidiary to that. And so religion was thought of primarily in terms of man's acts toward God, in the striving toward justification, much less in terms of God's acts for man which put him in the right with God once and for all.
>
> ...Salvation is wrought, they thought, certainly by divine pardon but on the ground of repentance, not apparently on the ground of the death of Christ alone...It was not seen that the whole of salvation is centred in the person and death of Christ, for there God has Himself come into the world and wrought a final act of redemption which undercuts all our own endeavours at self-justification, and places us in an entirely new situation in which faith alone saves a man, and through which alone is a man free to do righteousness spontaneously under the constraining love of Christ. That was not understood by the Apostolic Fathers, and it is the primary reason for the degeneration of their Christian faith into something so different from the New Testament. (133, 138, emphasis supplied)

Thus the early post-apostolic church's sub-Christian soteriological deliverances launched the church on a doctrinal trajectory that moved the entire church away from the pristine Pauline teaching on salvation by pure grace and justification by faith alone, a trajectory that would eventually harden in the work of Thomas Aquinas and become the official position of the Roman Catholic Church at the Council of Trent.

The Current Debate Over the Specific Character of the Teaching Paul Opposed by His Doctrine of Justification by Faith

I have not yet addressed what is currently the most debated topic among Paul scholars, namely, Paul's understanding of the law and more specifically the meaning of his key phrase, 'works of law' (ἔργα νόμου),[36] by which phrase he summarily characterized what he was so strongly setting off over against his own doctrine of justification by faith in Jesus Christ, namely, justification by 'works of law'. Obviously we will not be able fully to comprehend the precise nature of the doctrine Paul wants to put in its place if we do not grasp the precise nature of the teaching he so vigorously opposed. This debate is raging today between Protestant Pauline scholars, particularly German Lutheran scholars such as Rudolf Bultmann's followers, on the one hand, and the 'new perspective' views of E. P. Sanders, James D. G. Dunn and their followers, on the other.

The former view – the 'traditional Reformation view' – contends that Jews in general in Paul's day and the Pharisees in particular were obeying the law to accumulate merit before God for themselves and thereby to earn salvation, and that this is the reason Paul appears at times to inveigh against the law: his kinsmen according to the flesh or at least a large portion of first-century world Jewry (not all Jews, of course, since there was always 'a remnant chosen by grace', Rom 11:5) had come to view the law *legalistically* as the instrument for the acquisition of righteousness. C. E. B. Cranfield has argued that Paul's criticism of the law was a criticism of its then-current *perversion* into the legalism of works-righteousness; it is thus the 'legalistic misunderstanding and perversion of the law', not the law itself, which kills.[37]

---

36. Paul uses the phrase eight times: he affirms that no one can be justified by 'works of law' (Gal 2:16 [3 times]; Rom 3:20, 28), that the Spirit is not received by 'works of law' (Gal 3:2, 5), and that all those whose religious efforts are characterized by 'works of law' are under the law's curse (Gal 3:10). The simple ἔργα in Romans 4:2, 6; 9:12, 32; 11:6; and Ephesians 2:9 almost certainly has the same meaning. I will argue that Paul intended by the phrase 'things done in accordance with whatever the law commands – the moral law no less than the ritual, the ritual laws no less than the moral, with the intention of achieving right standing before God'. See τὸ ἔργον τοῦ νόμου in Romans 2:15.

Although C. E. B. Cranfield argued in his essay, 'St. Paul and the Law,' in *Scottish Journal of Theology* 17 (1964), 43-68, that Paul coined this Greek phrase because no designation was available in Greek to represent the idea of 'legalism', close equivalents have been found in the Qumran material, for example, מעשׂי תורה ('works of law') in 4QFlor 1.1-7 (= 4Q174); מעשׂין בתורה ('works in the law') in 1QS 5:20-24; 6:18; and מקצת מעשׂי התורה ('some of the works of the law') in 4QMMT 3:29, all which seem to denote the works that the Community thought the law required of it in order to maintain its separate communal existence.

The traditional Protestant view had not gone unchallenged, of course. For example, in 1894 C. G. Montefiore, a distinguished Jewish scholar, had argued that the rabbinic literature of the time speaks of a compassionate and forgiving God and of rabbis whose daily prayer was 'Sovereign of all worlds! not because of our righteous acts do we lay our supplications before you, but because of your abundant mercies' (*b. Yoma* 87b).[38] And in 1927 G. F. Moore had urged in his *Judaism in the First Centuries of the Christian Era*[39] that the earliest literature of rabbinic religion spoke constantly of grace, forgiveness and repentance. But the implications of such studies had been largely ignored by New Testament theologians. The publication of E. P. Sanders' programmatic *Paul and Palestinian Judaism*[40] in 1977, however, brought a 'rude awakening' to what Dunn calls the 'quiet

---

37. C. E. B. Cranfield, 'St. Paul and the Law,' 43-68; see also his response to his critics, ' "The Works of the Law" in the Epistle to the Romans' in *Journal for the Study of the New Testament* 43 (1991), 89-101. Of course, Paul's criticism of 'covenantal legalism' was not an innovation: both the Old Testament prophets, by their denunciation of a preoccupation with the niceties of sacrificial ritual while obedience from the heart expressed in humility, compassion, and justice for the oppressed was non-existent (1 Sam 15:22-23; Pss 40:6-8; 51:16-17; Isa 1:10-20; Amos 2:6-8; 4:4-5; 5:21-24; Mic 6:6-8), and later Jesus himself, by his denunciation of the concern of the hypocritical scribes and Pharisees for their external, presumably merit-amassing observance of the law while their hearts were far from the Lord (Matt 5:21-6:18; 23:1-39; Mark 7:1-13; Luke 11:37-54), had spoken against such a perversion of the law's purpose.

So also Ridderbos, 'Section 21: The Antithesis with Judaism' in *Paul: An Outline of His Theology*, 130-35, who insists that for the Judaism of Paul's day

> the law is the unique means to acquire for oneself merit, reward, righteousness before God, and the instrument given by God to subjugate the evil impulse and to lead the good to victory...for the Jews the law was the pre-eminent means of salvation, indeed the real 'substance of life'...Judaism knew no other way of salvation than that of the law, and...it saw even the mercy and the forgiving love of God as lying precisely in the fact that they enable the sinner once more to built for his eternal future on the ground of the law...It is this redemptive significance that Judaism ascribed to the law against which the antithesis in Paul's doctrine of sin is directed. (132-34)

38. C. G. Montefiore, 'First Impressions of Paul,' *Jewish Quarterly Review* 6 (1894), 428-75; 'Rabbinic Judaism and the Epistles of St. Paul,' *Jewish Quarterly Review* 13 (1900-1901), 161-217.

39. G. F. Moore, *Judaism in the First Centuries of the Christian Era: The Age of the Tannaim* (2 vols.; Cambridge, Mass.: Harvard University, 1927).

40. E. P. Sanders, *Paul and Palestinian Judaism, A Comparison of Patterns of Religion* (Philadelphia: Fortress, 1977); see also his more important *Paul, the Law, and the Jewish People* (Philadelphia: Fortress, 1983), his *Paul* (Oxford: University Press, 1991), and his *Judaism: Practice and Belief, 63BCE-66CE* (London: SCM, 1992), all four of these works unified by their common conviction concerning the non-legalistic nature of first-century Palestinian Judaism and their corresponding rejection of the traditional Lutheran Reformation

cul-de-sac' that the field of New Testament study had become, making it necessary for anyone earnestly desiring to understand Christian beginnings in general or Pauline theology in particular to reconsider the traditional view.[41]

Sanders, in the name of what he terms 'covenantal nomism', challenged the traditional view as being simply a myth. He argues, firstly, that traditional Protestantism, particularly Lutheranism, has been guilty of reading back into New Testament times late Jewish sources (such as those from the fifth century A.D. that picture the final judgment as a matter of weighing up merits and demerits) and thereby inappropriately construing the conflict between Paul and his Jewish opponents in terms of debates that occurred at the time of the magisterial Reformation between Luther and Rome. Secondly, he argues that conversely first-century Palestinian Judaism had not been seduced by merit theology into becoming a religion of legalistic works-righteousness wherein right standing before God was earned by good works in a system of strict justice. He contends rather

(1) that the covenant, the law, and the Jews' special status as the elect people of God were all gifts of God's grace to Israel and that the Jews did not have to earn – and knowing this were not trying to earn – what they already had received by grace;

(2) that Judaism did not teach that 'works of law' were the condition for entry into the covenant but only for continuing in and maintaining covenant status (that is to say, that salvation comes not from meritorious works but through belonging to the covenant people of God),[42] which 'pattern of religion', Sanders contends, *is also found in Paul*; and

(3) that the only real bone of contention between an (at times) incoherent and inconsistent Paul (who was not unwilling to distort his opponents' positions at times in order to safeguard his own) and

---

understanding of the law/gospel antithesis as the key to Paul's view of the law and the theology of his Jewish opposition. See also W. D. Davies, *Paul and Rabbinic Judaism: Some Rabbinic Elements in Pauline Theology* (1948; fourth edition; Philadelphia: Fortress, 1980), who argues that Paul's doctrine of justification by faith apart from 'works of law' was only one metaphor among many of the time (221-23) and that Paul was simply a Pharisee for whom the messianic age had dawned (71-73).

41. The reason Sanders' effort was heard while the previous efforts were largely ignored is traceable to the new historical situation and social climate which obtained at the time as the result of, first, the Holocaust in the aftermath of which the traditional denigration of Judaism as the negative side of the debate with the Protestant doctrine of justification could no longer be stomached, and second, Vatican II which absolved the Jewish people of deicide.

42. Sanders, *Paul and Palestinian Judaism*, 422.

his Jewish contemporaries was not soteriology (what one must do in order to be saved) but purely and simply *Christology* (what one thinks about Christ).

Which is just to say that Paul saw Christianity as superior to Judaism only because while the Jews thought they had in the covenant a *national* charter of privilege, Paul viewed covenantal privilege as *open to all* who have faith in Christ and who accordingly stand in continuity with Abraham. Or to put it more simply, Paul viewed Christianity as superior to Judaism only because Judaism was not Christianity.

It is indeed true, as Sanders demonstrates from his in-depth examination of the Qumran literature, the Apocryphal literature, the Pseudepigraphal literature, and the rabbinic literature of the first two-hundred years after Christ that one can find many references in this material to God's election of Israel and to his grace and mercy toward the nation. And, of course, if Sanders is right about the non-legalistic nature of Palestinian Judaism in Paul's day, then Douglas J. Moo is correct when he asserts that the traditional Reformation view of Paul's polemic 'is left hanging in mid-air, and it is necessary either to accuse Paul of misunderstanding (or misinterpreting) his opponents, or to find new opponents for him to be criticizing'.[43]

Regarding the first of these possibilities, I can only say that the modern scholar, whether Christian or Jew, who supposes that he understands better or interprets more accurately first-century Palestinian Judaism than Paul did, is a rash person indeed! Moreover, Sanders makes too much of his, in my opinion, methodologically flawed findings on the 'non-legalistic' character of first-century Palestinian Judaism, since first-century Palestinian Judaism, as he himself recognizes, also taught that the elect man was obligated, even though he would do so imperfectly (for which imperfections the law's sacrificial system provided the remedy), to obey the law in order to *maintain* his covenant status and to *remain* in the covenant. But this is to acknowledge, as Moo notes, that

---

43. Douglas J. Moo, 'Paul and the Law in the Last Ten Years' in *Scottish Journal of Theology* 40 (1987), 293. See also Moo's '"Law," "Works of the Law," and Legalism in Paul,' *Westminster Theological Journal* 45 (1983), 73-100; and his *The Epistle to the Romans* (Grand Rapids: Eerdmans, 1996), particularly his comments on Romans 3:20 and the following 'Excursus: Paul, "Works of the Law," and First-Century Judaism' (206-17), that take these developments into account, and Mark A. Seifrid, 'Blind Alleys in the Controversy over the Paul of History' in *Tyndale Bulletin* 45.1 (1994), 73-95.

even in Sanders's proposal, works play such a prominent role that it is fair to speak of a "synergism" of faith and works that elevates works to a crucial salvific role. For, while works, according to Sanders, are not the means of "getting in," they are essential to "staying in." When, then, we consider the matter from the perspective of the final judgment—which we must in Jewish theology—it is clear that "works," even in Sanders's view, play a necessary and instrumental role in "salvation."[44]

Moo goes on to note in the same connection:

---

44. Moo, *The Epistle to the Romans*, 215. In his somewhat dated but nonetheless very insightful *Biblical Theology* (Grand Rapids: Eerdmans, 1948), Geerhardus Vos also affirms that Judaism contained a large strain of legalism, stating that the Judaic 'philosophy asserted that the law was intended, on the principle of meritoriousness, to enable Israel to earn the blessedness of the world to come' (142). He then explains why and how the Judaizers went wrong:

It is true, certain of the statements of the Pentateuch and of the O. T. in general may on the surface seem to favor the Judaistic position. That the law cannot be kept is nowhere stated in so many words. And not only this, that the keeping of the law will be rewarded, is stated once and again. Israel's retention of the privileges of the berith is made dependent on obedience. It is promised that he who shall do the commandments shall find life through them. Consequently, writers have not been lacking, who declared, that, from a historical point of view, their sympathies went with the Judaizers, and not with Paul. Only a moment's reflection is necessary to prove that...precisely from a broad historical standpoint Paul had far more accurately grasped the purport of the law than his opponents. The law was given after the redemption from Egypt had been accomplished, and the people had already entered upon the enjoyment of many of the blessings of the berith. Particularly, their taking possession of the promised land could not have been made dependent on previous observance of the law, for during their journey in the wilderness many of its prescripts could not be observed. It is plain, then, that law-keeping did not figure at that juncture as the meritorious ground of life-inheritance. The latter is based on grace alone, no less emphatically than Paul himself places salvation on that ground. But, while this is so, it might still be objected, that law-observance, if not the ground of receiving, is yet made the ground for retention of the privileges inherited. Here it can not, of course, be denied that a real connection exists. But the Judaizers went wrong in inferring that the connection must be meritorious, that, if Israel keeps the cherished gifts of Jehovah through observance of His law, this must be so, because in strict justice they had earned them. The connection is of a totally different kind. It belongs not to the legal sphere of merit, but to the symbolico-typical sphere of appropriateness of expression. ...the abode of Israel in Canaan typified the heavenly, perfected state of God's people. Under these circumstances the ideal of absolute conformity to God's law of legal holiness had to be upheld. Even though they were not able to keep this law in the Pauline, spiritual sense, yea, even though they were unable to keep it externally and ritually, the requirement could not be lowered. When apostasy on a general scale took place, they could not remain in the promised land. When they disqualified themselves for typifying the state of holiness, they *ipso facto* disqualified themselves for typifying that of blessedness, and had to go into captivity.... And in Paul's teaching the strand that corresponds to this Old Testament doctrine of holiness as the indispensable (though not meritorious) condition of receiving the inheritance is still distinctly traceable. (142-44)

...there is reason to conclude that Judaism was more "legalistic" than Sanders thinks. In passage after passage in his scrutiny of the Jewish literature, he dismisses a "legalistic" interpretation by arguing that the covenantal framework must be read into the text or that the passage is homiletical rather than theological in intent. But was the covenant as pervasive as Sanders thinks? Might not lack of reference in many Jewish works imply that it had been lost sight of in a more general reliance on Jewish identity? And does not theology come into expression in homiletics? Indeed, is it not in more practically oriented texts that we discover what people *really* believe? Sanders may be guilty of underplaying a drift toward a more legalistic posture in first-century Judaism. We must also reckon with the possibility that many "lay" Jews were more legalistic than the surviving literary remains of Judaism would suggest. Certainly the undeniable importance of the law in Judaism would naturally open the way to viewing doing the law in itself as salvific. The gap between the average believer's theological views and the informed views of religious leaders is often a wide one. If Christianity has been far from immune to legalism, is it likely to think that Judaism, at any state of its development, was?[45]

---

45. Moo, *The Epistle to the Romans*, 216-17. See also Jacob Neusner, *Rabbinic Judaism: Structure and System* (Minneapolis: Fortress, 1995), 7-13, 20-23, who heaps scorn upon Sanders' literary efforts, not so much for his conclusions but because he tends by his method to join all Judaic religious systems into a single, harmonious 'Judaism'. While Neusner appreciates the methodology of Sanders' *Paul and Palestinian Judaism* much more than the methodology and conclusions reflected in his *Judaism: Practice and Belief 63 B.C.E.–66 C.E.*, he still faults Sanders' earlier handling of the Mishna and the other rabbinic sources because, says Neusner, the Pauline-Lutheran questions he brings to it are simply not these sources' central concerns: 'Sanders's earlier work is profoundly flawed by the category formation that he imposes on his sources; that distorts and misrepresents the Judaic system of these sources' (22). He explains:

Sanders quotes all documents equally with no effort at differentiation among them. He seems to have culled sayings from the diverse sources he has chosen and written them down on cards, which he proceeded to organize around his critical categories. Then he has constructed his paragraphs and sections by flipping through these cards and commenting on this and that. So there is no context in which a given saying is important in its own setting, in its own document. This is Billerbeck scholarship.

The diverse rabbinic documents require study in and on their own terms...[But Sanders's] claim to have presented an account of "the Rabbis" and their opinions is not demonstrated and not even very well argued. We hardly need to dwell on the still more telling fact that Sanders has not shown how systemic comparison is possible when, in point of fact, the issues of one document, or of one system of which a document is a part, are simply not the same as the issues of some other document or system; he is oblivious to all documentary variations and differences of opinion. That is, while he has succeeded in finding rabbinic sayings on topics of central importance to Paul (or Pauline theology), he has ignored the context and authentic character of the setting in which he has found these sayings. He lacks all sense of proportion and coherence, because he has not even asked whether these sayings form the center and core of the rabbinic system or even of a

In support of Moo's contentions one could cite, as samplings of Judaic thought in this regard, Sirach (also known as Ecclesiasticus) 3:3, 14-15, 30-31, a second century B.C. Jewish writing, that teaches quite clearly that human good deeds atone for sins:

> ³Whoever honors his father atones for sins,...
> ¹⁴For kindness to a father will not be forgotten,
>   and against your sins it will be credited to you;
> ¹⁵In the day of your affliction it will be remembered in your favor,
>   as frost in fair weather, your sins will melt away....
> ³⁰Water extinguishes a blazing fire:
>   so almsgiving atones for sin.
> ³¹Whoever requites favors gives thought to the future;
>   at the moment of his falling he will find support.
> (See also Sirach 29:11-13 and Tobit 4:7-11)

Sanders also ignores Flavius Josephus' frequent insistence that God's grace is meted out in response to merit,[46] and he simply discounts the argument of 2 Esdras[47] as an atypical exception here.[48] And Qumran document 1QS 11:2, 3 states: 'For I belong to the God

---

given rabbinic document. To state matters simply, how do we know that "the Rabbis" and Paul are talking about the same thing, so that we can compare what they have to say? If it should turn out that "the Rabbis" and Paul are not talking about the same thing, then what is it that we have to compare. I think, nothing at all. (22-23)

46. In his *Against Apion*, II, 217b-218, for example, Josephus writes: 'For those...who live *in accordance with our laws* [νομίμως] the prize is not silver or gold, no crown of wild olive or of parsley with any such public mark of distinction. No; each individual, relying on the witness of his own conscience and the lawgiver's prophecy, confirmed by the sure testimony of God, is firmly persuaded that *to those who observe the laws* [τοῖς τοὺς νόμους διαφυλάξασι] and, if they must needs die for them, willingly meet death, God has granted a renewed existence [γενέσθαι πάλιν] and in the revolution of the ages the gift of a *better life* [βίον ἀμείνων].'

In his *Discourse to the Greeks on Hades* Josephus says that 'to those that have done well [God will give] an everlasting fruition', and more specifically that 'the just shall remember only their righteous actions, whereby they have attained the heavenly kingdom'.

47. 2 Esdras is 4 Esdras in the appendix of the Roman Catholic Vulgate Bible, with chapters 3-14 being a late first-century A.D. work written by an unknown Palestinian Jew in response to the destruction of Jerusalem in A.D. 70.

48. See, for example, the following statements in 2 Esdras:
7:77: 'For you have a treasure of works laid up with the Most High.'
7:78-94: 'Now, concerning death, the teaching is: When the decisive decree has gone forth from the Most High that a man shall die...if [the spirits are] those...who have despised his law...such spirits shall not enter into habitations, but shall immediately wander about in torments, ever grieving and sad...because they scorned the law of the Most High...Now this is the order of those who have kept the ways of the Most High, when they shall be separated

of my vindication and the perfection of my way is in his hand with the virtue of my heart. And *with my righteous deeds* he will wipe away my transgressions.'[49] 1QS 3:6-8; 8:6-10; 9:4 also attribute an atoning efficacy to the community's deeds. One may also cite here the opinion of the 'believers who belonged to the party of the Pharisees' (Acts 15:5) who declared: 'Unless you [Gentiles] are circumcised, according to the custom taught by Moses, you cannot be saved' (Acts 15:1). I grant that the focus of these Acts verses is directed toward what the Pharisee party in the church thought Gentiles had to do in order to be saved, but it is surely appropriate to conclude, first, that they would have believed that they themselves had to do the same thing in order to be saved, and second, that they were apparently reflecting what at least the Pharisees – the strictest sect of Judaism – would also have believed.

Moreover, in Paul's 'allegory' in Galatians 4:21-31, he first declares that 'Hagar stands for Mount Sinai in Arabia and corresponds to *the present city of Jerusalem* [lit. 'the now Jerusalem', τῇ νῦν Ἰερουσαλήμ], because she is in slavery with her children'. He thereby places 'the now Jerusalem', which stands within his 'Hagar-Sinai-law-bondage' matrix, in bondage to the law (4:25), and then contrasts 'the now Jerusalem' with 'the Jerusalem that is above' [lit. 'the above Jerusalem', ἡ ἄνω Ἰερουσαλήμ] that is 'free' and the Christian's 'mother'. It is apparent, then, that Paul's expression, 'the now Jerusalem', goes beyond the Judaizers who were troubling his churches. In the words of Ronald Fung, it 'stands by metonymy for Judaism,

---

from their mortal bodies. During the time that they lived in it, they...withstood danger every hour, that they might keep the law of the Lawgiver perfectly. Therefore...they shall see with great joy the glory of him who receives them...because...while they were alive they kept the law which was given them in trust.'

7:105: '...no one shall ever pray for another on that day...for then every one shall bear his own righteousness or unrighteousness.'

7:133: '[The Most High] is gracious to those who turn in repentance to his law.'

8:33: 'For the righteous, who have many works laid up with thee, shall receive their reward in consequence of their own deeds.'

8:55-56: 'Therefore do not ask anymore questions about the multitude of those who perish. For they also received freedom, but they despised the Most High, and were contemptuous of his law.'

9:7-12: 'And it shall be that every one who will be saved and will be able to escape on account of his works...will see my salvation in my land...and as many as scorned my law while they still had freedom...these must in torment acknowledge it after death.'

See also B. W. Longenecker, *2 Esdras* (Sheffield: Sheffield Academic, 1995).

49. For the defense of 'with my righteous deeds' and not 'and in his righteousness' as the more likely original reading see Mark A. Seifrid, 'Blind Alleys,' 81-82, fn. 28.

with its trust in physical descent from Abraham and reliance on legal observance as the way of salvation'.[50] In sum, Paul by this allegory is saying that the nation of Israel because of its unbelief and bondage to the law is in actually a nation of spiritual Ishmaelites, sons of the bondwoman Hagar, and not true Israelites at all!

Finally, if the foregoing data are not sufficient to show Sanders' error, and if one is willing as I am to give Paul his rightful due as an inspired apostle of Christ, then as the *coup de grace* to his 'new perspective' on first-century Palestinian Judaism, Paul writes in Romans 9:30-32, 10:2-4:

> What then shall we say? That the Gentiles, who did not pursue righteousness, have obtained it, a righteousness that is by faith; but Israel, *who pursued law [as a means to] righteousness*,[51] did not attain [the requirements of that] law. Why not? Because *they pursued it not by faith but as if it were by works* [of law[52]].... For I can testify about [the Israelites] that they are zealous for God, but their zeal is not based on knowledge. Since they did not know the righteousness that comes from God and *sought to establish their own*, they did not submit to God's righteousness. Christ is the end of 'law-keeping' [lit. 'law'] as a means to [εἰς[53]] righteousness to all who believe.[54] (emphasis supplied)

In sum, while both Judaism and Paul viewed obedience to the law as having an appropriate place in the covenant way of life, there was

---

50. Ronald Y. K. Fung, *The Epistle to the Galatians* (New International Commentary on the New Testament; Grand Rapids: Eerdmans, 1988), 209; see also C. K. Barrett, 'The Allegory of Abraham, Sarah, and Hagar in the Argument of Galatians' in *Rechtfertigung, Festschrift für Ernst Käsemann*, edited by Johannes Friedrich, Wolfgang Pöhlmann, and Peter Stuhlmacher (Göttingen: Vandenhoeck & Ruprecht, 1976); republished in *Essays on Paul*, 154-70.

51. I construe δικαιοσύνης to be an ablative of means. Moo virtually says this when he concludes his discussion of the phrase νόμον δικαιοσύνης here by saying: ' "Law," therefore, remains the topic of Paul's teaching throughout this verse and a half [Rom 9:31-32a], but law conceived as a means to righteousness' (625-26).

52. I have added this prepositional phrase only to bring out what I think is Paul's intended meaning and not because I think that it reflects the originality of the textual variant ἔργων νόμου supported by ℵ² D K P Ψ 33 81 104 etc., a few church fathers, and a few versions.

53. By construing the εἰς here as denoting 'means', I have conformed Paul's statement here with his earlier phrase, 'law [as a means to] righteousness,' in 9:31.

54. C. K. Barrett, in 'Romans 9:30-10:21: Fall and Responsibility of Israel' in *Essays on Paul*, correctly explains Paul's intention in these verses this way: '...the only way to achieve righteousness (which is what the righteous law requires) is by faith. This way the Gentiles, who really had no choice in the matter, had adopted, when they were surprised by the gospel.... Israel had not done this. They had been given the law...and had sought to do what they understood it to mean; *but they had misunderstood their own law, thinking that it was to be obeyed on the principle of works*, whereas it demanded obedience rendered in, consisting of, faith' (141, emphasis supplied).

this difference: whereas Paul viewed the Christian's obedience as (at best) the *fruit* and *evidential sign* of the fact that one is a member of the covenant community, Judaism saw obedience to the law as the *instrumental basis* for continuing in salvation through the covenant. Thus the legalistic principle—even though it occurred within the context of the covenant as a kind of 'covenantal legalism'—was still present and ultimately that principle came to govern the soteric status of the individual. This is just to say that Second Temple Judaism apparently over time became focused more and more on an 'instrumental nomism' and less and less on a 'gracious covenantalism of faith'. Paul rightly saw that *any* obligation to accomplish a works-righteousness to *any* degree on the sinner's part would negate the principle of *sola gratia* altogether (Rom 11:5-6), obligate him to obey the whole law (Gal 3:10; 5:3), and make the cross-work of Christ of no value to him (Gal 2:21; 5:2).[55] Finally, Paul does not represent Christianity as superior to Judaism only because of a kind of dispensational shift within salvation history from Judaism to Christianity. As we have seen in Part I, his differences with Judaism were far more radical and passionate than that.

James D. G. Dunn, who accepts, not without some qualifications, Sanders' understanding of first-century Palestinian Judaism, in his *Jesus, Paul and the Law*[56] urges that Paul's 'works of law' phrase does not refer to works done to achieve righteousness, that is, to legalism, but to the Mosaic law particularly as that law came to focus for Israel in the observance of such Jewish 'identity markers' as circumcision, food laws and Sabbath-keeping. That is to say, Paul's 'works of law' phrase refers to a subset of the law's commands, encapsulating *Jewish* existence in the nation's covenant relationship with God or, to quote Dunn himself, 'the self-understanding and

---

55. For a detailed critical analysis of Sanders' thesis, see M. A. Seifrid, *Justification by Faith: The Origin and Development of a Central Pauline Theme* (*NovTSup* 68; Leiden: Brill, 1992); S. Westerholm, *Israel's Law and the Church's Faith: Paul and His Recent Interpreters* (Grand Rapids: Eerdmans, 1988); C. G. Kruse, *Paul, the Law and Justification* (Leicester: InterVarsity, 1996); and Karl T. Cooper, 'Paul and Rabbinic Soteriology' in *Westminster Theological Journal* 44 (1982), 123-39.

56. James D. G. Dunn, *Jesus, Paul and the Law: Studies in Mark and Galatians* (Louisville: Westminster/John Knox, 1990), 183-206, 215-36; see also his 'The New Perspective on Paul' in *Bulletin of the John Rylands University Library of Manchester* 65 (1983), 95-122. Moo, *The Epistle to the Romans*, provides the 'Dunn bibliography' on the issue (207, fn. 57), to which must be added his *The Theology of Paul the Apostle* (Grand Rapids: Eerdmans, 1998), 334-71.

obligation accepted by practicing Jews that E. P. Sanders encapsulated quite effectively in the phrase "covenantal nomism." "[57]

In sum, for Dunn the heart issue for Paul was the inclusion of Gentile Christians in the messianic community on an equal footing with Jewish Christians. In other words, for Paul his bone of contention with Judaism was not with an imagined attempt to acquire a merit-based righteousness before God as much as it was with Israel's *prideful* insistence on its covenantal racial exclusiveness: Israel shut Gentiles out of the people of God because they did not observe *their* ethno-social 'identity markers'. And apparently many Jewish Christians wanted Gentile Christians to observe these Jewish 'identity markers' before they would or could share table fellowship with them. Paul by his 'works of law' phrase was opposing then the Old Testament *ritual* laws that kept Israel in its national identity (see Num 23:9) apart from Gentiles.

Whereas Sanders' conclusions, in my opinion, go too far, Dunn's interpretation of Paul's concern, in my opinion, is reductionistic and does not go far enough. Paul was indeed concerned with—and vigorously opposed—the spirit of racial exclusiveness within Messiah's community, but this does not appear to be his concern in his sermon in the synagogue at Pisidian Antioch when he declared that 'through [Jesus] *everyone who believes* [πᾶς ὁ πιστεύων] *is justified* [δικαιοῦται] *from all things* [ἀπὸ πάντων], from which you could not be justified by [keeping] the [whole] law of Moses' (Acts 13:39). Nor does he hesitate to relate his 'works of law' terminology universally to 'no flesh' (lit. 'not...all flesh', οὐ...πᾶσα σάρξ) in Romans 3:20,[58] which surely includes both Gentiles (see Rom 3:9) who obviously *were not obligated to observe Israel's circumcision or food laws* but who, according to Paul, were nonetheless regarded by God as transgressors of his law (see Rom 1)

---

57. In his essay, 'Echoes of Intra-Jewish Polemic in Paul's Letter to the Galatians' in *Journal of Biblical Literature* 112 (1993), Dunn states that the phrase refers to 'acts of obedience required by the law of all faithful Jews, all members of the people with whom God had made the covenant at Sinai – the self-understanding and obligation accepted by practicing Jews that E. P. Sanders encapsulated quite effectively in the phrase "covenantal nomism" ' (466). In his more recent *The Theology of Paul the Apostle* Dunn declares quite forcefully: 'I do not (and never did!) claim that "works of the law" denote only circumcision, food laws, and Sabbath. A careful reading of my "New Perspective" should have made it clear that, as in Galatians 2, these were particular focal or crisis points for (and demonstrations of) a *generally nomistic attitude*' (358, fn 97, emphasis supplied).

58. Note too his universalistic phrases, 'every mouth' [πᾶν στόμα] and 'the whole world' [πᾶς ὁ κόσμος] in Romans 3:19.

and the people of Israel who *were obligated to observe and who were in fact observing their national identity markers* (see Rom 2:25-29) but who also, according to Paul, were still regarded by God as transgressors of his law (see Rom 2:21-24), both accordingly standing under the law's condemnation.[59] In short, Paul's 'works of law' phrase in Romans 3:20 intended more than simply observance (or in the case of Gentiles, non-observance) of Israel's national identity markers. *The phrase included observance of God's moral law too.*

But if the phrase in 3:20 includes observance of the moral law of God as well, it surely means the same in 3:28 where Paul declares: 'For we maintain that a man [any man; see 3:29-30] is justified by faith apart from [legalistic] works of law.' And immediately after he establishes mankind's guilt before God in terms of the inability of the 'works of law' to justify anyone (3:20) Paul places those 'works of law' as the false way to righteousness over against and in contrast to faith in Christ's saving work as the true way to righteousness (3:21-25: δικαιοσύνη θεοῦ διὰ πίστεως Ἰησοῦ Χριστοῦ). When one then takes into account Paul's reference to *human* 'boasting' both in 3:27 (καύχησις) and 4:2 (καύχημα) and his insistence in Romans 4 that Abraham was not justified by his 'works' (ἐξ ἔργων, 4:2) or by his 'working' (ἐργαζομένῳ, 4:4-5)—which words, given their proximity to Romans 3:20 and 3:28, are almost certainly his theological shorthand for his earlier 'works of law' expression—it should be again apparent that Paul's 'works of law' phrase intends more than the observance (or in the case of Gentiles, non-observance) of certain Jewish identity markers *since Abraham lived before the giving of the Mosaic Law.*[60]

Then to Peter who, after enjoying table fellowship with Gentiles for a time at Antioch, succumbed to the pressures of the Judaizers Paul said:

---

59. Moo, *The Epistle to the Romans*, writes: 'The "works" mentioned [in Rom 3:20] must...be the "works" Paul has spoken of in chap. 2. But it is not circumcision—let alone other "identity markers" that are not even mentioned in Rom. 1–3—that the Jew "does" in Rom. 2; it is, generally, what is demanded by the law, the "precepts" (v. 26; cf. vv. 22-23, 25, 27). Therefore, 3:20 must deny not the adequacy of Jewish identity to justify, but the adequacy of Jewish works to justify.' (214).

60. W. Gutbrod, νόμος (and the νομ- word cluster), *Theological Dictionary of the New Testament*, translated by Geoffrey W. Bromiley (Grand Rapids: Eerdmans, 1967), IV:1072, also declares that Paul 'works out his position' in regard to the law 'primarily with ref. to the ethical commandments, esp. those of the Decalogue which apply to all men'.

We [apostles] who are Jews by birth and not 'Gentile sinners' know that a man is not justified *by observing the law* [ἐξ ἔργων νόμου], but by faith in Jesus Christ. So we, too, have put our faith in Christ Jesus that we may be justified by faith in Christ and not *by observing the law* [ἐξ ἔργων νόμου], because *by observing the law* [ἐξ ἔργων νόμου] no one [note again, οὐ...πᾶσα σάρξ, 'not...all flesh'] will be justified. (Gal 2:15-16)

Then, after asking the 'Judaized' Gentile Christians of Galatia the twin questions: 'Did you receive the Spirit *by observing the law* [ἐξ ἔργων νόμου], or *by believing what you heard* [ἐξ ἀκοῆς πίστεως]' (Gal 3:2), and 'Does God give you his Spirit and work miracles among you because you *observe the law* [ἐξ ἔργων νόμου] or because you *believe what you heard* [ἐξ ἀκοῆς πίστεως]' (Gal 3:5), he avers:

> *All who* [ὅσοι, 'As many as'] *rely on observing the law* [ἐξ ἔργων νόμου εἰσίν] are under a curse, for it is written: 'Cursed is *everyone* [πᾶς] who does not continue to do *everything* [πᾶσιν] written in the Book of the Law.' Clearly *no one* [οὐδεὶς] is justified before God by the law, because, 'The righteous will live by faith.' (Gal 3:10-11; see also Rom 3:21-28; 4:1-5; Titus 3:5)

Who are these people who are 'relying on observance of the law' for their salvation? Once again we are struck by Paul's universalistic language. It is true that in his letter to the Romans Paul describes the Jew as one who '*relies* [ἐπαναπαύῃ] on the law' (2:17). And it is also true that in the context of the Galatians letter his most immediate opponents are the Judaizers and his Gentile converts who had succumbed to the teaching of the Judaizers. But Paul's 'no flesh' (οὐ...πᾶσα σάρξ) expression in Galatians 2:16 appears once again to be applicable to anyone and everyone[61] – Jew or Gentile, *the latter of whom had no obligation to observe circumcision or Israel's food laws* – who trusts in his own law-keeping for salvation. And the same must be said for his 'as many as' (ὅσοι), his 'everyone' (πᾶς), and his 'no one' (οὐδεὶς) in Galatians 3:10-11. Finally, his descriptive '*everything* [πᾶσιν] written in the Book of the Law' in Galatians 3:10 suggests once again that he intended by his 'works of law' expression not just Israel's identity markers of circumcision, food

---

61. Observe his universalistic *everyone* [πᾶς] and *no one* [οὐδεὶς] in Galatians 2:16.

laws, and Sabbath-keeping but also the moral law.

It would appear then from these biblical references, firstly, that the 'new perspective' theologians have not done adequate justice to Paul's teaching when they insist that first-century Palestinian Judaism was *not* a religion of legalistic works-righteousness for it clearly was (as were, of course, the religions of the Gentiles), even though its legalism expressed itself within the context of God's gracious covenant with them in terms of a 'maintaining' of covenantal status; secondly, that by his 'works of law' expression Paul intended not just the ceremonial aspects of the law but the whole law in its entirety; and thirdly, that 'there is more of Paul in Luther'[62] and the other Reformers with respect to the critical salvific matters that concerned them in the sixteenth century than some of the 'new perspective' theologians are inclined to admit.[63] In conclusion, these 'new perspective' suggestions that would have Paul saying either more or other than he should have said (Sanders) or less than he actually and clearly intended (Dunn) are 'blind alleys' which the church must reject if it hopes to understand Paul's doctrine of justification.[64]

Summary of the Doctrine

Paul defines the 'gospel of God', which is also the 'gospel of Christ' (Rom 1:1, 9), specifically in terms of justification by faith—faith alone – in the accomplishments of Christ's obedience and cross work, completely apart from law-keeping (Rom 1:16-17; 3:21-22, 27-28; 4:5-8; 5:1, 9, 17-19). And the manner in which he employs the term

---

62. S. Westerholm, *Israel's Law and the Church's Faith: Paul and his Recent Interpreters* (Grand Rapids: Eerdmans, 1988), 173.

63. One would not be too surprised if Roman Catholic scholars, given their historical opposition to the Reformation interpretation of Romans, embraced Sanders' and Dunn's 'new perspective', but Joseph A. Fitzmyer in his *Romans: A New Translation with Introduction and Commentary* (Anchor Bible; New York: Doubleday, 1993), rejects the views of Sanders and Dunn, even arguing that Paul opposes merit theology. B. Byrne, also a Roman Catholic, who holds a view of the law that is similar to Fitzmyer's view, like Fitzmyer dismisses the views of Sanders and Dunn in his *Romans* (Collegeville: Glazier, 1996).

64. For readers who are interested in pursuing these topics for themselves, I recommend that they begin with E. Earle Ellis, 'Pauline Studies in Recent Research' in *Paul and His Recent Interpreters* (Grand Rapids: Eerdmans, 1961), 11-34; Herman Ridderbos, *Paul: An Outline of His Theology*, translated by John R. De Witt (Grand Rapids: Eerdmans, 1975), 13-43; Scott J. Hafemann, 'Paul and His Interpreters', and Thomas R. Schreiner, 'Works of the Law', these last two articles appearing in *Dictionary of Paul and His Letters*, 666-79 and 975-79 respectively, and Thomas R. Schreiner, ' "Works of Law" in Paul' in *Novum Testamentum* 33 (1991), 217-44.

indicates that he regarded justification as an objective divine acquittal respecting the sinner's status before the condemning law of God and not as the subjective improvement of the sinner through the infusion of sanctifying grace. This was the gospel which Paul not only explicated in Galatians and Romans but also the gospel which he preached – '...through him forgiveness of sins is proclaimed to you, and through him *everyone who believes* [πᾶς ὁ πιστεύων] *is justified* [δικαιοῦται] from all things, from which you could not *be justified* [δικαιωθῆναι] by the law of Moses' (Acts 13:38-39). And he invoked a curse[65] upon any and all who would muddy the streams of grace which make glad the city of God by the legalistic teaching that the Christian's own efforts are essential to his justification before God (Gal 1:6-9; 2:11-21; 3:1-14; 5:1-4; 6:12-16). James I. Packer writes summarily of the biblical doctrine of justification:

> It defines the saving significance of Christ's life and death by relating both to God's law (Rom. 3:24ff.; 5:16ff.). It displays God's justice in condemning and punishing sin, his mercy in pardoning and accepting sinners, and his wisdom in exercising both attributes harmoniously together through Christ (Rom. 3:23ff.). It makes clear what faith is – belief in Christ's atoning death and justifying resurrection (Rom. 4:23ff.; 10:8ff.), and trust in him alone for righteousness (Phil. 3:8-9). It makes clear what Christian morality is – law-keeping out of gratitude to the Savior whose gift of righteousness made law-keeping needless for acceptance (Rom. 7:1-6; 12:1-2). It explains all hints, prophecies, and instances of salvation in the OT (Rom. 1:17; 3:21; 4:1ff.). It overthrows Jewish exclusivism and provides the basis on which Christianity becomes a religion for the world (Rom. 1:16; 3:29-30). It is the heart of the gospel.[66]

Quite correctly did Martin Luther declare that Paul's doctrine of justification by faith alone is the article of the standing or falling church (*articulus stantis vel cadentis ecclesiae*),[67] asserting:

---

65. Paul's 'anathema' (ἀνάθεμα) in Galatians 1:8-9 (see Rom 9:3; 1 Cor 16:22), derived as it is from the preposition ἀνά, 'up', τίθημι, 'to place or set', and μα, a noun-ending with passive significance, hence 'something set or placed up [before God]', is simply the New Testament expression of the Old Testament חֵרֶם ('devoted') principle of handing something or someone over to God for destruction. See BAGD, ἀνάθεμα, *A Greek-English Lexicon of the New Testament* (Chicago: University of Chicago Press, 1958), 54, no. 2.

66. James I. Packer, 'Justification' in *Evangelical Dictionary of Theology*, 593.

67. See Luther's exposition of Psalm 130:4 in his *Werke* (Weimar: Böhlau, 1883 to present), 40.3.352, 3: '...quia isto articulo stante stat Ecclesia, ruente ruit Ecclesia.'

The article of justification is the master and prince, the lord, the ruler, and the judge over all kinds of doctrines; it preserves and governs all church doctrine and raises up our consciences before God. Without this article the world is utter death and darkness...If the article of justification is lost, all Christian doctrine is lost at the same time...This doctrine is the head and the cornerstone. It alone begets, nourishes, builds, preserves, and defends the church of God; and without it the church of God cannot exist for one hour...In short, if this article concerning Christ – the doctrine that we are justified and saved through Him alone and consider all apart from Him damned – is not professed, all resistance and restraint are at an end. Then there is, in fact, neither measure nor limit to any heresy and error...Whoever departs from the article of justification does not know God and is an idolater...For when this article has been taken away, nothing remains but error, hypocrisy, godlessness, and idolatry, although it may seem to be the height of truth, worship of God, holiness, and so forth.[68]

John Calvin, declaring justification by faith alone to be 'the main hinge on which religion turns'[69] and 'the first and keenest subject of controversy' between the Reformers and Rome, unequivocally states:

Whenever the knowledge of [justification by faith alone] is taken away, the glory of Christ is extinguished, religion abolished, the Church destroyed, and the hope of salvation utterly overthrown.[70]

By expressly rejecting this teaching as it did at the Council of Trent (see Sixth Session, Canons 9-12), the Roman Catholic Church testifies to its fallen condition. This rejection it not only has never repudiated but also has even reaffirmed as recently as its 1994 *Catechism of the Catholic Church*, concerning which teaching Pope John Paul II declared as recently as his 1995 address commemorating the 450th anniversary of the Council of Trent: 'Thus, with the Decree of Justification—one of the most valuable achievements for the formulation of Catholic doctrine—the council intended to safeguard

---

68. Martin Luther, *What Luther Says*, compiled by Ewald M. Plass (St. Louis: Concordia, 1959), 2.703-04 (2192, 2194, 2195, 2196, 2197). Luther also asserted in his *Works*, edited by Helmut T. Lehmann (Philadelphia: Fortress, 1967) 54.340: 'If the article on justification hadn't fallen, the brotherhoods, pilgrimages, masses, invocation of saints, etc., would have found no place in the church. If it falls again (which may God prevent!) these idols will return.'
69. John Calvin, *Institutes*, 3.11.1.
70. John Calvin, 'Calvin's Reply to Sadoleto,' *A Reformation Debate* (Reprint; Grand Rapids: Baker, 1976), 66.

the role assigned by Christ to the Church and her sacraments in the process of sinful man's justification.'[71] And in rejecting this doctrine, as Luther so clearly saw, Rome has fallen heir to a hundred other evils, including its indulgence system and its doctrine regarding the works of supererogation of those whom it has determined have become 'saints'. Their 'congruent merit' is placed in Rome's 'treasury of merit', which merit is then dispensed through papal indulgences to the 'faithful' as they submit to the Romish priesthood and its sacraments and the confessional and as their prayers are offered in behalf of souls suffering in a humanly contrived, non-existent purgatory.

One has only to visit the great cathedrals of Europe, hear the Masses being said, and witness for himself the rows of burning candles 'praying' for the souls in purgatory and then to try to find a Protestant church in those cities to realize that a doctrinal reformation is as sorely needed today within Christendom as it was in the sixteenth century in order to capture once again the glorious truth of the Pauline gospel of justification by grace alone through faith alone in Christ's active and passive obedience. Indeed, never has the need been greater than right now for such a sweeping doctrinal reformation within Christendom! And never has the need been greater than right now for the Lord of the harvest to raise up a generation of missionaries who are thoroughly trained to propagate Paul's law-free gospel which alone saves men for heaven!

---

71. Pope John Paul II, 'Trent: A Great Event in Church History,' *The Pope Speaks* 40/5 (September-October 1995), 291.

CHAPTER TWENTY-ONE

THE PAULINE ETHIC: THE CHRISTIAN AND THE DECALOGUE

The law of God is good and wise
    And sets his will before our eyes,
Shows us the way of righteousness,
    And dooms to death when we transgress.

Its light of holiness imparts
    The knowledge of our sinful hearts,
That we may see our lost estate
    And seek deliv'rance ere too late.

To those who help in Christ have found
    And would in works of love abound,
It shows what deeds are his delight
    And should be done as good and right.

When men the offered help disdain
    And wilfully in sin remain,
Its terror in their ear resounds
    And keeps their wickedness in bounds.

The law is good; but since the fall
    Its holiness condemns us all;
It dooms us for our sin to die
    And has no power to justify.

To Jesus we for refuge flee,
    Who from the curse has set us free,
And humbly worship at his throne,
    Saved by his grace through faith alone.
            – Matthias Loy, 1863

That Paul expressly teaches that Christ in his cross-work of justifying Christians has liberated them from the condemnation of the Decalogue is beyond all reasonable doubt: 'Christ redeemed us from the curse of the law by becoming a curse for us, for it is written: "Cursed is everyone who is hung on a tree" ' (Gal 3:13; see also Gal 2:16; Rom 1:16-17; 3:21-26; 4:1-8; 5:1, 9-10; 2 Cor 5:21). But F. F. Bruce has argued, against the Reformed tradition, in his *Paul: Apostle of the Heart Set Free* that the gospel liberates the Christian from the law not only with respect to its condemning character but also with respect to it as a rule of life. He writes:

> In the Reformed tradition derived from Geneva, it has frequently been said that, while the man in Christ is not under law as a means of salvation, he remains under it as a rule of life. In its own right, this distinction may be cogently maintained as a principle of Christian theology and ethics, but it should not be imagined that it has Pauline authority. According to Paul, the believer is not under law as a rule of life – unless one thinks of the law of love, and that is a completely different kind of law, fulfilled not by obedience to a code but by the outworking of an inward power. When Paul says, 'sin will have no dominion over you, since you are not under law but under grace' (Romans 6:14), it is the on-going course of Christian life that he has in view, not simply the initial justification by faith.[1]

He holds this conviction because he believes that the 'law of Christ' under which Paul declared that he lived and served (1 Cor 9:21)

> is a promulgation of the injunction of Leviticus 19:18, 'You shall love your neighbor as yourself' (Galatians 5:14). But when 'law' is used in this way, it cannot be understood 'legally': *the law of love is incapable of being imposed or enforced by external authority*. Rather, it is *the spontaneous principle of thought and action in a life controlled by the Spirit of Christ*; it is willingly accepted and practised. Paul was persuaded that the freedom of the Spirit was a more powerful incentive to the good life than all the ordinances or decrees in the world. ...['Living according to the Spirit' meant for Paul that] the will of God had not changed; but *whereas formerly it was recorded on tablets of stone it was now engraved on human hearts*, and inward impulsion accomplished what external compulsion could not.... So far as Paul is concerned, *guidance for the church is provided by the law of love, not*

---

1. F. F. Bruce, *Paul: Apostle of the Heart Set Free* (Grand Rapids: Eerdmans, 1996 reprint of 1977 edition), 192.

by the 'law of commandments and ordinances' (Ephesians 2:15). ...unlike Paul's contemporary critics, Christian moralists since Paul's day have tended to hold that, in insisting on prudential rules and regulations, they are following the implications of his teaching, if not his express judgements. But we should appreciate that Paul conforms no more to the conventions of religious people today than he conformed to the conventions of religious people around A.D. 50; it is best to let Paul be Paul. And when we do that, we shall recognize in him the supreme libertarian, the great herald of Christian freedom, insisting that man in Christ has reached his spiritual majority and must no longer be confined to the leading-strings of infancy but enjoy the birthright of freeborn sons of God. Here if anywhere Luther entered into the mind of Paul: 'A Christian man is a most free lord of all, subject to none. A Christian man is a most dutiful servant of all, subject to all.' 'Subject to none' in respect of his liberty; 'subject to all' in respect of his charity. This, for Paul, is the law of Christ because this was the way of Christ.[2]

Divine revelation – indeed, Paul himself – however, defines that likeness to God according to which Christians' lives are to be patterned more concretely than Bruce would have us believe, couching that likeness in terms of conformity to *God's preceptive will* for them, which is simply the moral law of God as that law comes to verbal expression in the Ten Commandments (Ex 20:1-17; Deut 5:6-21) and to living expression in Christ's life of obedience to it (Rom 5:18-19; Phil 2:8; Heb 5:8). That is to say, it is the Decalogue, being obeyed in love for God, which is the ethical norm for the Christian's covenant way of life.

Of course, for many Christians today, to speak about Christian ethics and the Ten Commandments in the same breath is to graze the rim of, if not actually to enter into, *legalism*. This, of course, is a mistaken notion. The proper definition of legalism is given by the *Shorter Oxford Dictionary*: 'adherence to law as opposed to the gospel; the doctrine of justification by works, or teaching which savors of it.' This historic meaning of the term should be kept in mind, for it is all too common in the twentieth century to find the term being used for 'adherence to God's precepts as the norm of morality' which is something altogether different. By such misuse of the term the negative connotations of legalism are transferred to the morality of orthodox Protestantism. The doctrine of justification by faith alone

---

2. Bruce, *Paul*, 187, 200, 201, 202, emphasis supplied.

clearly relieves the latter from the charge of legalism. Still, an ethical position might 'savor' of legalism if it failed to give adequate attention to union with Christ as the ethical dynamic of the Christian life (see Rom 6:1-14) and to the enabling work of the Holy Spirit in sanctification. Such a charge cannot be leveled against the *Westminster Confession of Faith* which affirms the necessity of 'the Spirit of Christ subduing and enabling the will of man to do that freely, and cheerfully, which the will of God, revealed in the law, requireth to be done' (XIX/vii). A truly biblical ethic is concerned with obedience to God's precepts made possible by the Spirit of life in Christ Jesus (Rom 8:4). It is this 'manner of life and behaviour which the Bible requires and which the faith of the Bible produces'.[3]

The Third Use of the Law

The use of the Decalogue for Christian ethics has come to be referred to as 'the third use of the law' and is captured in the words of the third stanza of Loy's poem. The other two uses are, first, its moral standards which serve as the rule and norm of all true civil righteousness (Loy's fourth stanza), and second, its 'tutorial' work of convicting sinners, through the agency of the Holy Spirit, of their sins and thus driving them to Christ that they may be justified by faith (Gal 3:24; Loy's second stanza).

Some Lutherans, applying their law-gospel paradigm, reject this third use of the law (though it is clearly taught by Melanchthon and the *Formula of Concord*, Article VI), fearing that it intrudes legalism into the Christian experience.

Dispensationalists, fearing the heresy of 'Galatianism', also reject the notion that Christians are under the so-called 'Mosaic law'. For example, Lewis Sperry Chafer declares that Christians are not obligated to obey the Decalogue as such and cites Paul's statement that 'we are not under law but under grace' to prove it (Rom 6:15; see Gal 3:24-25).[4] These Christians argue that Paul teaches that the law has been fulfilled and hence done away in Christ. They are bound to Christ, they declare, and therefore are obligated only to serve him

---

3. John Murray, *Principles of Conduct* (Grand Rapids: Eerdmans, 1957), 12.

4. Lewis Sperry Chafer, *Systematic Theology* (Grand Rapids: Kregel, 1993 reprint of 1947 edition), IV, 209, writes: 'Must Christians turn to the Decalogue for a basis of divine government in their daily lives? Scripture answers this question with a positive assertion: "Ye are not under the law, but under grace." ' F. F. Bruce would concur.

out of love for him. I have been afforded the opportunity on several occasions to speak to dispensational thinkers who were contending, because they were 'not under law but under grace', that they were bound only to the 'law of Christ'[5] and were under no obligation to obey the Decalogue. My first question has always been, 'Can Christians sin?' Their answer, of course, has always been unequivocally in the affirmative. My second question has always been, 'What is the nature of their sin?' Their answer, of course, has always been, 'Sin is disobedience to the law of Christ.' I have then asked them to give me examples of the law of Christ against which Christians can sin. They have usually said: 'Simply Christ's two great love commandments, which are: "You shall love the Lord your God with all your heart, and with all your soul, and with all your mind, and with all your strength," and, "You shall love your neighbor as yourself." ' (Of course, the Old Testament said these things before Jesus did, and of course these are divine commandments under which they acknowledge that they stand. They must believe that they are under obligation to obey these

---

5. Paul uses the phrase 'the law of Christ' (ὁ νόμος τοῦ Χριστοῦ) as such only once (Gal 6:2) and the related expression 'subject to the law of Christ' (ἔννομος Χριστοῦ) only once (1 Cor 9:21). F. F. Bruce and R. Y. K. Fung suggest that this law is the law of love, C. H. Dodd argues that it refers to the dominical teachings of Jesus; O. Hofius, seeing in the Galatians context an allusion to the 'burden-bearing' Servant of Isaiah 42:1-4 and 52:13-53:12, urges that this law's referent is a similar 'burden-bearing' quality in Christians; R. B. Hays suggests that it intends the 'pattern' of Christ's life as the Christian's paradigm for living; and H. D. Betz argues that Paul is simply employing his opponents' expression. But there is nothing in either context to warrant any other conclusion than that Paul intended by the expression to refer to the moral norms of the Old Testament as those norms are obeyed in love to Christ and to one's neighbor.

In 1 Corinthians 9:21, even before he declares about himself that he is 'under Christ's law', that is, 'in law [that is, 'subject to law'] toward Christ', Paul writes: 'though I am not free from God's law [μὴ ὢν ἄνομος θεοῦ; lit. "not being lawless toward God"],' that is to say, he was not free from 'keeping God's commands [τήρησις ἐντολῶν θεοῦ]' (see 1 Cor 7:19 and my later comments on this verse). He says this precisely to make it clear that he was not antinomian.

Regarding the expression, 'the law of Christ', as it is found in Galatians 6:2, since it is a *hapax* it is best to interpret it within the section of the letter within which it occurs, namely, within Galatians 5:13-6:10. In 6:2 Paul declares that by bearing another Christian's burden with him, 'you will fulfill [ἀναπληρώσετε] the law of Christ.' But when Paul refers in 5:14 to 'the entire law [ὁ πᾶς νόμος]' being fulfilled (πεπλήρωται), while he finds this fulfillment in love, it is clear that he is thinking of the Old Testament law because he cites the love commandment of Leviticus 19:18: 'Love your neighbor as yourself.' This implies that one must fulfill the moral requirements of the Old Testament law relative to one's neighbor if one is to fulfill the 'law of Christ' that Paul has in mind.

See T. R. Schreiner, 'Law of Christ,' *Dictionary of Paul and His Letters*, edited by Gerald F. Hawthorne, Ralph P. Martin, and Daniel G. Reid (Downers Grove, Ill.: InterVarsity, 1993), 542-44.

commandments because Christ placed them under them and not because the God of the Old Testament did so.) I have then asked: 'How does one show concretely his love to God and to his neighbor, as Christ commands?' On every occasion, their response to my fourth question has become essentially a recitation of the laws of the Decalogue; as they must, they have regularly responded: 'One shows his love to God by worshiping God only and by never putting anything before him, by never making any image of him, by never taking his name in vain, that is, by keeping his commandments, as John says in 1 John 5:2-3 [dispensationalists usually omit his fourth commandment]. And one shows his love for his neighbor by honoring his parents, by not murdering his neighbor, by not committing adultery against him, by not stealing from him, by not bearing false witness against him, and by not coveting that which belongs to him.' So much for the dispensational contention that Christians are not under the Decalogue as the moral law of God for all men.

But does the New Testament repeal the Decalogue's normative character for Christian life and practice? Because it is Paul in particular who is credited with teaching this, it is important that we address this matter of Paul's teaching on the Christian's relation to the law of God.[6] At the outset, it is striking to note that the great Apostle of justification by faith alone completely apart from the works of the law can still speak of the law of God as holy, just, spiritual, and good (Rom 7:12, 14, 16) and can contend that all the world is accountable to God because all men are 'under the law' (Rom 3:19). He makes it clear that obedience is conformity to God's will and that God's will provides the specific norms or standards for Christian obedience. Here, as in the case of the content of the gospel message itself, the norms or standards are sometimes presumed or assumed and not always specifically stated. At times, however, the basis or standard is stated in very significant ways. In *these* places it becomes clear that the foundational character of Paul's ethic is God's revealed preceptive will or law.

The norm or standard in Paul's ethic is, first, the law of God known by all men because they are made in the image of God: 'Although they know the *righteous ordinance* [τὸ δικαίωμα] of God, that those

---

6. I am indebted to George W. Knight, III, for several of the following insights on Paul's teaching on the Christian's relation to the law. See also John Murray, *Principles of Conduct*, Chapter VIII, 'Law and Grace,' 181-201, for a superb treatment of this topic.

who practice such things [as he lists in Rom 1:29-31] are worthy of death, they not only do the same, but also give hearty approval to them who practice them' (Rom 1:32). Paul's foundational premise here is that men are aware of the basic moral teaching of God made known through God's general revelation to them (see Rom 1:26, 27; 2:14ff; 1 Cor 11:14). Thus it is that Paul speaks of conscience (συνείδησις)—the self-conscious self-evaluative process of assessing the degree of one's moral success or integrity—within men because they are made in God's image (see Rom 2:15). This is not to say that man's conscience is an independent norm but only that man's conscience is a scale which registers or reflects within him his own awareness of God's standard. *His conscience bears witness to the presence of God's norm within him.*

It is not very often, however, that Paul utilizes this perspective, regarding men in general, of Christians. Of the latter Paul speaks of informing their conscience by God's written word-revelation. He does not presume that their conscience does not need more instruction. But Romans 1:32 does indicate that at the most rudimentary level of human existence, the ordinance or law of God is understood to be the norm of human ethics or conduct. This aspect of the ordinance or law of God Paul develops from its most rudimentary and implicit presence to an explicit unfolding of the normative character of God's law.

For Paul the moral law of God, which Christians are to obey, is revealed in the Scriptures—especially (but not exclusively) in the Decalogue:

Romans 7:7: '...I would not have come to know sin except through the law; for I would not have known about coveting if the law had not said, *"You shall not covet."* '

Romans 8:4f: The work of Christ and of the Spirit in reference to sanctification and obedience is described here in terms, *not* of the requirements of Christ, but of the 'requirements of the law being fulfilled *in* [or *by*] us' (ἐν ἡμῖν). Here we see Paul placing ethics in this principial framework: Christ has redeemed us in order to enable us to obey the moral requirements of the law, and the Holy Spirit is enabling us to walk in the law's requirements. From Paul's statement in 8:7 that the ungodly mind cannot subject itself to the law of God, we should infer, I would submit, that the godly can. All the moral teaching that follows in Romans may in a real sense be seen as a statement of the law's requirements.

Romans 12:1-2: When Paul, beginning in Romans 12, takes up the matter of the moral outworking of justification, he does so by picking up on his earlier emphasis on God's law. Only now he does so by speaking of the law under the synonym of 'the will of God' (τὸ θέλημα τοῦ θεοῦ), describing God's will here in terms similar to those which he had used earlier to describe the law (see his 'good and acceptable and perfect will of God' here and his earlier description in 7:13 of the law as 'holy and just and good'). Here Paul calls on the Christian to use his renewed mind to discern and to obey God's law.

Romans 13:9ff: Before he turns to the specific problem of meat offered to idols, Paul brings to a conclusion his general section on ethics by quoting most of the second half of the Ten Commandments: '...he who loves his neighbor has fulfilled the law. For this, *"You shall not commit adultery, You shall not murder, You shall not steal, You shall not covet," and if there is any other commandment* [and we may be sure that Paul knew that there were other commandments], it is summed up in this saying, "You shall love your neighbor as yourself." Love does no wrong to a neighbor; love therefore is the fulfillment of the law.' Paul indicates that the four commandments he mentions (the sixth, seventh, eighth, and tenth) do not comprise the whole law by adding the words, 'and if there is any other commandment.' And his appeal to the Decalogue in the way which he does, as that which the law of love fulfills, demonstrates the permanent and abiding relevance of the law. Paul's specific appeal to the love obligation also reminds the Christian that his (Paul's) standard is the same as Jesus had indicated in his summary of the Ten Commandments: 'You shall love your neighbor as yourself' (he quotes Lev 19:18 in Rom 13:9; see Mark 12:31; Matt 7:12). He correlates 'love' and 'law' by saying in 13:10 that 'love is the fulfillment of the law'. Paul says again here then that the standard of ethics is the law. The very way in which it may be carried out or fulfilled is by the attitude and action of love. As Paul says in Galatians 5:6, 13, it is out of the Christian's 'new life' in Christ that faith works through love. In sum, *the norm or standard of the Christian life is the law, and the motive power to keep it is the new life in Christ, that is, life in the Spirit, which exhibits itself as a life of obedience which is the expression of love.*

Love finds its direction and its parameters in the law of God. Love is not contentless or only a warm and undefined feeling, nor is it something that may be set in opposition to the law. The law does not need to be a 'dead letter', but neither is it an entity which has its own inherent strength. Love expresses the true intent and direction of the law as God's good for man and as the way in which men properly express their love to God and man in the ethical realm.

1 Corinthians 7:19: Here Paul exhorts Christians to understand that 'circumcision is nothing and uncircumcision is nothing. *Keeping God's commands is what counts* [ἀλλὰ τήρησις ἐντολῶν θεοῦ]'. He says essentially the same thing in Galatians 5:6 when he writes: 'In Christ Jesus neither circumcision nor uncircumcision has any value. The only thing that counts is *faith expressing itself through love,*' love being viewed here as active obedience to God's commandments.

Contrary to what most studies have concluded, by setting circumcision, which was itself a ceremonial command of God, in contrast to the 'commandments of God' (ἐντολῶν θεοῦ), as he does in 1 Corinthians 7:19, Paul distinguishes here between the ethical and the ceremonial, that is, between the permanent and the temporary aspects of the Law, insisting on the essentiality of keeping God's moral law while at the same time insisting on the non-essentiality and insignificance of keeping the ceremonial law.

1 Timothy 1:8-11: Paul insists here that the purpose of the law, indeed, its continuing purpose, is ethical. It is not to be construed as the false teachers were doing. Thus the law is not 'made' for the 'righteous', that is, for the obedient man who is already molding his life in accordance with them. Of course, in saying this, Paul is not denying the law's relevance for Christians but rather is insisting on its *ethical* dimension. In 1:9-10 he virtually summarizes the Ten Commandments in their Old Testament order,[7] and with the strongest and clearest application – following the example of the Old Testament application in Exodus 21 and elsewhere – states the worst expression of the violation of each commandment to remind the reader of the

---

7. See George W. Knight, III, *The Pastoral Epistles* (Grand Rapids: Eerdmans, 1992), 82-87, for his insightful argument.

focus of these commands, that is, to the sinner. For example, to those whom sin tempts to be immoral in the sexual realm, the command says, 'You shall not commit adultery.' So Paul reminds his readers of the ethical and lawful use of the law. Therefore, to seek to use this passage in reference to the righteous or obedient man in other than in its ethical significance is quite erroneous. Finally, Paul closes this section by saying that law rules to restrain whatever is contrary to the sound teaching of the gospel (1:10-11). Thus again we see that the law's ethic and the gospel ethic are essentially one and the same.

Ephesians 6:2-3: Here Paul quotes the fifth commandment that children must honor their parents: 'Children, obey your parents in the Lord, for this is right. "*Honor your father and mother* (which is the first commandment with a promise), *that it may be well with you, and that you may live long on the earth.*" ' He does this with the assumption that the Christian community would recognize and accept the abiding significance of the law. He does not quote the law to make it binding but because it is binding. And he quotes this commandment as part of a whole, one among others (see his 'which is the *first* commandment with a promise'), which they would know, recognize, and follow. He quotes the commandments with the same ease and assumption with which he refers to the gospel (which also is not always named by name or repeated but assumed).

The focus of the 'second table' of the Ten Commandments (Fifth through Tenth) on disobedience can often be found in Paul's admonitions against sin, for example, against sexual immorality, stealing, coveting, and bearing false witness (see Eph 4:25, 28; 5:3, 5; Col 3:5, 9; 1 Cor 6:9-10), but of course not in a wooden or simply citational way.

The law's focus on disobedience Paul also underscores by citing other Old Testament passages to state his ethical teaching (see, for example, the end of Romans 12, not to mention earlier allusions; see also Eph 4:25-26; 5:31; 1 Cor 9:8ff, 11:8, 9; 14:34; 1 Tim 5:17ff). In fact, much of Paul's positive teachings he simply finds in the Old Testament and reiterates for his readers. In this approach he has followed Jesus' practice in the Sermon on the Mount who in his Beatitudes and in his correction of Judaism's misuse of the law was teaching the standards of his Father, the moral law of the Old Testament.

The Pauline Ethic

1 Corinthians 9:20-21: Here Paul declares that he is 'not free from the law of God but under the law of Christ'. That is to say, in terms of its ceremonial requirements Paul was not under the law; in terms of its moral code as the law of God and of Christ, he was under it.

2 Timothy 3:16-17: Here Paul informs Timothy that the *entirety of Scripture*, in a real sense *the* law (torah) of God, is profitable for teaching, rebuking, correcting, and training in righteousness, so that the man of God may be thoroughly equipped for every good work.

George E. Ladd is quite correct then when he concludes that Paul

> never thinks of the Law as being abolished. It remains the [ethical] expression of the will of God... The permanence of the Law is reflected...in the fact that Paul appeals to specific commands in the Law as the norm for Christian conduct...[For example, from Rom 13:8-10 and Eph 6:2] it is clear that the Law [in its ethical demands] continues to be the expression of the will of God for conduct, even for those who are no longer under the Law...the Law as the expression of the will of God is permanent.[8]

While we are primarily concerned with Paul's understanding of the relation between the Christian and the Decalogue, it would not be out of place to consider what the other New Testament writers say about this relationship. James cites the sixth and seventh commandments: 'For whoever keeps the whole law and yet stumbles in one point, he has become guilty of all. For he who said, "*Do not commit adultery*," also said, "*Do not commit murder*." Now if you do not commit adultery, but do commit murder, you [his Christian readers] have become a transgressor of the law' (James 2:10-11).[9]

Paul and the other New Testament writers also allude to every commandment in some one place or other in their letters to the churches:

the *first, second, and third* commandments lie behind many of the statements in Romans 1:21-30, 2:22, 1 Corinthians 6:9, Ephesians 5:5, Colossians 3:5, James 2:7, 19, and Revelation 21:7;

---

8. George Eldon Ladd, *Theology of the New Testament* (Grand Rapids: Eerdmans, 1974), 509-10.

9. It is significant to our present purpose to emphasize the fact that James in verse 10 enunciates the principle of the law's *unitary wholeness*. This certainly implies that if the sixth and seventh commandments are still normative for Christ's church and for society in general, so are the other eight.

the *fourth* commandment lies behind the designation of the first day of the week—the Christian's day of worship—as 'the Lord's day' (Acts 20:7, 1 Cor 16:2, and Rev 1:10; cf. Isa 58:13)[10];

the *fifth* commandment lies behind statements in Romans 1:30, Ephesians 6:2-3, Colossians 3:20, and 1 Timothy 1:9;

the *sixth* commandment lies behind statements in Romans 1:29, 13:9, 1 Timothy 1:9-10, James 2:11, 1 John 3:15, and Revelation 21:8;

the *seventh* commandment lies behind statements in Romans 2:22, 13:9, 1 Corinthians 6:9, Ephesians 5:3, 1 Thessalonians 4:3, 1 Timothy 1:10, James 2:11, Revelation 21:8;

the *eighth* commandment lies behind statements in Romans 2:21, 13:9, 1 Corinthians 6:10, Ephesians 4:28, 1 Timothy 1:10;

the *ninth* commandment lies behind statements in Romans 13:9, Ephesians 4:25, Colossians 3:9, 1 Timothy 1:10, and Revelation 21:8; and

the *tenth* commandment lies behind statements in Romans 1:29; 7:7-8, 13:9, 1 Corinthians 6:10, Galatians 5:26, Ephesians 5:5, Colossians 3:5, and Hebrews 13:5.

In addition, the two great Old Testament love commandments – to love God with all one's heart, soul, mind and strength and to love one's neighbor as oneself (Deut 6:5; Lev 19:18), which are beautifully New Testament as well in scope and concept—are declared to be summary statements of the Ten Commandments (see Matt 22:37-40; Mark 12:29-31; Romans 13:8-19), which love commandments no Christian should suggest have been abrogated for this age. Surely the Christian is to obey *these* two commandments! Indeed, Jesus said to his disciples: 'If you love me, you will keep my commandments' (John 14:15), and again, 'You are my friends, if you do what I command you' (John 15:14). And John declared: 'We know that we have come to know him if we keep his commandments'

---

10. See my extended argument, 'Lord's Day Observance: Man's Proper Response to the Fourth Commandment,' *Presbyterion: Covenant Seminary Review* (XIII, 1 [Spring 1987]), 7-23. See also Richard B. Gaffin, Jr., 'A Sabbath Rest Still Awaits the People Of God,' *Pressing Toward the Mark*, edited by C. G. Dennison and R. C. Gamble (Philadelphia: Committee for the Historian of the Orthodox Presbyterian Church, 1986), 33-51, who argues against the view that the Sabbath commandment has been done away in Christ by showing that the weekly Sabbath is the sign of the future Sabbath rest of Hebrews 3:7-4:13: 'To deny this is to suppose that for the writer the weekly sign has ceased, even though the reality to which it points is still future – again, an unlikely supposition. What rationale could explain such a severing, by cessation, of sign and unfulfilled reality?' (47).

(1 John 2:3), going on then actually to define love for God in terms of obedience to his law: 'This is love for God, that we keep his commandments' (1 John 5:3).

Ernest F. Kevan, British theologian and author of *The Grace of Law*, quite correctly concludes regarding the continuing normativity of the law:

> There is no hint anywhere in the New Testament that the Law has lost its validity in the slightest degree, nor is there any suggestion of its repeal. On the contrary, the New Testament teaches unambiguously that the Ten Commandments are still binding upon all men.[11]

Reformed Christians then deny that 'the third use of the law' places the Christian under the law as a covenant of works, insisting rather that

> The moral law doth for ever bind all, as well justified persons as others, to the obedience therefore; and that, not only in regard of the matter contained in it, but also in respect of the authority of God the Creator, who gave it. Neither doth Christ, in the Gospel, any way dissolve, but much strengthen this obligation.
>
> Although true believers be not under the law, as a covenant of works, to be thereby justified, or condemned; yet is it of great use to them, as well as to others; in that, as a rule of life informing them of the will of God, and their duty, it directs and binds them to walk accordingly; discovering [revealing] also the sinful pollutions of their nature, hearts, and lives; so as, examining themselves thereby, they may come to further conviction of, humiliation for, and hatred against sin, together with a clearer sight of the need they have of Christ, and the perfection of his obedience. It is likewise of use to the regenerate, to restrain their corruptions, in that it forbids sin: and the threatenings of it serve to show what even their sins deserve; and what afflictions, in this life, they may expect for them, although freed from the curse thereof threatened in the law. The promises of it, in like manner, show them God's approbation of obedience, and what blessings they may expect upon the performance thereof: although not as due to them by the law as a covenant of works. So as, a man's doing good, and refraining from evil, because the law encourageth to the one, and deterreth from the other, is no evidence of his being under the law; and not under grace.

---

11. Ernest F. Kevan, 'The Evangelical Doctrine of Law', *Tyndale Biblical Theology Lecture*, July 4, 1955. See also Herman Ridderbos's discussion of and similar conclusion concerning the 'Tertius Usus Legis' in his *Paul: An Outline of His Theology*, translated by John R. DeWitt (Grand Rapids: Eerdmans, 1975), 278-88.

Neither are the forementioned uses of the law contrary to the grace of the Gospel, but do sweetly comply with it; the Spirit of Christ subduing and enabling the will of man to do that freely, and cheerfully, which the will of God, revealed in the law, requireth to be done. (*Westminster Confession of Faith*, XIX/v-vii; see also the extended expositions of the law of God in both the *Westminster Larger Catechism* and *Westminster Shorter Catechisms.*)

Christian Intuitionism

Bruce's proposal and proposals resembling it – heard so often today that the position has acquired among Christian ethicists its own special designation, namely, 'Christian Intuitionism' – is that the renewed consciousness of the Christian has an intuitive sense of what is right and wrong. A popular version of this ethical theory is expressed by the words, 'As a Christian I don't need a written code of regulations. The law of love, infused within me by the Holy Spirit, will lead me to do the right thing.' This proposal urges that since the heart of the believer is renewed after the image of God in knowledge, righteousness, holiness, and love, the renewed person will spontaneously respond in the only way that bespeaks the divine exemplar after which the heart has been renewed. Of course, since the same renewal occurs over time in the hearts of a great number of individuals, which renewal dictates similar responses to similar situations, these 'common responses' produce a 'moral convention' which can become codified and systematized. If there are any objective norms of acceptable behavior, this is the explanation for their appearance. That is to say, any objective norms are human conventions which flow out of the renewed spirit, not objective norms revealed by God that exist objectively prior to the *palingenesis* to which the renewed spirit must give heed. In sum, the renewed heart does not require objective laws in order to know what to do or not to do.

Masquerading as a Christian ethic, an extreme contemporary humanistic example of this same rejection of all objective norms for human behavior in deference to love alone is *situation ethics*. The command of love, J. A. T. Robinson, late Bishop of Woolwich, avers, is such that 'apart from this there are no unbreakable rules'.[12] The various ethical injunctions of the New Testament are indeed

---

12. J. A. T. Robinson, *Christian Morals Today* (Philadelphia: Westminster, 1964), 16.

'comprehended under the one command of love and based upon it'. But

> in Christian ethics the only pure statement is the command to love: every other injunction depends on it and is an explication or application of it. There are some things of which one may say that it is so inconceiveable that they could ever be an expression of love—like cruelty to children [what about abortion on demand?] or rape—that one might say without much fear of contradiction that they are for Christians always wrong. But they are so persistently wrong *for that reason*.[13]

Robinson acknowledges that the whole class of actions prohibited by the second table of the Decalogue are 'fundamentally destructive of human relationships'. But he goes on to say that this does not mean that any of them cannot be right in certain circumstances.[14]

A little later Robinson states the key principle of the new morality: 'It starts from persons rather than principles, from experienced relationships rather than revealed commandments.'[15] Leaving comment aside on the fact that Robinson himself appeals to at least *one* revealed command – the command to love – there are two other problems with his principle. The first clause posits an antithesis between persons and principles without considering whether principles may not in fact embody personal concerns—principles having to do with things like cruelty to children and rape. The second clause is a self-conscious rejection of revelation for empiricism (see his 'from experienced relationships'), thus insuring epistemological uncertainty for his ethic. This 'uncertainty' problem surfaces concretely in Robinson's treatment of pre-marital sex. He says: 'Outside marriage sex is bound to be the expression of less than unreserved sharing and commitment of one person to another.' Now, one might say something like this on the basis of divine revelation, but what is the *empirical* basis for the assertion? Robinson must be able to demonstrate that pre-marital sex has the evil consequences he alleges before his principle is justified. But Robinson offers no argument; he is simply conservative on the issue, having held on to some of his borrowed orthodox capital. 'The one thing that finally counts is treating persons as persons with unconditional seriousness.'[16]

---

13. Robinson, *Christian Morals Today*, 16, emphasis original.
14. This would imply, of course, that the circumstance or situation would determine whether murder, adultery, theft, and lying under oath are morally right or wrong.
15. Robinson, *Christian Morals Today*, 35.

The problem with this is the assumption that we ourselves know what love is and can act on it in any situation. This involves an unrealistic view of man who not only has only a finite perspective on such things but also a deceitful heart.

Joseph Fletcher also holds that the ruling norm of Christian ethical decision making is love alone. 'Any ethical system is unchristian,' he writes. 'Jesus had no ethics, if...ethics [is] a system of values and rules intelligible to all men.' Whereas Paul wrote that love is the summary of the law, Fletcher exclaims: 'Only the summary of the law [that is, love] is the law!'[17] Love may find itself in fact pitted against the Decalogue. Principles may serve as illuminating maxims of conduct, but they are to be set aside if love is served by doing so in a particular situation. 'Act responsibly in love' is the sole ethical demand.

Fletcher once stated the central issue in the debate over situation ethics this way: 'Are there any moral principles, other than to do the most good possible, which oblige us in conscience at all times?'[18] To answer in the negative, as Fletcher does, is to place oneself with ethical utilitarians (and all the objections to it),[19] as Fletcher himself later confesses:

---

16. Robinson, *Christian Morals Today*, 37.

17. Fletcher, *Situation Ethics: The New Morality* (Philadelphia: Westminster, 1966), 77.

18. Fletcher, 'Situation Ethics Under Fire' in *Storm Over Ethics*, edited by John C. Bennett (Philadelphia: United Church, 1967), 151.

19. Ethical utilitarianism is the view that the good life is the one that provides the greatest good for the greatest number. This thesis envisages that at least some people, the smaller number, will suffer for the benefit of the majority's good. Associated with the name of Oxford-trained Jeremy Bentham (1748-1832), this hedonistic theory urges that one ought to seek, not only his own pleasure (egoistic hedonism), but also the greatest pleasure of the greatest number, this pleasure to be measured and determined by the seven parameters of its intensity, its duration, its certainty, its propinquity (or remoteness), its fecundity (that is, the chance a pleasureable act has of being followed by sensations of pleasure of the same kind), its purity (that is, the chance a pleasureable act has of not being followed by sensations of the opposite kind), and its extent (that is, the number of persons to whom the pleasurable act extends, that is, the number or persons who are affected by it) (Bentham). Regarding just this last parameter, Bentham writes:

> Take an account of the *number* of persons whose interests appear to be concerned; and repeat the above processes with respect to each. *Sum up* the numbers expressive of the degrees of *good* tendency, which the act has, with respect to each individual, in regard to whom the tendency of it is *good* upon the whole: do this again with respect to each individual, in regard to whom the tendency of it is bad upon the whole. Take the *balance*; which, if on the side of *pleasure*, will give the general *good tendency* of the act, with respect to the total number or community of individuals concerned; if on the side of pain, the general *evil tendency*, with respect to the same community.

Let's say plainly that *agape* is utility; love is well-being; the Christian who does not individualize or sentimentalize love is a utilitarian.... Then what remains as a difference between the Christian and most utilitarians is only the language used, and their different answers given to the questions: 'Why be concerned, why care?'[20]

A Biblical Theistic Response to Christian Intuitionism

There is a surface appearance of truth in these antinomian positions on two grounds: First, Paul does teach that even in the hearts of those who have never received special revelation the works of the law are written so that Gentiles (sometimes) do by nature[21] the things of the law (Rom 2:14-15). How much more significant, powerful, and intuitive then may we assume that inner inscription of the law to be in the hearts of those who have been regenerated. Second, the requirements of the entire law admittedly are fulfilled in the outflowing of one's love toward God and his neighbor (Matt 22:37-40). It would seem to follow then that to the extent to which love governs one, just to that same extent he fulfills the demands of the

---

Accordingly, one is to do that which brings the greatest pleasure to the greatest number of people. When one has to choose before two courses of action, he should calculate the amounts of pleasure and of pain each course of action would produce for him personally. Then he should make the same calculation for every other human being. One course of action would produce x units of pleasure for y number of people while the other course of action would produce w units of pleasure for z number of people. The same calculations should be done for pain.

As has been often noted, however, to calculate the sum total of pleasures and pains two incompatible courses of action will produce even for oneself is an impossibility. And to suppose that one can calculate units of pleasure and of pain accruing to the whole human race is nothing short of utter madness (Gordon Clark – '...how much pleasure or pain will my action today produce for a Chinese peasant a few hundred years from now?'). Were it possible to calculate such abstractions, as Kant noted, only mathematical geniuses (and I might add, mathematical geniuses with omniscience and eternal longevity) could be moral.

Second, this principle for determining one's choices is one by which dictators can justify any cruelty since the rights of minorities are given no place in such an ethic. In fact, this ethical theory has been used to justify massacre, for example, Stalin's murder of millions of Ukrainians and the suppression of the Hungarians. Apparently, these actions caused considerable pain to many people but their pain was 'over-balanced' by the pleasures of the greater number of happy communists who benefited from Stalin's oppression.

Third, utilitarianism can offer no reason why anyone should be concerned for the good of all society. In fact, no descriptive science, which is what Bentham's utilitarianism purports to be, can justify why anyone should govern his actions by the good of others.

20. Fletcher, 'What's in a Rule?: A Situationist's View' in *Norm and Context in Christian Ethics*, edited by Gene H. Outka and Paul Ramsey (New York: Charles Scribner's Sons, 1967), 332.

21. Paul is very careful not to say that Gentiles always conform to the demands of the law. He says: 'When Gentiles...do by nature things required by the law....'

biblical ethic, and where love is perfected, there ethical behavior is perfected. It could be argued then that the intuited 'readings' of love's dictates are all the 'norms' that one needs to have a biblical ethic.

Against both Decalogue-rejecting Christian intuitionists such as F. F. Bruce and Decalogue-rejecting situation ethicists such as Robinson and Fletcher I want to insist that the 'law written inwardly' and the outflow of love toward God and one's neighbor which springs naturally from every renewed heart cannot and do not do away with the need for objective norms for approved behavior. I say this for the following reasons.

I. The Insufficiency of 'Natural Law Theory'

With respect to the first of these two conditions (the 'law written inwardly'), the first question that must be addressed is this: *Is natural law theory, grounded as it is in the presumption of the 'inwardly written law', sufficient to ground ethical behavior?* Natural law theory contends that 'there is, by the very virtue of human nature, an order or a disposition which human reason can discover.... The unwritten law, or Natural Law, is nothing more than that' (J. Maritain). This law of nature is considered superior to the statutes of the state; it is a norm for legislation; and a state is under obligation to confine its legislation within the limits prescribed by nature. But can human reason discover in human nature an order of morality that sets the norms for statutory law? Are Thomas Jefferson's 'unalienable rights', for example, 'self-evident' in the laws of nature, as he claimed?[22] He himself owned slaves. DNA testing has shown that he may have fathered the fifth child of one of these slaves, Sally Hemings by name.

---

22. When Thomas Jefferson, as a man of the Enlightenment who rejected the divine authority of Holy Scripture and called the Gospel writers 'groveling authors' who displayed 'vulgar ignorance' and transmuted 'superstitions, fanaticisms, and fabrications' and the apostles a 'band of dupes and imposters', and who cited belief in the Trinity as proof that 'man, once surrendering his reason, has no remaining guard against absurdities the most monstrous', referred in the Declaration of Independence to the separate and equal station to which 'the Laws of Nature and of Nature's God' (a deist reference) entitle a people to assume, and when he declared certain 'truths to be *self-evident*', the first such truth being that 'all men are created equal, that they are endowed by their Creator with certain unalienable rights' (in the original draft Jefferson's phrase was 'are created equal and independent; that from that equal creation they are...'; a committee prevailed upon him to alter it to the present phrase), he was hardly providing adequate justification for the American revolution. For what are these laws of nature which support his 'self-evident truths', and how are they to be universally and unambiguously discerned? They cannot be so discerned. Hence his 'self-evident truths', grounded as they are only in Enlightenment theory, are more an assertion than the conclusion of a logically impeccable, demonstrable argument.

And the United States Constitution, as originally written, did not recognize slaves as full persons. Can limitations on governments, can the protection of minorities against the actions of majorities, can individual rights and liberties be established and maintained on natural law? Can these things be established and maintained by an observation of nature?

It is interesting to note that political theorists who were untouched by Christian revelation, almost without exception advocated some form of totalitarianism. If Plato was a communist, Aristotle was a fascist: private parental education was to be forbidden because education has as its aim the production of citizens for the good of the state. The number of children a family may have was to be controlled by the government, and surplus children were to be fed to the wolves. And everybody must profess the state religion. But if individual liberties were as self-evident as Jefferson supposed and if they can be learned by nature, would not Aristotle have recognized them?

Jean Jacques Rousseau (1712-1778) is equally totalitarian: 'There is,' he writes in his *Social Contract*, '...a purely civil profession of faith of which the Sovereign should fix the articles...If anyone, after recognizing these dogmas, behaves as if he does not believe them, let him be punished by death.' Again, if individual liberties were as self-evident as Jefferson supposed and if they can be learned by nature, would not Rousseau have recognized them? And in any case, would there not be a fairly widespread agreement on the details of these laws?

Thomas Aquinas argued that all things to which men have a natural inclination are naturally apprehended by reason as being good, but Duns Scotus replied that this leaves no method for determining whether an inclination is natural or unnatural. David Hume, in his critique – based upon the existence of injustices in the world – of the argument for God's existence, throws serious doubt on the natural law theory and demonstrates the difficulty, or rather the impossibility, of discovering by human reason any perfect justice in nature.

Now no orthodox Christian wants to deny that God at creation wrote the basic moral law on man's heart and that remnants of that law still remain stamped on human nature. But man fell into sin, corrupting his entire psyche thereby, and even though conscience still acts after a fashion, experiences of guilt occur all too infrequently and self-commendation occurs all too frequently, and both are all too frequently improperly assigned. Caesar, Napoleon, and Stalin took pride in their crimes, and looking carefully at nature and seeing nature 'red in tooth and claw', they could conclude that the universe is indifferent to the fate of the individual and that it is the law of nature for the brutal to rule the meek. There is evidence of natural inclinations for domination and a will to power on every hand in nature.

These brief considerations indicate that the theory of natural law is not a satisfactory theoretical defense of minority or individual rights. Human observation of nature (which includes the behavior of men) leads more naturally to totalitarian conclusions than to anything else other than anarchy. When, therefore, natural law advocates try to deduce normative conclusions from descriptive premises, they commit a major logical blunder, for no matter how carefully or how intricately they describe what men do, or what the provisions of nature are, or how natural inclinations function, it is a logical impossibility to conclude that this is or is not what men *ought* to do. The *is* never implies the *ought*. When the Thomist argues that it is a natural law to seek what is good, because as a matter of fact everybody seeks what is good, he reduces the term good to the several objects of human desire, which is hardly the biblical definition of the good. When he further states: 'No one calls in doubt the need for doing good, avoiding evil, acquiring knowledge, dispelling ignorance,'[23] he is simply closing his eyes to the massacre of the Huguenots and the massacre of the Covenanters by the Catholic Stuarts, Nietzsche's philosophy of the 'superman', the beatniks, the Mafia, the tribal wars of the Congo, and Stalin and his Communist regime.

I recognize, of course, that what I have been describing is the attitudes and actions, by and large, of the unregenerate heart and of fallen men in general. And, of course, the regenerate heart has been delivered from sin's mastery. But it does not follow from the fact of this new state that the regenerate heart instinctively knows, in its regenerate state, what it ought to do. Those who think so must not merely assert the fact; they must demonstrated it to be so.

---

23. Etienne Gilson, *The Christian Philosophy of St. Thomas Aquinas* (New York: Random House, 1956), 329.

II. The Inadequacy of 'Christian Intuitionism'

Against the second condition – the Christian intuitionist's insistence that the outflow of love toward God and one's neighbor which springs naturally from every renewed heart does away with the Christian's need for objective norms for approved behavior and his insistence that the intuited 'readings' of love's dictates are the only 'norms' that one needs to develop a biblical ethic—I would advance the following four arguments:

First, with John Murray I would urge that 'the thought of the passages [where the law is said to be written on the heart of the renewed person, Jer 31:33; Heb 8:10; 10:16] is not that we come to know what the law is by reading the inscription upon the heart. The thought is rather that there is generated in the sinful heart a new affinity with and a love to the law, to the end that there may be cheerful, spontaneous, loving fulfilment of it.' Surely Adam in the state of original integrity had the law of God inscribed upon his heart, but 'this inscription did not obviate the necessity of giving to Adam positive directions respecting the activity which was to engage interest, occupation, and life in this world'.[24] Murray explains:

> The procreative mandate, for example, had respect to the exercise of one of his fundamental instincts. Adam as created must have been endowed with the sex impulse which would have sought satisfaction and outlet in the sex act. But he was not left to the dictates of the sex impulse and of the procreative instinct; these were not a sufficient index to God's will for him. The exercise of this instinct was expressly commanded and its exercise directed to the achievement of a well-defined purpose. Furthermore, there was the marital ordinance within which alone the sex act was legitimate.
>
> These original mandates...show unmistakably that native endowment or instinct is not sufficient for man's direction even in the state of original integrity. The exercise of native instincts, the institutions within which they are to be exercised, and the ends to be promoted by their exercise are prescribed by specially revealed commandments. If all this is true in a state of sinless integrity, when where was no sin to blind vision or depravity to pervert desire, how much more must expressly prescribed directions be necessary in a state of sin in which intelligence is blinded, feeling depraved, conscience defiled, and will perverted![25]

---

24. Murray, *Principles of Conduct*, 25-26; see also Gen 1:27, 28; 2:2, 3, 15, 24.
25. Murray, *Principles of Conduct*, 26.

Second, I would say that while it is true that love is the fulfillment of the law (Matt 22:37-40; Rom 13:10), it must never be forgotten that

> love to God with all our heart and soul and strength and mind and love to our neighbor as ourselves are themselves commandments. We are *commanded* to love God and our neighbor. The antithesis which is oftentimes set up between love [as the only proper norm for action] and commandments [depicted as a sub-Christian norm for biblical ethics] overlooks this elementary fact. Love itself is exercised in obedience to a commandment: 'Thou shalt love.'[26]

Love then is not ultimate but is dictated by a divine command that is its logical prius. Love then is itself obedience to a commandment which comes from a source (namely, God) other than itself, and not to love is sin because it is the transgression of this commandment of God. We do not, by taking refuge in love as the only proper 'norm' of biblical ethics, totally escape thereby the norm of law.

Third, while again it is true that Jesus declares that on the two commandments of love hang all the law and the prophets (Matt 22:37-40) and Paul affirms that love is the fulfillment of the law (Gal 5:14), these very statements draw

> an obvious distinction between love and the law that hangs on it, and between love and the law that it fulfils.... In neither case do love and law have the same denotation. Hence there must be content to the law that is not defined by love itself. We may speak, if we will, of the law of love. But, if so, what we must have in view is the commandment to love or the law which love fulfils. We may not speak of the law of love if we mean that love is itself the law. Love cannot be equated with the law nor can law be defined in terms of love.[27]

Fourth, the consistent witness of Scripture is to the effect that love is never allowed to discover or dictate its own standards of conduct. The renewed heart is simply never allowed spontaneously to define the ethic of the saints of God. To the contrary, the Bible confronts us with objectively revealed precepts—all either explicit commandments or implicates of the Ten Commandments—to be

---

26. Murray, *Principles of Conduct*, 23.
27. Murray, *Principles of Conduct*, 24.

regarded as the norms for human behavior. Neither Adam in Paradise was permitted nor even the most committed saint since the Fall has been permitted to chart for himself the path he would take. Nor has the love which is the fulfillment of the law ever existed in a situation that is absent from the revelation of God respecting his will for mankind. To think so amounts to an abstraction that has never been true of the human experience. Rather, from the beginning—even from the state of innocence—into the New Testament era itself which extends to the present, the norms of human behavior have come in the form of divinely revealed objective commandments and precepts. After setting forth the doctrinal bases for the Christian life, the writers of the New Testament letters follow them with ethical imperatives addressed to the Christian mind and heart. They clearly understand that it is not enough to explicate the glories of our 'so great salvation' and to conclude their letters with such explication. They do not assume that the Holy Spirit will simply lead believers to see what they must do in light of their 'so great salvation'—the error of the Anabaptists in the sixteenth century who separated the Spirit of God from the written Word of God. To the contrary, they provide their readers detailed, at times highly detailed, moral instructions—this moral instruction, as we have seen, being nothing more than the Decalogue and/or its implicates (see the extended treatments of ethical behavior in Romans 12–16 and Ephesians 4–6).

To conclude, according to Murray, 'the notion...that love is its own law and the renewed consciousness its own monitor is a fantasy which has no warrant from Scripture and runs counter to the entire witness of biblical teaching.'[28] In sum, I would urge that the uniform biblical witness in this regard is that the Decalogue is the covenant norm and way of life for all human behavior, Christian no less than non-Christian.

---

28. Murray, *Principles of Conduct*, 26.

CHAPTER TWENTY-TWO

THE CHURCH

The church's one foundation is Jesus Christ, her Lord;
    She is his new creation by water and the Word:
From heav'n he came and sought her to be his holy bride;
    With his own blood he bought her, and for her life he died.

Elect from ev'ry nation, yet one o'er all the earth,
    Her charter of salvation one Lord, one faith, one birth;
One holy name she blesses, partakes one holy food,
    And to one hope she presses, with every grace endued.

The church shall never perish! Her dear Lord to defend,
    To guide, sustain, and cherish, is with her to the end;
Though there be those that hate her, and false sons in her pale,
    Against or foe or traitor she ever shall prevail.

'Mid toil and tribulation, and tumult of her war,
    She waits the consummation of peace forevermore;
Till with the vision glorious her longing eyes are blest,
    And the great church victorious shall be the church at rest.

Yet she on earth hath union with God the Three in One,
    And mystic sweet communion with those whose rest is won:
O happy ones and holy! Lord, give us grace that we ,
    Like them, the meek and lowly, on high may dwell with thee.
               – Thomas Benson Pollock, 1871

With the conversion of Saul of Tarsus and his subsequent missionary labors the gospel's advance throughout the northeastern provinces of the Roman world, as we have noted, enjoyed unprecedented success, with local churches (ἐκκλησίαι) being founded throughout Asia Minor, Macedonia, Greece, and even perhaps as far west as Spain (see Acts 14:23; 20:17; Gal 1:2; 1 Thess 1:1; 2 Thess 1:1; 1 Cor 1:2; 2 Cor 1:1; Col 4:16; Phlm 2; Rom 15:24).

In the course of reporting on Paul's ministry in Acts 13-28 Luke reports several striking things about Paul and the church. He reports that the church at Antioch commissioned Paul and Barnabas and sent them to their work (Acts 13:1-3); that Paul and Barnabas 'appointed elders *church-wide* [κατ᾽ ἐκκλησίαν]' throughout Galatia (Acts 14:23); that the church at Antioch sent Paul's party to the council at Jerusalem and that the church at Jerusalem received the Antioch party (Acts 15:3, 4); that Paul traveled through Syria and Cilicia, strengthening the church (15:41); and that churches were increasing in number daily (16:5). He reports as the aftermath of the Jerusalem Conference that once the church, through its representatives, had determined upon the course of action the church should follow with regard to the question of Gentile circumcision (here we see church government by the eldership in action), Paul and Silas delivered the Conference's Apostolic Decree (see 15:22-31) as 'decrees' or 'commands' (Acts 16:4; τὰ δόγματα) to the local churches and that they expected universal congregational compliance because of the connectionalism and mutual submission assumed to exist between the local gatherings of Christians.

Perhaps the most pregnant single notice about the nature of the church in Acts 13–28 occurs in Luke's report of Paul's farewell address to the Ephesian elders in Acts 20 in which Paul describes the city-church at Ephesus as a 'flock' and the elders themselves as 'overseers' (ἐπίσκοποι, plural of ἐπίσκοπος from which our word 'bishop' is derived) whom the Holy Spirit had appointed 'to shepherd [ποιμαίνειν] the church of God which he acquired through his own blood [or "the blood of his own (Son)"]' (Acts 20:28). From this statement we learn that the church belongs to God; he acquired it through the blood of his Son. In character, it is like a flock of sheep that needs shepherds because savage wolves (false teachers) will come in to draw disciples away after them. Elders, appointed by the Holy Spirit as overseers, are to be those shepherds to care for the church.

The Nature of the Church

While Paul employed many figurative expressions in his letters to refer to the church,[1] the study of any one of which richly rewarding its researcher, with the rest of the New Testament his most common

---

1. In addition to ἐκκλησία, his most common term, Paul employs many other images and metaphors to describe the church such as the following: the body of Christ (1 Cor 12:27;

term is ἐκκλησία,[2] with sixty-four of the one hundred and fourteen occurrences, that is, over one half of the occurrences, in the New Testament to be found in the Pauline corpus. One could easily write a dissertation on the church in Paul's theology; here we can only provide a summary.[3] To begin, local congregations of believers – often fellowships which met in homes belonging usually to wealthy persons (Rom 16:5; 23; 1 Cor 16:19; Col 4:15; Phlm 2) – stand alongside one another in Paul's mind as 'churches', as may be seen by his willingness to use the noun in the plural (Rom 16:4;, 16; 1 Cor 7:17; 14:33; 2 Cor 8:18; 11:8, 28; 12:13). He speaks of the 'church' at a certain place, such as 'the church at Cenchrea' (Rom 16:1), 'the church at Corinth' (1 Cor 1:2; 2 Cor 1:1), 'the church at Laodicea' (Col 4:16), and 'the church at Thessalonica' (1 Thess 1:1; 2 Thess

---

Eph 1:23; Col 1:18); the temple of God (or of the Holy Spirit) (1 Cor 3:16-17; 2 Cor 6:16-18; Eph 2:20-22; 2 Thess 2:4); God's household (1 Tim 3:15; Heb 3:1-6) in which God is 'Father' (Rom 8:15; Gal 4:9; Eph 3:14-15) of his 'adopted children' who have been redeemed by Christ (Rom 8:14-17; Gal 4:1-7) and in which Christ is the 'Firstborn' among many 'brothers', all of whom are 'heirs' of God (Rom 8:17, 29); the Jerusalem that is above (Gal 4:26); the new Jerusalem (Heb 12:22); the pillar and ground of the truth (1 Tim 3:15); a letter from Christ (2 Cor 3:2-3); the olive tree (Rom 11:13-24); God's field (1 Cor 3:9); God's building (1 Cor 3:9); the wife of Christ (Eph 5:22-31); fellow citizens with the saints (Eph 2:19); aliens and strangers on earth (Heb 11:13); ambassadors for Christ (2 Cor 5:18-21); the circumcision (Phil 3:3-11); Abraham's sons (Gal 3:29; Rom 4:16); the remnant (Rom 9:27; 11:5-7); the Israel of God (Gal 6:15-16); God's elect (Rom 8:33); the faithful in Christ Jesus (Eph 1:1); a new creation (2 Cor 5:17); a new man (Col 3:10); slaves of God, of Christ, and of righteousness (Rom 6:18, 22); and Christians (Acts 12:26). See Paul Minear, *Images of the Church in the New Testament* (Philadelphia: Westminster, 1977), for additional New Testament descriptions and figures of the church.

2. The English word 'church' is a poor translation of ἐκκλησία. As is true of the Scottish *kirk* and the German *Kirche*, the word 'church' is derived from the Greek word κυριακός which means 'belonging to the Lord'. The Greek phrase τό κυριακόν came to be used to designate first the place where Christians met to worship and in time was transferred also to the people themselves as the 'spiritual building' of the Lord. As a result of this transfer, the word 'church' has come to be used in our English Bibles to translate not the Greek word from which it is derived, which word by the way occurs only twice in the Greek New Testament (1 Cor 11:20; Rev 1:10) and in neither case does it describe God's people, but rather the Greek word ἐκκλησία which means something else entirely, namely, 'assembly'. By doing so, English translations have lost the rich connection between the Old and New Testament people of God fostered by the Septuagint's use of ἐκκλησία to translate עֵדָה and קָהָל, both of which roughly mean 'assembly'. For further discussion of this translation phenomenon see my *A New Systematic Theology of the Christian Faith* (Nashville: Thomas Nelson, 1998), 805-10.

3. Herman Ridderbos, *Paul: An Outline of His Theology*, translated by John R. DeWitt (Grand Rapids: Eerdmans, 1975), insightfully treats Paul's theology of the church, first, as the continuation and fulfillment of the historical people of God that in Abraham God chose to himself from all peoples, and to which he bound himself by making the covenant and the promises (327-61); second, as the body of Christ (362-95); and third, as an edifice—in general a building, in particular the temple of God (429-86).

1:1). He also speaks of the 'churches' within entire provinces such as 'the churches in Judea'(Gal 1:22; 1 Thess 2:14), 'the churches in Galatia' (Gal 1:21; Cor 16:1), 'the churches in Asia' (1 Cor 16:19), and 'the churches in Macedonia' (2 Cor 8:1).

These local and regional gatherings of saints Paul views in turn as making up the one church throughout the world (1 Cor 10:32; 11:22; 12:28), which church is the 'one body' of Christ (Eph 1:22; Col 1:18, 24; Rom 12:4-5; 1 Cor 12:12-27; Eph 4:4) and the 'wife' of Christ (Eph 5:25-27, 31-32). Within this one body there are diversities of spiritual gifts, abilities, and mandates (1 Cor 1:13; 12:12ff., Rom 12:4-5, Eph 4:15-16, 25; Col 3:14-15). But these diversities are intended to enhance the unity of the body. To the degree that their use fractures the unity of the visible body of Christ, to that same degree their use must be adjudged a misuse. For this reason Paul believes it entirely appropriate to ask Christians in every church to pattern their lives according to the same standards of conduct (1 Cor 4:17; 7:17; 14:33), and he expects Christians living in one area who are able to do so to assist poor Christians living in another area (1 Cor 16:1-3; 2 Cor 8:1-4).

Finally, he can use the term 'church' to denote the entire number of Christian faithful who have been or shall be united to Christ as their Savior, both in heaven and on earth – what theologians refer to as the 'invisible church' (Eph 1:22; 3:10, 21; 5:23-25, 27, 32; Col 1:18, 24).

Paul occasionally attaches an attributive or predicate definition to the noun 'church', primarily the genitive τοῦ θεοῦ ('of God') which is added both to the singular 'church' (Gal 1:13; 1 Cor 1:2; 10:32; 11:22; 15:9; 2 Cor 1:1; Acts 20:28; 1 Tim 3:5, 15) and to the plural 'churches' (2 Thess 1:4; 1 Cor 11:16). But he also speaks of 'the churches of Christ [τοῦ Χριστοῦ]' (Rom 16:16), 'the churches...which [are] in Christ [ἐν Χριστῷ]' (Gal 1:22), and 'the churches of God [τοῦ θεοῦ]...in Christ Jesus [ἐν Χριστῷ Ἰησοῦ]' (1 Thes 2:14). Once he speaks of 'the churches of the saints [τῶν ἁγίων]' (1 Cor 14:33). In his expression, 'to the church of God which is at Corinth [τῇ ἐκκλησίᾳ τοῦ θεου τῇ οὔσῃ ἐν Κορίνθῳ]' (1 Cor 1:2a), because three phrases later he links the saints at Corinth 'together with all those who in every place call on the name of our Lord Jesus Christ' (1 Cor 1:2d), there is the intimation that Paul is thinking of the 'church of God' in 1:2a in universalistic terms with

Corinth being only one place where it is manifested.

Paul employs a particularly rich and striking characterization of the church in 1 Timothy 3:15 where he speaks of the 'house of God, which is the church of the living God, the pillar and ground of the truth [οἴκῳ θεοῦ...ἥτις ἐστὶν ἐκκλησία θεοῦ ζῶντος, στῦλος καὶ ἑδραίωμα τῆς ἀληθείας]'. As such, the church is to 'hold high' as on a 'pillar' the absolute truth of Christianity upon which it itself is 'grounded'.

It is specifically in Ephesians and Colossians that we find Paul's most fully developed theology of the church as the body of Christ with Christ as its Head (Eph 1:22, 23; 2:16; 4:4, 12, 16; 5:30; Col 1:18, 24; 2:19; 3:15) and with the church as the wife of Christ and Christ as her Husband (Eph 5:22-32).

In Hebrews the church is the 'house of God' (3:6), the 'wandering people of God' for whom there yet remains a Sabbath-rest (see the 'wilderness' theme in Heb 3:7-4:13; 11:9, 13; 13:14), and 'brethren' of the great High Priest (2:17). His Jewish Christian readers have not assembled at Mount Sinai, as did the Old Testament church (12:18-21), but they have come 'to Mount Zion and to the city of the living God, the heavenly Jerusalem, and to myriads of angels in joyful assembly [πανηγύρει], to the church of firstborn men [ἐκκλησίᾳ πρωτοτόκων] whose names are written in heaven, and to God the Judge of all, and to the spirits of righteous men made perfect [see Heb 12:1], and to Jesus the mediator of a new covenant and to the sprinkled blood, which speaks a better word than the blood of Abel' (12:22-24).

What does he mean when he tells his readers that they have come to 'myriads of angels in joyful assembly' and to 'the church of firstborn men whose names are written in heaven'? These expressions require some comment if we are to appreciate all that he intended.

With reference to the 'myriads of angels in joyful assembly', one should recall that when Moses spoke of 'the assembly of Jacob' (συναγωγαῖς ᾽Ιακωβ) in Deuteronomy 33:4, he prefaced his remarks by declaring that 'God came from Sinai...with myriads of holy ones' (33:2; see also Acts 7:53; Gal 3:19; Heb 2:2 where we are informed that God gave the Law to Israel through the mediation of angels). Here we see the holy angels and the people of Israel brought together in one great assembly. Again, in Psalm 68, in David's description of Israel's march through the wilderness, we read that God, 'the One of

Sinai' who chooses to reign from that mountain (68:8, 16), 'has come from Sinai into his sanctuary' with 'tens of thousands and thousands of thousands of the chariots of God' (68:17). In his procession are his people Israel who are commanded: 'In the assembly bless God [ἐν ἐκκλησίαις εὐλογεῖτε τὸν θεόν]' (68:26). So we see God, as King reigning from Sinai, surrounded by the heavenly assembly of angels and summoning the earthly assembly to convene before him at his sanctuary. It is just this same great assembly of heavenly and earthly 'holy ones', only now in a more glorious sense than ever before because the assembly is before Mount Zion, which Paul has in mind when he says that the Christian church has come to 'myriads of angels in joyful assembly'.[4]

To come as well to 'the church of firstborn men whose names are written in heaven' highlights the truth that the church—comprised of 'firstborn' ones, that is, of those who in Christ occupy the place of highest honor in heaven—stands in the heavenly assembly before the King of that assembly as sole heir with Christ (see Gal 4:7; Rom 8:17). The fact that the names of these 'firstborn' are said to be written on the assembly roles in heaven indicates that they are *permanent* members and heirs in the kingdom assembly (recall here the enrollment of the assembly taken at Sinai in Numbers 1 and the enrollment of the Gentiles in the assembly described in Psalm 87). Entrance into this assembly follows upon repentance from dead works and faith in God and entails baptism (Heb 6:1; see 10:22-23 which also appears to be an allusion to Christian baptism). While he says little in Hebrews about formal worship in the church, Paul does exhort his readers not to forsake the assembling (ἐπισυναγωγὴν) of themselves together (10:25). When they do come together, they should do so with the consciousness that Christ himself will sing God's praise 'in the midst of the church [ἐν μέσῳ ἐκκλησίας]' (2:12) and for the purpose of mutual encouragement (10:25). Nor does he says anything in Hebrews about the government of the church beyond the fact that the church has 'leaders' (ἡγούμενοι) who are (1) to proclaim the Word of God to those for whom they are responsible, (2) to set a godly example of

---

4. Paul's insistence that women wear coverings in the public assembly 'because of the angels' (1 Cor 11:10) almost certainly means that he viewed the church, when assembled, as assembled in the presence of the angels of God who expect to see everything being done decently and in order. See the *Damascus Document* 4QDb, XV:15-17: 'Fools, madmen, simpletons and imbeciles, the blind, the maimed, the lame, the deaf, and minors, none of these may enter the midst of the community, for the holy angels [are in the midst of it].'

faith before the gathered assemblies, and (3) to watch over the souls under their care as those who must give account and who in return are to be obeyed (13:7, 17).

The Upbuilding of the Church

Concerned as we have been throughout this work to portray Paul in his role as the pioneer missionary-theologian to the nations, we should particularly note that for Paul the church is not to be a static entity. To the contrary, it is to experience, to employ the terminology of Herman Ridderbos, both extensive-missionary and intensive-confirmatory upbuilding and growth.[5]

For Paul the extensive progress of the church was and is to be clearly geographic. Not only did this perception drive him in his own missionary labors (Rom 15:19-21) but it governed his understanding of the progress of the gospel in the world as well. The gospel must bear fruit throughout the whole world (Rom 1:5, 16; Col 1:6, 23); no spatial or ethnic boundaries are be erected to hedge in the proclamation of the gospel which is to be catholic in its goals and aims (Gal 3:28; Col 3:11; 1 Cor 12:13). As Ridderbos observes in this connection, 'everything works toward the *pleroma*, the full number intended by God both of Jews and gentiles (Rom. 11:12, 25),'[6] which number will finally be reached in the Eschaton. This necessitates, of course, that not only must he as Christ's apostle be involved in the expansion of the church but that the church at large, which comes to expression in individual churches that have already been brought to salvation, must be engaged in the spread of the gospel throughout the world. Indirectly, the church's missionary involvement consists in its own sanctification:

> It...rejoices when people elsewhere come to conversion (1 Thess. 1:9; 2 Thess. 1:4). Its intercession for Paul and his missionary labor is repeatedly requested (2 Thess. 3:1; Eph. 6:18; Col. 4:3)...The church is also called to tangible assistance...(1 Cor 16:6, 11; 2 Cor 1:16; Rom 15:24; Titus. 3:13).
>
> ...It must be mindful of what is good, acceptable, and commends itself to all men (Rom 12:17); its friendliness and gentleness of spirit must be known to all men (Phil. 4:5); it must walk in wisdom toward those who are without.... Its word is always to be gracious, seasoned

---

5. Ridderbos, *Paul: An Outline of His Theology*, 432-38.
6. Ridderbos, *Paul: An Outline of His Theology*, 433.

with salt (Col. 4:5). The members of the church are to...walk decently, respectably, before those who are without... (1 Thess. 4:12). They must be in the forefront in good deeds, for these are good and profitable to men (Tit. 3:8). The whole life of the church is to be such that an opponent to his shame has nothing adverse to say of us (Tit. 2:8). ...the life of the church must be a recommendation of its faith, in conformity with, 'worthy of,' the Lord (Col. 1:10) and the gospel of Christ (Phil. 1:27).[7]

More directly and deliberately, the church itself lives under its Lord's missionary calling. While it is true that Paul does not say much directly about this missionary mandate, probably because it was for him a 'given', he does aver that the church is to 'imitate' the apostles and Christ (1 Cor 4:16; 11:1; 1 Thess 1:6), surely with the intention of saving others thereby.[8] Surely, too, when Paul states, 'Whatever you have...seen in me, put into practice' (Phil 4:9), the implication is there that he expected his converts at Philippi to emulate him in his mission efforts to reach the lost Gentile world. In Ephesians 6:15 ('feet fitted with the readiness') and 6:17 ('Take...the sword of the Spirit, which is the word of God') Paul declares that all Christians are involved in spiritual warfare in which they are to stand firm against the onslaughts of the evil one apparently by both resistance and proclamation. To Philemon Paul writes: 'I pray that you may be active in sharing your faith [ἡ κοινωνία τῆς πίστεως σου ἐνεργὴς γένηται, lit. 'the sharing of your faith may be active (or "effective")]' (6). He urges his churches that have a partnership in the gospel (Phil 1:5) to join him in contending for the faith of the gospel (Phil 1:27). And passages such as 1 Thessalonians 1:7-8, Romans 1:8, and Philippians 1:14 clearly imply that Paul's churches were sounding forth the gospel.

For Paul the church's intensive-confirmatory upbuilding is also a prerequisite for its final *pleroma*: '...all the gifts of Christ to his church serve to build up the body of Christ, the destiny of which he then describes as follows: "till we all attain to the unity of the faith, and of the knowledge of the Son to God, to mature manhood, to the measure of the stature of the fulness of Christ" (Eph. 4:13).'[9] Paul does not want his converts to remain spiritual infants (Gal 4:3; 1 Cor 3:1; Eph

---

7. Ridderbos, *Paul: An Outline of His Theology*, 433-434.
8. For the exegetical argument drawn from these passage and their larger contexts that Paul expected his churches to be engaged in evangelism as he was, see P. T. O'Brien, *Gospel and Mission in the Writings of Paul* (Grand Rapids: Baker, 1995), 89-107.
9. Ridderbos, *Paul: An Outline of His Theology*, 435.

4:14). To the contrary, he desires that they, living out of the abundance and fullness of Christ, may eventually come to apprehend the dimensions of Christ's love which surpasses knowledge and thus be filled to the measure of all the fullness of God (Eph 3:18-19). And his converts are to grow both in unity and in their mutual love for each other (Eph 4:3-6, 13-15; Col 2:2). Those who have attained deeper spiritual maturity (the 'strong') must bear with those who have not yet attained such maturity (the 'weak') (1 Cor 8; Rom 14:1-15:2). Finally, love is the key to this intensive upbuilding (Rom 14:15, 19; 1 Cor 8:1): of all Christ's gifts love is the 'most excellent' (1 Cor 13), the bond that alone makes the church 'perfect' (Col 3:14), and expresses itself in mutual admonition, encouragement, warning, and patience (1 Thess 5:11; 1 Cor 14:3). Without love the other gifts will fail to profit their possessors (1 Cor 13).

The Government of the Church

If he is generally silent elsewhere about these matters, Paul's first letter to the Corinthians (11-14), his two letters to Timothy, and his letter to Titus provide full and explicit instructions concerning how the people of God are to utilize their spiritual gifts for the edification of each other, 'how people [both officers and laity] ought to conduct themselves in God's household, which is the church of the living God' (1 Tim 3:15) and, more specifically, how the church should govern itself.

In the Old Testament Moses, the priests and Levites, the judges, and even the kings of Israel, were all assisted in their governance of the nation by the 'elders of Israel [or most striking, 'elders of the congregation']' (Ex 3:16, 18; 4:29; 17:5-6; 18:13-27; 19:7; 24:1, 9-11; Lev 4:15; 9:1-2; Num 11:14-25; Deut 5:23; 22:15-17; 27:1; Josh 7:6; 8:33; Judg 21:16; 1 Kgs 8:1-3; 1 Chr 21:16; Ps 107:32; Ezek 8:1, etc.). This practice continued within Israel into the New Testament era, as is evident from Luke 22:66 where we are informed that Jesus was brought before the Jewish 'presbytery' in Jerusalem:

> At daybreak *the council of the elders* [πρεσβυτέριον] of the people, both the chief priests and teachers of the law, met together, and Jesus was led before them. (cf. also Acts 22:5)

Beyond all reasonable doubt, it was this practice of governance by elders, begun in and present from the days of Mosaism onward, that lay behind Paul's practice to appoint (χειροτονήσαντες[10]) in every church he planted a plurality of elders (Acts 14:23) to govern and oversee it in accordance with the Word of God. He would later instruct Titus to appoint (καταστήσης[11]) elders 'in every city' (Tit 1:5; see also Acts 11:30; 15:2; 20:17; Jam 5:14; 1 Pet 5:1-2). And as his lists of qualifications for the eldership in 1 Timothy 3 and Titus 1 imply, he instructed the churches that they were to continue to be governed throughout this age by councils of elders chosen by the people.

I. The Duties of the Eldership

Just as their Savior, the Good Shepherd (Ps 23; John 10:11, 14), looked with compassion on the multitudes and saw them as sheep having no shepherd (Matt 9:36), so also, according to Paul's instructions to the Ephesian elders, elders are to 'take heed to yourselves and to all the flock, among which the Holy Spirit has made you overseers, *to shepherd* [ποιμαίνειν] the church of God' (Acts 20:28).[12] Here Paul clearly implies that elders, as shepherds of God's flock, are responsible to

A. Keep the members of their flock from going astray. This implies instruction and warning. An elder must be able and ready to teach those under his care.[13] This means, of course, that he must faithfully labor to acquire a knowledge of God's Word in order to teach it.

B. Go after their members when they go astray. This implies reproof,

---

10. The verb χειροτονέω literally means 'choose, elect by raising hands'. The action described here probably means that Paul as an apostle simply appointed elders when he first planted a church just as missionaries often do today when they first plant a church. This 'appointing' did not preclude, however, his seeking the church's will in the matter by asking the congregation for a show of hands.

11. The verb καθίστημι means simply 'to appoint'.

12. I have often thought, and stated almost as often to my students in more recent years, that pastors and pastors-to-be would benefit greatly from reading some books on just what sheep are like, what their needs are, and what is involved in shepherding them, for it is just a fact that under one shepherd sheep will struggle, starve and suffer endless hardship while under another those same sheep will flourish and thrive contentedly. I would recommend, first, a careful study of Ezekiel 34, then W. Phillip Keller's *A Shepherd Looks at Psalm 23* (Grand Rapids: Zondervan, 1970) and J. Douglas MacMillan's *The Lord our Shepherd* (Bryntirion: Evangelical Press of Wales, 1983).

13. Basing his study on Acts 20:28, Richard Baxter (1615-1691) in his *The Reformed Pastor* (Edinburgh: Banner of Truth, 1974 reprint) urges that pastors should diligently catechize not only the children of their flocks but also all the adults of their flocks who are willing to accept such training.

correction and in some cases the exercise of church discipline. Of course, elders should attempt by private instruction and admonition to correct an erring member of their flock at the earliest stage of a spiritual or moral defection before open and censurable sin breaks forth which would require harsher measures of discipline.

C. Protect their members from the wolves of false doctrine and evil practice which would enter in among them. This implies meticulous, careful application of the admission requirements for church membership and a constant effort to cultivate in their people a discerning apprehension of the distinction between truth and error.

D. Lead their flock to the fold and pour oil into their wounds and give them pure water to quench their thirst. This implies pastoral concern and consolation. Elders should be keenly aware of the fact that many of their people will be broken in spirit and wounded for many and varied reasons. They should be ready, whenever the need becomes known, to visit the sick, bind up the broken reed, lift up the fallen hand, strengthen the weakened knee, and fan the smoking flax back into a bright and healthy flame.[14]

II. Qualifications of the Eldership

To facilitate faithful shepherd-care for the flock of God, Paul lists the qualifications of the elder (overseer, bishop) in 1 Timothy 3:2-7 and Titus 1:6-9. In a word, the elder is to be a godly man. The elder, he insists,

A. must live a life which is *above reproach* (ἀνεπίλημπτον); that is, he must be *blameless* (ἀνέγκλητος) and have *a good reputation with non-believers* (μαρτυρίαν καλὴν...ἀπὸ τῶν ἔξωθεν) (1 Tim 3:2, 7; Tit 1:6);

B. must be the *husband of but one wife* (μιᾶς γυναικὸς ἄνδρα) (1 Tim 3:2; Tit 1:6);[15]

---

14. I adapted these four points from John Murray, 'Government in the Church of Christ,' *Collected Writings of John Murray* (Edinburgh: Banner of Truth, 1976), 1.265-67.
15. This qualification (1 Tim 3:2, 12; Tit 1:6; lit. 'a one-woman-[kind of]-man,' μιᾶς γυναικὸς ἄνδρα) has been variously interpreted. Some interpreters insist that its intent is to mandate that an office holder in the church must be married. Others declare that it means that an office holder can only be married *once*, that is to say, a man who has been widowed or

C. must be *temperate* (νηφάλιον), *self-controlled* (σώφρονα), *respectable* (κόσμιον), *hospitable* (φιλόξενον), *gentle* (ἐπιεικῆ), *upright* (δίκαιον), *holy* (ὅσιον), and *disciplined* (ἐγκρατῆ), and one who *loves what is good* (φιλάγαθον) (1 Tim 3:2; Tit 1:8);

D. must not be given to drunkenness, or be violent, over-bearing, quick-tempered, quarrelsome, a pursuer of dishonest gain, or a lover of money (1 Tim 3:3; Tit 1:7);

E. must manage his own family *well* (καλῶς), and see that his children, who are to be *believers* (ἔχων πιστά), obey him with proper respect and are not open to the charge of being wild and disobedient (1 Tim 3:4; Tit 1:6);

F. must be able to *take care of* (ἐπιμελήσεται) God's church and oversee God's work (1 Tim 3:5; Tit 1:7);

G. must not be a *recent convert* (νεόφυτον) (1 Tim 3:6);

H. must *hold firmly* to (ἀντεχόμενον) the trustworthy message *as it has been taught* (κατὰ τὴν διδαχὴν) (Tit 1:9); and

I. must be able *to teach* (διδακτικόν) and thereby *to encourage* (παρακαλεῖν) others by sound doctrine and *to refute* (ἐλέγχειν) those who oppose this teaching (1 Tim 3:2; Tit 1:9).

III. Qualifications of the Deacon

Deacons, first chosen to assist the apostles (Acts 6:1-7), were thereafter appointed to assist the elders. Paul's list of qualifications for the deacon may be found in 1 Timothy 3:8-12. The deacon, he commands,

A. must be *worthy of respect* (σεμνούς) and *sincere*, literally, not 'two-faced' (μὴ διλόγους) (3:8);

B. must not indulge in much wine (3:8);

C. must not pursue dishonest gain (3:8);

D. must be the *husband of one wife* (μιᾶς γυναικὸς ἄνδρες) (3:12), whose wife in turn must also be *worthy of respect* (σεμνάς), *not a*

---

divorced and then has remarried is not to hold office. The most likely intent of this qualification is the prohibition of a polygamist from holding church office.

malicious talker (μὴ διαβόλους) but *temperate* (νηφαλίους) and *trustworthy in everything* (πιστὰς ἐν πᾶσιν) (3:11)[16];

E. must manage his children and his household *well* (καλῶς) (3:12);

F. must *keep hold of* (ἔχοντας) the deep truths of the faith with a clear conscience (3:9); and

G. must first be *tested* (δοκιμαζέσθωσαν) before given the diaconal task (3:10).

* * * * *

Thus, according to Paul, the Christian church is comprised of the people of God who in a special manner are also the body of Christ and the temple of God. As the people of God it has its roots as the seed of Abraham in the Old Testament. As the body of Christ it enjoys the same close relationship to Christ that a body, unified in its oneness though it has many members, has with its single head. And as the temple of God it knows growth, both extensively and intensively.

The church is to be governed by spiritually qualified councils of elders and served by spiritually qualified deacons who were to be chosen by the people.[17] And given the connectionalism between the churches that is evident in Acts 8:14, 13:1-3, 14:27, and the entire

---

16. Edmund P. Clowney in his *The Church* (Downers Grove, Ill.: InterVarsity, 1995), basing his argument on Paul's description of Phoebe in Romans 16:1 as 'a διάκονον ["servant, helper, 'deacon'"] of the church in Cenchrea', and on Paul's reference to 'women' (γυναῖκας) in 1 Timothy 3:11, concludes that women may legitimately hold the office of deacon (231- 35). Other scholars as well, such as C. E. B. Cranfield (*A Critical and Exegetical Commentary on the Epistle to the Romans* [Edinburgh: T. & T. Clark, 1986], 2.781), make the same case.

While I feel the force of their argument, I am not persuaded that these verses endorse the position that women may hold official diaconal office because Paul expressly states in 1 Timothy 3:12 that deacons are to be 'one-woman-kind of men' who are to manage their children and their own households well. I believe that Phoebe was a godly 'servant' and 'helper' of the church in Cenchrea and that the women referred to in 1 Timothy 3:11 are best understood to be deacons' wives.

17. While Christian men and women both bear the image of God (Gen 1:26-27) and both are heirs together of the grace of life (1 Pet 3:7), only men are to be elected to the offices of elder and deacon in Christ's church. This is evident from the following data:

Elder: First, Paul expressly forbids women to teach or to exercise authority over men; rather, they are to be quiet in the churches (1 Tim 2:12; 1 Cor 14:33b-36). Since elders are to carry out these very functions, women necessarily are prohibited from holding this office. Second, the lists of qualifications for the elder in both 1 Timothy 3:2-7 and Titus 1:6-9 assume that elders are going to be men: an elder must be 'a one-woman-kind-of-man' (μιᾶς γυναικὸς ἄνδρα) and 'must manage his own family well and see that his children obey him with proper respect'. Third, with only rare exceptions under unusual circumstances (for

episode of the Jerusalem Conference in Acts 15, in which Paul was vitally involved, the church should ever seek to replicate the same connectionalism by series of church courts such as local church sessions, presbyteries, and general assemblies.

---

example, Deborah and Huldah; see Judg 4–5 and 2 Kgs 22:14-20), there is a consistent pattern of male leadership among God's people throughout the entire Bible. Jesus himself appointed only men as his apostles. A church that would ordain a woman to the eldership is flying in the face of the consistent testimony of Scripture and the consentient practice of the churches throughout church history.

Deacon: First, when the problem of the equitable distribution of food to widows arose in the early church, the apostles expressly directed the church to choose seven men (ἄνδρας) to oversee the distribution of food (Acts 6:1-6). Second, as with the elder's lists of qualifications, Paul's list of qualifications for the deacon in 1 Timothy 3:8-13 assumes that the deacon is going to be a man: he is to be 'a one-woman-kind-of-man' and 'must manage his children and his household well' (1 Tim 3:12).

See George W. Knight, III, *The Role Relationship of Men and Women* (Revised ed., Chicago: Moody, 1985) and *Recovering Biblical Manhood and Womanhood*, edited by John Piper and Wayne Grudem (Wheaton: Crossway, 1991), chaps. 9 and 20, for the full argument. See also Benjamin B. Warfield, 'Paul on Women Speaking in Church,' *The Presbyterian* (Oct 30, 1919), 8-9, for an unapologetic insistence on the necessity of women to be absolutely silent in all of the church's public worship meetings.

CHAPTER TWENTY-THREE

BAPTISM AND THE LORD'S SUPPER

> Baptized into your name most holy,
> O Father, Son, and Holy Ghost,
> I claim a place, though weak and lowly,
> Among your seed, your chosen host.
> Buried with Christ and dead to sin:
> Your Spirit e'er shall live within.
> – Johann J. Rambach

> At the Lamb's high feast we sing
> Praise to our victorious King,
> Who has washed us in the tide
> Flowing from his pierced side.
> Praise we him whose love divine
> Gives his sacred blood for wine,
> Gives his body for the feast,
> Christ the victim, Christ the priest.
> – Latin hymn, 6th century

During his earthly ministry Jesus Christ, as Lord of the church, instituted baptism and the Lord's Supper. He instituted the former on the eve of his ascension[1] when he gave to his disciples the Great Commission:

> All authority in heaven and on earth has been given to me. Therefore go and make disciples of all nations, *baptizing* [βαπτίζοντες] them in the name of the Father and of the Son and of the Holy Spirit, teaching them

---

1. John's Gospel records that during John the Baptist's ministry 'Jesus and his disciples went out into the Judean countryside, where he spent some time with them, and baptized' (3:22, 26); indeed, John reports that Jesus 'was...baptizing more disciples than John, although in fact it was not Jesus who baptized, but his disciples' (4:1-2). But his baptism at that time was not what was later to be Christian baptism 'in the name of the Father and the Son and the Holy Spirit'. As a short-term disciple of John (he had received baptism at John's hands), he was assisting John at that time in carrying out his mission of preparing a people for the coming of the Lord, that is to say, his baptism was John's baptism unto repentance.

to obey everything I have commanded you. And surely I am with you always, to the very end of the age. (Matt 28:18-20)

The church has then the sanction of the Son of God himself to baptize its members; indeed, not to baptize them is disobedience. As an adverbial participle βαπτίζοντες ('baptizing') connotes the idea of 'means'. That is to say, Jesus represents the outward ordinance of baptism as the first of the two specified means whereby the church is to make the nations his disciples, the second being his 'teaching [διδάσκοντες] them to obey everything I have commanded'. I do not mean to suggest here that Jesus was teaching that the outward rite of baptism as such *effects* discipleship but rather that it is the public ceremony in connection with which Christians to whom the gospel has cognitively come formally confess 'Jesus is Lord' as they initially come into the church.

Just as Jesus personally and expressly instituted the ordinance of baptism (Matt 28:19), so also he personally and expressly instituted the ordinance of the Lord's Supper during his last Passover meal with his disciples just hours before his crucifixion.[2] All three Synoptic

---

2. Many theologians contend that the language of 'eating Christ's flesh' and 'drinking his blood' in John 6 is an earlier allusion to the Lord's Table. But it is extremely unlikely that Jesus either intended his words in John 6 to be construed as eucharistic language or was referring to the Lord's Table at all. I say this for the following four reasons:

(1) The context is against it. Jesus was speaking in John 6 not to committed disciples (6:66) but to people, including opponents (6:41, 52, 59), who, if he was referring to the Lord's Supper, would not have understood that he was referring to an ordinance that he had not yet even instituted and about which John himself, in his later lengthy account of Jesus' upper room discourse in John 13-17, says nothing.

(2) 'Flesh' (σάρξ)is not the word he later used when he instituted the Lord's Table. There He employed 'body' (σῶμα). Also, when he instituted the Lord's Supper never did he speak of 'chewing' (ὁ τρώγων; lit. 'he who continually munches [or chews] on,' John 6:54, 56, 57, 58) his body or 'drinking' his blood; he spoke rather of eating the bread (1 Cor 11:26) which, he said, is his body and drinking the cup which, he said, is his blood.

(3) Jesus' words are absolute; without the specific eating and drinking of which he speaks one has no life in him (6:53). But it is impossible to believe that Jesus was teaching the people here that the observance of a particular ordinance, which he had not yet even instituted and about which John says nothing in his Gospel, is necessary for eternal life.

(4) The blessings of eternal life and the eschatological resurrection which he declares result from 'eating his flesh' and 'drinking his blood' (6:54-58), Jesus teaches in this very same passage, flow from his words (v. 63) and from believing in him (6:35, 40, 47). 'Coming to him' and 'believing in him', Jesus says, relieves one's spiritual hunger and thirst (6:35). Accordingly, Jesus is not binding eternal life here to a liturgical ordinance. To 'eat his flesh', answering to the hunger of 6:35, and to 'drink his blood', answering to the thirst of 6:35, is his metaphorical way of urging his auditors to hear his words and

Evangelists (Matt 26:26; Mark 14:22; Luke 22:19) and Paul (1 Cor 11:24) record that Jesus, on the night he was betrayed, took bread and gave it to his disciples and said: 'This is my body' (Synoptics: τοῦτό ἐστιν τὸ σῶμά μού Paul: Τοῦτό μού ἐστιν τὸ σῶμα). Luke (22:19) and Paul (1 Cor 11:24) both record that Jesus then said in connection with the bread: '...do this in remembrance of me [τοῦτο ποιεῖτε εἰς τὴν ἐμὴν ἀνάμνησιν].' Both Matthew (26:28) and Mark (14:24) record that Jesus then took the cup and said: 'This is my blood of the covenant which is poured out for many' (τοῦτο...ἐστιν τὸ αἷμά μου τῆς διαθήκης [Matthew: τὸ περὶ πολλῶν ἐκχυννόμενον, with Matthew adding, '...for the forgiveness of sins [εἰς ἄφεσιν ἁμαρτιῶν]; Mark: τὸ ἐκχυννόμενον ὑπὲρ πολλῶν).' Luke (22:20) and Paul (1 Cor 11:25) both report that Jesus then said: 'This cup is the new covenant in my blood' (Luke: Τοῦτο τὸ ποτήριον ἡ καινὴ διαθήκη ἐν τῷ αἵματί μου, with Luke adding, "which is poured out for you [τὸ ὑπὲρ ὑμῶν ἐκχυννόμενον]'; Paul: Τοῦτο τὸ ποτήριον ἡ καινὴ διαθήκη ἐστὶν ἐν τῷ ἐμῷ αἵματι). Paul alone records that Jesus then said in connection with the cup: 'do this, whenever you drink it, in remembrance of me [τοῦτο ποιεῖτε, ὁσάκις ἐὰν πίνητε, εἰς τὴν ἐμὴν ἀνάμνησιν]' (1 Cor 11:25). Though there are some minor variations between the accounts, it is still quite clear from Jesus' imperatives, 'do this in remembrance of me,' that he did indeed institute the sacrament and intend his church to observe the rite after he had departed from them and gone back to heaven.

Paul's Teaching on Baptism

I. Paul's references to baptism

Since Ananias baptized Paul some three days after his Damascus Road encounter with Jesus Christ (Acts 9:18; see 22:16), it comes as no surprise to find Paul writing about baptism in his letters. What is somewhat surprising is the paucity of references to the ordinance in his writings, indeed in the entire New Testament.[3] In fact, the references to baptism in the New Testament epistles are relatively few, with only one non-Pauline instance (1 Pet 3:21), and with none in

---

to trust with all their heart in his forthcoming atoning death to which he alludes in 6:51: 'This bread is my flesh, which I will give for the life of the world.'
    3. There are relatively few instances—only eleven—of actual Christian baptisms recorded in the New Testament. This is remarkable since actual baptisms must have been

the Apocalypse. The Pauline instances are as follows: Galatians 3:27, 1 Corinthians 1:13-17 (6 times); 10:2; 12:13; 15:29 (2 times); Romans 6:3-4; Ephesians 4:5; Colossians 2:12, and Hebrews 6:2, 9:10.[4] We will consider each reference in turn.

A. Galatians 3:26-27. 'For all of you are sons of God through faith in Christ Jesus; *for as many as have been baptized into Christ have put on Christ* [ὅσοι γὰρ εἰς Χριστὸν ἐβαπτίσθητε, Χριστὸν ἐνεδύσασθε].'

Paul has in mind here Christ's baptismal work of baptizing the elect by his Spirit (for surely not all who have been baptized by water have actually 'put on Christ'), by which work they are brought into union with him through faith, their union with him being described here metaphorically as their having 'put on Christ' in the sense that one would robe oneself in a garment.

B. 1 Corinthians 1:13-17; 10:2. The six references to baptism in 1 Corinthians 1 confirm the apostolic practice of baptism as it is reflected in Acts,[5] and are significant theologically in that they presuppose the *relational* import of Christian baptism (εἰς τὸ ὄνομα) which is also expressed in 1 Corinthians 10:2 (εἰς τὸν Μωυσῆν ἐβαπτίσθησαν).

---

very frequent in the days of the apostles. The recorded instances are the following: three thousand Jews at Pentecost, Acts 2:37-41; some Samaritans, Acts 8:12-17; the Ethiopian eunuch, Acts 8:35-38; Paul after his conversion, Acts 9:18, see 22:16; Cornelius' household, Acts 10:44-48; Lydia, Acts 16:13-15; the Philippian jailer, Acts 16:30-34; many Corinthians, Acts 18:8; John's disciples, Acts 19:1-7; Crispus and Gaius, 1 Cor 1:14; and Stephanas' household, 1 Cor 1:16.

4. The paucity of references to baptism in Paul's epistles should not be construed to mean that Paul held the ordinance in low esteem. Though he will say that Christ did not send him to baptize but to evangelize (1 Cor 1:17), when he expounds the significance of baptism he gives it high meaning (Rom 6:3-4) and places 'one baptism' in sixth place in the series of the seven 'ones' that undergird the unity of the people of God: 'one body', 'one Spirit', 'one hope', 'one Lord', 'one faith', 'one baptism', and 'one God and Father of all' (Eph 4:4-5).

5. The baptisms recorded in Acts are administered 'upon, into, or in the name of Jesus' (Acts 2:38, ἐπὶ τῷ ὀνόματι Ἰησοῦ Χριστοῦ; Acts 8:16, εἰς τὸ ὄνομα τοῦ κυρίου Ἰησοῦ; Acts 10:48, ἐν τῷ ὀνόματι Ἰησοῦ Χριστου; Acts 19:5, εἰς τὸ ὄνομα τοῦ κυρίου Ἰησου; see also Gal 3:27; Rom 6:3) and not in the name of the triune God as specified in the Matthew 28:19 formula. While some critics believe this proves that Matthew 28:19 is 'a later Matthean redaction of a more primitive apostolic commissioning', I would suggest that Luke's Acts is simply giving an abbreviated form of the words actually used in the baptismal ceremony, highlighting by his use of Jesus' name alone both the fact that it is through Jesus' mediation that one enters into union with the triune God and the fact that these persons were being admitted to the *Christian* church.

The primacy of the proclamation of the gospel over the ordinance of baptism is evident in Paul's statement: 'Christ did not send me to baptize, but to preach the gospel' (1 Cor 1:17), although he did, of course, baptize some initial converts such as Crispus (see Acts 18:8) and Stephanas (see 1 Cor 16:15).

C. 1 Corinthians 12:13. 'For we were all baptized by one Spirit into one body [καὶ γὰρ ἐν ἑνὶ πνεύματι ἡμεῖς πάντες εἰς ἓν σῶμα ἐβαπτίσθημεν].'

There is no reason why the preposition ἐν should not be translated 'with' rather than 'by'. Christ is the one who baptizes with the Holy Spirit (Matt 3:11); he is the baptizing Agent and the Holy Spirit is the 'element' with whom he is baptized. The preposition εἰς—'*into* one body'—underscores the relational character of this baptismal work rather than the goal or purpose of this work. I concur with David C. Jones when he writes in his classroom syllabus:

> That Christ rather than the Holy Spirit is the agent of this baptism is confirmed by the succeeding clause: '...and we were all given one Spirit to drink.' This passage is thus not a direct reference to water baptism; it refers rather to the outpouring of the Holy Spirit on the day of Pentecost as a definitive historico-redemptive event of which subsequent generations of believers partake as they are incorporated into the body of Christ. Water baptism, of course, is the outward sign of the [cleansing] work of the Holy Spirit in the life of the individual believer, but that does not seem to be the main point of this text.

While Jones does not provide us with the full reasoning behind his assertions, I think his point is borne out by both the passive voice and the punctiliar tense of the verb ἐποτίσθημεν, 'were given to drink.'

D. 1 Corinthians 15:29. 'Now if there is no resurrection, what will those do who *are baptized for the dead* [οἱ βαπτιζόμενοι ὑπὲρ τῶν νεκρῶν]? If the dead are not raised at all, why are people *baptized for them* [βαπτίζονται ὑπὲρ αὐτῶν]?'

The two references in this verse to baptism for the dead are puzzling, to say the least. Many are the suggestions made by commentators as to Paul's meaning here, but no exegetical solution presently on the scene is carrying the field.[6] Therefore, since it is

---

6. Of the more than two hundred interpretations (!) that have been placed on this verse John D. Reaume in 'Another Look at 1 Corinthians 15:29, "Baptized for the

impossible to know for certain what Paul meant by it, there is no warrant in the text or in the context for anyone to conclude that Paul places the practice in a positive light. One can only conclude that, whatever was the purpose behind the practice he alludes to in the Corinthian church, at the very least he is surely employing it as an *ad hominem* argument for the physical resurrection against those in the church there who denied it.

E. Romans 6:3-4. 'Or don't you know that *all of us who were baptized into Christ Jesus were baptized into his death* [ὅσοι ἐβαπτίσθημεν εἰς Χριστὸν Ἰησοῦν, εἰς τὸν θάνατον αὐτοῦ ἐβαπτίσθημεν]? *We were therefore buried with him through baptism into death* [συνετάφημεν οὖν αὐτῷ διὰ τοῦ βαπτίσματος εἰς τὸν θανατον].'

Here Paul teaches that when the believer is united to Christ through Christ's spiritual baptism by his Spirit into his body, that is, into union with him, a decisive change occurs in him of which the ordinance of baptism is the outward sign and seal, namely, he dies to sin's reign and lives for righteousness. If then the import of water baptism is symbolically that of union with Christ, it follows that baptism confirms, that is, serves as the seal of, our union with him in his crucifixion, death, burial, and resurrection. John Murray writes:

> ...the fact of having died to sin is the fundamental premise of the apostle's thought.... What [he] has in view is the once-for-all definitive breach with sin which constitutes the identity of the believer [concerning which breach baptism is the sign and seal].[7]

'In demonstration of his premise [that the Christian is in vital spiritual union with Christ],' David Jones notes, 'Paul appeals to the import of baptism. Baptism "into Christ" signifies union with Christ and participation in all the privileges and blessings that reside in him— union with him in all aspects of his work as Mediator, including his death, of which his burial was the unambiguous confirmation.'

Dead," ' *Bibliotheca Sacra* 152 (October-December 1995), 457-75, considers the nine most likely views and opts for the view which takes the ὑπὲρ in the sense of 'because of': 'because of the influence of deceased Christians.' See also BAGD, 'βαπτίζω,' 2bg, p. 132, for the pertinent literature.

7. Murray, *The Epistle to the Romans* (The New International Commentary on the New Testament; 2 vols.; Grand Rapids: Eerdmans, 1959, 1965), I, 213.

F. Ephesians 4:5. '...one Lord, one faith, one baptism [εἷς κύριος, μία πίστις, ἓν βάπτισμα].'

Here Paul's 'one baptism' seems to refer to the ordinance of water baptism inasmuch as the preceding verse has already spoken of 'one body and one Spirit'. The significance which Paul attaches to the ordinance is seen in his willingness to place it within the venue of the remarkable series of the church's 'ones' which undergird the church's unity: one body, one Spirit, one hope, one Lord, one faith, and one God and Father of all, who is over all and through all and in all. And his point appears to be that all who participate in Christian baptism rightly administered are subjects of one and the same ordinance with the same spiritual import. Baptism thus stands (along with the other six things mentioned as a summons to Christian unity) as a witness against disunity in the church.

G. Colossians 2:11-12. In these verses Paul expressly relates Old Testament circumcision and New Testament baptism:

> ...in him *you were also circumcised* [περιετμήθητε], in the putting off of the sinful nature, not with a circumcision done by the hands of men but with the circumcision done by Christ, *having been buried with him* [συνταφέντες αὐτῷ] *in* [the Spirit's] *baptism* and raised with him through faith.

The relation between Old Testament circumcision and New Testament baptism may be seen by simply reading the italicized words: '...in him you were also circumcised..., having been buried with him in baptism.' Clearly, for Paul the spiritual import of New Testament baptism—the outward sign and seal of the Spirit's inner baptismal work—is tantamount to that of Old Testament circumcision.[8] By the authority of Christ and his apostles then, the church in this age administers baptism in lieu of circumcision. But it should do so with the understanding that the spiritual significance of baptism as a sign

---

8. Paul King Jewett, the noted Reformed Baptist theologian, acknowledges as much, although he immediately thereafter aborts the significance of his acknowledgement, when he writes in *Infant Baptism and the Covenant of Grace* (Grand Rapids: Eerdmans, 1978), 89.

> ...the only conclusion we can reach is that the two signs [circumcision and baptism], as outward rites, symbolize the same inner reality in Paul's thinking. Thus circumcision may fairly be said to be the Old Testament counterpart of Christian baptism. So far the Reformed argument, in our judgment, is biblical. In this sense baptism, to quote the Heidelberg Catechism, 'occupies the place of circumcision in the New Testament.'

and seal is essentially the same as the former Old Testament ceremony, namely, a covenantal sign of the Spirit's act of cleansing from sin's defilement.

H. Hebrews 6:2. '...instruction about baptisms [βαπτισμῶν διδαχῆς].' Many are the commentary suggestions of the meaning of the phrase 'instruction about baptisms' which Paul represents here as one of the elementary or foundational teachings of Christianity. Given the two facts that the teaching spoken of here about such baptisms is said to be foundational and that the same word is used, again in the plural, in Hebrews 9:10 in reference to the ceremonial washings of the Old Testament, most likely the 'instruction' here refers to the catechesis which would have been carried out in a Jewish Christian environment concerning the typical character of the Old Testament ceremonial washings that pointed forward to the antitypical work of Christ (see comments on Heb 9:10 following) in the same way that the typical character of the priesthood of Melchizedek, referred to in the immediately preceding and following contexts (5:6, 10; 7:1-8:2), pointed forward to Christ's antitypical high priesthood. Reference to such instruction as foundational suggests in turn Paul's sense of continuity between the old and new dispensations.

I. In Hebrews 9 Paul characterizes the ceremonial washings of the Old Testament – the sprinkling (ῥαντίζουσα) of those who were ceremonially unclean with the blood of goats and bulls and the ashes of a heifer (9:13), Moses' sprinkling (ἐράντισεν) of the scroll and all the people with the blood of calves mixed with water and scarlet wool (9:19), and his sprinkling (ἐράντισεν) of the tabernacle and everything used in its ceremonies with blood (9:21) – all as *baptisms* [βαπτισμοῖς]', that is, as 'ceremonial washings' (9:10). Moreover, immediately thereafter he speak of Christians as being 'sprinkled' with Christ's blood:

Hebrews 10:22: 'Let us draw near to God with a sincere heart in full assurance of faith, *having our hearts sprinkled* [ῥεραντίσμενοι] to cleanse us from a guilty conscience and having our bodies washed with pure water.' (see Ezek 36:25)

Hebrews 12:24: '[You have come] to Jesus the mediator of a new covenant, and *to the sprinkled blood* [αἵματι ῥαντισμοῦ] that speaks a better word than the blood of Abel.'

Surely the contextual universe of discourse here would warrant the conclusion that Paul would have regarded the Christian's 'sprinkling' with Christ's blood – the New Testament fulfillment of the Old Testament typical sacrifice – as a spiritual 'baptism' as well. And just as surely, 'it would be strange if the baptism with water which represents the sprinkling of the blood of Christ could not properly and most significantly be performed by sprinkling.'[9]

II. The import of baptism

Following John Murray,[10] I would urge that the import of baptism should be derived primarily from the terms that Christ employed when he instituted it and then from the subsequent references to it which appear mainly in the Pauline letters. When we take our point of departure from the formula which Jesus used when he instituted it, namely, 'baptizing into the name' (βαπτίζοντες εἰς τὸ ὄνομα) (see 1 Cor 1:13, 15 – 'baptized into the name of Paul'; 10:2 – 'baptized into Moses'), it becomes apparent that the formula expresses a relationship to the person into whom or into whose name the person is being baptized.[11] Baptism then basically denotes the fact of a relationship. What kind of relationship? When such Pauline passages as Galatians 3:27-28, 1 Corinthians 12:13, Romans 6:3-6, and Colossians 2:11-12 are taken into account (see expositions above), it becomes plain that the nature of the relationship is one of *union with Christ*, more particularly, union with Christ in his crucifixion, death, burial, and resurrection (Note: not just union with him in the last two). Of this basic union baptism is the sign and seal. Baptism's basic and central import, that is, baptism's basic signification, then is one of union with Christ. But since Jesus speaks of being baptized into the name of the Father, and of the Son, and of the Holy Spirit, baptism also

---

9. John Murray, *Christian Baptism* (Philadelphia: Presbyterian and Reformed, 1962), 24.
10. John Murray, *Christian Baptism*, 5.
11. Edmund P. Clowney in *The Church* (Downers Grove, Ill.: Inter-Varsity, 1995) says in this regard: 'Christian baptism is a naming ceremony. The baptized is given a name,...the name of the triune God. ...Baptism gives Christians their family name, the name they bear as those called the children of God (Is. 43:6b-7)' (278). He refers his reader to the Aaronic blessing in Numbers 6:24-27 and to Paul's statement in Ephesians 3:14-15 for support.

signifies union with the Father and the Son and the Holy Ghost, and this means with the three persons of the Trinity, both in the unity expressed by their joint possession of the one name and in the richness of the distinctive relationship which each person of the Godhead sustains to the people of God in the economy of the covenant of grace.[12]

There is another aspect of the import of baptism which must not be overlooked—the ordinance involves the visible use of the element of water and the observable action of applying that water to the person. In view of the teaching of Ezekiel 36:25-26, John 3:5, 1 Corinthians 6:11, and Titus 3:5 concerning the ceremonial use of water and washing for cleansing, as well as the teaching of Colossians 2:11-12 where circumcision which is a sign of cleansing from sin's defilement is related to baptism, baptism signifies more specifically the *cleansing* or purification from sin's defilement and guilt which results from the sinner's union with the three persons of the Godhead in their respective labors in the *ordo salutis*.

Finally, because the very name of the ordinance is what it is, namely, baptism (βάπτισμα), it obviously symbolizes the spiritual work given that same name in the New Testament epistles, namely, Christ's work of baptizing his people with the Holy Spirit (see Matt 3:11; Mark 1:8; Luke 3:16; John 1:33; Acts 1:5; 2:33; 1 Cor 12:13), which work unites them to himself and to the other persons of the Godhead in their saving labors of regenerating, purifying, justifying, and cleansing.

Herman Ridderbos has correctly rejected the notion of some Roman Catholic scholars, taking Romans 6 as their point of departure, that in baptism time is made to fall away, Christ's death is made contemporary with the baptized party, and the baptized party is taken up into his death and is made to die with him in baptism. He argues that, according to Paul,

> baptism is not the moment or the place of dying together, etc., with Christ...In baptism the death of Christ as an event is not made to be renewed in the present and represented as a death in which believers are to 'die' with him, but believers are so involved in what took place once and for all [at Golgotha] that it can be said of his death [at Golgotha] that it is their death as well...the death of Christ is not prolonged in baptism and brought to believers, but [by faith] believers are in baptism brought

---

12. John Murray, *Christian Baptism*, 7.

to Christ's death, that is to say, made to share in what has occurred once for all....

The specific character of baptism into Christ's death is not that time falls away, or that the one baptized is made contemporaneous with Christ in his death, but that by baptism the believer [through faith] becomes a sharer in what has taken place with Christ. Baptism does not make us die anew with Christ, but rather rests on the fact that he has died for us and we with him....

We must conclude...that to have died and [to have] been buried with Christ neither comes about in baptism in the sense of the mystery theology [of these Roman Catholic thinkers], nor becomes an actual occurrence in baptism in the sense of the doctrine of contemporaneity, but that dying with Christ has been given with incorporation into Christ, and is thus appropriated to the one baptized as a given reality by baptism as the rite of incorporation. That is to say, therefore, that to have died once with Christ on the cross and to be baptized into his death do not coincide....[13]

In Paul's thought, in other words, just as Old Testament circumcision was a sign and seal of imputed righteousness received through faith apart from the rite of circumcision (Rom 4:11), so also New Testament baptism, circumcision's sacramental successor (Col 2:11-12) and thus the sign and seal of the spiritual verities of the new covenant, both signifies and confirms the graces of salvation which have been already accomplished for the believer at Calvary and which are received through faith apart from the ordinance of baptism. This means, and it bears repeating, that while baptism is an 'effectual means' of salvation in that it represents Christ and his saving benefits, confirms the Christian's interest in him, puts a visible difference between the baptized party and the unbeliever, and engages him to the service of God in Christ, it becomes such not by any intrinsic power within it but only by the blessing of Christ resting upon it and by the working of the Holy Spirit in him who by faith receives it (*Westminster Larger Catechism*, Question 161, and *Westminster Shorter Catechism*, Question 91).

III. The mode of baptism

Christ's baptismal work (see Matt 3:11; Mark 1:8; Luke 3:16; John 1:33; Acts 1:5; 2:33), by which he baptizes the elect *by* or *with* his Spirit, is invariably described in terms of the Spirit 'coming upon'

---

13. Herman Ridderbos, *Paul: An Outline of His Theology*, translated by John R. DeWitt (Grand Rapids: Eerdmans, 1975), 406-09, emphasis supplied.

(Acts 1:8, ἐπελθόντος; 19:6, ἦλθε ἐπ'), being 'poured out upon' (Acts 2:17, 33, ἐκχεῶ ἐπί, ἐξέχεεν), or 'falling upon' (Acts 10:44, 11:15, ἐπέπεσεν ἐπί). In the same vein Paul writes: 'God *has poured out* [ἐκκέχυται] his love into our hearts by the Holy Spirit' (Rom 5:5). We have already suggested that the outward ordinance of baptism signifies Christ's spiritual baptismal work. When he then represents the various ceremonial acts of sprinkling in the old dispensation as 'baptisms',[14] the conclusion would seem to be warranted, if the ordinance of baptism is to signify Christ's baptismal work (which is uniformly described in terms of affusion or sprinkling), that the ordinance's mode should reflect the affusionary pattern of Christ's baptismal work.

With reference to the alleged pattern of baptism in Romans 6:2-6 and Colossians 2:11-12 as being that of burial and resurrection, a careful analysis of these passages will show that Paul's basic thesis is the believer's union with Christ in his crucifixion, death, burial, and resurrection as the antidote to antinomianism. Baptism by immersion does not reflect our crucifixion and death with Christ which are as much aspects of our union with Christ as his burial and resurrection which Baptists tend to emphasise in the Romans passage. Murray is right when he affirms:

> It is arbitrary to select one aspect [of our union with Christ, namely, burial] and find in the language used to set it forth the essence of the mode of baptism. Such procedure is indefensible unless it can be carried through consistently. It cannot be carried through consistently here [since baptism by immersion does not and cannot visually reflect our being hung on the cross with Christ, which is as much an aspect of our union with Christ in the passage as our burial with him] and therefore it is arbitrary and invalid.[15]

---

14. The Hebrew verb root נזה, which occurs twenty-four times in the Old Testament, is a technical ritual word found mainly in the Levitical legislation (see Ex 29:21; Lev 4:6, 17; 5:9; 6:27 (2); 8:11, 30; 14:7, 16, 27, 51; 16:14 (2), 15, 19; Num 8:7; 19:4, 18, 19, 21) and denotes ceremonial sprinklings with oil, with oil and blood, or with water. The verb root זרק, which occurs thirty-five times in the Old Testament, like נזה, is also used to describe ceremonial sprinklings and seems to denote a heavier sprinkling than נזה, executed with the whole hand rather than with the finger (Ex 9:8; 29:20-21). It too is found mainly in the Levitical legislation (Ex 24:6, 8; 29:16, 20; Lev 1:5, 11; 3:2, 8, 13; 7:2, 14; 8:19, 24; 9:12, 18; 17:6; Num 18:17; 2 Kings 16:13, 15; 2 Chron 29:22 (3); 30:16; 35:11; Ezek 36:25; 43:18). Combined, these approximately sixty references to various sprinklings in the Old Testament, according to Hebrews 9:10, may all be described as 'baptisms'.

15. John Murray, *Christian Baptism*, 31.

It should also be noted that Christ was not 'buried' in the sense that the Baptist's mode of baptism requires. That is to say, his body was not placed *under* the ground. Rather, his body was temporarily deposited in a new tomb preparatory to what his disciples thought would be a permanent burial after the Passover festivities. These facts show that we should no more single out our union with Christ in his burial and resurrection and make these two aspects of our union with him the pattern for the mode of baptism than we should argue on the basis of Paul's statement in Galatians 3:27 ('For all of you who were baptized into Christ have clothed yourselves with Christ'; see also Col 3:9-14) that baptism should be carried out by requiring the new Christian to don a white robe, that is, by a 'baptism by donning'.

The simple fact of the matter is that the Baptist practice of baptism by immersion is simply based upon faulty exegesis of Scripture. The ordinance should not be represented as signifying Christ's burial and resurrection (aspects of the *accomplished* phase of his saving work, which the sacrament of the Lord's Supper memorializes) but rather his baptismal work (the *applicational* phase of his saving work). I would conclude therefore, as the *Westminster Confession of Faith* states, that 'dipping of the person into the water is not necessary; but baptism is *rightly* administered by pouring, or sprinkling water upon the person' (XXVIII.iii).

V. The subjects of baptism

Because we are limiting our discussions on baptism primarily to Paul's thought and not ranging freely over the entirety of Scripture, we do not have much material upon which to base our conclusions regarding this topic. But it goes without saying that Paul presumed, in accordance with Christ's words of institution (Matt 28:19-20), that all believers in Christ will have been or should be baptized. This may be inferred from Acts 9:18, 18:8, 19:1-3, 22:16 and Romans 6:3-5.

With respect to the question of the baptism of infants of believers, we have less Pauline material upon which to base a conclusion, but what evidence we do have would suggest that Paul was a paedobaptist. What is this evidence?

A. At least twice in Acts (16:15, 33, 34; see 11:14; 16:31) and once in 1 Corinthians (1:16) Paul is involved in what has come to be termed 'household baptisms' where the adult who came to faith presumably had his or her family also baptized, irrespective of the family's faith. Luke reports that after Lydia responded to Paul's message, 'she *and the members of her household* were baptized' (Acts 16:15). While Luke declares that the Lord opened *her* heart to receive the things spoken by Paul, he says nothing about the faith of her household, and yet the members of her household were baptized as well.

In the case of the Philippian jailer, there is a sustained emphasis in the Acts pericope (16:31-34) upon the jailer's faith alone. Luke informs us that, after Paul and Silas had instructed him, 'Believe [Πίστευσον – first aorist active imperative *second masculine singular*] in the Lord Jesus, and *you* will be saved – you and your household,' they spoke the word of the Lord *to him* (αὐτῷ), with all who were in his 'house' being present at that time (vs 32). Then after he had washed the prisoners' wounds, '...immediately he *and all his family* were baptized, and bringing them up into his house, he set a meal before them and he greatly rejoiced with all his house *because he had believed* [πεπιστευκὼς – perfect active participle nominative *singular* used causally] in God.' While it is virtually certain that the jailer's entire family heard the gospel, Luke says nothing at all about his family's believing (they may have; we simply do not know). Rather, he pointedly highlights only the jailer's faith, and yet his entire household was baptized as well.[16]

B. Paul expressly declares that the children of even one Christian parent are holy (ἅγια) (1 Cor 7:14). Paul's concern in this passage is to show that 'mixed' marriages, that is, marriages between a believer and an unbeliever, are 'holy', and he proves the sanctifying effect of the believing spouse on the marriage relationship (which was the thing in question) by appealing to the sanctifying effect of the believing parent upon the children of the marriage union (which was not in question). Since the children are 'holy', the marriage cannot be regarded as unholy. And since he cannot mean by this exceptional word 'holy' that these children are actually saved by the relation which they sustain to the believing parent, Paul doubtless intended by

---

16. I would counsel paedobaptists not to put much weight on these 'household' baptisms for the paedobaptist view, for even if they could convince the anti-paedobaptist that in these cases the believer's household was baptized on the basis of the faith of the household head, while such a view surely underscores the covenantal character of the Christian family, he cannot prove beyond a shadow of doubt that any of these households had infants or small children in them.

his striking description to ascribe covenant status to children of parents who are themselves members of the church of Jesus Christ – the New Testament form of the community rooted spiritually in the covenant with Abraham.

C. Paul presupposes the covenant status of children when he includes them among the 'saints' at Ephesus (Eph 1:1; 6:1; see also Col 3:20).[17] Given then

(1) the undeniable fact that infant males received the covenantal sign of circumcision (Gen 17:10-14)—the Old Testament type of New Testament baptism (Col 2:11-12) – in the old dispensation,

(2) the undeniable fact of the organic unity and continuity of the covenant of grace and the oneness of the people of God in all ages,

(3) the undeniable fact of the covenant status of children of believing parents in the new dispensation, and

(4) the undeniable fact that one can find no repeal in the New Testament of the nineteen-hundred-year-old Old Testament practice of placing the sign of the covenant of grace upon covenant children,

one may fairly infer that paedobaptism would have been practiced in Paul's Gentile churches. Accordingly, 'the absence of an express mention of infant baptism in the New Testament is rather to be explained from its "self-evidentness" than from its not yet having come into existence.'[18]

Paul's Teaching on the Lord's Supper

I. The terminology of the Lord's Supper
The church has come to refer to the Lord's Supper in the following ways because of the Pauline terminology associated with it:

(1) the 'breaking of bread [κλάσις τοῦ ἄρτου]' (1 Cor 10:16; see Acts 2:42),

(2) '[holy] communion' because Paul states that 'the cup of thanksgiving' and 'the bread we break' are 'communion [κοινωνία]' with the blood and body of Christ (1 Cor 10:16),

(3) the 'table of the Lord [τράπεζα κυρίου]' (1 Cor 10:21),

---

17. For Ridderbos's carefully nuanced discussion of this matter, see his *Paul: An Outline of His Theology*, 412-14. He concludes that Paul would have taken for granted that children, 'holy' by virtue of their solidaric relation to their Christian parents, would have been incorporated into the church by baptism.

18. Ridderbos, *Paul: An Outline of His Theology*, 414.

(4) the 'Lord's Supper [κυριακὸν δεῖπνον]' (1 Cor 11:20), and
(5) the 'Eucharist', on the basis of Paul's use of the aorist participle εὐχαριστήσας in 1 Corinthians 11:24.

Instituted as it was by Christ at the last Passover meal he celebrated with his disciples before his death, it is surely appropriate to infer a direct connection between the Passover meal and the Lord's Supper, namely, the latter is the antitype of the former in its theological significance. Not only is the Passover setting of this institution significant for its meaning but it is also noteworthy that our Lord used elements already normally employed in the Passover celebration when he instituted the Lord's Supper. R. T. Beckwith correctly observes:

> ...the only new thing which Christ instituted was his interpretation of the elements, i.e. his words of institution; for the thanksgivings, breaking of the bread and distributing of the elements took place at any formal Jewish meal, as the rabbinical literature shows. There were, indeed, interpretative words at the Passover meal, but they interpreted the elements in relation to the deliverance of the exodus, not in relation to the new deliverance through Christ's death. All that our Lord instituted needs to be performed, but the distinctive thing is his new interpretative words.[19]

II. The observance and liturgy of the Lord's Supper

With regard to the question of frequency of observance, the New Testament does not specify how often a congregation should observe the Lord's Supper. Paul states that Jesus simply said: 'Do this, *whenever* [ὁσάκις ἐάν] you drink it, in remembrance of me' (1 Cor 11:25).

With respect to the liturgy to be followed, while Rome has embellished the ordinance with a great deal of humanly devised pomp and circumstance, reflecting the 'transubstantiational theology' underlying the Roman Mass, Protestant churches, following Christ's and Paul's examples, have kept their liturgy, generally speaking, quite simple and scriptural:

1 Corinthians 10:14-17, 21: 'Therefore, my dear friends, flee from idolatry. I speak to sensible people; judge for yourselves what I say. *Is not the cup of thanksgiving for which we give thanks a participation* [κοινωνία] *in the blood of Christ? And is not the bread*

---

19. Beckwith, 'Eucharist,' *New Dictionary of Theology* (Downers Grove: InterVarsity, 1988), 236. For further information about the first-century Passover seder (order of service) and its relation to the Lord's Supper, see Ceil and Moishe Rosen, *Christ in the Passover* (Chicago: Moody, 1978).

that we break a participation [κοινωνία] *in the body of Christ?* Because there is one loaf, we, who are many, are one body, for we all partake of the one loaf...*You cannot drink the cup of the Lord and the cup of demons too; you cannot have a part in both the Lord's table and the table of demons.*'

1 Corinthians 11:23-30: 'I received from the Lord what I passed on to you: The Lord Jesus, on the night he was betrayed took bread, and when he had given thanks, he broke it and said, "This is my body, which is for you; do this in remembrance of me." In the same way, after supper he took the cup, saying, "This cup is the new covenant in my blood; do this, whenever you drink it, in remembrance of me." For whenever you eat this bread and drink this cup, you proclaim the Lord's death until he comes. Therefore, whoever eats the bread or drinks the cup of the Lord in an unworthy manner will be guilty of sinning against the body and blood of the Lord. A man ought to examine himself before he eats of the bread and drinks of the cup. For anyone who eats and drinks without recognizing the body of the Lord eats and drinks judgment on himself. That is why many among you are weak and sick, and a number of you have fallen asleep.'

With regard to the question of who are proper communicants at the Supper, Paul makes it clear that the Lord's Supper is not a 'converting ordinance'. It is for Christians only. The presiding minister must

(1) caution all against partaking of the elements *unworthily* (ἀναξίως, 1 Cor 11:27, 29), which in the Corinthians context probably had reference to that church's factiousness and selfishness, lest they bring judgment upon themselves;

(2) caution that all who participate must 'recognize the Lord's body' as they commune, that is to say, must view the elements in the context of the ordinance, not as food and drink for the physical body but as the sign and seal of *spiritual* verities; and

(3) summon all to self-examination (δοκιμαζέτω, 1 Cor 11:28), to insure among other things that those who commune are in the faith (see 2 Cor 13:5).

I should say in passing that while the classic Reformed position has restricted communion, precisely because of these apostolic admonitions, 'only to such as are of years and ability to examine themselves' (*Westminster Larger Catechism*, Question 177), a contemporary Reformed challenge has been mounted against this restriction in favor of paedocommunion primarily on the three grounds of (1) the analogy between the Passover and the Lord's Supper, (2) the analogy between baptism and the Lord's Supper, and (3) the insistence that Paul's summons to self-examination should be restricted to its contextual 'universe of discourse', namely, to adults. But because the Lord's Supper seems to require *active* participation on the part of the one receiving the elements (he or she is urged to 'take, eat, drink, do this'), while baptism by its very nature requires the recipient to be *passive* (no one, not even an adult, baptizes himself), I would urge that it is appropriate to draw a distinction between the two sacraments in this regard and to include infants and young children in baptism but to require them to mature sufficiently to the point where they are able to examine themselves before they are permitted to come to the Lord's Table.

III. The import of the Lord's Supper

The import of the Lord's Supper, according to Paul, can be addressed under the following five headings:

A. *A commemorative celebration.* Just as the Passover was to be a commemorative celebration of the Old Testament church's typical redemption from Egypt (Ex 12:11-14, 24-27; 13:8-10; Deut 16:1-8), so also the Lord's Supper, its New Testament antitype, is to be the commemorative celebration of the church's redemption which 'Christ our Passover' (1 Cor 5:7; see Ex 12:46) accomplished when he died as our sacrifice at the time of the Passover (John 18:28; 19:36). By it the church looks back to the historical actuality of Christ's cross work and remembers (ἀνάμνησις, 1 Cor 11:24), *not* reenacts as Rome contends, and proclaims (καταγγέλλετε, 1 Cor 11:26) Christ's sacrificial death for the church. Christ's summons to 'remember' here is addressing not so much the psychic defect of man's memory whereby he may forget something he has learned as the unbelief and ungratefulness in which the heart neglects and allows to be superseded what should never be superseded.

B. *An eschatological anticipation.* At the same time that the Lord's Supper looks back to the historical reality of Christ's Passion, it looks forward to the coming of the eschatological kingdom. Jesus specifically linked the Lord's Supper with the eschatological perspective of the kingdom of God when he informed his disciples that he would not eat the Passover again with them 'until it finds fulfillment in the kingdom of God' (Luke 22:16), and then, after taking the cup, he gave thanks and said: 'I will not drink again of the fruit of the vine until the kingdom of God comes' (22:18). In keeping with these expressions of his Lord, Paul's assertion that 'whenever you eat this bread and drink this cup, you proclaim the Lord's death *until he comes*' (1 Cor 11:26) also gives to the Lord's Supper an eschatological orientation.

The Lord's Supper is given then to the church on its pilgrimage through the world and is intended to kindle the eschatological hope that *then*, in the Eschaton, the knowledge of the glory of the Lord will cover the earth as the waters cover the places of the sea. The 'worthy' communicant also anticipates that glorious time in the Eschaton, at the return of Christ, when the church as the perfected Bride of Christ will sit down with Abraham, Isaac, and Jacob in the kingdom of heaven at the 'wedding supper of the Lamb' (Rev 19:9) and drink anew with Christ of the fruit of the vine in his Father's kingdom (Matt 26:29; Mark 14:25; Luke 22:18).

C. *A means of grace*. By his 'worthy' participation in the Lord's Supper, the celebrant 'communes' by faith with his Lord's body and blood (that is, his sacrificial death) which were offered up for him as his sacrifice for sin (1 Cor 10:16), thereby experiencing spiritual nourishment, growth in grace, and renewal of thanksgiving and engagement to God. In other words, the communion envisioned is more than a mere mental bringing to mind of Christ's death; it is a renewed impartation by Christ and appropriation by the believer of the spiritual benefits of Christ's redemption represented by the elements. *Westminster Larger Catechism*, Question 170, enlarges upon this aspect of the Lord's Supper in the following words:

> As the body and blood are not corporally or carnally present in, with, or under the bread and wine in the Lord's Supper, and yet are spiritually present to the faith of the receiver, no less truly and really than the elements themselves are to their outward senses; so they that worthily communicate in the sacrament of the Lord's Supper, do therein feed upon the body and blood of Christ, not after a corporal and carnal, but in a spiritual manner; yet truly and really, while by faith they receive and apply unto themselves Christ crucified, and all the benefits of his death.

D. *A demanding ordinance.* Larger Catechism, Question 171, in keeping with Paul's instructions, urges those who would come to the Lord's Table to prepare themselves *before* they come to it

> by examining themselves of their being in Christ, of their sins and wants; of the truth and measure of their knowledge, faith, repentance; love to God and the brethren, charity to all men, forgiving those that have done them wrong; of their desires after Christ, and of their new obedience; and by renewing the exercise of these graces, by serious meditation, and fervent prayer.

Question 174 admonishes those who are receiving the Lord's Supper *during* the time of its administration, that

> with all holy reverence and attention they wait upon God in that ordinance, diligently observe the sacramental elements and actions, heedfully discern the Lord's body, and affectionately meditate on his death and sufferings, and thereby stir up themselves to a vigorous exercise of their graces; in judging themselves, and sorrowing for sin; in earnest hungering and thirsting after Christ, feeding on him by faith, receiving of his fulness, trusting in his merits, rejoicing in his love, giving thanks for his grace; in renewing of their covenant with God, and love to all the saints.

Finally, Question 175 urges Christians *after* they have received the sacrament of the Lord's Supper

> seriously to consider how they have behaved themselves therein, and with what success; if they find quickening and comfort, to bless God for it, beg the continuance of it, watch against relapses, fulfil their vows, and encourage themselves to a frequent attendance on that ordinance: but if they find no present benefit, more exactly to review their preparation to, and carriage at, the sacrament; in both which, if they can approve themselves to God and their own consciences, they are to wait for the fruit of it in due time; but if they see they have failed in either, they are to be humbled, and to attend upon it afterward with more care and diligence.

E. *A vindicating apologetic.* In the life-and-death struggle between Christianity and Liberalism, indeed against all anti-supernaturalism, the Lord's Supper, both by its sign character (bread broken, fruit of the vine poured out, recipient participation) and by the words of institution ('This is my body which is *for you*'; 'This cup is the new covenant in my blood'), stands as a vindicating apologetic that the Pauline interpretation of the death of Christ as a substitutionary, atoning death by sacrifice (over against the portrayal of his death as that of a martyr in a noble cause or as that of a misguided fanatic) is the only true and proper view of Christ's death work. It too preaches the substitutionary atonement! It too proclaims the Lord's sacrificial death in our behalf! It too proclaims his final return to judgment!

* * * * *

We have completed our discussion of Paul's teaching on the two divinely-instituted sacraments of baptism and the Lord Supper. 'Both of them...according to the nature of the means of salvation concomitant with preaching, establish contact with Christ—baptism as baptism-into-his-death, the Supper as communion with the body and blood of Christ.'[20] Paul's Gentile churches' observance of them was much less ritualistic than is practiced today. For example, believers were baptized immediately upon their initial profession of faith and not, as is regularly done today, only after lengthy periods of instruction and observation of the believer's life. And the Lord's Supper, after the proper Pauline warnings had been issued, seems to have been celebrated in a very simple way, usually in connection with the eating together of the common meal (the Agape feast) and unaccompanied by the tinkling of bells, the swinging of censors of incense, and priestly and lay genuflection before the elements.

Simple, faithful, 'worthy' submission to and observance of them, as outlined by Paul, will strengthen Christians and equip them for living the Christian life. They should faithfully attend upon these gracious 'helps' which the wise God has determined is essential to and good for their growth and spiritual health. Their willful neglect can only result in spiritual loss.

---

20. Ridderbos, *Paul: An Outline of His Theology*, 424.

CHAPTER TWENTY-FOUR

THE PAULINE ESCHATOLOGY

>Rejoice, the Lord is King:
>>Your Lord and King adore!
>
>Rejoice, give thanks, and sing,
>>And triumph evermore!
>
>Jesus the Savior reigns,
>>The God of truth and love;
>
>When he had purged our stains,
>>He took his seat above.
>
>His kingdom cannot fail,
>>He rules o'er earth and heav'n;
>
>The keys of death and hell
>>Are to our Jesus giv'n.
>
>He sits at God's right hand
>>Till all his foes submit
>
>And bow to his command
>>And fall beneath his feet.
>
>Rejoice, in glorious hope!
>>Our Lord, the Judge, shall come,
>
>And take his servants up
>>to their eternal home.
>>>— Charles Wesley, 1746

We argued in Chapter Four that, in a very real sense, to speak about Paul's eschatology is to speak about his theology in its entirety. For Paul the fact that the Messianic kingdom had already come in one sense colored all his thinking. Nevertheless, there is a need to say something more about what Paul believed would occur after death and in the Eschaton. Accordingly, we will treat these biblical 'eventualities' here.

Eschatology is normally associated with the events surrounding the end of the world and the events of human history such as the return of Christ, the resurrection of men, and the final judgment. This is quite appropriate for in a real sense such events are the ultimate 'last things' in the 'last times'. But if we look at history from the perspective of the Old Testament, we see that its 'last times' are the 'complex times' of the Messiah, and the Messianic Age is the coming 'end time age'. However, as we noted in Chapter Four, Jesus Christ, the church's Prophet *par excellence*, gave to his church the key to unraveling the complexities of Old Testament eschatology. That key is what we termed there as his 'eschatological dualism': the kingdom of God has already come in its grace modality with his first appearance (this is the truth in what C. H. Dodd called 'realized eschatology') but the kingdom of God will yet come in its power and judgment modality when he comes again. By this eschatological duality Jesus provided the eschatological trajectory which set the direction for all of the New Testament writers, including Paul. As did our Lord, Paul maintained this perspective of the 'already/not yet' of eschatology. Consequently, there are stages or sequences in his eschatology. These stages or sequences may be indicated by the terms, 'present', 'intermediate', and 'future'. Within the future stage there are also subordinate items in that complex of events. We will look at each of these in turn.

The Present

Paul speaks of Christ's work as accomplishing the final victory, and he speaks of us participating here and now in essential, although not in full, completeness of that final victory.

I. Christ's work
About as completely and compactly as is possible for one verse to do (2 Tim 1:10), Paul declares that in his action in history Christ has abolished death, the end-time specter, and brought life and immortality to life through the gospel (see Col 2:14ff).

II. Our participation in that work
We, here and now, enter into eschatological life and immortality and escape death (see again 2 Tim 1:10). Our inward man experiences now, in this life, an 'end time death' to sin and death and a spiritual resurrection to newness of life (Rom 6:3-4). Even now we can speak

of already having been transferred from the dominion of darkness, and having been transferred to the kingdom of God's own beloved Son (Col 1:13). Paul can speak of our being seated with Christ now in heavenly places (Eph 2:6; see Col 3:3, where we are informed that our lives 'are hid with Christ in God').

The reality of the newness of the Christian's existence is so tremendous that he may be described as a 'new creation', in language reflecting the eschatological hope of the Old Testament: 'If anyone is in Christ, he is a new creation; the old things passed away; behold, the new things have come' (2 Cor 5:17; see Isa 65:17; 66:22). The Messianic Age has come and we are in it, and it has given us new life which will never perish.

But this new life, as wonderful as it is, is not all that we will have or be. There is more of blessing yet to come. Our inward man is renewed, but the mortal body and the whole universe await the resurrection (2 Cor 4:16-18; Rom 8:10-11, 18-22). Neither we nor any other Christians are ruling and reigning now in the way that we shall (1 Cor 4:8). Thus our perspective must be that of humble and thankful participation in the victory of the inward man on the one hand and expectant anticipation of the victory of the body and that of body and soul together in the Eschaton on the other.

The Intermediate State

Paul has as the hope for himself and all other believers the great triumph of Christ's return and the resurrection. This is the primary comfort he extends to those who are sorrowing (1 Thess 4:13-18). Without diminishing this perspective, he also speaks of the provision for believers between their death and future physical resurrection, and it is this to which we refer as the 'intermediate state', so named 'simply and only because it is temporary, and it is such both for the just and the unjust'.[1] Paul readily admits that the intermediate state is a lesser glory than the final state, and that it has its lacks when compared to the final glory accompanying the complex of events occurring at the return of Christ. The two key passages in Paul pertaining to the intermediate state are Philippians 1:21-23 and 2 Corinthians 5:1-10.

---

1. John Murray, 'The Last Things' in *Collected Writings of John Murray* (Edinburgh: Banner of Truth, 1977), 2, 401.

Philippians 1:21-23: 'For to me, to live is Christ and to die is gain. If I am to go on living in the body, this will mean fruitful labor for me. Yet what shall I choose? I do not know! I am torn between the two: I desire to depart and be with Christ, which is better by far.'

Here Paul speaks of wanting to die and being with Christ at death and he informs us that this state is only 'gain' (κέρδος) and very much better or better by far (πολλῷ μᾶλλον κρεῖσσον) than our present state. Since it is a state 'with Christ' and one of 'gain' which is 'very much better' than this one, it must at least have as great an aspect of self-consciousness as we have now or the significance of our being 'with Christ' and our being 'very much better' would seem to have little or no significance. Cullmann's argument from the 'pleasure of dreams' for a state of soul sleep as the condition of the blessed dead is not persuasive.[2]

2 Corinthians 5:1-10: 'Now we know that if the earthly tent we live in is destroyed, we have a building from God, an eternal house in heaven, not built by human hands. Meanwhile we groan, longing to be clothed with our heavenly dwelling, because when we are clothed,[3] we will not be found naked. For while we are in this tent, we groan and are burdened, because we do not wish to be unclothed but to be clothed with our heavenly dwelling, so that what is mortal may be swallowed up by life.... Therefore we are always confident and know that as long as we are at home in the body we are away from the Lord. We live by faith, not by sight. We are confident, I say, and

---

2. So also Herman Ridderbos, *Paul: An Outline of His Theology*, translated by John R. DeWitt (Grand Rapids: Eerdmans, 1975), 498-99, in his exposition of Philippians 1:20-23.

3. The United Bible Societies Greek text (fourth edition) offers the reading ἐκδυσάμενοι ('unclothed') in 2 Corinthians 5:3. Textually, it appears to be supported only by the original hand of D, the Old Latin versions a and (corrected) f, and the Fathers Tertullian and the Speculum Pseudo-Augustine. Bruce M. Metzger (*Textual Commentary*, 579) informs us that a majority of the Editorial Committee, while acknowledging that on the basis of external attestation ἐνδυσάμενοι ('clothed'), supported as it is by P[46], ℵ, B, C, D[2], Ψ, and most versions, has the much better external support, opted for the weaker 'vivid and paradoxical' reading ('inasmuch as we, though unclothed, shall not be found naked') to avoid what it perceived to be an otherwise banal tautology ('because when we are clothed, we will not be found naked'). (They do give their choice, however, a D rating ['very high degree of doubt']). This is a classic example of the Committee's openness to subjective conjectural emendation. I concur with Metzger's private opinion that 'in view of its superior external support the reading ἐνδυσάμενοι should be adopted, the reading ἐκδυσάμενοι being an early alteration to avoid apparent tautology' (580). The NASV, NIV, and NKJV adopt the better attested external reading.

would prefer to be away from the body and at home with the Lord. So we make it our goal to please him, whether we are at home in the body or away from it. For we must all appear before the judgment seat of Christ, that each one may receive what is due him for the things done while in the body, whether good or bad.'

This passage comprises the lengthiest and clearest reflective treatment of the intermediate state in the Pauline corpus. Here Paul states again that he 'prefer[s] to be away from the body and at home with the Lord' and speaks of 'being absent from the body and being at home with the Lord' (5:8). This would seem to speak of the time between death and the resurrection. The *crux interpretum* centers around this latter phrase and the correlative terms, 'house', 'building', and 'eternal in the heavens' (5:1), and the concepts of 'clothed' and 'naked' (5:2-4).

It is my understanding that the present tense 'we have'[4] (ἔχομεν, 5:1) and the references to 'house', 'building', and 'eternal in the heavens' refer to the resurrection body which we certainly 'have' in the sense that it is a promised and sure possession.[5] The terms 'naked' (5:3) and 'desiring to be clothed' (5:2) refer to us as those who are with the Lord with reference to our spirits but without resurrection bodies. The intermediate state is then one of being with the Lord but without our resurrection bodies. Again the language, 'absent from the body' and 'at home with the Lord' (5:8) over against the phrases 'absent from the Lord' and 'at home in the body' (5:6) and the note of preference for that condition over our present earthly existence (5:8) points to the reality of personal communion with the Lord (versus a state of soul sleep). For if we are now 'absent from the Lord' and are aware of personal communion with him, what will 'at home with the Lord' be if not in some sense an enhanced personal communion with him.

What Paul would most prefer would be that he might be alive at the return of the Lord and be clothed with the resurrection body without

---

4. Alfred Plummer, *A Critical and Exegetical Commentary on the Second Epistle of St. Paul to the Corinthians* (International Critical Commentary; Edinburgh: T. & T. Clark, 1915), affirms: 'The present tense is often used as a future, which is absolutely certain' (144).

5. So also Herman Ridderbos, *Paul: An Outline of His Theology*, 499-506, in his exposition of 2 Corinthians 5:1-10: '...what is meant by this "new building" is the glorified counterpart of the earthly body, and in the whole of Paul's proclamation this is to be understood in no other way than as that which will take place at Christ's coming... "have" thus has an anticipatory significance....' (501).

laying the mortal body down in death (5:2-4). But even the intermediate state is better than this present existence, beset as the present condition is with sin in which we have less direct communion with the Lord (5:6). Here, in this vale of tears, we do not yet love him with an unsinning heart as we will when we are actually in his presence. There we will know more intense joy, greater knowledge of, and closer communion with our exalted Savior and Lord. The love relationship between us and him there will be inexpressibly rhapsodic.

The Future State

I. The goal
For Paul 'the goal of God's redemptive purpose is the restoration of order to a universe that has been disturbed by evil and sin. This includes the realm of human experience, the spiritual world (Eph. 1:10), and...even nature itself. God will finally reconcile all things to himself through Christ.'[6]

II. All creation to pay homage to Christ
This will involve every knee bowing, in heaven, on earth, and under the earth, and every tongue confessing that Jesus Christ is Lord, to the glory of God the Father (Phil 2:10-11). This will come about as a result of Christ subduing all his enemies including death itself (1 Cor 15:25-27). Then, having accomplished his Messianic task, he will subject himself, in his Messianic role, to God the Father who had himself subjected all things to his Son, that God may be all in all (1 Cor 15:28).

III. Creation to be set free
This triumph will involve the final liberation of the creation from its state of bondage because of man's sin into the freedom of the glory of the children of God (Rom 8:19-23).

---

6. George Eldon Ladd, *A Theology of the New Testament* (Grand Rapids: Eerdmans, 1974), 567.

IV. Immortality either by bodily resurrection or by bodily transformation

For the believer the final Eschaton will involve either being physically resurrected from the dead or being physically transformed to incorruption while living. In either case it will involve the reception of an immortal body and a glorious state of eternity and glory ever with the Lord (Rom 8:23; Phil 3:21; 1 Thess 4:13-18; 1 Cor 15:51-54; 2 Cor 5:4-5).

V. Plight of the unbeliever

Unbelievers too are to be resurrected (Acts 24:15).[7] For the wicked the time of consummation is one of judgment, when Christ, having raised them at his coming, 'will punish those who do not know God and do not obey the gospel.... They will be punished with everlasting destruction and shut out from the [favorable] presence of the Lord and from the majesty of his power on the day he comes to be glorified in his holy people and to be marveled at among all those who have believed' (2 Thess 1:8-10). Paul elsewhere declares that 'in the day of wrath and revelation of the righteous judgment of God', to those who are self-seeking and who do not obey the truth but obey unrighteousness, that is, to those who do evil, God will render *wrath* (ὀργή—the objective product or issue in act of a 'thumotic' state of mind) and *anger* (θυμός—the subjective state of mind giving vent to ὀργή), trouble (θλῖψις) and distress (στενοχωρία) (Rom 2:8-9).

VI. Believers to be judged according to their works and to receive rewards accordingly

Paul teaches that not only unbelievers but believers as well will be judged in the judgment of the Eschaton (Rom 14:10, 12; 1 Cor 3:12-15; 2 Cor 5:10). To those who, by persistence in doing good, seek glory, honor, and immortality, that is, to those who do good, God will grant eternal life (ζωή αἰώνιον), glory (δόξα), honor (τιμή), and peace (εἰρήνη) (Rom 2:7, 10). The criteria of this judgment will be their works. With respect to how the apostle's teaching of judgment according to works is compatible with salvation by grace, John Murray declares that the following things need to be said:

---

7. Paul does not make this feature of the Eschaton explicit in his letters. In fact, as F. F. Bruce writes: '[*Acts* 24:15] is the only place in the New Testament where Paul is unambiguously credited with believing in a resurrection for the unrighteous as well as the righteous dead' (*Acts*, 444). But Paul implies it in 2 Corinthians 5:10.

(1) The distinction between judgment according to works and salvation on account of works needs to be fully appreciated. The latter is entirely contrary to the gospel Paul preached, is not implied in judgment according to works, and is that against which the burden of [Paul's letter to the Romans] is directed. Paul does not even speak of judgment on account of works in reference to believers. (2) Believers are justified by faith alone and they are saved by grace alone. But two qualifications need to be added to these propositions. (a) They are never justified by a faith that is alone. (b) In salvation we must not so emphasize grace that we overlook the salvation itself. The concept of salvation involves what we are saved to as well as what we are saved from. We are saved to holiness and good works (see Eph. 2:10). And holiness manifests itself in good works. (3) The judgment of God must have respect to the person in the full extent of his relationship and must therefore take into account the fruits in which salvation issues and which constitute the saved condition. It is not to faith or justification in abstraction that God's judgment will have respect but to these in proper relationship to the sum-total of elements comprising a saved state. (4) The criterion of good works is the law of God and the law of God is not abrogated for the believer. He is not without law to God; he is under law to Christ (see I Cor. 9:21 [see also Rom 6:14]). The judgment of God would not be according to truth if the good works of believers were ignored. (5) Good works as the evidences of faith and of salvation by grace are therefore the criteria of judgment and to suppose that the principle, 'who will render to every man according to his works' (Rom 2:6), has no relevance to the believer would be to exclude good works from the indispensable place which they occupy in the biblical doctrine of salvation.[8]

James Buchanan certainly would have concurred with Murray's judgment, writing in his famous work on justification:

> All faithful ministers have made use of both [doctrines – a present Justification by grace, through faith alone – and a future Judgment according to works], that they might guard equally against the peril of self-righteous legalism on the one hand and of practical Antinomianism on the other.[9]

The issue to be determined at the Final Judgment with respect to believers will be, not their justification *per se*, but their rewards for

---

8. John Murray, *Romans* (Grand Rapids: Eerdmans, 1968), I, 78-79; see also Leon Morris, *The Biblical Doctrine of Judgment* (London: Tyndale, 1978), 66f.
9. James Buchanan, *The Doctrine of Justification* (Edinburgh: T. & T. Clark, 1867), 238-39.

good works as the index to and evidence of their salvation which they procured through faith in Jesus Christ. With respect to this issue of believers' rewards, Murray writes in another place:

> While it makes void the gospel to introduce works in connection with justification, nevertheless works done in faith, from the motive of love to God, in obedience to the revealed will of God and to the end of his glory are intrinsically good and acceptable to God. As such they will be the criterion of reward in the life to come. This is apparent from such passages as Matthew 10:41; 1 Corinthians 3:8-9, 11-15; 4:5; 2 Corinthians 5:10; 2 Timothy 4:7. We must maintain therefore, justification complete and irrevocable by grace through faith and apart from works, and at the same time, future reward according to works. In reference to these two doctrines it is important to observe the following:
>
> (i) This future reward is not justification and contributes nothing to that which constitutes justification. (ii) This future reward is not salvation. Salvation is by grace and it is not as a reward for works that we are saved. (iii) The reward has reference to the degree of glory bestowed in the state of bliss, that is, the station a person is to occupy in glory and does not have reference to the gift of glory itself. (iv) This reward is not administered because good works earn or merit reward, but because God is graciously pleased to reward them. That is to say it is a reward of grace. (In the Romish scheme good works have real merit and constitute the ground of the title to everlasting life.) The good works are rewarded because they are intrinsically good and well-pleasing to God. They are not rewarded because they earn reward but they are rewarded only as labour, work or service that is the fruit of God's grace, conformed to his will and therefore intrinsically good and well-pleasing to him. They could not even be rewarded of grace if they were principally and intrinsically evil.[10]

VII. The 'triggering mechanism'

The 'triggering mechanism' and beginning point for this complex of events, this collective eschatology, is the bodily, visible, public return of Jesus Christ (1 Thess 4:13-18; 2 Thess 1:5-10 (esp. 1:7); Phil 3:20-21; 1 Cor 15:23). Paul speaks of 'the appearing of the glory of our great God and Savior Jesus Christ' as the Christian's 'blessed hope' (Tit 2:13). When he comes, he will resurrect the Christian dead, transform the Christian living, and catch both groups up in one body 'to the meeting of the Lord' (εἰς ἀπάντησιν τοῦ κυρίου) (1 Thess 4:13-18), these saints then returning immediately with him to earth to

---

10. John Murray, 'Justification' in *Collected Writings of John Murray*, 2, 221-22.

participate in the judgment of the resurrected and transformed wicked (1 Cor 6:2). Two analogies to the saints going up and then returning immediately with him to the judgment of the wicked may be seen, first, in the movement of the wise virgins who went out 'to meet the bridegroom' (εἰς ὑπάντησιν τοῦ νυμφίου) and who then accompanied him back to the wedding banquet (Matt 25:1-13) and, second, in the movement of the Roman Christians who came 'to meet [Paul and his companions]' (εἰς ἀπάντησιν ἡμῖν) as he approached Rome and who then returned with him to Rome (Acts 28:15).

VIII. The focal point of Paul's teaching on eschatology

The return of Jesus Christ is the focus of Paul's teaching on eschatology and it must be ours as well. No other problems, queries, doubts, disagreements, diversities of viewpoint, unresolved questions, and controversies respecting the relation of other events to the advent of Christ in glory can be permitted to set this one great fact aside or blur its significance and centrality for the Eschaton. Christ is coming back, and we shall be raised (or transformed) to imperishability, honor, power, and immortality (1 Cor 15:42-43)! This gives us comfort for ourselves and for those who have already died (1 Thess 4:13-18), and it gives us an ethical perspective to live expectantly and carefully (1 Thess 5:1-11). Such is always the by-product of the resurrection hope. It makes for godly living (1 Cor 15:56-58).

In a real sense the return of Christ and the resurrection and transformation of his people is the next important Messianic event on the horizon. It overshadows all else. So Paul may speak of all Christians as those who are not only serving the living and true God but as those who also 'wait for his Son from heaven' (1 Thess 1:10).

IX. A pre-tribulation rapture of the church?

Pre-tribulation rapturists customarily refer to the 'catching up' of the saints spoken of 1 Thessalonians 4:15-17 as the 'secret rapture' and place its occurrence seven years before Christ's actual coming. All kinds of bizarre, highly dramatic, and overdrawn descriptions of the effects of this secret rapture on the world community – all intended to strike fear into the unbeliever – can be found in their books and sermons. But when one takes Paul's description of the rapture seriously it is anything but 'separate' or 'secret'. From Paul's declaration that 'relief' from its troubles and persecutions will come to the church not seven years before but 'when the Lord Jesus is revealed [ἐν τῇ ἀποκαλύψει] from heaven with his holy angels with blazing fire' (2 Thess 1:7). One should also note 2 Thessalonians 2:1 which places the Lord's 'coming' (παρουσία) and our 'gathering together' (ἐπισυναγωγή) unto him under the regimen of the same article, thereby uniting the two ideas; see also Titus 2:13 which places the 'blessed hope', customarily construed by dispensationalists as a reference to the rapture, and the 'appearing of the glory' of Christ also under the regimen of the same article, again uniting the two ideas), which 'revealing' he describes only verses later as the 'appearing [ἐπιφάνεια] of his coming [παρουσία]' (2:8); it becomes quite clear that his coming and the ensuing rapture spoken of in 1 Thessalonians 4:15-17 is no secret, hidden event but a very visible breaking into history of the glory of God. The Lord's (Jesus') 'loud command' (κέλευσμα), the voice of the archangel, and the trumpet-blast (σάλπιγξ) of God all announcing Christ's coming make this one of the 'loudest' pericopes in the Bible! I say again, his coming and our rapture to him will be anything but secret!

X. The ingathering of 'all Israel' – the remnant throughout this age or the nation in the future?

The question of the time and nature of the restoration of Israel is a central aspect of the much larger and very complex issue concerning two major streams of tradition which developed during the Second Temple period which differed radically in their understanding of the postexilic situation. According to one view, the return from exile and the rebuilding of Jerusalem and the temple under the authority of Cyrus' decree in 539 B.C. (Isa 44:28; Ezra 1:1-4) and the rebuilding of the walls of Jerusalem under the authority of Artaxerxes I's decree in 445 B.C. (Neh 2:1-6), and the rebuilding there of the Jewish community under the Levitical legislation brought an end to the Jewish exile. In sum, according to this view, God's promised restoration of his people to his favor had already occurred. According to the second view, because a restoration of all twelve tribes to the land had not occurred, because Israel lived in the promised land at the behest of foreign rulers and existed there at the pleasure of these Gentile rulers, and because the rebuilt temple only modestly reflected the Solomonic Temple's former splendor, was never inhabited by the Shekinah Glory, and in no way served as the center of a unified people in its own land, the Jewish exile still continued. That is to say, according to the second view, the Jewish people were still under God's judgment and disfavor and God's promised restoration of his people to his favor and full blessing was still a hope to be fulfilled at some point in the future, indeed, in the eschatological future.[11] Accordingly, a wide strand of Second-Temple Jewish theology looked forward to a full return of all exiled Jews, the appearance of a Davidic heir who would throw off the shackles of foreign domination, and the gathering of one people around a new and glorified future temple.

There is good evidence that the New Testament writers in general and Paul in particular espoused the latter tradition. Indeed, Paul seems to espouse it in a more radical way than did even its Second Temple advocates. For he teaches that Israel's rejection of its Messiah in the person of Jesus of Nazareth only initiated Israel's continuing exile anew with intensified divine disfavor. The Messiah was in fact Israel's 'true Temple', in whom the church is rising to become the Lord's holy temple (Eph 2:21). He did indeed inaugurate the Kingdom of God in its grace modality which, except for the true remnant within Israel, official Israel promptly rejected. Paul writes about Israel's present state in the following passages:

Galatians 4:22-30: '...Abraham had two sons, one by the slave woman and the other by the free woman. His son by the slave woman was born in the ordinary way; but his son by the free woman was born as the result of a promise.

'These things may be taken figuratively, for *the women represent two covenants*. One covenant is from Mount Sinai and *bears children who are to be slaves*: This is Hagar. Now Hagar stands for Mount Sinai in Arabia and corresponds to *the present city of Jerusalem*, because *she is in slavery with her children*. But the Jerusalem that is above is free, and she is our mother....Now you, brothers, like Isaac,

---

11. In support of this view that the restoration of Israel involved more than just a return to the land, see O.J. Steck, *Israel und gewaltsame Geschick der Propheten* (Neukirchen-Vluyn: Neukirchener Verlag, 1967); N.T. Wright, *The New Testament and the People of God* (Philadelphia: Fortress, 1992), esp. 268-72; C.A. Evans, 'Aspects of Exile and Restoration in the Proclamation of Jesus and the Gospels,' in *Exile: Old Testament, Jewish and Christian Conceptions*, edited by J. M. Scott (Netherlands: Brill, 1997), esp. 311; and A. Ido, 'Romans 2: A Deuteronomistic Reading,' *JSNT* (1995). For the opposing view see A.T. Kraabel, 'The Roman Diaspora: Six Questionable Assumptions,' *JJS* 33: 445-62. See also James M. Scott, 'Restoration of Israel' in *Dictionary of Paul and His Letters*, edited by Gerald F. Hawthorne, Ralph P. Martin, and Daniel G. Reid (Downers Grove, Ill.: InterVarsity, 1993), 796-99, for literary evidence from the period for these views.

The Pauline Eschatology

are children of promise. At that time the son born in the ordinary way persecuted the son born by the power of the Spirit. *It is the same now.* But what does the Scripture say? "Get rid of the slave woman and her son, for the slave woman's son will never share in the inheritance with the free woman's son." Therefore, brothers, we are not children of the slave woman, but of the free woman'.[12] (emphasis supplied)

1 Thessalonians 2:14-16: 'For you, brothers, became imitators of God's churches in Judea, which are in Christ Jesus: You suffered from your own countrymen the same things those churches suffered from the Jews, who killed the Lord Jesus and the prophets and drove us out. *They displease God* and are hostile to all men in their effort to keep us from speaking to the Gentiles so that they may be saved. In this way *they always heap up their sins to the limit. The wrath of God has come upon them at last.*' (emphasis supplied)

Romans 9:27: 'Isaiah cries out concerning Israel: "Though the number of the Israelites be like the sand of the sea, only the remnant will be saved." '

Romans 9:33: 'See, I lay in Zion a stone that causes men to stumble and a rock that makes them fall.'

Romans 10:21: '...concerning Israel [Isaiah] says: "All day long I have held out my hands to a disobedient and obstinate people." '

Romans 11:8-10: '...as it is written [in Isaiah 29:10]: "God gave [non-elect Israel] a spirit of stupor, eyes so that they could not see and ears so that they could not hear *to this very day*." And David says: "May

---

12. I remain unpersuaded by those Paul scholars who urge that Paul also intended in the earlier Galatians passage, Galatians 4:1-7, directly to teach Israel's continuing exile. In my opinion their *heilsgeschichtliche* exegesis is highly strained and their conclusion an untenable theological reach.
    I prefer to read the passage *existentially* as referring to all Christians, both Jews and Gentiles, with its descriptive referent in 4:1-3 being their pre-Christian state of enslavement to whatever 'fundamental principles of this world' (see Paul's τὰ στοιχεῖα τοῦ κόσμου in 4:3, 9) to which they had ultimately entrusted themselves religiously (in the case of Jews it was adherence to the law; in the case of Gentiles it was anything and everything except the true God). Of course, from this reading of the text the implication follows that all those outside of Christ, including both Jews and Gentiles, *continue* in their 'minority' under their chosen στοιχεῖα ('elementary principles'), and thus this minority status makes them 'no different from a slave [οὐδὲν διαφέρει δούλου]' (Gal 4:1). Only indirectly then does this passage teach unbelieving Israel's continuing captivity and enslavement to sin, but then it teaches the same about all other people as well.

their table become a snare and a trap, a stumbling block and a retribution for them. May their eyes be darkened so they cannot see and their backs be bent forever" ' (see also Jesus' teaching in Matthew 21:42-43; 23:29-38; 24:1-35).

In fact, 'the disobedience with which Paul charges Israel represents not just a continuation, but a repetition of Israel's earlier refusal of God's saving mercies.'[13]

His apostolic understanding of God's attitude toward Israel gave Paul a special insight into Israel's future and the nature of Israel's restoration. God has, according to Paul, something of a 'love/hate' attitude today toward ethnic Israel: 'As far as the gospel is concerned, [Jews] are [regarded as his] enemies[14] for [the salvific sake of Gentiles]; but as far as election is concerned, they are loved on account of the patriarchs' (Rom 11:28). Today non-Christian ethnic Israel (ἡ νῦν 'Ἱερουσαλήμ, Gal 4:25), because they are Jews 'only outwardly' (Rom 2:28-29), that is to say, because they pursue a righteousness before God 'not by faith but as if it were by works' (Rom 9:31-32; 10:3), are not really sons of Isaac and hence not the true 'Israel' at all (Rom 9:6-9). Rather, because of their unbelief and rejection of Christ 'the present city of Jerusalem' is as much the 'son of Hagar' as Ishmael himself was (Gal 4:25)! And just as Ishmael persecuted Isaac (Gen 21:9; Gal 4:29), Paul writes, ethnic Israel, as the spiritual 'son of Hagar' in its unbelief, as we already noted,

> killed the Lord Jesus and the prophets, and also drove us out. They displease God and are hostile to all men in their effort to keep us from speaking to the Gentiles so that they may be saved. In this way they always heap up their sins to the limit [see Matt 23:32]. The wrath of God has come upon them at last [εἰς τέλος[15]]. (1 Thess 2:15-16)

He says still further that God has given them 'a spirit of stupor, eyes so that they could not see and ears so that they could not hear, to this very day' (Rom 11:8).[16]

---

13. Mark A. Seifrid, 'Blind Alleys in the Controversy Over the Paul of History' in *Tyndale Bulletin* 45.1 (1994), 91.

14. That it is God who is regarding Israel as his enemy for the sake of the gospel and not Israel who is regarding God as their enemy is plain from the parallel thought in 11:28b that it is God who also loves Israel as far as election is concerned.

15. See BAGD, τέλος, *A Greek-English Lexicon of the New Testament and Other Early Christian Literature*, 812, 1.d.g, for other possible translations of this phrase: 'finally', 'utterly', 'decisively', 'until the end', 'forever'.

Yet Paul also speaks in Romans 11 of a saving ingathering of ethnic Jews in some sense of such proportions that he can speak of 'all Israel' being saved (Rom 11:26). Consider these Pauline statements:

Romans 11:2a: 'God did not reject his people, whom he foreknew.'
Romans 11:12: '...how much greater riches will their *fullness* [τὸ πλήρωμα] bring!'
Romans 11:15: '...what will their *acceptance* [πρόσλημψις] be but life from the dead?'
Romans 11:23: 'And if they do not persist in unbelief, they will be grafted in, for God is able to graft them in again.'
Romans 11:24: '...how much more readily [than the wild uncultivated branches] will these, the natural [cultivated] branches, be grafted into their own olive tree.'
Romans 11:25-26: 'Israel has experienced a hardening [only] in part until the *full number* [τὸ πλήρωμα] of the Gentiles has come in. And so all Israel will be saved....'

From these verses it is clear that God intends to save the elect remnant of Israel. But when? Throughout this age or at some time in the future *after* the full number of elect Gentiles has been saved? And what will be the nature of Israel's 'restoration'?

Classic dispensationalists teach that after the rapture of the church,

---

16. The *Catechism of the Catholic Church* (1994) is hardly saying everything that should be said when it declares that 'Jews are not collectively responsible for Jesus' death' (153), stating that
> ...we cannot lay responsibility for the trial [of Jesus] on the Jews in Jerusalem as a whole, despite the outcry of a manipulated crowd and *the global reproaches contained in the apostles' calls to conversion after Pentecost*.... Still less can we extend responsibility to other Jews of different times and places, based merely on the crowd's cry: 'His blood be on us and on our children!' a formula for ratifying a judicial sentence. As the Church declared at the Second Vatican Council: '...[N]either all Jews indiscriminately at that time, nor Jews today, can be charged with the crimes committed during his Passion.... *[T]he Jews should not be spoken of as rejected or accursed as if this followed from holy Scripture*' (para 597, emphasis supplied).

Paul's statements in Romans 11:28 and 1 Thessalonians 2:15-16 as well as his description of God's attitude toward Israel as a nation in Romans 11:7-10 belie Rome's catechesis here. In this age, while Israel's blindness is not total (elect Jews are excluded, Rom 9:27-29; 11:5), Israel *as a nation* stands under God's wrath and curse and *as a nation* has no salvific covenant with God today. Nevertheless, when 'the full number of the Gentiles' has come (Rom 11:25), the 'full number' of Jewish elect will also have been grafted 'by faith in Jesus Christ' into the church which is both 'the true Israel' and the 'covenant people of God', and in that relationship these elect Jews are no longer 'Ishmaelites' but, in the church, are the true 'Israel of God'.

either during the entire last half of their so-called seven-year Tribulation or just before Christ's return at the end of the Tribulation or at his return itself, he will save 'all Israel' and reign for a thousand years over the restored nation from a throne in Jerusalem. Even some non-dispensational scholars, such as George E. Ladd (a historic premillennialist) and John Murray (a postmillennialist), place the time of Israel's 'full number' in the future after the 'full number' of the Gentiles has been accomplished. Basing his view on Romans 11:12, 15, 26-32, which he describes as the 'most relevant passages', Murray asserts:

> ...Paul envisions a restoration of Israel as a people to God's covenant favour and blessing. In Romans 11:15 this viewpoint is inescapable. The casting away of Israel (*apobole*) is the rejection of Israel as a people collectively (see Matt 21:43). The rhetorical question which follows implies that there is to be a reception of them again (*proslempsis*), a restoration of that from which they had been rejected. But the same collective aspect must apply to the restoration; otherwise the contrast would lose its force.[17]

Commenting on Romans 11:26 Murray states:

> The apostle is thinking of a time *in the future* when the hardening of Israel will terminate. As the fulness, receiving, ingrafting have this time reference, so must the salvation of Israel have.[18]

As a result of ethnic Israel's future salvation, basing his remarks on Romans 11:12 Murray insists that

> ...there awaits the Gentiles, in their distinctive identity as such, gospel blessing [which he interprets to mean 'the expansion of the success attending the gospel and of the kingdom of God'] far surpassing anything experienced during the period of Israel's apostasy, and this unprecedented enrichment will be occasioned by the conversion of Israel on a scale commensurate with that of their earlier disobedience.[19]

But if the 'full number' of the Gentiles, which surely speaks of the totality of the Gentile elect, has already been salvifically realized prior to the 'full number' of 'all Israel', how will Israel's subsequent corporate salvation result in even greater salvific blessing to the Gentiles, which 11:12 and 11:15 seems to envision? Regarding this seeming discrepancy in his interpretation Murray writes:

---

17. John Murray, 'The Last Things,' *Collected Writings*, 2, 409.
18. Murray, *Romans*, 2, 98, emphasis supplied.
19. Murray, *Romans*, 2, 79.

It could be objected that [this] interpretation brings incoherence into Paul's teaching. On the one hand, the "fulness" of Israel brings unprecedented blessing to the Gentiles (vss. 12, 15). On the other hand, "the fulness of the Gentiles" marks the terminus of Israel's hardening and their restoration (vs. 25). But the coherence of these two perspectives is not prejudiced if we keep in mind the mutual interaction for the increase of blessing between Jew and Gentile. We need but apply the thought of verse 31 that by the mercy shown to the Gentiles Israel may also obtain mercy. By the fulness of the Gentiles Israel is restored (vs. 25); by the restoration of Israel the Gentiles are incomparably enriched (vss. 12, 15). The only obstacle to this view is the unwarranted assumption that the "fulness of the Gentiles" is the consummation of blessing for the Gentiles and leaves room for no further expansion of gospel blessing. "The fulness of the Gentiles" denotes unprecedented blessing for them but does not exclude even greater blessing to follow. It is to this subsequent blessing that the restoration of Israel contributes.[20]

I am not persuaded that Murray's reasoning here is exegetically sustainable. It empties the phrase, 'the full number of the Gentiles', which surely intends the salvific totality of Gentile elect, of all significance if unprecedented gospel blessing 'far surpassing anything experienced during the period of Israel's apostasy' throughout this age yet awaits the Gentile world following upon the 'full number of the Gentiles'. Murray's exegetical construction appears to be erected here simply in the interest of his postmillennial vision of the conversion of the entire world before Christ's return.

For five reasons I would urge that Paul's intention seems rather to be that just as God throughout this age brings the divinely determined full number (τὸ πλήρωμα) of elect Gentiles to faith in Christ and thus into the church, so he is also bringing the divinely determined full number (τὸ πλήρωμα) of elect Jews (the 'remnant', 'all Israel') also to faith in Christ throughout this same age so that both 'full numbers' are reached simultaneously.[21]

---

20. Murray, *Romans*, 2, 95-96.
21. So L. Berkhof, *Systematic Theology* (Grand Rapids: Eerdmans, 1939), 698-700; William Hendriksen, *Israel in Prophecy* (Grand Rapids: Baker, 1974), 39-52; G. C. Berkouwer, *The Return of Christ*. trans. James Van Oosterom (Grand Rapids: Eerdmans, 1972), 323-58; Herman Ridderbos, *Paul: An Outline of His Theology* (Grand Rapids: Eerdmans, 1975), 354-61; Anthony A. Hoekema, *The Bible and the Future* (Grand Rapids: Eerdmans, 1979), 139-47; O. Palmer Robertson, 'Is There a Distinctive Future for Ethnic Israel in Romans 11?' *Perspectives on Evangelical Theology*, edited by K. Kantzer and S. Gundry (Grand Rapids: Baker, 1979), 209-27.

The first reason is the implication in Paul's employment of the one cultivated olive tree in Romans 11:17-24 that the Jewish 'cultivated' branches, though 'broken off,' can and will be grafted into the same olive tree again. 'Every thought of a separate future, a separate kind of salvation, or a separate spiritual organism for saved Jews is here excluded. Their salvation is here pictured in terms of becoming one with the saved totality of God's people, not in terms of a separate program for Jews!'[22]

Second, the phrase which is rendered 'until' (ἄχρις οὗ) in Romans 11:25 has the force of a *terminus ad quem* with no implication that a prevailing circumstance will then be reversed.[23] What this phrase intends in Romans 11:25 is that the partial blindness of Israel extends to the coming of the fulness of the Gentiles. It implies nothing about a reversal of that condition after that fulness comes.

Third, Paul does not say in Romans 11:25-26 that 'Israel has experienced a hardening in part until the full number of the Gentiles has come in. And then [τότε, εἶτα or ἔπειτα] all Israel will be saved', teaching thereby that the salvation of 'all Israel' temporally follows upon the salvation of the full number of elect Gentiles. He says rather in verse 26: 'And so [οὕτως—'thus', 'in this way'] all Israel will be saved', teaching thereby that in and by the remarkable process of calling the full number of elect Gentiles to himself—which 'provokes [the elect Jews] to jealousy'—God also brings them to himself.

Fourth, Paul clearly appears to teach this by his strategic placement of a third 'now' in Romans 11:30-31:

---

22. Hoekema, *The Bible and the Future*, 139-47.
23. See the use of 'until' or 'unto' in Matthew 24:38; Acts 22:4; 1 Corinthians 11:26, 15:25; and Hebrews 4:12. The point of the 'until' in Matthew 24:38 is not that the eating and drinking, the marrying and giving in marriage going on in the days of Noah were replaced by a different circumstance on the day that Noah entered the ark; rather, the 'until' stresses the people's constant practice of these things until the flood came. These things ceased in the destruction of the flood but began again after the flood. The point of the 'unto' in Acts 22:4 is not that Paul's persecution ceased after the persecuted Christians died; rather, it stresses that Paul's persecution continued to the very point of the Christian's death. The 'until' in 1 Corinthians 11:26 does not lay stress on the fact that a day is coming when Christians will no longer celebrate the Lord's Supper; rather, it emphasizes that this celebration will continue until Christ returns. The 'until' in 1 Corinthians 15:25 does not mean that a day will come when the Lord Christ will no longer reign; rather, it stresses that he must continue to reign now until he has put all of his enemies under his feet. Finally, the 'unto' in Hebrews 4:12 does not mean that the Word's piercing ceases and that another condition will prevail from that time onward; rather, it stresses that the piercing process continues as far as possible.

Just as you [Gentiles] who were at one time disobedient to God have *now* received mercy as a result of their [the Jews'] disobedience, so they too have *now* become disobedient in order that they too may *now* [νῦν] receive mercy as a result of God's mercy to you.

The third 'now' in this two-verse statement, supported by ℵ, B, the original hand (and the third 'corrector' hand) of D and several other lesser witnesses,[24] declares that the divine mercy is being shown to elect Jews *now*, throughout *this* age.

Finally, Paul's concluding summary statement in 11:32, 'For God has bound all men over to disobedience so that he may have mercy on them all,' strengthens the current significance of the gospel for Jew as well as for Gentile.

This view still allows for enough Jewish conversions to Christianity throughout this age to meet the demands of the 'riches' (πλοῦτος, 11:12) and the 'life from the dead' (ζωὴ ἐκ νεκρῶν, 11:15) which Paul envisions 'all Israel's' salvation will bring to the world.

Thus I would urge that the 'all Israel' of Romans 11:26 refers to the totality of elect Jews taken as a whole from their initial election to their ultimate salvation, and the nature of their 'restoration' is their spiritual ingrafting throughout this age into the 'Israel of God' whose roots are in the faith of Abraham and whose current expression is the church of Jesus Christ.

The only question that remains is the specific instrumentality that God will employ to bring this ingathering to pass. Dispensational scholars suggest that the return of Christ itself will be the instrumentality which will effect this ingathering of Jews. They call attention to Paul's statement in Romans 11:26: 'The Deliverer will come from Zion; he will turn godlessness away from Jacob.' But it is not at all certain that Zion here is heaven or that the Deliverer's 'coming' is the second coming of Christ. In Hebrews Paul declares that the church is Zion (Heb 11:22), and Paul intimates in Romans 11 that *whenever* (ὅταν) God takes away Jacob's sins, he may be said to have 'come from Zion' to them and to have kept his covenant with them. So Israel's

---

24. The Fourth Revised Edition of the UBS *Greek New Testament*, places this νῦν in brackets and gives it a C rating, indicating that it 'may be regarded as part of the text, but that in the present state of New Testament textual scholarship this cannot be taken as completely certain' (2*). Bruce M. Metzger in his *Textual Commentary on the Greek New Testament* states that 'external evidence and internal considerations are rather evenly balanced' for the retention or deletion of the third νῦν in 11:31 but adjudges that, after all things are considered, 'it seemed best to retain νῦν in the text' (527).

conversion through the instrumentality of the church's proclamation of the gospel meets all the details of Romans 11:26 as well as (I think better than) the instrumentality of Christ's coming. Particularly does this appear so when one recalls that when Paul describes the effects of Christ's return, he does not represent Christ's coming as a 'saving event' in the sense that it converts unconverted men to him. It is a saving event only in the sense that it delivers those who are already his own from their final enemies who are judged in and by Christ's coming (see 2 Thess 1:6-10, esp. 1:8: 'He will punish those who do not know God and do not obey the gospel of our Lord Jesus').

On the basis of Paul's statements that 'salvation has come to the Gentiles to make Israel envious' (Rom 11:11; Deut 32:21) and that the design behind his own ministry to the Gentiles was to 'arouse my own people to envy and save some of them' (Rom 11:14), I would suggest that the tangible, concrete, visible salvific mercies effecting *the fulness* [τὸ πλήρωμα] of the Gentiles' (11:25) will be the instrumentality God will use to effect also *the fulness* [τὸ πλήρωμα] of Israel' (11:12; see 11:31). By doing the former (see Paul's καὶ οὕτως, 'and accordingly', 'and in this manner', 11:26), God will make the elect Jews 'righteously jealous' of the multitude of Gentiles enjoying the blessings rightfully theirs, and will thereby quicken their interest in gospel issues, leading to their 'fulness' as well and accordingly to even futher blessing for the Gentiles.

XI. The apostasy and the man of sin

For all his expectancy of the 'blessed hope', Paul indicates nonetheless that there are other eschatological events which must occur first, namely, the apostasy and the revelation of the man of lawlessness (2 Thess 2:1-11) who is 'a distinct personage who will appear on the scene of this world just prior to the advent of Christ'.[25] Paul, somewhat cryptically, declares that while the secret power of lawlessness is already at work, 'that which restrains'[26] will restrain the power of lawlessness 'until he [the man of lawlessness] comes out of the midst [of men] [ἄρτι ἕως ἐκ μέσου γένηται].'[27] At that time the man of lawlessness will be revealed. He will oppose and exalt himself over

---

25. Murray, 'Last Things,' *Collected Writings*, 2, 410; so also Ridderbos, *Paul: An Outline of His Theology*, 515-16.
26. Does Paul intend by this phrase (1) the rule of civil law or (2) the need for the gospel to be proclaimed to all nations or (3) an angelic personage such as Michael or (4) the divinely determined time in the eternal counsel of God? I prefer the first suggestion.

everything that is called God or is worshiped, and even set himself up in God's temple (the church), proclaiming himself to be God.[28] But Christ will slay the lawless one with the breath of his mouth and bring him to an end by the appearance of his coming (2 Thess 2:8).

How are we to relate the salvation of Israel and the resultant blessing which their salvation will be to the Gentile church (Paul's 'world') (Rom 11:11, 12, 15), which we treated above, with these negative eschatological events? I would respond with this scenario: Through the preaching of the gospel the day will come when the full tale of the Gentile elect will be reached. In the course of God's bringing this to fulfillment, God's ancient 'people whom he foreknew' (Paul's 'all Israel') will also be stirred to a degree of 'fulness' to put their trust in their Messiah and be grafted again into their own olive tree, the church of Jesus Christ (Rom 11:23-24), whose presence in the church will prove to be a source of still richer blessing to the church at large. Only *after* this will appear the apostasy and the man of lawlessness who will assume the role of God in the church, whom Christ will then slay with the breath of his mouth at his coming.

Paul's stress on the expectancy of the return of our Lord might seem on the surface to be contradictory to these negative end-time events. But as a matter of fact Paul wrote about *these* events to correct just such a misconstruction by the Thessalonian Christians, and it should serve the same purpose now. The perspective of expectancy of Christ's return should continue undiminished, but no erroneous deductions, such as the notion that no evil event will precede it, should be drawn.

XII. The question of a millennial reign before the final state

The concept of a millennial reign as such is found only in Revelation 20, a book with extensive symbolism. It is most likely that this Johannine millennial reference should be construed symbolically either of the present spiritual reign of Christians with Christ (Rom 5:17; 14:17; Eph 2:6; Col 1:13) or the present reign of the martyred saints in the intermediate state, or both rather than construed literally as an aspect

---

27. George Eldon Ladd, *The Blessed Hope* (Grand Rapids: Eerdmans, 1956), 94-95.
28. Perhaps the Reformers were not wrong when they saw the Papal power in general as 'antichrist' and the last Pope in particular as the Antichrist. The Papacy and the Popes already claim in turn to be the Vicars of Christ on earth and through their doctrinal pronouncements are already leading the vast majority of professing Christendom away from reliance in Christ alone for salvation.

of the Eschaton. But whatever John intended by his teaching, *it is beyond dispute that there is no clearly delineated millennial period in Paul's eschatology.*

The most appropriate place where he might have spoken about it, if, in fact, he had advocated the millennial position, is the pericope in 1 Corinthians 15:20-26, but he makes no mention of it there.[29] Premillennialists claim that Paul does indeed allude to the millennial kingdom in 1 Corinthians 15:24 ('the kingdom') and in 15:25 ('he must reign'). They urge, on the basis of what they refer to as the 'order' (τάγμα, 15:23) phrases, 'Christ the *firstfruits*' (ἀπαρχή), '*then* [ἔπειτα] those who are Christ's at his coming [παρουσία]', and '*then* [εἶτα] comes the end', that the millennial kingdom occurs between the resurrection of Christ's own at the time of the first 'then' and the coming of the 'end' at the time of the second 'then'. They call attention to the usage of εἶτα and ἔπειτα in 1 Corinthians 15:5, 7 and the usage of εἶτα in 1 Timothy 2:13 and 3:10 to support the notion of a gap of 1000 years between 1 Corinthians 15:23 and 15:24.

How does the amillennialist respond to the premillennial interpretation that would insert the millennium of the Apocalypse between verses 23 and 24? Vos observes:

> Much is made of the argument that εἶτα at the beginning of vs. 24 proves a *substantial* interval between the parousia and 'the end'. It must be granted that, had the Apostle meant to express such a thought, εἶτα would have been entirely appropriate for the purpose. But it is not true that εἶτα is out of place on the [amillennial] view, viz, if Paul means to affirm *mere succession without any protracted interval*. Εἶτα can be used just as well as τότε to express *momentary sequence of events*, as may be verified from a comparison with vss. 5, 6, 7 in this same chapter, and with Jno. xiii.4,5. Of course, a brief interval in logical conception at least, must be assumed: 'τὸ τέλος' comes, speaking in terms of strict chronology, after the rising of οἱ τοῦ χριστοῦ. But that by no means opens the door to the intercalation of a rounded-off chiliad of years.[30]

---

29. I should say in passing that in the same way if Peter too had believed in a millennial kingdom following this age, an excellent place where he might have made reference to it is in 2 Peter 3, but he makes no mention of it either, placing the entirety of earth history within three time frames: 'the world of that time [which was destroyed by the flood]' (3:6), 'the present heavens and earth [which will be destroyed by fire at the Day of the Lord]' (3:7, 10-11, 12), and 'a new heaven and a new earth [for which Christians are to look, 3:12, 13, 14]'.

30. Geerhardus Vos, *The Pauline Eschatology* (Princeton, N. J.: Princeton University Press, 1930), 243, emphasis supplied.

BAGD also states that 'in enumerations [εἶτα] often serves to put things in juxtaposition without reference to chronological sequence', thus becoming 'in general a transition word' (e. g., 'next', 'then').[31]

Accordingly, the 'order' words as such cannot bear the weight that the premillennialist wishes to place upon them. To those premillennialists who urge that these 'order' words are essential as time-sequence words in order to make room for the resurrection of the unjust at the 'end' after the millennium, the amillennialist observes that the pericope addresses only the issue of the resurrection of those who are in Christ ('So in Christ all will be made alive. But each in his own turn: Christ, the firstfruits of those who have fallen asleep [that is, of Christians]; then, when he comes, those who belong to him'). Paul assumes that his readers understand that unbelievers will be raised at the same time; see his 'there will be a resurrection, both of just and unjust' (Acts 24:15). For those premillennialists who, while not urging that a second resurrection is before the mind of the apostle here, still insist nonetheless that the 'kingdom' referred to in 15:24 is the millennial kingdom, the amillennialist points out that according to 15:51-55 Christ destroys death, his last enemy, at his coming by effecting the resurrection. This means that the reign in question in 15:25 occurs *before* his coming (see 'he must reign *until* [ἄχρι] he has put all his enemies [including his last enemy, death] under his feet'), and reaches its consummation *with* his coming and the eschatological judgment which immediately ensues, at which time (the εἶτα phrase) he then delivers up his Messianic reign to the Father that God might be all in all. Murray says essentially the same thing:

> ...in verses 54, 55, the victory over death is brought into conjunction with the resurrection of the just, which in turn is at the *parousia* (vs. 24), while in verses 24-26 the bringing to nought of death is at the *telos*. It is not feasible to regard the swallowing up of death in victory (vs. 24), and the destruction of death (vs. 26), as referring to different events.[32]

Some premillennialists have urged that amillennialists cannot stop with their amillennial stance but are compelled by the same line of argument they have opposed to premillennialism to move all the way to postmillennialism. For if Christ is presently reigning and must

---

31. BAGD, *A Greek-English Lexicon of the New Testament*, 233.
32. Murray, 'Last Things,' *Collected Writings*, 2, 406; I would urge students to read also Ridderbos' discussion of premillennialism in his *Paul*, 556-59.

continue to reign without interruption until he has put all his enemies under his feet, they argue, then the world of necessity must be brought to a state of virtual moral perfection – the major contention of postmillennialism – by the effects of the gospel and by the judgment of its rejectors *prior* to his return, a position which amillennialists reject. But this line of reasoning does not follow. If it did, it would teach more than the premillennialist himself would want, for if Paul is referring to the millennial kingdom in 1 Corinthians 15:24 and declares of that kingdom that Christ must reign until he has put all of his enemies under his feet, then their objection against amillennialism would apply with equal force to their own position. For the millennium would be a state which would not allow the apostasy which the premillennialist himself affirms is to occur at the end of the kingdom age to begin or to continue. Christ would have to put down that apostasy while he reigned, that is, he could not return until he had put down that apostasy. But if the premillennialist admits, as he must if he is to maintain his own view, that sinful opposition to Christ could continue to exist for a short time after Christ returns to conclude his reign at the end of the millennium, then his point loses its force and he should acknowledge that Christ could return, not only to resurrect his own, but also (as a related aspect of the eschatological complex of events) to destroy the reprobate who would also have been raised to stand before him in judgment, which point the amillennialist does makes.

XIII. The 'new heaven and the new earth' state

A. The 'earthly' habitat of our eternal state

As the final aspect of the future state, in Romans 8:19-23 Paul speaks of the final redemption (or 're-creation') of the created order. Ladd writes:

> The final state of the Kingdom of God is a new heaven and a new earth. This expresses a theology of creation that runs throughout the Bible...a fundamental theology underlies [the Old Testament] expectations, even though they must be clarified by progressive revelation: that man's ultimate destiny is an earthly one. Man is a creature, and God created the earth to be the scene of his creaturely existence. Therefore, even as the redemption of man in the bodily aspect of his being demands the resurrection of the body, so the redemption of the very physical creation requires a renewed earth as the scene of his perfected existence.[33]

B. Christ in the eternal state

As we have already noted, after Christ subdues all of his enemies at his coming, he will deliver up his Messianic kingship with its commission and the authority pertaining to it to the Father. What will his self-subjection to the Father mean for the Son?

> [It will] not mean that from that moment he is really no longer to be spoken of as the Son, or that no power or dominion is any longer due him.... Christ's kingly power need not end at the point he transfers to God the subjection of all powers.[34]

After all, as God he is the second person of the holy Trinity and will continue to be the Son of God forever. While retaining his native divine kingship and lordship, he will transfer his invested *Messianic* lordship to the Father that the triune God might commence 'undisturbed dominion...over all things'.[35] His tranference of authority simply 'throws light on the fact that Christ has *completed* his task in perfection and that the glory of God, no longer clouded by the power of sin and death, can now reveal itself in full luster'.[36]

C. The redeemed in the eternal state

The redeemed in the eternal state will 'be *with the Lord* forever' (1 Thess 4:17). This is a major Pauline description of their condition. But Paul employs other phrases as well to 'give expression to the content of this life with Christ and the "all" with which God will fill all in various ways: it is being saved by his life (Rom. 5:10); salvation with eternal glory (2 Tim. 2:10); honor and immortality (Rom. 2:7; 1 Cor. 15:42ff.; 2 Tim. 1:10); eternal glory (2 Cor 4:17); seeing face to face (1 Cor. 13:12); fulfillment of righteousness and peace and joy in the Holy Spirit (Rom. 14:17); perfect knowing (1 Cor. 13:12). All [of these characterizations] are concepts of salvation, descriptions of God's imperishable gift, every one of which has its own context, origin, and nuance, and offers its own special contribution in order to make what is [now] unutterable (2 Cor 12:4) nevertheless known even now in part.'[37]

---

33. Ladd, *Theology of the New Testament*, 631.
34. Ridderbos, *Paul*, 561-62.
35. Ridderbos, *Paul*, 561.
36. Ridderbos, *Paul*, 561, emphasis supplied.
37. Ridderbos, *Paul*, 562, emphasis supplied.

D. The nature of the final glorification (Rom 8:30)

While the intermediate state of believers in heaven, brought to pass in his will when God calls his children to himself through death, is a more blessed state than their present one, it is not their best and most glorious state. Accordingly, death is not the ultimate experience to which they should longingly look. Rather, their blessed hope is the 'glorious appearing [or "the appearing of the glory"] of their great God and Savior Jesus Christ' (Tit 2:13), at whose coming those who have died in the faith and those who are alive at the time of his coming

> will all be changed – in a flash, in the twinkling of an eye, at the last trumpet. For the trumpet will sound, the dead will be raised imperishable, and we will be changed. For the perishable must clothe itself with the imperishable, and the mortal with immortality. When the perishable has been clothed with the imperishable, and the mortal with immortality, then the saying that is written will come true: 'Death has been swallowed up in victory.' Where, O death, is your victory? Where, O death, is your sting? The sting of death is sin, and the power of sin is the law. But thanks be to God! He gives us the victory through our Lord Jesus Christ (1 Cor 15:51-57).

'At the resurrection, believers, being raised up in glory, shall be openly acknowledged, and acquitted in the day of judgment, and made perfectly blessed in the full enjoying of God to all eternity' (*Shorter Catechism*, Question 38). As we have already observed, all the more will their state of blessedness, as the consequence of their full and open acquittal in the judgment, be evident by its contrast to the state of those 'vessels of wrath fitted for destruction, even in order that [God] might make known the riches of his glory upon the vessels of mercy, which he prepared beforehand unto glory' (Rom 9:22-23). For whereas they will enter into everlasting life and receive that fullness of joy and refreshing which shall come from the presence of the Lord, the wicked who know not God and who obey not the gospel of our Lord Jesus will pay the penalty of eternal destruction away from the approving presence of the Lord and from the glory of his power.

At this point Christians will enter upon their glorified state, the goal toward which the triune Godhead, in all of their salvific exercises, have been relentlessly driving from the moment of creation, and that ultimate end which was the first of the decrees in the eternal plan of salvation.

We thus see how, in the final realization of the goal of sanctification, there is exemplified and vindicated to the fullest extent, an extent that staggers our thought by reason of its stupendous reality, the truth inscribed upon the whole process of redemption, from its inception in the electing grace of the Father (see Eph. 1:4; Rom 8:29) to its consummation in the adoption (Rom 8:23; Eph. 1:5), that Christ in all his offices as Redeemer is never to be conceived of apart from the church, and the church is not to be conceived of apart from Christ. There is correlativity in election, there is correlativity in redemption once for all accomplished, there is correlativity in the mediatorial ministry which Christ continues to exercise at the right hand of the Father, and there is correlativity in the consummation, when Christ will come the second time without sin for those that look for him unto salvation.[38]

And so with the church's glorification and the accompanying – yet more ultimate – glorification of Christ himself we come to that moment in the execution of God's work toward which all of history is moving. God will not be finally satisfied until Christ and his church are fully and finally glorified, to the praise of his Son and his own most holy name (Phil 2:11), and that to all eternity.

---

38. Murray, *Collected Writings*, 2, 316-17.

CHAPTER TWENTY-FIVE

LESSONS FROM PAUL'S MINISTRY FOR TODAY'S MISSIONARIES

Would I describe a preacher, such as Paul,
Were he on earth, [one I] would hear, approve, and own –
Paul should himself direct me. I would trace
His master-strokes, and draw from his design.
I would express him simple, grave, sincere;
In doctrine uncorrupt; in language plain,
And plain in manner; decent, solemn, chaste,
And natural in gesture; much impressed
Himself, as conscious of his awful charge,
And anxious mainly that the flock he feeds
May feel it too; affectionate in look,
And tender in address, as well becomes
A messenger of grace to guilty men.
                From 'The Task' – William Cowper

We have completed our walk with Paul and his several missionary teams through their five missionary journeys. We have witnessed their tragedies and their triumphs. We have wept with them in their sorrows and sufferings and we have rejoiced with them in their conquests and victories. We have overviewed the gospel they joyously proclaimed and the theology which they taught and which sustained them when they were persecuted. What lessons should we now take away from our study of the Apostle Paul, the great pioneer missionary to the nations, to better prepare us for whatever pastoral and missionary tasks God may call us to? How should we emulate him?

We should begin, of course, by noting several respects in which we will never be like Paul.

First, Christ will never actually reveal himself directly to us as he did to Paul, convert us thereby, and call us immediately to the work. The gospel, and the authority to proclaim it, which came to Paul came in connection with Jesus Christ's unique personal disclosure to him (Gal 1:11-12).

Second, Paul was the last apostle to see the risen Lord (1 Cor 15:8), and as such his teachings became part—indeed, a very significant part—of the church's doctrinal foundation (Eph 2:20). We will never be apostles in that sense because the apostolic office in that sense passed out of the life of the church by the end of the first century, and accordingly we will never write inspired Scripture as Paul did.

Third, it is apparent from Ephesians 3:1-13 that one aspect of Paul's missionary message was a unique, unrepeatable aspect of redemptive history: he was called to make known to the Gentiles the 'mystery' that 'through the gospel the Gentiles are heirs together with Israel, members together of one body, and sharers together in the promise in Christ Jesus' (3:3-6). And we learn from 1 Corinthians 15:51 (among other 'mystery' texts that could be cited) that he was called to disclose the 'mystery' that 'we will not all sleep, but we will all be changed—in a flash, in the twinkling of an eye, at the last trump'. We will never receive directly from God, or be inspired to inscripturate, such revelatory 'mysteries' as Paul received and revealed. Nor will we ever be caught up to the 'third heaven', that is, to 'paradise', and 'hear inexpressible things that man is *not* permitted to tell' (2 Cor 12:1-4). Today we must rely on the canonical Scriptures of the Old and New Testaments for our word from 'another world'.

Fourth, we will never be able to perform signs, wonders and miracles as he did; these supernatural powers were reserved for the apostolic age as 'marks of the apostle' to authenticate the apostolic message (2 Cor 12:12; see Acts 15:12; Heb 2:3-4). Today we must trust God to accomplish his *extraordinary* works such as revival and the reformation of cultures and societies through his appointed *ordinary* means of grace – preaching the Word of God in the power of the Spirit, administering the sacraments, and prayer. And for the authentication of our message we must look back, as did John Calvin in his *Institutes of the Christian Religion*,[1] to the miracles of the New Testament age.[2]

In other respects, however, we can and should emulate him. Readers may think of other ways, in addition to the ones that I will

---

[1]. John Calvin, 'Prefatory Address to King Francis I of France' in *Institutes of the Christian Religion*.

[2]. See my *A New Systematic Theology of the Christian Faith* (Nashville: Thomas Nelson, 1998), 56-59, 407-13, for the argument.

mention, but in the following respects, at least, we who would be pastor/teachers and pastor/teacher-missionaries should be like him:

1. We should be, as was Paul, students primarily of one book, even the Holy Scriptures, 'correctly handling the Word of truth' in order to be approved by God (2 Tim 2:15).

This means that as 'people of the Book', since the Holy Scriptures are the Word of Christ, we are to live in obedience under the lordship of Christ as that lordship is explicitly expressed in the words of Holy Scripture. This also means that we are to derive the doctrines we proclaim from his written Word and endeavor to protect their purity with the same zeal Paul exhibited both in Galatians 1:8-9 and throughout his life when protecting the 'deposit' of truth against all false teaching which would muddy in any way and to any degree the pure waters of grace which make glad the hearts of the people of God. This means too that mission agencies must make sure that their missionaries' evangelistic preaching conforms to the apostolic model exhibited in Luke's Acts, and that all the mission strategies which they devise to proclaim the gospel are to be in accord with and to honor both the specific and the general principles of the Holy Scriptures.

2. We should, as did Paul, uncompromisingly proclaim God's law-free gospel (Gal 1:8-9; 2 Tim 4:1-6).

By 'law-free gospel' I do not mean an antinomian gospel. I mean what Paul meant when, elucidating the 'gospel of God' to which he had been set apart and of which he was not ashamed, he declared that 'in the gospel a righteousness from God is revealed, a righteousness that is by faith, from first to last' (Rom 1:17). In other words, Paul elucidated the gospel precisely in terms of the doctrine of justification by faith apart from works of law and so should we. Consequently, great care must be taken when the missionary proclaims this doctrine lest he wind up declaring 'another gospel'. To illustrate, one occasionally hears justification popularly defined as simply God 'looking at me "just if I'd" never sinned'. This is an example of a (very) partial truth becoming virtually an untruth since nothing is said in such a definition concerning the ground of justification (the 'what' or the 'why?') or the instrumentality (the 'how?') through which justification is obtained. Much more accurately, in a superb abridgment of the *Westminster Confession of Faith*, the *Westminster Shorter Catechism* defines justification as 'an act of God's free grace, wherein he pardoneth all our sins, and accepteth us as righteous in his sight, only for the righteousness of Christ, imputed to us, and received by faith alone' (Question 33).

Thus defined over against Rome's tragically defective representation of justification,[3] justification *per se* says nothing about the subjective transformation that necessarily begins to occur within the inner life of the Christian through the progressive infusion of grace that commences with the new birth (which subjective transformation Scripture views as progressive sanctification). Rather, justification refers to God's *wholly* objective, *wholly* forensic judgment concerning the sinner's standing before the law. By this forensic judgment God declares that the sinner is righteous in his sight because of the imputation of his sin to Christ on which ground he is pardoned, and the imputation of Christ's perfect obedience to him on which ground he is constituted righteous before God. In other words, 'for the one who does not work but believes in him who justifies the ungodly' (Rom 4:5), God *pardons* him of all his sins (Acts 10:43; Rom 4:6-7) and *constitutes* him righteous by imputing or reckoning the righteousness of Christ to him (Rom 5:1, 19; 2 Cor 5:21). And on the basis of his *constituting* the ungodly man righteous by his act of imputation, God also *declares* the ungodly man to be righteous in his sight. The now-justified ungodly man is then, to employ Luther's famous expression, *simul iustus et peccator* ('simultaneously just and sinner').

Paul's gospel of justification by faith means then, as we have already argued, that in God's sight the ungodly man, now 'in Christ', has perfectly kept the moral law of God, which means in turn that 'in Christ' he has perfectly loved God with all his heart, soul, mind, and strength and his neighbor as himself. It means as well that saving faith is directed to the doing and dying of Christ alone and not to the good works or inner experience of the believer. It means that the Christian's righteousness before God is *in heaven* at the right hand of God in Jesus Christ and *not on earth* within the believer. It means

---

3. The *Catechism of the Catholic Church* (1994), citing the Council of Trent (Sixth Session, Chapter VII, 1547), declares: 'Justification is not only the remission of sins, but also *the sanctification and renewal of the interior man*' (para. 1989, emphasis supplied). It also states: 'Justification is conferred in Baptism' and by it God '*makes us inwardly just* by the power of his mercy' (para. 1992, emphasis supplied).

that the ground of our justification is the vicarious work of Christ *for* us, not the gracious work of the Spirit *in* us. It means that the faith-righteousness of justification is not personal but vicarious, not infused but imputed, not experiential but judicial, not psychological but legal, not our own but an alien righteousness external to us, not earned but graciously given through faith in Christ which is itself a gift of grace. It means also in its declarative character that justification possesses an eschatological dimension for it amounts to the divine verdict of the Eschaton being brought forward from the Great Assize and rendered here and now concerning the sinner who trusts Christ. By God's act of justifying him through faith in Christ, the sinner, as it were, has been brought, 'before the time', to the Final Assize and has already passed successfully through it, having been acquitted of any and all charges brought against him! Justification then, properly conceived, contributes in a decisive way to the biblical doctrine of the eternal security and assurance of the believer.

The two recent, shall I say, concordats, 'Evangelicals and Catholics Today' (March 1994) and 'The Gift of Salvation' (November 1997), both of which, their signers say, set forth 'what the Reformation traditions have meant by the doctrine of justification by faith alone (*sola fide*),' only underscore the supreme need on the church's part for constant vigilance regarding this doctrine which is so central to the biblical faith. For how can the signers make this claim when the word 'alone' after the word 'faith' in the first document's affirmation that 'we are justified by grace through faith because of Christ' is deafening by its absence. How can they make this claim when the second document in the sentence immediately following its declaration that it was setting forth what the Reformers meant by justification states: 'In justification we receive the gift of the Holy Spirit, through whom the love of God is poured forth into our hearts,' and when toward the end of the second document the signers acknowledge that there are urgent questions that still remain unresolved by them, among them being

> the meaning of baptismal regeneration, the Eucharist and sacramental grace, the historic uses of the language of justification as it relates to imputed and transformative righteousness, the normative status of justification in relation to all Christian doctrine,...diverse understandings of merit, reward, purgatory, and indulgences; Marian devotion and the assistance of the saints in the life of salvation; and the possibility of salvation for those who have not been evangelized?

In my opinion, the Protestant signatories, in their zeal for church unity, have both bewitched themselves and betrayed the Reformation cause. For as recently as his 1995 address commemorating the 450th anniversary of the Council of Trent, Pope John Paul II stated: 'Thus, with the Decree of Justification—one of the most valuable achievements for the formulation of Catholic doctrine—the council intended to safeguard the role assigned by Christ to the Church and her sacraments in the process of sinful man's justification.'[4]

The following remarks of Donald A. Carson should be heeded by these signatories if they intend to produce a third document. Carson rightly states that for most evangelicals,

> our understanding of justification is tied to a rejection of purgatory, indulgences, and claims that Mary may properly be called a coredemptrix. For us the doctrine of purgatory (to go no further) implicitly asserts that the death of Christ on the cross for sinners was in itself insufficient or inadequate. Catholics, within a quite different framework, draw no such conclusion. Sooner or later, of course, the dispute over purgatory gets tracked farther back to the dispute over the locus of revelation. It is very difficult [I would say impossible – RLR] to substantiate purgatory from the Protestant Bible. Catholics themselves commonly appeal to the Apocrypha (especially 2 Macc 12:46) and tradition [and even here it is worth observing that the notion of purgatory receives no prominence in the Western church until the twelfth and thirteenth centuries, which with respect to a doctrine drawn primarily from tradition the doctrine of purgatory seems like a remarkably loose use of the Vincentian canon that the church should believe only those doctrines that have been believed by everyone everywhere and at all times – RLR]. Suddenly our reflections on justification become inextricably intertwined with complex debates not only over purgatory but also over Scripture and tradition, papal authority, and so forth. This is not an attempt to blow smoke over an already confusing terrain. It is simply a way of saying that...to formulate a shared statement on justification without recognizing that the two sides bring diametrically opposed sets of baggage to the table, with the baggage intact when we walk away from the table, is to construct a chimera.[5]

3. We should be willing, as was Paul, to proclaim this 'good news' of justification by faith alone to *all the nations of the world* and to

---

4. Pope John Paul II, 'Trent: A Great Event in Church History,' *The Pope Speaks* 40/5 (September-October 1995), 291.

5. D. A. Carson, 'Reflections on Salvation and Justification in the New Testament,' *JETS* 40/4 (December 1997), 604.

everyone – rich and poor alike – within them to whom we may have recourse. This is but an application of the new 'universalism' which governed Paul in his ministry: whereas 'in the past [ἐν ταῖς παρῳ - χημέναις, lit., "in the having passed by"] [God] let all nations go their own way' (Acts 14:16), whereas 'in the past God overlooked [the nations'] ignorance [τοὺς χρόνους τῆς ἀγνοίας, lit., 'the times of ignorance'] [of him, in the sense that he did nothing to reach them with his saving revelation],...now [with the appearance of the Messiah and the Messianic Age] he commands all people everywhere to repent' (Acts 17:30).

Of course, we must understand that Paul's universalism was actually a redefined particularism, for whereas access to the covenant community of Judaism depended on *ethnic* distinctions such as circumcision and observance of certain ritual food laws, what we actually find in Paul is the universal invitation to the nations to enter the one particular saving covenant community, represented by its local assemblies existing in those nations, through faith in Christ that is in no way tied to ethnic exclusiveness or ethnic 'identity markers'. In sum, we should be willing, as was Paul—though we are free in Christ and belong to no man (1 Cor 9:19), yet because we are 'debtors to all men' (Rom 1:14)—to make ourselves slaves to all men in order to win as many as possible to Christ, and to become all things to all men, as long as we do not compromise the purity of the law-free gospel, so that by all possible means we may save some of them (see 1 Cor 9:19 23).

4. Not only should we preach to the lost world; we should also take seriously, as did Paul, the 'watchman' principle of Ezekiel 33:7-9, apply it to our mission labors today, and faithfully declare the whole counsel of God to Christ's church (Acts 20:27), rebuking her for her sin and warning her against apostasy, and doing so regardless of the cost to our physical safety, our reputations, and our earthly fortunes.

What is the nature of this 'watchman' principle? In the words of the Lord God Almighty himself, it is this:

> Son of man, I have made you a watchman for the house of Israel; so hear the word I speak and give them warning from me. When I say to the wicked [among Israel], 'O wicked man, you will surely die,' and you do not speak out to dissuade him from his ways, that wicked man will die for his sin, and I will hold you accountable for his blood. But if you do

warn the wicked man to turn from his ways and he does not do so, he will die for his sin, but you will have saved yourself." (Ezek 33:7-9)

When Paul then reaches back into Ezekiel and by a straight-line extension in hermeneutical application applies the watchman principle of this passage to himself in the following words to the Jews at Corinth: 'Your blood be on your own heads! I am clear of my responsibility. From now on I will go to the Gentiles' (Acts 18:6), and to the Ephesians elders at Miletus, 'I declare to you today that I am innocent of the blood of all men. For I have not hesitated to proclaim to you the whole counsel of God' (Acts 20:26), we cannot argue dispensationally that the 'watchman' principle enunciated by Ezekiel was for an earlier age. To the contrary, the principle is equally and directly normative today and makes it incumbent upon every missionary to proclaim the whole counsel of God to the church, 'in season and out of season', that is, when the church wants to hear it and when the church does not want to hear it.

5. We should take seriously the sovereignty of God in the salvation of mankind, as did Paul, and in the spread of the gospel avoid all the gimmickry, such as Charles G. Finney's 'new measures' in modern market evangelism. To the Thessalonians Paul testified concerning his ministry practice:

> You know, brothers, that our visit to you was not a failure. We had previously suffered and been insulted in Philippi, as you know, *but with the help of our God we dared to tell you his gospel in spite of strong opposition. For the appeal we make does not spring from error or impure motives, nor are we trying to trick you. On the contrary, we speak as men approved by God to be entrusted with the gospel. We are not trying to please men but God, who tests our hearts. You know we never used flattery, nor did we put on a mask to cover up greed – God is our witness. We were not looking for praise from men, not from you or anyone else.*
>
> As apostles of Christ we could have been a burden to you, but we were gentle among you, like a mother caring for her little children. We loved you so much that we were delighted to share with you not only the gospel of God but our lives as well, because you had become so dear to us. Surely you remember, brothers, our toil and hardship; we worked night and day in order not to be a burden to anyone while we preached the gospel of God to you.
>
> You are witnesses, and so is God, of how holy, righteous, and

blameless we were among you who believe. For you know that we dealt with each of you as a father deals with his own children, encouraging, comforting and urging you to live lives worthy of God, who calls you into his kingdom and glory. (1 Thess 2:1-12)

To the Corinthians he affirmed of his ministry practice:

When I came to you, brothers, I did not come with eloquence...as I proclaimed to you the testimony of God. For I resolved to know nothing while I was with you except Jesus Christ and him crucified. *I came to you in weakness and fear, and with much trembling. My message and my preaching were not with wise and persuasive words*, but with a demonstration of the Spirit's power, so that your faith might not rest on men's wisdom, but on God's power. (1 Cor 2:1-5)

To the same Christians he also described his ministry practice this way:

...we have renounced secret and shameful ways; we do not use deception, nor do we distort the word of God. On the contrary, by setting forth the truth plainly we commend ourselves to every man's conscience in the sight of God.... For we do not preach ourselves, but Jesus Christ as Lord, and ourselves as your servants for Jesus' sake. (2 Cor 4:2-3, 5)

Finally, he described the nature of his own evangelistic weaponry this way:

For though we live in the world, *we do not wage war as the world does. The weapons we fight with are not the weapons of the world.* On the contrary, they [our weapons] have divine power to demolish strongholds. We demolish arguments and every pretension that sets itself up against the knowledge of God, and we take captive every thought to make it obedient to Christ. (2 Cor 10:3-5)

How different was Charles Finney's weaponry! Regrettably, most contemporary evangelicals know little to nothing about Charles G. Finney (1792-1875). This revivalist of the last century, and virtually the 'patron saint' for Billy Graham and most other contemporary evangelists, introduced into American revivalism a number of what were called 'new measures' – that is, new evangelistic techniques – such as the 'anxious bench' (which was the precursor to the modern 'altar call') and 'excitements', that is, emotional tactics that led to weeping and fainting.

He wrote his own *Systematic Theology* and in it he denied the doctrines of original sin, the substitutionary atonement, the supernatural character of the new birth, that is, the need for regeneration by the Holy Spirit, and justification as a legal or forensic verdict, saying in regard to this last doctrine:

> The doctrine of an imputed righteousness is another gospel. For sinners to be forensically pronounced just is impossible and absurd. The doctrine of an imputed righteousness is founded on a most false and nonsensical assumption, representing the atonement, rather than the sinner's own obedience, as the ground of his justification, which has been a sad occasion of stumbling for many.

Simply put, Finney was a Pelagian. Because he believed that there is no fallen nature in man he held that there is no need for a man's nature to be changed, and that mankind possesses the native gifts to do what God requires of men in order to be saved. Accordingly, he taught that the evangelist should orchestrate the psychological climate and emotional mood of the audience in order to move their wills to a visible response to his preaching. Not surprising, therefore, one of his most popular sermons was titled, 'Sinners Bound to Change Their Own Hearts.'

In sum, the Bible would regard him, not as a great Christian evangelist, but as a heretic, indeed, an *arch*-heretic, and the fact that he is esteemed so highly by so many evangelists and pastors in the modern church is simply an indication of the theological illiteracy that pervades the so-called evangelical church today.

6. We should, as did Paul, in our propagation and defense of the Faith refuse to compromise with unbelief and employ an apologetic method which would distort and compromise the gospel or dishonor the self-authenticating character of Scripture.

Today's so-called 'enlightened' pagans need to have the facade of their feigned sovereignty and knowledge stripped away, the barrenness of their atheistic world-and-life-view exposed for what it is, and their rebellion against God, truth, and holiness uncovered by a sound apologetic method. With Paul we may and should assume, wherever we go in the nations of the world with the truth of the gospel, that all men know God and know a good deal about him by virtue of the fact that they bear his image (Gen 1:26-27). Men do not need to have their

Creator's existence proven to them since they know at some level of consciousness or unconsciousness that he exists because (1) *he has revealed himself to them* through natural revelation (Ps 19:1; Rom 1:19-20) and (2) *they understand* (νοούμενα, *nooumena*) that revelation because it is clearly seen (καθορᾶται, *kathoratai*) (Rom 1:20-21, 32; 2:14-15). Of course, because they are sinners, they neither glorify him as God nor are they thankful to him and are therefore without excuse before him (Rom 1:20).[6] And far from being religiously neutral, they are now doing everything they can in their sinfulness, because it is now their nature to do so, to suppress their knowledge of him, bringing God's wrath down upon them as the result (Rom 1:18, 28).

All this means that there is no person anywhere in the nations of the world who is an actual atheist. There are only theists, some of whom *claim* to be atheists. God's Word declares that these 'atheists' are not real atheists; they only attempt to live as though there is no God, and they attempt to suppress their knowledge of God in many unrighteous ways. But they know in their hearts that he is 'there' and that he will someday judge them for their sin. As we have said, they are theists who hate their indelible, ineradicable theism and attempt to do everything they can to suppress their innate theism. Any 'intellectual problems' they may have with Christianity are in reality only masks or rationalizations to cover up their hatred of God and

---

6. Some theologians have argued on the basis of the aorist (punctiliar) tense of the participle γνόντες ('knowing') in Romans 1:21 that, while the entire race may have known God at some point in the past, that knowledge has not continued into the present and therefore the aorist participle does not describe everyone today. John Frame has responded to this argument in his *Apologetics to the Glory of God* (Phillipsburg, N. J.: Presbyterian and Reformed, 1994), 8, fn. 12, as follows:

Paul's purpose in this passage...is part of his larger purpose in 1:1-3:21, which is to show that all have sinned and therefore that none can be justified through the works of the law (3:19-21). In chap. 1 he shows us that even without access to the written law, Gentiles are guilty of sin before God (chap. 2 deals with the Jews). How can they be held responsible without access to the written law? Because of the knowledge of God that they have gained from creation. If that knowledge were relegated to the past, we would have to conclude that the Gentiles in the present are not responsible for their actions, contrary to 3:9. The past form is used (participially) because the past tense is dominant in the context. That is appropriate, because Paul intends to embark on a 'history of suppressing the truth' in vv. 21-32. But he clearly does not regard the events of vv. 21-32 merely as past history. He clearly is using this history to describe the present condition of Gentiles before God. Therefore, the aorist *gnontes* should not be pressed to indicate past time exclusively. As the suppression continues, so does the knowledge that renders the suppression culpable.

their love of and bondage to sin. These 'practicing atheists' insist that the burden of proof lies with the Christian missionary to prove his God's existence to them. But the burden of proof actually is theirs to prove that the physical world is the only reality and that no supernatural spiritual divine being anywhere exists. This, of course, they cannot do. Thus their 'atheism' is their unproved 'grand assumption'—an assumption or presupposition, by the way, with which they cannot consistently live!

The God of Scripture calls upon men to begin with or to 'presuppose' him in all their thinking (Exod 20:3; Prov 1:7). But beginning as the non-Christian does in his quest for knowledge, not with God as his ultimate standard and basic reference point for all human predication, but either with no particular criteria at all or with his own 'provisional' criteria, with 'the facts' viewed simply as 'brute, uninterpreted facts', he never arrives at God or gets the facts either. Such a beginning is out of the question for the Reformed missionary for whom 'the fear of the Lord is the beginning of knowledge'.

Believing that 'the fear of the Lord is the beginning of knowledge' (Prov 1:7), that 'all the treasures of wisdom and knowledge are hidden in Christ' (Col 2:3), and *therefore* that the triune God (and/or the self-attesting Christ) is the *transcendental* ground of all meaning, intelligibility and predication, the Christian missionary may and should presuppose the truth of God's self-authenticating Word from start to finish throughout his witness effort. While he values logic he understands that apart from God there is no reason to believe that the laws of logic correspond universally to objective reality. While he values science he understands that apart from God there is no philosophical basis for doing any science. While he values ethics he understands that apart from God moral principles are simply changing conventions and today's vices can and often do become tomorrow's virtues. While he affirms the dignity and significance of human personhood he understands that apart from God man is simply a biological machine, an accident of nature, a cipher. And while he values the concepts of purpose, cause, probability and meaning he understands that apart from God these concepts have no real basis or meaning. Therefore, he will regard any other witness effort as untrue to the biblical faith if it grants to the non-Christian the hypothetical possibility of a non-theistic world that can successfully function and be rightly understood in terms of the laws of logic, the law of causality, the basic reliability of human sense perception, and the human sciences. For to do this is to deny the existence of the sovereign God of the universe 'for whom and through whom and to whom are all things' (Rom. 11:36) and whose lordship extends over every square inch of the universe and over every second of time. To do so is also to abandon the Christ who 'is before all things, in whom all things consist', 'in whom are hidden all the treasures of wisdom and knowledge' (Col. 1:17; 2:3), who 'gives light to every man coming into the world' (John 1:9), and without whom man can do nothing (John 15:5). The informed Christian knows that it is not God who is the felon on trial here; men are the felons. It is not God's character and word which are questionable; men's are (Job 40:1, 8; Rom 3:4; 9:20). And it is not the Christian who is the trespasser in this world: this is his Father's world, and the Christian is 'at home' in it. Sinful men who deny his claim upon their lives are the trespassers. It is not then primarily the Christian who should feel he must justify his presence in the world but the non-Christian who must be made to feel the necessity of justifying his non-Christian views living as he does in this Christian-theistic world.

The Christian missionary will work out his propagation and defense of the faith in this hostile world in a way which is consistent with his most fundamental commitment to Scripture lest they become ineffective and incoherent. Accordingly, he does not believe that he can improve upon the total message that God has commanded him to give to fallen men. Taking very seriously all that the Scriptures say about the inability of non-Christians to understand the things of the Spirit (1 Cor 2:14; see also Rom 8:7-9; Eph 4:17-18), he will proclaim and argue the case for God's message, not before the so-called 'rational, neutral person' who claims to be standing before him, but before the spiritually blind, spiritually hostile, and spiritually dead person who God says is standing before him. And he does this with the confidence that God's Spirit, working by and with God's Word, will regenerate the elect sinner and call him to himself.

In his apologetic argumentation with the non-Christian the informed missionary should and will employ all the biblical data and all their implications for nature and history as (divinely-preinterpreted) *evidence* for the truthfulness of the Christian position. And it is powerful evidence indeed. But he should not and will not answer the 'biblical fool' (that is, the non-Christian) according to his folly, that is, he should not and will not argue the case for Christian theism utilizing the tests for truth of the unbeliever's 'world-and-life-view', lest 'he become like the fool' (Prov 26:4). When he does 'answer the fool according to his folly', he should and will do so only as an *ad hominem*, to show him the unintelligibility of this world apart from the Christian God and the dire results of living consistently with his non-Christian world-view, and he should and will do so in order to keep the non-Christian from 'becoming wise in his own eyes' (Prov 26:5).

In sum, he should be able to say with Paul: 'My message and my preaching were not with wise and persuasive words, but with a demonstration of the Spirit's power, so that your faith might not rest on men's wisdom, but on God's power' (1 Cor 2:4-5).

He should also say, '...we have renounced secret and shameful ways; we do not use deception, nor do we distort the word of God. On the contrary, by setting forth the truth plainly we commend ourselves to every man's conscience in the sight of God....For we do not preach ourselves, but Jesus Christ as Lord, and ourselves as your servants for Jesus' sake' (2 Cor 4:2-5).

And he should affirm, 'What, after all, is Apollos? And what is Paul? Only servants, through whom you came to believe – as the Lord has assigned each his task. I planted the seed, Apollos watered it, but God made it grow. So neither he who plants nor he who waters is anything, but only God, who makes things grow' (1 Cor 3:5-7).

In humble reliance upon God, he should, as I said earlier, look to the ordinary but powerful means of grace which God has given to his church to fulfill the mission task.

7. We should be willing, as was Paul, to endure loneliness, pain and suffering, loss of friends, persecution, insults, misunderstanding, physical affliction, even death itself, if necessary, for the cause of Christ. That is to say, we should be willing to go anywhere, at any time, at any cost for Christ's sake (see Acts 20:24; 1 Cor 4:9-13; 2 Cor 11:23-28; Phil 3:7-9; 2 Tim 4:6-8). Simply put, if Christ is God and if he died for us, then nothing he would demand of us should we regard as too great a thing for him to ask or too high a sacrifice for us to make in his service.

8. We should be willing, as was Paul, both to become ourselves transcultural communicators of the gospel and to send and assist

others to go everywhere—not only to the villages but to the large cities of the world—to proclaim the law-free gospel of Christ. Regarding Paul's ministry to the large cities of the Empire Derek J. Tidball observes:

> The mission undertaken by Paul led to a remarkable social shift in the early Christian church. It moved away from being a predominantly Palestinian and rural movement to being a Gentile and urban movement. Paul's horizons were dominated by the ethos of the city not the countryside.[7]

An examination of Paul's mission practice will reveal that apparently

> cities had much greater potential for the Pauline mission than villages. This is not only because of their obvious value in terms of communication, as a result of their common language and favorable location on the trade routes for spreading the good news, but for deeper reasons to do with their character. Villages were more conservative in character and evinced little openness. They were subsistence economies with no opportunities for upward social mobility. Cities were much more open. They possessed both power and potential for change. They would have within them more independently minded people who were open to the new message of the gospel of Jesus Christ.[8]

Although it is true that Paul was not a 'foreign' missionary in the sense that, in the time God allotted him, his labors were restricted primarily to several large cities (Tarsus, Damascus, Antioch, Corinth, Ephesus, Rome) in certain provinces in the northeastern arc of the Roman Empire of which he was a citizen, nevertheless he was willing to leave his friends and home church for lengthy periods of time and to travel great distances to unknown places in order to 'preach to the Gentiles the unsearchable riches of Christ' (Eph 3:8). And should Christ call us, we should be willing to do the same.

9. We should be willing, as was Paul, to nurture our converts by forming them into communities in which both mutual respect for other Christians (see Rom 14:1-15:13) and the sharing of spiritual

---

[7]. Derek J. Tidball, 'Social Setting of Mission Churches' in *Dictionary of Paul and His Letters*, edited by G. F. Hawthorne, R. P. Martin, D. G. Reid (Downers Grove, Ill.: InterVarsity, 1993), 883-84.
[8]. Tidball, 'Social Setting of Mission Churches' in *Dictionary of Paul and His Letters*, 884.

gifts with the other members of the brotherhood (1 Cor 14) are encouraged and achieved. W. Paul Bowers writes:

> It is hardly accidental that Paul did not picture himself as a maker of bricks but as a builder of buildings (cf. 1 Cor 3:10). His mission was focused on corporate achievement.... A distinguishing dimension of the Pauline mission is that it found its fullest sense of completion neither in an evangelistic preaching tour nor in individual conversions but only in the presence of firmly established churches.[9]

While it is true that our churches should be marked by a high degree of member participation and a strong sense of belonging (1 Cor 14:26-33),[10] one thing we must do in carrying out this nurturing function is to teach doctrine to these communities of believers. Declaring that 'the Lord's servant must be able to teach' (2 Tim 2:24), Paul said of his own ministry: 'I am a teacher of the true faith' (1 Tim 2:7), 'I was appointed...a teacher' (2 Tim 1:11), 'I teach everywhere in every church' (1 Cor 4:17), and 'We proclaim him,...teaching...so that we may present everyone perfect in Christ' (Col 1:28).[11]

In this day of woeful theological illiteracy throughout the world, and in our own 'nation of biblical illiterates' (George Gallup's expression, not mine) –

where, according to George Barna, 30% of teenagers who regularly attend church do not know why Easter is celebrated,

where 35% of professing evangelical Protestants agreed with the proposition proposed to them: 'God will save all good people when they die, regardless of whether they have trusted in Christ,'

where 66% of the same group found nothing objectionable to the statement: 'Christians, Jews, Muslims, Buddhists, and others all pray to the same God, even though they use different names for that God,'

where 50% of the same group thought that the statement, 'God

---

9. W. Paul Bowers, 'Mission' in *Dictionary of Paul and His Letters*, 609, 610 (emphasis supplied).

10. I would commend the following to the reader who is interested in learning more about the *communitas* in the Pauline churches of the first century: J. P. Sampley, *Pauline Partnership in Christ: Christian Community and Commitment in Light of Roman Law* (Philadelphia: Fortress, 1980); R. F. Hock, *The Social Context of Paul's Ministry: Tentmaking and Apostleship* (Philadelphia: Fortress, 1980); A. J. Malherbe, *Social Aspects of Early Christianity* (Baton Rouge: Louisiana State University, 1977); and W. A. Meeks, *The First Urban Christians: The Social World of the Apostle Paul* (New Haven: Yale University, 1983).

11. Roy B. Zuck's encyclopedic *Teaching as Paul Taught* (Grand Rapids: Baker, 1998), 14-15, lists thirty-two aspects of Paul's teaching that we can emulate.

Lessons from Paul's Ministry for Today's Missionaries

helps those who help themselves' (which is the modern version of Ockham's medieval declaration, 'God will not deny his grace to those who do what they can'), was a direct biblical quotation, and where over 84% of those asked thought that it was a biblical idea,

where Clark H. Pinnock denies that 'one must confess the name of Jesus Christ to be saved' and urges the Arminian/Wesleyan tradition to embrace the notion of purgatory because 'most believers [Most? How about all!] end their lives imperfectly sanctified and far from perfect',

where Russell Spittler, a Pentecostal theologian at Fuller Seminary, reflecting on Luther's 'simultaneously just and sinner' statement, queries:

> ...can it really be true? I wish it were so. Is [it correct to say]: 'I don't need to work at becoming. I'm already declared to be holy. No sweat needed'? It looks wrong to me. I hear moral demands in Scripture. *Simul iustus et peccator*? I hope it's true. I simply fear it's not.

where Robert Schuller states that the Reformation 'erred because it was God-centered rather than man-centered',

and where Norman Geisler declares: 'God would save all men if he could. He will save the greatest number actually achievable without violating their free will' –

where, I say, these disheartening statistics are rung up and these kinds of statements from theologians who ought to know better are out there doing their destructive work in the church, it is quite evident that the truly Reformed church must stop 'playing school' and place the highest priority on rigorously teaching its laity biblical content and Reformed systematic theology lest it too become prey to such false teaching as I just cited and add its numbers to these frightening statistics.

We should, like Paul, also fulfill this nurturing function by our example and our personal contacts with our converts and congregations through every means available, including writing them letters when we are absent from them. Indeed, Paul's commitment to nurturing his churches is most immediately apparent to us today by the existence of his letters to them which were not intended to be evangelistic pieces. W. Paul Bowers observes: 'The Paul who is available to us at first hand is available almost exclusively in the community-nurturing dimension of his missionary role' as a letter-writer.[12] And Derek J. Tidball notes that Paul's letters are full of the language of kinship ('children of God', 'brothers') and positive descriptions of their recipients ('saints', 'beloved', 'coworkers with God').[13]

10. We should instruct these communities of believers, as did Paul (1 Cor 11–14), to worship God with reverence and fear (Heb 12:28) and in accordance with what has come to be known as the Reformation's 'regulative principle of worship', that is, only in those ways that God himself has expressly prescribed.

All too often in the past have missionaries from some church communions, notably, the Roman Catholic Church, permitted their converts from paganism to bring into their worship of Christ accoutrements and worship methods of their pagan past. But the Scriptures provide ample warning against worshiping God in ways which he has not expressly prescribed. For example, Moses instructed Israel:

> ...when you have driven [the nations] out and settled in their land, and after they have been destroyed before you, be careful not to be ensnared by inquiring about their gods, saying, 'How do these nations serve their gods? We will do the same.' *You must not worship the LORD your God in their way*, because in worshiping their gods, they do all kinds of detestable things the LORD hates. They even burn their sons and daughters in the fire as sacrifices to their gods. *See that you do all I command you; do not add to it or take away from it* (Deut 12:29-32).

Nadab and Abihu were consumed by the fire of the Lord because they 'offered unauthorized fire...contrary to his command' (Lev 10:1-2). Korah, Dathan, Abiram, and On were swallowed up in an earthquake because they had insisted on their right to burn incense before God without priestly mediation, after which judgment God instructed Eleazar to take the censers of 'the men who sinned' and hammer them into sheets and overlay the bronze altar with them as a sign to Israel that 'no one except a descendant of Aaron should come to burn incense before the LORD' (Num 16:36-40). King Uzziah was smitten with leprosy because he attempted to usurp the priestly privilege to burn incense in the temple (2 Chr 26:16-19). Israel's sin

---

12. Bowers, 'Mission,' 610.
13. Tidball, 'Social Setting of Mission Churches' in *Dictionary of Paul and His Letters*, 885.

in building high places and offering her sons on them to Baal was due to their doing 'something [God says] I did not command or mention, nor did it enter my mind' (Jer 19:5). Jesus himself declared that when men 'let go of the commands of God' and 'hold on to the traditions of men' in their worship of God, their worship is 'in vain' (Mark 7:7-8)! To the Samaritan woman, he spoke of the character of true worship: 'You Samaritans worship what you do not know; we worship what we do know, for salvation is from the Jews. Yet a time is coming and has now come when the *true worshipers will worship the Father in spirit and truth*, for they are the kind of worshipers the Father seeks. God is spirit, and *his worshipers must worship in spirit and in truth*' (John 4:22-24).[14]

Accordingly, knowing these things, Paul laid down broad regulations to be followed by the Corinthians in their worship assemblies (1 Cor 14) and admonished the Colossians against self-willed asceticism in worship:

> Since you died with Christ to the basic principles of this world, why, as though you still belonged to it, do you submit to its rules: 'Do not handle! Do not taste! Do not touch!'? These are all destined to perish with use, *because they are based on human commands and teachings*. Such regulations indeed have *an appearance of wisdom, with their self-imposed worship*, their false humility and their harsh treatment of the body, but they lack any value in restraining sensual indulgence. (Col 2:20-23)

11. We should be willing, as was Paul, to be accountable to the church and to spurn the 'lone ranger' attitude toward ministry. Paul was willing to labor with some one hundred coworkers that we know of,[15] and he regularly reported back to Antioch after his journeys and gave an account of his labors to his 'sending church'.

To facilitate this spirit of accountability, we should follow Paul's practice of appointing (χειροτονήσαντες[16]) or electing pluralities

---

14. To worship God 'in spirit and in truth' means, according to Leon Morris, that he 'must be worshipped in a manner befitting [him as the life-giving Spirit]. Man cannot dictate the "how"...of worship. He must come only in the way that the Spirit of God opens to him' (*The Gospel According to John* [Grand Rapids: Eerdmans, 1971], 272).

15. See E. Earle Ellis, 'Coworkers, Paul and His' in *Dictionary of Paul and His Letters*, 183-89. Ellis finds in Acts and the Pauline letters some one hundred individuals, under a score of titles and activities, who were actively associated with Paul at one time or another during his ministry.

16. The verb χειροτονέω literally means 'choose, elect by raising hands'. The action described here probably means that Paul as an Apostle simply appointed elders

of elders (Acts 14:23) in the churches we plant to govern and to oversee them in accordance with the Word of God. This accords with Paul's instruction to Titus to appoint (καταστήσης[17]) elders 'in every city' (Tit 1:5; see also Acts 11:30; 15:2; 20:17; Jam 5:14; 1 Pet 5:1-2). Finally, anticipating the day when the apostles would have passed from the scene, Paul instructed the churches to choose councils of elders, according to his lists of qualifications for the eldership in 1 Timothy 3 and Titus 1, to govern them and fulfill their office according to his description of their responsibilities in Acts 20.

Beyond this—and most important is it to note—the churches throughout the Empire were connected or bound together by a spirit of mutual accountability, dependency, and submission. This principle of mutual accountability, dependency, and submission among the churches is taught at several places in Scripture, for example, in Acts 8:14 where the Jerusalem church sent Peter and John to investigate Philip's work in Samaria and in Acts 13:1-3 and 14:27 where the Antioch church dispatched its mission teams which then upon the completion of their tour returned to Antioch and reported on the state of the Gentile churches which they had founded. But the primary text in demonstrating the connectional nature of the early church is Acts 15 where we are informed of the appeal made by the Antioch church to the apostles and elders in Jerusalem who met with them in a deliberative council and then *together* rendered a decision in the form of a 'letter', called in Acts 16:4 τὰ δόγματα (*ta dogmata*, 'rules, regulations, laws, decrees'),[18] which the Jerusalem council sent not just to the 'asking' church at Antioch but to the churches in Syria and Cilicia as well, with every expectation that its instructions would be heeded and viewed as church law by all these churches. Clearly, these congregations were not independent and autonomous. Rather, they were mutually submissive, dependent, and accountable to each other.

It is virtually acknowledged by all church authorities that it was the Presbyterian form of church government—one that was both

---

when he first planted a church just as missionaries often do today when they first plant a church. This 'appointing' did not preclude, however, his seeking the church's will in the matter by asking the congregation for a show of hands.

17. The verb καθίστημι means simply 'to appoint'.

18. John Murray in his article, 'The Government of the Church', in *Collected Writings of John Murray* (Edinburgh: Banner of Truth, 1977), 2, 344, writes: 'It is all the more striking that the church should have resorted to such deliberation, and to this method of resolving an issue, since it was the era of special revelation.'

conciliar and connectional – which prevailed until the end of the third century[19] when under the influence of Cyprian (195-258), bishop of Carthage, episcopal forms began to take over. But the earliest form of church government was Presbyterian. *So if one is really looking for a form of church government which is biblical and apostolic, Presbyterianism is it.*[20]

12. We should live before our converts and congregations, as did Paul, model lives of reliance upon God for all things, of discipline, holiness, truth, honesty, consistency, industry, humility and joy. In sum, we should live godly lives among them.

Over time among them, with Paul we should be able to say to them: 'In everything I did, I showed you...' (Acts 20:35); 'You became *imitators* [μιμηταί] of us and the Lord' (1 Thess 1:6); 'For you yourselves know how you ought to follow our *example* [μιμεῖσθαι]. We were not idle when we were with you...On the contrary, we worked night and day...We did this, not because we do not have the right to such help, but in order to make ourselves *a model* [τύπον] for you *to follow* [μιμεῖσθαι]' (2 Thess 3:7, 9); 'Even though you have ten thousand guardians in Christ, you do not have many fathers, for in Christ Jesus I became your father through the gospel. Therefore I urge you to *imitate* [μιμηταί] me' (1 Cor 4:15-16); 'Do not cause anyone to stumble...– even as I try to please everybody in every way. For I am not seeking my own good but the good of many, so that they may be saved. *Follow my example* [μιμηταί], as I follow the example of Christ' (1 Cor 10:32-11:1);[21] 'Join with others in following [our]

---

19. Ignatius of Antioch (d. ca. 107) is possibly the lone dissenting voice during this period in presenting a distinction between the bishop and elder, but 'even his writings are arguably nonprelatic' (so Joseph H. Hall, 'History and Character of Church Government,' *Paradigms in Polity: Classic Readings in Reformed and Presbyterian Church Government*, edited by David W. Hall and Joseph H. Hall [Grand Rapids: Eerdmans, 1994], 5).
20. See Joseph H. Hall, 'History and Character of Church Government,' Thomas Witherow, 'The Apostolic Church: Which Is It?,' and 'Earliest Textual Documentation,' *Paradigms in Polity*, 3-11, 35-52, 55-61, for bibliographic and biblical support respectively for early Presbyterianism.
21. For the exegetical argument drawn from this passage and its larger context that Paul expected his churches to be engaged in evangelism as he was, see P. T. O'Brien, *Gospel and Mission in the Writings of Paul* (Grand Rapids: Baker, 1995), 89-107. See also Ephesians 6:15, 17 where Paul seems to suggest that all Christians are involved in spiritual warfare in which they are to stand firm against the onslaughts of the evil one by both resistance and proclamation. To Philemon Paul writes: 'I pray that *you may be active in sharing your faith* [ἡ κοινωνία τῆς πίστεως σου ἐνεργὴς γένηται; lit. 'the

example [Συμμιμηταί], brothers, and take note of those who live according to the *pattern* [τύπον] we gave you' (Phil 3:17); and finally, '*Whatever you have learned or received or heard from me, or seen in me – put it into practice*. And the God of peace will be with you' (Phil 4:9).[22]

It was for this reason among others – that he might become a role model to others – that Paul instructed Timothy: 'Train yourself to be godly' (1 Tim 4:7). Given the times in which we live, all the more urgently must Paul's advice be pressed upon missionaries today, for godliness or holiness of life is a necessary prerequisite of any true fragrance of spiritual prosperity in Christian service. What John Owen of Coggeshall said of true godliness in the mid-seventeenth century must be truer still today: 'It is a comely thing,' he writes, 'to see a Christian weaned from the world, minding heavenly things, green and flourishing in spiritual affections, and it is the more lovely because it is so rare.'[23]

However much the earnest and systematic cultivation of the spiritual life may be the deepest aspiration of Christian saints generally, even more is it a duty to be impressed upon him who would aspire to the missionary task of Christ's church. For without that inner life which is produced only by much time spent in the consideration of and meditation upon the Word of God in purposeful self-examination, and before the presence of the Lord in earnest prayer, he will never obtain that blessed ministry which the Puritan writers described as 'powerful', 'painful' (that is, laborious), and 'useful' –

---

sharing of your faith may be active (or "effective")]' (6). Surely, too, when Paul states, 'Whatever you have...seen in me, put into practice' (Phil 4:9), the implication is there that he expected his converts at Philippi to emulate him in his mission efforts to reach the lost Gentile world.

22. The question has often been asked how Paul's calls to imitate him comport with the Christian virtue of humility. Contrary to E. A. Castilli, *Imitating Paul: A Discourse of Power* (Literary Currents in Biblical Interpretation; Louisville: Westminster, 1991), who contends that all such 'imitate me' language should be seen as both a Greco-Roman rhetorical device employed by Paul both to build his own authority and to define his social group and a power tool of social control intended to promote 'sameness', both W. P. de Boer, *The Imitation of Paul* (Kampen: Kok, 1962) and Andrew D. Clarke, ' "Be Imitators of Me," Paul's Model of Leadership' in *Tyndale Bulletin* 49.2 (November 1998), 329-60, argue that Paul's 'imitate me' language is his sincere call to Christians to emulate his own self-sacrificing efforts to express the fruit of the Spirit as he in turn seeks to imitate Christ's self-sacrificing character. Paul's understanding of Christ's earthly work and his own entire Christian experience as they are reflected in Luke's Acts and his own letters support the latter representation.

23. John Owen, *The Works of John Owen*, edited by William H. Goold (Edinburgh: Banner of Truth, 1965), 7, 453.

that high ministry to which one must eagerly aspire if the call of Almighty God to the teaching and missionary ministry has truly been written large upon his heart. This is so for the following three reasons:

First, only a flourishing spiritual life and a genuine walk before God in holiness will fortify the missionary in times of discouragement. The ministerial 'burnout' and 'dropout' about which one reads and hears all too often today is to be traced directly to the minister's failure to maintain personal intimate fellowship with the triune God. Because of the press of his myriad other ministerial duties, all too often he allows the cultivation of his spiritual walk with God – this training of self in godliness – to drop out of his daily vocational routine. And the missionary who eliminates this exercise from his daily round immediately places his ministry in peril. For of this he can be sure: he will have so many separate occasions of failure and discouragement in the gospel ministry that he will be no stranger to grief. The burdens are so great, the troubles so constant, the failures so painful, that unless he is personally thriving in his devotion to the Lord, delighting in his Savior's love and fellowship, enjoying intimacy with him in prayer, and generally having the gospel proven to him again and again in the secret places of his own heart, his ministry will not well endure the shocks that will come to it. But if he is walking closely with his Lord and if he is surrounded and protected by daily experiences of God's love and presence, he *will* find strength to endure every trial and to overcome every obstacle, and his ministry will not be undone by the discouragements, but rather he will persevere in the midst of difficulty and in this way bring even greater honor to Christ.

Second, only a flourishing spiritual life and a genuine walk before God in holiness will protect the missionary from the perils of success in the ministry. The success and popularity that will attend his ministry will certainly increase the opportunities to be useful in the kingdom of God, but *such success will also expose him to the great temptation of pride*. However much he may admit that it is necessary for ministers to remain humble, alas, it remains true, as the godly John Newton once wrote:

> There will be almost the same connection between popularity and pride, as between fire and gunpowder; they cannot meet without an explosion, at least not unless the gunpowder [of pride] is kept very damp.[24]

---

24. John Newton, *The Works of John Newton* (Edinburgh: Banner of Truth, 1985), 1, 52.

And unless his heart is being constantly impressed through self-examination and meditation in God's Word with the true and odious darkness of his old man, with the weakness of his will, with the utter necessity of the mercies of God and the aid of his Spirit upon which one must depend if any good is to come from his ministry, his successes will lead him astray, turn his eyes away from the Lord to himself, and spoil his ministry insofar as it would have any capacity to exalt Christ and to build his church. For the Lord himself has said in both the Old and New Testaments: 'I resist the proud, but give grace to the humble' (Prov 3:34; Jam 4:6). But if by earnest and regular devotional times with his Lord the missionary cultivates that pure poverty of spirit and meekness of heart in which the Lord of grace and mercy delights, the successes that attend his labors will not undo his ministry but will simply give him cause to praise the name of the Lord and to trust him to use him even more.

Third, only a flourishing spiritual life and a genuine walk before God in holiness will lend the power and effectiveness necessary to the missionary's labor in the gospel. The work of many talented missionaries today produces little or no fruit because God is blowing a cold wind across their efforts. The problem with these men and women is not that they have no natural gifts, for they are sometimes eminent in such gifts; nor is the problem necessarily that they are proud or harboring some other great sin in their hearts for reason of which God is withholding blessing. The problem is that they are personally simply spiritually cold and listless; there is no Spirit-wrought animation in their devotion to God, no earnestness, no zeal, no inexpressible joy in God, and no tears shed over their people's sin.

The missionary may have the highest academic and professional competence, but his labors cannot be sustained by any aggregate of natural gifts, however splendid. Such gifts alone cannot compensate for the lack of a Spirit-kindled heart. The missionary must be perennially 'charismatic' in the sense that he is to be continually 'fanning into flame' the Spirit's engiftings by his longing for holiness and a personal spiritual walk before God (2 Tim 1:6). For if he has a dull listless walk with God his auditors will not take his teaching very seriously. He may tell them all he wants that sin is terrible, but his own indifferent example, if it is there, will neutralize the desired effect of his words. He may tell them that the love of God ought to make their hearts sing for joy, but his own listless demeanor, if there, will undo his exhortations. He may say that there ought to be a deep abiding love among the brethren in the church, but his own arid experience, if there, will prevent them from rejoicing with their brothers and sisters who rejoice or from truly weeping with their brothers and sisters who weep in distress and sorrow. No, God honors that ministry that blazes with the passion and fire of a Spirit-filled heart, and he pours out his power upon that ministry in which the teaching and pleading come from the broken heart and are accompanied by tears, that ministry in which the encouragement is not in promises only but in the sharing of the servant's own experiences of God's faithfulness and mercy, that ministry in which the counsel is animated by a deep and obvious devotion to God, by true love for people, and by genuine concern for their eternal state and the salvation and sanctification of their souls.

But whence comes that tender, earnest, zealous heart which so powerfully animates the greatly used servant of the gospel? The spiritually informed missionary knows that it does not reside natively in his breast. *It comes from many experiences with God* – from great exercises of heart and mind in heavenly things, in the cultivation of spiritual affections in the Word of God and in prayer, or, in Paul's simple words, in 'training oneself to be godly'. He knows that before everything else he needs a daily personal walk with God – a walk which will so inspire him by the awesomeness of the divine face that no human face will frighten him, a walk which will so fire him by the divine holiness that he will hate sin as God hates sin, a walk which will so thrill and engage him by ever-new revelations of God's immeasurable love and gracious ways toward men that he will proclaim with rhapsodic delight both to God's flock and to those outside the church the mercies of God in Christ, a walk which will so humble him before the divine majesty that he will always give all the glory to God for whatever he enables him to accomplish in and through his labors, a walk which will enable him to say with Paul: 'Neither count I my life dear unto myself, if only I may finish my race with joy, and fulfill the ministry which I received from the Lord Jesus, to testify to the gospel of the grace of God,' a walk which will compel him to lose himself in his concern for the glory of Christ and the good of Christ's body, the church. But the spiritually informed missionary knows that such a walk will not be naturally his. He knows that in himself he is spiritually dead and cold before God. So he will humbly beseech the faithful God again and again to quicken the desire in his heart for that walk in godliness which alone will bring heaven's beauty to rest upon the work of his hands and the fragrance of Christ to perfume his life and ministry.

Robert Murray McCheyne declared: 'The greatest need my flock will ever have is to see their pastor walking before them in holiness.' The apostle Paul himself puts all the above ministrations this way in 1 Timothy 4:15-16: 'Be diligent in these matters, give yourself wholly to them, so that everyone may see your progress. Watch your life and doctrine closely. Persevere in them, because if you do, you will save both yourself and your hearers.' If the missionary does these things, his labors will be fruitful and his converts and congregations will ever bless God for allowing his servant to walk among them and to teach them not only by his word but also by his godly example.

13. In our daily lives we should glory, as did Paul, only in the cross of Christ (Gal 6:14). There is no place for boasting in ourselves.

About himself Paul affirmed: 'I cannot boast' (1 Cor 9:6), 'I will not boast about myself' (2 Cor 12:5), 'We do not preach ourselves' (2 Cor 4:5), and 'May I never boast except in the cross of our Lord Jesus Christ' (Gal 6:14). He described himself as 'the least of the apostles' (1 Cor 15:9), the worst of sinners (1 Tim 1:15), and 'less than the least of all God's people' (his 'less than the least' here is ἐλαχιστότερος, a comparative piled on top of a superlative, suggesting deep self-abasement) (Eph 3:8). He regarded himself as a slave of Christ (Rom 1:1; Gal 1:10; Phil 1:1), of God (Titus 1:1), and of the saints (2 Cor 4:5).

If we would glory in anything about ourselves, we should glory not in our strengths but in our weaknesses so that Christ's power may rest upon us: 'That is why, for Christ's sake,' writes Paul, 'I delight in weaknesses, in insults, in hardships, in persecutions, in difficulties. For when I am weak, then I am strong' (2 Cor 12:9-10). God does not need or want men, regardless of the number and strength of the talents with which he has engifted them, who believe they can and must conduct their ministries in their strength. What God wants is a few weak men, for when they are weak in themselves, then he can make them strong in him.

More than natural talents and a sound seminary education, more than winsome ways and relentless doggedness in the pursuit of ministerial success, the spiritually informed missionary, as I have already underscored, knows that he needs God's blessing and power upon his life. He knows that if he would lead God's flock effectively he needs an intimate personal knowledge of the Great Shepherd's ways, for only those who know their God will be strong and do great exploits for him.

14. We should strive, accordingly, as did Paul, to give all glory to God for everything that God by his grace and power enables us to accomplish for the cause of Christ (1 Cor 1:26-31; 10:31).

This simply means, echoing the first answer of the *Westminster Shorter Catechism*, 'Man's chief end is to glorify God and enjoy him forever,' that *our greatest passion in life should be to learn to know God better than we know anyone or anything else in this world and to enjoy God more than we enjoy anyone or anything else in this world*, for only in such devotion will our lives publicly display as they should the glory of God and thus give as they should all glory to him. Only by such devotion will the missionary martyr's love for Christ be cultivated which kind of love is absolutely essential if the church is to fulfill its Lord's Great Commission.

This also means that we should seek to impart this same great passion for God to the nations that do not know and do not enjoy him. In sum, the engine that should drive us in all our mission activity is the realization that mission activity exists because the worship of God among the unreached nations does not. Mission activity is not the first duty of the church. The worship of the triune Savior God is man's first duty, and it is also our blessed privilege to do so. Someday mission activity will cease, but our duty and privilege to worship our God will never cease. It is this concern – to bring the nations of the world to the foot of the cross in worship of the one living and true triune Savior God – that should energize us in the church's mission enterprise.

15. Finally, we should be, as was Paul, missionary statesmen, and carefully strategize about mission policy and procedure and carefully plan our courses of action. This will entail much reading and prayerful reflection on the part of church mission agencies, mission teams, and individual missionaries.

This topic of mission strategy is so involved, given the cultural differences among the nations and national needs, and the literature is so immense, with literally hundreds of volumes on the subject, that I can do little more here than recommend the following as only a few of the better works on the topic:

Roland Allen, *Missionary Methods: St Paul's or Ours? A Study of the Church in the Four Provinces* (London: World Dominion, 1912)

Roland Allen, *Missionary Principles* (Grand Rapids: Eerdmans, 1964)

Robert Banks, *Paul's Idea of Community: The Early House Churches in their Historical Setting* (Grand Rapids, Eerdmans, 1988)

J. H. Bavinck, *An Introduction to the Science of Missions* (Philadelphia: Presbyterian and Reformed, 1961)

J. Blauw, *The Missionary Nature of the Church: A Survey of the Biblical Theology of Missions* (London: Lutterworth, 1962)

David J. Bosch, *Transforming Mission: Paradigm Shifts in Theology of Mission* (Maryknoll, N. Y.: Orbis, 1992)

Harvey M. Conn, *Eternal Word and Changing Worlds: Theology, Anthropology, and Mission in Trialogue* (Phillipsburg, N. J.: Presbyterian and Reformed, 1984)

N. A. Dahl, *Studies in Paul: Theology for the Early Christian Mission* (Minneapolis: Augsburg, 1977).

Edward R. Dayton and David F. Fraser, *Planning Strategies for World Evangelization* (Grand Rapids: Eerdmans, 1990)

E. Earle Ellis, *Pauline Theology: Ministry and Society* (Grand Rapids: Eerdmans, 1989)

Dean S. Gilliland, *Pauline Theology and Mission Practice* (Grand Rapids: Baker, 1983)

Dean S. Gilliland, *The Word Among Us: Contextualizing Theology for Mission Today* (Dallas: Word, 1989)

Arthur F. Glasser and Donald A. McGavran, *Contemporary Theologies of Mission* (Grand Rapids: Baker, 1983)

Arthur F. Glasser, Paul G. Hiebert, C. Peter Wagner and Ralph D. Winter, *Crucial Dimensions in World Evangelization* (Pasadena, California: William Carey, 1976)

Michael Green, *Evangelism in the Early Church* (Grand Rapids: Eerdmans, 1970)

F. Hahn, *Mission in the New Testament* (London: SCM, 1965)

Paul G. Hiebert, *Anthropological Insights for Missionaries* (Grand Rapids: Baker, 1985)

Paul G. Hiebert, *Anthropological Reflections on Missiological Issues* (Grand Rapids: Baker, 1994)

E. G. Hinson, *The Evangelization of the Roman Empire: Identity and Adaptability* (Macon, Georgia: Mercer University, 1981)

R. F. Hock, *The Social Context of Paul's Mission* (Philadelphia: Fortress, 1980)

J. Herbert Kane, *Christian Missions in Biblical Perspective* (Grand Rapids: Baker, 1976)

J. Herbert Kane, *Understanding Christian Missions* (Grand Rapids: Baker, 1974)

Harold Lindsell, *An Evangelical Theology of Missions* (Grand Rapids: Zondervan, 1949)

Sherwood G. Lingenfelter, *Agents of Transformation: A Guide for Effective Cross-Cultural Ministry* (Grand Rapids: Baker, 1996)

W. A. Meeks, *The First Urban Christians: The Social World of the Apostle Paul* (New Haven: Yale University, 1983)

John L. Nevius, *The Planting and Development of Missionary Churches* (Nutley, N. J.: Presbyterian & Reformed, 1958 reprint)

P. T. O'Brien, *Gospel and Mission in the Writings of Paul* (Grand Rapids: Baker, 1995)

William M. Ramsay, *St. Paul the Traveller and Roman Citizen* (eleventh edition; London: Hodder & Stoughton, 1895)

D. Senior and C. Stuhlmueller, *The Biblical Foundations for Mission* (Maryknoll: Orbis, 1983)

Johannes Verkuyl, *Contemporary Missiology: An Introduction* (Grand Rapids: Eerdmans, 1978)

C. Peter Wagner, *Frontiers in Missionary Strategy* (Chicago: Moody, 1971)

Roy Zuck, *Teaching as Paul Taught* (Grand Rapids: Baker, 1998)

Most of these works will provide additional valuable bibliography for readers interested in studying mission methods in depth and determining mission strategy.

These are some of the lessons we should learn from our study of this great missionary and missionary statesman.

* * * * *

As I bring our study of Paul as the outstanding pioneer missionary of the Christian church to a close, I would now urge the reader to consider whether God may be calling him to some missionary or cross-cultural ministry. Noting that there are more unsaved people in the world today than there were even people living in the world when our Lord gave to his church the Great Commission two thousand years ago (I thank God that there are more Christians too!), I would say to the many graduates of the Reformed (and other evangelical) seminaries in the West that I believe that they should ask themselves, before they begin to seek pastoral positions in established pulpits in their own countries, whether they should not first present themselves to the world-mission agencies of their churches and give those agencies first opportunity to use them. Only when these agencies, for whatever reasons, decline their services – only then should they consider serving Christ at home.

The Psalmist declares: 'He who goes out weeping, carrying seed to sow, will return with songs of joy, carrying sheaves with him' (Ps 126:6). The wise man of Proverbs informs us: 'He who wins souls is wise' (Prov 11:30). Daniel teaches: 'Those who are wise will shine like the brightness of the heavens, even those who lead many to righteousness, like the stars for ever and ever' (Dan 12:3). And Christ, the Lord of the church, states: 'The harvest is plentiful but the workers are few. Ask the Lord of the harvest, therefore, to send out workers into his harvest field' (Matt 9:37; see Luke 10:2). He also says: 'Do you not say, "Four months more and then the harvest"? I tell you, open your eyes and look at the fields! They are ripe for harvest. Even now the reaper draws his wages, even now he harvests the crop for eternal life, so that the sower and the reaper may be glad together' (John 4:35).

Let us be clear about the spiritual condition of those 'fields ripe for harvest'. We may not like it, we may instinctively recoil against it, but the Bible wants us to understand (and to act on this understanding) that these 'ripe fields' are lost, unsaved people, perishing without a knowledge of Christ. They are under divine condemnation, not just because they have never heard about Christ but more primarily because they are already sinners by nature and sinners by practice. Some readers may already be doing what they can to reach the lost, and I thank God for them. But we all must be involved, if we are Christians, in witnessing to our friends and neighbors about Christ

Lessons from Paul's Ministry for Today's Missionaries

and doing what we can to get the good news of the gospel to the ends of the earth, for repentance and forgiveness of sins must be preached in Christ's name to all nations (Luke 24:47), and salvation is to be found in no other name under heaven than his (Acts 4:12). Moreover, we must be faithful in supporting with our prayers and money, even more than we have in the past, Christ-preaching, Bible-believing missionaries on the mission fields of the world. Which is just to say, if we cannot go ourselves, we must help others to go.

In closing I want to relate a story. Some time ago I viewed the 1993 Academy Award movie of the year, *Schindler's List*, the Steven Spielberg story of Oskar Schindler, the Nazi war profiteer, who shortly after the German invasion of Poland in 1939 began to use the Jews of the Krakow ghetto as workers in his pots and pans factory. At first he saw them only as chattel to be used to line his own pockets, which he did quite successfully, becoming exceedingly rich. But as the war dragged on, and as he increasingly witnessed Nazi atrocities being inflicted against the Jews of Poland, increasingly did he begin to use his own wealth to bribe Nazi officials and army officers to give him more and more Jews for his factory which the Nazis had turned into a munitions factory, which became a model of non-productivity in the Nazi war effort. Though it virtually bankrupted him personally, he saved over twelve hundred Jews from certain death in the gas chambers.

I recount this story line only to say that I was struck by some statements put in his mouth toward the end of the movie. The war has just ended, and having worked for the Third Reich, both he and his Jewish factory workers realize that the Allied authorities might search for him. As he bids farewell to them, they present him with a letter signed by each of them which they hope will help him before the Allied authorities.

At this moment Schindler suddenly becomes very sober and quietly says: 'I could have done more. I could have done more!' He begins to sob. 'I could have done more. I didn't do enough. This car – why did I keep the car? Ten people right there. Ten people. Ten more people.' Pulling off his lapel pin, he exclaims, 'The pin. Two people. This is gold. Two more people. One more. I could have bought more people! But I didn't.' His knees crumble and he sobs heavily.

As his words – 'I could have done more! Why did I keep the car? Ten people right there. The pin. This is gold. Two people. One more.

I could have bought more people. But I didn't'—seared themselves into my mind as I sat in the darkness of that theater, I suddenly became convicted that many Christians—I among them—are going to be asking similar questions at the Great White Throne Judgment: 'Why did I not do more to reach the lost for Christ? Why did I think I had to have that more expensive house, that more expensive car? Why did I not use more of my resources for the cause of Christ?' More poignantly, 'Why was I not willing to go myself?' In that Great Day I fear that many of us will have no answers to salve our smitten consciences.

May God raise up in our day, while divine patience still grants us time, a multitude of men and women who will follow in Paul's footsteps and boldly dare to go into this lost and dying world where no man has ever gone before with the liberating gospel of God!

Appendix

Representative Greek Words Describing Paul's Preaching Activity

I. As a new convert to Christianity

A. Immediately preached (ἐκήρυσσεν) Jesus in Damascus, that he is the Son of God (Acts 9:20)

B. Baffled (συνέχυννεν) the Jews living in Damascus, offering proof (συμβιβάζων) that Jesus is the Christ (Acts 9:22)

C. Preached boldly (ἐπαρρησιάσατο) in Damascus in the name of Jesus (Acts 9:27)

D. Preached boldly (παρρησιαζόμενος) in the name of the Lord in Jerusalem and talked (ἐλάλει) and debated with (συνεζήτει) the Hellenists there (Acts 9:28-29)

E. Preached (εὐαγγελίζεται) the faith in Syria and Cilicia (Gal 1:23) and taught (διδάξαι) many people in Antioch (Acts 11:26)

II. As a missionary on his first missionary journey

A. Proclaimed (κατήγγελλον) the Word of God in the synagogues of the Jews in Salamis on Crete (Acts 13:5)

B. Said (εἶπεν) and preached good news (εὐαγγελιζόμεθα) in the synagogue at Pisidian Antioch (Acts 13:32)

C. Proclaimed (καταγγέλλεται) the forgiveness of sins in the synagogue at Pisidian Antioch (Acts 13:38)

D. Addressed (προσλαλοῦντες) and urged (ἔπειθον) the believing Jews in Pisidian Antioch to continue in the grace of God (Acts 13:43)

E. Spoke (λαληθῆναι) the Word of God to the unbelieving Jews at Pisidian Antioch (Acts 13:46).

F. Spoke (λαλῆσαι) in Iconium to a great number of Jews and Greeks (14:1)

G. Preached boldly (παρρησιαζόμενοι) in Iconium (14:3)

H. Preached the gospel (εὐαγγελιζόμενοι ἦσαν) directly to the Gentiles in Lystra since apparently there was no synagogue there (14:6-7)

I. Preached the gospel (εὐαγγελισάμενοί) in Derbe and made many disciples (14:20-21)

J. Encouraged (παρακαλοῦντες) the Christians of Lystra, Iconium, and Antioch to continue in the faith (14:21-22)

K. Preached the word (λαλήσαντες τὸν λόγον) in Perga (14:25)

L. According to Galatians, he preached the gospel (εὐηγγελισάμεθα, 1:8; τὸ εὐαγγέλιον τὸ εὐαγγελισθὲν ὑπ᾽ ἐμου᾽, 1:11; εὐηγγελισάμην, 4:13) to the Galatian churches, preached (εὐαγγελίζωμαι) Christ to the Galatian churches (Gal 1:16), proclaimed the gospel (τὸ εὐαγγέλιον ὃ κηρύσσω (Gal 2:2), was entrusted to preach the gospel (πεπίστευμαι τὸ εὐαγγέλιον) among the Gentiles (Gal 2:7), portrayed (προεγράφη) Christ as crucified before the Galatian churches (Gal 3:1), told the truth (ἀληθευών) to the Galatians (Gal 4:16), told (λέγω) the Galatians that if they let themselves be circumcised Christ would be of no value to them (Gal 5:2), bore witness (μαρτύρομαι) that every Christian who lets himself be circumcised in order to be saved is obligated to keep the whole law (Gal 5:3), warned (προλέγω) the Galatians that those who live according to the sinful nature will not inherit the kingdom of God (Gal 5:21), and boasted (καυχᾶσθαι) only in the cross of Christ (Gal 6:14)

M. Reported (ανήγγελλον) to the church at Syrian Antioch what God had done through them (Acts 14:27)

N. Reported in detail (ἐκδιηγούμενοι) to the Phoenicians and Samaritans the conversion of the Gentiles (Acts 15:3)

O. Preached (κατηγγείλαμεν) the word of the Lord to the Galatian churches (Acts 15:36)

III. **As a missionary apologist at the Jerusalem Conference and afterward as a teacher at Antioch**

A. Reported to (ἐξηγουμένων) the assembly of apostles and elders about the miraculous signs and wonders God had been doing among the Gentiles (Acts 15:12)

B. Taught (διδάσκοντες) and preached (εὐαγγελιζόμενοι) the Word of the Lord in Antioch (Acts 15:35)

Appendix

IV. As a missionary on his second missionary journey

A. Strengthened (ἐπιστηρίζων) the churches in Syria and Cilicia (Acts 15:41)

B. Strengthened (ἐστερεοῦντο) the Galatian churches in the faith (Acts 16:5)

C. Preached the gospel (εὐαγγελίσασθαι) in Macedonia (Acts 16:10)

D. Spoke (ἐλαλοῦμεν, λαλουμένοις) to women in Philippi (Acts 16:13, 14)

E. Spoke the word of the Lord (ἐλάλησαν τὸν λόγον τοῦ κυρίου) to the Philippian jailer (Acts 16:32)

F. Reasoned from the Scriptures (διελέξατο ἀπὸ τῶν γραφῶν) with the Jews of Thessalonica, explaining and proving (διανοίγων καὶ παρατιθέμενος) to them that the Messiah had to suffer and rise from the dead (Acts 17:2-3)

G. Proclaimed (καταγγέλλω) Jesus as the Christ to the Jews of Thessalonica (Acts 17:3)

H. According to 1 Thessalonians, Paul was bold to speak the gospel of God (ἐπαρρησιασάμεθα λαλῆσαι τὸ εὐαγγέλιον τοῦ θεοῦ) to the Thessalonians (1 Thess 2:2), shared (μεταδοῦναι) not only the gospel of God but also himself with them (1 Thes 2:8), encouraged, comforted, and urged (παρακαλοῦντες, παραμυθούμενοι, μαρτυρόμενοι) them to live lives worthy of God (1 Thess 2:12), and asked and urged (ἐρωτῶμεν καὶ παρακαλοῦμεν) them to live in order to please God (1 Thes 4:1)

I. According to 2 Thessalonians Paul told (ἔλεγον) the Thessalonians about end-time matters (2 Thess 2:5), and taught (ἐδιδάχθητε) 'the traditions' to them (2 Thess 2:15)

J. Preached the word of God (κατηγγέλη...ὁ λόγος τοῦ θεοῦ) at Berea (Acts 17:13)

K. Reasoned (διελέγετο) with the Jews and God-fearers in the synagogue at Athens and with those who happened to be in the marketplace (Acts 17:17)

L. Preached (εὐηγγελίζετο) about Jesus and the resurrection in Athens (Acts 17:18)

M. Said (ἔφη) his argument to the philosophers on Mars' Hill (Acts 17:22)

N. Proclaimed (καταγγέλλω) the 'unknown God' to the philosophers in his meeting with the Areopagus (Acts 17:23)

O. Reasoned (διελέγετο) in the synagogue at Corinth and persuaded (ἔπειθεν) both Jews and Greeks (Acts 18:4)

P. Devoted himself to the Word (συνείχετο τῷ λόγῳ) and testified (διαμαρτυρόμενος) to the Jews of Corinth that Jesus was the Messiah (Acts 18:5)

Q. Taught the Word of God (διδάσκων τὸν λόγον τοῦ θεοῦ) to the Corinthian (Acts 18:11)

R. Reasoned (διελέξατο) with the Jews in the synagogue at Ephesus (Acts 18:19)

V. As a missionary on his third missionary journey

A. Strengthened (ἐπιστηρίζων) all the disciples throughout the region of Galatia and Phrygia (Acts 18:23)

B. Preached boldly (ἐπαρρησιάζετο) in the synagogue at Ephesus, arguing and persuading (διαλεγόμενος καὶ πείθων) about the kingdom of God (Acts 19:8)

C. Had daily dialogues (διαλεγόμενος) at Ephesus in the lecture hall of Tyrannus (Acts 19:9), giving them the Word of the Lord (Acts 19:10)

D. Preached (κηρύσσει) Jesus (Acts 19:13)

E. Spoke many words of encouragement (παρακαλέσας) throughout Macedonia (Acts 20:2)

F. Dialogued (διελέγετο) with the people of Troas, talking (παρέτεινεν τὸν λόγον) (Acts 20:7), dialoguing at length (διαλεγομένου) into the night (Acts 20:9), and talking (ὁμιλήσας) until daylight (Acts 20:11)

G. Preached (ἀναγγεῖλαι) and taught (διδάξαι) the Ephesians, bearing witness to (διαμαρτυρόμενος) both Jew and Gentile that they must repent and have faith in Jesus Christ (Acts 20:20:21)

H. Testified to (διαμαρτύρασθαι) the gospel of God's grace (Acts 20:24)

I. Preached (κηρύσσων) the kingdom (Acts 20:25)

J. Proclaimed (ἀναγγεῖλαι) the whole counsel of God (Acts 20:27)

Appendix 593

K. Never stopped warning (οὐκ ἐπαυσάμην νουθέτων) the Ephesian elders night and day for three years about false teaching (Acts 20:31)

L. Committed (παρατίθεμαι) the Ephesian elders to God and to the Word of his grace (Acts 20:32)

M. Reported (ἐξηγεῖτο) in detail to the Jerusalem elders what God had done among the Gentiles through his ministry (Acts 21:19)

N. Confessed (ὁμολογῶ) his faith in the Way before Felix (Acts 24:14)

O. Shouted out (ἐκέκραξα) before the Sanhedrin his faith in the resurrection (Acts 24:21)

P. According to 1 Corinthians, Paul was sent not to baptize but to preach the gospel (εὐαγγελίζεσθαι) (1:17), proclaimed (καταγγέλλων) the mystery about God (2:1), spoke (λαλοῦμεν) the wisdom of God (2:6, 7), fed (ἐπότισα) them the milk of the Word (3:2), planted (ἐφύτευσα) the seed of the Word (3:6), blessed (εὐλογοῦμεν) in the face of persecution (4:12), begat (ἐγέννησα) the Corinthians through the gospel (4:15), sowed (ἐσπείραμεν) spiritual seed among them (9:11), preached the gospel (εὐαγγελίζομαι) (9:16), passed on (παρέδωκα) the traditions he had received from the Lord (11:2, 23), showed (δείκνυμι) them a more excellent way (12:31), prophesied (προφητεύομεν) to them (13:9), wanted to instruct (κατηχήσω) others (14:19, wrote (γράφω) the Lord's command (14:37), preached the gospel (τὸ εὐαγγέλιον ὃ εὐαγγελισάμην) (15:1), passed on (παρέδωκα) (15:3) and proclaimed (κηρύσσομεν) the 'tradition' (15:11), and testified (ἐμαρτυρήσαμεν) that God raised Jesus from the dead (15:15).

Q. According to 2 Corinthians, to the Corinthians Paul had preached (κηρύχθεις) the Son of God, Jesus Christ (1:19), did not adulterate (δολοῦντες) the Word of God but plainly set forth (φανερώσει) the truth (4:2), proclaimed (κηρύσσομεν) not himself but Jesus Christ as Lord (4:5), persuaded (πείθομεν) (5:11), implored (πρεσβεύομεν) on Christ's behalf (5:20), requested (δέομαι) that they not make it necessary for him to be bold among them when he came (10:2), and preached (εὐηγγελισάμην) the gospel of God free of charge (11:7).

R. According to Romans, Paul was set apart (ἀφωρισμένος) for the gospel of God (1:1), served (λατρεύω) God in the gospel of his Son (1:9), desired to impart (μεταδῶ) some spiritual gift to Christians there (1:11) and to preach the gospel (εὐαγγελίσασθαι) in Rome

(1:15), bore witness (μαρτυρῶ) to the Jews' zeal for God (10:2), saw it as his "priestly" duty to proclaim the gospel of God (ἱερουργοῦντα τὸ εὐαγγέλιον τοῦ θεοῦ) so that the Gentiles might become an acceptable offering to God (15:16), had fully proclaimed the gospel of Christ (πεπληρωκέναι τὸ εὐαγγέλιον) from Jerusalem to Illiricum (15:19), and had always made it his ambition to preach the gospel (φιλοτιμούμενον εὐαγγελίζεσθαι) where Christ was not known (15:20)

VI. As a missionary on trial in Jerusalem and Caesarea

A. Defended (ἀπολογίας) his ministry before the mob at the Jerusalem temple (Acts 22:1), testifying (διεμαρτύρω) to the Lord (Acts 23:11)

B. Discoursed (διαλεγομένου) on righteousness, self-control, and the judgment to come (Acts 24:25) before Felix

C. Defended (ἀπολογουμένου) himself against the Sanhedrin's false charges before Festus (Acts 25:8) and before Agrippa (ἀπελογεῖτο) (Acts 26:1)

D. Stated before Agrippa that he preached (ἀπήγγελλον) to those in Damascus, to those in Jerusalem, and in all Judea, and to the Gentiles that they should repent and turn to God (Acts 26:20)

E. Testified (μαρτυρόμενος) before Agrippa that throughout his entire ministry he had never said anything beyond what the prophets and Moses said would happen—that the Messiah would suffer and, as the first to rise from the dead, would proclaim light to his own people and to the Gentiles (Acts 26:22-23)

VII. As a missionary under house arrest in Rome

A. Explained (ἐξετίθετο) and declared (διαμαρτυρόμενος) the kingdom of God to the Jewish leaders at Rome and persuaded (πείθων) them about Jesus (Acts 28:23)

B. Preached (κηρύσσων) the kingdom of God and taught (διδάσκων) about the Lord Jesus Christ boldly and without hindrance in Rome for two whole years (Acts 28:30-31)

C. To the Colossians, Paul writes that, as a servant of the gospel (1:23), he was commissioned by God to present in its fullness (πληρῶσαι) the Word of God (1:25), proclaimed (καταγγέλλομεν) Christ, admonishing (νουθετοῦντες) and teaching (διδάσκοντες) everyone with all wisdom (1:28), and still desired to speak (λαλῆσαι) the mystery of Christ for which he was in chains (4:3)

D. To the Ephesians, Paul writes that, as a servant of the gospel (3:7), he was commissioned to preach the gospel (εὐαγγελίσασθαι) to the Gentiles and to make plain (φωτίσαι) to everyone the administration of the mystery that the Gentiles are heirs together with Israel, members together of the one body, and sharers together in the promise in Christ Jesus (3:8-9), and that he desired to make known (γνωρίσαι) fearlessly the mystery of the gospel for which he was an ambassador in chains (6:19:20)

E. To the Philippians, Paul writes that, in chains for the gospel, he was set (κεῖμαι) for the defense (ἀπολογίᾳ) and confirmation of (βεβαιώσει) the gospel (1:7, 16)

VIII. As the author of the Pastoral Letters

A. According to 1 Timothy, Paul was entrusted (ἐπιστεύθην) with the gospel of the glory of the blessed God (1:11)

B. According to Titus, Paul was entrusted with preaching (κηρύγματι, ὃ ἐπιστεύθην) (1:3)

C. According to 2 Timothy, Paul suffered (συγκακοπάθησον) for the gospel (1:8) because with regard to this gospel he had been appointed a herald and an apostle and a teacher (ἐτέθην ἐγὼ κῆρυξ καὶ ἀπόστολος καὶ διδάσκαλος) (1:11).

Bibliography

Abbreviations:
HNTC   Harper's New Testament Commentaries
NICNT   New International Commentary on the New Testament
NIGTC   New International Greek Testament Commentary
TNTC   Tyndale New Testament Commentary
WBC   Word Bible Commentary
Ed, eds   editor, editors
Edition, revised, translated are all written out in full.

Alford, Dean. *Edinburgh Review* (Jan-Apr 1853).
Allen, Roland. *Missionary Methods: St Paul's or Ours? A Study of the Church in the Four Provinces*. London: World Dominion, 1912.
Anderson, H. George, A. Murphy, & J.A. Burgess (eds). *Justification by Faith: Lutherans and Catholics in Dialogue VII*. Minneapolis: Augsburg, 1985.
Arnold, Clinton E. 'Ephesians, Letter of' in Gerald F. Hawthorne *et al* (eds), 1993.
Arnold, Clinton E. *The Colossian Syncretism: The Interface between Christianity and False Belief at Colossae*. Grand Rapids: Baker, 1996.
Barclay, William. *The Acts of the Apostles*. Philadelphia: Westminster, 1955.
Barclay, William. *The First Epistle to the Corinthians*. HNTC. New York: Harper & Row, 1968.
Barclay, William. *The Second Epistle to the Corinthians*. HNTC: New York: Harper & Row, 1973.
Barnett, P.W. 'Opponents of Paul' in Gerald F. Hawthorne *et al* (eds), 1993.
Barrett, C.K. 'Paul and the Pillar Apostle' in J.N. Sevenster & W.C. van Unnik (eds), *Studia Paulina in honorem J. de Zwaan*. Haarlem: Erven F. Bohn, 1953.
Barrett, C.K. 'Cephas and Corinth' in Otto Betz, Martin Hengel, Peter Schmidt (eds), *Abraham unser Vater: Juden und Christen im Gesprach uber die Bibel*. Festschrift für Otto Michel zum 60 Geburtsta. Leiden: E.J. Brill, 1963. Reprinted in C.K. Barrett, 1992.
Barrett, C.K. 'Christianity at Corinth' in C.K. Barrett, 1992.
Barrett, C.K. 'Paul's Opponents in II Corinthians' *New Testament Studies* 17 (1971). Reprinted in C.K. Barrett, 1992.
Barrett, C.K. 'ΨΕΥΔΑΠΟΣΤΟΛΟΙ (2Cor.11: 13)' in C.K. Barrett, 1992.
Barrett, C.K. *Essays on Paul*. Philadelphia: Westminster, 1992.
Barrett, C.K. *Paul: An Introduction to his Thought*. Louisville, Kentucky: Westminster/John Knox, 1994.
Barrett, C.K. *The Acts of the Apostles*. 2 vols. ICC. Edinburgh: T. & T. Clark, 1994.
Baxter, Richard. *The Reformed Pastor*. Edinburgh: Banner of Truth, 1974 reprint.
Beckwith, R.T. 'Eucharist' in Sinclair B. Ferguson and David F. Wright, *New Dictionary of Theology*. Downers Grove, Illinois: Intervarsity, 1988.

Bibliography

Beitzel, Barry J. *The Moody Atlas of Bible Lands*. Chicago: Moody, 1985.
Beker, Jürgen C. *Paul the Apostle: the Triumph of God in Life and Thought*. Philadelphia: Fortress, 1980.
Berkhof, Louis. *Systematic Theology*. Grand Rapids: Eerdmans, 1941.
Berkouwer, G.C. *The Return of Christ*. Translated by James Van Osterom. Grand Rapids: Eerdmans, 1972.
Bloesch, Donald G. 'Betraying the Reformation? An Evangelical Response' *Christianity Today* 54 (Oct. 1996).
Bornkamm, Günther. *Jesus of Nazareth*. New York: Harper & Brothers, 1960.
Bornkamm, Günther. *Paul*. Translated by D.M.G. Stalker. New York: Harper & Row, 1971.
Bowers, W. Paul. 'Mission' in Gerald F. Hawthorne *et al* (eds), 1993.
Brown, Raymond E. 'Does the New Testament call Jesus "God"?' *Theological Studies* 26. 1965
Brown, Raymond E. *An Introduction to the New Testament*. Anchor Bible Reference Library. New York: Doubleday, 1997.
Bruce, F.F. *Commentary on the Book of Acts*. Grand Rapids: Eerdmans, 1954.
Bruce, F.F. *Commentary on the Epistle to the Hebrews*. Grand Rapids: Eerdmans, 1964.
Bruce, F.F. *New Testament History*. London: Nelson, 1969.
Bruce, F.F. *I & II Corinthians*. NCBC. Grand Rapids: Eerdmans, 1971.
Bruce, F.F. *1 and 2 Thessalonians*. WBC. Waco: Word, 1982.
Bruce, F.F. *The Epistle to the Galatians*. NICGT. Grand Rapids: Eerdmans, 1982.
Bruce, F.F. *The Epistles to the Colossians, to Philemon and to the Ephesians*. NICNT. Grand Rapids: Eerdmans, 1984.
Bruce, F.F. *The Book of the Acts*. NICNT, revised edition, Grand Rapids: Eerdmans, 1988.
Bruce, F.F. *The Canon of Scripture*. Downers Grove, Illinois: Intervarsity, 1988.
Bruce, F.F. *Paul: Apostle of the Heart Set Free*. Exeter: Paternoster, 1977. Reprinted Grand Rapids: Eerdmans, 1996.
Buchanan, James. *The Doctrine of Justification*. Edinburgh: T. & T. Clark, 1867.
Büchsel, F. ἱλάσκεσθαι in *Theological Dictionary of the New Testament*. Grand Rapids: Eerdmans, 1965.
Bultmann, Rudolph. *Theology of the New Testament*. Translated by Kendrich Grobel. London: SCM, 1971.
Burton, E. de W. *A Critical and Exegetical Commentary on the Epistle to the Galatians*. ICC. Edinburgh: T. & T. Clark, 1921.
Byrne, B. *Romans*. Collegeville: Glazier, 1996.
Calvin, John. 'Calvin's Reply to Sadoleto' in *A Reformation Debate*. Reprint, Grand Rapids: Baker, 1976.
Calvin, John. *Institutes of the Christian Religion*, Translated by Ford Lewis Battles. Philadelphia: Westminster 1960.
Carson, D.A. 'Reflections on Salvation and Justification in the New Testament' *JETS* 40/4 (Dec.1997).

Carson, Donald A. *From Triumphalism to Maturity: An Exposition of 2 Corinthians 10-13*. Grand Rapids: Baker, 1984.

Carson, D.A., D.J. Moo, & Leon Morris *An Introduction to the New Testament*. Grand Rapids: Zondervan, 1992.

Castilli, E.A. *Imitating Paul: A Discourse of Power*. Literary Currents in Biblical Interpretation. Louisville: Westminster, 1991.

Cerfaux, L. *Christ in the Theology of St Paul*. New York: Herder & Herder, 1959.

Chafer, Lewis Sperry. *Systematic Theology*. Grand Rapids: Kregel, 1993. reprint of 1947 edition.

Chase, F.C. *The Credibility of Acts*. London: Macmillan, 1902.

Clarke, Andrew D. ' "Be Imitators of Me": Paul's Model of Leadership' *Tyndale Bulletin* 49.2 (Nov. 1998).

Clowney, Edmund P. *The Church*. Downers Grove, Illinois: Intervarsity, 1995.

Cole, R.A. *The Epistle of Paul to the Galatians*. TNTC. Grand Rapids: Eerdmans, 1977.

Conybeare, W.J. & J.S. Howson. *The Life and Epistles of St Paul*. Reprint, Grand Rapids: Eerdmans, 1971.

Cooper, Karl T. 'Paul and Rabbinic Soteriology' *Westminster Theological Journal* 44 (1982).

Corley, Bruce. 'Interpreting Paul's Conversion – Then and Now' in Richard N. Longenecker (ed), *The Road to Damascus: the Impact of Paul's Con-version on his Life, Thought and Ministry*. Grand Rapids: Eerdmans, 1997.

Cranfield, C.E.B. 'St Paul and the Law' *Scottish Journal of Theology* 17 (1964).

Cranfield, C.E.B. *Romans*. 2 vols. ICC. Edinburgh: T. & T. Clark, 1975, 1979.

Cranfield, C.E.B. ' "The Works of the Law" in the Epistle to the Romans' *Journal for the Study of the New Testament* 43 (1991).

Cullman, Oscar. *Christ and Time*. Translated by Floyd V. Filson. Philadelphia: Westminster, 1950.

Cullman, Oscar. *Peter: Disciple – Apostle – Martyr*. Translated by Floyd V. Filson. Philadelphia: Westminster, 1953.

Cullman, Oscar. *The Christology of the New Testament*. Translated by Shirley C. Guthrie & Charlesall. London: SCM, 1959.

Dana, H.E. & J.R. Mantey. *A Manual Grammar of the Greek New Testament*. (1927). Reprinted New York: Macmillan, 1954.

Davies, W.D. *Paul and Rabbinic Judaism: Some Rabbinic Elements in Pauline Theology*. (1948). 4th edition. Philadelphia: Fortress, 1980.

De Boer, W.P. *The Imitation of Paul*. Kampen: Kok, 1962.

Demerest, Bruce A. 'Hebrews, Letter to the' *Baker Encyclopaedia of the Bible*. Grand Rapids: Baker, 1988.

Denney, James. *The Death of Christ*. London: Hodder & Stoughton, 1900.

Dittenberger, W. *Sylloge Inscriptionum Graecarum*. 3rd edition. Hildesheim: Georg Olms, 1960.

Dodd, C.H. ' Ἱλασκεσθαι, Its Cognates, Derivatives & Synonyms in the Septuagint' *Journal of Theological Studies* 32 (1931).

Dodd, C.H. *New Testament Commentary on Romans*. Moffatt Commentary Series. London: Hodder & Stoughton, 1932.

Bibliography

Dodd, C.H. *The Johannine Epistles*. London: Hodder & Stoughton, 1946.

Dodd, C.H. *The Apostolic Preaching and its Developments*. New York: Harper & Row, 1964.

Drane, John W. 'Why did Paul write Romans?' in Donald A. Hagner & Murray J. Harris (eds), *Pauline Studies: Essays presented to F.F. Bruce on his 70th Birthday*. Grand Rapids: Eerdmans, 1980.

Dunn, James D.G. *Jesus and the Spirit*. Philadelphia: Westminster, 1975.

Dunn, James D.G. *Unity and Diversity of the New Testament*. Philadelphia: Westminster, 1977.

Dunn, James D.G. *Christology in the Making: a New Testament Inquiry into the Origins of the Doctrine of the Incarnation*. London: SCM, 1980.

Dunn, James D.G. 'The New Perspective on Paul' *Bulletin of John Rylands University Library of Manchester* 65, (1983).

Dunn, James D.G. *Jesus, Paul and the Law*. Louisville, Kentucky: Westminster/John Knox, 1990.

Dunn, James D.G. 'Echoes of Intra-Jewish Polemic in Paul's Letter to the Galatians' *Journal of Biblical Literature* 112 (1993).

Dunn, James D.G. 'Romans, Letter to the' in Gerald F. Hawthorne *et al* (eds), 1993.

Dunn, James D.G. 'Pauline Legacy and School' in R.P. Martin & P.H. Davids (eds), *Dictionary of the Later New Testament and its Development*. Downers Grove, Illinois: Intervarsity, 1997.

Dunn, James D. G. *The Theology of Paul the Apostle*. Grand Rapids: Eerdmans, 1998.

Dupont, Jacques. 'The Conversion of Paul, and its Influence on his Understanding of Salvation by Faith' in W. Ward Gasque & Ralph P. Martin, *Apostolic History and the Gospel*. Exeter: Paternoster, 1970.

Dupont, Jacques. *The Sources of Acts*. Translated by K. Pond. London: Darton, Longman & Todd, 1964.

Ellingworth, Paul. *The Epistle to the Hebrews: A Commentary on the Greek New Testament*. NIGTC. Grand Rapids: Eerdmans, 1993.

Ellis, Earle E. 'Pauline Studies in Recent Research' in *Paul and His Recent Interpreters*. Grand Rapids: Eerdmans, 1961.

Ellis, Earle E. 'Coworkers, Paul and his' in Gerald F. Hawthorne *et al* (eds), 1993.

Everts, Janet Meyer 'Conversion and Call of Paul' in Gerald F. Hawthorne *et al* (eds), 1993.

Elwell, Walter A. (ed), *Evangelical Dictionary of Theology*. Grand Rapids: Baker, 1984.

Fee, Gordon D. *The First Epistle to the Corinthians*. NICNT. Grand Rapids: Eerdmans, 1987.

Fee, Gordon D. *The Pastoral Epistles*. Peabody, Mass.: Hendricksen, 1988.

Fee, Gordon D. *Paul's Letter to the Philippians*. NICNT. Grand Rapids: Eerdmans, 1995.

Feine, P. & J. Behm. *Introduction to the New Testament*. Translated by A.J. Mattill jr. Revised edition; Nashville: Abingdon, 1975.

Fitzmyer, J.A. *Pauline Theology: A Brief Sketch*. Englewood Cliffs, New Jersey: Prentice-Hall, 1967.

Fitzmyer, J.A. *Romans: A New Translation with Introduction and Commentary*. Anchor Bible Commentary. New York: Doubleday, 1993.

Fletcher, Joseph. *Situation Ethics: the New Morality*. Philadelphia: Westminster, 1966.

Fletcher, Joseph. 'What's in a rule?: A Situationist's View' in Gene H. Outka & Paul Ramsey (eds), *Norm and Context in Christian Ethics*. New York: Charles Scribner's Sons, 1967.

Fletcher, Joseph. 'Situation Ethics under Fire' in John C. Bennett (ed), *Storm over Ethics*. Philadelphia: United Church, 1967.

Forsyth, P.T. *The Cruciality of the Cross*. London: Hodder & Stoughton, 1909.

Frame, J.E. *A Critical and Exegetical Commentary on 1 and 2 Thessalonians*. ICC. Edinburgh: T. & T. Clark, 1912.

Frame, John. *Apologetics to the Glory of God*. Phillipsburg, New Jersey: Presbyterian & Reformed, 1994.

Franzmann, Martin. *The Word of the Lord Grows*. St Louis: Concordia, 1961.

Fung, Ronald Y.K. *Epistle to the Galatians*. NICNT. Grand Rapids: Eerdmans, 1988.

Gaffin, Richard B. Jr. 'A Sabbath Rest Still Awaits the People of God' in C.G. Dennison & R.C. Gamble (eds), *Pressing Towards the Mark*. Philadelphia: Committee for the Historian of the Orthodox Presbyterian Church, 1986.

Gaffin, Richard B. Jr. 'The New Testament as Canon' in Harvey M. Conn (ed), *Inerrancy and Hermeneutics*. Grand Rapids: Baker, 1988.

Gaffin, Richard B. Jr. ' "Life-Giving Spirit": Probing the Center of Paul's Pneumatology' *JETS* 41/4 (Dec. 1998).

Gerstner, John H. 'Aquinas was a Protestant' *Tabletalk* (May 1994).

Gibbs, J.G. *Creation and Redemption*. Leiden: E.J. Brill, 1971.

Gifford, E.H. *The Epistle of St Paul to the Romans*. London: John Murray, 1886.

Grant, Michael. *Saint Paul*. New York: Charles Scribner's Sons, 1976.

Green, Joel. 'Acts of the Apostles' in R.P. Martin & Peter H. Davids (eds), *Dictionary of the Later New Testament and its Development*. Downers Grove, Illinois: Intervarsity, 1997.

Gundry, Robert H. 'The Moral Frustration of Paul Before his Conversion: Sexual Lust in Romans 7: 7-25' in Donald A. Hagner & Murray J. Harris (eds), *Pauline Studies: Essays presented to F.F. Bruce on his 70th Birthday*. Grand Rapids: Eerdmans, 1980.

Gutbrod, W. νόμος (νομ- -word cluster)' *Theological Dictionary of the New Testament*. Translated by G.W. Bromiley. Grand Rapids: Eerdmans, 1967.

Guthrie, Donald. *New Testament Introduction*. Downers Grove, Illinois: Intervarsity, 1970.

Guthrie, Donald. *Galatians*. NCBC. London: Marshall, Morgan & Scott, 1973.

Guthrie, Donald. *New Testament Theology*. Downers Grove, Illinois: Intervarsity, 1981.

Guthrie, Donald. *The Pastoral Epistles*. TNTC. 2nd edition. Grand Rapids: Eerdmans, 1990.

Habermas, Gary R. *Ancient Evidence for the Life of Jesus*. Nashville: Thomas Nelson, 1984.

Bibliography

Hafemann, Scott J. 'Paul and his Interpreters' in Gerald F. Hawthorne *et al* (eds), 1993.

Hagner, Donald A. *Hebrews*. New International Bible Commentary. Peabody, Mass.: Hendricksen, 1990.

Hall, David W. & Joseph H. Hall (eds), *Paradigms in Polity: Classic Readings in Reformed and Presbyterian Church Government*. Grand Rapids: Eerdmans. 1994.

Hall, Joseph H. 'History and Character of Church Government' in David W. Hall & Joseph H. Hall (eds), 1994.

Hansen, G. Walter. 'Galatians' in Gerald F. Hawthorne *et al* (eds), 1993.

Hansen, G. Walter. *Galatians*. IVP New Testament Commentary. Downers Grove, Illinois: Intervarsity Press, 1994.

Harris, Murray J. 'The Translation of אלהים in Psalm 45: 7-8' *Tyndale Bulletin* 35 (1984).

Harris, Murray J. 'The Translation and Significance of ὁ θεός in Hebrews 1: 8-9' *Tyndale Bulletin* 36 (1985).

Harris, R. Laird. *Inspiration and Canonicity of the Bible*. Grand Rapids: Zondervan, 1957.

Harrison, Everett F. 'Redeemer, Redemption' in Walter A. Elwell (ed), 1984.

Hawthorne, Gerald F., Ralph P. Martin & Daniel G. Reid (eds), *Dictionary of Paul and his Letters*. Downers Grove, Illinois: Intervarsity, 1993.

Hawthorne, Gerald F. *Philippians*. WBC 43. Waco: Word, 1983.

Hawthorne, Gerald F. 'Philippians, Letter to the' in Gerald F. Hawthorne *et al* (eds), 1993.

Hemer, C.J. 'Acts and Galatians Reconsidered' *Themelios*. New Series 2. (1976-7).

Hemer, C.J. *The Book of Acts in the Setting of Hellenistic History*. edited by C.H. Gempf; Wissen-schaftliche Untersuchungen zum Neuen Testament 49. Tubingen: J.C.Mohr, 1989.

Hendriksen, William. *New Testament Commentary: I & II Thessalonians*. Grand Rapids: Baker, 1955.

Hendriksen, William. *Israel in Prophecy*. Grand Rapids: Baker, 1974.

Hendriksen, William. *Exposition of Ephesians*. Grand Rapids: Baker, 1979.

Hengel, M. 'Die Ursprünge der christlichen Mission' *New Testament Studies* 18 (1971-2).

Hengel, M. *The 'Hellenization' of Judaea in the First Century after Christ*. Philadelphia: Trinity, 1989.

Hengel, M. *The Zealots: An Investigation into the Jewish Freedom Movement in the Period from Herod I until 70 A.D.* translated by David Smith. Edinburgh: T. & T. Clark, 1989.

Hengel, Martin. *Acts and the Earliest History of Christianity*. Philadelphia: Fortress, 1979.

Hengel, Martin. 'The Origins of the Christian Mission' in *Between Jesus and Paul: Studies in the Earliest History of Christianity*. London: SCM, 1983.

Hengel, M. & Anna Maria Schwerner. *Paul between Damascus and Antioch: the Unknown Years*. Translated by John Bowden. Louisville, Kentucky: Westminster/ John Knox, 1997.

Héring, J. *The Epistle to the Hebrews*. London: Epworth, 1970.

Hickling, C.J.A. 'Centre and Periphery in Paul's Thought' in E.A. Livingstone (ed), *Papers on Paul and Other New Testament Authors. Studia Biblica* III. Sheffield: Sheffield University Press, 1978.

Hock, R.F. *The Social Context of Paul's Ministry: Tentmaking and Apostleship*. Philadelphia: Fortress, 1980.

Hoekema, Anthony A. *The Bible and the Future*. Grand Rapids: Eerdmans, 1979.

Hooker, M.D. 'Were there False Teachers in Colossae?' in B. Lindars & S.S. Smalley (eds), *Christ and Spirit in the New Testament: Studies in honour of Charles Francis Digby Moule*. Cambridge: Cambridge University Press, 1973.

Horsley, G.H.R. *New Documents Illustrating Early Christianity*. North Ryde: Ancient History Documentation Centre, 1981.

Howard, G. *Paul: Crisis in Galatia: A Study in Early Christian Theology*. Society for New Testament Studies Monograph Series 35. Cambridge: Cambridge University Press, 1979.

Hughes, Philip E. *Paul's Second Epistle to the Corinthians*. NICNT. Grand Rapids: Eerdmans, 1962.

Hughes, Philip Edgecombe. *A Commentary on the Epistle to the Hebrews*. Grand Rapids: Eerdmans, 1977.

Jewett, Paul King. *Infant Baptism and the Covenant of Grace*. Grand Rapids: Eerdmans, 1978.

Jewett, Robert. 'Paul, Phoebe and the Spanish Mission' in J. Neusner, S.S. Frerichs, P. Borgen & R. Horsley (eds), *The Social World of Formative Christianity and Judaism. Essays in tribute to H.C. Kee*. Philadelphia: Fortress, 1988.

Käsemann, Ernst. *New Testament Questions of Today*. London: SCM, 1979.

Keller, W. Phillip. *A Shepherd Looks at Psalm 23*. Grand Rapids: Zondervan, 1970.

Kelly, J.N.D. 'Creedal Elements in the New Testament' in *Early Christian Creeds*. London: Longman Green, 1950.

Kelly, J.N.D. *Early Christian Doctrine*. London: Adam & Charles Bloch, 1958.

Kelly, J.N.D. *The Pastoral Epistles*. London: Black, 1963.

Kevan, Ernest F. 'The Evangelical Doctrine of Law.' *Tyndale Biblical Theology Lecture* July 4, 1955.

Kim, Seyoon. *The Origin of Paul's Gospel*. 2nd edition. Tübingen: J.C.B. Mohr, 1984.

Kirk, Kenneth Escott. *The Vision of God: the Christian Doctrine of the Summum Bonum*. 1928 Bampton Lectures. London: Longman Green, 1931.

Kistemaker, Simon J. *New Testament Commentary: Exposition of the Epistle to the Hebrews*. Grand Rapids: Baker, 1984.

Kistemaker, Simon J. *New Testament Commentary: Exposition of the Second Epistle to the Corinthians*. Grand Rapids: Baker, 1997.

Knight, George W. III. *The Role Relationship of Men and Women*. Revised edition; Chicago: Moody, 1985.

Knight, George W. III. *The Pastoral Epistles* NIGTC. Grand Rapids: Eerdmans, 1992.

Knox, J. 'Romans 15: 14-33 and Paul's Concept of his Apostolic Ministry' *Journal of Biblical Literature* 83 (1964).

Kruse, C.G. *Paul, the Law and Justification*. Leicester: Intervarsity, 1996.

Bibliography

Ladd, G. E. *A Theology of the New Testament.* 1987 reprint; Grand Rapids: Eerdmans, 1974.
Ladd, G.E. 'Revelation and Tradition in Paul' in Ward Gasque & R.P. Martin (eds), *Apostolic History and the Gospel.* Exeter: Paternoster, 1970.
Ladd, George Eldon. *The Blessed Hope.* Grand Rapids: Eerdmans, 1956.
Lane, William L. *Hebrews.* 2 vols. WBC 47a, b. Dallas: Word, 1991.
Lane, William L. 'Hebrews' in Gerald F. Hawthorne *et al* (eds), 1993.
Lightfoot, J.B. *St Paul's Epistle to the Galatians.* London: Macmillan, 1890. Reprinted Grand Rapids: Zondervan, 1957.
Lincoln, A.T. *Ephesians.* WBC 42. Dallas: Word, 1990.
Lock, Walter. *A Critical & Exegetical Commentary on the Pastoral Letters.* ICC. Edinburgh: T. & T. Clark, 1924.
Longenecker, B.W. *2 Esdras.* Sheffield: Sheffield Academic Press, 1995.
Longenecker, R. N. *The Ministry and Message of Paul.* Grand Rapids: Zondervan, 1971.
Longenecker, Richard N. *Paul, Apostle of Liberty.* New York: Harper & Row, 1964.
Longenecker, Richard N. *Galatians.* WBC 41. Dallas: Word, 1990.
Lovelace, Robert. 'A Call to Historic Roots and Continuity' in Robert Webber & Donald Bloesch (eds), *The Orthodox Evangelicals.* Nashville: Thomas Nelson, 1978.
Luther, Martin. *What Luther Says.* Edited by Ewald M. Plass. St Louis: Concordia, 1959.
Machen, J. Gresham. *The Origin of Paul's Religion.* Reprint of 1925 edition. Grand Rapids: Eerdmans 1965.
Machen, J. Gresham. *Machen's Notes on Galatians.* Edited by John H. Skilton. Philadelphia: Presbyterian and Reformed, 1972.
Macmillan, J. Douglas. *The Lord our Shepherd.* Brytirian: Evangelical Press of Wales, 1983.
Macrae, Allan A. 'עלם in R. Laird Harris, Gleason L. Archer Jr. & Bruce K. Waltke (eds), *Theological Word Book of the Old Testament.* Chicago: Moody, 1980.
Malherbe, A.J. *Social Aspects of Early Christianity.* Baton Rouge: Louisiana State University Press, 1977.
Malina, Bruce & Jerome H. Neyrey. *Portraits of Paul: An Archaeology of Ancient Personality.* Louisville, Kentucky: Westminster/John Knox, 1996.
Marshall, I. H. *The Acts of the Apostles.* TNTC. Grand Rapids: Eerdmans, 1980.
Marshall, I. Howard. 'Incarnational Christology in the New Testament' in Harold Rowden (ed), *Christ the Lord.* Leicester: Intervarsity, 1982.
Marshall, I. Howard. *1 & 2 Thessalonians.* NCBC. Grand Rapids: Eerdmans, 1983.
Martin, R.P. *The Epistle of Paul to the Philippians.* TNTC. Grand Rapids: Eerdmans, 1959.
Martin, R.P. *Philippians.* NCBC. Grand Rapids: Eerdmans, 1976.
Martin, R.P. *Colossian and Philemon.* NCBC. Grand Rapids: Eerdmans, 1981.
Martin, R.P. *Carmen Christi: Philippians 2: 5-11* in *Recent Interpretation in the Setting of Early Christian Worship.* Grand Rapids: Eerdmans, 1983.

Martin, R.P. *Reconciliation: A Study of Paul's Theology*. Grand Rapids: Zondervan, 1990.

Martin, R.P. *Ephesians, Colossians and Philemon*. Interpretation Commentary. Louisville: John Knox, 1992.

Martin, R.P. 'Center of Paul's Theology' in Gerald F. Hawthorne *et al* (eds), 1993.

Martin, Ralph P. *Second Corinthians*. WBC 40. Waco: Word, 1986.

Meeks, W.A. *The First Urban Christians: the Social World of the Apostle Paul*. New Haven: Yale University Press, 1983.

Metzger, Bruce M. *A Textual Commentary on the Greek New Testament*. New York: UBS, 1971.

Metzger, Bruce M. *Index to Periodical Literature on the Apostle Paul*. 2nd edition. Leiden: E.J. Brill, 1970.

Metzger, Bruce. 'The Punctuation of Romans 9: 5' in Stephen Smalley and Barnabas Lindars (eds) *Christ and Spirit in the New Testament*. Cambridge: Cambridge University Press, 1973.

Mills, Watson E. *An Index to Periodical Literature on the Apostle Paul*. Leiden: E.J. Brill, 1990.

Minear, Paul. *Images of the Church in the New Testament*. Philadelphia: Westminster, 1977.

Moffatt, James. *Introduction to the Literature of the New Testament*. 3rd edition. New York: Charles Scribner's Sons, 1918.

Moffatt, James. *A Critical and Exegetical Commentary on the Epistle to the Hebrews*. ICC. Edinburgh: T. & T. Clark, 1924.

Montefiore, C.G. 'First Impressions of Paul' in *Jewish Quarterly Review* 6 (1894).

Montefiore, C.G. 'Rabbinic Judaism and the Epistles of Saint Paul' *Jewish Quarterly Review* 13 (1900-1).

Moo, Douglas J. ' "Law", "Works of the Law" and Legalism in Paul' *Westminster Theological Journal* 45 (1983).

Moo, Douglas J. 'Paul and the Law in the Last Ten Years' in *Scottish Journal of Theology* 40 (1987).

Moo, Douglas J. *The Epistle to the Romans*. NICNT. Grand Rapids: Eerdmans, 1996.

Moore, G.F. *Judaism in the First Centuries of the Christian Era: the Age of the Tannaim*. 2 vols. Cambridge, Mass.: Harvard University Press, 1927.

Morris, Leon. *The Apostolic Preaching of the Cross*. London: Tyndale, 1955.

Morris, Leon. 'The Meaning of HILASTERION in Romans III.25' *New Testament Studies* 2. XXX

Morris, Leon. 'The use of ἱλασκεσθαι etc. in Biblical Greek' *Expository Times* LXII 8 (1951).

Morris, Leon. *The First and Second Epistles to the Thessalonians*. NICNT. Grand Rapids: Eerdmans, 1959.

Morris, Leon. *The Cross in the New Testament*. Leicester: Paternoster, 1965.

Morris, Leon. *The Biblical Doctrine of Judgement*. London: Tyndale, 1978.

Morris, Leon. *Hebrews*. Bible Study Commentary. Grand Rapids: Eerdmans, 1983.

Morris, Leon. 'Propitiation' in Walter A. Elwell (ed), 1984.

Morris, Leon. *New Testament Theology*. Grand Rapids: Zondervan, 1986.
Moulton, James Hope. *A Grammar of New Testament Greek*, vol. I. 3rd edition. Edinburgh: T. & T. Clark, 1930.
Murray, John. *Redemption Accomplished and Applied*. Grand Rapids: Eerdmans, 1955.
Murray, John. *Principles of Conduct*. Grand Rapids: Eerdmans, 1957.
Murray, John. *The Imputation of Adam's Sin*. Grand Rapids: Eerdmans, 1959.
Murray, John. *Christian Baptism*. Philadelphia: Presbyterian & Reformed, 1962.
Murray, John. *The Epistle to the Romans*. NICNT. Grand Rapids: Eerdmans, 1968.
Murray, John. *Collected Writings of John Murray*. Edinburgh: Banner of Truth, 1977.
Murray, John. 'The Atonement' in John Murray, 1977.
Murray, John. 'The Goal of Sanctification' in John Murray, 1977.
Murray, John. 'The Plan of Salvation' in John Murray, 1977.
Narborough, F.D.V. *The Epistle to the Hebrews*. Oxford: Clarendon, 1930.
Neill, Stephen, C. *Jesus through Many Eyes: Introduction to the Theology of the New Testament*. Philadelphia: Fortress, 1976.
Neusner, Jacob. *Rabbinic Judaism: Structure and System*. Minneapolis: Fortress, 1995.
Neve, J.L. *A History of Christian Thought*. Philadelphia: Muhlenberg, 1946.
Newton, John. *The Works of John Newton*. Edinburgh: Banner of Truth, 1985.
Nicole, Roger R. 'C.H. Dodd and the Doctrine of Propitiation' in *Westminster Theological Journal* XVII.2 (May, 1955).
O'Brien, P.T. *Colossians, Philemon*. WBC 44. Waco: Word, 1982.
O'Brien, P.T. *The Epistle to the Philippians*. Grand Rapids: Eerdmans, 1991.
O'Brien, P.T. 'Colossians, Letter to the' in Gerald F. Hawthorne *et al* (eds), 1993.
O'Brien, P.T. *Gospel and Mission in the Writings of Paul*. Grand Rapids: Baker, 1995.
Osborne, Grant. *The Resurrection Narratives: A Redactional Study*. Grand Rapids: Baker, 1984.
Owen, John. *The Works of John Owen*. Edited by William H. Goold. Edinburgh: Banner of Truth, 1965.
Packer, J.I. 'Justification' in Walter A. Elwell (ed), 1984.
Pannenberg, Wolfhart. *Jesus – God and Man*. Philadelphia: Westminster, 1968.
Patzia, Arthur. *Ephesians, Colossians and Philemon*. Peabody, Mass.: Hendricksen, 1991.
Patzia, Arthur. 'Philemon, Letter to' in Gerald F. Hawthorne *et al* (eds), 1993.
Pinnock, Clark E. *Grace Unlimited*. Minneapolis: Bethany, 1975.
Piper, John & Wayne Grudem (eds). *Recovering Biblical Manhood and Womanhood*. Wheaton: Crossway, 1991.
Plevnik, J. 'The Center of Paul's Theology' *Catholic Biblical Quarterly* 51 (1989).
Plummer, Alfred. *A Critical and Exegetical Commentary on the Second Epistle of St Paul to the Corinthians*. ICC. Edinburgh: T. & T. Clark, 1925.
Räisänen, Heikki. *Paul and the Law*. Philadelphia: Fortress, 1983.

Ramsay, William M. *A Historical Commentary on St Paul's Epistle to the Galatians.* New York: G.P. Putnam's Sons, 1900.

Reaume, John D. 'Another Look at 1 Corinthians 15: 29: "Baptized for the Dead" ' in *Bibliotheca Sacra* 152 (Oct – Dec 1995).

Reid, D.G. 'Elements/Elemental Spirits of the World' in Gerald F. Hawthorne *et al* (eds), 1993.

Reid, D.G. 'Satan, Devil' in Gerald F. Hawthorne *et al* (eds), 1993.

Reymond, Robert. 'Lord's Day Observance: Man's Proper Response to the Fourth Commandment' *Presbuterion: Covenant Seminary Review* XIII (Spring, 1987).

Reymond, Robert. *Jesus, Divine Messiah: the New Testament Witness.* Phillipsburg, New Jersey: Presbyterian & Reformed, 1990.

Reymond, Robert. 'Dr. John H. Gerstner on Thomas Aquinas as a Protestant' *Westminster Theological Journal* 59 (1997).

Reymond, Robert. *A New Systematic Theology of the Christian Faith.* Nashville: Thomas Nelson, 1998.

Ridderbos, Herman. *The Epistle of Paul to the Churches of Galatia.* NICNT. Grand Rapids: Eerdmans, 1953.

Ridderbos, Herman. *When the Time had Fully Come: Studies in New Testament Theology.* Grand Rapids: Eerdmans, 1957.

Ridderbos, Herman. 'The Canon of the New Testament' in Carl F.H. Henry (ed), *Revelation and the Bible.* Grand Rapids: Baker, 1958.

Ridderbos, Herman. *Paul: an Outline of his Theology.* Translated by John R. De Witt. Grand Rapids: Eerdmans, 1975.

Ridderbos, Herman. *Paul and Jesus.* Translated by David H. Freeman. Nutley, New Jersey: Presbyterian & Reformed, 1977.

Ridderbos, Herman. *Redemptive History and the New Testament Scriptures.* 2nd edition. Phillipsburg, New Jersey: Presbyterian & Reformed, 1988.

Robertson, A.T. *A Grammar of the Greek New Testament in the Light of Historical Research.* Nashville: Broadman, 1934.

Robertson, O. Palmer. 'Is There a Distinctive Future for Ethnic Israel in Romans 11?' in K. Kantzer & S. Gundry (eds), *Perspectives on Evangelical Theology.* Grand Rapids: Baker, 1979.

Robinson, J.A.T. *Christian Morals Today.* Philadelphia: Westminster, 1964.

Robinson, J.A.T. *The Human Face of God.* London: SCM, 1973.

Rodkinson, Michael, (ed), *New Edition of the Babylonian Talmud.* Boston: New Talmud Society, 1918.

Rosen, Ceil & Moshe Rosen. *Christ in the Passover.* Chicago: Moody, 1978.

Sampley, J.P. *Pauline Partnerships in Christ: Christian Community and Commitment in Light of Roman Law.* Philadelphia: Fortress, 1980.

Sanday, William & A.C. Headlam. *A Critical and Exegetical Commentary on the Epistle to the Romans.* ICC. Edinburgh: T. & T. Clark, 1902.

Sanders, E.P. *Paul and Palestinian Judaism.* Philadelphia: Fortress, 1977.

Sanders, E.P. *Paul, the Law and the Jewish People.* Philadelphia: Fortress, 1983.

Sanders, E.P. *Paul.* Past Masters. Oxford: Oxford University Press, 1991.

Sanders, E.P. *Judaism: Practice and Belief 63 BCE – 66CE.* London: SCM, 1992.

Bibliography

Sanders, J. Alvin. 'Dispersion' in *Interpreter's Dictionary of the Bible*. Nashville: Abingdon, 1962.

Schaff, Philip. *A History of the Christian Church*. New York: Charles Scribner's & Sons, 1910.

Schreiner, Thomas R. ' "Works of the Law" in Paul' *Novum Testamentum* 33 (1991).

Schreiner, Thomas R. 'Circumcision' in Gerald F. Hawthorne *et al* (eds), 1993.

Schreiner, Thomas R. 'Law of Christ' in Gerald F. Hawthorne *et al* (eds), 1993.

Schreiner, Thomas R. 'Works of the Law' in Gerald F. Hawthorne *et al* (eds), 1993.

Schreiner, Thomas R. *Romans*. Baker Exegetical Commentary on the New Testament. Grand Rapids: Baker, 1998.

Schweitzer, Albert. *The Mysticism of Paul the Apostle*. London: Black, 1931.

Scott, James M. 'Restoration of Israel' in Gerald F. Hawthorne *et al* (eds), 1993.

Segal, Alan F. *Paul the Convert: the Apostolate and Apostasy of Saul the Pharisee*. New Haven: Yale University Press, 1990.

Seifrid, Mark A. 'Blind Alleys in the Controversy over the Paul of History' *Tyndale Bulletin* 45, 1 (1994).

Seifrid, Mark A. *Justification by Faith: the Origin and Development of a Central Pauline Theme*. Novum Testamentum Supp. 68. Leiden: E.J. Brill, 1992.

Shaw, R.D. *The Pauline Epistles*. Edinburgh: T. & T. Clark, 1910.

Silva, Moises 'Old Testament in Paul' in Gerald F. Hawthorne *et al* (eds), 1993.

Smith, Wilbur M. 'Resurrection' in Everett F. Harrison (ed), *Baker's Dictionary of Theology*. Grand Rapids: Baker, 1960.

Souter, A. 'Did Paul Speak Latin?' *Expositor* 8 (1911).

Sproul, R.C. *Essential Truths of the Christian Faith*. Wheaton, Illinois: Tyndale, 1992.

Stalker, James. *The Life of St Paul*. Edinburgh: T. & T. Clark, 1989.

Steele, David N. & Curtis C. Thomas. *Romans: An Interpretive Outline*. Philadelphia: Presbyterian & Reformed, 1963.

Stein, R.H. 'Jerusalem' in Gerald F. Hawthorne *et al* (eds), 1993.

Stendahl, Krister. *Paul among Jews and Gentiles and Other Essays*. Philadelphia: Fortress, 1976.

Stern, M. 'The Jewish Diaspora' in S. Safrai & M. Stern (eds), *The Jewish People in the First Century: Historical, Geographical, Political History, Social, Cultural and Religious Life*. 2 vols. Philadelphia: Fortress, 1974.

Stott, John. *The Cross of Christ*. Downers Grove, Illinois: Intervarsity, 1986.

Stuhlmacher, Peter. *Biblische Theologie des Neuen Testaments, Bd 1: Grundelegung. Von Jesus zu Paulus*. Göttingen: Vandenhoek & Ruprecht, 1992.

Taylor, Vincent. *The Person of Christ in New Testament Teaching*. London: Macmillan, 1959.

Tenney, Merrill C. *New Testament Survey*. Grand Rapids: Eerdmans, 1961.

Thrall, Margaret. 'The Origin of Pauline Christology' in W. Ward Gasque & Ralph P. Martin (eds), *Apostolic History and the Gospel*. Exeter: Paternoster, 1970.

Tidball, Derek J. 'Social Setting of Mission Churches' in Gerald F. Hawthorne *et al* (eds), 1993.

Torrance, Thomas F. *The Doctrine of Grace in the Apostolic Fathers*. Grand Rapids: Eerdmans, 1959.

Turner, Nigel. *A Grammar of New Testament Greek*. Edinburgh: T. & T. Clark, 1963.

Turner, Nigel. *Grammatical Insights into the New Testament*. Edinburgh: T. & T. Clark, 1965.

Van Unnik, W.C. *Tarsus or Jerusalem: the City of Paul's Youth*. Translated by G. Ogg. London: Epworth, 1962.

Vos, Geerhardus. *Biblical Theology*. Grand Rapids: Eerdmans, 1948.

Vos, Geerhardus. *The Pauline Eschatology*. Princeton University Press, 1930. Reprinted Grand Rapids: Eerdmans, 1979.

Warfield, B.B. *The Person and Work of Christ* Philadelphia: Presbyterian & Reformed, 1950.

Warfield, B.B. 'Paul and Women Speaking in Church' *The Presbyterian* (Oct. 30, 1919).

Warfield, B.B. *The Inspiration and Authority of the Bible*. Philadelphia: Presbyterian & Reformed, 1948.

Warfield, B.B. 'Faith' in *Biblical and Theological Studies*. Philadelphia: Presbyterian & Reformed, 1952.

Warfield, B.B. 'The Westminster Doctrine of the Holy Spirit' in John E. Meeter (ed), *Selected Shorter Writings of Benjamin B. Warfield*. Nutley, New Jersey: Presbyterian & Reformed, 1973.

Warfield, B.B. *The Lord of Glory*. Reprint, Grand Rapids: Baker, 1974.

Warfield, B.B. 'Imputation' in *New Schaff-Herzog Encyclopaedia of Religious Knowledge*. Reprint, Grand Rapids: Baker, 1977.

Warren, M.A.C. *The Gospel of Victory*. London: SCM, 1995.

Wells, David F. *The Person of Christ*. Westchester, Illinois: Crossway, 1984.

Wenham, David. *Paul: Follower of Jesus or Founder of Christianity?* Grand Rapids: Eerdmans, 1995.

Westcott, B.F. *The Epistle to the Hebrews*. 1892. Reprinted Grand Rapids: Eerdmans, 1970.

Westerholm, S. *Israel's Law and the Church's Faith: Paul and his Recent Interpreters*. Grand Rapids: Eerdmans, 1988.

Witherington, Ben, III. *The Paul Quest: the Renewed Search for the Jew of Tarsus*. Downers Grove, Illinois: Intervarsity, 1998.

Witherow, Thomas. 'Earliest Textual Documentation' in David W. Hall & Joseph H. Hall (eds), 1994.

Witherow, Thomas. 'The Apostolic Church: Which is it?' in David W. Hall & Joseph H. Hall (eds), 1994.

Wright, N.T. *What Saint Paul Really Said*. Grand Rapids: Eerdmans, 1997.

Wright, N.T. 'Harpagmos and the Meaning of Philippians ii 5-11' *Journal of Theological Studies* 37 (Oct. 1986).

Wright, N.T. *Colossians and Philemon*. TNTC. Grand Rapids: Eerdmans, 1986.

Zuck, Ray B. *Teaching as Paul Taught*. Grand Rapids: Baker, 1998.

Persons Index

Alford, Dean 22
Allen, Roland 213, 584
Anslem 448
Aquinas 444, n. 28, 439, n. 24, 448, 451, n.35, 487
Aristotle 487
Arnold, Clinton E. 233, n.23,n.24, 239, n.31
Athanasius 297, 448
Augustine 60, 212, 276, 298, 4 4 8, 450, n.35
Banks, Robert 584
Barclay, John 11,n.9
Barclay, William 99, n.21, 302
Barker, Glenn W. 303, n.13
Barnett, P.W 13, n.14, 217, 218, n.3
Barrett, C.K 9, 12, 13, n. 14, 26, n. 18, 36, n.9, 192, n. 28, 193, n.29, 194, n.32, 196, n.37, 201, n.52, 207, n.55, 459, n.50, 460, n.54
Baur, Ferdinand Christian 12, 13
Bavinck, J.H. 584
Baxter, Richard 502, n.13
Beitzel, Barry 117
Beckwith, R.T 522
Beker, J.C. 308
Bentham, Jeremy 484, n.19, 4 8 5, n.19
Berkhof, Louis 320, n.4, 328,4 3 6, n.22, 545, n.21
Berkouwer, C. G. 545, n.21
Betz, H.D. 473, n.5
Blauw, J 584
Bloesch, Donald G. 429, 430, 431, 432
Boer de ,W.P. 578, n.22
Bonar, Horatius 421, 440
Bornkamm, Gunther 9, 51, n. 20, 58, 67, n.27, 94, n. 13, 106, 207, n.55
Bosch, David J. 584
Bousset, W 12, 306, n.1
Bowers W. Paul 572, 573, 574

Bowring, John 373
Brown, Raymond 141, 367, n.18
Bruce, F. F 11, n. 9, 18, 23, 24, 31,32, 34, 42, 46, n.5,6, 47, 49, n. 16, 50, n.17, 52, 53, 55, 56, n.2, 58, n.8,n.9, 60, n.16, 65, n.26, 67, n.27, 69, n.28, 72, 73, n.33, 80, n.48, 90, n.2, n.4, 91, n.6, 93, n.9, n.10, 94, 95, n.14, n.16, 99, 100, n.25, 101, n.29, n.30, n.31, 102, 103, 104, 105, n.37, 106, 110, 111,n.48, 112, n.49, 114, 115, n.1, 116, n.2, 119, 123, n.14, 124, n.18, 125, n.19, 127, 128, 129, n.30, 132, n.32, 140, n.2, 155, n.3, 156, n.7, 158, 159, n.12, 160, n.14, 163, 164, n.22, 166, n.23, 167, n.24, 169, n.27, 177, n.1, 181, n.5, 182, n.7, 184, n.11, 185, 186, 187, 188, 193, n.28, 194, 196, n.36, n.37, 207, n.55, 222, n.7, 223,n.9, n.11, 224, n.12-14, 225, n.15, n.16, 227, n.17, 228, n.18, 236, n.29, 238, n.31, 246, 248, n.5, 263, 265, 266, 282, n.55, 296, n.3, 298, n.6, 302, 303, 384, 470, 471, 472, n.4, 473, n.5, 482, 486, 535, n.7
Buchanan, James 536
Buchsel, Fredrich 390
Bultmann, Rudolph 13, 63, 452
Burkitt, F.C 110, n.47
Burton, E, DeW 132, n.32
Byrne, B 465, n.63
Calvin, John 212, 265, n.28, 427, 446, 467, 558
Carson, Donald A. 188, n.22, 303, 562
Castilli, E.A 578, n.22
Cerfaux, L 307, n.3
Chafer, Lewis Sperry 472
Chase, F.C 162, n.17
Chrysotom 212
Clark, Andrew 485, n.19, 578, n.22
Clarkson, Margaret 343
Clayton, Norman 421
Clement of Alexandria 275
Clowney, Edmund P. 505, n.16, 515, n.11
Cole, R.A., 106

Conn, Harvey 584
Conybeare, W.J 56,n.5, 161, n.15, 166, n,.23, 181, n.5, 227, n.17, 229, n.19, 248, n.4
Cooper, Karl T. 65, n. 25, 461, n.55
Corley, Bruce 59, n.11
Cranfield, C. E. B. 207, n.55, 218,n.4, 452, 453, 505, n.16
Cullman, Oscar 109, 262, 303, 356, n.2, 367, 532
Cyprian 577
Dahl, N.A. 584
Dana, H.E 261, n.15
Davies, W.D. 389, n. 1, 454.
Dayton, Edward R. 584
Deissmann, Adolf 307
Demarest, Bruce 269
Denney, James 391
Dibelius, Marin 125, n.19
Dittenberger, W 365, n.14
Dodd, C.H. 36, 40, 123, 124, n.17, 231, 389, 390, 473, n.5, 530
Drane, John W 207, n.55
Dunn, James. D. G. 13, 18, 63, 64, 93,n.11, 102, 103, 111, n.47, 207, n.55, 264, 266, 277, n.44, 307, n.2, 408, n.2, 420, 452, 453, 461, 462, 465
Dupont, Jacques 35, n.8, 65, n. 25
Ellerton, John 55
Ellingworth, Paul 279, n.45
Ellis, E. Earle 465, n.64, 575, n.15, 584
Epicurus 161, n.16
Epimenedes 47
Eusebius 142, 274, 275, 297
Evans, C.A., 294, 343, 348, 540, n.11
Everts, Janet Meyer 62, n.20
Fadus, Cuspius 65
Fee, Gordon D. 196, n.37, 242, n.32, 253, n.8
Finney, Charles G. 564, 565, 566
Fitzmyer, J.A. 307,n.4, 465, n.63
Fletcher, Joseph 484, 485, n.20, 486
Forsyth, P.T. 394
Frame, J.E 169, n. 27, 567, n.6

Franzmann, Martin 10, n. 6, 32, 54, n.27, 99, n.24, 100, n.28, 106, 132, n.32, 133, n.33, 137, 138, n.36, 150, 151, n.20, 169, n.26, 170, n.28, 173, n.29, 174, 182, n.6, 187, n.20, 196, n.38, n.39, 197, n.40-43, 198, n.44-47, 199, n.48, n.49, 200, n.50, 202, n.53, 204, 205, n.54, 211, n.58, 216, 231, n.21, 234, 242, n.33, 250, 252, 253, n.9, 256, n.11, 269, 281, n.51, 283, n.56, 288, 295, 303, 304
Fraser, David 584
Fung, Ronald,Y.K 106, 110, n.46, 132, n.32, 381, 382, n.9, 459, 460, n.50, 473, n.5
Gaffin, Richard B. 76, 299, 300, 301, 304, 480, n.10
Geisler, Norman 573
George, Timothy 448, n.33, 450
Georgi, Dieter 12
Gerstner, John H. 439, n.24
Gibbs, J.G. 307, n. 2
Gifford, E.H 360, 361
Gilliland, Dean S. 584
Gilson, Etienne 488
Glasser, Arthur 584
Graham, Billy 565
Grant, Michael 9, 17, 18, n.3
Green, Joel. B 32, n.1, 35, n.9
Green, Michael 584
Gundry, Robert H. 59, n.12
Gutbrod, W 463, n.60
Guthrie, Donald 106, 132, n.32, 253, n.8, 259, 269, 274, 280, n.48, 281, n.52, 282
Habermas, Gary 94, n. 13
Hafemann, Scott. J 465, n.64
Hagner, Donald, A 282, n.55
Hahn, F 584
Haldane, Robert 316, n.1
Hall, Joseph H. 577, n.19
Hanson, Walter 132,n.32
Harris, Murray, J 260, n. 14, 365, n.15
Harris, Laird 274, n.42, 279, n.48, 299, n.7

Persons Index

Harrison, Everett F. 398
Hawthorne, Gerald 242, n.32
Hays, R.B 473, n.5
Headlam, Arthur 207, n.55
Hegesippus 142
Hemer, C.J. 36,n.9, 106
Hemings, Sally 487
Hendricksen, William 169, n. 27, 230, n.20, 545, n.21
Hengel, Martin 19, 36, n. 9, 46, n.3, 47, 48, 49, n.15, 51, 57, n.5, 91, n.6, 92, 95, n.16
Héring, J. 269
Hickling, C.J.A 308
Hiebert, Paul 584, 585
Hinson, E.G. 585
Hock, Robert 117, 572, n.10, 585
Hodge, Charles 316, n.1, 327, 328
Hoekema, Anthony, A. 545, n.21, 546, n.22
Hofius ,O 473, n.5
Hooker, M.D. 233, n.24
Hooker, Richard 448, 449
Horsley, G. H. R. 85,n.56
Howard, G 132, n.32
Howson, J.S 56, n.5, 161,n.15, 166, n.23, 181, n.5, 229, n.19, 248, n.4
Hughes, Philip E. 201, n.52, 263, 264, 265, n.27, 272, n.38
Hume, David 487
Ignatius 577, n. 19
Jefferson, Thomas 486, 487
Jerome 276, 298
Jewett, Paul King 513, n.8
Jewett, Robert 19
Jones, David C. 511, 512
Josephus 45, n.3, 46, n.3, 49, n.16, 90, n.3, 97,n.20, 98, 100, n.27, 107, n.41, 143, 390, 458
Kane, Herbert J. 585
Kant 485, n.19
Kasemann, Ernst 307
Kellar, W. Phillip 502, n.12
Kelly, J.N.D 253, n.8, 311, n.15, 450, n.35

Kevan, Ernst F. 481
Kim, Seyoon 56, n.3
Kirk, Kenneth Escott 450, n.35
Kistemaker, Simon J. 201, n.52, 277, n.45, 282, n.55
Knight, George W 253, n.8, 474, n.6, 477, n.7, 506, n.17
Knox, J 246, n.2
Kraabel, A.T., 540, n.11
Kruse, C.G. 461, n.55
Kummel, W,G 106
Kuyper, Abraham 424, n.5
Ladd, George Eldon 42, 43,n.15, 60, n.16, 72, 73, 75, 76, 77, 81, 82,n.51, 94, n. 13, 270, 271,n.37, 281,n.51, 317, 390, n.10, 448, n.32, 479, 534, n.6, 544, 549, n.27, 552, 553, n.33.
Laertius, Dogenes 31, n.1
Lane, William, L 279, 282, n.55, 303, n.13
Landis, R.W 326
Leary, T.J. 121, n.11
Liddle, H.G. 85, n.56
Lightfoot, J. B 12, 19, 106, 207, n.55
Lincoln, A.T. 238, n.31
Lindsell, Harold 585
Lingenfelter, Sherwood G. 585
Lock, Walter 253, n.8, 365
Longenecker, Richard 56, n.3, 64, 65, n.25, 115, n.1, 116, n.3, 123, 127, 132, n.32, 147, 150, 233, n.24, 459, n.48
Loy, Matthias 469, 472
Lutgert, W 12
Luther, Martin 22, 60, 138, 212, 302, 307, 427, 433, 454, 465, 466, 467, 468, 471, 560, 573
Lyttleton, George 55, n.1, 56
Machen, Gresham. J 11, n. 8, 17, 56, n.3, 62 ,n.21, 63, 70, n.29, 95, 106, 118, 119, n.7,n.8
MacMillan, J. Douglas 502, n.12
Macrae, Allan. A 74, n.35
Malalas, John 45
Malherbe, A.J 572, n.10
Malina, Bruce 45, n.1
Manson, T.W. 110, 127

Mantey, J.R. 261, n.15
Marcion 294, 296, 384
Maritain, J 486
Marshall, Howard 36,n.9, 169, n.27, 264
Martin, Ralph P. 201, n.52, 233, n.24, 236, n.29, 239, n.31, 242, n.32, 308
Martyr, Justin 295
Marxsen, Willi 106
McCheyne, Robert Murray 582
Meeks, W.A 572, n.10, 585
Melanchthon 472
Metzger, Bruce M. 9, n. 1, 148, n.17, 362, 363, 532, n.3, 547, n.24
Michaels, J. Ramsey 303, n.13
Mills, Watson E 9, n. 1
Milton, John 159, n.13, 215, 245
Minear, Paul 495, n.1
Moffat, James 106, 282, n.55
Montefiore, C.G. 453
Moo, Douglas 207, n.55, 303, 316, n.1, 376, 377, 378, 455, 456, 457, n.45, 458, 460, n.51, 461, n.56, 462, n.59
Moore, G.F. 453
Morris, L 169, n.27, 266, 283, n.55, 303, 316, n.1, 389, 390, 391, 392, 434, 575, n.14
Moulton, James, H. 364
Munck, Johannes 186, n.16
Muratori, Lodovico 296
Murray, Gilbert 23
Murray, John 207, n.55, 316, n.1, 323, 327, 328, 341, 352, 353, 354, n.3, 391, 399, 434, 438, 439, n.23, 442, n.26, 444, 445, n.29, 472, n.3, 474, n.6, 489, 490, n.26, n.27, 491, 503, n.14, 512, 513, n.9, n.10, 515, 516, n.12, 518, 531, n.1, 535, 536, 537, 544, 545, 548, n.25, 551, 555, n.38, 576, n.18
Myers, Fredrick 45, 56, 139, 1 5 3 , 177, 245
Narborough, F.D.V. 269, n.31
Neander, August 12

Neill, Stephen 257
Neusner 457, n.45
Neve, J.L 450, n.35
Nevius, John L. 585
Newman, John Henry 17, 115, 215
Neyrey, Jerome 45, n.1
Nicator, Seleucus 97
Nicole, Roger R. 389, 390
O'Brien P.T. 233, n.24, 234, 236, n.29, 242, n.32, 500, n.8, 577, n.21, 585
Origen 274
Osborne, Grant 94, n.13
Owen, John 578
Packer, J.I. 466
Pannenberg, Wolfhart, 94, n.13
Patzia, Arthur G. 236, n.29
Paul, Pope John 11 467, 468, n.71, 562
Philo 46, n. 3, 390
Picirilli, Robert 117, n.4, 232, n.22
Pinnock, Clark 323, n.8, 573
Plato 487
Plevnik, J 306, 307
Plummer, Alfred 201, n.52, 533, n.4
Pollock, Thomas Benson 493
Raisanen, Heikki 308
Rambach, Johann J. 507
Ramsay, William 106, 585
Reaume, John D. 511, n.6
Reitzenstein, R 11
Rex, Maricus 98
Ridderbos, Herman 12, n. 10, 75, 82, 83, n.52, 106, 132, n.32, 296, 300, 301, 317, 356, n.2, 358, n.4, 421, n.1, 422, n.3, 453, n.37, 465, n.64, 481, n.11, 495, n.3, 499, 500, n.7, n.9, 516, 517, n.13, 521, n.17, n.18, 527, n.20, 532, n.2, 533, n.5, 545, n.21, 548, n.25, 551, n.32, 553, n.34, n.37
Robertson, A.T. 425, n.6
Robertson, O.Palmer 545, n.21
Robinson, J.A.T 263, 264, n.21, 266, 482, 483, 484, n.16, 486
Robinson, Robert 355
Rodkinson, Michael 96, n.17
Rosen, Moishe 522, n.19

Persons Index

Sampley, J.P 572, n.10
Sanday, William 207, n.55
Sanders, E.P 13, 51, n.19, 65, n.25, 308, 316, n.1, 356, n.1, 452, 453, 454, 455, 456, 457, 458, 460, 461, 462, 465
Schaff, Philip 20, 22, 23, n.14, 47, 56, n.3, 89, 142, n.6, 143, 280, 281, 282, n.53
Schreiner, Thomas. 155, n.3, 207, n.55, 465, n.64, 473, n.5
Schwemer, Anna Maria 91, n.6, 92, 95, n.16
Scofield, C.I 145, 383, n.11
Scott, James M. 107, n.41, 540, n.11
Scott, R. 85, n.56
Scotus, Duns 487
Segal, Alan 308, n.8
Seifrid, Mark A. 455, n.43, 459, n.49, 461, n.55, 542, n.13
Senior, D 585
Sharp, Granville 364, n.12
Shaw, R. D 20, 22, n.12
Shedd, W.G.T. 326
Sheler, Jeffrey L. 9
Silva, Moises 310, n.13
Smith, Wilbur. M 42
Souter, A 47
Spielberg, Steven 587
Spittler, Russell 573
Sproul, R.C. 300, n. 10, 429, 430, 431, 432
Stalker, James 70
Stanley, Dean 21
Steck, O.J. 540, n.11
Steele, David 339, n.6
Stein, Robert 103, 104, n.35, 149, 150, n.18
Stendahl, Krister 60
Stern, M 51, n. 19
Stott, John 394
Stuhlmacher, P. 307, n.6

Stuhlmueller, C 585
Tacitus 100, n.26
Taylor, Vincent 262, 367
Tenney, Merrill 99, 106, 108, 112, 133, n.33, 137, 163, n.18, 190, 191, n.27, 201, n.51, 244
Theodore of Mopsuestia 276
Thomas, Curtis 339, n.6
Thornwell, James Henley 326
Thrall, Margaret 70, n.30
Tidball, Derek J. 571, 574
Torrance, Thomas F. 451, n.35
Turner, Nigel 48, n. 12, 261, 363, 366
Valentinus 276, 294, n.1
van Unnik, W.C 48
Verkuyl, Johannes 585
Vos, Geerhardus 17, 83, 277, n. 43, 338, n.5, 339, 340, 388, 455, n.44, 550
Wagner, Peter C. 584
Warfield, B.B. 263, 265, n.28, 299, n.7, 326, 358, 359, n.5, 370, 371, 375, n.3, 398, 399, 406, n.1, 423, n.4, 506, n.17
Warren, M.A.C. 394
Wells, David F. 359, n.6
Wenham, David 11, n.8, 27, n.19
Westcott, B.F 283, n.55, 398
Westerholm, Stephen 461, n.55, 465, n.62
Wickham, E.C. 262
Witherington III, Ben 20, n.10, 45, n.1, 46, n.4, 48, n.14, 61, n.18, 121, n.11, 279, n.47
Witherow, Thomas 577, n.20
Wright, N.T 86, n.57, 233, n.24, 236, n.29, 242, n.32, 439, n.25, 448, 449, 450, 540, n.11
Zeno, Cypriote 161, n.16
Zinzendorf, Nikolaus Ludwig von 421
Zuck, Roy B. 572, n.11, 585

Scripture Index

Genesis
1:26-27 505, 566
1:27 489
1:28 489
2:2 489
2:3 489
2:15 489
2:24 489
3 329, 374
4:1 338
12:1-3 374
12:3 374, 375, 376, 377
13:14-16 374
13:15 376
14:18-20 267, 392
15:6 74, 77, 383, 422, 437, 438, 442, 443
15:18-21 374
17:1-16 374
17:7 374
17:8 376
17:9-14 73
17:10-14 122, 139, 521
17:23-24 74
18:19 338
21:9 335, 542
22:9-10 443
22:12 443
22:16-18 374
22:17 377
22:18 375, 376
25:22-23 337
32:20 390
34:25-26 48

Exodus
2:25 338
3:16 501
3:18 501
4:24-26 73
4:29 501
9:8 518
12:11-14 524
12:17 74
12:24-27 524
12:46 524
13:8-10 524
15:26 359
17:5-6 501
17:8-16 359
18:13-27 501
19:7 501
20:1-17 471
20:3 568
20:5 48
20:5-6 444
21 477
23:7 432, 433
24:1 501
24:6 518
24:8 518
24:9-11 501
25:16 10
29:16 518
29:20 518
29:20-21 518
29:21 518
31:13 359
32:10 389
32:30 390
34:14 48

Leviticus
1:4 388
1:5 518
1:11 518
3:2 388, 518
3:8 388, 518
3:13 388, 518
4:4 388
4:6 518
4:15 388, 501
4:17 518
4:24 388
4:29 388
4:33 388
5:9 518
6:27 518
7:2 518
7:14 518
8:11 518
8:19 518
8:24 518
8:30 518
9:1-2 501
9:12 518
9:18 518
10:1-2 574
12:3 74
14:7 518
14:16 518
14:27 518
14:51 518

16:5 10
16:14 518
16:15 518
16:19 518
16:21-22 388
17:6 518
19:18 470, 473, 476, 480
24:10-16 58
26:11-12 407

Numbers
6:24-27 515
8:7 518
8:12 388
11:14-25 501
15:37-41 118
16:35-40 574
16:41-50 390
18:17 518
19:4 518
19:18 518
19:19 518
19:21 518
23:9 462
25:6-13 48
25:11-13 390

Deuteronomy
4:24 48, 258, 273
5:6-21 471
5:9 48
5:23 501
6:4-9 118
6:5 480
6:15 48
9:3 258, 273
11:13-21 118
12:29-32 574
16:1-8 524
17:7 58
21:22-23 53
22:15-17 501
25:1 434, 435
27:1 501
28:58-59 96
29:9 96
32:21 548
33:2 497
33:4 497

Joshua
5:2-9 73
7:6 501

8:33 501
Judges
4–5 506
6:24 359
21:16 501
1 Samuel
15:22-23 453
1 Kings
2:38-39 92
8:1-3 501
8:32 435
18:40 49
2 Kings
10:16-17 48
10:30 48
16:13 518
16:15 518
17:6-23 45
22:14-20 506
24:14-15 45
25:11 45
1 Chronicles
21:16 501
2 Chronicles
6:23 435
26:16-19 574
29:22 518
30:16 518
35:11 518
Ezra
1:1-4 539
9–10 34
Nehemiah
2:1-6 539
8–10 34
13 34
Job
32:2 434
40:1 569
40:8 569
Psalms
1:6 338
2:8 264
5:9 318
8 285
10:7 318
14:1-3 318
19:1 567
23 502
24:1 358
32:1-2 383, 422

614

Scripture Index

Psalms, cont.
36:1   318
40:6-8   453
45:4   261, 366
45:6   261, 365, 366
45:6-7   260, 313, 365
51:16-17   453
62:12   444
68   497
68:8   498
68:16   498
68:17   498
68:18   358
68:26   498
69:9   49
78:2   78
78:38-39   96
80:3   423
80:7   423
80:19   423
83:5-6   335
87   498
102   262, 367
102:25-27   260, 261, 263, 313, 358, 365, 366
106:30-31   48
107:32   501
110:1-4   267, 392
110:4   267, 392
126:6   586
130:4   466
139:7-10   359
140:3   318
143:2   435
144:3   338

Proverbs
1:7   568
3:34   580
11:30   586
13:13   444
15:8   445
16:14   389
17:15   434, 435
17:23   435
21:4   445
25:21-22   444
26:4   570
26:5   570

Ecclesiastes
12:14   444

Isaiah
1:9   120
1:10-20   453
5:23   432, 434
6:9-10   228, 310, 407
8:14   358
10:22   120
13:6   359
29:10   541
40-55   440
40:9   83
40:13   358
42:1-4   473
42:6   51
42:10   80
43:6-7   515
43:10-12   51
43:21   51
43:19   80
44:28   539
45:23   358
45:24-25   439
49:1-2   54
49:6   310
52:7   83, 310
52:13–53:12   473
53:4   388
53:5   388
53:6   388
53:7   388
53:8   388
53:10   388
53:11   388
53:12   388
55:3-5   377
55:11   175
58:13   480
59:7-8   318
61:1-2   84
61:10   439
65:17   80, 531
66:22   531

Jeremiah
1:5   54, 338
19:5   575
23:6   359
31:18   423
31:31   380
31:31-34   61, 74, 380
31:33   489
41:17-18   46
44:1ff   46

Lamentations
5:21   423

Ezekiel
8:1   501
33:7-9   563, 564
34   502
35:5   335
36:25   514, 518
36:25-26   516
36:26-27   74
43:18   518
44:9   146

Daniel
1:1-14   45
12:3   586

Hosea
13:5   338

Joel
2:28-32   76
2:32   358

Amos
2:6-8   453
3:2   338
4:4-5   453
5:21-24   453
5:26-27   34
9   145
9:11-12   144, 146, 148
9:12   145

Micah
6:6-8   453

Nahum
1:15   84

Habakkuk
2:4   77, 422
2:14   81

Zechariah
7:2   390
8:22   390

Malachi
1:2-3   335
1:9   390
3:1   77
4:4-6   34
4:5-6   77

Matthew
3:11   511, 516, 517
5:12   444
5:21–6:18   453
6:1   444
6:2   444
6:4   444
6:12   447
6:16   444
6:18   444
6:20   444
7:12   476
7:22-23   338
9:13   344
9:36   502
9:37   586
10:17   118
10:33   271
10:41   444, 537
11:10   77
12:21   272
12:37   10, 435
13   80
13:3-9   77
13:12   271
13:17   78
13:18-23   77
13:20-21   76
13:21   271
13:24-30   77
13:31-33   77
13:34-35   78
13:36-43   77
13:44-45   77
13:47-50   77
13:55   142
15:3-9   61
16:17   345
16:18   81
16:21   44
16:27   444
19:28   77
19:29   444
20:28   10
21:42-43   541
21:43   544
22:37-40   480, 485, 489, 490
23   61
23:1-39   453
23:15   25, 51
23:29-38   541
23:32   542
24:1-35   541
24:38   546
25:1-13   538
25:26-30   271
25:31-46   77, 444
26:26   509
26:28   10, 509
26:29   525
28:18-20   508
28:19   508, 510
28:19-20   519

Mark
1:1   85
1:8   516, 517
1:15   36, 78
2:7   344
4:11-12   75, 82
4:26-29   77
6:3   142
7:1-13   453
7:5   50
7:6-8   61
7:7-8   575
7:13   61
10:45   10, 399
12:29-31   480
12:31   476
13:9   118
14:22   509
14:24   10, 509
14:25   525
14:58   44

Luke
1:1   31, 35
1:13-17   54
1:17   77
1:35   406
2:34   124
3:16   516, 517
4:16-21   118
4:17-21   84
5:8   406
5:32   344
6:37-38   444
7:29   435
7:36-50   442
10:2   586
10:29   435
11:4   447
11:20   78, 80
11:37-54   453
12:11   33
16:15   435
17:20-21   78
18:9-14   10
19:9   349
21:28   400
22:16   525
22:18   524, 525
22:19   509
22:19-20   10
22:20   509
22:66   501
24:46-47   42
24:47   11, 587

John
1:9   320, 569
1:33   516, 517
2:12   142
2:17   49
2:19   44
2:21   44
3:5   516
3:8   345
3:14-16   11
3:18   12
3:22   507
3:26   507
4:1-2   507
4:21-24   57
4:22-24   575
4:35   13, 586
5:24-25   76
5:28-29   44
5:29   444
6:29   11
6:35   508
6:40   11, 508
6:41   508
6:44   345
6:45   345
6:47   11, 508
6:51   509
6:52   508
6:53   508
6:54   508
6:54-58   508
6:56   508
6:57   508
6:58   508
6:59   508
6:63   508
6:66   508
6:69   406
7:3   142
7:5   142
7:10   142
7:17   149
7:39   183
10:11   10, 502
10:14   502
10:15   10
11:25-26   11
13-17   508
14:6   89
14:15   480
15:5   569
15:14   480
17:2   320

18:13   143
18:28   524
19:36   524

Acts
1-12   191
1:1   31, 32, 35
1:1-6:7   33
1:5   516, 517
1:8   518
1:13   32, 216
1:14   142
1:15ff   216
1:22   43
2   11, 411
2:9-11   46
2:12   127
2:14-36   42, 216
2:14-39   37
2:17   518
2:17-21   76
2:22   42
2:22-36   75
2:24   43
2:24-32   42
2:30   43
2:31   43
2:33   516, 517, 518
2:36   42, 43
2:37-41   510
2:38   43, 123, 510
2:42   29, 521
3:1-4:23   32
3:1   57
3:1ff   216
3:13-26   37
3:15   42, 43
3:26   43
4:2   43
4:8ff   216
4:10   42, 43
4:10-12   38
4:12   44, 587
4:19ff   216
4:33   43
4:36   92, 116, 154, 280
5:3ff   216
5:20   57
5:29ff   216
5:30   42, 43
5:30-32   38
5:31   423
5:34-39   52
6:1   56

6:1-6   506
6:1-7   504
6:5   56
6:7   32, 219
6:8–9:31   33
6:9-10   52, 57
7:43   34
7:53   497
7:56   73
7:58   31, 46, 58
8   100, 190
8:1   31, 58
8:2   218
8:3   31, 58
8:12-17   510
8:14   32, 505, 576
8:16   510
8:35-38   510
9   59, 64
9:1ff   31
9:1-2   58
9:1-9   278
9:1-19   59
9:1-28   64
9:2   89
9:3-4   64
9:7   64, 71
9:9   72
9:11-16   92
9:15-16   86
9:18   509, 510, 519
9:20   61, 68, 90, 91
9:20-22   89
9:22   61, 68, 90
9:23   90, 92
9:23-24   33
9:23-25   91
9:26-28   68, 94
9:26-30   92, 216
9:27   68, 90, 94, 95
9:29   33, 56, 93
9:30   95, 117
9:31   32, 93
9:32–12:24   33
10   220
10:9   57
10:9ff   216
10:14   57
10:19   148
10:27-28   57
10:30   57
10:36-43   38
10:39   42
10:40   43

Scripture Index

Acts, cont.
10:42 43
10:43 123, 432, 560
10:44 518
10:44-45 74
10:44-47 148
10:44-48 510
10:48 126, 140, 510
11 109
11:2-3 57
11:12 148
11:14 157, 519
11:15 518
11:15-17 148
11:15-18 74
11:18 140, 423
11:19 99
11:19-21 99, 218
11:20 58, 99
11:20-21 99
11:25-26 97, 117
11:26 95, 100
11:27-30 68, 100, 101, 216
11:28 65, 100
11:29 28
11:29-30 65
11:30 100, 101, 106, 502, 576
11:30–12:25 117
12 100, 101
12:2 32, 142
12:17 109, 142
12:19 126
12:24 32, 97
12:25 28, 100, 101, 216
12:25–16:5 33
12:26 495
13 11, 100
13–28 493, 494
13:1 101, 148
13:1-3 494, 505, 576
13:1–14:28 115
13:2 407
13:2-3 116
13:3 154
13:4-12 116
13:4-14:26 28
13:4–14:28 117
13:6-12 34
13:7 116
13:9 121, 148
13:11 116
13:13 123
13:14-16ff 118
13:15-41 123
13:17-41 39
13:27-30 380
13:27-36 357
13:27-30 378
13:29 42
13:30 43
13:30-31 94
13:30-41 75
13:33 43
13:34 43
13:37 43
13:38-39 10, 14, 92, 123, 309, 422, 466
13:39 108, 141, 439, 462
13:40-41 44
13:42-43 124
13:43-50 119
13:44 124
13:45 124
13:45 33
13:46 120
13:46-47 44, 124, 310
13:46-48 423
13:48-49 124
13:50 33, 124
13:51-52 124
13:52 44
14:1 124
14:2 33
14:3 124
14:4-6 125
14:4 32
14:6-7 125
14:8-10 125
14:11-18 125
14:12 121
14:14 32
14:15-17 125
14:16 563
14:17 312
14:19 33
14:19-20 125
14:20-21 125
14:21-23 126
14:22 175
14:23 493, 494, 502, 576
14:24-25 126
14:25 123
14:26 116, 126
14:26-27 126
14:26-28 28
14:27 148, 506, 576
14:28 126
15 105, 106, 107, 108, 109, 110,
15 111, 114, 117, 122, 129, 130, 131, 139, 217, 220, 506, 576
15:1-2 110, 112
15:1 112, 122, 127, 139, 194, 217, 459
15:2 109, 111, 130, 502, 576
15:3 140, 148, 494
15:4 141, 494
15:5 122, 127, 141, 194, 217, 219, 459
15:6 141
15:5 94
15:7 94
15:7-11 69, 144
15:8 148
15:12 74, 121, 124, 141, 144, 148, 558
15:13-17 145
15:13-19 148
15:13-21 145
15:13-22 217
15:13 142, 143
15:15 145, 146
15:16-17 146
15:21 149
15:22 148, 153, 154
15:22-31 494
15:23 143
15:23-29 110, 112
15:24 122, 139, 193, 217, 493
15:24-29 147
15:25 121
15:25-26 111
15:28 149
15:31 151
15:32 148, 153, 154
15:32-36 152
15:36 151
15:36-40 154
15:36–18:22 29, 153
15:37-39 121, 123
15:39 113
15:39–18:22 117
15:41 155, 238, 494
16:1 125, 155, 250
16:1-3 150
16:1-6 153
16:3 155, 185
16:4 147, 151, 155, 494, 576
16:5 32, 151, 155, 494
16:6 107
16:6-19:20 33
16:8-10 154
16:9 155
16:10 155, 191
16:10-17 35, 156
16:12 156
16:12-40 154
16:13-15 156, 510
16:14 119, 424
16:15 157, 520
16:16 157
16:16-21 34
16:17 89, 156
16:21 156
16:25-34 157
16:30-34 510
16:31 157, 519
16:31-34 157, 520
16:32 520
16:33 157, 519
16:34 157, 519
16:37 148, 154, 157
16:37-39 34
16:38 154, 157
16:40 158, 231
17:1-9 154
17:2-3 158, 357, 378, 380
17:3 43
17:4 119, 159
17:5 33, 159
17:6 43, 158
17:7 159
17:8 158
17:10-14 154, 159
17:11 159

Acts, cont.
17:12 159
17:13 33
17:13-15 159
17:16 28, 161
17:16-17 161
17:16-34 154
17:17 119
17:18 43, 161, 162
17:18-21 162
17:21 160, 162
17:22-31 39, 125
17:23 161
17:24 312
17:25 312
17:26 47
17:28 47
17:29 312
17:30 85, 563
17:31 43, 44
17:32 43
18:1 28
18:1-18 153, 164
18:2 164, 185
18:2-3 182
18:3 46, 96, 164
18:4 164
18:5 164, 168, 169
18:5-8 28
18:6 33, 564
18:7 119
18:8 510, 511, 519
18:9ff 96
18:11 29, 164, 167
18:12-13 33
18:12-17 34
18:18-22 165
18:18 29, 150, 164
18:19-21 154, 184
18:19 178, 182, 192
18:22 154, 217
18:23 107, 113, 178
18:23–21:15 29
18:23–21:16 177
18:23–21:17 117
18:24-25 182
18:25-26 89
18:26 182
18:27 182, 424
18:28 182
19:1 28, 182
19:1-3 519
19:1-7 182, 510
19:2 183

19:4 183
19:5 510
19:6 518
19:8 184, 185
19:8-10 183
19:9 89, 184
19:10 28, 177, 184, 185
19:11-20 184
19:13 184
19:20 32, 184
19:20-21 29
19:21 185, 191
19:21-22 185
19:21–28:31 33
19:22 178, 185, 191, 192, 247
19:23-27 34
19:23-41 181, 185
19:23 89
19:27 181
19:30-41 179
19:31 34, 179
19:35-41 34
19:35 180
20 576
20:1 247
20:1-2 29
20:1-3 188
20:2-3 205, 247
20:3 29, 34, 183
20:3-4 189
20:4 206, 222, 224
20:5–21:18 35, 156
20:5 189, 222, 247
20:6 156, 189, 206, 232
20:7 480
20:7-12 189
20:13-16 189
20:15 247
20:16 28, 189
20:17-38 189
20:17 493, 502, 576
20:18-21 184
20:22 190
20:24 13, 25, 291, 570
20:25 184
20:26 564
20:27 184, 563
20:28 10, 42, 400, 401, 407, 494, 496, 502

20:31 177, 185
20:34-35 46
20:35 577
21:1-3 190
21:4 190
21:8-9 190
21:8 190
21:10-16 190
21:11 34
21:17–28:16 215
21:17-40 222
21:17 217
21:18ff 143
21:18 142, 191
21:18-25 219
21:18ff 143
21:19 218
21:20 218
21:20-21 219, 282
21:20-24 248
21:20-25 281
21:21-24 57
21:23-24 57
21:24 219
21:25 219
21:26 150
21:27 34, 219
21:37 47
21:40 47
22 64
22:1-21 64
22:1-29 223
22:2 47
22:3 47, 48, 66
22:3-4 50
22:3-16 59
22:4 58, 89, 546
22:5 58, 501
22:6-7 64
22:8 369
22:9 64, 70
22:14 64
22:15 86
22:16 509, 510, 519
22:17-21 92, 93
22:18 86
22:19 58
22:20 58
22:21 86
22:28 46
22:30 223
23:1-9 223

23:6 42, 43, 49, 223
23:11 96, 223
23:12-35 223
23:16 47
23:23–28:31 29
23:26 220
23:31-32 117
24:1-9 34
24:5-6 223
24:10-21 223
24:14, 22 89
24:15 42, 44, 535, 551
24:17 216, 218
24:21 43
24:22-23 34, 223
24:24-25 224
24:26-27 224
24:27 29
25:1-12 34, 224
25:2-3 34
25:7 34
25:9 42
25:11-12 232
25:13–26:1 224
25:19 43
25:24 34
26 64
26:2-18 59
26:2-23 224
26:4-5 50, 66
26:4-23 64
26:5 49, 50
26:6-7 87, 379
26:8 42, 43
26:10 49, 58
26:10-12 58
26:11-12 59
26:13-14 64, 70
26:14 47, 62
26:15-18 87
26:16 64
26:19 64
26:22-23 87, 379, 380
26:24-27 224
26:23 42, 43
26:28 100
26:28-29 224
26:30-32 34
26:31-32 224
27 117
27:1–28:16 35, 117, 156

Scripture Index 619

Acts, cont.
27:1 224, 232
27:2 224
27:3-44 225
27:7-8 247
27:14 225
28:1-10 225
28:11-15 225
28:14 225
28:15 211, 538
28:16-31 228
28:16 35, 228, 231
28:17-20 228
28:20 379
28:21-22 228
28:22 310
28:23 228, 379
28:24-28 228
28:25-27 407
28:25-28 44
28:28 310
28:30 29, 34, 228
28:30-31 229, 231
28:31 29, 32, 34

Romans
1 315, 329, 462
1:1 288, 359, 421, 465, 582
1:1-3 357
1:1-7 208
1:1-17 208
1:1–3:21 567
1:2 384
1:2-3 378
1:2-4 40
1:3-4 311, 360, 370, 406
1:3 27, 313, 356
1:4 43,73,313, 406
1:5 85, 499
1:1-5 85
1:7 312, 345, 358
1:8-15 208
1:8 500
1:9-15 189
1:9 313, 359, 465
1:14 563
1:16-17 10, 208, 465, 470
1:16 120, 421, 466, 499
1:17 60, 422, 438, 439, 450, 466, 559

1:18–3:20 208, 315, 390
1:18-28 318
1:18-32 208
1:18 315, 320, 322, 390, 391, 393, 567
1:18ff 321
1:19-20 567
1:20-21 567
1:20-25 312
1:20 321, 567
1:21-23 397
1:21-30 479
1:21 320, 321, 567
1:24-31 26
1:24-28 315
1:24 316, 391
1:25 321, 362
1:26 316, 391, 475
1:27 475
1:28 49, 316, 390, 567
1:29-31 475
1:29-32 318
1:29 480
1:30 480
1:32 320, 321, 322, 391, 475, 567
2 315, 321
2:1–3:8 316
2:1-16 208
2:5-10 444
2:5 322, 391, 393
2:6 536
2:7 535, 553
2:8-9 535
2:8 322
2:9-10 120
2:10 535
2:11 313
2:14ff 475
2:14-15 485, 567
2:15 320, 475
2:16 40, 391
2:17-3:8 208
2:17 464
2:17ff 329
2:19-20 51
2:21-24 462
2:21 480
2:22-23 452, 463
2:22 479, 480
2:24 51

2:25-29 375, 463
2:25-27 74, 463
2:28-29 74, 542
3 322, 425
3:1-20 315
3:1-2 54
3:2 295, 384
3:4-6 313
3:4 435, 451, 569
3:5 322, 391, 393
3:8 206, 441
3:9-18 316
3:9-20 208
3:9-23 318
3:9 462, 567
3:10-18 316
3:19-21 567
3:19-20 316, 436
3:19 462, 474
3:20-22 425
3:20 426, 452, 462, 463
3:21-4:25 316
3:21 384, 466
3:21-22 439, 465
3:21-23 208
3:21-25 463
3:21-26 470
3:21-28 464
3:21-31 208, 390
3:21-32 567
3:22 10, 438, 440
3:23ff 466
3:24 313, 399
3:24ff 387, 466
3:24-25 10, 439
3:24-26 208
3:24-27 399
3:25 10, 389, 391, 395, 401, 438
3:25-26 387, 432
3:26 313
3:27 463
3:27-28 208, 429, 465
3:28 10, 69, 425, 438, 450, 452, 462, 463
3:29-30 208, 463, 466
3:30 311, 355, 438
3:31 208
4 425
4:1 54

4:1ff 466
4:1-3 383
4:1-5 359, 464
4:1-8 208, 470
4:1-25 208
4:2 426, 452, 463
4:2-3 422
4:3 425, 436, 437
4:3-8 378
4:4 436
4:4-5 463
4:5 10, 346, 425, 432, 436,437, 450, 560
4:5-8 465
4:6 436, 452
4:6-7 346, 383, 433, 560
4:6-8 422, 447
4:8 436
4:9 436, 437
4:9-12 74, 208
4:10 436
4:10-11 375
4:11 74, 122, 139, 437, 517
4:11-12 377
4:13 347, 349, 374, 377
4:13-14 426
4:13-17 208
4:14 347, 349
4:15 322, 329
4:16 428, 438, 495
4:18-25 208
4:22 437
4:23 437
4:23ff 466
4:23-24 437
4:24 432
4:25 44, 76, 385
5 327, 328, 329, 408
5:1 76, 346, 433, 438, 439,465, 470, 560
5:1-7 246
5:1-11:36 208
5:1 77
5:1-11 209
5:2 359, 438
5:5 518
5:6 10, 388

Romans, cont
5:8   10, 313, 387, 388, 395
5:9   10, 76, 77, 322, 350, 439, 465, 470
5:10   313, 350, 356, 387, 395, 470, 553
5:10-11   395
5:11   395, 398
5:12   323, 324, 325, 326, 386
5:12-19   317, 323, 327
5:12-18   324
5:12-21   209, 316
5:13-14   324, 325
5:13-17   324
5:14   325, 327
5:14ff   386
5:15   313, 324, 325, 386
5:15-17   324
5:16   325, 326, 435
5:16ff   466
5:17   325, 549
5:17-19   440, 465
5:18   324, 325, 326
5:18-19   386, 471
5:19   324, 325, 326, 346, 388, 433, 437, 560
5:20   329
5:21   322, 324, 326
6   408, 409, 417, 418, 515
6-7   441
6:1-10   402
6:1-14   442, 472
6:1–7:6   209
6:1–7:25   208, 209
6:2   409
6:2ff   409
6:2-6   518
6:2-7   329
6:3   510
6:3-4   82, 510, 512, 530
6:3-5   519
6:3-6   515
6:4   82, 324, 385, 408
6:5   408

6:6   322, 408, 409, 410
6:8   408
6:11   410
6:13   418
6:14   69, 322, 470, 536
6:15   472
6:17   80, 322
6:17-22   382
6:18   322, 495
6:19   322
6:20   322
6:21-22   401
6:22   418, 495
6:23   322
7   418
7:1-6   466
7:4-6   402
7:5   329
7:7   475
7:7-8   480
7:7-13   329
7:7-25   59, 63, 209
7:9-11   51, 52
7:12   474
7:13   476
7:14   474
7:14-25   51, 59, 60, 209, 322
7:16   474
7:18   323
7:24   398
8   323, 347, 417, 418
8:1   401, 439
8:1-4   209
8:1-39   208
8:2-4   329
8:2ff   409
8:3   276, 313, 356, 388
8:3f   323
8:4   418, 472, 475
8:5-11   209
8:7   475
8:7-8   319
8:7-9   569
8:9   405, 407, 414, 419, 420
8:9-10   404, 407
8:9-11   407
8:10-11   531
8:11   405, 407, 414
8:12-17   209

8:13   410, 418
8:14   346, 348, 418, 420
8:14-17   495
8:15   346, 405, 495
8:15-16   347, 407
8:16   346, 349
8:17   347, 349, 352, 408, 495, 498
8:17-25   209
8:18   353
8:18-22   531
8:19   346
8:19ff   44
8:19-21   351
8:19-23   403, 534, 552
8:20-22   329
8:21   346, 349
8:23   346, 347, 351, 352, 353, 399, 407, 535, 555
8:26-27   210, 407
8:28   210, 332, 334
8:28-29   345
8:28-30   210, 343
8:28-39   337
8:29   313, 332, 339, 348, 352, 353, 356, 395, 408, 495, 555
8:29-30   49, 338, 340
8:30   332, 344, 349, 350
8:32   313, 356, 388
8:33   332, 338, 436, 495
8:33-34   435, 439
8:34   40, 277
8:35   210, 359
8:38-39   210
9   334
9–11   313
9:1-5   54
9:1–11:36   208, 210
9:1-33   210
9:3   466
9:4   54, 346
9:5   10, 40, 265, 313, 357, 360, 361, 362, 363, 365, 368, 369, 406
9:6   120, 334, 382
9:6-9   542
9:7-9   334
9:8   346, 349
9:10   54
9:11   332, 340
9:11-12   340
9:11-13   332, 335, 337, 339
9:11-23   312
9:12   338, 452
9:13   335
9:14   340
9:16   336
9:17   337, 375
9:18   336
9:20   569
9:22   322
9:22-23   351, 554
9:23   332
9:25   348
9:26   348
9:27   495, 541
9:27-29   120, 543
9:30–10:21   460
9:30   438
9:30-32   460
9:31   460
9:31-32   460, 542
9:32   358, 452
9:33   358, 541
10:1-21   210
10:2-4   439, 460
10:3   73, 439, 542
10:4   73, 401, 426, 450
10:5-8   139
10:6   438
10:6-9   122
10:8-9   40
10:8ff   466
10:9   311
10:9-13   358
10:11-15   310
10:12-13   358
10:15   83
10:21   541
11:1-36   210
11:2   332, 543
11:5   332, 338, 340, 452, 543

Scripture Index

Romans, cont.
11:5-6   450, 461
11:5-7   495
11:6   65, 428, 452
11:7   332
11:7-10   543
11:8   542
11:8-10   541
11:11   548, 549
11:12   499, 543, 544, 545,547, 548, 549
11:13   30
11:13-24   495
11:14   548
11:15   395, 543, 544, 545, 547, 549
11:16-24   382
11:17-24   546
11:18   382
11:23   543
11:23-24   549
11:24   543
11:25   499, 543, 544, 545, 546, 548
11:25-26   543, 546
11:26   382, 398, 544, 546, 547, 548
11:26-32   544
11:28   332, 382, 542, 543
11:29   345
11:30   324
11:30-31   546
11:31   545, 547, 548
11:32   547
11:33   340
11:33-34   313
11:36   276, 312, 362, 569
12–16   491
12:1   419
12:1-2   466, 476
12:1-21   210
12:1–15:13   210
12:2   81, 410
12:4-5   496
12:6-8   415
12:17   499
12:19   277, 322

13:1-5   320
13:1-7   210, 416
13:2   419
13:3   419
13:4   419
13:8-10   479
13:8-19   480
13:8–15:13   210
13:9   417, 476, 480
13:10   417, 476, 489
13:11   82, 350, 419
13:13-14   212
13:14   323
14–15   417
14:1-2   220
14:1-15   149
14:1–15:2   501
14:1–15:13   207, 571
14:10   535
14:12   535
14:15   388, 501
14:17   414, 549, 553
14:19   501
15:1   220, 419
15:3   27
15:8   275
15:8-9   376
15:8-12   310
15:13   406, 414
15:14-33   210, 246
15:16   407
15:19   47, 113, 188, 246, 407
15:19-21   499
15:20   13
15:22-29   189
15:24   47, 206, 493, 499
15:25-26   29, 205
15:28   246
15:30   358
15:30-31   276
15:31   218
16:1   29, 189, 206, 495, 505
16:1-27   211
16:3   182, 211
16:4   495
16:5   183, 495
16:13   332
16:16   359, 495, 496
16:18   357
16:20   317, 358, 402

16:21   206
16:23   164, 206, 495
16:25-26   78, 79
16:26   313
16:27   311

1 Corinthians
1–4   196
1:2   345, 358, 410, 493, 495, 496
1:3   312, 358
1:8   349, 359
1:8-9   345
1:9   313, 344, 345
1:11   186
1:12   101, 182
1:13   496, 515
1:13-17   510
1:14   164, 206, 510
1:14-16   164
1:15   515
1:16   157, 510, 519
1:17   510, 511
1:18-25   400
1:18   350
1:20   47
1:23   53
1:24   387
1:26-30   345
1:26-31   583
1:28-31   429
1:30   359, 399, 400, 401
2:1-4   49
2:1-5   565
2:2   25, 163, 164
2:4   43
2:4-5   570
2:6-13   294
2:7   332
2:7-8   78
2:8   265, 387
2:10-11   406, 407
2:12-13   293
2:13   27
2:14   319, 569
2:16   358
3:1   500
3:4   182
3:5-7   570
3:8-9   537
3:9   495
3:10   572
3:10-11   192
3:10-17   12, 192

3:11-15   537
3:12-15   419, 535
3:13   444
3:15   350
3:16   414
3:16-17   495
3:17   49
3:18-20   194
3:22   101, 350
4:5   444, 537
4:8   195, 330, 531
4:8-13   196
4:9   276
4:9-13   570
4:12   46
4:15-16   577
4:16   500
4:17   186, 251, 496, 572
5   194
5–6   197
5:1-13   197
5:2   195
5:5   317
5:7   10, 74, 382, 388, 524
5:9   30, 186, 299
6:2   538
6:6   424
6:8   424
6:9   479, 480
6:9-10   478
6:10   480
6:11   80, 197, 407, 410, 439, 516
6:12   149, 194
6:12-20   185, 194, 197
6:14   385
6:19   414
6:19-20   400
6:20   401, 419
7   195
7:1   186, 197
7:2-5   197
7:5   317, 345
7:8   50
7:9   197
7:10   197
7:11   395, 419
7:14   520
7:17   495, 496
7:17ff   419
7:19   417, 473, 477

1 Cor., cont.
7:22 344
7:23 197, 400, 401
7:25 197
7:30 400
7:36 197
7:38 197
8 501
8-10 417
8:1 197, 501
8:1-3 194
8:1-13 149
8:1-11:1 198
8:3 338
8:4 312, 355
8:5 167, 312
8:6 26, 198, 311, 312
8:9-11 220
8:10 194
8:11 194, 198, 388
8:13 221
9:1 59, 64
9:1-18 46
9:5 101, 142, 311
9:6 113, 154, 582
9:8ff 478
9:16 103
9:19 563
9:19-20 218
9:19-23 150, 563
9:20-21 479
9:21 470, 473, 536
9:22 219
9:24 166
9:26 166
9:27 166
10:1 54
10:1-13 198
10:2 510, 515
10:11 80
10:13 313
10:14-17 522
10:14-22 198
10:16 521, 525
10:20 312, 317, 402
10:21 521, 522
10:21-22 358
10:23 149, 194
10:23-33 149
10:23–11:1 198
10:25-33 149
10:26 358
10:31 583
10:31–11:1 221
10:32 496
10:32–11:1 577
11 416
11-14 574
11:1 419, 500
11:2 186, 197, 419
11:2-16 195, 198
11:2–14:40 198
11:3 198
11:7-10 198
11:8 478
11:9 478
11:10 498
11:12 312
11:14 475
11:16 496
11:17-34 198
11:19 149
11:20 495, 522
11:22 496
11:23-25 27
11:23-30 523
11:24 388, 509, 522, 524
11:25 125, 509, 522
11:26 508, 524, 525, 546
11:27 523
11:28 523
11:29 523
11:30-32 322
12-14 195, 198
12:1 197
12:1-11 407
12:2 312
12:3 311, 407
12:3-6 313
12:4-6 358, 407
12:7-11 415
12:11 406
12:12ff 496
12:12-27 496
12:13 411, 499, 510, 511, 515, 516
12:27 494
12:28 496
12:28-30 415
12:31 49, 414
13 22, 417, 501
13:4-7 414
13:6 204
13:9 194
13:12 553
13:13 414
14 416, 572, 575
14:1, 12, 39 49
14:3 501
14:26-33 572
14:33 416, 495, 496
14:33-36 195, 198, 505
14:34 478
14:40 416
15 195, 199
15:1 197
15:1-34 199
15:2 350
15:3 10, 41, 385, 386, 388
15:3-4 40, 357, 379
15:3-5 94, 95, 311, 370
15:3-7 94
15:4 385
15:4-8 27
15:5 101, 550
15:5-7 68, 95
15:7 142, 550
15:8 60, 558
15:8-10 59, 64
15:9 359, 496, 582
15:11 124, 193, 311
15:14-19 385
15:20 385
15:20-26 550
15:20ff 44
15:21 386
15:21-22 323
15:21-23 76
15:22 386
15:23 537, 550
15:23-25 75
15:24 550, 551, 552
15:24-26 551
15:24-28 266
15:25 546, 550, 551
15:25-27 534
15:26 551
15:28 313, 534
15:29 510, 511
15:33 47
15:35-38 199
15:42ff 553
15:42-43 538
15:44-49 386
15:45 406
15:50 82
15:51 558
15:51-54 535
15:51-55 551
15:51-57 351, 554
15:54 551
15:55 551
15:56-58 538
16:1 197, 496
16:1-2 178
16:1-3 496
16:1-4 199
16:2 480
16:5 29, 113, 191
16:5-6 186, 187
16:5-9 199
16:6 499
16:8 29, 192
16:10 29, 186, 251
16:10-12 199
16:11 499
16:12 182, 186
16:15 164, 511
16:15-20 199
16:17 186
16:19 192, 495, 496
16:21-24 199
16:22 371, 466
2 Corinthians
1–7 202
1:1 201, 276, 493, 495, 496
1:1-11 202
1:2 312, 358
1:3 312, 362
1:8 200
1:8-10 231
1:12–2:17 202
1:15 187
1:16 499
1:17 201
1:18-20 313
1:19 148, 154, 313
1:21-22 412

ical Index

Scripture Index

2 Cor., cont
1:22 76, 407, 412
2:1 187
2:2 187
2:3-11 188
2:4 187, 299
2:5-8 188
2:6 322
2:9 187, 299
2:11 317
2:12 29, 187, 200
2:13 29, 200, 255
2:14 403
2:15 350
2:16 82
3 61, 277
3:1 194, 201
3:1-3 202
3:2 49
3:2-3 495
3:3 405
3:4-4:6 202
3:6 277
3:7 54
3:8 54
3:11 54, 276
3:14 277
3:15 384
4:2-3 565
4:2-5 570
4:4 82, 312, 317, 402
4:5 202, 565, 582
4:6 82, 359
4:7-12 202
4:13-5:5 202
4:16 330
4:16-18 203, 531
4:17 353, 553
5 330
5:1 533
5:1-10 531, 532, 533
5:2 533
5:2-4 533, 534
5:3 532, 533
5:4 82
5:4-5 535
5:5 76, 387, 412
5:6 533, 534
5:6-10 202
5:7 304
5:8 350, 533
5:9 419

5:10 419, 444, 535, 537
5:11-15 203
5:14 419
5:14-15 402, 441
5:15 387, 388, 442
5:16-21 203
5:17 80, 82, 329, 409, 495, 531
5:17-21 395
5:18 395
5:18ff 387
5:18-21 495
5:19 395, 398
5:20 395
5:20-21 439
5:21 387, 388, 433, 437, 439, 448, 470, 560
6:1-2 203
6:2 80
6:3 49
6:3-10 203
6:5 46
6:9 49
6:11-7:1 203
6:14 185
6:15 317, 402
6:16 407
6:16-18 495
6:18 346
7:2-4 203
7:5 200
7:5-7 29
7:5-16 188, 203
7:6ff 256
7:7 49
7:11 49
7:13-14 29
8:1 200, 496
8:1-4 496
8:1-7 203
8:6 29, 256
8:8-15 203
8:9 265, 356, 388
8:16-9:5 203
8:17-18 256
8:18 495
8:19 359
8:20-23 201
8:23 359
9:2 49, 200
9:6-15 203
10–13 203

10:1 26, 201
10:1-12 204
10:1-18 204
10:2 201
10:3-5 565
10:6 322
10:8 201
10:10 201
10:12-18 192
10:13-18 204
10:15-16 47
11:1-6 204
11:1-12:21 204
11:2 49
11:3 317
11:4-5 194
11:5 12, 192
11:7 201
11:7-15 204
11:8 495
11:12-15 317
11:12 192
11:13 96, 192, 193, 194, 221
11:14 312, 317, 402
11:15 193, 194
11:16-33 204
11:16-12:10 91
11:19 195
11:19-20 194
11:22-23 194
11:23f 192, 194
11:24 118, 216
11:25 117
11:23-27 46, 96
11:23-28 570
11:26 194, 216, 221
11:28 495
11:31 362, 363
11:32-33 67, 89
11:32ff 91
12:1-4 558
12:1-10 204
12:2-9 96
12:4 553
12:5 582
12:7 123, 317, 402
12:8-9 358
12:9-10 91, 582
12:11 192
12:11-18 204
12:12 74, 116, 558
12:13 495

12:14 187, 200
12:16 201
12:18 29, 256
12:19-21 204
13:1 200
13:1-2 187
13:1-10 204
13:2 187, 188, 205
13:5 523
13:11-14 204
13:14 313, 358, 407

Galatians
1–2 72, 111
1 103
1:1-5 133
1:1 103, 278, 294, 310, 385
1:2 105, 107, 493
1:3 133, 312, 358
1:4 75, 81, 359, 388
1:5 362
1:6 133, 359
1:6-7 104, 422, 450
1:6-9 466
1:6-10 133
1:6-2:21 111, 133
1:7 359
1:8-9 422, 450, 466, 559
1:8 137
1:10 359, 582
1:11-12 294, 557
1:11-24 133
1:11 103
1:12 69, 103, 278
1:13 49, 60, 359, 496
1:13-14 50, 60, 66
1:13-17 64
1:13-2:21 66
1:14 48
1:15 54, 344, 359
1:15-16 59, 310
1:15-17 67
1:16 65, 90, 313
1:17 72, 89, 90
1:17-18 117
1:18 86, 92, 94, 95, 101
1:18-19 68, 92, 93, 94, 216, 278, 311

Galatians, cont.
1:19 94, 142
1:20 67
1:21 93, 153, 496
1:22 68, 496
1:22-23 95
1:23 68
1:21-24 109
1:24 359
2 92, 105, 109, 110, 113, 140, 220, 408
2:1 65, 68, 95, 109, 112, 114, 255
2:1-3 150
2:1-10 28, 65, 100, 101, 102, 105, 106, 109, 110, 114, 117, 134, 216, 220, 278
2:2 68, 102, 103, 109, 193, 216, 217, 371
2:3 110, 255
2:3-5 111
2:4 111, 127, 139, 194, 221
2:4-5 110
2:5 128, 140
2:6 68, 102, 110, 193, 217
2:6-9 371
2:7 68
2:7-8 30, 101
2:7-9 101, 192
2:8 68
2:8-9 311
2:9 12, 101, 102, 112, 142, 193, 217, 278
2:10 68, 110
2:11f 112
2:11-13 112, 140
2:11-14 69, 101, 126
2:11-21 126, 134, 466
2:12 57, 112, 122, 126, 139, 142, 217
2:12-13 128
2:13 112, 113, 141
2:14 128, 140
2:14-21 129
2:15-16 464
2:16 10, 69, 76, 426, 438, 440, 450, 452, 464, 470
2:17 439
2:19 408
2:19-20 129
2:20 313, 388, 408, 410
2:20-21 426
2:21 450, 461
3–4 347, 348, 408
3:1 107
3:1-5 74, 134, 441
3:1-14 134, 466
3:1–4:31 134
3:1–5:12 129
3:2 464
3:3 131
3:5 124, 148, 464
3:6 375, 437
3:6-9 134
3:7 348, 375
3:8 359, 375, 384, 438
3:9 375
3:10 387, 452, 461, 464
3:10ff 329
3:10-11 450, 464
3:10-14 74, 134
3:11 422, 426, 438
3:13 53, 387, 388, 400, 401, 470
3:13-14 377
3:14 349
3:15-18 134
3:15-29 134
3:15-4:7 74
3:16 27, 376
3:16-17 377
3:19 276, 497
3:19-24 134
3:20 311
3:22 319, 359
3:23 77, 401
3:24 438, 472
3:24-25 472
3:25 77
3:25-29 134
3:26 346, 348, 450
3:26-27 510
3:27 510, 519
3:27-28 515
3:28 128, 499
3:29 347, 349, 376, 377, 495
4 61
4:1 347, 541
4:1-2 348
4:1-3 541
4:1-6 221
4:1-7 495, 541
4:1-11 135
4:1-31 135
4:2-5 401
4:3 233, 500, 541
4:4 27, 77, 313, 356
4:4-5 347, 400
4:5 346, 401
4:6 313, 348, 356, 405, 407
4:6-7 346
4:7 347, 498
4:8 312, 359
4:9 233, 495, 541
4:12-20 135
4:13 125
4:13-15 123
4:20 130
4:21-31 135, 335, 459
4:22-30 540
4:25 90, 91, 276, 459, 542
4:26 276, 495
4:29 335, 542
5 323
5:1 401
5:1-4 466
5:1-12 135
5:1-24 135
5:1-6:10 135
5:2 450, 461
5:3 450, 461
5:2-6 74
5:4 426, 428, 450
5:6 417, 443, 476, 477
5:10 130
5:11 25, 51, 52
5:12 193
5:13 151, 323, 345, 476
5:13-15 135
5:13-6:10 473
5:14 417, 470, 473, 490
5:16 418, 419
5:16-18 407
5:16-24 135
5:18 416
5:22 359, 413, 414
5:22-23 407
5:25-26 135
5:25–6:6 135
5:26 480
6:1-5 135
6:2 419, 473
6:6 135
6:7-9 444
6:7-10 135, 419
6:8 82
6:11-18 135
6:12-16 381, 466
6:14 25, 582
6:15 381
6:15-16 495
6:16 120, 381
6:17 125
6:18 359

Ephesians
1–3 238
1:1 495, 521
1:1-2 239
1:2 312, 347, 358
1:3 347, 362
1:3-4 423
1:3-5 359
1:3-14 312, 313, 344, 395
1:4 339, 353, 555
1:4-5 341, 347
1:5 332, 341, 346, 353, 555
1:7 10, 238, 399, 400, 401
1:9 332, 333, 341
1:9-10 79
1:10 534
1:11 332, 334, 341, 359
1:13 405

Scripture Index

Ephesians, cont.
1:13-14   407, 412
1:14   76, 239, 399, 400, 411
1:15-23   239
1:17   312, 347, 405
1:17-18   344
1:17-23   344
1:18   238
1:20   385
1:22   496, 497
1:23   495, 497
2:1   322
2:1-3   239, 319, 409
2:1-7   402
2:1-10   239, 329
2:1-22   239
2:2   312, 317, 329, 402
2:2-3   322
2:3   322, 323
2:4   238
2:4-5   345, 409
2:4-6   239
2:4-10   313, 344
2:5   82, 322, 408, 409
2:6   82, 408, 531, 549
2:7   238
2:8   349, 359, 409
2:8-9   424
2:8-10   239, 443
2:9   359, 452
2:10   239, 332, 418, 536
2:11   382
2:11-12   239
2:11-13   380
2:11-21   104
2:11-22   239
2:12   395
2:12-13   322
2:13-18   239
2:14   359
2:14-17   396
2:15   80, 470, 471
2:16   395, 497
2:17   379
2:18   314, 347, 407
2:19   276, 381, 495
2:19-22   239
2:20   415, 558
2:20-22   495
2:21   540
2:22   407
3:1   29, 229, 230
3:1-13   558
3:1-19   239
3:2-13   239
3:3-5   78, 79
3:3-6   558
3:5   415
3:6   411
3:8   238, 571, 582
3:9   312
3:9-10   333
3:10   338, 496
3:11   332, 333, 395
3:14   347
3:14-15   312, 495, 515
3:14-19   239
3:14-21   344
3:16   238, 406
3:17   417
3:18-19   501
3:21   362, 496
3:26   239
4–6   239, 347, 491
4:1   29, 229, 230, 239, 345
4:1ff   419
4:1-16   240
4:3-6   501
4:4   345, 496, 497
4:4-5   510
4:4-6   314, 358, 407
4:5   510, 513
4:6   347
4:8-9   356
4:8-10   358
4:9-10   360
4:11   415
4:11-13   70
4:12   497
4:13   313, 500
4:13-15   501
4:14   501
4:15   359
4:15-16   496
4:16   417, 497
4:17   239
4:17ff   416
4:17-18   569
4:17-19   319
4:17-24   240
4:18   395
4:21   379
4:22   416
4:22-24   329, 410
4:23   410
4:24   416
4:25   478, 480, 496
4:25-26   478
4:25-5:2   240
4:27   317
4:28   478, 480
4:30   76, 399, 400, 407
4:32   400
5   416
5:1   346, 347
5:2   10, 239, 276, 388, 400
5:3   478, 480
5:3-14   240
5:5   359, 478, 479, 480
5:6   322
5:8   239, 347
5:15   239
5:15-20   240
5:16   400
5:17   359
5:18   410
5:18-21   412
5:19-21   413
5:20   347
5:21-6:9   240
5:22-31   495
5:22-32   497
5:22-33   240
5:22-6:9   414
5:23   360
5:23-25   496
5:25   388, 417
5:25-27   496
5:25-29   417
5:26   410
5:27   496
5:30   497
5:31   478
5:31-32   496
5:32   496
6:1   521
6:1ff   416, 419
6:1-4   240
6:2   479
6:2-3   478, 480
6:5-9   240
6:9   358
6:10-17   403
6:10-18   240
6:11   317, 402
6:12   317, 402
6:12-13   317, 402
6:15   500, 577
6:16   317, 402
6:17   403, 407, 500, 577
6:18   499
6:19-20   229, 276
6:19-24   240
6:20   29
6:21   29
6:21-22   230
6:23   347, 358

Philippians
1:1   582
1:1-2   242
1:1-11   242
1:2   312, 358, 359
1:3-8   242
1:4   244
1:5   500
1:6   359
1:7   29, 229, 241
1:9-11   242
1:10   359
1:12-13   242
1:12-14   229
1:12-26   241, 242
1:13   29, 229, 241
1:14   500
1:14-18   242
1:16   29, 241
1:18   65, 244, 497
1:19   359, 405
1:19-26   242
1:20   232, 241
1:21   25, 249
1:21-23   350, 531, 532
1:23   249
1:24   497
1:25   29, 244
1:26   244
1:27   419, 500
1:27-30   241, 242
1:27-2:2   243
1:27-2:18   243
1:28   424
1:29   425
2:1   65

Philippians, cont.
2:1-10   65
2:1-18   242
2:3-11   243
2:5-7   27
2:6   10, 313
2:6-7   356
2:6-11   26, 311, 350, 370
2:7   388
2:8   388, 471
2:9   276, 277
2:9-11   85
2:10   358
2:10-11   534
2:11   354, 555
2:12-13   410, 418, 419, 447
2:12-18   243
2:13   332
2:15   346
2:16   244, 359
2:17   244
2:18   244
2:19   497
2:19-23   243
2:19-30   243
2:20-22   251
2:24   29, 243, 247
2:25   241
2:25-30   243
2:26   241
2:27   241
2:28   244
2:29   241, 244
3:1   244
3:1-11   243
3:1-21   241
3:1-4:1   243
3:2   193
3:3   244, 382
3:3-11   495
3:4-6   50, 66
3:4-8   61
3:4-11   59
3:5   47
3:6   48
3:7-9   25, 291, 570
3:8   96
3:8-9   437, 466
3:9   10, 426, 438, 439
3:10   408
3:10-14   70

3:12   60, 65
3:12, 14   49
3:12-17   243
3:13-14   25
3:14   166, 330, 345
3:15   497
3:17   578
3:18-4:1   243
3:20   360, 408
3:20-21   537
3:21   352, 535
4:1   166, 244
4:2-3   241, 243
4:2-9   243
4:3   158
4:4   241, 244
4:4-7   243
4:5   499
4:7   359
4:8-9   243
4:9   359, 500, 578
4:10   244
4:10-18   241
4:10-20   244
4:11-13   244
4:14   241
4:14-18   244
4:18   241
4:19-20   244
4:20   362
4:21-23   244
4:22   29, 33, 35, 229, 241

Colossians
1:1   276
1:1-14   234
1:2   312, 359
1:4-8   232
1:6   359, 499
1:7   177
1:9   233
1:10   419, 500
1:13   75, 76, 81, 82, 234, 313, 317, 355, 357, 359, 398, 402, 531, 549
1:14   398, 399, 401
1:15   353
1:15-18   235
1:15-19   26
1:15-20   9, 313, 360, 369, 370
1:15-23   235

1:15-2:23   234
1:16   233, 312
1:16-17   313, 357
1:17   321, 569
1:18   25, 353, 495, 496
1:19   368, 369
1:19-22   396
1:19-23   235
1:20   10, 395, 403
1:21   395
1:22   395
1:23   499
1:24   496
1:24-25   235
1:24-2:5   235
1:25   359
1:25-26   78, 79
1:26-27   235
1:27   359
1:28   233, 572
2:1-5   235
2:2   368, 501
2:3   233, 368, 568, 569
2:6-7   235
2:6-23   235
2:8   233, 235
2:9   9, 313, 360, 361, 368, 369
2:9-10   235
2:10   233
2:11   233
2:11-12   74, 382, 513, 515, 516, 517, 518, 521
2:11-14   74
2:11-15   235
2:12   234, 385, 408, 510
2:13   408
2:13-15   403
2:14   530
2:14f   81
2:15   233, 317, 402
2:16-17   233
2:16-19   235
2:17   276, 277, 368
2:18   233
2:19   358
2:20-23   235, 575
2:23   233, 323

3:1   234, 408
3:1-4   234, 402
3:1-11   235
3:1-17   235
3:3   234, 531
3:5   478, 479, 480
3:5ff   416
3:6   322
3:8   416
3:9   478, 480
3:9-10   329, 409, 410
3:9-14   519
3:10   416, 495
3:11   233, 499
3:12   332
3:12-17   235
3:14   501
3:14-15   496
3:15   345, 359
3:15-17   412, 413
3:16   233, 410, 413
3:18-4:1   235
3:20   480, 521
3:23-24   444
3:24   357
4:1   358
4:2-6   236
4:3   230, 499
4:5   233, 400, 500
4:7-9   236
4:7-10   29, 230
4:7-18   236
4:10   101, 123, 154, 230
4:10-14   230
4:12-13   177
4:14   29, 222, 231
4:15   495
4:16   27, 30, 238, 240, 293, 294, 299, 493, 495
4:17   29, 230
4:18   230

1 Thessalonians
1:1   28, 148, 154, 168, 312, 358, 493, 495
1:1-10   170

Scripture Index

1 Thess., cont.
1:1-2:12 170
1:1-3:13 170
1:3 443
1:4 332
1:6 168, 500, 577
1:7-8 500
1:8 359
1:9 312, 359, 499
1:9-10 159
1:10 172, 313, 322, 359, 391, 398, 538
1:14 399
2:1-8 170
2:1-12 170, 172, 565
2:2 359
2:3-12 159
2:6-9 359
2:9 46
2:9-12 170
2:12 172, 345, 359, 419
2:13 27, 159, 294, 359
2:13-16 171
2:14 168, 496
2:14-16 541
2:15 27, 293
2:15-16 542, 543
2:16 172, 322
2:17 168, 171
2:17-18 168
2:17-3:5 171
2:18 317, 402
2:18-20 171
2:19 172
3:1 28, 168
3:1-2 164, 251
3:1-5 171
3:2 28, 276, 359
3:5 168, 317, 402
3:6 28, 168, 169
3:6-10 171
3:11 358
3:11-13 171
3:13 172, 416
4:1-8 171
4:1-12 171
4:1-5:28 171
4:3 172, 359, 416, 480
4:5 359
4:6 322
4:7 345
4:8 359
4:9-10 171
4:11-12 171
4:12 500
4:13-18 171, 172, 531, 535, 537, 538
4:13-5:11 171
4:14 44
4:15 359
4:15-17 538, 539
4:17 553
5:1-11 171, 172, 538
5:9 322
5:10 388
5:11 501
5:12-13 171
5:12-22 171
5:14-15 171
5:16-18 171
5:17 293
5:18 350, 359
5:19-22 171
5:23 172
5:23-24 172, 344, 345
5:23-28 172
5:25 276
5:25-27 172
5:27 27, 294
5:28 172, 359

2 Thessalonians
1:1 29, 148, 154, 172, 493, 496
1:1-2 358
1:1-12 173
1:2 312
1:3-10 173
1:4 173, 496, 499
1:4f 168
1:4-10 174
1:5-10 537
1:6-10 548
1:7 537, 539
1:8 548
1:8-10 535
1:10 553
1:11-12 173
1:12 358
2:1 173, 539
2:1-11 174, 548
2:1-12 173
2:1-17 173
2:2 173
2:4 495
2:8 539, 549
2:9 317
2:10 553
2:13 341, 416
2:13-14 314, 344
2:13-15 173, 174
2:14 345, 352
2:15 27, 293, 294
2:16-17 173
2:17 174
3:1 174, 499
3:1-5 174
3:1-14 174
3:3 317, 402
3:6-12 173
3:6-15 174
3:7 577
3:8 46
3:9 577
3:11-12 174
3:13 174
3:16 174
3:16-18 174
3:17 21, 174
3:18 174

1 Timothy
1:1 360
1:1-2 253
1:2 312, 358
1:3 30, 245, 247, 250, 253
1:3-7 253
1:3-3:16 253
1:4 252
1:4-5 253
1:5 417
1:7 253
1:8-11 252, 253, 477
1:9 480
1:9-10 477, 480
1:10 480
1:10-11 478
1:11 253
1:12-16 59
1:12-17 253
1:13 63, 67
1:13-16 58
1:14 414
1:15 250, 252, 311, 316, 360, 370, 582
1:17 311, 313, 362
1:18 251
1:18-20 253
1:19 252
1:20 317
2 416
2:1 252
2:1-7 253
2:3 360
2:4 252
2:5 252, 311, 355
2:6 252, 388, 399, 401
2:7 572
2:8 254
2:9-15 254
2:12 505
2:13 550
3 502
3:1 250, 311
3:1-7 382
3:1-13 252
3:1-16 254
3:2 503, 504
3:2-7 503, 505
3:3 504
3:4 504
3:5 496, 504
3:6 317, 504
3:7 317, 503
3:8 504
3:8-12 504
3:8-13 506
3:9 505
3:10 505, 550
3:11 505
3:12 503, 504, 505, 506
3:15 495, 496, 497
3:16 252, 311, 360, 369, 370
4:1 407
4:1-6:2 254
4:2 321
4:4 252
4:6-7 252
4:6-16 254
4:7 252, 578
4:7-8 166
4:7-9 311
4:9 250

1 Timothy, cont.
4:10 360
4:14 251
4:15-16 582
5 416
5:1-2 254
5:1-6:2 254
5:3-16 254
5:15 317, 402
5:17ff 478
5:17-25 254
5:18 31
5:20 322
5:21 332
6:1-2 254
6:3-10 255
6:3-12 252
6:11-12 255
6:11-21 255
6:12 345
6:13 252
6:13-16 255
6:15-16 311
6:17 252
6:17-19 255
6:20-21 255

2 Timothy
1:1-2 288
1:2 312, 358
1:3-5 288
1:4 288
1:5 155, 250
1:6 580
1:6-7 289
1:6-18 289
1:7 407
1:8-12 289
1:9 332, 334, 338, 339, 345, 349, 395
1:9b-10 80
1:10 82, 360, 530
1:11 572
1:13 251
1:13-14 289
1:15-18 289
1:16 288
1:16-17 245, 248
1:16-18 30
2:1-7 289
2:1-13 289
2:1-4:5 289
2:5 166
2:8 44

2:8-10 289
2:10 332
2:11 408
2:11-13 289, 311
2:12 271, 408
2:14 289
2:14-26 289
2:15 559
2:15-18 289
2:17 288
2:19 289, 338
2:20-23 290
2:24 572
2:24-26 290
2:25 423
2:26 317, 402
3:1-8 290
3:9 290
3:9-17 290
3:10-13 290
3:10-14 251
3:12 175
3:14 290
3:14-15
3:15 155, 250, 383
3:15-17 290
3:16 31, 293, 294
3:16-17 27, 479
4:1-5 290
4:1-6 559
4:5 85
4:6 248
4:6-8 291, 570
4:7 537
4:7-8 444
4:8 166
4:9 248, 280, 288, 290
4:9-18 290
4:11 123, 154, 222, 248, 278
4:13 245, 247, 248
4:16-17 248, 288
4:18 362
4:18-19 30
4:19 182, 211, 247
4:19-22 290
4:20 206, 245, 247
4:21 248, 288, 290
4:22 291

Titus
1:1 332, 582
1:1-4 256
1:2-3 78, 80

1:3 360
1:4 312, 358, 360
1:5 30, 245, 247, 250, 502, 576
1:5-9 256, 382
1:6 503, 504
1:6-9 503, 505
1:7 504
1:8 504
1:9 504
1:10-16 256
1:12 47, 163
1:14 256
2:1-15 256
2:1-3:8 256
2:8 500
2:10 360
2:13 10, 265, 313, 351, 360, 361, 363, 364, 365, 368, 369, 537, 539, 554
2:14 49, 388, 399, 401
3:1 416
3:1-7 256
3:4 360
3:4-6 314
3:4-8 311
3:5 349, 407, 410, 426, 439, 464, 516
3:6 360, 410
3:7 347, 349
3:8 250, 257, 500
3:9 256
3:9-11 257
3:12 245, 247
3:12-15 257
3:13 182, 499
3:15 256

Philemon
1 29, 230, 276
1-3 237
2 230, 493, 495
3 312
4-7 237
6 500
8-21 237
9 29, 229, 230
10 29
13 29, 230
17 237
18 237

22 247
22-25 237
23 230
23-24 230
24 29, 123, 154, 231

Hebrews
1 9
1:1 258
1:1-2 258, 260
1:1-3 284
1:1-4:13 284
1:2 258, 259, 262, 264, 265, 272, 283, 284, 312, 313, 367
1:2-3 260
1:2-8 312
1:3 258, 262, 264, 265, 273, 284, 312, 367
1:4 260, 264, 265, 276, 277, 283, 284, 285, 365
1:4-14 284, 313
1:5 259, 313
1:6 260, 262, 353, 367
1:6-7 258
1:7 261, 366
1:8 258, 259, 260, 261, 262, 263, 273, 313, 360, 365, 366, 367, 368, 369
1:8-9 260, 261, 365, 366
1:9 264
1:10 258, 259, 262, 367
1:10-12 261, 358, 366
1:11 258
1:11-12 262, 263, 273, 367
1:13 261, 264, 273, 366
1:14 260
2:1-4 271, 283
2:1-3 271
2:1-4 285
2:2 276, 284, 497
2:2-3 259, 273

Scripture Index

Hebrews, cont.
2:3   259, 266, 277, 278
2:3-4   558
2:5   273
2:5-18   285
2:6ff   285
2:7   258, 259, 312
2:9   259, 264, 265, 272
2:10   264, 276
2:12   498
2:12f   264
2:14   259, 317
2:16   264
2:17   259, 272, 389, 392, 497
2:18   259
3:1   259, 275, 285
3:1-6   495
3:2f   264
3:2-6   285
3:3-6   283
3:4   258, 312
3:5-6   260, 285
3:6   259, 272, 285, 313
3:7   407
3:7-19   271, 285
3:7-4:11   283
3:7-4:13   272, 480, 497
3:12   258, 271, 281, 285, 312
3:14   259
4:1   286
4:1-11   283
4:1-13   285
4:3-4   258, 312
4:8   285
4:9   273
4:9-10   285
4:11   271, 273
4:11-16   271
4:12   546
4:14   259, 268, 285, 313, 393
4:14-5:10   286
4:14-12:29   286
4:15   259
5:1-6   264
5:5   259, 261, 313, 366
5:6   266, 392, 514
5:7   259
5:8   259, 264, 265, 313, 388, 471
5:10   264, 266, 392, 514
5:11-6:12   283
5:11-6:20   271, 286
5:12   233, 281
6:1   259, 272, 498
6:1-2   294
6:1-8   294
6:1-14   281
6:2   510, 514
6:3   258, 312
6:4-6   76
6:4-8   272, 276
6:5   76, 273, 283
6:6   259, 271, 313
6:9   272, 283
6:9-12   286
6:13   258
6:13-20   286
6:18   258
6:20   259, 266, 392
7:1-8:2   514
7:1-8:6   266, 392
7:1-10:19   286
7:1   258, 312
7:3   259, 267, 313, 392
7:7   267, 283, 392
7:11   267, 268, 273, 392, 393
7:13-14   267, 393
7:14   259
7:18   267, 276, 392
7:19   267, 283, 392
7:20   267, 392
7:20-21   393
7:21   261, 366
7:22   259, 283
7:23   267, 392
7:24   267, 393
7:24-25   44, 385
7:25   268, 393
7:27   267, 268, 270, 276, 392, 393
7:28   259, 264, 313
8:1   273
8:4   281
8:5   267, 268, 392
8:6   267, 283, 284, 392, 393
8:8-13   380
8:10   489
8:13   281
9   514
9:1-10:18   286
9:5   10
9:7   267, 392
9:8   267, 392
9:9   267, 392
9:10   510, 514, 518
9:11   259, 268, 393
9:11-14   382
9:12   268, 270, 393
9:13   268, 273, 393, 514
9:14   258, 259, 268, 273, 312, 393, 405
9:15   267, 277, 380, 393
9:19   514
9:21   514
9:23   268, 270, 283
9:24   259, 268, 393
9:26   267, 270, 272, 283, 393
9:27   259, 273
9:28   259, 268, 273, 393
10:1   277, 281, 283
10:1ff   267, 392
10:2-4   267, 268, 392, 393
10:4   267, 392
10:8   281
10:10   259, 268, 270, 273, 393
10:11   267, 281, 392
10:12   268, 393
10:12-13   268, 273, 393
10:14   268, 273, 393
10:15   258, 407
10:16   489
10:16-18   268, 393
10:17   407
10:19   259
10:19-25   286
10:19-39   271, 283
10:19-12:29   286
10:22   268, 393, 514
10:22-23   272, 498
10:25   272, 273, 283, 498
10:26   272
10:26-31   286
10:27   273
10:29   258, 259, 313, 405
10:30   277
10:31   258, 273, 312
10:32-12:3   287
10:33   276
10:34   283
10:37   273
10:38   422, 438
10:39   271
11   77, 258
11:3   258, 312
11:7   438
11:9   272, 497
11:13   272, 276, 495, 497
11:16   283
11:22   547
11:26   259, 444
11:32   274, 283
11:35   283
11:40   283
12:1   497
12:2   259
12:3   259
12:4-11   287
12:6-8   322
12:9   258, 312
12:12-29   271
12:14   259
12:15-16   271
12:18-21   258, 497
12:22   272, 276, 495
12:22-24   497
12:23   258, 313, 350
12:24   259, 283, 515
12:26-28   273
12:28   574
12:29   258, 273, 287
13:1-6   287
13:1-19   287
13:5   480
13:7   272, 280, 282, 499

Hebrews, cont.
13:7-19 287
13:8 259, 262, 263, 367
13:10 281
13:11 281
13:12 259, 268, 273, 393
13:14 272, 497
13:15-16 382
13:17 272, 382, 499
13:18-24 274
13:20 259
13:20-25 287
13:21 259, 263
13:22 123, 280, 283
13:23 248, 276, 280
13:24 30, 245, 279, 280
James
1:1 143
2:1 142
2:2 120
2:5 143
2:7 479
2:10-11 479
2:11 480
2:14-17 443
2:14-26 112, 141, 442
2:17 443
2:18 443
2:19 443, 479
2:21 443
2:22 443
2:23 437
2:24 426, 427, 442, 443
2:26 443
4:6 580
5:14 502, 576
1 Peter
1:3-4 44
1:5 350
1:17 444
3:7 505
3:21 509
4:16 100
5:1-2 502, 576
5:12 148, 154
2 Peter
1:3 344
3:6 550
3:7 550
3:10-11 550
3:11 80
3:12 550
3:13 550
3:14 550
3:15 69
3:15-16 27, 293, 294
1 John
2:2 10
2:3 481
2:19 272
3:15 480
4:10 10
5:2-3 474
5:3 481
Revelation
1:3 294
1:5 353
1:10 480, 495
2-3 178
3:14-22 238
4:10-11 446
5:9 80
7:9 353
14:3 80
17:9 226
19:9 525
20 76, 549
21:1 80
21:7 479
21:8 480

SUBJECT INDEX

Part One, 15-304

Acts of the Apostles (see Luke's Acts)
Antioch on the Orontes, excursus on 97-9
Areopagitica 162-63
Areopagus 162
Athens, excursus on 159-61
Barnabas: accompanied Paul on first journey 116-26; attended Jerusalem Conference 139; brought Saul to Antioch 100; disagreement with Paul over John Mark 154; introduced Saul to Peter 92-93; led astray by Peter's hypocrisy 128; testified at Jerusalem Conference 144; vindicated by Jerusalem Conference 147-51
Baur, F. C. (see Tübingen School) 11-3
Circumcision, Paul's argument's against necessity of for salvation 73-4, n 35
Colossians, Epistle to the: content of 234-6; date of writing of 232; dominant theme of 236; occasion of 232-4; place of origin of 230-3
Conversion of Saul 59-72; apologetic for historicity of 66-72; biblical evidence for 64-5; conversion or 'call'? 60-1; date of 65-6; demographic extent of his apostolic call 86-7; his theological deductions from 72-5; rationalizing explanations of 62-4
Corinth, excursus on 165-6; C. K. Barrett's view of Paul's opponents at 192, n 28
Corinthians, First Epistle to the: content of 196-9; date of writing of 192; dominant themes of 199; occasion of 192-6; place of origin of 191-2
Corinthians, Second Epistle to the: content of 202-4; date of writing of 200; dominant themes of 204; occasion of 201; place of origin of 200
Diaspora, meaning of 45, n 3
Ephesians, Epistle to the: content of 238-40; date of writing of 238; dominant themes of 240; occasion of 238; place of origin of 237
Ephesus, excursus on (see Third Missionary Journey) 179-81
Epicurean school 161, n 16
'Eschatological dualism', meaning of 75-83
'Famine relief visit' 100-14; identical with visit of Galatians 2:1-10 101-14; mission fields defined at 104-5
Fifth missionary journey (to Spain?, Crete, Nicopolis, Ephesus, Macedonia, Nicopolis, Troas, Corinth, Miletus, Rome) 245-9
First Corinthians (see *Corinthians, First Epistle to the*)
First missionary journey (to South Galatia) 115-26; results of 136-37
First Thessalonians (see *Thessalonians, First Epistle to the*)
First three missionary journeys, results of 213

631

First Timothy (see *Timothy, First Epistle to*)
Fourth missionary journey (to Rome) 215-29
Galatians, Epistle to the: content of 132-35; date of writing of 130; dominant themes of 136; 'Magna Charta of Christian liberty' 130, 36; occasion of 130-32; place of origin of 130
'God-fearers', meaning of 119
Hebrews, Epistle to the: content of 283-7; date of 280-1; dominant theme of 287; its alleged Philonic Platonism 268-70; its doctrine of apostasy 271-2; occasion of 281-2; place of origin of 280; question of authorship 273-9; theology of 257-73
'Hellenist', meaning of 56, n 4
Jerusalem Conference 139-52; 'conciliar decree' of 147-51; issue addressed at 140; occasion of 139-40; proceedings at 141-47; theological positions present at 140-41
Jesus and Paul, comparison of teachings of 10-11; Machen on 11, n 8
James ('the Just'), excursus on 142-3; his deliverance at the Jerusalem Conference 144-7
Jerusalem, Paul's relationship to the Jerusalem church 216-22; Visits to, Paul's post-conversion: fifth 190, 216-23; first 92-5; fourth 167; second (see 'Famine relief visit') 100-5; third (see Jerusalem Conference) 139-52
John Mark, accompanied Paul on first missionary journey 116; left Paul 121, 123; Paul's ultimate words of approval of 123, n 15
'Judaism': distinction between and Yahwism 61, n 19; meaning of 60, n 17
Kerygma, primitive: Acts record of 35-41; primary emphasis in 41-4
Luke, accompanied Paul on his second journey 155-8; third journey 189-91; fourth journey 224-5; with Paul during second imprisonment 248
Luke's Acts, its purpose 33-5; its record of the primitive *kerygma* 35-41; its title 31-3
Missionary journeys, Paul's: importance of 17-9; method of presenting 16; sources for 16
'Painful visit' to Corinth 186-87
Pastoral letters 249-91
Pauline correspondence, divine authority and canonicity of 293-304
Paul's execution, reasons for 248
Paul's first imprisonment, outcome of 244
Paul's letters, missionary character of 19-26; relationship of to Luke's Acts 28-30
Paul, life of (see also Saul of Tarsus): demographic extent of his apostolic call 86-7; fifth missionary journey 245-9; fifth post-conversion visit to Jerusalem 190, 216-23; first evangelistic efforts 89-92; first missionary journey 115-26; first post-conversion visit to Jerusalem 92-5; first Roman imprisonment 228-9; fourth missionary journey 215-29; fourth post-conversion visit to Jerusalem 167; his conversion 59-72; his gospel 83-6;

his involvement in Stephen's martyrdom 56-8; his maryrdom 248-9; his new 'eschatological dualism' 75-83; his Roman citizenship 46, n 5; his Syria/Cilicia evangelization 95-7; introduction to 17-9; preaching, 39-41; product of three civilizations 45-9; rebuke of Peter 126-30; relationship to the Jerusalem church 216-22; right man for the Gentile mission 54; second missionary journey 153-67; second post-conversion trip to Jerusalem 100-114; third missionary journey 177-91; third post-conversion trip to Jerusalem 139-52; two-year imprisonment at Caesarea 223-4

Paul's relationship to the Jerusalem church, excursus on 216-22

Peter: hypocrisy at Antioch, 126-30; preachimg, 37-39; speech at the Jerusalem Conference 141-4

Pharisees, distinction from Sadducees 49, n 16

Philemon, Epistle to: content of 237; date of writing of 236; dominant theme of 237; occasion of 236; place of origin of 236

Philippians, Epistle to the: content of 242-4; date of writing of 241; dominant theme of 244; occasion of 241-2; place of origin of 241

Philippi, excursus on 156

Prison letters, discussion of 230-44

Reasons (four) for writing this book 9-14

Resurrection of Christ, primary feature of the primitive *kerygma* 41-3, implications of in primitive *kerygma* 43-4

Romans, Epistle to the: content of 208-11; date of writing of 206; dominant theme of 211; occasion of 206-7; place of origin of 205-6; its effect 211; its value 211-13

Rome, excursus on 226-7

Saul of Tarsus (see Paul, life of): Antiochene labours 97-100; change of name from to 'Paul' 121; demographic extent of his apostolic call 86-7; first evangelistic efforts 89-92; first missionary journey 115-26; first post-conversion visit to Jerusalem 92-5; his conversion 59-72; his gospel 83-6; his involvement in Stephen's martyrdom 56-8; his new 'eschatological dualism' 75-83; his Phariseeism 49-52; his religion 48-9; his Roman citizenship 46, n 5; his Syria/Cilicia evangelization 95-7; his 'zeal', meaning of 48-9; product of three civilizations 45-9; right man for the Gentile mission 54; second post-conversion trip to Jerusalem 100-114; visionary persecutor 52-3; zealot Jew 45-54

Second missionary journey (to Asia, Macedonia, Achaia) 153-67; results of 174-75

Second Corinthians (see *Corinthians, Second Epistle to the*)

Second Thessalonians (see *Thessalonians, Second Epistle to the*)

Sergius Paulus, significance of conversion of for Paul's mission strategy 116-20

South Galatia: destination of Paul's *Letter to the Galatians*, 105, fn 38; defense of the 'South Galatia' hypothesis 105-14

Stephen's martyrdom, Saul's involvement in 56-8
Silas 154, n 1
'Stern letter' to Corinthians 187-88
Stoic school 161-2, n 16
Synagogue, the Jewish 118-19
Thessalonica, excursus on 158
Thessalonians, First Epistle to the: content of 170-2; date of 168; dominant themes of 172; occasion of 168-9; place of origin of 168
Thessalonians, Second Epistle to the: content of 173-4; date of 172; dominant themes of 174; occasion of 173; place of origin of 172
Third missionary journey (to Ephesus, Macedonia, Achaia) 177-91; Luke's depiction of Paul's ministry at Ephesus 178-85; Paul's additional details about his activities at Ephesus 185-7
Timothy, conversion of 125, chief aide to Paul 250-1
Timothy, First Epistle to: content of 253-5; date of 250; dominant themes of 255; occasion of 250-3; place of origin of 250
Timothy, Second Epistle to: content of 288-90; date of 287; dominant themes of 290; occasion of 288; place of origin of 287
Titus, description of 255-6
Titus, Epistle to: content of 256-7; date of 255; dominant themes of 257; occasion of 255-6; place of origin of 255
Travel in Paul's day, excursus on 117
Tübingen School (see F. C. Baur), theory of 11-3
Visits to Jerusalem, Paul's post-conversion: fifth 190, 216-23; first 92-5; fourth 167; second (see 'Famine relief visit') 100-5; third (see Jerusalem Conference) 139-52.

Part Two, 305-588

Abrahamic covenant, significance of for nations 374-78
Baptism 507-21; import of 515-7; mode of 517-9; instituted by Christ 507-8; Paul's teaching on 509-21; Paul's references to 509-15; subjects of 520-1
Christ, person of 355-71; entails Jesus as 'Savior' 360; entails Jesus' divine Lordship 357-9; E. P. Sanders's low view of 356, n 1; Jesus as the 357; preexistence of 356-57; seven great passages concerning 360; three uses of as a title for 360-67
'Christian Intuitionism' 482-5; a biblical theistic response to 485-91; inadequacy of 489-91; J. A. T. Robinson's version of 482-4; Joseph Fletcher's version of 484-5
Church 493-506; government of 501-5; nature of 494-9; offices of open only to men 505 n 16, n17; upbuilding of 499-501
Colossians 2:9, exposition of 368-9

Subject Index

'Covenantal nomism', E. P. Sanders's 453-61; Douglas Moo on 455-7; Jacob Neusner on 457 n 45; James D. G. Dunn's 461-2

Deacon, qualification of the 504-5

Death and resurrection of Christ, Old Testament prophets' references to 378

Eldership, duties of the 502-3; qualifications of the 503-4

Eschatology (see Pauline eschatology)

Ethical utilitarianism, criticism of 484 n 19

'Eternal purpose' 332-41; anticipated charge of arbitrariness in, excursus on 339-40; election of men in 341; God's foreknowledge and predestination of the elect in 338-9; person and work of Christ central to 333; soteric issues central to 333-4

Faith in Jesus Christ 422-29; alone comports with a salvation by grace that excludes all human boasting 428-9; diametrical opposite of law-keeping 425-7; instrumental to justification 422-3; in its 'gift' character procured by Christ's cross work and effected by the Spirit's regeneration 423-5

Glorification of Christian, nature of 350-4; significance of for Christians 352-3; significance of for creation 351-2; significance of for Christ 353-4

God the Father (see Salvific work of)

God the Holy Spirit (see Holy Spirit, the person of and Salvific work of)

God the Son (see Christ, person of and Salvific work of)

Hebrews 1:8, exposition of 365-7

Holy Spirit, the person of 405-20; distinct person of 406-7; co-equal with the Father and the Son 407; does divine works 407; names and titles of in Pauline literature 405; possesses divine attributes 407; relation of to the Father and the Son 407; Yahweh of Old Testament 407. See also Salvific work of the Holy Spirit.

Israel, see Pauline eschatology

Justification (right standing with God) 421-68; a juridical or forensic determination 434-7; current debate over the specific chacter of the teaching Paul opposed by his doctrine of 452-65; faith alone in Jesus Christ instrumental to 422-3; its righteousness the alien righteousness of Jesus Christ 437-40; James and Paul on 442-3; nature of 429-40; six objections to Protestant representation of 441-51; summary of doctrine of 465-8

Law, see Pauline ethic

'Law of Christ', 473 n 5

Lord's Supper 521-7; import of 524-27; instituted by Christ 508-9; Paul's teaching on 521-27; Pauline terminology of 521-2; observance and liturgy of 522-4

'Man in Adam' 323-9

'Natural law theory', insufficiency of 486-8

'New perspective on Paul', see pages 451-65; James D. G. Dunn's 461-5

Pauline eschatology 529-55; **future** state (entailing the apostasy and the man of sin 548-9, freedom of creation 534, goal of eschatology 534, immortality 534, judgment 535-7, new heaven and new earth state 552-5, plight of the unbeliever 535, questions concerning the ingathering of 'all Israel' 539-48, the millennial reign 549-52, the time of the rapture 538-9; 'triggering' mechanism 537-8) 534-55; **intermediate** state 531-4; **present** state 530-1

Pauline ethic 469-91; F. F. Bruce opposed to Reformed understanding of 470-1; the 'third use' of the law 472-82

Pauline gospel, Old Testament roots of 373-84

Paul's ministry, lessons from for today's missionaries 557-85

Paul's missionary theology God of 309-13; presenting 306-8; sources of 308-9

People of God, church as present day expression of 380-81

Romans 9, exposition of 334-8

Romans 9:5, exposition of 360-3

Salvation, identical requisites for the same in both Testaments 383-4

Salvific work of **God the Father** 343-54; salvation ultimately to be traced to 343-4; includes adoption of sinner 346-9; includes effectual summons of sinner 344-45; includes glorification of Christian (see Glorification of Christian) 349-54; includes justifying the sinner 345-6; includes quickening of the sinner and engifting of faith to 345; of **God the Holy Spirit** 405-20; Christians baptized by 411, engifted by 415, filled with 412-4, sanctified by 414, sealed by 412; creates men anew 409-10; unites men with Christ 408-9; works obedience in Christians 415-9; of **God the Son** 385-404; entailed his death as a destructive sacrifice, 402-3, an expiatory sacrifice 388, a propitiatory sacrifice 389-93, a reconciling sacrifice 395-8, a redemptive sacrifice 398-402; entailed work of a high priest 391-3; E. P. Sanders's low view of Paul's understanding of 388, n 1; includes the application of the atonement 404; significance of his obedience for 388

Satan 317, n 2

Second Corinthians 5:1-10, exposition of 532-4

Sin 315-30; as 'flesh' 323; as moral depravity and inability to please God 318-21; background to the Incarnation and Calvary 315-6; consequences of 322; continuing effects of on the body 330; law's function in regard to 329; man's accountability for, 321; present deliverance from 329; Sanders's view of Paul's thought on 316, n 1; vocabulary 317-8

Sovereignty of God in salvation 331-42; exposition of pertinent passages concerning 332-41; Pauline terminology with regard to 331-2

Titus 2:13, exposition of 363-5

Union with Christ 408-9

Wrath of God 393-5

Paul's First Missionary Journey

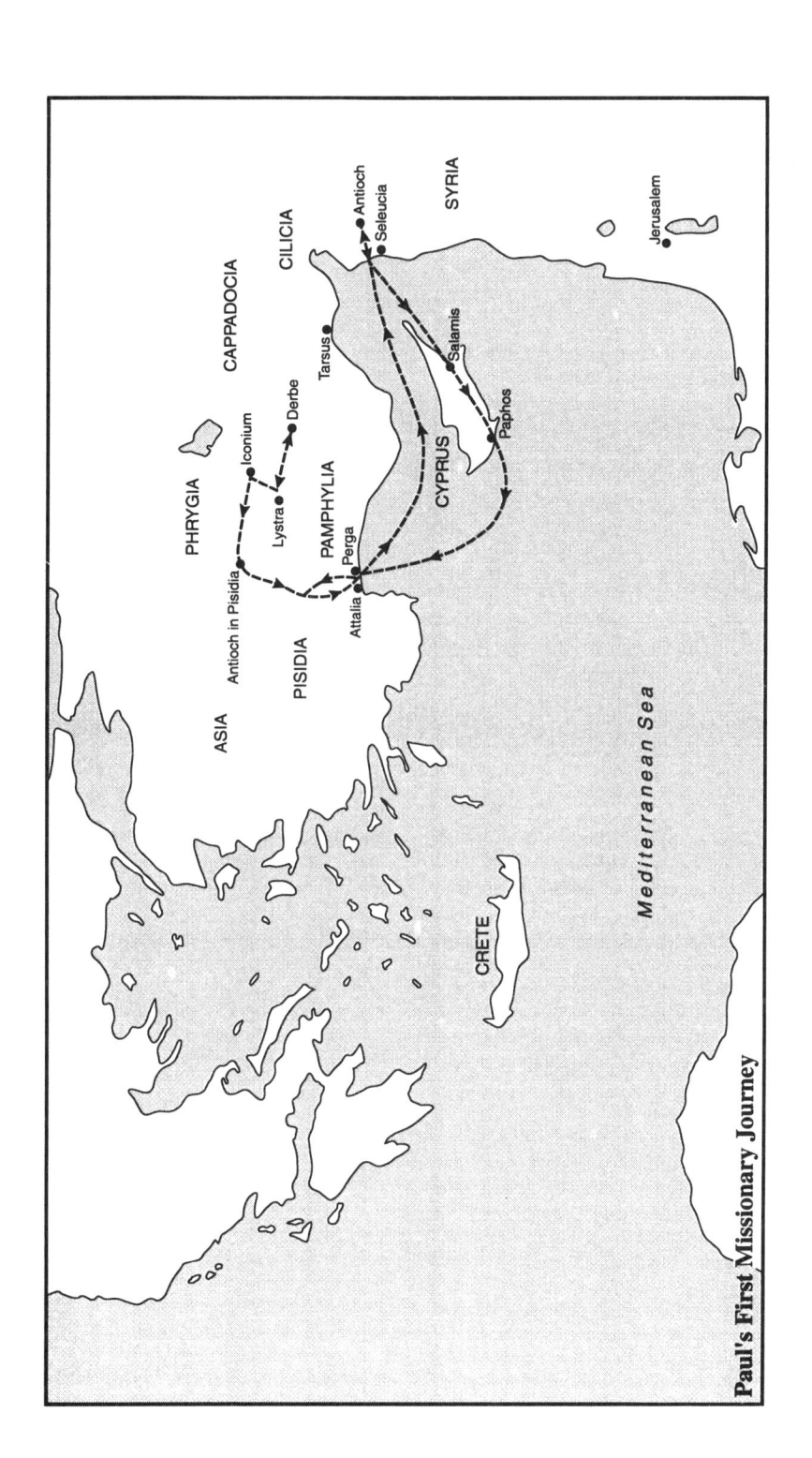

Paul's Second Missionary Journey

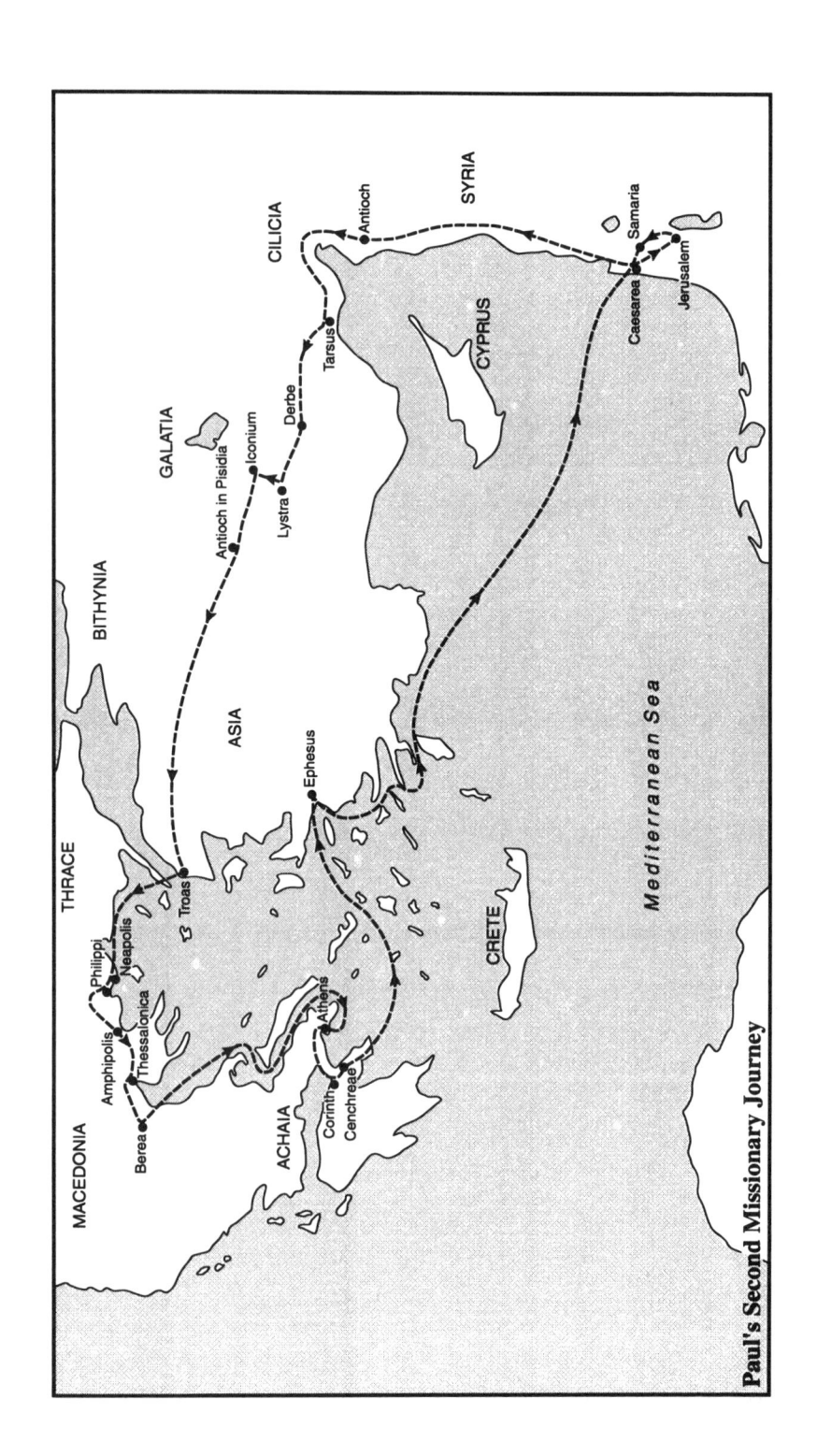

Paul's Third Missionary Journey

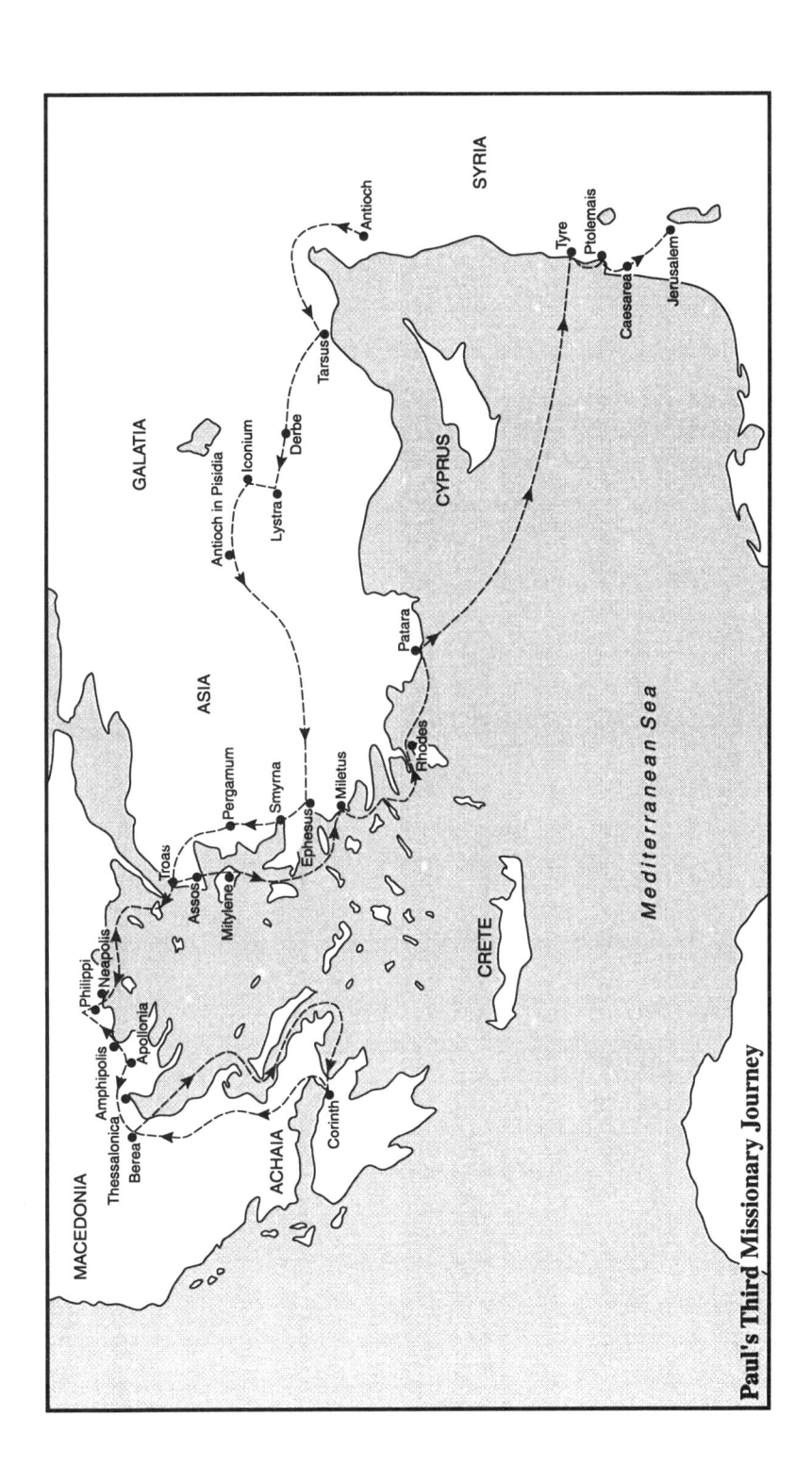

Christian Focus Publications publishes biblically-accurate books for adults and children. The books in the adult range are published in three imprints.

Christian Heritage contains classic writings from the past.

Christian Focus contains popular works including biographies, commentaries, doctrine, and Christian living.

Mentor focuses on books written at a level suitable for Bible College and seminary students, pastors, and others; the imprint includes commentaries, doctrinal studies, examination of current issues, and church history.

For a free catalogue of all our titles, please write to
Christian Focus Publications,
Geanies House, Fearn,
Ross-shire, IV20 1TW, Great Britain

For details of our titles visit us on our web site
http://www.christianfocus.com